Social Issues Primary Sources Collection

Terrorism

Essential Primary Sources

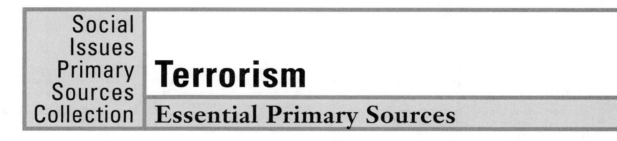

Social
Issues
Primary
Sources
Collection

Terrorism

Essential Primary Sources

K. Lee Lerner and **Brenda Wilmoth Lerner,** Editors

THOMSON
━━━ ✳ ━━━ ™
GALE

Detroit • New York • San Francisco • San Diego • New Haven, Conn. • Waterville, Maine • London • Munich

Terrorism: Essential Primary Sources

K. Lee Lerner and Brenda Wilmoth Lerner, Editors

Project Editor
Dwayne D. Hayes

Editorial
Luann Brennan, Angela Doolin, Grant Eldridge, Jennifer Greve, Anne Marie Hacht, Joshua Kondek, Gillian Leonard, Andy Malonis, John McCoy, Mark Milne, Rebecca Parks, Mark Springer

Permissions
Susan J. Rudolph, Emma Hull, Andrew Specht

Imaging and Multimedia
Dean Dauphinais, Leitha Etheridge-Sims, Lezlie Light, Michael Logusz, Dan Newell, Christine O'Bryan, Kelly A. Quin, Denay Wilding, Robyn Young

Product Design
Pamela A. Galbreath

Composition and Electronic Capture
Evi Seoud

Manufacturing
Wendy Blurton

Product Manager
Carol Nagel

LIBRARY OF CONGRESS CATALOGING-IN-PUBLICATION DATA

Terrorism : essential primary sources / K. Lee Lerner and Brenda Wilmoth Lerner, editors.
    p. cm. — (Social issues primary sources collection)
    Includes bibliographical references and index.
    ISBN 1-4144-0621-5 (hardcover : alk. paper)
    1. Terrorism—History—Sources. I. Lerner, K. Lee. II. Lerner, Brenda Wilmoth. III. Series.
HV6431.T4432 2006
303.6'25—dc22   2005024002

This title is also available as an e-book.
ISBN 1414406223
Contact your Thomson Gale sales representative for ordering information.

Printed in the United States of America
10 9 8 7 6 5 4 3 2

Table of Contents

2 POLITICAL TERRORISM

7 GLOBAL TERRORIST MOVEMENTS

8 SPECIAL-INTEREST TERRORISM

10 TERRORISM AND SOCIETY

Advisors and Contributors

While compiling this volume, the editors relied upon the expertise and contributions of the following scholars, journalists, and researchers who served as advisors and/or contributors for *Terrorism: Essential Primary Sources:*

Steven Archambault (Ph.D. Candidate)
University of New Mexico
Albuquerque, New Mexico

William Arthur Atkins, M.S.
Normal, Illinois

Annessa Ann Babic (Ph.D. Candidate)
SUNY at Stony Brook
Stony Brook, NY

Alicia Cafferty
Auburn University
Auburn, Alabama

James Anthony Charles Corbett
Journalist
London, UK

Bryan Davies, J.D.
Ontario, Canada

Amit Gupta, Ph.D.
Ahmedabad, India

Stacey N. Hannem
Journalist
Quebec, Canada

Brian D. Hoyle, Ph.D.
Nova Scotia, Canada

Alexandr Ioffe, Ph.D.
Russian Academy of Sciences
Moscow, Russia

Lynda Joeman
Fmr Principal Research Officer, Analytical Services
Agency, UK Ministry of Defence
Sabah, Malaysia

Kenneth T. LaPensee, Ph.D., MPH
Hampton, New Jersey

S. Layman, M.A.
Abingdon, MD

Adrienne Wilmoth Lerner (J.D. Candidate)
University of Tennessee College of Law
Knoxville, Tennessee

Eric v.d. Luft, Ph.D., M.L.S.
SUNY Upstate Medical University
Syracuse, New York

Pamela V. Michaels, M.A.
Santa Fe, New Mexico

Caryn Neumann, Ph.D.
Ohio State University
Columbus, Ohio

Michael J. O'Neal, Ph.D.
Moscow, Idaho

Mark Phillips, Ph.D.
Abilene Christian University
Abilene, Texas

Shelley Ann Wake
Journalist
Wishart, Queensland, Australia

Simon Wendt, Ph.D.
John F. Kennedy Institute for North American
Studies
Berlin, Germany

Steve Wilson, Ph.D.
Houston, Texas

Jeremy Wimpfheimer, Ph.D.
Beit Shemesh, Israel

Melanie Barton Zoltán, M.S.
Amherst, Massachusetts

Because they are actively working in criminal investigations or other sensitive areas, some advisors and contributors requested the release of a minimum of personal and/or affiliation information.

When the only verifiable or attributable source of information for an entry comes from documents or information provided by a governmental organization (e.g., the U.S. Department of State), the editors endeavored to carefully note when the language used and perspective offered was that of a governmental organization.

As publishing deadlines loomed, *Terrorism: Essential Primary Sources* was well served by a research staff dedicated to incorporating the latest relevant events prior to publication deadlines—especially information related to bombings in London during July 2005. The editors wish to thank Mr. Lee Wilmoth Lerner for his IT and engineering assistance that facilitated efficient communications and information exchange among a multi-platform, multi-lingual global group of scholars, researchers, and writers.

The editors gratefully acknowledge and extend thanks to Mr. Peter Gareffa and Ms. Carol Nagel at Thomson Gale for their faith in the project and for their sound content advice. The tenacious work of Thomson Gale copyright research staff, literally right up to publication deadlines, made this book possible. The editors also wish to acknowledge the contributions of the Thomson Gale Imaging Team, Ms. Amanda Wilmoth Lerner, and Ms. Marcia Schiff at the Associated Press for their help in securing images. Most directly, the editors wish to acknowledge and thank the Thomson Gale Project Editor, Mr. Dwayne Hayes, for his steady, experienced, and reassuring oversight of both content and technical matters.

Acknowledgements

Copyrighted Excerpts in *Terrorism: Essential Primary Sources* were reproduced from the following periodicals:

Agence France Presse, December 23, 1991; March 13, 2004. All republished with permission of *Agence France Presse,* conveyed through Copyright Clearance Center, Inc.- *AP Newswire,* March 30, 1985. Copyright © 1985 Associated Press. All rights reserved. Distributed by Valeo IP. Reprinted with permission of the Associated Press. —*AsiaSource,* June 6, 2002. Copyright © 2002, Asia Society. All rights reserved. Reproduced by permission.—*Associated Press,* January 25, 1975; April 3, 1986; September 12, 1988; September 2, 2000; January 27, 2002; April 16, 2003. Copyright © 1975, 1986, 1988, 2000, 2002, 2003 Associated Press. All rights reserved. Distributed by Valeo IP. All reprinted with permission of the Associated Press./November 22, 1979; December 3, 1979; April 23, 1983; April 26, 1983; October 23, 1983; July 22, 1985; July 31, 1989; April 23, 1997. Copyright © 1979, 1983, 1985, 1989, 1997 Associated Press. All reprinted with permission of the Associated Press.—*The Atlanta Journal and Constitution,* July 28, 1996. Republished with permission of The Atlanta Journal and Constitution, conveyed through Copyright Clearance Center, Inc.— *BBC News at bbcnews.com,* January 16, 2002; October 4, 2002; January 7, 2003; July 16, 2004; March 9, 2005. All reproduced by permission.—*Chemical & Engineering News,* November 4, 1996 for "FBI Takes Lead In Developing Counterterrorism Effort" by Lois R. Ember. Copyright © 1996 American Chemical Society. Reproduced with permission of the publisher and author.—*Christian Science Monitor,* April 6, 2003 for "How Did Eric Rudolph Survive?" by Patrik Jonsson. Copyright © 2003 The Christian Science Publishing Society. All rights reserved. Reproduced by permission of the author.—*Computing,* April 21, 2005. Copyright 2005 VNU Business Media. www.computing. co.uk. Reproduced by permission.—*Contemporary Review,* v. 263, October, 1993. Reproduced by the permission of Contemporary Review Ltd.—*The Daily Telegraph,* April 1, 2002; October 28, 2002; September 8, 2004. All reproduced by permission.—*The Economist,* November 1, 2003. © 2003 The Economist Newspaper Ltd. All rights reserved. Further reproduction prohibited. www.economist.com.—*Financial Times,* August 6, 1998. Reproduced by permission.— *The Guardian,* August 17, 1998. Copyright © 1998 by Guardian Newspapers Limited. Reproduced by permission of Guardian News Service, LTD.—*The Independent (London),* May 16, 2001. Copyright © 2001 Independent Newspapers (UK) Ltd. Reproduced by permission.—*International Herald Tribune,* September 22, 2000; March 5, 2003; December 29, 2003. All reproduced by permission.—*Knight Ridder Washington Bureau,* March 12, 2004. © 2004, Knight Ridder/Tribune. Reprinted with permission.—*Latin American Newsletters,* June 2, 1967. Reproduced by permission.—*Latin American Newsletters,* v. 2, January 26, 1968; June 5, 1970; v. 4, December 11, 1970; v. 6, September 11, 1972; v. 7, November 8, 1974; v. 8, December 13, 1974. All reproduced by permission.—*Maclean's Magazine,* October 21, 1985. © 1985 by Maclean's Magazine. Reproduced by permission.—*Moscow Times,* August 30, 2004. © Copyright 2004 The Moscow Times. All rights reserved. Reproduced by permission.—*New York Times,* November 2, 1950; December 2, 1956; July 25, 1961; July 23, 1972; March 2, 1973; January 25, 1975; December 2, 1979; December 2, 1987; November 5, 1995; May 9, 1998; October, 2001. Copyright © 1950,

1956, 1961, 1972, 1973, 1975, 1979, 1987, 1995, 1998, 2001 by The New York Times Company. All reproduced by permission.—*Newsweek*, July 19, 1976; May 2, 1988. Copyright © 1976, 1988 Newsweek, Inc. All reproduced by permission.—*The Observer*, May 6, 2001. Copyright © 2001 by Guardian Publications Ltd. Reproduced by permission of Guardian News Service, LTD.—*The Officer*, October, 2003. Copyright © 2003 Reserve Officers Association of the United States. Reproduced by permission.—*The Times*, April 29, 1977; March 2, 1988. All reproduced by permission.—*The Times of India*, September 9, 2000. © Bennett, Coleman & Co. Ltd. Reproduced by permission.—*Toronto Star*, November 26, 1986; July 31, 1988. All reproduced by permission.—*U.S. News & World Report*, October 18, 1993. Copyright © 1993 U.S. News and World Report, L.P. Reprinted with permission.—*United Press International*, April 2, 1986; October 21, 1992. Copyright © 1986, 1992 by United Press International. Both reproduced by permission.—*Washington Post*, July 15, 1980; October 8, 1981; November 25, 1986; October 16, 2001; October 14, 2002; April 25, 2005. Copyright © 1980, 1981, 1986, 2001, 2002, 2005 Washington Post Book World Service/Washington Post Writers Group. All reproduced by permission.—*Washington Times*, October 19, 2003. Copyright © 2003 Washington Times. All rights reserved. Distributed by Valeo IP. Reproduced by permission.—*World Tribune.com*, June 14, 2002. Reproduced by permission.

Copyrighted Excerpts in *Terrorism: Essential Primary Sources* were reproduced from the following books:

Bin Laden, Usama. From "Declaration of War (August 1996)," in *Anti-American Terrorism and the Middle East*. Edited by Barry Rubin and Judith Colp Rubin. Oxford University Press, 1996. Copyright © 1996 by Oxford University Press. Used by permission of Oxford University Press.—Bower, Anne, "A soldier in the Army of God," *http://www.monitor.net/monitor/abortion/abortionsoldier.html*, February 18, 1996. Reproduced by permission of the author.—Ben Artzi-Pelossof, Noa. From *In the Name of Sorrow and Hope*. Random House, 1997. Copyright © 1996 by Editions Robert Laffont. Used by permission of Alfred A. Knopf, Inc., a division of Random House, Inc.—Brace, Richard and Joan. From *Algerian Voices*. D. van Nostrand Company, Inc., 1965. Copyright © 1965 by Richard and Joan Brace. This material is used by permission of John Wiley & Sons, Inc.—Klee, Ernest. From "Testimony of gas-van driver Walter Burmeister," in *"The Good Old Days": The Holocaust as Seen by Its Perpetrators and Bystanders*. Edited by Ernest Klee, Willi Dressen, Volker Riess. Translated by Deborah Burnstone. The Free Press, 1991. Copyright © 1988 by S. Fischer Verlag GmbH. Translation copyright © 1991 by Deborah Burnstone. All rights reserved. Reprinted with the permission of The Free Press, a Division of Simon & Schuster Adult Publishing Group. In the United Kingdom by the author.—Mamdani, Mahmood. From *When Victims Become Killers*. Princeton University Press, 2001. Copyright © 2001 by Princeton University Press, 2002 paperback edition. Reproduced by permission of Princeton University Press.—Masry, Mohammed O. "A Muslim US Soldier's Diary, Entry#1," *http://www.islamonline.net/english/In_Depth/Iraq_Aftermath/2003/12/article_06.shtml*, November 9, 2003. Reproduced by permission.—McCauley, Clark, "The Psychology of Terrorism," *http://www.ssrc.org/sept11/essays/mccauley.htm*, 2005. Reproduced by permission of the author.—Ong, Betty, "Witness to Terror: The 9-11 Hearings: A Voice From The Sky," *http://americanradioworks.publicradio.org/features/911/ong.html*, September 11, 2001. Reproduced by permission.—Reid, Richard, and Judge William Young, "Reid: 'I Am at War with Your Country,'" *http://www.cnn.com/2003/LAW/01/31/reid.transcript/*, January 31, 2003. Reproduced by permission.—Sarajlic, Izet. From "Former Yugoslavs/The Jewish Cemetery (poem)," in *AFTER AUSCHWITZ, AFTER SARAJEVO. . . .* English translation by C. Polony, http://www.leftcurve.org/lc18-20pgs/aftersarajevo.html, 1994. Reproduced by permission of C. Polony.—Society for Russian-Chechen Friendship, "Declaration on the hostage-taking in Moscow," *http://www.ishr.org/press/pr2002/oct02/021025chechnya.htm*, October 25, 2002. Reproduced by permission.—Williams, Maj. (Res.) Louis, "Entebbe Diary," *http://www1.idf.il/DOVER/site/mainpage.asp?sl=EN&id=5&from=history&docid=23016&Pos=23&bScope=false*, July 4, 1976. Reproduced by permission.

Photographs and Illustrations Appearing in *Terrorism: Essential Primary Sources* were received from the following sources:

Abdo Hussam, Palestinian youth and would-be suicide bomber, March 24, 2004, photograph by Lefteris Pitar. AP/Wide World Photos.— Aftermath of a bomb detonated on Wall Street in 1920. © Corbis.— Aircraft about to fly into the World Trade Center in New York, September 11, 2001, by ABC via APTN. AP/Wide World Photos.—al-Islambouli, Lt. Col. Khaled, at his trial for the assassination of President Anwar al-Sadat, Cairo, Egypt, March 6, 1982, photograph by Foley. AP/Wide World Photos.—al-Jiaydi, Saja, draws pictures of Israeli tanks and soldiers firing at Palestinians, at the Dheisheh refugee camp in Behlehem in 2002, photograph. AP/Wide World Photos.—al-Molqi, Youssef Magied, shown behind the bars at the time of the trial in Genoa, May 6, 1986, photograph. AP/Wide World Photos.—American hostage led by young militants to a mob in front of the United States Embassy in Tehran, Iran, November 8, 1979, photograph. AP/Wide World Photos.— American soldiers take a rest while inspecting a cave complex, April 2, 2004, photograph by Emilio Morenatti. AP/Wide World Photos.—Arab commando group member, photograph by Kurt Strumpf. © AP/Wide World Photos.—Armed search team enters the forest near Nantahala, N.C., July 16, 1998, photograph by Alan Marler. AP/Wide World Photos.—Lincoln, Abraham, assassination of, drawing. AP/Wide World Photos.—Assassination of Archduke Franz Ferdinand of Austria-Hungary and his wife, Czech Countess Sophie Chotek, drawing. AP/Wide World Photos.—Australian forensic team collects evidence at the bombing site of a nightclub in Kuta, Bali, that killed nearly 200 people, photograph. AP/Wide World Photos.—Auto burns after bomb explodes in front of Saigon's Hotel De Ville, 1952, photograph. AP/Wide World Photos.—Ayatollah Khomeini's portrait hangs from the roof inside the compound of the United States Embassy in Tehran, photograph. AP/Wide World Photos.—bin Laden, Osama, handling a Kalashnikov rifle at an undisclosed location, image. AP/Wide World Photos.—bin Laden, Osama, statement as provided on Monday, Sept. 24, 2001, by the Al-Jazeera television news network, based in Doha, Qatar, AP Photo/Al-Jazeera. AP/Wide World Photos.—Bin Laden, Osama, with imposed graphics, photograph. AP/Wide World Photos.—Blood stained barber's chair, evidence of damage wrought by terrorist explosion, Israel, November, 1968, photograph. AP/Wide World Photos.—Blood stains on lyrics of a song about peace carried by former Israeli Premier Yitzhak Rabin on the day he was assassinated in 1995, photograph. © Reuven Kastro/Corbis Sygma.—Body of blast victims at the explosion site outside the National Hotel in Moscow, December 9, 2003, photograph by Kommersant Dmitry Lebedev. AP/Wide World Photos.—Bodies of school children killed in a school seizure, Beslan, North Ossetia, September 3, 2004, photograph by Sergey Ponomarev. AP/Wide World Photos.—Body of an explosion victim on the commemorative bricks in Atlanta's Olympic Centennial Park after a blast early July 27, 1996, photograph. AP/Wide World Photos.—Bomb blast destruction at South Quay in London's Docklands, February 10, 1996, photograph by Alastair Grant. AP/Wide World Photos.—Burning of the Frigate Philadelphia in the Harbor of Tripoli on February 16, 1804, painting. © New York Historical Society, New York/Bridgeman Art Library.—"Bury Them and Keep Quiet," etching by Francisco Goya from his "Disasters of War" series.

© Burstein Collection/Corbis.—Bush, George, delivering remarks on the Patriot Act in Buffalo, New York, 2004, photograph. AP/Wide World Photos.—Bush, George W., during his State of the Union address, January 29, 2002, photograph. AP/Wide World Photos.—Bushnell, Prudence, U.S. Ambassador, center, evacuated from the area of the U.S. Embassy following an explosion in downtown Nairobi, August 7, 1998, photograph by Sayyid Azim. AP/Wide World Photos.— Car bomb explosion scene, Dublin, Ireland, May 18, 1974, photograph. AP/Wide World Photos.—Chreidi, Yasser Mohammed, center, escorted by Lebanese police to a court in Beirut, Lebanon, March, 1994, photograph. AP/Wide World Photos.—Colombia's National Police officers taking the finger prints of Ricardo Palmera, Bogota, Colombia, December 31, 2004, photograph by Carlos Pinto. AP/Wide World Photos.— Colombian activists protest in front of a hotel, Bogota, Colombia, January 29, 2004, photograph. AP/Wide World Photos.—"Cowboy," a search canine for the Federal Emergency Management Agency (FEMA) standing atop a pile of rubble at the World Trade Center site in New York, September, 2001, photograph. AP/Wide World Photos.—Crater 35 feet deep and 85 feet wide made by a truck bomb, June 26, 1996 at the Khobar Towers in Dhahran, Saudi Arabia, photograph. AP/Wide World Photos.—Dohrn, Bernardine, 1969, photograph. AP/Wide World Photos.—Dy, Vince, right, a K-9 officer with the Nashville airport, directs his search dog, photograph by Mark Humphrey. AP/Wide World Photos.—Egyptian security policeman on the scene, as Islamic militant gunmen attacked tourists entering the Hatshepsut Temple complex, November 17, 1997, photograph. AP/Wide World Photos.—Elderly Jew harassed by Hitler's Brown Shirts in a Berlin, Germany, street, April 4, 1933, photograph. AP/Wide World Photos.—Emergency personnel walk past an automobile destroyed in a pre-dawn arson fire at an auto California dealership, 2003, photograph. © Reuters/Corbis.—Envelope with an anthrax-laced letter that was sent to Senate Majority Leader Tom Daschle, Washington, October 23, 2001, photograph. © Reuters/Corbis.—EPA and United States Coast Guard cleanup crew members prepare to enter the American Media Inc., office building in Boca Raton, Florida, photograph. AP/Wide World Photos.— Ethiopian hijacker identified as Shamsu Kabret holds a knife to the throat of flight attendant Sofia Mastelou while talking to TV crews through the door of an Olympic Airways 747 on the tarmac at Athens, November 9, 1995, photograph. AP/Wide World Photos.—Execution of King Louis XVI, illustration after a painting by Edouard Manet. © Bettman/ Corbis.—False passport and disguise used by Lenin to escape into Finland after an order for his arrest was issued by the Russian Provisional Government, July, 1917, photograph. © Hulton-Deutsch Collection/ Corbis.—FBI agents view the damage caused by the 1993 terrorist bombing of the parking garage at the World Trade Center towers in New York, photograph. © Reuters NewMedia Inc./Corbis.—FBI and ATF agents entering the World Trade Center parking garage in New York after the 1993 bombing, photograph. © Reuters/Corbis.—FBI Special Agent Edward Hegerty displaying items captured during a news conference, photograph. AP/Wide World Photos.— "Fenian Outrage," an illustration of the explosion of the Clerkenwell prison in 1867. © Corbis.—Firefighters in a crane examine the damage after terrorists blew themselves up in a building, Legenes, Spain, Saturday, April 3, 2004, photograph. AP/Wide World Photos.—Firefighters search through debris after a bomb attack at the Berlin discotheque "La Belle," photograph by Hans Edinger. AP/Wide World Photos.— Fiumicino Airport in Rome, December 17, 1973, photograph. AP/Wide World Photos.—Five-level, color-coded terrorism warning system, enacted in 2002, photograph. AP/Wide World Photos.—"For This You Were Born," etching by Francisco Goya from his "Disasters of War" series. © Burstein Collection/ Corbis.—Fragment that proved crucial in tracking down the bombers of Pan AM flight 103, shown on the tip of a finger, photograph. Justice Department/AP Wide World Photos.—Funeral ceremony for Yulia and Yelena Nelimov, Tel Aviv, June 3, 2001, photograph by Eitan Hess-Ashkenazi. AP/Wide World Photos.— Gadhafi, Moammar, during a news conference in Tripoli, February 5, 2001, photograph by Amr Nabil. AP/Wide World Photos.—Galal, Capt. Hani, pilot of the hijacked EgyptAir Flight 648, receiving medical attention, Malta, November 25, 1985, photograph. AP/Wide World Photos.—German poster for the Nazi party, with the phrase "National Socialism: The Organized Will of the Nation." Bridgeman Art Library.—"Great deeds! Against the Dead!" etching by Francisco Goya from his "Disasters of War" series. © Burstein Collection/Corbis.—Guhfron, Ali, alias Mukhlas, during his trial in Denpasar, Bali, Indonesia, July 9, 2003, photograph by M.M. Palinggi. AP/Wide World Photos.—Hamas suicide bombers, photograph by Mohammed Zaatari. © AP/Wide World Photos.— Haymarket Massacre in Chicago, illustration. © Chicago Historical Society, Chicago/Bridgeman Art Library.—Hearst, Patricia, posing in front of the Symbionese Liberation Army symbol, photograph. © Bettmann/Corbis.—Hearst, Patricia, carrying a weapon, photograph. AP/Wide World Photos.—Hermes the robot exiting an empty cave, July 29, 2002, photograph by Wally Santana. AP/Wide World Photos.— Hezbollah's suicide bomber squad members with colored faces during a rally in a suburb of Beirut, May 7, 1996, photograph by Ali Mohamed. AP/Wide World Photos.—Higgins, William, Marine Lt. Colonel, photograph. AP/Wide World Photos.—Hostages in a school in Beslan, Russia, photograph. AP/Wide World Photos.—Hostages return from Uganda after being freed during raid of Israeli forces on Entebbe airport, 1976, photograph. AP/Wide World Photo.—Hostages sit below explosives strung from basketball hoops in the gymnasium of a school in Beslan, Russia, September 7, 2004, photograph. AP/Wide World Photos.—Hostages taken by Chechen gunmen who stormed a crowded Moscow theater in 2002, photograph. AP/Wide World Photos.—Hyon-hui, Kim, North Korean Communist agent, Seoul, Korea, April 25, 1989, photograph by Liu Heung Shing. AP/Wide World Photos.—International Workers of the World pamphlet, 1927. University of Washington Libraries, Special Collections, UW 25329z.—International Workers of the World pamphlet, 1927. University of Washington Libraries, Special Collections, UW 25612z.—Internet page allegedly showing pictures of the beheaded body of kidnapped American Paul M. Johnson, Jr., photograph. AP/Wide World Photos.—Iraqi National Guard soldiers aiming guns in a raid, Baghdad, Iraq, September 29, 2004, photograph by Imad Akrawi. AP/Wide World Photos.—Iraqis firing their machine guns into the air during the funeral of slain Iraqi policemen in Fallujah, Sept. 13, 2003, photograph by Karel Prinsloo. AP/Wide World Photos.—Israeli soldier hugging child, July 4, 1976, photograph. AP/ Wide World Photos.—Israeli team's headquarters at the Olympic Village in Munich, West Germany, where Israeli weightlifter Moshe Romano was killed, photograph. © AP/Wide World Photos.—Israelis scattering after three terrorist bombs explode in a crowded bus station, Tel Aviv, September 4, 1968, photograph. AP/ Wide World Photos.—Italian policeman holding an undated photo of 33-year-old Egyptian suspect Rabie Osman Ahmed during a press conference in Milan, Italy, June 8, 2004, photograph. AP/Wide World Photos.—Kennedy, Jacqueline, cradling her husband President John F. Kennedy seconds after he was fatally shot, November 22, 1963, photograph. AP/Wide World Photos.—Kennedy, Senator Robert F., talking to campaign workers in Los Angeles minutes before he was shot, June 5, 1968, photograph by Dick Strobel. AP/Wide World Photos.—Khaled, Leila, toting a submachine gun at a Palestinian refugee camp in Lebanon, November 29, 1970, photograph by Eddie Adams. AP/Wide World Photos.—King David Hotel, Jerusalem, Israel, British headquarters in Palestine, after bombing by Zionist terrorists, photograph. Getty Images.—Letter that was sent to Senate Majority Leader Tom Daschle containing anthrax, photocopy. AP/Wide World Photos.—Lifeboats rescuing surviving crewmen of the wrecked USS Maine anchored in Havana, Cuba, after an explosion destroyed the battleship in 1898, photograph. AP/Wide World Photos.—Local language leaflets dropped over Afghanistan by the U.S. military advertising rewards of up to $25 million for information leading to the capture of Osama bin Laden or his lieutenant Aiman al-Zawahiri, photograph. AP/Wide World Photos.— "Maid of the Seas," nose section lies in a field near Lockerbie, Scotland, December, 1988, photograph. AP/Wide World Photos. —Man carrying the body of his child killed by a blast which completely destroyed the two-story building housing the office of the Federal Security Service at the site of the explosion, Znamenskoye, May, 2003, photograph by Musa Sadulayev. AP/Wide World Photos.—Manhattan financial district blast damage, 1975, photograph. AP/Wide World Photos.—Masked protesters, proclaiming to be supporters of the Earth Liberation Front, photograph by Don Ryan. AP/Wide World Photos.—McVeigh, Timothy James, photograph. AP/Wide World Photos.—McKinley, William, shot by Leon Czolgosz, October 29, 1901, drawing. AP/Wide World Photos.—Mercenaries of the French Foreign Legion operating south of Saigon hold a Communist Viet Minh fighter at gunpoint, photograph. AP/Wide World Photos.—Mohammed, Khalid Shaikh, photograph. AP/Wide World Photos.— "MRTA, surrender is not the way of Tupac Amaru," sign hung by Tupac Amaru rebels on the roof of the Japanese ambassador's residence in Lima, Peru, January 22, 1997, photograph by Ricardo Mazalan. AP/Wide World Photos.—Muslim woman at a checkpoint, 2001, photograph by Elizabeth Dalziel. AP/Wide World Photos.—Navy patrolman and his dog searching seats at the Utah Olympic Oval in Salt Lake City at the 2002 Winter Olympics, photograph. AP/Wide World Photos.—Oswald, Lee Harvey, shot by Dallas nightclub owner Jack Ruby, Dallas, Texas, November 25, 1963, photograph. © Topham/The Image Works. Reproduced by permission.—Pakistani soldier walking past a burned U.S. embassy vehicle, 1979, photograph. AP/Wide World Photos.—Palestinian boy holding a Palestinian flag on a rooftop in Hebron, photograph by Greg Marinovich. AP/Wide World Photos.—Palestinian boy assembling an AK-47 assault rifle blindfolded, photograph. AP/Wide World Photos.—Palestinian demonstrators hurling rocks at Israeli troops during the Palestinian uprising in Nablus, Occupied West Bank, on December 13, 1987, photograph by Max Nash. AP/Wide World Photos.—

Palestinian member of Islamic Jihad holding up a Holy Koran and a grenade, Gaza City, Gaza Strip, February 21, 2003, photograph by Brennan Linsley. AP/Wide World Photos.—Palestinian youth hit in the head by a rubber bullet fired by Israeli soldiers during clashes in Hebron, photograph by Khaled Zighari. AP/Wide World Photos.—Passenger standing opposite an anti terrorism poster at London's Embankment tube station, March 15, 2004, photograph by Richard Lewis. AP/Wide World Photos.—Passersbys looking at damaged buildings in Nairobi, Kenya, after a huge explosion ripped apart a building in the Kenyan capital, August 7, 1998, photograph by Sayyid Azim. AP/Wide World Photos.—Pedestrian looking at the wreckage of a Jewish shop in Berlin, November 10, 1938, the day after the "Kristallnacht" rampage, photograph. AP/Wide World Photos.—People run from the collapse of World Trade Center Tower, New York, September 11, 2001, photograph by Suzanne Plunkett. AP/Wide World Photos.—Police investigate burned-out tourists bus with the remains of a body in the front seat after it was attacked in front of the Egyptian museum in Cairo, September 18, 1997, photograph. AP/Wide World Photos.—Poster on a wall in Jenin refugee camp in the West Bank glorifying Palestinian suicide bomber Shadi Zakaria, photograph by Greg Baker. AP/Wide World Photos.—Princips, Gavrilo, arrested for the assassination of Archduke Ferdinand, photograph. © Bettman/Corbis.—Puerto Rican nationalist Oscar Collazo wounded at the base of the steps to Blair House, November 1, 1950, photograph by Harvey Georges. AP/Wide World Photos.—Raiyshi, Reem, photograph by Hamas Ho/AP/Wide World Photos.—Reid, Richard Colvin, photograph by Elise Amendola. AP/Wide World Photos.—Remains of severely burned bodies of U.S. Marines amidst the wreckage of U.S. aircraft, failed attempt to rescue hostages, April 24, 1980, photograph. AP/Wide World Photos.—Rescue workers looking for remains from a Bologna blast site, 1980, photograph. AP/Wide World Photos.—Rescue workers covering bodies by a bomb blast on passenger train, Madrid, Spain, March 11, 2004, photograph. AP/Wide World Photos.—Rescue workers pulling injured man from ruins of a neighboring building after a powerful blast detonated next to the U.S. Embassy in Nairobi, Kenya, 1998, photograph. Ken Karuga/AP Wide World Photos.—Rescue workers sifting through rubble of the U.S. Marine base in Beirut, Lebanon, October 23, 1983, photograph. AP/Wide World Photos.—Rescue workers sorting through the rubble at the bombed Alfred P. Murrah Federal Building, April 24, 1995, photograph. AP/Wide World Photos.—Reward flyer offering up to $2.5 million for information leading to the arrest and conviction of the individuals responsible for mailing anthrax-tainted letters in 2001 to members of congress and the media, photograph. AP/Wide World Photos.—Ricin, found in letter addressed to the Transportation Department discovered at a U.S. Postal facility in Greenville, S.C., October, 2003, photograph. AP/ Wide World Photos.—Royal Ulster Constabulary police officers and firefighters inspecting the damage caused by a bomb explosion in Market Street, Northern Ireland, August 15, 1998, photograph by Paul McErlane. AP/Wide World Photos.—RPG-7 Russian grenades seen with a "Contra" pamphlet that reads "Commandos," photograph by Oscar Navarrete. AP/Wide World Photos.—Rudolph, Eric, led into a federal courthouse, June 22, 2004, Huntsville, Alabama, photograph by Haraz Ghanbari. AP/Wide World Photos.—Russian sailors watching as crewmen of the Japanese Maritime Safety Agency cutter Tsugaru haul a crate of wreckage to their vessel at Nevelsk, September 26, 1983, photograph by Neal Ulevich. AP/Wide World Photos.—Sadat, Anwar, shot by a gunman wearing an Egyptian uniform, 1981, photograph. AP/Wide World Photos.—Salt Lake City police officers at the Salt Lake Ice Center in 2002, photograph by Amy Sancetta. AP/Wide World Photos.—Sanchez, Ilich Ramirez, photograph. AP/Wide World Photos.—Senior researcher at the Centers for Disease Control (CDC), photograph. AP/Wide World Photos.—Shifa Pharmaceutical factory, Khartoum, Sudan, photograph. AP/ Wide World Photos.—Shiite Moslem hijacker pointing his pistol toward an ABC news media crew at Beirut International Airport, Lebanon, June 19, 1985, photograph by Herve Merliac. AP/Wide World Photos.—Shiite Muslim Sheikhs addressing supporters of the Radical Hezbollah outside the bombed U.S. Embassy in West Beirut, Lebanon, 1986, photograph. AP/Wide World Photos.—Soldiers patrolling the crumbling remains of a school in Beslan, Russia, photograph. © Antoine Gyori/AGP/Corbis.—Spanish fireman extinguishing flames from a car, Madrid, January 21, 2000, photograph by Dani Duch/La Vanguardia. AP/Wide World Photos.—Subway passengers affected by Sarin gas planted in central Tokyo subways, photograph by Chikumo Chiaki Tsukumo. © AP/Wide World Photos.—Suspected Taliban and al-Qaida detainees sitting in a holding area at Camp X-Ray at Guantanamo Bay, Cuba, January 11, 2002, photograph. AP/Wide World Photos.—Taliban fighter, talks on a radio near the front-line of Jalrez, Afghanistan, June 1, 1997, photograph by Zaheerudding Abdullah. AP/Wide World Photos.—Taliban fighters at Aryana square in Kabul where the bodies of former Afghanistan President Najibullah, and his brother Shahpur Ahmedzai, hang from a traffic post, September 27, 1996, photograph by B. K. Bangash. AP/Wide World Photos.—Tamil man garlands the portraits of Black Tigers, Jaffna, Sri Lanka, July 5, 2004, photograph by Gemunu Amaras. AP/Wide World Photos.—"The 9/11 Commission Report," cover, photograph by Ric Francis. AP/Wide World Photos.—U.S. Army military police leading a Taliban detainee through fenced enclosure at Camp X-Ray at the U.S. Naval base in Guantanamo, Cuba, 2002, photograph. AP/Wide World Photos.—U.S. Army soldiers struggling to reach injured woman caught in the crossfire, Iraq, photograph. AP/Wide World Photos.—U.S. ballistics investigator looking for clues at the burned-out wreckage of the U.S. Embassy in Tanzania, August 8, 1998, photograph by Brennan Linsley. AP/Wide World Photos.—U.S. diplomat William Buckley's kidnappers distributing his picture to newspapers throughout Lebabon, October, 1985, photograph. AP/Wide World Photos.—U.S. Marines and an Italian soldier, digging through the debris at the Battalion headquarters in Beirut, Lebanon, in 1983, after a suicide car bomb attack, photograph. Bill Foley/AP Wide World Photos.—U.S. Marines guarding the wrecked U.S. Embassy annex in Aukar, September 22, 1984, photograph. AP/Wide World Photos.—U.S. soldier reaching for the body of a fellow Marine amid the rubble of the blasted command center of the U.S. contingent of the multinational force near Beirut airport on Oct. 23, 1983, Lebanon, photograph. AP/Wide World Photos.—Undated photo found in the burned-out ruins of the house in south-central Los Angeles, photograph. AP/Wide World Photos.—United Airlines flight 175 crashing into the South Tower of the World Trade Center in New York City during terrorist attacks on September 11, 2001, photograph. © Rob Howard/Corbis.—United States Navy and Marine Corps security personnel patroling past the damaged destroyer USS Cole, Aden, Yemen, photograph. © AFP/Corbis.—USS Cole, pulled out of Aden port by Yemeni tugboats, photograph by Hasan Jamali. AP/Wide World Photos.—Very light air traffic shown at 11:30 a.m. on September 11, 2001, in this image by the Federal Aviation Administration, photograph. AP/Wide World Photos.—Victims treated at the scene of a car bomb explosion in Market Street, Northern Ireland, August 15, 1998. AP/Wide World Photos.—Warner, Paul, U.S. attorney, holding a news conference Tuesday, Salt Lake City, Utah, September 28, 2004, photograph by Douglas C. Pizac. AP/Wide World Photos.—Warsame, Maryam, 5, watching as her mother, Fartun Farah, wipes away a tear during a news conference at the Somali Justice Advocacy Center, St. Paul, Minnesota, Friday, Dec. 11, 2003, photograph. AP/Wide World Photos.—White, Mary Jo, U.S. Attorney, and Lewis

Schiliro, assistant director in charge of the FBI's New York office, announcing the indictments of Osama Bin Laden, and Muhammad Atef for the 1998 U.S. Embassy bombings, photograph by Marty Lederhandler. AP/Wide World Photos.—Workers standing beside crater, June 26, 1996 after a truck bomb explosion at a U.S. military facility in Dhahran, Saudi Arabia, photograph by U.S. Navy. AP/Wide World Photos.—Wreckage of a Ford Sierra at the scene of a nail-bomb explosion in Brick Lane, east London, April 24, 1999, photograph by Toby Melville. AP/Wide World Photos.—Wrecked houses and a deep gash in the ground in the village of Lockerbie, Scotland, photograph by Martin Cleaver. AP/Wide World Photos.—Yemeni pilot boat carrying investigators from Yemen, France, and the United States, watching as Dutch divers gather evidence, Yemen, October, 2002, photograph. AP/Wide World Photos.—Yongbyon nuclear facility in North Korea, 2002, satellite image. AP/Wide World Photos.

About the Set

Essential Primary Source titles are part of a ten-volume set of books in the Social Issues Primary Sources Collection designed to provide primary source documents on leading social issues of the nineteenth, twentieth, and twenty-first centuries. International in scope, each volume is devoted to one topic and will contain approximately 160 to 175 documents that will include and discuss speeches, legislation, magazine and newspaper articles, memoirs, letters, interviews, novels, essays, songs, and works of art essential to understanding the complexity of the topic.

Each entry will include standard subheads: key facts about the author; an introduction placing the piece in context; the full or excerpted document; a discussion of the significance of the document and related event; and a listing of further resources (books, periodicals, Web sites, and audio and visual media).

Each volume will contain a topic specific introduction, topic-specific chronology of major events, an index especially prepared to coordinate with the volume topic, and approximately 150 images.

Volumes are intended to be sold individually or as a set.

THE ESSENTIAL PRIMARY SOURCE SERIES
- *Terrorism: Essential Primary Sources*
- *Medicine, Health, and Bioethics: Essential Primary Sources*
- *Environmental Issues: Essential Primary Sources*
- *Crime and Punishment: Essential Primary Sources*
- *Gender Issues and Sexuality: Essential Primary Sources*
- *Human and Civil Rights: Essential Primary Sources*
- *Government, Politics, and Protest: Essential Primary Sources*
- *Social Policy: Essential Primary Sources*
- *Immigration and Multiculturalism: Essential Primary Sources*
- *Family in Society: Essential Primary Sources*

Introduction

Terrorism: Essential Primary Sources provides insight into the scale and complexities of terrorism across a sweeping landscape of time, geography, act, and motive.

Despite the suffering inflicted on the innocent, it is an unarguable political reality that what constitutes terrorism is often contentious and heavily tied to cultural perspective. A suicide bomber labeled as a terrorist by one society may be referred to as a martyr in the news reports designed for more politically sympathetic audiences.

Groups and governments often resort to tortured language and labels as they attempt to either justify or dissociate themselves from often-horrific acts of violence. Moreover, as documents of early Nazi propaganda demonstrate, the label of terrorist is also used as propaganda to stir hatred against ideas, causes, or peoples.

Terrorism: Essential Primary Sources adopts the fundamental view that terrorism refers to an attempt to achieve a goal by violent or destructive acts intended to induce change through fear. The motives of terrorism are as diverse as the acts themselves and cover a range of religious, social, economic, and political passions.

As with the case of the Unabomber, the seed of terrorist acts may exist solely in the mind of an individual, or as in the case of al-Qaeda, may germinate into far-flung cells that operate globally. Although many definitions of terrorism restrict the label to sub-national groups, governments may water the seeds of terrorism with money or, as in the case of the former Taliban regime in Afghanistan, allow it to grow in fertile soil.

The roots of terrorism can also be buried in the history of countries now considered flowers of Western democracy. The term terrorism comes from the French *terrorisme* (in or under the Terror of the French Revolution), and finds ancient philosophical and linguistic origin in the Latin verbs *terrere* (to make one tremble) and *deterrere* (to frighten one from).

Terrorism as a tactic of revolutionaries is not a new phenomenon practiced only in distant and dusty lands. A description of a brutal tarring and feathering of a loyalist man by colonial revolutionaries provides evidence that America's own founding insurrectionists used physical intimidation against British noncombatant loyalists. Ironically, the Boston Tea Party—a 1773 raid by colonialists on British ships in protest of high taxes, long taught as a heroic prelude to the American Revolutionary War—could easily be classified under new FBI guidelines as an act of terrorism.

Terrorism is also a tool of economic repression. The excerpt from Ida B. Wells's 1892 "Southern Horrors" pamphlet provides evidence that nineteenth-century lynching of African-Americans was not the exclusive product of Klu Klux Klan hatred, but was also inflicted to preserve established economic interests. Evidence of similar motive is also provided for later terrorist attacks against Chinese immigrants.

Rather than attempt subjective judgment as to whether acts are those of freedom fighters, patriots, or terrorists, the editors have attempted to establish a logical basis for the selection of primary sources that independently hold conflicting views of terrorism.

As a foundation, the editors incorporate the definition of terrorism found in the United States Code as "premeditated, politically motivated violence perpetrated against noncombatant targets by subnational groups or clandestine agents, usually intended to influence an audience."

In order to allow a more culturally diverse and broader international perspective on terrorism, however, the editors also include resources devoted to terrorism deeply planted in religious or social fervor. Examples of such causes are found in resources related to anti-abortion murders and ecoterrorism.

Obviously, not all acts of terrorism or significant resources related to terrorism can be included in a single volume, nor can all viewpoints find voice. Copyright restrictions also prevented the inclusion of some desired source materials. However, the primary sources selected for inclusion in *Terrorism: Essential Primary Sources* provide a foundation for understanding the often-entangled branches of cool political calculation, cold indifference, and blinding rage that bud into brutal acts.

K. Lee Lerner & Brenda Wilmoth Lerner, editors
London, U.K.
July, 2005

About the Entry

The primary source is the centerpiece and main focus of each entry in *Terrorism: Essential Primary Sources*. In keeping with the philosophy that much of the benefit from using primary sources derives from the reader's own process of inquiry, the contextual material surrounding each entry provides access and ease of use, as well as giving the reader a springboard for delving into the primary source. Rubrics identify each section and enable the reader to navigate entries with ease.

ENTRY STRUCTURE

- Primary Source/Entry Title, Subtitle, Primary Source Type
- Key Facts—essential information about the primary source, including creator, date, source citation, and notes about the creator.
- Introduction—historical background and contributing factors for the primary source.
- Primary Source—in text, text facsimile, or image format; full or excerpted.
- Significance—importance and impact of the primary source related events.
- Further Resources—books, periodicals, websites, and audio and visual material.

NAVIGATING AN ENTRY

Entry elements are numbered and reproduced here, with an explanation of the data contained in these elements explained immediately thereafter according to the corresponding numeral.

Primary Source/Entry Title, Subtitle, Primary Source Type

---

[1] **"Easter, 1916"**

[2] Militants in the Irish Sinn Fein Party Form the Irish Republican Army (IRA)

---

[3] **Poem**

[1] **Primary Source/Entry Title:** The entry title is usually the primary source title. In some cases where long titles must be shortened, or more generalized topic titles are needed for clarity primary source titles are generally depicted as subtitles. Entry titles appear as catchwords at the top outer margin of each page.

[2] **Subtitle:** Some entries contain subtitles.

[3] **Primary Source Type:** The type of primary source is listed just below the title. When assigning source types, great weight was given to how the author of the primary source categorized the source.

Key Facts

[4] **By:** William Butler Yeats

[5] **Date:** September 25, 1916

[6] **Source:** "Easter, 1916," a poem by William Butler Yeats

[7] **About the Poet:** William Butler Yeats (1865–1939) was one of the twentieth century's most acclaimed

English-language poets. Born in Dublin, Ireland, themes of Irish rebellion and independence from England often featured prominently in his poetry.

[4] **Author, Artist, or Organization:** The name of the author, artist, or organization responsible for the creation of the primary source begins the Key Facts section.

[5] **Date of Origin:** The date of origin of the primary source appears in this field, and may differ from the date of publication in the source citation below it; for example, speeches are often delivered before they are published.

[6] **Source Citation:** The source citation is a full bibliographic citation, giving original publication data as well as reprint and/or online availability.

[7] **About the Author:** A brief bio of the author or originator of the primary source gives birth and death dates and a quick overview of the person's work. This rubric has been customized in some cases. If the primary source written document, the term "author" appears; however, if the primary source is a work of art, the term "artist" is used, showing the person's direct relationship to the primary source. For primary sources created by a group, "organization" may have been used instead of "author." Other terms may also be used to describe the creator or originator of the primary source. If an author is anonymous or unknown, a brief "About the Publication" sketch may appear.

Introduction Essay

[8] **INTRODUCTION**

On Easter Monday, April 24, 1916, as Padraig Pearse (Commander in Chief of Republican forces) read a "Proclamation of the Republic" declaring Ireland a nation separate from England, from the steps of Dublin's General Post Office, the silence of the surrounding crowd reflected the uncertainty of many Irish people. Such nationalist speeches of independence from Great Britain were not unfamiliar to Irish citizens. It would take action on behalf of the Irish Republican Brotherhood (IRB), the forerunner of the Irish Republican Army (IRA), and its political party Sinn Fein to convince the Irish people that freedom from the 750-year domination by the British was actually within their grasp.

The Proclamation's call for action was planned as the British were committing their troops to fight in Germany during World War I (1915–1918). Angered that the British were enlisting Irish men to fight in the war fueled a decision to rise up against the British. The IRB Military Council that was formed the previous year acted on the philosophy that "England's difficulty

is Ireland's opportunity." The council included seven members: Padraig Pearse (1879–1916), James Conolly (1868–1916), Joseph Mary Plunkett (1887–1916), Thomas MacDonagh (1878–1916), Eamonn Ceannt (1881–1916), Thomas J. Clarke (1857–1916), and Sean MacDermott (1884–1916), all of whom were revolutionaries who signed the Proclamation . . .

[8] **Introduction:** The introduction is a brief essay on the contributing factors and historical context of the primary source. Intended to promote understanding and equip the reader with essential facts to understand the context of the primary source.

To maintain ease of reference to the primary source, spellings of names and places are used in accord with their use in the primary source. According names and places may have different spellings in different articles. Whenever possible, alternative spellings are provided to provide clarity.

To the greatest extent possible we have attempted to use Arabic names instead of their Latinized versions. Where required for clarity we have included Latinized names in parentheses after the Arabic version. Alas, we could not retain some diacritical marks (e.g. bars over vowels, dots under consonants). Because there is no generally accepted rule or consensus regarding the format of translated Arabic names, we have adopted the straightforward, and we hope sensitive, policy of using names as they are used or cited in their region of origin.

Primary Source

[9] **PRIMARY SOURCE**

Easter, 1916
I have met them at close of day
Coming with vivid faces
From counter or desk among grey
Eighteenth-century houses.
I have passed with a nod of the head
Or polite meaningless words,
Or have lingered awhile and said
Polite meaningless words,
And thought before I had done
Of a mocking tale or a gibe
To please a companion
Around the fire at the club,
Being certain that they and I
But lived where motley is worn:
All changed, changed utterly:
A terrible beauty is born.

That woman's days were spent
In ignorant good-will,

Her nights in argument
Until her voice grew shrill.
What voice more sweet than hers
When, young and beautiful,
She rode to harriers?
This man had kept a school
And rode our winged horse;
This other his helper and friend
Was coming into his force;
He might have won fame in the end,
So sensitive his nature seemed,
So daring and sweet his thought.
This other man I had dreamed
A drunken, vainglorious lout.
He had done most bitter wrong
To some who are near my heart,
Yet I number him in the song;
He, too, has resigned his part
In the casual comedy;
He, too, has been changed in his turn,
Transformed utterly:
A terrible beauty is born.

Hearts with one purpose alone
Through summer and winter seem
Enchanted to a stone
To trouble the living stream.
The horse that comes from the road.
The rider, the birds that range
From cloud to tumbling cloud,
Minute by minute they change;
A shadow of cloud on the stream
Changes minute by minute;
A horse-hoof slides on the brim,
And a horse plashes within it;
The long-legged moor-hens dive,
And hens to moor-cocks call;
Minute by minute they live:
The stone's in the midst of all.

Too long a sacrifice
Can make a stone of the heart.
O when may it suffice?
That is Heaven's part, our part
To murmur name upon name,
As a mother names her child
When sleep at last has come
On limbs that had run wild.
What is it but nightfall?
No, no, not night but death;
Was it needless death after all?
For England may keep faith
For all that is done and said.
We know their dream; enough
To know they dreamed and are dead;
And what if excess of love
Bewildered them till they died?
I write it out in a verse -
MacDonagh and MacBride
And Connolly and Pearse

Now and in time to be,
Wherever green is worn,
Are changed, changed utterly:
A terrible beauty is born.

---

[9] **Primary Source:** The majority of primary sources are reproduced as plain text. The primary source may appear excerpted or in full, and may appear as text, text facsimile (photographic reproduction of the original text), image, or graphic display (such as a table, chart, or graph).

The font and leading of the primary sources are distinct from that of the context—to provide a visual clue to the change, as well as to facilitate ease of reading. As needed, the original formatting of the text is preserved in order to more accurately represent the original (screenplays, for example). In order to respect the integrity of the primary sources, content some readers may consider sensitive (for example, the use of slang, ethnic or racial slurs, etc.) is retained when deemed to be integral to understanding the source and the context of its creation.

Primary source images (whether photographs, text facsimiles, or graphic displays) are bordered with a distinctive double rule. Most images have brief captions.

The term "narrative break" appears where there is a significant amount of elided (omitted) material with the text provided (for example, excerpts from a work's first and fifth chapters, selections from a journal article abstract and summary, or dialogue from two acts of a play).

Significance Essay

[10] **SIGNIFICANCE**

William Butler Yeats' description "A terrible beauty is born" illustrates the violence of Ireland's fight for independence as well as the "beauty" of the prospect of independence from Great Britain. "Easter 1916" captures the monumental change in the Irish collaboration towards home rule for what is now the Republic of Ireland.

Fifteen of the Uprising participants were sentenced to death by firing squad, and the harsh sentences roused the Irish people. Connolly was taken from his deathbed to be strapped in a chair and shot, fueling anti-British sentiment throughout the streets of Dublin and echoing throughout Ireland. The Sinn Fein ("we ourselves") Party that had no seats in Britain's parliament in 1910 would hold 70% of the seats allotted to Ireland in the British Parliament after the elections of 1918 . . .

[10] Significance: The significance discusses the importance and impact of the primary source and the event it describes.

Further Resources

[11] FURTHER RESOURCES
Books
Yeats, William Butler. *Easter, 1916 and Other Poems.* Mineola, N.Y.: Dover, 1997.

Web sites
About.com. "History of Terrorism in Ireland." <http://terrorism.about.com/od/historyofterrorism/a/ireland.htm> (accessed July 16, 2005).

Ireland's Own.net. "Irish History: Easter 1916." <http://irelandsown.net/easterrising.html> (accessed July 16, 2005).

Political Information Net. "Sinn Féin." <http://www.politicalinformation.net/encyclopedia/Sinn_Fein.htm> (accessed July 16, 2005).

Roots Web. "Easter Rising 1916." <http://www.rootsweb.com/~fianna/history/east1916.html> (accessed July 16, 2005).

Wellington College Belfast GCSE History. "Irish Political Developments From 1916–1972." <http://websites.ntl.com/~wellclge/depts/history/module1/ni20_72.htm> (accessed July 16, 2005).

[11] Further Resources: A brief list of resources categorized as Books, Periodicals, Web sites, and Audio and Visual Media provides a stepping stone to further study.

SECONDARY SOURCE CITATION FORMATS (HOW TO CITE ARTICLES AND SOURCES)

Alternative forms of citations exist and examples of how to cite articles from this book are provided below:

APA Style

Books:
Creelman, James. (1901). *On the Great Highway: The Wanderings and Adventures of a Special Correspondent,* Boston: Lothrup. Excerpted in K. Lee Lerner and Brenda Wilmoth Lerner, eds. (2006) *Terrorism: Essential Primary Sources,* Farmington Hills, MI: Thomson Gale, 75.

Periodicals:
Ember, Lois R. (1996, November 4). FBI Takes Lead in Developing Counterterrorism Effort. *Chemical & Engineering News,* vol. 74, no. 27. Excerpted in K. Lee Lerner and Brenda Wilmoth Lerner, eds. (2006) *Terrorism: Essential Primary Sources,* Farmington Hills, MI: Thomson Gale, 75.

Web sites:
U.S. Department of State. (2002, June 27) The G-8 Global Partnership Against the Spread of Weapons and Materials of Mass Destruction. Retrieved July, 10, 2005, from http://www.state.gov/e/eb/rls/othr/11514.htm. Excerpted in K. Lee Lerner and Brenda Wilmoth Lerner, eds. (2006) *Terrorism: Essential Primary Sources,* Farmington Hills, MI: Thomson Gale, 75.

Chicago Style

Books:
Creelman, James. *On the Great Highway: The Wanderings and Adventures of a Special Correspondent.* Boston: Lothrup, 1901. Excerpted in K. Lee Lerner and Brenda Wilmoth Lerner, eds., *Terrorism: Essential Primary Sources,* Farmington Hills, MI: Thomson Gale, 2006, 75.

Periodicals:
Ember, Lois R., "FBI Takes Lead in Developing Counterterrorism Effort." *Chemical & Engineering News,* November 4, 1996, vol. 74, no. 27. Excerpted in K. Lee Lerner and Brenda Wilmoth Lerner, eds., *Terrorism: Essential Primary Sources,* Farmington Hills, MI: Thomson Gale, 2006, 75.

Web sites:
U.S. Department of State. "The G-8 Global Partnership Against the Spread of Weapons and Materials of Mass Destruction" June 27, 2002. <http://www.state.gov/e/eb/rls/othr/11514.htm> (accessed July 10, 2005). Excerpted in K. Lee Lerner and Brenda Wilmoth Lerner, eds., *Terrorism: Essential Primary Sources,* Farmington Hills, MI: Thomson Gale, 2006, 75.

MLA Style

Books:
Creelman, James. *On the Great Highway: The Wanderings and Adventures of a Special Correspondent,* Boston: Lothrup, 1901. Excerpted in K. Lee Lerner and Brenda Wilmoth Lerner, eds., *Terrorism: Essential Primary Sources,* Farmington Hills, MI: Thomson Gale, 2006, 75.

Periodicals:
Ember, Lois R. "FBI Takes Lead in Developing Counterterrorism Effort." Chemical & Engineering News, 4 November 1996, vol. 74 no. 27. Excerpted in K. Lee Lerner and Brenda Wilmoth Lerner, eds., *Terrorism: Essential Primary Sources,* Farmington Hills, MI: Thomson Gale, 2006, 75.

Web sites:
"The G-8 Global Partnership Against the Spread of Weapons and Materials of Mass Destruction." U.S. Department of State. 4 November 1996. 5 July 2005 <http://www.state.gov/e/eb/rls/othr/11514.htm>. Excerpted in K. Lee Lerner and Brenda Wilmoth Lerner, eds., *Terrorism: Essential Primary Sources,* Farmington Hills, MI: Thomson Gale, 2006, 75.

Turabian Style

Books:

Creelman, James. *On the Great Highway: The Wanderings and Adventures of a Special Correspondent.* Boston: Lothrup, 1901. Excerpted in K. Lee Lerner and Brenda Wilmoth Lerner, eds., *Terrorism: Essential Primary Sources* (Farmington Hills, MI: Thomson Gale, 2006), 75.

Periodicals:

Ember, Lois R. "FBI Takes Lead in Developing Counterterrorism Effort." *Chemical & Engineering News,* 4 November 1996, vol.74, no. 27. Excerpted in K. Lee Lerner and Brenda Wilmoth Lerner, eds., *Terrorism: Essential Primary Sources* (Farmington Hills, MI: Thomson Gale, 2006), 75.

Web sites:

U.S. Department of State. "The G-8 Global Partnership Against the Spread of Weapons and Materials of Mass Destruction" available from http://www.state.gov/e/eb/rls/othr/11514.htm; accessed 10 July, 2005. Excerpted in K. Lee Lerner and Brenda Wilmoth Lerner, eds., *Terrorism: Essential Primary Sources* (Farmington Hills, MI: Thomson Gale, 2006), 75.

Using Primary Sources

The definition of what constitutes a primary source is often the subject of scholarly debate and interpretation. Although primary sources come from a wide spectrum of resources, they are united by the fact that they individually provide insight into the historical *milieu* (context and environment) during which they were produced. Primary sources include materials such as newspaper articles, press dispatches, autobiographies, essays, letters, diaries, speeches, song lyrics, posters, works of art—and in the twenty-first century, web logs—that offer direct, first-hand insight or witness to events of their day.

Categories of primary sources include:

- Documents containing firsthand accounts of historic events by witnesses and participants. This category includes diary or journal entries, letters, email, newspaper articles, interviews, memoirs, and testimony in legal proceedings.
- Documents or works representing the official views of both government leaders and leaders of terrorist organizations. These include primary sources such as policy statements, speeches, interviews, press releases, government reports, and legislation.
- Works of art, including (but certainly not limited to) photographs, poems, and songs, including advertisements and reviews of those works that help establish an understanding of the cultural milieu (the cultural environment with regard to attitudes and perceptions of events).
- Secondary sources. In some cases, secondary sources or tertiary sources may be treated as primary sources. For example, the 9/11 Commission report on the September 11, 2001 terrorist attacks on the United States contains a mixture of primary and secondary sources. Many historians argue that

the document should rightly be considered a primary source because it is a government report. However, the report also clearly contains retrospective analysis (analysis of past events) and comments on events far removed from the time of the subject event. In many cases, such material by itself would not be considered as primary source material. However, if such work contains first hand accounts of events—or material written or created near the time of the underlying event—most historians would agree that such material can be considered as primary source material.

ANALYSIS OF PRIMARY SOURCES

The material collected in this volume is not intended to provide a comprehensive overview of a topic or event. Rather, the primary sources are intended to generate interest and lay a foundation for further inquiry and study.

In order to properly analyze a primary source, readers should remain skeptical and develop probing questions about the source. As in reading a chemistry or algebra textbook, historical documents require readers to analyze them carefully and extract specific information. However, readers must also read "beyond the text" to garner larger clues about the social impact of the primary source.

In addition to providing information about their topics, primary sources may also supply a wealth of insight into their creator's viewpoint. For example, when reading a news article on a terrorist attack, consider whether the reporter's words also indicate something about his or her origin, bias (an irrational disposition in favor of someone or something), prejudices (an irrational disposition against someone or something), or intended audience.

Students should remember that primary sources often contain information later proven to be false, or contain viewpoints and terms unacceptable to future generations. It is important to view the primary source within the historical and social context existing at its creation. If for example, a newspaper article is written within hours or days of an event, later developments may reveal some assertions in the original article as false or misleading.

For example, in the newspaper article about the 2004 terrorist bombing of trains in Madrid, Spain—included herein and titled, "Investigators See ETA, not al-Qaeda (spelled al-Qaida in the primary source), behind Madrid Blasts"—the following assertions and quotes were made soon after the attack:

- " . . . Spanish officials remained adamant Friday that they believe that the Basque separatist group ETA, not the al-Qaeda terrorist network, was behind the morning rush-hour train bombings that rocked this capital city Thursday."
- " . . . the dynamite chemically matched 1,100 pounds of explosives seized in February from an ETA van heading toward Madrid, and that the satchel and cell phone setup matched that found on two ETA members when they were arrested at a northern Madrid commuter rail station on Christmas Eve."
- "This explosion had a very similar modus operandi used by the terrorist group ETA . . . "
- "Interior Minister Acebes was adamant that the evidence pointed to ETA. He noted that ETA has a history of creating havoc in the days before a national election."
- "He (Acebes) also said the explosives used—Goma II Eco—were made in Spain and that ETA had used the same brand in previous attacks."
- " . . . American intelligence agencies had detected no spike in 'chatter' among al-Qaeda-related groups before the attacks."
- "Other U.S. officials stressed that the group that claimed responsibility for the bombings, the Abu Hafs al Masri Brigades, is thought to exist in name only and has made implausible claims of responsibility before."

Despite the fact that ETA spokesmen denied involvement, the article clearly lays out strong evidence that suggests ETA responsibility. The issue was important because if al-Qaeda (also spelled al-Qaida) was responsible instead of ETA, it was argued that the more conservative Spanish political politicians who supported Spain's involvement as a coalition partner in the U.S. led war in Iraq would receive a boost in upcoming elections. The article even casts evidence against ETA involvement in this context:

- "Listen, ETA has never done a bombing like this without calling and warning the government beforehand," said Olga Gonzalez, a 32-year-old secretary. "Ninety percent of Spaniards were against the war in Iraq. If al-Qaida is involved and not ETA, this changes everything for the elections."

However, despite the Spanish Interior Minister Acebes being "adamant that the evidence pointed to ETA and his quote that "at this point there is mounting evidence that this was not the work of al-Qaida", evidence in the form of documents and tapes found soon thereafter made it clear that a group called the Moroccan Islamic Combatant Group, part of the al-Qaeda network, was responsible for the blasts.

The analytical reader will ask, "Why was the article wrong? Did it present best evidence known at the time, or were the errors a result of "slant" or motive to blame the incident on ETA instead of al-Qaeda? What was at stake? Who could have benefited from such deception?

TEST NEW CONCLUSIONS AND IDEAS

Whatever opinion or working hypothesis the reader forms, it is critical that they then test that hypothesis against other facts and sources related to the incident. For example, it might be wrong to conclude that factual mistakes are deliberate unless evidence can be produced of a pattern and practice of such mistakes with an intent to promote a false idea.

The difference between sound reasoning and preposterous conspiracy theories (or the birth of urban legends) lies in the willingness to test new ideas against other sources, rather than rest on one piece of evidence such as a single primary source that may contain errors. Sound reasoning requires that arguments and assertions guard against argument fallacies that utilize the following:

- false dilemmas (only two choices are given when in fact there are three or more options)
- arguments from ignorance (*argumentum ad ignorantiam*; because something is not known to be true, it is assumed to be false)
- possibilist fallacies (a favorite among conspiracy theorists who attempt to demonstrate that a factual statement is true or false by establishing the possibility of its truth or falsity. An argument where "it could be" is usually followed by an unearned "therefore, it is.")

- slippery slope arguments or fallacies (a series of increasingly dramatic consequences is drawn from an initial fact or idea)
- begging the question (the truth of the conclusion is assumed by the premises)
- straw man arguments (the arguer mischaracterizes an argument or theory and then attacks the merits of their own false representations)
- appeals to pity or force (the argument attempts to persuade people to agree by sympathy or force)
- prejudicial language (values or moral goodness good and bad are attached to certain arguments or facts)
- personal attacks (*ad hominem*; an attack on a person's character or circumstances);

- anecdotal or testimonial evidence (stories that are unsupported by impartial or unreproducable data)
- *post hoc* (after the fact) fallacies (because one thing follows another, it is held to cause the other)
- the fallacy of the appeal to authority (the argument rests upon the credentials of a person, not the evidence).

Despite the fact that primary sources can contain false information or lead readers to false conclusions based on the "facts" presented, they remain an invaluable resource regarding past events. Primary sources allow readers and researchers to come as close as possible to understanding the perceptions and context of events and thus, to more fully appreciate how and why misconceptions occur.

Chronology

During the French Revolution (1789–1799), Robespierre's informant networks denounced traitors to the new republic, and tracked down refugee aristocrats and clergy for trial and execution. The wide application of treason laws and charges (known as "the terror") gives rise to the modern use of the term terrorism.

1800–1849

c.1800: Colonial rulers and powers employ secret police and agents of espionage throughout their territorial holdings, hoping to quell anti-colonial rebellions and separatist movements.

1823: Monroe Doctrine declares Western Hemisphere a U.S. "sphere of influence".

1839: First Opium War begins between Britain and China. The conflict lasts until 1842. Imperial Chinese commissioner Lin Tse-Hsu seizes or destroys vast amounts of opium, including stocks owned by British traders. The result was a Chinese payment of an indemnity of more than twenty-one million silver dollars and Hong Kong being ceded to Britain under the Treaty of Nanking.

1845: Christian Friedrich Schönbein (1799–1868), German-Swiss chemist, prepares guncotton. He discovers that a certain acid mixture combines with the cellulose in cotton to produce an explosive that burns without smoke or residue.

1846: Ascanio Sobrero (1812–1888), Italian chemist, slowly adds glycerin to a mixture of nitric and sulfuric acids and first produces nitroglycerine. He is so impressed by the explosive potential of a single drop in a heated test tube and so fearful of its use in war that he makes no attempt to exploit it. It is another twenty years before Alfred Bernhard Nobel learns the proper formula and puts it to use.

1848: Unites States Congress passes Drug Importation Act that allows United States Customs Service inspection to stop entry of foreign drugs.

1850–1899

1856: Second Opium War begins between Britain and China. The conflict lasts until 1860. Also known as the Arrow War, or the Anglo-French War in China, the war broke out after a British-flagged ship, the *Arrow*, is impounded by China. France joins Britain in the war after the murder of a French missionary. China is again defeated, resulting in another large indemnity and the legalization of opium under the Treaty of Tientsin.

1858: A group of the Irish Republican Brotherhood (IRB), forms another revolutionary group, the Fenian Brotherhood with the goal of freeing Ireland from British rule.

1861: U.S. Civil War (1861–1865).

1861: President-elect Lincoln arrives secretly in Washington to foil assassination plot brewing in Baltimore.

1864: First Geneva Convention addresses "the amelioration of the condition of the wounded on the field of battle," resulting in principles for protecting noncombatant personnel caring for the wounded. The Convention also establishes the International Red Cross.

1865: President Abraham Lincoln is shot in Washington, D.C., by John Wilkes Booth. Lincoln dies the next day; Andrew Johnson assumes the Presidency.

1865: Molly Maguires, a secret society of Irish miners, attacked coal-mine operators and owners for mistreatment of workers.

1867: Alfred Bernhard Nobel (1833–1896), Swedish inventor, invents dynamite, a safer and more controllable version of nitroglycerine. He combines nitroglycerine with "kieselguhr," or earth containing silica, and discovers that it could not be exploded without a detonating cap.

1870: Lambert Adolphe Jacques Quetelet showes the importance of statistical analysis for biologists and provides the foundations of biometry.

1870: Congress creates Department of Justice.

1876: Robert Koch publishes a paper on anthrax that implicates a bacterium as the cause of the disease, validating the germ theory of disease.

1877: Congress passes legislation prohibiting the counterfeiting of any coin, gold, or silver bar.

1878: Charles–Emanuel Sedillot introduces the term "microbe." The term becomes widely used as a term for a pathogenic bacterium.

1878: In a backlash against twelve years of martial law in the southern United States, Congress passes the Posse Comitatus Act, which forbids the military from enforcing domestic law.

1881: President James A. Garfield is shot on July 2, 1881, in Washington, DC, by anarchist Charles J. Guiteau. Garfield dies September 19, 1881; Chester A. Arthur assumes the Presidency.

1883: Hiram S. Maxim invents the machine gun.

1894: U.S. Secret Service begins part-time protection of U.S. President Grover Cleveland.

1898: Spanish-American War.

1899: First Hague Conference establishes international laws of conduct in warfare.

1900–1949

1901: President William McKinley is assassinated by anarchist Leon Czolgosz.

1901: U.S. acquires rights from Cuba to use Guantanamo Bay indefinitely as a naval base.

1901: Henry Classification System was devised for fingerprint analysis by Sir Edward Henry.

1904: Roosevelt Corollary to the Monroe Doctrine asserts that the United States has the right to assume the defacto role of an international police power.

1905: Bloody Sunday incident in Russia. Czarist troops fire on marchers in St. Petersburg.

1905: Sinn Fein political movement for Irish independence is founded.

1907: Second Hague Conference establishes further international laws of conduct in warfare, with a focus on war in a maritime environment.

1908: Large deposits of petroleum are discovered in Middle East.

1908: Formal beginning of the Bureau of Investigation (BOI) that became the FBI in 1935.

1912: U.S. Marines invade Honduras, Cuba, and Nicaragua to protect American interests. U.S. troops will remain in Nicaragua until 1930s.

1912: Theodore Roosevelt (ex-president of U.S.) escapes assassination, although shot on October 14, 1912, in Milwaukee while campaigning for president.

1913: U.S. troops assist in pursuit of Mexican rebel leader Francisco Pancho Villa in Northern Mexico.

1914: The assassination of Austrian Archduke Francis (Franz) Ferdinand precipitates start of World War I.

1915: Germany uses poison gas at the Battle of Ypres.

1915: A U-boat sinks the passenger ship S.S. Lusitania, a passenger ship also carrying military supplies for Britain.

1916: The Black Tom explosion was the peak act of German sabotage on American soil during the First World War. On July 29, 1916, German agents set fire to a complex of warehouses and ships in the New York harbor that held munitions, fuel, and explosives bound to aid the Allies in their fight. Though America was technically a neutral nation at the time of the attack, their general policies greatly favored the Allies. The attack persuaded many that the United States should join the Allies and intervene in the war in Europe.

1916: The Home Section of the British Secret Service Bureau becomes MI5, or the Security Service.

1916: Mexican guerrilla leader Pancho Villa conducts a raid on Columbus, New Mexico, killing seventeen Americans.

1917: British issue declaration calling for a Jewish homeland in Palestine.

1917: Tsarist Russia's February Revolution (based upon the calendar used in Russia at the time, but March in the West) began with rioting and strikes in

St. Petersburg. Alexander Kerensky ultimately assumes control of democratic socialist Provisional government, exposes undercover agents of the Okhrana.

1917: U.S. declares war on Germany.

1917: The U.S. Army creates the Cipher Bureau within the Military Intelligence Division.

1917: United States Congress passes the Espionage Act, criminalizing the disclosure of military, industrial, or government secrets related to national security. The act also prohibits anti-war activism and refusal of conscription, sparking controversy.

1917: V.I. Lenin returns from exile to Russia following Romanov abdication of the Russian throne. Lenin leads a Bolshevik revolution in November.

1918: Bolsheviks execute former Czar and his family.

1918: Germany's Kaiser Wilhelm II abdicates and World War I ends in Europe after twenty million casualties and six million deaths.

1918: Sedition Act of 1918 amends Espionage and Sedition Acts to broaden the arrest powers granted to federal agents in apprehending and detaining individuals suspected of treason or antiwar activity.

1918: An influenza epidemic spreads across Asia and war-ravaged Europe to the Americas. The epidemic eventually kills twenty million people, including 500,000 Americans.

1919: U.S. fears increased after anarchist groups targeted several government and business leaders with bombs in April and May of 1919, a terrorist wave culminates in a series of bombings in eight American cities on June 2, 1919. Under the orders of Attorney General A. Mitchell Palmer, federal agents begin round up of suspected communists and anarchists in November 1919. The Palmer Raids, as they became known, last until March, 1920, and result in the arrest of 6,000 suspects.

1919: Anarchists Emma Goldman and Alexander Berkman are deported by the U.S. to Russia.

1920: Bolshevist or anarchist terrorists are accused of September 16 bombing on Wall Street in New York City that kills thirty-five people and injures hundreds more.

1920: Iraq is placed under British mandate.

1921: Except for six counties in Protestant Northern Ireland, the British Parliament grants Ireland dominion status.

1922: Militants in the Irish Sinn Fein party form the Irish Republican Army (IRA).

1923: Union of Soviet Socialist Republics (USSR) formed.

1923: Adolf Hitler, leader of the German Nazi party, attempts to seize power. Hitler is arrested and sentenced to prison.

1924: Lenin dies, to be succeeded by a triumvirate of leaders headed by Joseph Stalin.

1924: From prison, Adolf Hitler publishes *Mein Kampf*, in which he outlines the plan for conquest in eastern Europe, and the extermination of the Jews, that he will undertake as German leader less than a decade later.

1924: BOI establishes an Identification Division after Congress authorized "the exchange of identification records with officers of the cities, counties, and states . . . "

1926: U.S. forces intervene in Nicaragua against leftist nationalist insurgency led by Augusto Cesar Sandino.

1927: Chiang Kai-Shek defeats Communist Mao Zedong's "Autumn Harvest" rebellion.

1928: Sixty-two nations sign the Kellogg-Briand Pact (including the U.S, Great Britain, Japan, and Italy) and renounce war as a means to solve international disputes.

1929: Kingdom of Serbs, Croats, and Slovenes becomes Yugoslavia.

1929: Scottish biochemist Alexander Fleming (1881–1955) discovers penicillin. He observes that the mold *Penicillium notatum* inhibits the growth of some bacteria. This is the first antibiotic, and it opens a new era of "wonder drugs" to combat infection and disease.

1929: U.S. stock market crash in October ushers in Great Depression.

1930: U.S. Treasury Department creates Bureau of Narcotics, which will remain the principal anti-drug agency of the federal government until the late 1960s.

1930: Primitive anthrax vaccine developed.

1932: The Bureau of Investigation starts the international exchange of fingerprint data with friendly foreign governments. Halted as war approached the program was not re-instituted until after World War II.

1932: In response to the Lindbergh kidnapping case and other high profile cases Federal Kidnapping Act is passed to authorize BOI to investigate kidnappings perpetrated across state borders.

1932: Iraq declared an independent state.

1933: In January, Adolf Hitler and Nazi Party take power in Germany. By the end of the year, Hitler proclaims Third Reich.

1933: Franklin D. Roosevelt, the President-elect of United States, escapes assassination attempt in Miami.

1935: German Nazi party formalizes anti-Semitism with passage of Nuremberg laws.

1935: In violation of the Versailles Treaty, Germany begins to rearm and reconstitutes the German Air Force (Luftwaffe).

1935: Federal Bureau of Narcotics, forerunner of the modern Drug Enforcement Administration (DEA), began a campaign that portrayed marijuana as a drug that led users to drug addiction, violence, and insanity. The government produced films such as *Marihuana* (1935), *Reefer Madness* (1936), and *Assassin of Youth* (1937).

1935: Irish Protestants in Belfast riot against Catholics, provoking Catholic retaliation.

1935: On July 1, the DOI officially became the Federal Bureau of Investigation (FBI).

1936: Italy and Germany sign Axis Pact, to which Japan will become a signatory in 1940.

1936: President Roosevelt asks FBI to report on the activities of Nazi and communist groups.

1938: German Nazis attack Jews and Jewish businesses during night of violence termed Kristallnacht.

1938: Hitler annexes Austria.

1939: President Roosevelt assigns responsibility for investigating espionage, sabotage, and other subversive activities jointly to the FBI, the Military Intelligence Service of the War Department (MID), and the Office of Naval Intelligence (ONI).

1940: Germany launches a full-scale air war against England and extends persecution of the Jews into Poland, Romania, and the Netherlands.

1940: Winston Churchill succeeds Neville Chamberlain as Britain's prime minister.

1940: Ernest Chain and E.P. Abraham detail the inactivation of penicillin by a substance produced by *Escherichia coli*. This is the first bacterial compound known to produce resistance to an antibacterial agent.

1940: Leon Trotsky is assassinated in Mexico City by SMERSH (*SMERrt SHpionam* or "Death to Spies") agents (a KGB assassination team).

1940: The Federal Bureau of Investigation (FBI) participates in the growing Red Scare by conducting additional arrests of suspected Communist agents under powers granted by the 1940 Smith Act that permits the arrest of any individual inciting the overthrow of the government.

1940: The FBI establishes a Special Intelligence Service (SIS).

1941: U.S. President Franklin D. Roosevelt appoints William J. (Wild Bill) Donovan as "Coordinator of Information," a proto intelligence service.

1941: On December 7, the Japanese attack the U.S. naval base at Pearl Harbor, Hawaii. In response, the United States entered World War II. The FBI is authorized to act against dangerous enemy aliens and to seize enemy aliens and contraband (e.g. short-wave radios, dynamite, weapons, and ammunition.).

1942: German Nazi party makes Jewish extermination a systematic state policy, termed the "Final Solution."

1942: Alcohol Tax Unit (ATU) formed and given responsibility for enforcing the Firearms Act.

1942: The Manhattan Project is formed to secretly build the atomic bomb before the Germans.

1942: Four German saboteurs come ashore from a U-boat on the beach near Amagansett, Long Island. Within the week, a second team of German saboteurs lands in Florida. Some saboteurs surrender, and within two weeks the FBI captured the others.

1944: Assassination attempt on Hitler and several other high-ranking officials. Himmler suspects that the plot was the work of agents inside of the government, most especially the Abwehr.

1945: Italian dictator Benito Mussolini killed by partisans on April 28, Adolf Hitler commits suicide April 30, and Germany surrenders to the Allies on May 7.

1945: United States destroys the Japanese city of Hiroshima with a nuclear fission bomb based on uranium-235 on August 6. Three days later a plutonium-based bomb destroys the city of Nagasaki. Japan surrenders on August 14 and World War II ends. This is the first use of nuclear power as a weapon.

1946: Winston Churchill states that an "iron curtain" has come down across Europe.

1947: Three "pillars" of the containment policy are in place: Truman Doctrine (March 12), Marshall Plan (June 5), National Security Act (July 28). Supporting instruments include DOD, CIA, SAC, advance bases in Turkey and Libya. Stalin creates the Cominform, or Information Bureau of Communist parties in August, at the meeting in Poland of the Soviet, East European, French, and Italian communist parties. Andrei Zhadov reported to the conference that America and Russia were locked in a two-camp struggle for world domination.

By September, the Freedom Train begins traveling the U.S. through 1948.

1947: The National Security Act of 1947 establishes the National Security Council and the Central Intelligence Agency (CIA) to replace the National Intelligence Authority and the Central Intelligence Group.

1947: The United Nations proposes a division of what is now Israel almost equally between Israelis and Arabs. Arab countries reject this proposal.

1948: The state of Israel is created and prompts Arab-Israel conflict.

1948: Soon after Israel becomes a state in May, it is attacked by Egypt, Iraq, Jordan, and Syria. Though outnumbered, the Israelis defeat the Arab nations, and Israeli territory expands to encompass an area larger than that allotted in the original UN partition.

1949: Victory of Mao Zedong in China forces Nationalist government to flee to Formosa, where it establishes the Republic of China. Meanwhile, the world's largest population falls under Communist rule as the People's Republic of China.

1949: Russia announces that its first A-bomb was successfully tested on July 14.

1950–1999

1950: McCarran Internal Security Act enacted, stating that all communist-front organizations must register with Attorney-General, communists can be prohibited from working in national defense, and provides for no entry into the U.S. of anyone who was a member of a totalitarian organization.

1950: North Korea invades South Korea, igniting the Korean War. U.S. military troops sent to expel North Korean forces as part of a United Nations force.

1950: President Harry S. Truman escapes assassination attempt unhurt as two Puerto Rican nationalists attempted to shoot their way into Blair House in Washington. Officer Leslie Coffelt, White House Police, is shot and killed.

1950: North Korean troops gain easy victories against Allied forces, but when General Douglas MacArthur launches a bold offensive at Inchon, he cuts the North Korean army in half. By Thanksgiving, he promises that U.S. troops will be home by Christmas, but on November 25, China enters the war, and drives the Allies back to the 38th parallel. Allied bombing ensures that this

line remains the boundary between North and South Korea.

1951: Mossad, Israel's chief intelligence collection, counterterrorism, and covert action agency, established on April 1.

1952: First thermo-nuclear device is exploded successfully by the United States at the Eniwetok Atoll in the South Pacific. This hydrogen-fusion bomb (H bomb) is the first such bomb to work by nuclear fusion and is considerably more powerful than the atomic bomb exploded over Hiroshima on August 6, 1945.

1952: McCarran-Walter Act is revised. The new immigration quota laws allow more Asians, but not "subversives." and gives the Attorney-General the right to deport immigrants that were communist even after U.S. citizenship is acquired.

1953: Joseph Stalin dies and a political power struggle starts in the USSR.

1953: James D. Watson and Francis H. C. Crick publish two landmark papers in the journal *Nature*. The papers are entitled *Molecular structure of nucleic acids: a structure for deoxyribose nucleic acid* and *Genetic implications of the structure of deoxyribonucleic acid*. Watson and Crick propose a double helical model for DNA and call attention to the genetic implications of their model. Their model is based, in part, on the x-ray crystallographic work of Rosalind Franklin and the biochemical work of Erwin Chargaff. Their model explains how the genetic material is transmitted.

1954: A CIA-supported coup in Guatemala overthrows President Jacobo Arbenz.

1954: French garrison at Dien Bien Phu falls to Viet Minh on May 7, and in July, French agree to leave Vietnam.

1954: Atomic Energy Act is passed.

1954: Communist Control Act is passed, briefly outlawing the Communist Party in the U.S.

1956: Suez Crisis when Western powers, worried over Egyptian president Gamal Abdel Nasser's close ties with the Soviet bloc, refuse assistance in building Aswan High Dam. In response, Nasser seizes the Suez Canal. Britain and France form an alliance with Israel, which invades on October 26.

1956: Fidel Castro launches Cuban revolution against the Batista regime.

1956: Soviet Premier Nikita Khrushchev, speaking about the West, states "History is on our side. We will bury you . . ."

1956: Pakistan officially becomes an Islamic state.

1957: International Atomic Energy Agency (IAEA) is formed as an autonomous United Nations body to verify that nuclear materials are not used in a prohibited manner.

1957: The Soviet Union launches Sputnik.

1958: U.S. Department of Defense establishes Advanced Research Projects Agency (ARPA).

1958: Iraqi monarchy is overthrown in a military coup.

1959: Fidel Castro takes power in Cuba on January 1.

1960: Soviet Premier Nikita Khrushchev vows USSR will support "wars of national liberation . . . "

1963: Coup in Iraq led by the Arab Socialist Ba'th Party (ASBP).

1963: On November 22, Lee Harvey Oswald assassinates President John F. Kennedy in Dallas, Texas.

1964: North Vietnamese gunboats open fire on U.S. destroyer *Maddox* in the Gulf of Tonkin on August 2. This results in the Gulf of Tonkin resolution, passed by U.S. Senate, which gives President Lyndon B. Johnson power to vastly escalate U.S. commitment in Vietnam.

1965: American troops sent to the Dominican Republic to prevent a Communist takeover.

1965: First U.S. combat troops are sent to Vietnam in March.

1965: Anthrax vaccine adsorbed (AVA), is approved for use in the United States.

1965: First bombings against Israel by the Palestine Liberation Organization (PLO).

1966: France withdraws its troops from the North Atlantic Treaty Organization (NATO). French President de Gaulle argues for a Europe free from both American and Soviet intervention.

1967: FBI's National Crime Information Center (NCIC) becomes operational.

1967: In the Six-Day War, fought in the first week of June, Israel defeated a much larger Arab force, and gains control of the west bank of the Jordan River, which had been Jordanian territory.

1968: During testing exercise of VX nerve agent, 6,400 sheep killed near Dugway, Utah.

1968: Following passage of the Gun Control Act, the Alcohol and Tobacco Tax Division of IRS becomes the Alcohol, Tobacco, and Firearms (ATF) Division.

1968: James Earl Ray assassinates Dr. Martin Luther King, Jr. in Memphis, Tennessee on April 4. The FBI opened a special investigation based on the violation of Dr. King's civil rights so that federal jurisdiction in the matter could be established.

1968: As a result of Senator Robert F. Kennedy's assassination on June 5, Congress authorized protection of major Presidential and Vice Presidential candidates and nominees.

1969: On July 20, U.S. astronaut Neil Armstrong becomes the first man to walk on the moon.

1969: By Executive Order, the United States renounces first-use of biological weapons and restricts future weapons research programs to issues concerning defensive responses (e.g., immunization, detection, etc.).

1969: Microprocessor developed.

1969: Defense Department's Advanced Research Projects Agency (ARPA) established ARPANET, a forerunner to the Internet.

1969: Muammar Qaddafi seizes power from King Idris in Libya on September 1.

1970: Treaty on the Non-Proliferation of Nuclear Weapons (NPT), signed by 188 states, becomes operative.

1970: The U.N. assigns the International Atomic Energy Agency (IAEA) the task of NPT monitoring and for developing nuclear safeguards.

1970: In October, a group advocating the separation of Quebec from Canada kidnaps two government officials and murders one of them. The crisis causes the temporary imposition of martial law in the country and renews calls for a dedicated security agency.

1971: Chinese defense minister Lin Pao attempts a failed coup against Mao Zedong and is killed in a plane crash. China is officially seated in the United Nations and launches its first space satellite.

1972: U.S. Department of Defense directs Advanced Research Projects Agency (ARPA) name change to the Defense Advanced Research Projects Agency (DARPA) in March. DARPA is established as a separate defense agency under the Office of the Secretary of Defense.

1972: Biological and Toxin Weapons Convention (BWC) first signed. BWC prohibits the offensive weaponization of biological agents (e.g., anthrax spores). The BWC also prohibits the transformation of biological agents with established legitimate and sanctioned purposes into agents of a nature and quality that could be used to effectively induce illness or death.

1972: Termed "Bloody Friday," on July 21, an IRA bomb attack killed eleven people and injured 130 in Belfast, Northern Ireland. Ten days later, three additional IRA attacks in the village of Claudy left six dead.

1972: After eleven Israeli athletes are murdered by Palestinian terrorists with the Black September organization at the Munich Olympics in September, Israel's Mossad establishes an action team, Wrath of God (WOG). Over the next two years, WOG tracks down and kills a dozen members of Black September.

1973: Atmospheric Release Advisory Capability (ARAC) concept has its origins when the Department of Energy (DOE) seeks assistance from scientists at California's Lawrence Livermore National Laboratory in assessing potential and ongoing atmospheric hazards.

1973: Concerns about the possible hazards posed by recombinant DNA technologies, especially work with tumor viruses, leads to the establishment of a meeting at Asilomar, California. The proceedings of this meeting are subsequently published by the Cold Spring Harbor Laboratory as a book entitled *Biohazards in Biological Research.*.

1973: Oil embargo imposed by the Organization of Petroleum Exporting Countries (OPEC).

1973: Libya claims the Gulf of Sidra in defiance of international protocol.

1973: Arab-Israeli Yom Kippur War. Fourth Arab-Israeli war begins with a combined Egyptian and Syrian attack against Israel in October. When military efforts fail, the Organization of Petroleum-Exporting Countries (OPEC) announces a cutback in oil production, raising gasoline prices and precipitating an energy crisis in the United States.

1974: Members of the Symbionese Liberation Army (SLA) kidnap heiress Patricia Hearst on February 5. Hearst, allegedly brainwashed by the group, adopts the name "Tania" and participates in bank robberies. Most members, including leader Donald DeFreeze, are killed in a May 1974 shootout with authorities, and Hearst is captured by the FBI in September 1975. In January 2001, outgoing president William J. Clinton pardons her.

1974: Cuba's National Liberation Directorate (DLN), which is responsible for fomenting Communist revolutions worldwide, becomes the America Department (DA) of the Communist Party of Cuba Central Committee. During the years that follow, DA will provide support to Communist insurgents and terrorists in numerous locales.

1974: New era of congressional oversight in intelligence begins with passage of Hughes-Ryan Act amending the Foreign Service Act. Written in the wake of covert activities that helped bring down the Marxist regime of Salvador Allende in Chile,

Hughes-Ryan requires the President to submit plans for covert actions to the relevant congressional committees.

1974: British Prevention of Terrorism Act permits the arrest of suspected terrorists without a warrant and allows authorities to detain them for a week without bringing charges. While being interned, detainees are subject to a range of harsh practices that include "hooding"—being isolated and forced to wear a hood over their heads—noise bombardment, and sleep and food deprivation.

1975: Puerto Rican nationalists bombed a Wall Street bar, killing four and injuring sixty; Two days later, the Weather Underground claims responsibility for an explosion in a bathroom at the U.S. Department of State in Washington.

1975: U.S. Nuclear Emergency Support Team established to analyze and respond to cases involving nuclear threats.

1975: On April 30, Saigon falls to North Vietnamese. In the following year, Vietnam is united under a communist government.

1975: FBI Special Agents Jack R. Coler and Ronald A. Williams are murdered while conducting an investigation on an Indian reservation in South Dakota. American Indian Movement leader Leonard Peltier was subsequently convicted of committing the murders.

1975: President Gerald R. Ford escaped an assassination attempt September 5, in Sacramento, California, by Lynette Alice (Squeaky) Fromme, who pointed a gun, but did not fire. Ford again escaped an assassination attempt in San Francisco, California, on September 22, as Sara Jane Moore's shot was deflected.

1976: Chinese Premier Zhou Enlai dies of cancer and Central Committee Chairman Mao Zedong dies.

1976: On the night of July 3-4, members of Israel's Mossad conduct a raid on a French airliner, hijacked by Palestinian terrorists, in the Uganda city of Entebbe. The Israelis rescue all but four of the plane's ninety-seven passengers, losing a single officer, along with twenty Ugandan soldiers, in the process.

1977: The United States vetoes a United Nations Security Council resolution calling for a proposed total Israeli withdrawal from Arab areas.

1977: The United States Ambassador Francis E. Melroy is killed in Beirut.

1977: The last reported smallpox case recorded. Ultimately, the World Health Organization (WHO) declares the disease eradicated.

1978: A bomb disguised as a package goes off at Northwestern University. This is the first of sixteen attacks, over the course of seventeen years, by an individual dubbed the "Unabomber" for his principal targets, universities and airlines.

1978: Camp David meetings between President James E. Carter, Egyptian President Anwar Sadat, and Israeli Prime Minister Menachem Begin, offer hope for peace in Middle East.

1978: Department of Energy initiates its Nuclear Threat Assessment Program at Lawrence Livermore National Laboratory in September.

1978: Kidnapping of Italian Prime Minister on March 16: Premier Aldo Moro was seized by the Red Brigade and assassinated fifty-five days later.

1978: The United States cancels development of the neutron bomb, which would theoretically destroy life but cause minimal physical destruction. The bomb was initially developed, in part, to ensure the maximal survival of European cultural treasures in the advent of nuclear war and thus enhance the credibility of U.S. use of the bomb against a Soviet aggression into Europe.

1979: Sandinistas gain control of Nicaragua.

1979: Saddam Hussein becomes president of Iraq.

1979: The Iranian Shah flees Iran, and Shiite Muslim leader Ayatollah Khomeini assumes control of the fundamentalist Islamist revolution. The former Shah, suffering from cancer, seeks treatment and asylum in the United States. Islamist revolutionaries (mostly Iranian students) seize the American embassy and take sixty-six American diplomats hostage. Thirteen hostages were soon released, but the remaining fifty-three were held until their release on January 20, 1981. The hostage crisis consumes the remainder of U.S. President Jimmy Carter's term and critics claim that his failure to act decisively to secure the release of the hostages ultimately emboldens a generation of Islamist fundamentalist terrorism against the United States.

1979: Less than a month following the seizure of the U.S. Embassy in Tehran, Iran the United States Embassy in Tripoli, Libya is attacked.

1979: Less than a month following the seizure of the U.S. Embassy in Tehran, Iran the United States Embassy in Islamabad, Pakistan, is attacked, resulting in the killing of a U.S. Marine and another American.

1979: Soviets invade Afghanistan on December 24.

1980: CNN, the first twenty-four hours-a-day cable television news channel is launched. The Iranian hostage crisis and intense media coverage sparks "real-time" interest in American political, diplomatic, and security matters. For example, a nightly news program on ABC regarding the hostage crisis evolves into the modern news program, "Nightline."

1980: After Lech Walesa leads a strike by shipyard workers, Poland's Solidarity Party becomes an independent labor union, the first in the sphere of Soviet influence.

1980: More than five months after the seizure of the U.S. Embassy in Tehran, Iran, the United States mounts an attempt to rescue the American hostages held in Iran, but fails when helicopters collide in the desert. The crash forces leaders to abort the mission. Eight Americans die and five are injured in the attempt.

1981: AIDS (Acquired Immune Deficiency Syndrome) is recognized and tracked as an epidemic.

1981: Ronald Reagan inaugurated as President of the United States. Fearing Reagan's promise to renew and use American military strength to protect U.S. citizens and interests, Islamist militant revolutionaries in Iran release U.S. hostages held for 444 days under the Carter administration.

1981: President Ronald Reagan wounded in assassination attempt by John W. Hinckley, Jr.; three others also wounded.

1981: Israel launches air attacks to destroy an Iraqi nuclear research centre at Tuwaythah, Iraq (a city near Baghdad).

1981: In August, two U.S. F-14 Tomcat fighters dispatched by the U.S. Sixth Fleet shoot down two Libyan Su-22 fighter-bombers over the Gulf of Sidra.

1981: Egyptian President Anwar Sadat assassinated by Islamic militants on October 6.

1982: Israel invades Lebanon and ousts PLO forces.

1982: The FDA issues regulations for tamper-resistant packaging after seven people died in Chicago from ingesting Tylenol capsules laced with cyanide. The following year, the federal Anti-Tampering Act was passed, making it a crime to tamper with packaged consumer products.

1983: February 13 attack on law enforcement officers in Medina, North Dakota, by the Sheriff's Posse Comitatus is the first significant incident involving an anti-government right-wing terrorist group in the United States.

1983: Bombing of U.S. Embassy in Beirut on April 18: Sixty-three people, including the CIA's Middle

East director, were killed, and 120 were injured in a 400-pound suicide truck-bomb attack on the U.S. Embassy. The Islamic Jihad claimed responsibility.

1983: Reagan terms the Soviet Union the "evil empire" and announces the Strategic Defense Initiative (Star Wars), a satellite-based defense system that would destroy incoming missiles and warheads in space.

1983: The FBI Hostage Rescue Team (HRT) became fully operational.

1983: Simultaneous suicide truck-bomb attacks were made on American and French compounds in Beirut, Lebanon. A 12,000-pound bomb destroyed the U.S. compound, killing 242 Americans, while 58 French troops were killed when a 400-pound device destroyed a French base. Islamic Jihad claimed responsibility.

1984: The Islamic Jihad kidnaps and later murders CIA station chief William Buckley in Beirut, Lebanon. Other U.S. citizens not connected to the U.S. Government were subsequently seized over a two year period.

1984: Eighteen U.S. servicemen were killed, and 83 people were injured in a bomb attack on a restaurant near a U.S. Air Force Base in Spain. Responsibility was claimed by Hezbollah.

1984: Sikh terrorists seized the Golden Temple in Amritsar, India. One hundred people die as Indian security forces retake the Sikh holy shrine.

1984: Assassination of Prime Minister Gandhi on October 31. The Indian premier was shot to death by members of her security force.

1985: Mikhail Gorbachev becomes general secretary of the Communist Party in the USSR. Gorbachev institutes economic reforms and policies such as "glasnost" (openness) to ease Cold War tensions.

1985: Alec Jeffreys developed "genetic fingerprinting," a method of using DNA polymorphisms (unique sequences of DNA) to identify individuals. The method, which is subsequently used in paternity, immigration, and murder cases, is generally referred to as "DNA fingerprinting."

1985: The Global Positioning System becomes operational.

1985: Federal Radiological Preparedness Coordinating Committee, appointed by the Federal Emergency Management Agency (FEMA), completes the U.S. Federal Radiological Emergency Response Plan, a blueprint for the federal response to a hazard involving nuclear radiation.

1985: On June 14, a Trans-World Airlines (TWA) flight is hijacked en route to Rome from Athens by two Lebanese Hezbollah terrorists and forced to fly to Beirut. The eight crew members and 145 passengers were held for seventeen days, during which one American hostage, a U.S. Navy sailor, was murdered. After being flown twice to Algiers, the aircraft was returned to Beirut after Israel released 435 Lebanese and Palestinian prisoners.

1985: *Achille Lauro* Hijacking, October 7, 1985: Four Palestinian Liberation Front terrorists seize the Italian cruise liner in the eastern Mediterranean Sea, taking more than 700 hostages. One elderly U.S. passenger is murdered.

1986: The space shuttle Challenger explodes during lift-off.

1986: The Chernobyl nuclear plant in the Ukraine suffers explosions, severe radiation leakage, and causes an estimated 8,000 near-term deaths.

1986: U.S. sales of arms to Iran during its war with Iraq, and the use of profits to fund Contra forces in Nicaragua fuels the Iran-Contra scandal.

1986: DNA analysis conducted by the Scientific Intelligence Unit of England's Scotland Yard leads to the first conviction of a criminal—Colin Pitchfork, accused of rape and murder—on the basis of DNA evidence.

1986: U.S. forces in the Gulf of Sidra sink two Libyan vessels on March 24, and on April 5, after a bomb goes off in a German discotheque. Based on intelligence that Libyan strongman Muammar Qaddafi orchestrated the attack in retaliation (a fact confirmed fifteen years later by Qaddafi himself), America strikes back. On the night of April 15–16, U.S. forces launch a devastating 12-minute air strike on five strategic targets in Libya.

1986: United States Congress passes Anti-Drug Abuse Act. This federal law includes mandatory minimum sentences for first time offenders with harsher penalties for possession of crack cocaine than powder cocaine.

1986: Computer Fraud and Abuse Act is enacted, defining federal computer crimes.

1986: U.S. Defense Department establishes Chemical and Biological Defense Analysis Center.

1986: U.S. Congress passes Goldwater-Nichols Act. Goldwater-Nichols, which represents the fourth major reorganization of the U.S. Department of Defense since World War II, calls on the White House to issue an annual National Security Strategy.

1987: Congress passes the Computer Security Act, which makes unclassified computing systems the responsibility of the National Institute of Standards and Technology (NIST) and not the NSA with regard to technology standards development.

1987: Iraqi government uses nerve agents including sarin against Kurds in Northern Iraq.

1987: The PLO's terrorist campaign against Israel became acute during its first Intifada (or "shaking off") of Israeli authority in the Occupied Territories.

1987: North Korean agents planted a bomb that destroys Korean Air Lines Flight 858.

1988: U.S. Marine Corps Lt. Col. W. Higgins is kidnapped and murdered by the Iranian-backed Hezbollah group while serving with the United Nations Truce Supervisory Organization (UNTSO) in Lebanon.

1988: Iran-Iraq ceasefire begins (monitored by the UN Iran-Iraq Military Observer Group (UNIIMOG)).

1988: Libyan intelligence operatives plant a bomb aboard Pan-Am 103 that crashes into the village at Lockerbie, Scotland, killing all 259 aboard and eleven persons on the ground. Two Libyan intelligence officers are ultimately tried under Scottish law in The Hague. Abdelbaset Ali Mohmed Al Megrahi was found guilty in January 2001.

1989: After nine years of war, Soviet forces withdraw from Afghanistan.

1989: British Parliament passes Security Service Act, which for the first time confers legal status on MI5.

1989: The New People's Army (NPA) assassinated Col. James Rowe in Manila in April. The NPA also assassinated two U.S. government defense contractors in September.

1989: The Berlin Wall is torn down, as many communist governments in Eastern Europe collapse.

1989: In December, U.S. forces attack Panama to remove General Manuel Noriega in Operation Just Cause. The U.S. Army uses loud music as part of a psychological operation to dislodge Noriega from his refuge at the Papal embassy.

1989: Nicolae Ceausescu, communist dictator of Romania, is overthrown and executed.

1990: Yugoslavia overthrows communist party and ethnic tensions flourish.

1990: U.S. Embassy bombed in Peru by the Tupac Amaru Revolutionary Movement.

1990: Iraq invades Kuwait. United Nations Security Council (UNSC) passes resolution 660 that calls for full Iraqi withdrawal. President Bush vows "This aggression will not stand."

1990: U.S. military personnel receive vaccinations against anthrax prior to duty in the Persian Gulf War.

1990: U.N. (via resolution 661) imposes economic sanctions on Iraq.

1990: East and West Germany reunited.

1990: Former Solidarity union leader Lech Walesa becomes president of post-communist Poland.

1990: Iraq hangs Farzad Bazoft, an Iranian-born journalist with the London *Observer* newspaper, who Hussein accuses of spying on Iraqi military installations.

1991: Launch of Operation Desert Storm against Iraq on January 17. The initial bombing campaign lasts approximately one hundred hours, and the entire military operation takes only forty-two days. The result is overwhelming Iraqi defeat.

1991: Saddam Hussein orders Iraqi forces to brutally suppress Kurd and Shia rebellions in northern and southern Iraq.

1991: IAEA's Iraq Action Team begins inspecting suspect sites in Iraq under U.N. Security Council mandate.

1991: The Warsaw Pact is officially dissolved.

1991: The Baltic republics declare their independence and the USSR crumbles. A Commonwealth of Independent States takes the place of the former Soviet empire. Boris Yeltsin becomes president of Russia.

1993: Czechoslovakia dissolves into the Czech Republic and Slovakia.

1993: The Maastricht Treaty officially forms the European Union.

1993: World Trade Center Bombing, February 26, 1993: The World Trade Center in New York City was badly damaged when a car bomb planted by Islamic terrorists explodes in an underground garage. The bomb left six people dead and 1,000 injured. The men carrying out the attack were followers of Umar Abd al-Rahman, an Egyptian cleric who preached in the New York City area.

1993: After a 51-day siege by the Bureau of Alcohol, Tobacco, and Firearms, a federal team assaults a compound held by the Branch Davidians, a religious sect charged with hoarding illegal weapons. The Branch Davidians set the buildings on fire, killing seventy-six people, including cult leader David Koresh.

1993: On April 14, Iraqi intelligence agents attempt to assassinate former President George Bush during a visit to Kuwait. Two months later, the administration of William J. Clinton launches a cruise missile attack on the Iraqi capital of Baghdad.

1993: Explosive growth of Internet begins as a result of two factors: the full opening of the National Science Foundation's NSFNET, and the development of the first browsers, Mosaic (forerunner of Netscape Navigator) and Microsoft Internet Explorer.

1993: On October 3, eighteen U.S. Rangers, participants in a United Nations peacekeeping force in Somalia, are killed in a firefight on the streets of Mogadishu.

1994: Jewish right-wing extremist and U.S. citizen Baruch Goldstein kills Muslim worshippers at a mosque in West Bank town of Hebron, killing twenty-nine and wounding about 150.

1994: North Korea withdraws its membership from IAEA over dispute regarding nuclear inspections.

1994: Britain's Parliament passes Intelligence Services Act, which gives MI6 new statutory grounding. The Act defines the responsibilities and functions of MI6 and its chief, and sets in place a framework of government oversight for MI6 activities.

1994: After Rwandan dictator, Major General Juvenal Habyarimana, dies in a plane crash on April 6, his Hutu supporters blame the Tutsi-controlled Rwandan Patriotic Front, and launch a campaign of genocide that resulted in more than 800,000 deaths over a period of a few weeks.

1994: Russia invades Chechnya on October 11, launching a war that will last the better part of two years.

1995: U.N. Security Council resolution 986 allows partial resumption of Iraqi oil exports, with the original intent to allow Iraq to sell oil to buy food and medicine (the "oil-for-food program"). Iraq subsequently diverts funds from sales to additional weapons purchases and the building of offices and places for the Hussein government. Malnutrition and improper medical care becomes widespread in Iraq.

1995: After thwarting U.N. weapons inspectors, the government of Iraq admits to producing over 8,000 liters of concentrated anthrax as part of the nation's biological weapons program.

1995: Twelve persons were killed, and 5,700 were injured in a Sarin nerve gas attack on a crowded subway station in the center of Tokyo, Japan. Aum Shinrikyu cult is blamed for the attacks.

1995: A car bomb explodes outside the Alfred P. Murrah Federal office building in Oklahoma City, Oklahoma, on April 19, collapsing walls and floors.

169 persons were killed, including nineteen children and one person who died in the rescue effort. Timothy McVeigh and Terry Nichols are later convicted in the anti-government plot to avenge the Branch Davidian standoff in Waco, Tex., exactly two years earlier.

1995: Concerned by revelations that agents of the Central Intelligence Agency (CIA) in Guatemala had committed human rights violations, CIA draws up guidelines prohibiting the agency from hiring agents with records of human-rights violations.

1995: President William J. Clinton issues Presidential Decision Directive 39, "U.S. Policy on Counterterrorism," calling for a number of specific efforts to deter terrorism on America's shores, as well as that against Americans and allies abroad.

1995: Radical Sunni Muslims set off a bomb at a national guard facility in Riyadh, Saudi Arabia, which killed five Americans.

1996: An Irish Republican Army (IRA) bomb detonates in London on February 9, killing two persons and wounding more than 100 others, including two U.S. citizens.

1996: The Chemical and Biological Incident Response Force (CBIRF), a unit of the United States Marines devoted to countering chemical or biological threats at home and abroad, is activated.

1996: A fuel truck carrying a bomb exploded outside the U.S. military's Khobar Towers housing facility in Dhahran on June 25, killing nineteen U.S. military personnel and wounding 515 persons, including 240 U.S. personnel. Thirteen Saudis and a Lebanese, all alleged members of Islamic militant group Hezbollah, are indicted on charges relating to the attack in June 2001.

1996: Bombing at Atlanta's Centennial Olympic Park on July 27, during the Olympic Games, kills two people and injures 112. Eric Robert Rudolph is charged with the crime, but he evades capture for several years. Rudolph was later captured and sentenced in 2005.

1996: Twenty-three members of the Tupac Amaru Revolutionary Movement (MRTA) took several hundred people hostage at a party given at the Japanese Ambassador's residence in Lima, Peru on December 17. Among the hostages were several U.S. officials, foreign ambassadors and other diplomats, Peruvian Government officials, and Japanese businessmen. The group demanded the release of all MRTA members in prison and safe passage for them and the hostage takers. The terrorists released most of the hostages in December but held eighty-one Peruvians and Japanese citizens for several months.

1997: The corrupt regime of Mobutu Sese Seko, a long-time U.S. ally in Zaire, is overthrown by rebel forces under the leadership of Laurent Kabila. Kabila will change the country's name back to Congo, but his regime will bring few democratic reforms, and he will be killed by his own bodyguards in 2001.

1997: Tourist Killings in Egypt, November 17, 1997: Al-Gama'at al-Islamiyya (IG) gunmen shot and killed fifty-eight tourists and four Egyptians and wounded twenty-six others at the Hatshepsut Temple in the Valley of the Kings near Luxor.

1998: The Hebron Accord, designed to promote peace between Israel and Palestine, is undermined by both sides as terrorism breaks out and the building of new settlements defies non-expansionist agreements.

1998: India and Pakistan conduct underground nuclear tests.

1998: Controversy breaks out over the reported NSA "Echelon" project, which privacy groups describe as a worldwide surveillance network that eavesdrops on communications traffic and shares intelligence gathered by the United States, Great Britain, Canada, Australia and New Zealand.

1998: International Atomic Energy Agency Iraq Action Team withdraws from Iraq because of a lack of "full and free access" to Iraqi sites.

1998: Real IRA explodes a car bomb outside a store in Banbridge, North Ireland.

1998: U.S. Embassy Bombings in East Africa, August 7, 1998: A bomb explodes at the rear entrance of the U.S. embassy in Nairobi, Kenya, killing twelve U.S. citizens, thirty-two Foreign Service Nationals (FSNs), and 247 Kenyan citizens. About 5,000 Kenyans, six U.S. citizens, and thirteen FSNs were injured. The U.S. embassy building sustained extensive structural damage. Almost simultaneously, a bomb detonates outside the U.S. embassy in Dar es Salaam, Tanzania, killing seven FSNs and three Tanzanian citizens, and injuring one U.S. citizen and seventy-six Tanzanians. The explosion caused major structural damage to the U.S. embassy facility. The U.S. Government holds Osama Bin Laden responsible.

1998: Formation, in October, of the U.S. National Domestic Preparedness Office as the coordination center for all federal efforts in response to weapons of mass destruction.

1998: Iraq expels U.N. weapons inspectors on October 31.

1998: In December, 1998 following Iraq's expulsion of U.N. weapons inspectors, the U.S. and U.K. launch Operation Desert Fox to attempt to destroy Iraq's nuclear, chemical, and biological weapons programs.

1999: Vladimir Putin becomes Prime Minister of Russia.

1999: Beginning March 24, NATO forces conduct a 78-day campaign of air strikes against Yugoslavia. Operation Allied Force brings an end to Serb "ethnic cleansing" in the Albanian enclave of Kosovo, and helps to break the hold of Slobodan Milosevic on the country as a whole.

1999: Melissa virus (actually a form of malicious data wedded to a particular type of virus program, a macro virus) spreads through the e-mail systems of the world on March 26, causing $80 million worth of damage, primarily in the form of lost productivity resulting from the shutdown of overloaded mailboxes.

1999: Fugitives Abdel Basset Ali Al-Megrahi and Lamen Khalifa Fhimah were surrendered to Dutch authorities on April 5 for trial before a Scottish court for charges in connection with the 1998 bombing of Pan Am Flight 103, which exploded over Lockerbie, Scotland.

1999: Osama Bin Laden was added to the FBI's "Ten Most Wanted Fugitives" list in June, in connection with the U.S. Embassy bombings in East Africa.

1999: FBI personnel traveled to Kosovo on June 23 to assist in the collection of evidence and the examination of forensic materials in support of the prosecution of Slobodan Milosevic and others before the International Criminal Tribunal for the former Yugoslavia.

1999: As the year 2000 approaches, the world prepares itself for the possible deleterious effects of a computer shortcut (a protocol developed when memory was scarce) that used only the last two digits of a year to indicate the year. Termed the Y2K glitch or problem, fears approach near hysteria as people and governments prepare for computers to malfunction and adversely effect critical infrastructure. Adequate preparation, considerable investment in programming solutions, and monitoring turn the dawn of 2000 into a grand worldwide party but a non-event with regard to Y2K fears. Minimal disruptions are reported.

2000–

2000: Mokhtar Haouari and Abdel Ghani Meskini were charged with collaborating with Ahmed Ressam and others in a wide-ranging terrorist conspiracy to bomb American sites during the January 1, 2000, millennium celebrations. The FBI/New York Police Department Joint Terrorist Task Force, Royal Canadian Mounted Police, the Canadian Security and Intelligence Service, and Canada's Department of Justice assisted in the investigation.

2000: Asbat al-Ansar carries out a rocket-propelled grenade attack on the Russian Embassy in Beirut in January 2000.

2000: The Jaish-e-Mohammed (JEM) an Islamic extremist group based in Pakistan is formed by Masood Azhar upon his release from prison in India in early 2000.

2000: October 12, terrorist bombing of U.S.S. Cole kills seventeen of its crew and wounds thirty-nine others. Two suicide bombers, ultimately linked to al-Qaeda, pulled alongside the vessel near the port in Aden, Yemen, and detonated explosives near the Cole's hull.

2000: The PLO's terrorist campaign against Israel again intensifies with start of second Intifada.

2000: Former Senator Danforth, conducting an independent review of FBI actions in the 1993 FBI assault on the Branch Davidian compound in Waco, Texas, released his final report exonerating the FBI of wrongdoing. The Government Operations Committee reaches a similar conclusion.

2001: The complete draft sequence of the human genome is published in February. The public sequence data is published in the British journal *Nature* and the Celera sequence is published in the American journal *Science*. Increased knowledge of the human genome allows greater specificity in pharmacological research and drug interaction studies.

2001: In May, Libyan leader Muammar Qaddafi admits to a German newspaper that Libya was behind a Berlin discotheque bombing in 1986 that killed a U.S. serviceman and a Turkish civilian, and injured some two hundred others. At a trial in November, four defendants are convicted for roles in the bombing.

2001: Hamas claims responsibility for the bombing of a popular Israeli nightclub that causes more than 140 casualties.

2001: A U.S. grand jury indicts fourteen Hezbollah members on June 21 for the 1996 Khobar Towers bombing in Saudi Arabia.

2001: Ahmad Shah Massoud, the leader of the rebels in the Afghanistan Northern Alliance, widely regarded as the most popular opposition figure to the then ruling Taliban (the regime that provided asylum to al-Qaeda and its leader, Osama Bin Laden) is assassinated on September 9.

2001: September 11, Islamist terrorists mount a coordinated terrorist attack on New York and Washington. The World Trade Center Towers are destroyed, killing nearly 3,000 people. In Washington, a plane slams into the Pentagon, but passengers aboard another hijacked airliner, aware of the other terrorist attacks, fight back. During the struggle for the aircraft, it crashes into a Pennsylvania field, thwarting the terrorist's plans to crash the plane into either the U.S. Capital or White House.

2001: Letters containing a powdered form of *Bacillus anthracis*, the bacteria that causes anthrax, are mailed by an unknown terrorist or terrorist group (foreign or domestic) to government representatives, members of the news media, and others in the United States. More than twenty cases and five deaths are eventually attributed to the terrorist attack.

2001: On October 7, United States launches Operation Enduring Freedom against the al-Qaeda terror network and Afghanistan's Taliban regime.

2001: Natural and manmade caves are used by Al-Qaeda forces in Afghanistan.

2001: In conjunction with the U.S. Post Office, the FBI on October 18 offered a reward of $1,000,000 for information leading to the arrest of the person who mailed letters contaminated with Anthrax in October to media organizations and congressional offices. A further anthrax contaminated letter was postmarked to a U.S. senator on October 8, resulting in closure of the Hart Senate building and other government offices and postal facilities.

2001: On October 26, 2001, President George W. Bush signs the Patriot Act into law, giving the FBI and CIA broader investigatory powers and allowing them to share confidential information about suspected terrorists with one another. Under the act, both agencies can conduct residential searches without a warrant and without the presence of the suspect and allows immediate seizure of personal records. The provisions are not limited to investigating suspected terrorists, but may be used in any criminal investigation related to terrorism. The Patriot Act also grants the FBI and CIA greater latitude in using computer tracking devices such as the Carnivore (DCS1000) to gain access to Internet and phone records.

2001: On November 19, President George W. Bush signs into law the Aviation and Transportation Security Act (ATSA), which creates the Transportation

Security Administration (TSA), and authorizes TSA to direct a team of air marshals and federal airport security screeners.

2001: United Kingdom passes a new counter-terrorist bill in December, 2001, the Anti-Terrorism, Crime, and Security Act. The act allows British authorities to detain suspected terrorists for up to six months before reviewing their cases and for additional six-month periods after that. As in the United States, civil liberty advocate groups in the United Kingdom criticize the new law for potentially infringing upon a basic civil liberty, specifically the right to avoid unlawful detention and gain access to a speedy trial.

2001: The Chemical and Biological Incident Response Force (CBIRF) sends a 100-member initial response team into the Dirksen Senate Office Building in Washington on December 2 alongside Environmental Protection Agency (EPA) specialists to detect and remove anthrax. A similar mission was undertaken at the Longworth House Office Building in October, during which time samples were collected from more than 200 office spaces.

2001: FBI Director Mueller orders the reorganization of FBI operations on December 3 to respond to a revised agency mission that emphasizes terrorism prevention, internal accountability, and strengthens partnerships with domestic and international law enforcement.

2001: Enough closed-circuit television cameras (CCTV) are installed in public places in Britain that, on an average day in any large British city, security experts calculate that a person will have over 300 opportunities to be captured on CCTV during the course of normal daily activities.

2002: In the aftermath of the September 11, 2001 terrorist attacks on the United States, by the first few months of 2002, the United States Government dramatically increases funding to stockpile drugs and other agents that could be used to counter a bioterrorism attack.

2002: An explosives-laden boat rammed the French oil tanker *Limburg* off the coast of Yemen, killing one member of the tanker's crew, tearing a hole in the vessel, and spilling 90,000 barrels of oil. U.S. experts believe that the attack was linked to al-Qaeda.

2002: Industrialized nations pledge $10 billion to help Russia secure Soviet era nuclear weapons and materials.

2002: The planned destruction of stocks of smallpox causing Variola virus at the two remaining depositories in the U.S. and Russia is delayed over fears that large scale production of vaccine might be needed in the event of a bioterrorist action.

2002: More than 1,300 FBI personnel, along with representatives of other federal, state, and local law enforcement agencies ensure safety at the 2002 Winter Olympic Games in Salt Lake City. Preparations for the games had begun in May 1998 and included multiple training exercises involving weapons of mass destruction scenarios.

2002: Scientists at Russia's DS Likhachev Scientific Research Institute for Cultural Heritage and Environmental Protection successfully breed a new kind of highly efficient explosives sniffer dog. The new breed is a cross between a wild jackal and a Russian Husky.

2002: GAO reports that thirteen of the hijackers involved in the September 11, 2001 terrorist attacks on the U.S. had not been interviewed by U.S. consular officials prior to the granting of visas.

2002: The Defense Advanced Research Projects Agency (DARPA) initiates the Biosensor Technologies program in 2002 to develop fast, sensitive, automatic technologies for the detection and identification of biological warfare agents.

2002: Russian and NATO foreign ministers reach final agreement in May on the establishment of the NATO-Russia Council, in which Russia and the nineteen NATO countries will have an equal role in decision-making on counter terrorism policy and other security threats.

2002: U.S. President George Bush calls upon United Nations to confront the Iraqi threat and usurp potential Iraqi transfer of weapons of mass destruction to terrorist groups (some of which operate within Iraq).

2002: London police arrest seven men in connection with Ricin manufacture.

2002: On November 26, President George W. Bush signs into law the Terrorism Risk Insurance Act. Intended to cover the private sector in the event of terrorist attacks such as those that occurred on September 11, 2001.

2002: Congress passes and President George W. Bush signs the "Homeland Security Act of 2002" into law creating the Department of Homeland Security.

2002: In November, a CIA-operated Predator drone fires a missile that killed Bin Laden's top lieutenant in Yemen, Qaed Salim Sinan al-Harethi, and five other al-Qaeda suspects in Yemen.

2002: A group of Swiss researchers at the Lausanne-based Dalle Molle Institute for Perceptual Artificial Intelligence (IDIAP), claimed they were

95 percent certain that a tape purported to contain a message from Osama Bin Laden and played on Arabic television network Al-Jazeera was a fake. U.S. officials continued to assert that the tape was probably genuine. Investigators claim that the poor tape quality defeats sophisticated efforts using aural spectrogram machines that rely on biometric algorithms to analyze breath patterns, syllable emphasis, frequency of speech, rate of speech, and other factors. Over the next several months, additional tapes are released with experts generally agreeing only that the voice alleged to be that of Bin Laden could be genuine. The authenticity of the tapes was critical to determine if the al-Qaeda leader had survived the U.S. war against al-Qaeda in Afghanistan.

2002: Abd al-Rahim al-Nashiri—allegeded to be leader of al-Qaeda operations in the Persian Gulf is captured. Nashiri, also known as Abu Asim al-Makki, is suspected of masterminding the October 2000 attack on the American warship U.S.S. Cole.

2002: Anas al-Liby, one of the FBI's list of most-wanted, is captured in Afghanistan. Al-Liby was allegedly linked by to the 1998 bombings of American embassies in Kenya and Tanzania.

2002: Ramzi Binalshibh allegedly one of the most senior al-Qaeda members, is arrested in Pakistan.

2002: Trial of Mounir Al-Motassadek begins in Germany. al-Motassadek, a Moroccan, is the first man to stand trial over the September 11 terrorist attacks and is charged with being an accessory to more than 3,000 murders in New York and Washington, and of belonging to an al-Qaeda cell in Hamburg. Motassadek claimed he knew the hijackers, but only socially but is convicted and sentenced to fifteen years in prison for being a co-conspirator. Al-Motassadek's conviction related to involvement in the September 11 terrorist attacks is ultimately overturned but his conviction for belonging to a terrorist cell stands.

2002: Zacarias Moussaoui, a 34-year-old French citizen of Moroccan origin, is charged with six counts of conspiracy and faces a possible death sentence for alleged involvement in the September 11, attacks on New York and Washington. Moussaoui is referred to as the "20th hijacker" who was unable to participate in the mission because he was already under arrest. Moussaoui has denied involvement in the attacks but allegedly admitted to being a member of the al-Qaeda network.

2002: In December, 2002, North Korea expels IAEA inspectors, removes surveillance equipment from nuclear facilities, and announces an intent to make plants operational.

2002: In violation of a 1994 agreement with the U.S., North Korea claims to have a secret nuclear weapons program.

2002: Jemaah Islamiah organisation bombing of nightclub in Kuta, Bali leaves more than two hundred people dead—including many Australian tourists. In March 2005, JI leader Abu Bakar Bashir is found guilty of conspiracy in connection with the attacks in Bali.

2003: Office of Homeland Security becomes Department of Homeland Security on January 24.

2003: President George W. Bush announces formation of Project BioShield during his 2003 State of the Union Address.

2003: North Korea pulls out of the Treaty on the Non-Proliferation of Nuclear Weapons (NPT).

2003: United States Secretary of State Colin L. Powell presents to the United Nations Security Council evidence of Iraq's continued development of prohibited biological weapons. In 2005, Powell will state that he was subsequently embarrassed by his presentation and upset that intelligence officials who knew the information was not reliable never informed him.

2003: NATO's internal divisions are highlighted as France, Germany, and Belgium temporarily block U.S. moves to offer military support to Turkey in the event of war in Iraq.

2003: Ten suspected terrorists mysteriously vanished from a high-security prison in Yemen. Among the escapees are two top suspects in the bombing of the U.S.S. Cole.

2003: Richard Reid, the failed "shoe bomber" who attempted a suicide bombing of an American Airlines Paris-to-Miami flight in December 2001, plead guilty on all eight charges against him and declared himself a follower of Osama Bin Laden. Reid is sentenced to life in prison without possibility of parole.

2003: U.S. government officials claim that the capture of top al-Qaeda lieutenant Khalid Sheik Mohammed, allegedly al-Qaeda's chief operations planner also yields valuable documents and computer drives outlining al-Qaeda operations.

2003: Virtually all agencies scheduled for transfer to the new Department of Homeland Security are officially moved in a March 1 ceremony attended by President George W. Bush.

2003: Space shuttle Columbia is destroyed upon reentry.

2003: Carbon-graphite coils capable of generating an electromagnetic pulse or otherwise disabling electronics are used in U.S.-led raids on Baghdad, Iraq.

2003: United States intelligence sources indicate that at least seventeen nations around the globe have offensive biological weapons programs.

2003: On March 17 U.S. President George W Bush gives Saddam Hussein and his sons forty-eight hours to leave Iraq or face war.

2003: On March 20, American missiles hit "targets of opportunity" in Baghdad to mark the start of the war to oust Saddam Hussein. Intelligence sources on the ground in Iraq indicate that Hussein and other elements of the Iraqi leadership are meeting in a bunker in Baghdad. In less than forty-five minutes, a U.S. B-2 stealth bomber armed with "bunker-buster" munitions attempts to eliminate the Iraqi leadership. For several weeks the fate of Hussein is debated, with Iraqi television showing images of Hussein that do not verify his survival. Within days, U.S. and British ground troops enter Iraq from the south. Intelligence data will also drive a similar attack on potential Iraqi leadership targets as U.S. troops approach Baghdad.

2003: On April 9. U.S. forces advance into central Baghdad. Saddam Hussein government is toppled. With the assistance of U.S. troops, Iraqis celebrating liberation pull down a large statue of Saddam Hussein located in central Baghdad.

2003: Widespread looting in Iraqi threatens general security and plunders cultural treasures.

2003: PLF leader Abu Abbas, found guilty of the murder of an elderly American during the 1985 terrorist hijacking of the cruise ship *Achille Lauro* is discovered and arrested in Baghdad following Operation Iraqi Freedom.

2003: Al-Qaeda blamed for May bombings of United States housing compounds in Saudi Arabia that kill twenty-six and injure 160.

2003: Chechnya-based suicide bombers attack train in southern Russia and kill forty-six people.

2003: Chechnya-based terrorists blamed for blast in the center of Moscow that kills six people and wounds a dozen more.

2003: Chechnya-based terrorists blamed for blasts at Moscow rock concert that kill fifteen people.

2003: Chechnya-based terrorists blamed for bombing of passenger train near Kislovodsk in Russia

that kills seven people and injures nearly one hundred.

2003: Chechnya-based terrorists blamed for explosion at the Russian hospital in Mozdok that kills at more than fifty people.

2003: FARC rebels are blamed for car bomb that kills thirty-six and injures 150 in Bogot·, Colombia.

2003: Hotel Bombing in Baghdad, Iraq, kills twenty-two people (including the U.N. representative Sergio Vieira de Mello).

2003: Palestinian suicide bomber kills twenty-one and wounds fifty-one by bombing Haifa restaurant (Maxim restaurant massacre).

2003: Truck bombs in Turkey damage two synagogues, the British Consulate, and a bank in Istanbul. More than fifty killed and seven hundred wounded in the attacks.

2004: Abu Sayyaf group bombs ferry in Philippines, killing more than one hundred people.

2004: Australian embassy in Jakarta, Indonesia bombed.

2004: Bombing of commuter trains in Madrid, Spain, kills 191 people and injures more than 1,500. The attacks—initially blamed on ETA—are ultimately attributed to al-Qaeda.

2004: Chechnya-based suicide bombers attack Russian airplanes and kill ninety people.

2004: Chechnya-based Terrorists seize Beslan school near North Ossetia, Russia. More than three hundred hostages, including children, die during attack by Russian forces to liberate the hostages.

2004: Chechnya-based suicide bomber, kills ten people and injures thirty-three in Moscow subway entrance bombing.

2004: More than one hundred Kurds are killed in two suicide bombings near Arbil, Iraq.

2004: Moscow Metro bombing that kills forty-one is attributed to Chechnya-based terrorists.

2004: Suicide bombings at Shia holy sites in Iraq kill more than 175 people and injure at least five hundred additional pilgrims.

2005: Islamic Jihad conducts suicide bombing in Netanya, Israel, that kills five people.

2005: Suicide bomber in the predominantly Shiite town of Musayyib in Iraq, destroyed oil tanks and kills nearly one hundred people.

2005: Lebanese Prime Minister Rafiq Hariri and twenty others in Beirut killed by car bombs.

2005: More than one hundred Iraqis killed by a suicide car bomb outside a clinic south of Baghdad.

2005: Suicide bomber in Cairo market, kills three foreign tourists.

2005: Suicide bombers sympathetic to al-Qaeda mount coordinated attack on London Underground and bus transport, destroying one double-decker bus and damaging three London Underground trains. More than fifty people killed and more than seven hundred injured.

2005: Explosives fail to detonate during attempted follow-up attacks on London Underground.

2005: Car bombs explode at tourist sites in Sharm el-Sheikh, Egypt, more than eighty persons killed.

2005: Jewish terrorist wearing the uniform of the Israeli Defense Forces (IDF) kills four Arab Israelis on a bus in Shfaram, Israel.

Historical and Philosophical Underpinnings of Terrorism

Terrorism has age-old origins. Mentioned by the ancient Greek historian Xenophon, terrorism may well have been practiced by the first humans to walk the Earth. As a means of frightening the opposition into surrendering, it has been a popular tactic in every era. As defined by the U.S. State Department Office on Counterterrorism, terrorism is premeditated, politically motivated violence that targets noncombatants in an effort to influence an audience. It is propaganda dependent upon violence to maintain fear.

Although terrorism is a worldwide phenomenon, it has roots in the Middle East. The first terrorist organization appeared in the first century when a Jewish sect known as the Zealots (Sicarii) promoted revolution against the Romans by killing Roman soldiers and Jewish collaborators. The Zealots committed mass suicide at Masada in A.D. 70. In 1090, a terrorist organization formed in the mountains of Persia. This group of Islamic extremists included Shiites who sought to keep Islam pure by killing prominent men from the Sunni branch of Islam. The Abbaside dynasty targeted by the Isamailis insisted that the terrorists were "Hashshishin" or under the influence of hashish. The term became the source of the word assassin.

By the middle ages, terrorist violence had spread to Europe. In 1605, the most famous act of terrorism in this era occurred when a Catholic attempted to assassinate Protestant James I of England. James had issued an edict banishing Catholic priests from England. Guy Fawkes, a Catholic, attempted to kill the king by placing thirty-six barrels of gunpowder under the houses of Parliament. He was caught while unloading the barrels, one day before the king planned to appear before the assembly. Under torture, Fawkes revealed the names of fellow Catholic conspirators,

who were tried and executed. Guy Fawkes Day remains a popular British holiday.

In the New World, Europeans directed terrorism at Native Americans. Ethnic violence by the Dutch, Spanish, and British claimed many Native American lives with Native Americans retaliating by slaughtering some European colonists and kidnapping others. The Spanish conquistadors are known to have used rape as a weapon against Native American women. Rape as an instrument of terror had a long tradition in the Old World, with soldiers typically assaulting women in conquered areas. While there is no evidence that Native Americans sexually assaulted Europeans, colonists expected and feared such attacks. This fear of sexual assaults upon white women would continue to poison relations between Native Americans and the United States well into the nineteenth century.

With the end of the French and Indian War in 1763, the British needed to find a way to pay for the costs of the conflict. Unwilling to add to the burden of the British taxpayer, Parliament imposed the Stamp Act on the British colonies in America. The Americans did not want to be taxed without their consent. They tried peaceful protests and petitions before resorting to violence. Samuel Adams, a Bostonian opponent of the tax, decided to unite various city mobs as a weapon for demonstrating American opposition to the tax. He created the Sons of Liberty. Mobs that appeared in other cities were labeled Sons of Liberty, although they were not directly connected to the Boston group. These men roughed up tax collectors, invaded and wrecked the homes of British officials, and hanged tax collectors in effigy. The violence became so severe that few men could be found to serve as tax collectors. Conservatives who opposed the Sons of Liberty also

Execution of King Louis XVI, an illustration after a painting by Edouard Manet depicting the crowd surrounding a man on guillotine platform holding up the King's severed head. © BETTMAN/CORBIS

resorted to violence. The White Oaks and Hearts of Oak clubs consisted of men loyal to England who posted themselves throughout Philadelphia to break up Sons of Liberty demonstrations. As the American Revolution progressed, both sides employed terror. The Americans who supported the British suffered vandalism and physical assault, while the revolutionaries were tortured and had their fields burned.

The French Revolution that began in 1789 involved several episodes of terrorism as France underwent a profound political and social upheaval. The revolution had began in a comparatively moderate fashion but became radical in 1791, when Paris militants forced members of the Legislative Assembly to schedule new elections. The Paris masses continued to remain anxious about the Revolution and, in September 1792, responded violently to rumors of

counter-revolutionary plots. Crowds of workers, shopkeepers, and artisans stormed the prisons, from which they assumed thousands of royalists would escape in the event of a foreign invasion. Popular courts were improvised, which ordered the executions of more than 1,000 prisoners, many of whom were criminals and prostitutes.

These "September Massacres" were followed by the 1793–1794 "Reign of Terror." During the Terror, the Committee of Public Safety attempted to create a Republic of Virtue. All the people who did not measure up as sufficiently virtuous were to be executed. About 10,000 victims were arrested, interrogated, and guillotined. Most of the dead were politicians and aristocrats, including King Louis XVI and Queen Marie Antoinette of France, but the guillotined also included peasants who had refused to give food and farm animals to the revolutionary army. The execution of the king prompted the ruling monarchs throughout Europe to become much more autocratic in an attempt to prevent bloody revolutions in their own nations. When the Jacobins who conducted the Reign of Terror fell from power, they were attacked in the White Terror. This outburst of violence targeted the Jacobins and their supporters in the form of street fighting and massacres. More people died in the White Terror than in the Reign of Terror.

The United States, though horrified by the French violence, experienced its own terrors. While colonial America had been made up of diverse people, virtually all but the blacks and Native Americans possessed a northern European Protestant background. After the end of the Revolution, large numbers of Irish Catholics began to immigrate. These immigrants came under attack, both for religious reasons and for competing with native-born Americans for jobs. The Irish were quick to fight back. In New York in 1799, the Orangemen—Presbyterian Scots-Irish who had a long history of fighting with the Catholics in Ireland—mounted an anti-Catholic parade on St. Patrick's Day. In 1806, a New York Scots-Irish gang known as the Highbinders tried to storm a Catholic church. Both clashes resulted in deaths on both sides. In Boston in 1837, eight hundred state cavalry were needed to put down a street battle that began when a Protestant gang inadvertently bumped into an Irish funeral. And in Philadelphia in 1843, an anti-immigrant group formed to promote the idea of Protestant Bibles in the public schools. After much parading and counter-parading, a young Protestant was shot to death by Irish terrorists. A Protestant counterattack on a Sisters of Charity school the next day sparked a melee that killed two passersby and many combatants. In the next several days, the outnumbered Irish watched as two Catholic churches and a female seminary were burned to the ground, as rioters defied state troops. On July 7, 1843, a mob used battering rams to attack another Catholic church. Five thousand state troops were called in to halt the violence. The mob, unimpressed, fired a cannon at the soldiers with the soldiers firing volleys in return. The riot ended with two dead soldiers and thirteen dead civilians. Continuing violence between Protestant and Irish Catholics prompted many cities, including Philadelphia, to form police forces.

Meanwhile, Irish Americans combined with other whites to riot against the black presence in major Northern cities. African American communities in the North grew during the antebellum era as freed blacks and fugitive slaves fled from the South. This influx was resented by unskilled white workers and competition for jobs became more intense as the economy weakened in the 1830s. The growing abolition movement added to hostilities when black and white reformers, both male and female, gathered in public meetings. The mixing of the sexes and races in public raised sexual fears of miscegenation or race-mixing, and prompted mobs to burn down the halls in which the meetings were held. A July 1834 New York City riot set off by meetings to discuss the abolition of slavery turned into an orgy of violence that spread over several days and seemed designed to drive blacks out of New York City. The riot ended only when 1,000 militiamen answered an emergency call and were issued live ammunition with orders to shoot into the crowd. In Boston in 1835, Mayor Theodore Lyman was attacked and his office was stormed by a mob that also attempted to lynch abolitionist newspaper editor William Lloyd Garrison. This racial terrorism would ultimately culminate in the three-day-long New York City Draft Riots of 1863.

Terrorism is a popular political tactic because it often succeeds. Through the coming decades, terrorism would continue to be deployed around the world to influence politics, to end the perceived abuses of big business, and to remove the economic competition of minority groups.

Introduction to Anarchist Terrorism

Anarchism is a social and political movement that advocates the elimination of an organized government and social hierarchy. Most anarchists assert that, in the absence of centralized political structures—such as governments, corporations, legal codes, and private ownership of land and resources—people would form voluntary, cooperative, and community-based associations. Since its inception, the anarchist movement has debated the utility and morality of violence as a means of establishing anarchy.

The editors have chosen to distinguish historical incidences of anarchist terrorism from other forms of modern political terrorism. In the United States, anarchism, socialism, bolshevism, and communism were often conflated. Although most anarchists, communists, and socialists did not advocate terrorism, in the media of the day, the terms implied the threat of violence. Some actions attributed to anarchists were perpetrated by members of other political groups. As a consequence, socialist and communist groups suffered increased oppression during periods of anarchist terrorist activity. Anarchist violence added to public and government fears about so-called left-wing extremists, resulting in the panic of the first Red Scare after the end of the Russian Revolution and World War I (1915–1918). However, by the outbreak of World War II in 1939, the anarchist movement had all but disappeared.

While some modern definitions of terrorism exclude assassinations, the editors have chosen to include primary sources on the assassinations of Alexander II of Russia, United States President William McKinley, and Austrian Archduke Franz Ferdinand, all of whom were killed by anarchists or members of extremist groups who espoused anarchist principles. Between the years 1880 and 1915, nearly ten Western members of royal families or heads of state were assassinated by anarchists. Among those who advocated the use of violence to further anarchist principles, political assassinations were one of the most discussed and favored tactics of the era. Leading anarchist Emma Goldman, who claimed to abhor the use of violence within the movement, once quipped that political assassinations were inevitable actions so long as centralized governments continued to exist.

Articles on more recent incidences of terrorism perpetrated by groups with anarchist underpinnings are located elsewhere in the book. The actions of eco-anarchists, such as the Animal Liberation Front (ALF), and anarcho-primitivists, such as the Unabomber, are featured in the chapter titled "Special Interest Terrorism." An article on terrorist actions in the 1970s by the Baader-Meinhoff Group appears in the "Political Terrorism" chapter.

Edgar Bauer Promotes Anarchy

Critique's Quarrel with Church and State

Book Excerpt

By: Edgar Bauer

Date: 1843

Source: Edgar Bauer, *Der Streit der Kritik mit Kirche und Staat (Critique's Quarrel with Church and State)* (Charlottenburg: Egbert Bauer, 1843; Bern: Friedrich Jenni, 1844), excerpts from Chapter 4, "The Christian State," Part III, "The Christian State and the Free Human Being," Section 3, "The Political Revolution," newly retranslated by Eric v.d. Luft.

About the Author: Edgar Bauer (1820–1886) was the younger brother of the radical Hegelian theologian Bruno Bauer (1809–1882) and a friend of both Karl Marx (1818–1883) and Friedrich Engels (1820–1895).

INTRODUCTION

Edgar Bauer became involved with subversive groups in 1839 while a student at the University of Berlin. His first book, *Bruno Bauer and his Enemies* (1842), defended his brother against political persecution and called readers to total revolution and anarchy. Their brother Egbert published his second book, *Critique's Quarrel with Church and State*, in 1843. It was the world's first sustained theoretical justification of terrorism to advance political and social agendas. Prussian authorities quickly suppressed it and Berlin police soon believed that they had confiscated all copies. But Edgar had smuggled a copy to Switzerland, where Jenni republished it in 1844 and smuggled copies into Prussia. Because of this book, Edgar was imprisoned from September 1844 until Prussia's general amnesty for political prisoners in March 1848.

Edgar began his anarchist and terrorist theorizing in *Bruno Bauer and his Enemies*, but *Critique's Quarrel with Church and State* is concerned almost entirely with encouraging violent means of anarchic political action. He built his theory upon the ideas of Jean-Jacques Rousseau (1712–1778) and Georg Wilhelm Friedrich Hegel (1770–1831) and upon his construal of the Jacobin and Sansculotte influences on the French Revolution. Rousseau and Hegel would certainly have condemned his extrapolations or distortions of their respective philosophies. Rousseau was a Universalist who eschewed violence in any form. Hegel was a liberal constitutional monarchist, but Edgar held constitutions as too restrictive

In bombing the federal building in Oklahoma in 1995, Timothy McVeigh enacted theories set forth by Edgar Bauer in his writings. AP/WIDE WORLD PHOTOS

on human freedom and argued that to be a king in a free state was a capital crime that justified summary execution. While for Hegel the state was necessary and desirable, Edgar belabored the point that individual freedom is always impossible if government exists.

Edgar's revolutionary culture is starkly simple, and as such is its own contradiction. Modeled after the basest instincts of the Reign of Terror, it embodies the very inconsistencies that led to the downfall of Maximilien Robespierre (1758–1794) and the rise of Napoleon Bonaparte (1769–1821), which Edgar deplored. Adopting the Sansculotte view that human freedom is identifiable with and only achievable by abrogating all restraint, he thus paradoxically, and against his own wishes, ensured that such freedom would never be achieved, since lack of restraint leads inexorably to tyranny.

Yet Edgar's faith in anarchy as pure freedom was unshakable. He permitted any degree of violence toward achieving this goal. He believed that the only worthwhile freedom was absolute freedom. The very existence of any government, especially the nation-state, necessarily curtails or cancels freedom. The state is thus the natural enemy of the whole human spirit, whose only aspiration is freedom. Natural human freedom, Rousseauian freedom, is stifled by industrial capitalism, bourgeois society, and their accompanying mentalities. Edgar thus saw all modern government as his enemy because it pretends to enfranchise and liberate its citizens while in fact controlling them politically and enslaving them to the economy.

The selection below, mainly an interpretation of the French Revolutionary events of 1793, shows Edgar at his most vehement, and could have been titled "The First Principles of Terrorism." Political theorists of all persuasions in the nineteenth century typically took the French Revolution as their point of departure. For them it was the most significant event in world history, the unique and unprecedented reversal of the established order, not just the overthrow of a monarchy, but the introduction of new ideas that turned the world upside-down.

If Edgar had a hero, it was another wayward disciple of Rousseau, Robespierre, the effective dictator of France from the triumph of the Jacobins over the Girondists on June 2, 1793, until the coup d'état of 9 Thermidor and his death by guillotine on July 28, 1794. Although Edgar disagreed with Robespierre's authoritarian policies, he understood why they were necessary, sympathized with Robespierre's motives, and praised him for bringing violent purges into the revolutionary mix. Viewing the Reign of Terror through the lens of Hegelian historicism, i.e., the belief that historical forces shape events, Edgar saw Robespierre as an innocent victim of circumstance, forced into authoritarianism only because he needed a means to exterminate supporters of both the old regime and the new spirit of compromise. Edgar's Robespierre remained an idealist to the end, and killed only for the sake of promoting and safeguarding human freedom.

As a latter-day Jacobin and Sansculotte, Edgar, like most of the Young Hegelians, adored the French Revolution and thought he had it completely analyzed so that, if the word could be spread, the next revolution would not fail. Edgar thus took the short step from Bruno's idea of the rightful dominance of critical spirit over the phlegmatic masses to the self-righteousness of the terrorist. His books, pamphlets, and speeches in the early 1840s threatened the Prussian regime with a return to the French Revolution in general and the Reign of Terror in particular. As far as we know, he committed no violent political acts himself, but strongly encouraged them, especially during the 1848 revolutions.

■ PRIMARY SOURCE

They often enough reproach us that our loftiest fantasies indeed go no further than wanting to restore the French Revolution. They say that we seek our ideals here among the anarchists of 1793 and that our heroes are the Jacobins. But they are quite mistaken. Our project would then in fact be nothing but a reaction, and in all history no reaction has ever brought any good with it. Do they think we are blind? Do they think that we cannot see the consequences of the Revolution? The consequences of the Revolution were the empire of Napoleon and the restoration of Louis XVIII. An observant historian will notice that any new, merely political revolution will come to nothing but the restoration of legitimacy. . . .

. . . The Reformation taught us the great lesson that we cannot thoroughly heal any evil in any organism unless we subject that entire organism to new laws of life. . . . The French Revolution is a similar case. As the Revolution returned toward so-called primal human rights, it sought to realize these rights *within the state*, but that was nothing but the attempt to make humans free within the state, as if such a thing were possible, and the result proved that it is not possible. If revolution is to succeed, then we must understand freedom more broadly and must jettison its exclusively *political* character. . . .

. . . The Revolution resulted from the life of the state. . . . The freedom party took as its premise that everyone must take part in the life of the state, pretentiously displayed the word "people," and decreed that the people were the only legitimate power in the state. The individual would not be tolerated who called himself to a higher traditional right, who claimed all state power so that he exclusively would have the enjoyment of freedom and would make the people's living conditions dependent upon his mere grace. Let no law exist unless the people's reason has agreed to it. Let no right exist unless it finds its confirmation in the advantage of the state and in the demand of universal equality. The freedom party was in the right. But, for itself, on its own terms, the other party was also in the right. The other party proved that the natural representative of state power was the king, that the king's *right* to dominance could not be permitted, and that the *law* would be shaken if the king could no longer sustain the inherited rights of many citizens.

The beginning of the Revolution was . . . the constitutional mediation between these two parties, an armistice in which the rights of each were somewhat curtailed, i.e., in which injustice was done to each. Monarchy retained its hereditary privilege, but the king was now appointed by the people, no longer by God. . . .

. . . The Revolution went further. The internal contradiction of constitutional organization asserted itself. . . .

Monarchy was abolished. The execution of Louis XVI should have been a lesson to all peoples that in a free state it is a crime to be called "king." It should have taught them that nothing sacrosanct and inviolable may be placed ahead of the people. But now, they believed, they had achieved the free state and the true republic.

Anarchy, the start of all good things, was there at least. A hopeful demolition was approaching. Religion was abolished yet preserved and raised to a higher level. But that anarchy was an anarchy within the state. Could the state survive without stability, police rule, or severe military control? Of course not! And that was the revolutionaries' mistake, their only mistake. They believed that true freedom could become actual in the state and they failed to see that all the strivings toward freedom since the start of the Revolution had naturally moved against the state. Robespierre indeed wished for a universal equality, so that even the Sansculottes, the most deprived, could have a voice and take part in the life of the state. . . . But . . . the Revolution did not go far enough because it could not go far enough, and because of that it had to go very quickly backwards. Robespierre undoubtedly saw himself pushed in that direction . . . Even the splendidly striving yet despondent terrorists had to reach their end on the guillotine in order to maintain equality. The people deserted politics, which after all had not brought them any freedom. They returned to their dull, ordinary interests; and the reaction, i.e., the attempt to restore the state and make it sacred again, found every door open to it.

Thus Napoleon's tyrannical empire was a necessary consequence of the inconsistent Revolution. If we ever want to live in a state, then of course we must get used to its differences, its imperious police, its surveillance, its stability, its medals, and its privileges. Terrorists gladly accepted their medals from the emperor, incarnate republicans allowed him to make them counts and dukes, and almost without becoming inconsistent. At least it was the state and its particulars that made them inconsistent. Indeed even the reaction was not satisfied with the empire, for had not the empire been created by the Revolution? . . .

If the political revolution does not know how to overcome itself, then it does not understand how to banish the abstraction of the state or how to proceed to the comprehension of full communal freedom. Thus it will always, again and again, arrive only at legitimacy and the tyranny of stability. Always whatever exists will place itself above the freedom of the spirit—and with perfect right, since freedom is dangerous to whatever exists.

The political revolution serves us as nothing more than proof that it alone cannot get things done. It is an instructive example, and that may be enough. It is, in itself, a complete historical phenomenon. It can never, and should never, return *in its old form*. . . .

Indeed we do not deny that the eternal struggles of revolution in search of freedom continue to work themselves out in history. Nor do we deny that their course will be similar to that of the [French] Revolution. But we do deny that the lessons of the Revolution will pass away without a trace in history, and we deny that modern historical development will arrive at the same abstract goal at which the Revolution stopped in order to roll back downhill.

We hold that the new experiments that various peoples are making with political freedom are precisely useful to show humankind that there is nothing for them in political freedom or in the glorified constitutional and republican forms of the state. The attempts at a state, at which these peoples now toil, will eventually lead them beyond the state. History will teach them that the very word, "freedom," is hostile to the state. . . .

The state has more and more increased its power to stagnate. Rule is by the majority of property owners, who profit from no change. Ideas are suppressed. Free expression is persecuted by trials in the press, and the free spirit who loves the fresh air of movement groans under the burden of a dull, bourgeois, egoistic regime. That is what a constitution leads to—and must lead to. Just give a constitution enough time and it will become as oppressive as any other form of the state. Its laws will clothe themselves in the tyranny of law in general.

Freedom, which has grown smart through experience, certainly does not lack time to rebel against these laws. But the constitutional form of government will not sign its own death warrant. It will not voluntarily give up its laws to the progress that criticizes them.

Thus it is clear that nothing can exist except eternal struggle, namely, the life-and-death struggle by which those laws will be destroyed. But if freedom begins this annihilating struggle, will it contradict itself and sanctify new laws? Or will it finally tear everything down once and for all?

SIGNIFICANCE

Until the 1970s, Edgar Bauer was known only to a handful of academicians studying the Young Hegelians of the 1840s. As such, his direct impact on subsequent terrorist ideology has been minimal. His indirect impact, on the other hand, has been substantial, as his works were used by more famous anarchist or terrorist writers such as Max Stirner (1806–1856), Karl Heinzen (1809–1880), Mikhail Bakunin (1814–1876), Johann Joseph Most (1846–1906), and Sergei Nechaev (1847–1882). Marx and Engels each criticized the Bauer brothers severely, but these others generally agreed with Edgar's views on freedom and violence.

FURTHER RESOURCES
Books

Luft, Eric v.d. "Edgar Bauer and the Origins of the Theory of Terrorism," in *The Left-Hegelians: New Philosophical and Political Perspectives*, edited by Douglas Moggach and Andrew Chitty. Cambridge: Cambridge University Press, forthcoming.

Marx, Karl, and Friedrich Engels. *The German Ideology*, translated by S. Ryazanskaya. Moscow: Progress, 1964.

Marx, Karl, and Friedrich Engels. *The Holy Family, or, Critique of Critical Critique*, translated by R. Dixon. Moscow: Foreign Languages Publishing House, 1956.

Stirner, Max. *The Ego and His Own*, translated by Steven Byington, revised and edited by David Leopold. Cambridge: Cambridge University Press, 1995.

"Murder and Liberty"

Karl Heinzen Advocates Political Assassination

Pamphlet

By: Karl Peter Heinzen

Date: 1853

Source: Excerpts from Karl Heinzen, *Murder and Liberty, 1853, Reprinted as a Contribution for the "Peace League" of Geneva* (Indianapolis, Indiana: H. Lieber, 1881).

About the Author: Karl Peter Heinzen (1809–1880) was a radical German democrat, an active participant in the 1848 revolutions in Germany, and, for the last thirty-one years of his life, a political exile in America.

INTRODUCTION

Most of the earliest theorists of general class warfare terrorism were either German or Russian. Along with Edgar Bauer (1820–1886), Mikhail Bakunin (1814–1876), Wilhelm Weitling (1808–1871), Sergei Nechaev (1847–1882), and Johann Most (1846–1906), Heinzen formulated the terrorist approach to modern politics. These six authors typically worked independently of one another, sometimes drawing upon each other's work and sometimes rejecting it, and the relations among them were quite complex.

Heinzen experienced his first political exile in 1829 when he was a medical student at the University of Bonn. He returned to Germany in 1831 and thereafter worked in various civil service positions, secretly pamphleteering to urge violent uprising against the Prussian, Austrian, and Russian regimes. Friedrich Engels (1820–1895) considered him simple-minded and argued that his reduction of the problems of the common people to the existence of autocrats was not helpful to the proletarian revolution. In the 1848 revolutions, he fought alongside Friedrich Franz Karl Hecker (1811–1881), Gustav von Struve (1805–1870), and other leaders of the Baden republican uprising. After their defeat in the fall of 1848, he fled Germany and in 1849 settled in America as a refugee. From 1854 until his death, supported by several German immigrants—including the prominent woman physician, Marie Elizabeth Zakrzewska (1829–1902)—he edited his own radical German-language newspaper, *Der Pionier* (The Pioneer).

In 1848, Heinzen wrote a vigorous polemical essay, "*Der Mord*" (Murder), which advocated tyrannicide by claiming that monarchs and potentates were *ipso facto* murderers and thieves and that, therefore, to kill them is only to act in self-defense. After his friend and fellow revolutionist, Johann Philipp Becker (1809–1886), published the essay in Biel, Switzerland, in two installments in January and February 1849 (in his short-lived underground newspaper, *Die Evolution*), "*Der Mord*" became a rallying point for the most extreme opponents of established governments worldwide.

In 1853, Heinzen revised and expanded "*Der Mord*" into a 30-page pamphlet that appeared in English several times as "Murder and Liberty".

PRIMARY SOURCE

There are a number of technical expressions for the important manipulation by which one man destroys the life of another. . . . but the object is always the same, viz., the annihilation of a hostile or inconvenient human life. From the stand-point of justice and humanity, the destruction of the life of another is always unjust and barbarous, whether it occur on the scaffold or in battle, in the murderer's den or on the dueling grounds, in prison or on the street. The language of humanity has, therefore, no concern for the subtle differences by which the dominant barbarity claims on the one hand as permissible killing, what it condemns on the other hand as punishable murder. Humanity must absolutely condemn all killing, since she refers all hostile conflicts among men to the tribunal of reason, and not to that of force; she is, therefore, only consistent if she designates *every* voluntary annihilation of the life of another human being with the condemnatory term murder. Her only endeavor can be to abolish murder; yet, as long as murder offers the only means for the attainment of this object, Humanity is also compelled to draw the sword and to become the murderess of the murderers. If one man is permitted to murder, all must be permitted to do so, particularly those who practice it for the annihilation of the murderers by profession or "by the grace of God."

. . . The large, bloodstained picture which we call history shows us murder in a thousand forms, and the murderers under a thousand names. Sometimes it is called war, and the murderers' heroes; sometimes it is called insurrection, and the murderers are called the people; again it is called assassination, and the murderers are called bandits, etc. It is always the same simple object, viz: to neutralize opposition by destroying human life; according to the motives and circumstances, it meets with different criticism, which as a rule is wholly perverse and servile. The principles of justice remain unchanged in history; but their *recognition* is possible only to free judgment for which reason they are sometimes wholly obscured for long periods. The judgment of men is, usually ruled, nay, entirely suppressed, by the *prevailing fact,* so that they acknowledge even the prevailing murder, in spite of its injustice, while they condemn the conquered murder, in spite of all justice. . . .

. . . what signify the few thousand executions of the French Revolution in comparison with the millions of murders of the centuries of reactionary dominion which brought about that popular explosion? I remind the reader among other things of the fact that at the outbreak of that revolution *several million* victims of the despots and priests filled the dungeons of Europe. What signify the daggers of Harmodius [assassin of Hipparchus] and Brutus [assassin of Julius Caesar], or the arrow of [Wilhem] Tell [assassin of Hermann Gessler], or the attempt[s] of [Giuseppe Maria] Fieschi and [Louis] Alibaud [on the life of Louis-Philippe] in comparison with the numberless murders by which the tyrants put their opponents out of the way in all conceivable manners? . . . Caesar, Tiberius, Caligula, Claudius, Galba, Otho, Vitellius were murdered. From Commodus to Constantine the Great, 27 out of 36 emperors were murdered. Of all these assassinations of tyrants, only the smallest share is to be attributed to friends of freedom or revolutionists; but suppose, they were all committed by them,—are they worth mentioning in comparison, with the mass-destruction of human life that proceeded from these tyrants? How many human beings, did Sulla murder! But he went unpunished after he had laid down the dictatorship, and lice had to perform executioner's duty on him—men in their degeneracy had failed to do it. . . . weakness has always been the main fault of the revolutionists, that, in ill-conceived humanity and devoid of energy, they spared the lives of incurable reactionaries, or that, blinded by the unreasonable joy over the seeming victories of their cause, they failed to gain it in reality, or, at least, to secure it by the complete annihilation of their enemies. Called to exercise the functions of [the] Goddess of Justice towards all the enemies of the people, they dropped the sword of the Goddess from their hands at the first blow, and kept only her blindness. A revolutionist in whose power it lay to annihilate all the representatives of the system of violence and murder which rules the world and lays it waste, would deserve a thousand-fold the traitor's death, if he hesitated but a moment. . . .

. . . the assassin Tell was praised as liberator, because from safe ambush he shot down the slave of a tyrant . . . Switzerland which today celebrates the memory of the assassin Tell on the walls of every house, all Switzerland becomes the object of persecution for all the reactionary blood-hounds, when a German Tell discharges only a revolutionary thought arrow from his quiver. Make your own applications of this logic. Neither the despots nor the republicans reject murder as "immoral," but they hold it to be moral, only if they practice it themselves, or . . . if it serves their interest. . . .

Revolution is only *self-defense.* Murder in self-defense is not only permitted, but is also a duty to society, when it is directed against a professional murderer. The fault of self-defense, as well as of the revolution, usually lies in the fact that it is satisfied with the immediate results without using its victory to secure guarantees for the future. A bandit attacks a traveler and is disarmed by him, but allowed to live; this gives the bandit an opportunity to make surer work of the traveler next time, and jeopardizes also the lives of his friends. Just so with the revolution. It is folly and self-betrayal, if it limits self-defense to the result of the moment. It must *root out* the reaction in its carriers, its representatives; for its enemies are *incurable,* like the merely disarmed bandit, like the spared tiger. We *know* our enemies, we know them all and in every place personally. There will be no more excuse, if they are again spared. Whoever stands beyond the line that separates the ruling powers from the people, is doomed. Let the people execute the sentence, and let them spare only those who were misled, compelled, or powerless.

The road to humanity leads over the summit of cruelty. This is the inexorable law of *necessity* dictated to us by the reaction. We *cannot* evade it, unless we would renounce the future. If we would accomplish the end, we *must* use the means. If we would secure the life of the people, we *must* secure the death of its enemies; if we would vindicate humanity, we *must* not shrink—from murder. . . .

I preach the murder of despots openly, because it is a right, because it is a duty, because it is the only means to save humanity from the rule of murder, and because it must be acknowledged to be universally permitted and just. I know that the famous leaders [of the revolution] are not to be relied upon, that they care more for their reputation of gentility than for the radical revolution, and that the heads of the reactionaries are safest in their hands. Ther[e]fore, I endeavor to make the murder of despots a cause of the people, so that the people may without considering the genteel great men *murder democratically* on every *occasion,* if they would live democratically after the revolution. . . .

The doctrine of the murder of tyrants must be short, as the murder itself. Only one thing remains. It was not my object to shed blood and to annihilate tyrants on paper, in order to secure cheap alleviation for long-repressed wrath over a world full of unprecedented disgrace and disgraceful acts. It was my object, in the first place, to destroy that false ethical code, to annihilate the "moral scruples" by which thousands, especially of our country-men, are kept from decisive action, even when free opportunity is offered. It was my object to vindicate not only the aims of the revolution, but also its means, including assassination, and to render it as *legitimate* as the tyrants have done with their murder by war, their "legal" murder, their murder by "court-martial." My further task is to give hints concerning the augmentation and application of such means. The safety of the despots rests wholly on the preponderance of their means of destruction. Remove their soldiers, or only spike their guns, and they sink trembling into the dust and whine at the feet of their subjects. The first aim then, must be to do away with the preponderance of engines of mass-destruction, which we do not and cannot possess, by means of the homeopathic use, as it were, of powerful destructive substances which it would cost little to furnish and which might be obtained or prepared with little risk of discovery.

SIGNIFICANCE

Heinzen's influence has been mainly secret and subversive, but very powerful. Even though he apparently committed no violent acts himself, his calls to violence have inspired terrorists since the 1840s. Johann Most, likewise an exile in America, frequently cited Heinzen in his own radical periodical, *Die Freiheit* (Freedom). In sympathy with the attack of the anarchist Leon Czolgosz (1873–1901) on President William McKinley (1843–1901), Most reprinted Heinzen's 1849 essay on murder in *Die Freiheit*, no. 36 (September 7, 1901), the day after the shooting. Federal agents and local police nationwide, already busy rounding up anarchists after Czolgosz's immediate confession, took this opportunity to arrest Most and send him to prison for a year.

In a sense, Heinzen was typical of militant "ends-justify-the-means" theorists from Caligula to Stalin. In the name of humanity and peace, he advocated extreme levels of cruelty and violence. Not only the monarchs and potentates themselves, but also all who support them, from their willing henchmen to their unwilling servants, and even innocent passersby if they should happen to be present, must be killed without pity in order to build an anarchic society based on wisdom and justice. The essential contradiction and numerous internal inconsistencies of this line of reasoning are self-evident. Like most terrorists, Heinzen failed to see that killing unarmed, unprepared, or innocent civilians undermines the purity and authority of whatever cause the killer supports. His basic argument, expressed as a syllogism, will not withstand the scrutiny of even the simplest Aristotelian logic:

Premise 1: Murder is always wrong.
Premise 2: Murder occurs.
Conclusion: Therefore, to murder murderers is right.

FURTHER RESOURCES

Books

Alexander, Yonah, and Walter Laqueur, eds. *The Terrorism Reader: A Historical Anthology.* New York: Penguin, 1987.

Wittke, Carl Frederick. *Against the Current: The Life of Karl Heinzen (1809–80).* Chicago: University of Chicago Press, 1945.

Periodicals

Grob-Fitzgibbon, Benjamin, "From the Dagger to the Bomb: Karl Heinzen and the Evolution of Political Terror." *Terrorism and Political Violence*, vol. 16, no. 1 (Spring 2004): 97–115.

Haymarket Massacre

Illustration

By: Anonymous

Date: c. 1886

Source: An illustration of the scene following the Haymarket Massacre in Chicago from the Chicago Historical Society.

About the Artist: The artist of the illustration is unknown.

INTRODUCTION

The Haymarket affair represented the coming together of a number of important trends that were transforming the United States in the late nineteenth century. One trend was urbanization. At the beginning of the Industrial Revolution, the United States was largely a rural nation, but between 1870 and 1900 the number of cities with more than 100,000 people grew from just fourteen to thirty-eight, and fifteen of those cities had more than a quarter million people. In 1830, Chicago was so small that it was not even mentioned in the national census; by 1890 it was the nation's second-largest city.

Accompanying this rapid urbanization was an equally rapid growth in industrialization, which in turn led to deepening tensions between capital and labor. At one end of the economic spectrum were wealthy entre-preneurs, industrialists, stockholders, and managers; at the other was unskilled factory labor, which had migrated to the cities to become little more than a cog in the machine of industrialization. In between was a middle class that was increasingly suspicious of labor unioniza-tion, associating it with radical foreign immigrants, agi-tation, communism, anarchy, and social unrest. In the summer of 1877, when a national railroad strike sparked widespread conflict between labor and law enforcement, a riot broke out when Chicago labor agitators vandalized Burlington & Quincy locomotives.

By the early 1880s Chicago had become a center for radical, socialist, and anarchist thought. While some anarchists accepted the more moderate ideals of the International Working People's Association, others preached—often in Chicago's numerous socialist and anarchist newspapers—that violence was the only way that labor could redress its grievances. In April 1885, the anarchist newspaper *Alarm* wrote: "Dynamite is a peace-maker because it makes it unsafe to wrong our fellows." Other publications instructed anarchists in the art of bomb making.

In this climate, anxiety about labor unrest contin-ued to grow among civic leaders, newspaper editors, the police, and the public. It intensified in April 1885, when a bomb exploded during an anarchist rally protesting the opening of the downtown Board of Trade Building. In May 1885, the Illinois militia killed two striking work-ers in the nearby town of Lemont. In August, bystanders were beaten during a strike at the West Division Railway Company. Tensions remained high in 1886, when labor, lobbying for an eight-hour workday, called a general strike to begin on May 1. The police, Pinkerton detec-tives (a private agency hired by business owners), and the state militia were on high alert.

On May 3, four people were killed when the police fired on a crowd at a strike against the McCormick Harvesting Machine Company. To protest the killings, Chicago anarchists called a rally at Chicago's Haymarket Square on May 4. About 1,300 people showed up for the protest, but most left when it began to rain. A police

contingent of 180 officers had just arrived to disperse the remaining three hundred protestors when a bomb exploded in their midst, killing seven policemen and wounding dozens more. Rioting began as the panicked police opened fire into the crowd. Several people were killed and a hundred more were wounded, including as many as sixty police officers. No one was ever able to establish who was responsible for the bomb.

PRIMARY SOURCE

HAYMARKET MASSACRE
See primary source image.

SIGNIFICANCE

The Haymarket bombing induced the first "Red Scare" in the United States. The public was in a state of frenzy, convinced that foreign-born communist ter-rorists were bent on the overthrow of American ideals and institutions. The authorities embarked on a kind of witch hunt, less concerned with who had actually hurled the bomb than with rounding up hundreds of real and suspected anarchists. The Illinois state's attorney was reported to have ordered, "Make the raids first and look up the law afterward!"

Eventually, eight known anarchists were indicted for conspiracy in the bombing and one, Rudolph Schnaubelt, was charged with killing a police officer with a "certain deadly and destructive instrument, charged with divers dangerous and explosive sub-stances." Seven of the eight were German immigrants, and all were suspect not because of evidence pointing at them but because of their political beliefs.

The trial, during which any pretence of fairness was abandoned, began on June 21. After fifty-four days, including three weeks of jury selection, the eight men were convicted. Seven were sentenced to hang; the eighth was sentenced to prison. The executions were sched-uled for November 11, but on November 10, one of the men, Louis Lingg, hanged himself in jail and the Illinois governor commuted the sentences of two others to life imprisonment. Four of the men—George Engel, Adolph Fischer, Albert Parsons, and August Spies—were exe-cuted the next day.

In 1893 John Peter Altgeld (1847–1902), newly elected as governor, granted pardons to Samuel Fielden, Michael Schwab, and Oscar Neebe, seemingly putting an end to the tragedy, but the Haymarket affair fueled resistance to unionism and nativist fears of immigrants for years to follow.

Haymarket Massacre An illustration of the scene after the Haymarket Massacre in Chicago. © CHICAGO HISTORICAL SOCIETY, CHICAGO/BRIDGEMAN ART LIBRARY

FURTHER RESOURCES

Books

Avrich, Paul. *The Haymarket Tragedy*. Princeton, NJ: Princeton University Press, 1986.

Web sites

Chicago Historical Society and Northwestern University. "The Dramas of Haymarket." <http://www.chicagohistory.org/dramas/overview/over.htm> (accessed May 16, 2005).

Memoirs of a Revolutionist

Assassination of Alexander II, Tsar of Russia

Memoir

By: Peter Alexeievich Kropotkin

Date: 1899

Source: Excerpt from Peter Kropotkin's *Memoirs of a Revolutionist* (New York: Houghton Mifflin, 1899), chapter 32.

About the Author: Peter Kropotkin, the "Anarchist Prince," was born in Moscow on December 12, 1842, the son of a Russian prince. After several years in the military, he left in 1867 to pursue his interests in science (especially geography), and to study the condition of the Russian peasantry. In 1872, Kropotkin traveled to Switzerland, where he joined the International Workingmen's Association. During the 1870s and 1880s, he came to reject the Darwinian concept of "survival of the fittest" in favor of anarchist-communist principles based on mutual aid among members of society. He expressed these views in such books as *Memoirs of a Revolutionist* (1899) and *Mutual Aid: A Factor of Evolution* (1902). Kropotkin died on February 8, 1921.

INTRODUCTION

Tsar Alexander II (1818–1881) of Russia ascended to the throne in 1855. History will forever link his name

Forged passport with picture of himself in disguise enabled Lenin to escape to Finland in the fall of 1917. Warrant for his arrest had been issued in July of that same year.

The false passport Lenin (whose brother was a member of Narodnaya Volya) used to escape Russia in July 1917.
© HULTON-DEUTSCH COLLECTION/CORBIS

to the emancipation of the Russian serfs. In 1856, he famously stated that it would be "better to abolish serfdom from above than to wait until it begins to abolish itself from below." He carried through on his conviction in 1861, when he signed a manifesto freeing some 20 million Russian serfs.

This move met with little opposition, for among all classes of Russian society the conviction had been growing that the serf system was inefficient. Further, many of Russia's intellectuals and members of the higher classes, led by Alexander, wanted to forge a more modern Russia by adopting the liberal reforms of western Europe.

In the years that followed, Alexander initiated further reforms. In 1864, he reformed the judiciary, making it an independent branch of government and abolishing secret trials and corporal punishment. That year, too, he created the *zemstvo* system, granting autonomy and some measure of democracy to local government. Alexander advocated a free press, and he restructured the military, requiring military service of all social classes, not just of the lower classes.

In this more liberal climate, numerous anarchist, populist, and revolutionary groups began to flex their muscles. Many of these groups believed that the only way to reform Russian society was through violence and terrorism, including the assassination of top government officials. Alexander himself survived a number of assassination attempts. On April 4, 1866, an attempt on

his life was made in St. Petersburg; on April 20, 1879, the tsar fled on foot as a would-be assassin fired five shots at him; in December 1879, the anarchist group Narodnaya Volya (People's Will) tried unsuccessfully to bomb the tsar's train; on February 5, 1880, the same group detonated a bomb beneath the tsar's dining room at the Winter Palace, but he survived because he was late arriving to dinner. In response to these attempts on his life and to the spread of anarchist and revolutionary doctrines, Alexander adopted more repressive policies in the later years of his reign.

Narodnaya Volya finally succeeded on March 13, 1881. The tsar was in St. Petersburg when a bomb was thrown at the carriage in which he was riding near the Winter Palace. Alexander got out of the carriage to check on the condition of an injured bystander. When he approached the man who had thrown the bomb, a second terrorist threw a bomb that severely injured the tsar, who died a few hours later. Peter Kropotkin describes the scene in the excerpt from *Memoirs of a Revolutionist* that follows.

PRIMARY SOURCE

The person of the Liberator of the serfs was surrounded by an aureole, which protected him infinitely better than the swarms of police officials. If Alexander II had shown at this juncture the least desire to improve the state of affairs in Russia; if he had only called in one or two of those men with whom he had collaborated during the reform period, and had ordered them to make an inquiry into the conditions of the country, or merely of the peasantry; if he had shown any intention of limiting the powers of the secret police, his steps would have been hailed with enthusiasm. A word would have made him the Liberator again, and once more the youth would have repeated Hérzen's words: "Thou had conquered, Galilean." But just as during the Polish insurrection, the despot awoke in him, and, inspired by Katkóff, he found nothing to do but to nominate special military governors—for hanging.

Then and then only, a handful of revolutionists—the Executive Committee—supported, I must say, by the growing discontent in the educated classes, and even in the Tsar's immediate surroundings, declared that war against absolutism which, after several attempts, ended in 1881 in the death of Alexander II. . . .

It is known how it happened. A bomb was thrown under his iron-clad carriage, to stop it. Several Circassians of the escort were wounded. Rysakóff, who flung the bomb was arrested on the spot. Then, although the coachman of the Tsar earnestly advised him not to get out, saying that he could drive him still in the slightly damaged carriage, he insisted upon alighting. He felt that his military dignity required him to see the wounded Circassians, to condole with them as he had done with the wounded during the Turkish war, when a mad storming of Plevna, doomed to end in a terrible disaster, was made on the day of his fête. He approached Rysakóff and asked him something; and as he passed close by another young man, Grinevétsky, the latter threw a bomb between himself and Alexander II, so that both of them should be killed. They both lived but a few hours.

There Alexander II lay upon the snow, profusely bleeding, abandoned by every one of his followers! All had disappeared. It was cadets, returning from the parade, who lifted the suffering Tsar from the snow and put him in a sledge, covering his shivering body with a cadet mantle and his bare head with a cadet cap. And it was one of the terrorists, Emeliánoff, with a bomb wrapped in a paper under his arm, who, at the risk of being arrested on the spot and hanged, rushed with the cadets to the help of the wounded man. Human nature is full of contrasts.

SIGNIFICANCE

Narodnaya Volya was formed in 1879, and the members of its executive committee included some of the leading anarchist revolutionaries in Russia. Its program called for creation of a parliament and the drafting of a constitution; universal voting rights; freedom of the press, speech, and assembly; local self-government; a volunteer army; redistribution of land to the people; and self-determination for oppressed peoples.

An influential faction of the group believed that violence was the only way to spark a revolution and reform the government. The members of this faction, which included the brother of later Communist dictator Vladimir Lenin, made at least seven attempts on the life of Alexander II and his successor and son, Alexander III.

The government took severe countermeasures against Narodnaya Volya. In connection with the assassination of Alexander II, six members of the group were arrested (a seventh, who threw the bomb that killed the tsar, died in the attack), and five were sentenced to death. During the period 1879–1883, 2,000 members of the group were prosecuted in seventy trials, effectively breaking the back of the organization.

In later years, attempts were made to revive Narodnaya Volya, but these efforts failed, in large part because of the group's terrorist agenda. Meanwhile, Alexander III believed that the growing anarchist movement during his father's reign was the result of excess liberalization, so he adopted more autocratic, nationalist policies. In particular, he stripped the *zemstvos* of

their power and began a plan of Russification among his German, Polish, Finnish, and Jewish subjects.

FURTHER RESOURCES
Books
Kropotkin, Peter. *Anarchism: A Collection of Revolutionary Writings.* Mineola, NY: Dover, 2002.

Van der Kiste, John. *The Romanovs, 1818–1959: Alexander II of Russia and His Family.* Gloucester, UK: Alan Sutton, 2000.

Web sites
LaborLawTalk.com. "Peter Kropotkin." <http://encyclopedia.laborlawtalk.com/Peter_Kropotkin> (accessed May 16, 2005).

Story of an Eyewitness

Leon Czolgosz Assassinates President William McKinley

Newspaper article

By: Leon F. Czolgosz

Date: September 8, 1901

Source: *New York Times.*

About the Author: According to the *New York Times*, the article contains "a graphic account by an Exposition official who stood near the President when shots were fired."

INTRODUCTION

Leon F. Czolgosz, born in Detroit in 1873 to Polish immigrants, had a reputation as a quiet loner with a violent temper. While working as a blacksmith in a Cleveland wire mill in the 1890s, he began attending meetings of local socialists and anarchists. In 1898, Czolgosz quit his job at the mill and never again worked regularly. Czolgosz's family and friends, including fellow anarchists, later reported that they regarded him as mentally unbalanced. On September 6, 1901, Czolgosz fatally shot President William McKinley in a reception line at the Pan American Exposition in Buffalo, New York. Convicted of murder, he died in the electric chair at the prison at Auburn, New York, on October 29, 1901.

Anarchism appeared in Europe in the 1860s as a reaction to the perceived brutalities of unregulated capitalism. Seeing private property as the root cause of inequality, anarchists sought to eliminate private ownership. Arguing that government officials cooperated

Drawing depicting the assassination of President William McKinley by Leon Czolgosz on September 6, 1901. AP/WIDE WORLD PHOTOS

with property owners to exploit the workers, anarchists sought the elimination of the state. They believed that the abolition of the state would allow individuals to live full and free lives. To this end, some anarchists advocated revolutionary violence.

Political opponents had threatened President William McKinley with death, but the threats were not considered serious. On the hot afternoon of September 6, 1901, McKinley shook hands with people in a long line at the Pan American Exposition in Buffalo, New York. Thousands had waited for hours in the hope of shaking hands with the popular president. Exposition officials had deployed extra guards, but their position in the receiving area of the Temple of Music made it harder for the McKinley's three Secret Service men to scrutinize every outstretched hand.

Czolgosz waited in the long line. The handkerchief carried by Czolgosz, a short, slender man in a black suit, concealed a short-barreled .32 revolver. As McKinley reached forward to shake Czolgosz's empty left hand, the anarchist fired two bullets through the handkerchief in his right hand. The first hit a button on McKinley's jacket and the second lodged in the President's pancreas. Czolgosz was knocked to the ground and the crowd seemed ready to maul him. "Let no one hurt

him," said the wounded President. Moments later he turned to his secretary: "My wife, be careful how you tell her—oh, be careful."

McKinley's doctors thought that he would survive, but the medical technology of the era was poor. The doctors could not find the bullet, and gangrene set in. The President died at 2:15 A.M. on September 14, 1901.

▌ PRIMARY SOURCE

Buffalo, N.Y., Sept. 7.—

"A little girl was immediately ahead of him in the line," he said," and the President, after patting her kindly on the head, turned with a smile of welcome and extended hand.

"The assassin thrust out both of his hands, brushed aside the President's right hand with his left hand, lurched forward and, thrusting his right hand close against the President's breast, pulled the trigger twice. The shots came in such quick succession as to be almost simultaneous.

"At the first shot the President quivered and clutched at his chest. At the second shot he doubled slightly forward and sank back. It all happened in a moment.

"Quick as was Czolgosz he was not quick enough to fire a third shot. He was seized by a Secret Service man, who stood directly opposite the President, and hurled to the floor. Soldiers of the United States Artillery, detailed at the reception, sprang upon the pair, and Exposition police and Secret Service detectives also rushed upon them.

"A detective clutched the assassin's right hand, tore from it the handkerchief, and seized the revolver. The artillerymen, seeing the man with the revolver, grabbed him and held him powerless, and a private of the artillery got the pistol.

"Meanwhile the President, supported by Detective Geary and President Milburn, was assisted to a chair. . . . His face was deathly white. He made no outcry, but sank back with one hand holding his abdomen, the other fumbling at his breast. His eyes were open and he was clearly conscious of all that happened. . . .

"Then moved by a paroxysm of pain, he writhed to the left and his eyes fell upon the prostrate form of his would-be-murderer lying on the floor, bloodstained and helpless beneath the blows of the guard. The President raised his right hand, stained with his own blood, and placed it on the shoulder of his secretary.

"'Let no one hurt him,' he gasped.

"He sank back as . . . the guard bore the murderer out of the President's sight.

"They carried Czolgosz into a side room at the northwest corner of the temple."

SIGNIFICANCE

McKinley's murder fit into a pattern of anarchist attacks in the 1890s. Anarchists assassinated a number of European political leaders and monarchs, including French President François Sadi-Carnot in 1894, Prime Minister Antonio Canovas del Castillo of Spain in 1897, the Empress Elizabeth of Austria-Hungary in 1898, and King Umberto I of Italy in 1900. Most anarchists did not assume that such killings would necessarily lead to revolution, but saw them as the inevitable result of government oppression.

McKinley's death led to more government persecution of anarchists and did nothing to help the anarchist cause in the United States. In the aftermath of the McKinley attack, anarchism came under heavy assault from the government, the press, and the public. All anarchists, whether peaceful or violent, were demonized as scoundrels and deviants. Across the country, crowds vented their anger on any anarchists that they could find. The pressure forced anarchists to begin to shift away from individual acts of violence toward labor union activism on behalf of oppressed workers.

Perhaps more importantly, McKinley's death propelled Vice President Theodore Roosevelt into the White House. A much more dynamic leader than McKinley, Roosevelt was the first Progressive president. Along with other Progressives, he held that government had an obligation to protect the public by establishing laws in a range of areas that had been free of government control in the past. Roosevelt, focused on business activities, promoted a "Square Deal" to place workers and business owners on a level playing field. Roosevelt's reforms, ones that McKinley did not endorse, ended many of the abusive practices of industry and helped change public perception of government into an institution known for protecting the general public.

Czolgosz's assassination of McKinley, an example of anarchist terrorism, was among the most high-profile anarchist attacks on U.S. soil.

FURTHER RESOURCES
Books

Fisher, Jack. *Stolen Glory: The McKinley Assassination*. La Jolla, CA: Alamar Books 2001.

Seibert, Jeffrey W. *"I Done My Duty": The Complete Story of the Assassination of President McKinley*. Bowie, MD: Heritage Books 2002.

Gavrilo Princip's Arrest

Assassination of Archduke Ferdinand: Spur to World War

Photograph

By: Milos Oberajger

Date: June 28, 1914

Source: Photograph from the Croatian History Museum in Zagreb, Croatia, taken by Milos Oberajger and showing the arrest of Gavrilo Princip, the assassin of Austria's Archduke Franz Ferdinand.

About the Photographer: Milos Oberajger was an amateur photographer who was in the crowd at 11:00 on the morning of June 28, 1914, to greet Austrian Archduke Franz Ferdinand in the Bosnian city of Sarajevo. Oberajger worked as a forestry engineer in Sarajevo, but his avocation was taking photographs. His wife donated this photograph to the Croatian History Museum in 1988.

INTRODUCTION

Gavrilo Princip (1894–1918) was a young Bosnian revolutionary and a member of a secret society called Union or Death, commonly referred to as the Black Hand. On the morning of June 28, 1914, with the knowledge of Serbian officials, he fatally shot Archduke Franz Ferdinand, heir to the throne of the Austrian Empire, on the streets of the Bosnian capital city of Sarajevo. Princip also killed Ferdinand's wife, the Archduchess Sophie, who was at Ferdinand's side at the time.

In 1914, Europe was a powder keg of mutual alliances, fears, and suspicions. Ferdinand's assassination acted as a match, igniting tensions and ushering Europe into World War I.

The fuse had been laid in 1908 during the first Balkan crisis, when Austria annexed Bosnia. This move infuriated Serbia, which since the nineteenth century had been the center of a movement to form a unified Slavic state made up of Serbians, Bosnians, Croats, and Slovenes. The state that Slavic nationalists envisioned would be independent of the Russian Empire on the east, whose satellites included the Serbs and the Bosnians, and the Austro-Hungarian Empire

PRIMARY SOURCE

Gavrilo Princip's Arrest Gavrilo Princip's arrest on June 28, 1914 for the assassination of Archduke Ferdinand.
© BETTMAN/CORBIS

on the west, whose satellites included the Slovenes and the Croats. Austria saw Serbia as an adversary that was agitating to lay claim to a piece of its empire. Although the Eastern Orthodox Serbs were allies of Russia, Russia had been weakened by war with Japan and was unwilling to do more than protest the annexation of Serbia.

The second Balkan crisis occurred in 1912–1913, when warfare engulfed the Balkan region. Afterward, Austria—in concert with other European powers—backed the formation of an independent kingdom of Albania to block the Serbs from access to the Adriatic Sea. Again, Serbian nationalism was frustrated and its efforts to create a unified Slavic state were blocked; Russia again declined to intervene.

The assassination of Archduke Ferdinand constituted the third Balkan crisis. Amateur photographer Milos Oberajger caught the moment of Princip's arrest—after Princip's attempt to turn the gun on himself was foiled—in the following dramatic photo.

PRIMARY SOURCE

GAVRILO PRINCIP'S ARREST
See primary source image.

SIGNIFICANCE

Within little more than a month, Europe was at war. Austria was determined to put an end to Slavic agitation on its southern border. With the support of its major ally, Germany, it issued a sharp ultimatum to Serbia, demanding a roll in the investigation of the assassination and in the punishment of those responsible. Serbia counted on support from its Russian allies. Russia, in turn, counted on the support of France, which maintained strong ties with Russia because it had long been frightened by the prospect of having to fight a war alone against the larger and more heavily industrialized Germany. Just as Germany had backed Austria in its reprisals against Serbia, France—desperate to retain Russia as an ally—expressed support for Russia in its response to the crisis.

When Serbia rejected Austrian demands, Austria declared war on Serbia. Russia made preparations to defend Serbia, and expecting that Germany would join the fight, massed troops on the German border. Accordingly, on August 1, 1914, Germany declared war on Russia. Believing that France would support Russia, Germany also declared war on France on August 3. The wild card in this system of alliances was Great Britain. At the time Great Britain was bound by no formal ties but, like France, was wary of a growing and increasingly militarized Germany, especially of German naval power in the North Sea and the English Channel. Germany's actions against Russia and France were predicated on its hope that Great Britain would remain neutral. But when Germany invaded neutral Belgium on its way into France, England, in the face of German naval might, declared war on Germany on August 4.

World War I lasted for over four years, at a horrific cost. Ten million men were killed, and another twenty million were wounded. The stalemate in the trenches of western Europe was broken after Russia withdrew from the war and the United States declared war on Germany in April 1917. Although American troops fought for only four months in 1918, the increase in Allied troop strength was enough to tip the balance in favor of the Allies against the Central powers of Germany and Austria.

On November 12, 1918, at the close of the war, the last Austrian emperor, Charles I, abdicated; the next day Austria proclaimed itself a republic, and a week later Hungary did the same. The Treaty of Versailles, which formally ended the war, sought to weaken Germany by imposing on it financial reparations that devastated its economy. The resulting political instability in Germany formed the soil in which Nazism would take root and Adolf Hitler would rise to power. In 1939, the European nations were again at war.

FURTHER RESOURCES

Books

Dutton, David. *The Politics of Diplomacy: Britain, France and the Balkans in the First World War.* International Library of Historical Studies, 13. London: I.B. Tauris, 1998.

Fromkin, David. *Europe's Last Summer: Who Started the Great War in 1914?* New York: Knopf, 2003.

Hamilton, Richard F., and Holger H. Herwig, eds. *The Origins of World War I.* Cambridge, UK: Cambridge University Press, 2003.

Web sites

First World War.com. "How It Began." <http://www.firstworldwar.com/origins/index.htm> (accessed May 16, 2005).

"The Case Against the Reds"

Palmer Raids

Essay

By: A. Mitchell Palmer

Date: February 1920

Source: "The Case Against the 'Reds'" as published in *The Forum.*

About the Author: A. Mitchell Palmer (1872–1936) became an attorney in Pennsylvania after graduating from Swarthmore College in 1891. Elected to the U.S. House of Representatives in 1908 by a large majority, Palmer quickly rose in the ranks of the national Democratic Party. A Progressive, he authored a bill against child labor, supported women's suffrage, and earned a perfect rating by the American Federation of Labor. After losing a bid to enter the U.S. Senate, Palmer became President Woodrow Wilson's attorney general in 1919. In his most controversial action, Palmer led the so-called Palmer Raids against suspected political radicals in 1919 and 1920. After failing to win the 1920 Democratic nomination for president, Palmer retired from public life.

INTRODUCTION

A. Mitchell Palmer became a national political figure because of his support for the rights of workers. After organized labor failed to support his unsuccessful bid for the U.S. Senate, Palmer turned against labor. As attorney general in the administration of President Woodrow Wilson, he obtained injunctions stopping strikes by mine and railroad workers in 1919. His actions led American Federation of Labor president Samuel Gomper to denounce Palmer as an autocrat. When Wilson Administration officials objected to the injunctions, Palmer assured the members of the president's cabinet that his intelligence division had collected proof that the strike was part of a worldwide communist conspiracy.

In 1919, most middle-class Americans feared communism. The Red Scare ("red" refers to the color of the flag used by Bolshevik Russian revolutionaries) had its roots in the post-World War I (1915–1918) recession, labor unrest, and the difficulties of reintegrating millions of returning veterans. Unsettling events overseas also added to American anxieties. In March 1919, leaders of the young Soviet Union created the Comintern, a worldwide association of Communist leaders intent on promoting revolution in capitalist societies.

A Communist revolution in the U.S. was unlikely, but a series of isolated terrorist attacks convinced many nervous Americans that a revolution was imminent. Under pressure from the U.S. Senate, Palmer began to investigate radicals. Advised by J. Edgar Hoover of the Justice Department that radicals planned to overthrow the government, Palmer authorized raids on radical gatherings. In November 1919, the Justice Department with assistance from local police began to make arrests throughout the nation. The raids reached their peak on January 2, 1920 when 7,000 immigrants were arrested. Most arrests were made without warrants. Some of those arrested spent up to four months in prison awaiting trial or a deportation hearing.

■ PRIMARY SOURCE

In this brief review of the work which the Department of Justice has undertaken, to tear out the radical seeds that have entangled American ideas in their poisonous theories, I desire not merely to explain what the real menace of communism is, but also to tell how we have been compelled to clean up the country almost unaided by any virile legislation. Though I have not been embarrassed by political opposition, I have been materially delayed because the present sweeping processes of arrests and deportation of seditious aliens should have been vigorously pushed by Congress last spring. The failure of this is a matter of record in the Congressional files . . .

Like a prairie-fire, the blaze of revolution was sweeping over every American institution of law and order a year ago. It was eating its way into the homes of the American workmen, its sharp tongues of revolutionary heat were licking the altars of the churches, leaping into the belfry of the school bell, crawling into the sacred corners of American homes, seeking to replace marriage vows with libertine laws, burning up the foundations of society.

Robbery, not war, is the ideal of communism. This has been demonstrated in Russia, Germany, and in America. As a foe, the anarchist is fearless of his own life, for his creed is a fanaticism that admits no respect of any other creed. Obviously it is the creed of any criminal mind, which reasons always from motives impossible to clean thought. Crime is the degenerate factor in society.

Upon these two basic certainties, first that the "Reds" were criminal aliens and secondly that the American Government must prevent crime, it was decided that there could be no nice distinctions drawn between the theoretical ideals of the radicals and their actual violations of our national laws. An assassin may have brilliant intellectuality, he may be able to excuse his murder or robbery with fine oratory, but any theory which excuses crime is not wanted in America.

This is no place for the criminal to flourish, nor will he do so long as the rights of common citizenship can be exerted to prevent him . . .

The Government was in jeopardy; our private information of what was being done by the organization known as the Communist Party of America, with headquarters in Chicago, of what was being done by the Communist Internationale under their manifesto planned at Moscow last March by Trotzky, Lenin, and others addressed "To the Proletariats of All Countries," of what strides the Communist Labor Party was making, removed all doubt. In this conclusion we did not ignore the definite standards of personal liberty, of free speech, which is the very temperament and heart of the people. The evidence was examined with the utmost care, with a personal leaning toward freedom of thought and word on all questions.

The whole mass of evidence, accumulated from all parts of the country, was scrupulously scanned, not merely for the written or spoken differences of viewpoint as to the Government of the United States, but, in spite of these things, to see if the hostile declarations might not be sincere in their announced motive to improve our social order. There was no hope of such a thing . . .

Behind, and underneath, my own determination to drive from our midst the agents of Bolshevism with increasing vigor and with greater speed, until there are no more of them left among us, so long as I have the responsible duty of that task, I have discovered the hysterical methods of these revolutionary humans with increasing amazement and suspicion. In the confused information that sometimes reaches the people they are compelled to ask questions which involve the reasons for my acts against the "Reds." I have been asked, for instance, to what extent deportation will check radicalism in this country. Why not ask what will become of the United States Government if these alien radicals are permitted to carry out the principles of the Communist Party as embodied in its so-called laws, aims and regulations?

There wouldn't be any such thing left. In place of the United States Government we should have the horror and terrorism of bolsheviki tyranny such as is destroying Russia now. Every scrap of radical literature demands the overthrow of our existing government. All of it demands obedience to the instincts of criminal minds, that is, to the lower appetites, material and moral. The whole purpose of communism appears to be a mass formation of the criminals of the world to overthrow the decencies of private life, to usurp property that they have not earned, to disrupt the present order of life regardless of health, sex, or religious rights. By a literature that promises the wildest dreams of such low aspirations, that can occur to only the criminal minds, communism distorts our social law. . . .

It has been inferred by the "Reds." that the United States Government, by arresting and deporting them, is returning to the autocracy of Czardom, adopting the system that created the severity of Siberian banishment. My reply to such charges is that in our determination to maintain our government we are treating our alien enemies with extreme consideration. To deny them the privilege of remaining in a country which they have openly deplored as an unenlightened community, unfit for those who prefer the privileges of Bolshevism, should be no hardship . . .

It has been impossible in so short a space to review the entire menace of the internal revolution in this country as I know it, but this may serve to arouse the American citizen to its reality, its danger, and the great need of united effort to stamp it out, under our feet, if needs be. It is being done. The Department of Justice will pursue the attack of these "Reds." upon the Government of the United States with vigilance, and no alien, advocating the overthrow of existing law and order in this country, shall escape arrest and prompt deportation . . .

SIGNIFICANCE

The Palmer Raids constituted, at the time, perhaps the largest reinterpretation of civil liberties in U.S. history. Most constitutional scholars agree that the raids violated First Amendment rights of free assembly and free speech (especially political speech), as well as Fourth Amendment protections against unreasonable searches and seizures, and Fifth Amendment guards against the deprivation of liberty without due process. Nevertheless, the former critics of Palmer's inactivity now applauded him. The raids crippled such radical organizations as the Communist Party, the Communist Labor Party, and the Industrial Workers of the World (commonly known as the Wobblies). Palmer was the hero of the hour.

In March 1920, Secretary of Labor William B. Wilson stepped down because of illness to be replaced by Assistant Secretary Louis F. Post. Much more sympathetic to the plight of immigrants and citizens held without good cause or due process, Post investigated each person's case. He released detainees held on evidence seized improperly and those belonging to groups whose leaders had transferred their memberships to the Communist party without their knowledge. He lowered bail for those jailed radicals with jobs and families, despite protests from the Justice Department. By April, Post had decided 1,600 cases, canceling arrests in over 70 percent of them. Only 249 radicals suffered deportation.

The backlash against Palmer began within months. The House Committee on Rules, informed by Palmer

that Post was delaying deportations, began impeachment proceedings against the secretary of labor but ultimately took no action. Meanwhile, some of America's most prominent attorneys, including future Supreme Court Justices Charles Evans Hughes, Harlan Fiske Stone, and Felix Frankfurter spoke out against the Palmer Raids and signed a public petition criticizing the arrests.

By mid–1920 public opinion had turned against Palmer. His activities as Alien Property custodian and attorney general gave rise to numerous complaints of improper activity. After investigations by Congress and several grand juries, no indictments were ever brought against Palmer.

FURTHER RESOURCES
Books

Coben, Stanley. *A. Mitchell Palmer, Politician*. New York: Columbia University Press, 1963.

Dunn, Robert W. *The Palmer Raids*. New York: International Publishers, 1948.

Feuerlicht, Roberta Strass. *America's Reign of Terror: World War I, the Red Scare, and the Palmer Raids*. New York: Random House, 1971.

McCormick, Charles H. *Seeing Reds: Federal Surveillance of Radicals in the Pittsburgh Mill District, 1917–1921*. Pittsburgh: University of Pittsburgh Press, 1997.

Devastation on Wall Street

Bolshevist, Anarchist Terrorists Accused of Wall Street Bombing

Photograph

By: Unknown

Date: September, 1920

Source: Photograph showing bomb damage to Wall Street from a 1920 bomb attack.

About the Photographer: The photographer is unknown.

INTRODUCTION

Just after noon on September 16, 1920, a powerful dynamite bomb exploded in New York City's financial district on Wall Street near the intersection with Broad Street. Until the 1995 bombing of the Alfred P. Murrah federal office building in Oklahoma City, Oklahoma, the Wall Street bombing was the most devastating terrorist attack in U.S. history.

Devastation on Wall Street Photograph showing damage on Wall Street after a bomb exploded September 16, 1920.
© CORBIS

The bomb, which detonated just as the lunch hour was beginning, was carried in a horse-drawn cart. In the cart were hundreds of pounds of iron window-sash weights that acted as shrapnel. The scene was one of horrible devastation. At least thirty people were killed instantly, and some forty more would later die of their injuries. Hundreds more were wounded. Many of the victims were messengers crossing the streets or clerks eating lunch at their desks.

One witness described a mushroom cloud of greenish-yellow smoke rising a hundred feet in the air. Broken glass was everywhere, people were lifted into the air and then fell to the ground with their clothing on fire, and body parts were scattered on the street.

Windows shattered and canopies were burned up to a fourth of a mile away. A car was thrown twenty feet into the air. At the corner of Broad and Wall Street, scars from the bombing can still be seen on the J. P. Morgan Building, where the firm's chief clerk was decapitated as he sat at a front window eating his lunch.

Minutes later, some 1,700 New York City policemen and seventy-five nurses from the Red Cross descended on the scene by foot, subway, car, and on horseback. Rifles and bayonets at the ready, 22nd Infantry Army troops from Governors Island marched through Lower Manhattan.

The only real piece of usable evidence was two charred horse hooves that had landed in front of nearby

Trinity Church. Investigators showed the hooves to more than four thousand horseshoers and stable hands up and down the Atlantic coast, hoping that one would recognize his work and provide a clue to the identity of the bomber. One blacksmith on Elizabeth Street remembered a driver who had a Sicilian accent. Meanwhile, investigators carted away ten tons of broken glass and other debris, keeping it for two years as evidence.

The following photograph captures the devastation in front of the New York Stock Exchange.

▓ PRIMARY SOURCE

DEVASTATION ON WALL STREET
See primary source image.

▓▓

SIGNIFICANCE

Between 1892 and 1914, many of the seventeen million immigrants who had passed through New York's Ellis Island were from places such as Hungary, Greece, Romania, and southern Italy. Popular anti-immigrant sentiment wrongly associated these immigrants with disease, dirt, crime, communism, anarchism, and extremism. Secretary of Labor James J. Davis had referred to them as "rat people."

After the outbreak of the Russian Revolution of 1917, anti-immigrant sentiment and fears of communist insurgents led to the first wave of "Red scares" in the twentieth century. Those fears were stoked in 1919, when mail bombs had exploded in eight American cities, one at the home of U.S. Attorney General A. Mitchell Palmer (1872–1936), touching off the so-called Palmer raids in which ten thousand suspected subversives and anarchists were rounded up and hundreds were deported.

In response to the bombing, Palmer ordered the arrest of "Big Bill" Haywood (1869–1928), president of the labor union Industrial Workers of the World. The estates of financial magnates such as J. P. Morgan, John D. Rockefeller, and others were put under guard.

Postal workers later discovered circulars that had been mailed a block away in the half hour before the bombing. The circulars read "Remember/We will not tolerate/any longer/Free the political/prisoners or it will be/sure death for all of you." The circular was signed by the American Anarchist Fighters, a group linked to the bombings in 1919. One suspicion was that the bombing was an act of reprisal for the September 11, 1920, indictment of Italian immigrants Nicola Sacco and Bartolomeo Vanzetti, both with anarchist ties, in connection with a holdup in Massachusetts.

Despite the efforts of the Federal Bureau of Investigation and other investigators, no one was ever charged with the crime. Suspicion centered on Italian anarchist Luigi Galleani and his followers. The next day, the stock exchange opened for business and thousands of New Yorkers, led by the Sons of the American Revolution, gathered at the site to sing "America the Beautiful" and listen to patriotic speeches.

FURTHER RESOURCES
Books

Baritz, Loren, ed. *The American Left: Radical Political Thought in the Twentieth Century.* New York: Basic, 1971.

Lynd, Staughton. *Intellectual Origins of American Radicalism.* London: Faber and Faber, 1969.

Pope, Daniel, ed. *American Radicalism.* Malden, MA: Blackwell, 2001.

Periodicals

Ward, Nathan. "The Fire Last Time." *American Heritage* (December 2001). Available online from <http://www.freerepublic.com/focus/f-news/577915/posts> (accessed May 16, 2005).

"Red Record of Failure and of Innocent Victims"

Newspaper article

By: William L. Chenery

Date: September 19, 1920

Source: "Red Record of Failure and of Innocent Victims" as published by the *New York Times.*

About the Author: William L. Chenery was a reporter for the *New York Times* during the 1920s.

INTRODUCTION

Throughout 1919 and 1920, anarchists featured in news reports as the United States found itself gripped by fears of radical terrorism. Anarchist terrorists detonated a bomb that exploded in the heart of New York's financial district at Broad and Wall Streets on September 16, 1920. The bomb killed 28 people and injured more than 200. The victims were mostly low-paid secretaries and clerks, not the captains of industry that the bombers had intended to harm.

In November 1917, Bolsheviks seized control of Russia. Many Americans, equating communism and anarchism, feared that this revolution would come to U.S. shores. Labor disputes, race riots, heavy immigration, a recession, and the difficulties of returning to a peacetime economy after World War I, all added to American fears. Four million workers, one out of every five, went on strike in 1919, including the entire police force of Boston.

The actions of anarchists contributed to these fears for the future of America. Disillusioned by political repression in the U.S., especially the Ludlow Massacre of 1914, they dedicated themselves to a war on the oppressors that was preached as a duty by the anarchist writer Luigi Galeani.

Anarchists distributed pamphlets that threatened violent attacks throughout the country. In Milwaukee, an anarchist bomb killed ten people attending church in April. The next month, 36 packages mailed from New York to prominent Americans were found to contain explosives. In June 1919, anarchist Carlo Valdinoci blew himself up on the porch of the home of U.S. Attorney General A. Mitchell Palmer while attempting to place a bomb. On the same night that Valdinoci died, bombs were detonated in seven U.S. cities.

In response to the anarchist terror campaign, Palmer conducted raids in late 1919 and early 1920 that rounded up radicals for deportation. The raids, which captured some innocent people as well as the guilty, were ultimately halted because of the injustices inevitable in mass arrests.

The last major anarchist attack in the U.S. took place on September 16, 1920 when a bomb exploded on Wall Street in New York. Mario Buda, an associate of Nicola Sacco and Bartolomeo Vanzetti, is considered responsible for planting this bomb. Buda was part of an anarchist cell that also included Sacco and Vanzetti, radicals who were executed for participating in a 1920 Massachusetts armed robbery that cost the lives of two working men, a paymaster and a guard. Buda may also have participated in the Massachusetts robbery.

■ PRIMARY SOURCE

Supposing that the ultimate evidence allays the last doubt that the explosion which spread desolation from the very heart of Wall Street Thursday noon was an accident—the bomb which took so great a toll of life among unoffending men and women was the instrument of a characteristic crime in the long story of the Propaganda of the Deed . . .

It is a curious and sad chapter in the history of the human race that records the vain deeds of these deluded men and women who by dynamite and with even more powerful explosives have attempted to blast a road to their revolution. Little has been achieved by the misguided terrorism except the retardation of the causes they professed to serve and the destruction of many innocent people. The men aimed at have usually escaped. Folk outside any controversy have been killed. The bomb thrown at a King has more often hit a workman. The mortality among terrorists themselves has been exceedingly large. If ever insanity by public action has been shown by a class, the individual members of which seemed to be rational creatures, it has been shown in the record compiled by men and women here and there who have been exponents of this mad doctrine called in their own jargon the Propaganda of the Deed . . .

Since the Haymarket riot the teaching of the terrorist philosophy in this country has been isolated and clandestine. Even the anarchists, such as Benjamin Tucker, who eschewed violence from the very outset, became fewer. Not until the beginning of the present century did the old philosophy, the Propaganda of the Deed, appear in a new form. Then it emerged chiefly as sabotage rather than as terrorism. This happened when the I.W.W. [International Workers of the World] broke away from the Socialist Party. William D. Haywood and others in 1911 began to argue that, since "the present laws of property are made by and for the capitalists, the workers should not hesitate to break them."

The conflict of principle between progress in accordance with the law and terrorism, which two generations previously had exiled the anarchists from the Socialist International, was again fought out within the ranks of American socialism. Once more the advocates of violence were driven out. Morris Hilquit was the leader in the attack on the new advocacy of lawlessness. Hilquit insisted that a resort to law-breaking and violence was "ethically and tactically suicidal."

He pointed out that all of the various forms of lawlessness and violence, terrorism, direct action, Propaganda of the Deed, had served chiefly to injure the group which used this method. Criminals concealed their depradations under the cover of the revolutionary movement. Spies and agents provocateurs led simple workmen into senseless slaughter and destruction. "It has invariably served to demoralize and to destroy the movement, ultimately engendering a spirit of disgust and reaction," said Hilquit.

Such in fact is the history of terrorism not only in the United States, but in the world. But in spite of its suicidal consequences, in spite of the fact that terror has retarded rather than advanced social progress, there seems to be a continuing line of these weak-minded criminals who madly dream that by dealing out sudden death they can accomplish their ends. These uncontrolled individuals, sometimes isolated exponents of the philosophy of terrorism, and again merely desperate and unscrupulous advocates of some idea or cause, are chargeable with most of the outrages which have brought trouble to this land . . .

SIGNIFICANCE

By the time that the Wall Street bomb detonated, the panic of the Red Scare (an era of increased anticommunist, immigrant, anarchist, and socialist sentiment which prompted widespread repression of such groups) was in decline. Under the direction of Attorney General Palmer, the government had launched an all-out attack on radicals that had swept up many anarchists. When Palmer declared that radicals were planning to celebrate the Bolshevik Revolution on International Labor Day, May 1, 1920, government officials responded by calling out state militia, fortifying public buildings, and placing machine-gun nests at major city intersections. May 1st came and went without disturbance.

Even before the Palmer Raids, most Americans had shown a distinct lack of interest in left-wing political extremism. The membership in communist (known as "Red" for the color of the Bolshevik flag) and anarchist groups remained extremely small. The radicals who joined such organizations often spent their time debating the finer points of doctrine rather than planting bombs.

Nevertheless, the anti-radicalism of the Red Scare significantly altered legal protections on free speech and free assembly. The Alien and Sedition Acts of the World War I era (1914–1918) were invoked to arrest, detain, and punish radical activists and sympathizers. Several leading radicals were convicted in highly publicized trials and deported.

FURTHER RESOURCES

Books

Avrich, Paul. *Sacco and Vanzetti: The Anarchist Background.* Princeton, NJ: Princeton University Press, 1991.

Bose, Atinkranath. *A History of Anarchism.* Calcutta: World Press, 1967.

Reichert, William O. *Partisans of Freedom: A Study in American Anarchism.* Bowling Green, OH: Bowling Green Popular Press, 1976.

Sheehan, Sean. *Anarchism.* London: Reaktion, 2003.

Topp, Michael M. *The Sacco and Vanzetti Case: A Brief History with Documents.* Boston: Bedford/St. Martin's, 2005.

"Centralia Case: A Chronological Digest"

Aftermath of a Coordinated Series of Anarchist Bombings

Pamphlet

By: The Washington Branch of the General Defense Committee of the Industrial Workers of the World (IWW) labor union.

Date: 1927

Source: "The Centralia Case: A Chronological Digest," a pamphlet produced by the labor union Industrial Workers of the World.

About the Author: The General Defense Committee is an arm of the Industrial Workers of the World (IWW), or Wobblies, a radical labor union. Its purpose is to "provide support to any member of the working class who finds themselves in legal trouble due to their involvement in the class war."

INTRODUCTION

A series of events in Centralia, Washington, in 1919 was indicative of the tumult in American history in the months and years after World War I (1914–1918). During this period, a wave of labor strikes, many of them violent, rocked the country. Anarchists, socialists, and communists openly threatened to disrupt capitalism and the United States government. In April 1919, the mayor of Seattle received in the mail a package that contained a bomb; though the bomb did not detonate, a similar package sent the next day to U.S. Senator Thomas R. Hardwick did explode, seriously injuring Hardwick's maid.

Panic grew on June 3, 1919, when a bomb exploded at the home of U.S. Attorney General A. Mitchell Palmer (1872–1936) in Washington, D.C., and similar bombs exploded in seven other cities across the country. An alert New York City postal worker, who heard about the bombings, discovered sixteen more bombs that were addressed to prominent people but had remained undelivered because of insufficient postage. Some Americans assumed that communist and other alien terrorists, with their alleged "Bolshevist," communist doctrines, were plotting a revolution in the United States. Many Americans, their sense of nationalism and insecurity heightened by the war, looked upon immigrants as a threat to American security.

Intermingling with this fear was a mistrust of organized labor. One focus of this fear was the Industrial

Workers of the World (IWW), or "Wobblies," a labor union formed in 1905 by prominent socialist advocate Eugene V. Debs (1855–1926). Throughout World War I, vigilante groups repeatedly attacked the IWW and its members were arrested on espionage and sedition charges, brought in large part because of the union's opposition to the war. In this climate, the little town of Centralia, eighty-five miles south of Seattle, became the center of an incident that typified the negative perceptions held by some Americans on immigration, unionism, socialism, and anarchism.

In 1914, the IWW set up an office in Centralia, where they reportedly received a chilly reception. In 1918, locals raided and destroyed the union's hall during a parade in support of the Red Cross. After the IWW (which had openly supported the Bolshevist revolution in Russia) opened a new hall in 1919, just months after the June bombings in Washington and other cities, rumors began to circulate that their new hall would be attacked. IWW members armed themselves for the raid, which took place during an Armistice Day parade on November 11.

As the parade passed the IWW hall, a number of Centralia Legionnaires forced their way in and a gun battle erupted, leaving four Legionnaires dead and one seriously wounded. Several Wobblies were arrested, including one named Wesley Everest, who was mistakenly believed to be local IWW leader Britt Smith. That evening a mob broke into the jail, seized Everest, and dragged him outside of town, where they hanged, shot, and mutilated him.

Anxiety swept quickly through Centralia, the state, and the nation at large. Washington quickly passed a law making membership in the IWW illegal, and authorities throughout the nation were advised to hold suspected IWW members in jail. Fear grew that the "Centralia Massacre" was part of a widespread conspiracy to overthrow the government, and part of a larger plot connected to the earlier bombing.

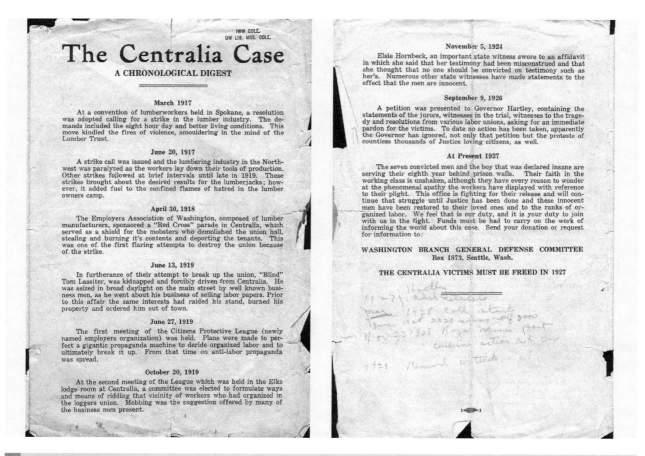

PRIMARY SOURCE

"Centralia Case: A Chronological Digest" Photograph of a pamphlet published by the International Workers of the World, outlining a chronology of the violence associated with the labor union's cause from 1917–1927. UNIVERSITY OF WASHINGTON LIBRARIES, SPECIAL COLLECTIONS, UW 25612Z, UW25329Z

The following document, published by the IWW's General Defense Committee in 1927, presents a timeline of the events in the Centralia case from the labor union's perspective.

CENTRALIA CASE: A CHRONOLOGICAL DIGEST

See primary source image.

SIGNIFICANCE

In 1920, ten Wobblies and the union's lawyer were put on trial for the murder of the Legionnaires. The judge dropped the charges against one defendant during the trial. After six weeks of testimony and two days of deliberations, the jury acquitted two of the remaining defendants, found one "guilty, but insane," and found the remaining seven guilty of second-degree murder. The convicted Wobblies were given sentences ranging from twenty-five to forty years in prison.

Throughout the 1920s and 1930s, allegations of jury intimidation surfaced, and several jurors signed affidavits recanting their verdict. Some investigators concluded that the trial was unfair and that the Wobblies had acted in justifiable self defense. A succession of state governors refused petitions for new trials, but throughout the 1930s, various surviving members of the group were granted parole. The case came to an official end in 1939, when the last parole was granted.

Anti-immigrant and anti-communist sentiment reached a high point throughout the 1920s. The Russian Revolution of 1917, as well as anarchist, socialist, and communist unrest within the United States stirred public fear. The period, known as the first "Red Scare," was marked by the arrest of prominent anarchists, socialists, labor organizers, and communist advocates.

Meanwhile, the IWW ceased to be a powerful force in organized labor, although it still exists with headquarters in Chicago. In 1924 the U.S. Congress passed the National Origins Act to sharply restrict immigration. President Warren G. Harding and his successor, Calvin Coolidge, made good on Harding's pledge to return the nation to "normalcy," and the booming economy of the 1920s effectively quieted the voices of anarchism and organized labor until the Great Depression.

FURTHER RESOURCES

Books

The Centralia Case: Three Views of the Armistice Day Tragedy at Centralia, Washington, November 11, 1919: The Centralia Conspiracy. Civil Liberties in American History. New York: Da Capo Press, 1971.

Web sites

University of Washington Libraries. "Centralia Massacre Collection." <http://content.lib.washington.edu/iwwweb> (accessed May 16, 2005).

2 Political Terrorism

Introduction to Political Terrorism

Political terrorism relies on violent acts to influence public opinion on political issues or to vie for political power. Political terrorists sometimes harbor nationalistic aims, but these motivations are more clearly considered as separatist terrorism. Political terrorism may be waged by extremist groups on either end of the political spectrum, more often described as "left wing" or "right wing" terrorist groups.

In the United States, right-wing groups are most often aligned with ideologies of religious fundamentalism or racism. Many right-wing extremists also view federal governments as unnecessarily intrusive on personal property rights, or are isolationist, calling for the withdrawal of the United States from global economic markets, treaties, and the involvement in the United Nations. Timothy McVeigh, the terrorist responsible for the 1995 bombing of the Murrah Federal Building in Oklahoma City, claimed that his attack was in retribution for a siege-ending deadly raid by federal agents against the Branch Davidian cult exactly two years earier. McVeigh also had contacts in several right-wing extremist groups.

Neo-fascists, neo-Nazis, or skinhead groups are also right-wing extremists. Neo-Nazism blends the desire to recreate a fascist state with a racist social hierarchy and strong anti-Semitism. The most violent neo-fascist groups operate in Western Europe.

Left-wing terrorists are most often aligned with ideologies of anarchism, anti-globalism, or anti-capitalism. Left-wing terrorists seek to destroy capitalist economic structures, most often with the intention of replacing them with socialist or communist systems. The most violent left-wing terrorists currently operate outside of the United States.

Globally, both right-wing and left-wing extremist groups are often paramilitary. Such paramilitary extremist groups often vie for power in regions torn by ethnic conflict or civil war; some are even state-sponsored by their own government or the governments of neighboring nations. Most of these groups conduct terror campaigns against civilians.

This chapter provides primary sources on both right-wing and left-wing terrorism. Extremist groups and terrorist organizations are not synonymous. Not all extremist groups have committed acts of terrorism, and only those that have are included in this volume. The representative sample of acts of political terrorism spans both the political spectrum and the globe.

As in the chapter on anarchist terrorism, the editors have included primary sources on the assassinations of heads of state. Although some definitions of terrorism exclude political assassinations, these acts are sometimes carried out by members of terrorist networks with the intent of supporting terrorist aims. The assassination of foreign leaders is prohibited under the Geneva Conventions. However, political assassinations sometimes carry similar social consequences as a terrorist act.

Warren Commission Report

Assassination of President John F. Kennedy

Commission report

By: Report of the President's Commission on the Assassination of President Kennedy

Date: September 27, 1964

Source: "Report of the President's Commission on the Assassination of President Kennedy," as published by the National Archives and Records Administration (NARA).

About the Author: On November 29, 1963, President Lyndon B. Johnson (1908–1973) established a committee, led by Chief Justice of the United States Supreme Court Earl Warren (1891–1974), to evaluate the assassination of President John F. Kennedy in Dallas, TX, on November 22, 1963, and the killing of his assassin Lee Harvey Oswald by Jack Ruby on November 24, 1963. "The Warren Commission" released its findings in September 1964 in an 888 page report.

INTRODUCTION

The assassination of President John F. Kennedy (1917–1963) on November 22, 1963 in Dallas, Texas, took the country by surprise. Kennedy was shot in the head during a parade while riding in an open convertible, seated next to his wife, Jacqueline. Within hours, Lee Harvey Oswald, a former Marine and vocal communist, was arrested and charged with the

First Lady Jacqueline Kennedy cradles her husband, President John F. Kennedy, seconds after he was fatally shot in Dallas, Texas on November 22, 1963. AP/WIDE WORLD PHOTOS

murder of the president. In addition to killing Kennedy, the shooter struck the Governor of Texas, John Connelly, who was riding in the front seat of the president's limousine, directly in front of Kennedy. Connelly received wounds to the back, chest, right wrist, and thigh.

On November 24, 1963, Jack Ruby murdered Lee Harvey Oswald as Oswald was being transported from the Dallas police station. The murder was the first to be viewed on national television, airing live on the National Broadcast Company (NBC). Ruby, a local nightclub owner with ties to the mafia, claimed to have killed Oswald simply because the opportunity presented itself. Oswald had been detained shortly after the shooting and was interrogated by Dallas police for fifteen hours. His answers were not documented.

In view of the Kennedy assassination and Oswald's murder, newly sworn-in President Lyndon B. Johnson called for the creation of an investigatory body, to look into the assassination of President Kennedy and surrounding events. Johnson appointed Chief Justice of the Supreme Court Earl Warren to head the operation. Other members of the investigation team included Richard B. Russell, a Democratic Senator from Georgia; John Sherman Cooper, Republican Senator from Kentucky; Hale Boggs, Democratic Representative from Louisiana and the majority whip in the House of Representatives; Gerald R. Ford, Republican Representative from Michigan and future President of the United States; Allen W. Dulles, former Director of the Central Intelligence Agency; and John J. McCloy, former President of the International Bank for Reconstruction and Development, and the former United States High Commissioner for Germany.

Dubbed "The Warren Commission," the group interviewed 552 witnesses and worked with ten different government agencies, including the FBI, CIA, and others. The investigation took ten months, and the official report was released on September 27, 1964.

PRIMARY SOURCE

Conclusions:

1. The shots which killed President Kennedy and wounded Governor Connally were fired from the sixth floor window at the southeast corner of the Texas School Book Depository. This determination is based upon the following:

    (a) Witnesses at the scene of the assassination saw a rifle being fired from the sixth floor window of the Depository Building, and some witnesses saw a rifle in the window immediately after the shots were fired.

    (b) The nearly whole bullet found on Governor Connally's stretcher at Parkland Memorial Hospital and the two bullet fragments found in the front seat of the Presidential limousine were fired from the 6.5-millimeter Mannlicher-Carcano rifle found on the sixth floor of the Depository Building to the exclusion of all other weapons.

    (c) The three used cartridge cases found near the window on the sixth floor at the southeast corner of the building were fired from the same rifle which fired the above-described bullet and fragments, to the exclusion of all other weapons.

    (d) The windshield in the Presidential limousine was struck by a bullet fragment on the inside surface of the glass, but was not penetrated.

    (e) The nature of the bullet wounds suffered by President Kennedy and Governor Connally and the location of the car at the time of the shots establish that the bullets were fired from above and behind the Presidential limousine, striking the President and the Governor as follows:

    President Kennedy was first struck by a bullet which entered at the back of his neck and exited through the lower front portion of his neck, causing a wound which would not necessarily have been lethal. The President was struck a second time by a bullet which entered the right-rear portion of his head, causing a massive and fatal wound.

    Governor Connally was struck by a bullet which entered on the right side of his back and traveled downward through the right side of his chest, exiting below his right nipple. This bullet then passed through his right wrist and entered his left thigh where it caused a superficial wound.

    (f) There is no credible evidence that the shots were fired from the Triple Underpass, ahead of the motorcade, or from any other location.

2. The weight of the evidence indicates that there were three shots fired.

3. Although it is not necessary to any essential findings of the Commission to determine just which shot hit Governor Connally, there is very persuasive evidence from the experts to indicate that the same bullet which pierced the President's throat also caused Governor Connally's wounds. However, Governor Connally's testimony and certain other factors have given rise to some difference of opinion as to this probability but there is no question in the mind of any member of the Commission that all the shots which caused the President's and Governor Connally's wounds were

fired from the sixth floor window of the Texas School Book Depository.

4. The shots which killed President Kennedy and wounded Governor Connally were fired by Lee Harvey Oswald. This conclusion is based upon the following:

   (a) The Mannlicher-Carcano 6.5-millimeter Italian rifle from which the shots were fired was owned by and in the possession of Oswald.

   (b) Oswald carried this rifle into the Depository Building on the morning of November 22, 1963.

   (c) Oswald, at the time of the assassination, was present at the window from which the shots were fired.

   (d) Shortly after the assassination, the Mannlicher-Carcano rifle belonging to Oswald was found partially hidden between some cartons on the sixth floor and the improvised paper bag in which Oswald brought the rifle to the Depository was found dose by the window from which the shots were fired.

   (e) Based on testimony of the experts and their analysis of films of the assassination, the Commission has concluded that a rifleman of Lee Harvey Oswald's capabilities could have fired the shots from the rifle used in the assassination within the elapsed time of the shooting. The Commission has concluded further that Oswald possessed the capability with a rifle, which enabled him to commit the assassination.

   (f) Oswald lied to the police after his arrest concerning important substantive matters.

   (g) Oswald had attempted to kill Maj. Gen. Edwin A. Walker (Retired, U.S. Army) on April 10, 1963, thereby demonstrating his disposition to take human life. . . .

9. The Commission has found no evidence that either Lee Harvey Oswald or Jack Ruby was part of any conspiracy, domestic or foreign, to assassinate President Kennedy. The reasons for this conclusion are:

   (a) The Commission has found no evidence that anyone assisted Oswald in planning or carrying out the assassination. In this connection it has thoroughly investigated, among other factors, the circumstances surrounding the planning of the motorcade route through Dallas, the hiring of Oswald by the Texas School Book Depository Co. on October 15, 1963, the method by which the rifle was brought into the building, the placing of cartons of books at the window, Oswald's escape from the building, and the testimony of eyewitnesses to the shooting.

   (b) The Commission has found no evidence that Oswald was involved with any person or group in a conspiracy to assassinate the President, although it has thoroughly investigated, in addition to other possible leads, all facets of Oswald's associations, finances, and personal habits, particularly during the period following his return from the Soviet Union in June 1962.

   (c) The Commission has found no evidence to show that Oswald was employed, persuaded, or encouraged by any foreign government to assassinate President Kennedy or that he was an agent of any foreign government, although the Commission has reviewed the circumstances surrounding Oswald's defection to the Soviet Union, his life there from October of 1959 to June of 1962 so far as it can be reconstructed, his known contacts with the Fair Play for Cuba Committee and his visits to the Cuban and Soviet Embassies in Mexico City during his trip to Mexico from September 26 to October 3, 1963, and his known contacts with the Soviet Embassy in the United States.

   (d) The Commission has explored all attempts of Oswald to identify himself with various political groups, including the Communist Party, U.S.A., the Fair Play for Cuba Committee, and the Socialist Workers Party, and has been unable to find any evidence that the contacts which he initiated were related to Oswald's subsequent assassination of the President.

   (e) All of the evidence before the Commission established that there was nothing to support the speculation that Oswald was an agent, employee, or informant of the FBI, the CIA, or any other governmental agency. It has thoroughly investigated Oswald's relationships prior to the assassination with all agencies of the U.S. Government. All contacts with Oswald by any of these agencies were made in the regular exercise of their different responsibilities.

   (f) No direct or indirect relationship between Lee Harvey Oswald and Jack Ruby has been discovered by the Commission, nor has it been able to find any credible evidence that either knew the other, although a thorough investigation was made of the many rumors and speculations of such a relationship.

   (g) The Commission has found no evidence that Jack Ruby acted with any other person in the killing of Lee Harvey Oswald.

   (h) After careful investigation the Commission has found no credible evidence either that Ruby and Officer Tippit, who was killed by Oswald, knew each other or that Oswald and Tippit knew each other.

Because of the difficulty of proving negatives to a certainty, the possibility of others being involved with either Oswald or Ruby cannot be established categorically, but if there is any such evidence it has been beyond the reach of all the investigative agencies and resources of the United States and has not come to the attention of this Commission.

10. In its entire investigation, the Commission has found no evidence of conspiracy, subversion, or disloyalty to the U.S. Government by any Federal, State, or local official.

11. On the basis of the evidence before the Commission it concludes that Oswald acted alone. Therefore, to determine the motives for the assassination of President Kennedy, one must look to the assassin himself. Clues to Oswald's motives can be found in his family history, his education or lack of it, his acts, his writings, and the recollections of those who had close contacts with him throughout his life. The Commission has presented with this report all of the background information bearing on motivation which it could discover. Thus, others may study Lee Oswald's life and arrive at their own conclusions as to his possible motives.

The Commission could not make any definitive determination of Oswald's motives. It has endeavored to isolate factors which contributed to his character and which might have influenced his decision to assassinate President Kennedy. These factors were:

(a) His deep-rooted resentment of all authority which was expressed in a hostility toward every society in which he lived;

(b) His inability to enter into meaningful relationships with people, and a continuous pattern of rejecting his environment in favor of new surrounding;

(c) His urge to try to find a place in history and despair at times over failures in his various undertakings;

(d) His capacity for violence as evidenced by his attempt to kill General Walker;

(e) His avowed commitment to Marxism and communism, as he understood the terms and developed his own interpretation of them; this was expressed by his antagonism toward the United States, by his defection to the Soviet Union, by his failure to be reconciled with life in the United States even after his disenchantment with the Soviet Union, and by his efforts, though frustrated, to go to Cuba.

Lee Harvey Oswald, alleged assassin of John F. Kennedy, being shot by Jack Ruby in Dallas, Texas on November 25, 1963. ©TOPHAM/THE IMAGE WORKS. REPRODUCED BY PERMISSION

Each of these contributed to his capacity to risk all in cruel and irresponsible actions.

SIGNIFICANCE

The seven-member panel split their decision, 4 to 3, in favor of the single-assassin theory, declaring that Lee Harvey Oswald acted as a "lone gunman," and that the injuries to the president and Governor Connally were caused by two bullets. Abraham Zapruder, a bystander at the parade, caught the assassination on 8mm film. "The Zapruder Film" is the best video document of the shooting, and has been studied in great detail for decades. Still images from the film are some of the most famous pictures of the assassination.

The Warren Commission report also noted the limitations of Secret Service security operations during the parade. The report contained recommendations for future measures that could be taken to protect the president and other government officials, such as better communication with local police, a bulletproof top for the president's limousine, and maintaining a steady driving pace (to hamper an assassin's ability to zero in on a target). These recommendations have become standard protocol for presidential public appearances.

The Warren Commission's interviews, research, and transcripts were initially sealed upon their release until 2039, by executive order of President Johnson, although many documents may be released to the public as soon as 2017.

FURTHER RESOURCES

Books

Semple, Robert B. *Four Days in November: The Original Coverage of the John F. Kennedy Assassination*. New York: St. Martin's Press, 2003.

Web sites

Archives.gov. "Report of the President's Commission on the Assassination of President Kennedy." <http://www.archives.gov/research_room/jfk/warren_commission/warren_commission_report.html> (accessed July 5, 2005).

Archives.gov. "Report of the Select Committee on Assassinations of the U.S. House of Representatives." <http://www.archives.gov/research_room/jfk/house_select_committee/committee_report.html> (accessed July 5, 2005).

Time.com. "TIME Magazine Cover: Lee Harvey Oswald—Oct. 2, 1964." <http://www.time.com/time/covers/0,16641,1101641002,00.html> (accessed July 5, 2005).

Audio and Visual Media

WKIC and WSGS Coverage: Hazard, KY. *John F. Kennedy Assassination Radio Broadcast*. <http://www.wsgs.com/1963.ram>

"Return of the Terrors"

Dominican Republic

News article

By: Latin American Newsletters

Date: June 2, 1967

Source: "The Dominican Republic: The Return of the Terrors" as published by *Intelligence Research*.

About the Author: This news report was originally published as part of the Latin American news series from Lettres, UK (now Intelligence Research, Ltd.), a London-based news agency. Established in 1967, the *Latin American Newsletters* were written by Latin American specialists in London, writing about political and social events throughout Latin America as they unfolded. Printed in both English and Spanish, the *Latin American Newsletters* were a compilation from a variety of sources, without author attribution.

INTRODUCTION

Following thirty-one years of dictatorship rule by Rafael Leonides Trujillo Molina, the Dominican Republic was rocked by a series of political events that included widespread terrorism, economic instability, and dramatic political change on the Caribbean island nation.

Trujillo's assassination on May 30, 1961 ended a 31-year reign that leaned toward fascism, but stabilized the country both economically and politically. Following Fidel Castro's toppling of dictator Fulgencio Batista in Cuba and Castro's subsequent communist rule, two opinions of Trujillo formed in Washington, D.C.: that he was either a stable influence in the Caribbean, or a Batista-like dictator who was vulnerable to a possible pro-communist revolutionary attack. Trujillo's assassination left those holding both opinions concerned about the island nation's future and the spread of communism throughout the region.

Joaquín Balaguer Ricardo, Trujillo's designated successor, was widely viewed as a "puppet" president by the opposition and international observers alike. When Juan Bosch Gaviño, head of the leftist Dominican Revolutionary Party, was elected to the presidency in 1962, Balaguer was forced into exile. Bosch instituted a wide range of democratic reforms, including a 1963 constitution that separated church and state, granted new civil and individual rights, and created civilian control over the military. A new policy of land redistribution, however, threatened elites and the

Catholic Church alike. The conservative upper class, military officials, and the church all feared a leftist revolution. Within a few months of Bosch's election military forces staged a coup and installed a military-backed civilian president. This triggered protests, assassinations, bombings, and attacks on the government. The instability caught Washington's eye; the recent communist revolution in Cuba was viewed as an urgent threat to the United States, and the prospect of another communist takeover in the Dominican Republic was considered unacceptable.

On April 24, 1965, Bosch supporters (calling themselves "Constitutionalists", a reference to the 1963 constitution) seized the National Palace and installed Rafael Molina Ureña as provisional president. The next day, military forces (calling themselves "Loyalists") struck back and attacked the Constitutionalists. On April 28, United States President Lyndon Johnson sent troops (eventually totaling 24,000) into the Dominican Republic to stabilize the country. The United States troops remained until October 1966, after elections were held and Balaguer, Trujillo's former protégé, had been voted into office.

At the beginning of Balaguer's administration, the country was plagued by repeated assassinations and assassination attempts on government and military officials. Balaguer fought to maintain a delicate balance to please anti-Trujillo forces, angry leftists, and the coalition of conservatives that had helped elect him into power.

◼ PRIMARY SOURCE

Political killings, always present in the Dominican Republic, are once again on the increase. President Balaguer is in less than firm control of events, and even the moderate right is now seriously concerned about the rising threat from the *Trujillistas*.

Six years ago this week *Generalissimo* Rafael Trujillo, the 'Benefactor' of the Dominican Republic, was assassinated. In the vacuum left by this abrupt end to a dictatorship of 31 years, the country has been in persistent turmoil ever since. Hopes that President Joaquin Balaguer could develop a new and stable political system have been fading fast in recent weeks. Today, just one year since Dr. Balaguer's election, the country's future looks more uncertain than ever.

The political temperature rose sharply on 21 March, when an attempt was made to murder General Antonio Imbert, one of the only two surviving assassins of Trujillo, and leader of the right-wing *junta* that opposed Colonel Caamano in the summer of 1965. Since the end of March,

a growing wave of terrorism has caused the main opposition party, the *Partido Revolucionario Dominicano* (PRD), to withdraw from congress in protest: has impelled President Balaguer to set up a five-man commission to investigate charges of police complicity; and has aggravated the already serious economic crisis.

This renewed tension hardly comes as a surprise. In the uneasy quiet of the past few months, the question has been when, rather than if, the crisis would break out again. Before he left the island for self-imposed exile in Madrid last November, Juan Bosch persuaded the PRD to play the game of 'loyal and constructive opposition.' But this game is totally alien to Dominican political tradition. Its rules have never been accepted by some of the extreme right-wing military groups, whose aim is the absolute defeat and, if necessary, the physical elimination, of their opponents. Nurtured by Trujillo, their stronghold is in the San Isidro air force base east of the capital, but there is good reason to believe that they have many friends elsewhere in the armed services, including the para-military national police.

Never subject to presidential control, these groups have been at the root of much of the political instability of the past six years. Many people were surprised that President Balaguer—to whom they are also a potential threat—did not neutralize them before US troops departed last September. He appears to have calculated that he could gradually tighten his hold over the armed forces, and eventually deal with them from a position of strength. But although he managed to appoint his supporters to a number of key positions, the events of the past two months (as well as the history of the last six years) make the success of this plan highly doubtful.

Alarm about the growing influence of *Trujillistas*, in both civil and military affairs, was initially confined to the political opposition. Members of the PRD in particular (which, to a great extent, is the heir to Colonel Caamano's constitutionalist government) have been the primary targets of terrorist groups for two years. The last straw, for the PRD, was the attack on 4 May on one of their leading senators, who was seriously injured by an incendiary bomb thrown into his car. The party then announced its withdrawal from both the house of congress, and from all normal political life, until such time as the government could guarantee civil liberties. One week later, another prominent party member was found dead in his car, riddled with bullets.

The inability of the government to control terrorism, and bring its perpetrators to justice, was dramatically demonstrated by the attempted assassination in March of General Imbert, almost certainly an act of vengeance on the part of the Trujillo family. President Balaguer immediately appointed as minister of the interior and police, Luis Amiama Tio, the other surviving Trujillo assassin, and thus the man with the greatest interest in bringing the culprits to justice.

This appointment was a move by the government to demonstrate its own innocence, as well as its determination to uncover the truth. But the truth has not been uncovered. The new minister started by demanding the replacement of the police chief, General Tejeda Alvarez (who, in fact, has been twice promoted since). The real reason was never published, but it is widely believed that the police allowed incriminating evidence to disappear. At any rate, Amiama Tio was reported to know full details of the plot, but to be unable to prove anybody's guilt through lack of evidence. Faced by obstruction and disrespect he resigned after only a month in office.

The alarm felt by the opposition then spread to the anti-Trujillo right, which has supported Dr Balaguer, but which began to feel threatened by the 'return to *Trujillismo*.' Criticism of the police became so widespread that on 14 May, the President announced the appointment of a commission to investigate it; its composition, however, gives little confidence that the full truth about the police will be revealed. It consists of the minister for the armed services, the three chiefs of staff, and the chief of police, General Soto Echavarria. General Soto, who replaced General Tejeda against the wishes of Amiama Tio (and even, it is said, without much enthusiasm from the President), was the last chief of Trujillo's military intelligence organization, *Servicios de Inteligencia Militar* (SIM), before it was disbanded.

President Balaguer has publicly recognized that the country's economy is being seriously damaged by the present tension. Previously, although far from healthy, it had shown some signs of picking up.

The question of the US role in Dominican affairs is, of course, still crucial. US influence is strong in all-important sectors, political, economic, military and educational. Washington has, however, chosen not to advise President Balaguer to aim at the elimination of the right-wing terrorist groups responsible for the present tension. Its representatives have instead, consistently counseled a policy of caution and conciliation. Partly this may be due to a desire not to provoke a military coup against the present government, but the impression remains that Washington fears that the elimination of the extreme right would fatally alter the balance of power in favor of the communists.

It is true that the population is still heavily armed, and there have been clashes between the armed forces and small, ineffectual guerilla groups. Undoubtedly, too, some of the 'communist plots' unearthed by the government have been genuine. But fear of the extreme left, divided and fragmented as it is, and cut off from outside support, seems exaggerated.

At present, the more serious problem seems to be the rapid radicalization of opinion in once relatively moderate opposition groups like PRD. More and more talk can be heard of another insurrection, because it is believed that democratic opposition has been shown to be futile, and wild and unrealistic phrases like 'a second Vietnam' are being used with increasing frequency.

SIGNIFICANCE

With violent political actions from both the far right and the far left, Balaguer inherited a country that was under the careful scrutiny of the United States government as well. The concern about the Dominican Republic becoming "another Vietnam" (specifically, a long-term military engagement) was palpable. The "domino effect" (a theory that held that if one nation in a region underwent a communist revolution then other nations would follow) was a great source of fear and consternation for United States government officials as the Dominican Republic's instability came on the heels of Cuba's newly established communist government. If communism spread to the Dominican Republic, United States officials feared Soviet involvement in the region would soon follow.

As the article notes, Balaguer's appointment of one of Trujillo's assassins was viewed as an attempt to distance himself from Trujillo's dictatorship, and also to show his ruthless side in bringing the Dominican Republic's political violence under control.

Balaguer used the military as a tool to maintain power for the next twelve years, winning elections in 1970 and 1974. By rewarding loyal officers, weeding out those less loyal, and never permitting higher-ranking officers to gain too much control, Balaguer side-stepped future coups. He used the military and the National Police to control leftists as well, though not to the degree that Trujillo used during his dictatorship. The balance was enough to satisfy the U.S. government. Favorable sugar prices in the early 1970s helped the Dominican Republics economy, and encouraged foreign investment.

By the 1978 elections, however, economic conditions had changed. As oil prices increased and sugar prices fell, Balaguer's support among the middle class diminished. With high voter turnout at the election signaling a possible leftist win, Balaguer had security forces seize ballots at the Central Electoral Board. After United States President Jimmy Carter threatened intervention by U.S. naval forces, Balaguer permitted the ballots to be counted. Balaguer lost the election.

FURTHER RESOURCES

Books

Moya Pons, Frank. *The Dominican Republic: A National History.* New York: Marcus Weiner Publishers, 1998.

Web sites

Combined Arms Research Library. "U.S. Intervention in the Dominican Republic, 1965–1966." <http://cgsc.leavenworth.army.mil/carl/resources/csi/yates/yates.asp> (accessed June 23, 2005).

Guatemala Extremists

"Guatemala: Extremists Squeeze Out the Moderates"

News article

By: Latin American Newsletters

Date: January 26, 1968

Source: "Guatemala: Extremists Squeeze Out the Moderates," as published by *Intelligence Research*.

About the Author: This news report was originally published as part of the Latin American News series from Lettres, UK (now Intelligence Research, Ltd.), a London-based news agency. Established in 1967, the *Latin American Newsletters* were written by Latin American specialists in London, writing about political and social events throughout Latin America as they unfolded. Printed in both English and Spanish, the *Latin American Newsletters* were a compilation from a variety of sources, without author attribution.

INTRODUCTION

The United States-owned United Fruit Company had a long history in Guatemala as a fruit grower and exporter. When voters elected Jacobo Guzman Arbenz to the presidency in 1951, his appointment of communists to key positions in his administration was cause for concern for United Fruit Company. Fearing government seizure of privately held crop lands, the United Fruit Company appealed to the United States government for help. In 1954, rebels overthrew Arbenz with help from the United States military and the Central Intelligence Agency (CIA).

Carlos Castillo Armas assumed the presidency, with approval of United Fruit Company and other conservative interests. Castillo prohibited activity on the part of political parties, labor unions, and other groups as he conducted an exhaustive search for remaining communists. Although most leftist leaders had fled to Mexico after the 1954 change in power, Castillo continued to search for any remains of communist activity. In 1957, Castillo was assassinated.

Anti-communist concerns from Washington D.C. reached fever pitch by 1959, following Fidel Castro's overthrow of Fulgencio Batista and the establishment of communist rule in Cuba. In Guatemala, remaining leftists continued a campaign of political violence, while right-wing reactionary groups fought back, many with the support of the Guatemalan government, the United States government, and the United Fruit Company.

In 1960, a civil war began in Guatemala. The conflict lasted for thirty-six years, leaving more than 200,000 citizens dead by the end of the war. Throughout the early 1960s, Guatemala was used as a base for training anti-communist forces, while at the same time, leftist-leaning military officers joined with students to form a guerilla movement. In 1963, Enrique Peralta Azurdia, the defense minister, was put into power by a military coup. Yet more instability wracked Guatemala as leftists fought against the president, in turn provoking right-wing opposition. By 1968, when the United States ambassador to Guatemala was assassinated, chaos in the region seemed entrenched.

PRIMARY SOURCE

Guatemalan *guerrilla* sources are claiming that the assassination of two senior US military advisers last week was not merely a reprisal, but the start of a new campaign, in response to heightened right-wing terrorism, following the unification of the two left-wing guerrilla groups. Both the pro-Moscow communists, and President Mendez Montenegro himself, are being left behind as helpless spectators of the carnage.

The gunning down of two senior US military advisers in a street of Guatemala City last week was at first attributed to an act of vengeance on the part of the *Fuerzas Armadas Rebeldes* (FAR), who claimed responsibility. Certainly there was every reason to expect reprisals for the wave of right-wing terrorism, culminating in the brutal killing the week before of a former Guatemalan beauty queen with left-wing connections, Rogelia Cruz Martinez.

But sources close to the Guatemalan guerrillas claim that there was a great deal more than that to the assassination of the Americans. They admit that the guerrillas have suffered serious setbacks in recent months at the hands of extremist right-wing organizations with close connections in the army and police, particularly the *Mano Blanca* and the *Nueva Organizacion Anticomunista* (NOA). Successful attacks on their groups in the countryside and their friends in the cities had 'practically liquidated' their hopes of armed revolutionary warfare, these sources recognize.

But, they claim, this situation was radically altered by the recent unification of the two guerrilla groups: the FAR, led by Cesar Montes, and the *Movimiento Revolucionario 13 de Noviembre* (MR–13), headed by Yon Sosa. This union opened the way to a decisive counter-attack on the Right, which was in any case the only alternative to total defeat. The attack on the American officers, it is suggested, represents only the first move in the new operation.

Whether the guerrillas can so easily recover their waning fortunes must be a matter of doubt; virtually the whole weight of the armed forces is behind the Right. And in any case the Left itself is still not wholly united. Left-wing sources have been predicting an early split between the pro-Moscow communists of the *Partido Guatemalteco del Trabajo* (PGT) and the guerrillas, who accuse PGT leaders of irrelevant activities such as promoting the sale of more coffee to socialist countries, instead of helping the weakened guerrilla movement.

In fact this is not the first serious difference among Guatemalan revolutionaries. When Fidel Castro, at the Tricontinental Conference in Havana two years ago, acclaimed the late Turcios Lima as leader of the Guatemalan revolution, PGT leaders complained of his interference in Guatemala's internal affairs. But some of the younger Party members sided with Fidel, and many of the senior leaders felt obliged to make a clandestine return from their exile in Mexico for a full scale meeting to sort matters out. As a result, more than 20 PGT leaders, including the chief ideologist, Victor Manuel Gutierrez, were caught by the police, tortured and liquidated, and there were dark whispers of betrayal. This time, the FAR are understood to have prepared a document condemning the 'lame' activities of PGT leaders, despite the fact that Montes is a member of the central committee. It may be, however, that the guerrillas will once again win the sympathy of some younger PGT members who favour armed warfare.

But if the pro-Moscow communists are being left behind in the struggle, President Julio Cesar Mendez Montenegro is in an even more unenviable position. The army only allowed him to come to power in 1965 under strong US pressure, and after he had accepted a number of stringent conditions. One of these was that the fight against the guerrillas should go on; another, much more important, was that not he, but the army, should select the minister of defense. This ensured that the ultimate source of power in the country, the armed forces, would not be under his control except in a purely formal sense.

Now the President has had to declare a state of siege again, transferring responsibility for national security from the ministry of the interior and the police to the ministry of defense and the army. This blatant evidence of his impotence indicates, in the opinion of most observers, that Mendez Montenegro's middle-of-the-road regime has lost all hope of effective action by the squeeze exerted upon it from the extremes of Left and Right.

SIGNIFICANCE

The union between FAR and MR-13 provoked right-wing fears of increased leftist power in Guatemala. Successful assassinations from both sides rocked the country and its government, and instability threatened the United Fruit Company's holdings as well. Although the left was not a united front, the appearance of leftist rebel consolidation was enough to provoke the military and right-wing supporters to work to break up leftist insurgent power. The increased violence and terrorism in Guatemala provoked a military crack down.

As this article notes, "But if the pro-Moscow communists are being left behind in the struggle, President Julio Cesar Mendez Montenegro is in an even more unenviable position. The army only allowed him to come to power in 1965 under strong US pressure, and after he had accepted a number of stringent conditions. One of these was that the fight against the guerrillas should go on; another, much more important, was that not he, but the army, should select the minister of defense. This ensured that the ultimate source of power in the country, the armed forces, would not be under his control except in a purely formal sense." With leftists viewing Mendez as a United States "puppet" president, and military forces maintaining true control while considering him a figurehead, his administration was shaky at best.

In 1970, the military went from behind the scenes control to being front and center: General Carlos Arana Osorio assumed the presidency and now completed armed forces control over Guatemala. Arana's rule put Guatemala into a state of siege, suspending civil liberties while reducing political violence between opposing revolutionary groups. As one of the Central American "Banana Republics," countries controlled by generally right-wing rulers propped up by U.S. and European governments and corporate interests, Guatemala's bloody history in the latter half of the twentieth century presents a case study in tensions between corporate interests, communism, and sovereign rule.

FURTHER RESOURCES
Books

Grandin, Greg. *The Last Colonial Massacre: Latin American in the Cold War*. Chicago: University of Chicago Press, 2004.

Web sites

George Washington University National Security Archive. "U.S. Policy in Guatemala, 1966–1996." <http://www.gwu.edu/~nsarchiv/NSAEBB/NSAEBB11/docs/> (accessed June 24, 2005).

"The Kidnappers Strike Again"

Leftists Interrupt Investment in Brazil

News article

By: Latin American Newsletters

Date: December 11, 1970

Source: Intelligence Research, Ltd.

About the Author: This news report was originally published as part of the *Latin American News* series from Lettres, UK (now Intelligence Research, Ltd.), a London-based news agency. Established in 1967, the *Latin American Newsletters* were written by Latin American specialists in London, writing about political and social events throughout Latin America as they unfolded. Printed in both English and Spanish, the *Latin American Newsletters* were a compilation from a variety of sources, without author attribution.

Similar to ALN tactics, Iranian students held fifty-two Americans hostage for 444 days in this compound in Iran. AP/WIDE WORLD PHOTOS

INTRODUCTION

In the early 1960s, Brazil experienced a rapid industrialization that changed its population demographics. As rural citizens flocked to urban areas in search of jobs and new opportunities in the factories, the economy shifted. The rapid growth was halted in 1962, however, as external forces lowered foreign investment and led to stagnation and inflation, affecting all financial classes but hurting the urban poor disproportionately. Economic problems led to unrest throughout the country, and on April 1, 1964, a military coup, led by General Humberto Castello Branco, took control of Brazil.

The military immediately enacted a number of economic reforms to stabilize the economy, such as controlling inflation, encouraging foreign and domestic investment, balancing trade, increasing markets for industrial goods from Brazil, and developing the country's infrastructure to help with internal trade and business development in general. These changes paved the way for the "economic miracle" of the late 1960s and early 1970s, when Brazil's GDP went from an average of 4.0 percent (1962–1967) to 11 percent (1968–1973).

At the same time, the military instituted civil changes, such as granting security forces broad powers in controlling political or social unrest. Two leftist groups formed in 1968, both with a mission to fight the military government. The National Liberation Alliance (ALN) and the People's Revolutionary Vanguard (VPR), two separate leftist groups with similar philosophies, formed within one month of each other. These urban guerillas sought to destabilize the military government through bombings and kidnappings.

When the Swiss ambassador was kidnapped in late 1970, the police arrested more than 8,000 people with suspected ties to the ALN and VPR. With each insurgent act, the military's response was swift and thorough, breeding further discontent among some leftist interests.

PRIMARY SOURCE

The kidnapping of the Swiss ambassador to Brazil, Giovanni Enrico Bucher, has put in question the claims by the

Brazilian authorities that the terrorist campaign is now 'under control'.

The kidnapping of the Swiss ambassador on Monday appears to have been carried out by the National Liberation Alliance (ALN) and as we went to press unconfirmed reports said that the kidnappers were demanding the release of 69 political prisoners in exchange for the ambassador's release. This kidnapping, which is the fourth diplomatic kidnapping in Brazil in the last 18 months, is most notable as an indication that the ALN—the last viable terrorist organisation in Brazil—is still active. Last year its legendary leader, Carlos Marighela, was shot by the police and this year in October, almost a year to the day later, his successor, Joaquim Camara Ferreira, was also shot. It was then felt that the ALN was without leadership and therefore incapable of effective activity, but Monday's kidnapping was carried out with military precision. The ambassador's guard was machine-gunned down and the ambassador himself is believed to have been hit. The police escort never appears to have got a look in.

Assuming that the only demands are for the release of political prisoners, previous experience indicates that the Brazilian government will release the prisoners with expedition and send them to whatever country the kidnappers indicate. The Brazilian government has already developed a face-saving formula which is that 'the sooner we are rid of these people the better'. This attitude has in the past resulted in the almost immediate release of kidnapped diplomats without the drawn-out bargaining which has in other countries resulted in the death of the person kidnapped. Such an attitude is typical of the compromising attitude of Brazilians in general; 'the Portuguese don't kill the bull', Spanish- speaking Americans say.

It is this attitude, too, which has, up till now, stopped the Brazilians from applying the death penalty which was placed on the statute book last year but has not been used. At the trial last week of three hijackers, before a military court, the prosecutor argued that their crime fell under section 28 of the criminal code, the penalty for which is a maximum of death and a minimum of life imprisonment. Although, on the evidence, the offence clearly fell within the terms of section 28, the air force officers who were acting as judges refused to accept the prosecutor's argument and doled out prison sentences ranging from five to 25 years.

There is, however, a danger that the terrorists' demands may increase. Some observers are of the opinion that the Swiss ambassador was particularly chosen because Switzerland recently expelled two Brazilian exiles, Apolino de Carvalho and Ladislaw Dowber, who had been sent to Algeria in exchange for the kidnapped Japanese consul in March, and had been conducting a campaign of anti-Brazilian propaganda from Switzerland. It is possible that the kidnappers may try to exert some pressure on the Swiss government, which will be outside the control of the Brazilian government.

There is a further problem. In the past released prisoners have, at the request of the kidnappers, been sent either to Algeria or to Cuba. But the Algerian and Cuban governments have recently revealed some hesitation at receiving any more of these exiles, most of whom do not appear to be prepared to do any work in their country of exile. There is a serious possibility that the kidnappers may have difficulty in finding a country that will accept the prisoners when they are released by the Brazilian authorities.

SIGNIFICANCE

Before the 1964 coup, the United States had become increasingly concerned about Brazil's instability and leftist efforts. Alarmed that Brazil might become a large communist or socialist stronghold with great influence over Latin and Central America, President Lyndon B. Johnson's military and intelligence agencies offered behind-the-scenes assistance in the Brazilian coup. As economic development progressed under Brazilian military control throughout the mid and late 1960s, the United States and other foreign interests were more willing to invest in Brazil.

The leftist kidnappings from 1968 onward were related to foreign investment; diplomats from the United States, Japan, Germany and Switzerland were kidnapped in the order of the amount of money they had invested in Brazil, from largest investor to the second-largest, and so on. The subtlety of this planned order of attack was lost on the Brazilian authorities; the insurgents pointed out this strategy after the fact. The use of kidnapping diplomats as a leftist attack on foreign investment foreshadowed Tupac Amaru's 1996 capture and detention of the Japanese ambassador and other diplomats in Peru as a protest against foreign investment in that country.

In response to the kidnappings, the Brazilian government gave in to the kidnappers' demands, but also increased restrictions on civil life. The Department of Social and Political Order was created within the War Department to manage political violence and insurgents. In December 1968, the government enacted Institutional Act Number Five, which strengthened the president's powers and gave the executive branch more authority than ever before. Death squads, vigilante groups made up largely of off-duty police officers and soldiers, were responsible for more than one thousand deaths from 1968 to 1970. According to human rights observers, Brazil's military and security forces established a "dirty war" similar to other activities in Chile and Argentina in the 1970s, as the government used detention, torture, and disappearances while routing out leftists. As the conflicts between leftist groups and right-wing vigilantes escalated, urban guerilla activity increased across the board.

The official government response to the kidnappings was to give in to the captors' demands, which normally involved releasing political prisoners and sending them to Cuba or Algeria. The kidnappings became, in the eyes of some international observers, a successful tool on the part of the opposition to win concessions from the Brazilian government. However, as the economy improved, guerilla activity lessened. In addition, as this article notes, both Cuba and Algeria wavered in permitting released rebels into their countries. By the end of 1971, all of the leaders of the ALN and VPR were imprisoned, dead, or no longer active in these groups.

FURTHER RESOURCES

Books

Schneider, Ronald M. *The Political System of Brazil: Emergence of a Modernizing Authoritarian Regime, 1964–1970,* 1973.

Web sites

MIPT Terrorism Knowledge Base. "Popular Revolutionary Vanguard." <http://www.tkb.org/Group.jsp?groupID=4213> (accessed July 9, 2005).

The National Security Archive. "Brazil Marks 40th Anniversary of Military Coup." <http://www.tkb.org/Group.jsp?groupID=4213> (accessed July 9, 2005).

"Mexico: Conflict on the Campus"

News article

By: Latin American Newsletters

Date: August 11, 1972

Source: "Mexico: Conflict on the Campus," as published by Intelligence Research.

About the Author: This news report was originally published as part of the Latin American News series from Lettres, U.K. (now Intelligence Research, Ltd.), a London-based news agency. Established in 1967, the *Latin American Newsletters* were written by Latin American specialists in London, writing about political and social events throughout Latin America as they unfolded. Printed in both English and Spanish, the *Latin American Newsletters* were a compilation from a variety of sources, without author attribution.

INTRODUCTION

In the late 1960s and early 1970s, Mexico was rocked by a series of protests by middle-class university students, who joined with labor organizers and a small number of peasants to form a fluid movement that argued for greater democratic reforms in Mexican government. The Partido Revolucionario Institucional (PRI) had controlled Mexican politics as the ruling party since 1929. By the mid-1960s, a series of economic problems led to unrest in the populace, especially among the poor, middle-class students, and labor organizers.

As protestors took to the streets in gatherings as large as 500,000 people, the PRI, unaccustomed to such opposition, instituted security crackdowns. The 1968 Summer Olympics were being held in Mexico City, and student protestors sought to use the international exposure to gain attention for their cause. In September, one month before the Olympics, President Gustavo Díaz Ordaz ordered the Mexican Army to occupy Latin America's largest university, the National Autonomous University of Mexico (UNAM).

On October 2, 1968, more than 15,000 students had protested throughout the day. By evening, their numbers had dwindled to 5,000 students and workers, some with spouses and children present. As the protestors gathered in Plaza de las Tres Culturas in the Tlaltelolco section of Mexico City, they chanted "Mexico! Liberty! Mexico! Liberty!"

Security forces, with armored tanks and guns, surrounded the protestors. What happened next remains a source of conflict to this day. Eyewitnesses among the protestors report that at sunset, the security forces began firing on the crowd indiscriminately, killing as many as three hundred protestors. The police claim that armed protestors began firing, and that the police returned fire in self-defense. An official report in 2002 set the death toll at thirty-eight, although some protest groups claim the figure is much higher.

The "massacre at Tlaltelolco" gained international attention. It also led to the PRI's launch of the "Dirty War," with security forces secretly targeting suspected insurgents, university activists, labor organizers, and many political opponents of the PRI. The covert campaign, which lasted roughly from 1971 until 1978, led to accusations from abroad of widespread human rights abuses in Mexico. Throughout the 1970s, other Latin American countries, such as Chile and Argentina, experienced their own "dirty wars" against suspected leftists. Under military dictators such as Augusto Pinochet in Chile and Argentina's Leopoldo Galtieri, tens of thousands of *desaparecidos* (disappeared) protestors were arrested, imprisoned, and remained missing after the military was granted broad, sweeping powers in an effort to stop all leftist activity.

With the election of Luis Echeverria as Mexican president in 1970, it was thought that a fragile peace might develop between protestors and the government. As this dispatch from Latin American Newsletters shows, by 1972, tension was again on the rise as right-wing paramilitary groups, suspected of having links to the Mexican government, began to fight against leftist protestors.

■ PRIMARY SOURCE

Tension is growing on university campuses, with right-wing paramilitary groups becoming more aggressive, and left-wing students trying to establish links with peasants and workers.

Mexican university students, who have suffered heavy losses in clashes with the authorities over the past few years, once more seem to be set on a collision course with the powers that be. It is less than four years since several hundred students were gunned down by the army in the "Tlaltelolco massacre" of 1968, and only just over a year since 30 or more were killed by paramilitary bands of thugs during a Corpus Christi day demonstration. It would surprise no one if a similar massacre were to occur again at any moment.

Tension has been rising as a result, more than anything, of the growing aggressiveness of these right-wing terrorist groups, known in general as *Las Porras,* though sometimes sporting a particular name, such as *Los Halcones* in Mexico City. The latter are armed, trained for street fighting, and have the use of radio-equipped cars similar to those used by the police. In Puebla, some 65 miles southeast of the capital, these bands are trained by serving army officers, and march through the streets, often carrying Nazi flags. Nobody doubts that they are all linked with one or another government agency, but the mystery is always: which, and by whose authority?

The left-wing militants, on the other hand, have realized that one of the student movement's greatest weaknesses has been its lack of support among workers' and peasants' organizations. This is hardly surprising, since in the first place students are almost all from middle class families, and in the second, workers' and peasants' organizations are strictly controlled by some of the most conservative members of the "establishment." Furthermore most peasants, particularly in the more populous parts of central Mexico, are deeply imbued with the conviction that all left-wingers are communists, and that communists are agents of the devil—thanks to the anti-communist proselytizing action of parish priests.

Although militant students have so far made little headway in obtaining the support of workers and peasants, they have made a start. In Mexico City, students from the National University (UNAM) seized a number of buses and held them in a campus car park as security for compensation which they demanded from the city's bus company, on behalf of the family of a worker run over by a bus. A group of *Porras* then attacked the faculty of law and history in an apparent attempt to recover the buses, but the attempt failed, although a number of students were wounded. The atmosphere in the university remains highly charged.

In Culiacan, capital of the northwestern state of Sinaloa, two students were killed, many wounded and 200 arrested in demonstrations which followed four months of agitation on the campus. This was a result of attempts by police, with the help of the local *Porras,* to reinstate the unpopular rector, Armienta Calderon, who had been expelled by the students last April. In the end, the federal minister of education Victor Bravo Ahuja had to intervene with the state authorities to secure the release of the gaoled students, while such normally staid bodies as the local chamber of commerce, the chamber of manufacturing industry and the employers' association protested publicly against police brutality.

But the most inflammatory incident recently took place in Puebla, where the left-wing director of the university's preparatory school, Joel Arriaga Navarro, was gunned down one night at the end of last month as he drove home from a party. The reaction was explosive. Students organized a joint demonstration of protest with railway and electrical workers, employees of the local Volkswagen factory, teachers, and the *Confederacion Campesina Independiente* (CCI), which Echeverria has been surreptitiously encouraging as a counterbalance to the more conservative, but official, *Confederacion Nacional de Campesinos* (CNC).

The position of President Echeverria in this growing conflict remains obscure. He is undoubtedly sincere in wanting a "dialogue" with students, and knows this cannot happen without the "democratic opening" he has repeatedly spoken of. Equally, he wants to avoid at all costs the use of the army against students, as at Tlaltelolco. Last year Echeverria and his aides put the word out that the Los Halcones had perpetrated the Corpus Christi day massacre, and indeed were operating as a group, without his authorization or knowledge. It hardly seems likely, however, that this could still be true for all the universities where these terrorist bands are still active 14 months later. Either the President is not strong enough to challenge those in the "establishment" who control these groups, or he does not want to. The growing tension in the universities may soon smoke him out of this ambiguous position.

■□

SIGNIFICANCE

The killings of student protestors in 1968 and 1971 weighed heavily on the minds of political observers, government officials, and students. In response to the leftist protestors, a backlash developed, resulting in the formation of right-wing terrorist groups.

Echeverria's secret "Dirty War" had just been launched, and the right-wing paramilitary groups were a public display of these private activities. While observers noted the mystery of the paramilitary's backers, the assumption of the government's involvement was a given.

In addition, the conflicts involved a wide cross-section of the population, including middle-class students, peasants, right-wing paramilitary groups, parish priests, and labor organizers. As the article notes, the peasants distrusted the left-wingers, believing them to be communists and "agents of the devil—thanks to the anti-communist proselytizing action of parish priests." One of the major sources of protestors' anger was the government's seizure of *ejido* lands, land collectively held by peasants in the countryside. One reason for the students' failure to bring more peasants into their cause was the priests' involvement; church teachings have a strong role in the daily life of Catholic peasants. The students' inability to reach these peasant groups in a meaningful way, and to communicate their role in trying to fight the land reform, was a crucial failure that led to a lack of support for the protests among the Mexican peasantry.

By 1972, the spotlight was on Echeverria's actions in handling the conflicts between students and right-wing paramilitary groups. Behind the scenes, the PRI and Echeverria conducted the dirty war against protestors and suspected leftists, with Mexico's Federal Security Directorate in charge of operations. The PRI's goal of eliminating the leftist opposition led to widespread human rights abuses and the stripping of legal protections for the accused. In 2000, Vicente Fox's election to the presidency of Mexico ended the PRI's seventy-one-year reign. In 2001, a 2,000-page report on the "Dirty War", written by Mexico's human rights ombudsman, detailed the documented disappearance of 275 detainees during the 1970s and the torture of 523 persons, with as many as thirty-seven different government agencies implicated in the disappearances and human rights abuses. President Fox appointed special prosecutor Ignacio Carrillo to investigate the disappearances and human rights abuses; on June 19, 2005, four former government officials were charged with the 1974 disappearances of six peasants from the Mexican state of Hidalgo.

FURTHER RESOURCES

Books

Preston, Julia, and Samuel Dillon. *Opening Mexico: The Making of a Democracy.* New York: Farrar, Straus and Giroux, 2004.

Web sites

George Washington University NSA Archives. "Mexico: An Emerging Internal Security Problem?" State Department Bureau of Intelligence and Research, secret intelligence note. <http://www.gwu.edu/~nsarchiv/NSAEBB/NSAEBB105/Doc2.pdf> (accessed June 21, 2005).

"Life as 'Tania' Seems So Far Away"

The Symbionese Liberation Army (SLA)

Newspaper article

By: Maureen Orth

Date: July 31, 1988

Source: *Toronto Star.*

About the Author: Maureen Orth began writing for *Vanity Fair* in 1988. She advanced to contributing editor in 1989 and to special correspondent in 1993. Among her investigative articles was a story on the funding of terrorism activities through Afghanistan's illegal opium trade. Orth has also written for the *Washington Post, New York Times*, and the *Toronto Star.*

INTRODUCTION

The Symbionese Liberation Army (SLA) was a small, but violent group of radicals in the 1970s opposed to what they perceived as powerful influences of wealthy corporate interests over the United States government. Two activists, Russell Little and Robyn Sue Steiner, originally created the loosely based group in Berkeley, California to recognize the issues involved with poverty, prison reform, and race. Shortly after its inception, the group was taken over by Donald DeFreeze, an escaped prisoner, and Patricia Soltysik, a radical activist. The name Symbionese was adopted from the word symbiosis, which DeFreeze applied within his manifesto to refer to different types of people living together in peace and harmony.

DeFreeze and Soltysik gathered together the original members of the SLA: Nancy Ling Perry, Russell Little, William Wolfe, Bill and Emily Harris, Joe Remiro, Camilla Hall, and Angela Atwood. DeFreeze

Photo found in the burned-out ruins of the house in Los Angeles where six Symbionese Liberation Army (SLA) members died on May 17, 1974. AP/WIDE WORLD PHOTOS

soon convinced the members to burglarize and kidnap wealthy capitalists and rob banks in order to raise money for a self-described revolution of the underprivileged. Their plan involved high-profile crimes in order to receive regional, if not national, media coverage of their rebellion.

Their first deadly action was the November 6, 1973 killing of Marcus Foster, the superintendent of Oakland, California's public school system. A statement delivered to a radio station communicated that the SLA was responsible for the assassination because Foster allegedly agreed to use compulsory photograph identification cards for high school students, which the group believed was a covert plan by the federal government to place surveillance cameras inside schools.

The SLA's next target became its most notorious crime. DeFreeze, Atwood, and Bill Harris kidnapped Patricia (Patty) Hearst on February 4, 1974, from her apartment while she was a student at the University of California, Berkeley. The kidnapping became a national media event as Patty was the daughter of newspaper magnate Randolph Apperson Hearst, son of William Randolph Hearst. According to a statement given to a radio station, the SLA kidnapped Hearst to exchange her for SLA members (Little and Remiro) held in jail. However, when the exchange did not succeed, its second demand was for the Hearst family to give free food to the poor.

In response, Hearst's father, chairman of the Hearst Corporation, formed the People In Need program in the San Francisco Bay area, to which he donated almost $2 million. However, Hearst went from SLA hostage to SLA member when she announced that after the SLA released her, she decided to stay and fight for its cause. Her family and the police asserted that she had been brainwashed.

Then, on April 15, 1974, Hearst was photographed holding an assault rifle while robbing the Sunset District branch of the Hibernia Bank in San Francisco. Later, it was learned she had adopted her SLA name, Tania. At this time, Hearst was considered a criminal and, at one time, was on the Federal Bureau of Investigation's Ten Most Wanted list.

In May 1974, six members of the SLA died in a confrontation with police officers and FBI agents. However, Hearst and Bill and Emily Harris, the last remaining SLA members, were not involved. They vowed to keep the SLA alive and continued robbing banks.

In August 1975, with weapons and explosive materials purchased with stolen money, they began a series of bombings against law enforcement and other government agencies. Hearst was eventually arrested in San Francisco in September 1975, along with Bill and Emily Harris and several other associates. At that time, the police declared the SLA to be no longer functioning.

Hearst's trial began on January 15, 1976 when her defense attorney, F. Lee Bailey, claimed she had been blindfolded, locked in a closet, brainwashed, physically and sexually abused, forced to join the SLA cause, and coerced into committing crimes. However, the jury did not believe Patty Hearst's testimony. Hearst was convicted on March 20, 1976. She served nearly two years of a seven-year prison sentence, and was released on February 1, 1979, after having her sentence commuted by President Jimmy Carter. Later, on January 20, 2001, Patty Hearst (now Patty Hearst Shaw) was pardoned by President Bill Clinton.

PRIMARY SOURCE

On Feb. 4, 1974, the SLA broke into the house Patricia Hearst, 19, shared with her boyfriend and kidnapped her at gunpoint. A month later she embraced her captors, renounced her family as "fascist pigs" and took the name "Tania," a female guerrilla who died in Bolivia fighting with Che Guevara. That seminal media event of the '70s is about to bob up in the national consciousness again, this time in the movie *Patty Hearst,* directed by Paul Schrader and starring Natasha Richardson as Patty. The film, scheduled for release in August, is based on Hearst's 1982 book, *Every*

Secret Thing. But rather than being the final word on this extraordinary tale, the film is bound to unleash a whole new debate because at crucial moments it begs the key questions: Was Patty Hearst's conversion for real or did she feign allegiance to the SLA to ensure her survival? And why didn't she ever try to escape? The film has already provoked anger and controversy from major players in the real-life drama, people who have remained silent for a decade. "She could have gone home; she could have killed us in our sleep if she wanted to," says one of her former SLA captors. "She wasn't imprisoned for the 19 or 20 months she was with us. The point is, she started out a victim and then a process took place. You can't say it was psychological coercion and you can't say it was 100 per cent free will. We ourselves were fooled by a lot of the dynamics of the conversion."

Was it, in fact, a conversion experience? How else to explain a kidnapping victim who, within two months, emerged with a gun and a new identity to rob a bank with the SLA and then shoot up a Los Angeles store with a submachine gun in a second SLA holdup? Hearst watched on TV as the Los Angeles police fired 9,000 rounds of ammunition into the SLA hideout, killing everyone inside including her lover "Cujo" (William Wolfe). Hearst herself would have been in the house that day, but she was hiding out in a Disneyland motel with Bill and Emily Harris, the two surviving members of the SLA, who each served five years for her kidnapping.

One of the country's most-wanted women, Hearst used a dozen disguises as she crisscrossed the country on the lam and took part in another bank robbery during which a mother of four was killed—all before the FBI finally caught up with her 19 months after her kidnapping. When Hearst was arrested she gave her profession as "urban guerrilla." The star of a sensational trial, she took the Fifth 42 times. Her lawyers offered brainwashing (referred to as "duress") as her defense; the jury did not buy it and the heiress was convicted on bank robbery charges and sentenced to seven years in jail. During her two years of incarceration, Hearst and her family launched a major media campaign to influence public opinion in her favor. President Carter finally commuted her sentence on Jan. 29, 1979, nearly five years to the day after her kidnapping.

The film, told strictly from Patty Hearst's point of view, tries to convince the audience of what director Schrader calls the horrendous "psychological reality" with which she had to cope and the living hell she writes of in her book: a numbing isolation; the belief that her parents had abandoned her ("There was no one out there who could help me," she writes), her firm conviction that the SLA was "suicidal," and that the FBI would shoot her on sight.

Schrader shot much of the first half hour of *Patty Hearst* in near darkness, a stylistic simulation of the terror of being kidnapped, blindfolded, locked in a closet for much of the time and subjected to regular propaganda sessions for more than a month before Hearst told Cinque, the ex-convict leading the SLA, that she chose to join them.

For a good part of the film Natasha Richardson plays the forceful Patty like a scared doe; The film doesn't take into account the rage that may have fueled Hearst's decision. After all, although her parents Randolph and Catherine Hearst paid $2 million for the abortive food giveaway program the SLA had demanded, they turned down a second set of ransom demands, claiming, according to a source close to the family, it was "throwing good money after bad." Then, at a delicate moment in the negotiations, Catherine Hearst not only defied the SLA when they demanded that she resign as a regent of the University of California, but renewed her term for another 10 years— without telling even her husband. "My father was furious and insisted she shouldn't do it. And she just insisted it was the right thing to do," says Shaw today.

The effect on Patty then, says someone who knew her, was that "she started to see her mother as the enemy."

When she finally was able to get out of the closet— off "death row," as she puts it—and convince the SLA that she was sincere in wanting to join them, she felt tremendous relief and something else as well. Hearst writes in her book: "In trying to convince them, I convinced myself. I felt that I had truly joined them; my past life seemed to have slipped away . . . Somewhere in the jumble of my reasoning was the hope, reborn, that the essential thing was that I would survive. I would stay with this horrible group for a while and the day would come when I would be rescued or perhaps be able to escape."

But the day never came. Instead, Hearst participated in escalating acts of violence and never once tried to escape. Why?

Her SLA captors were convinced that Hearst was a genuine convert when she joined them in robbing the Hibernia Bank in San Francisco. "She never would have been taken to do such a thing if she was not felt to be 100 percent with us," says one of them. "You do not give a person who's a captive a loaded weapon, an automatic weapon." Shaw protests; she says that the bolt on the weapon was turned. But could she have turned the bolt? Today she is evasive. "I don't know," she says. One of her kidnappers contends that due to Hearst's inexperience she jammed the gun and could not get it unjammed while she was in the bank. "She wasn't coerced. She was freely involved in it— I don't know how else to put it."

Shaw argues that she was controlled by other people the whole time and in her mind was unable to distinguish right from wrong. "At Mel's Sporting Goods Store I really began to notice I was no longer in control when, without a thought, I just did what I had been trained to do—fire the machine gun and the other guns in sequence." Given her overall fear—and her fear of SLA members Bill and Emily Harris in particular (she calls them "evil")—Shaw says she never believed she could escape.

Not even months later when she and a radical boyfriend, a house painter named Steven Soliah, were mistakenly thought to be stranded on some rocks near San Francisco Bay and some friendly sheriff's deputies rescued them. She didn't give herself up, she says, because she genuinely believed she was without options—still in terror of the police because of the way they had decimated the SLA hideout in Los Angeles. "Everybody asked me why didn't I go to the police?" says Shaw. "Why would I? A police station! That's about the last place I would have thought would be safe to walk into."

But according to some of the country's leading terrorism experts, brainwashing—deliberate coercive persuasion—cannot account for the depth of Hearst's conversion. Not even the Stockholm or "survivor" syndrome can explain 19 months of sustained rage at the system. A conversion process like hers is complex, they claim, and had a great deal to do with her age, sex, and personality development at the time of the kidnapping.

In prep school Hearst's IQ was measured at 130. Among Randolph and Catherine Hearst's five daughters, "She was the iconoclast, the individualist," says lawyer Coblentz. "Patty was known to be rebellious." Her first cousin William Randolph Hearst III, publisher of The San Francisco Examiner, agrees: "She was certainly someone capable of expressing her own mind. She tended to challenge people and ideas." At the time of her kidnapping Patty Hearst was 19, living with and engaged to be married to someone her family didn't like, Steven Weed, her former math tutor and a graduate philosophy student at the University of California at Berkeley where she was a student. (In her book, Hearst contends she had doubts about going through with the wedding.)

One of her SLA captors says that, ironically, it was Hearst's large engagement picture in the San Francisco Chronicle that triggered the kidnapping plan; "You rarely see that much information about someone in the ruling class." At first, the captor says, the SLA viewed her merely as a "rich bitch," but as time and the propaganda sessions wore on they began to view her as "exceptional, a diamond in the rough. She had spunk." The SLA seemed almost flattered when she decided to join.

Other ties began to develop as well. At her trial, Hearst testified that she was forced to have sex in the closet with both Cinque, the ex-convict leading the SLA, and William Wolfe ("Cujo"), the son of a doctor, a National Merit Scholar finalist and a prep-school graduate like Hearst.

One of her captors vehemently disputes this, saying the women in the group, radical feminists, would never

have condoned rape. Although it was considered "comradely" to have sex with everyone within the group, Hearst spurned the four female SLA members in favor of Wolfe. After he died in the SLA shootout in Los Angeles, Hearst issued an emotional communique (she later said she was forced to write it) that eulogized him as "the gentlest, most beautiful man I've ever known . . . Neither Cujo or I had ever loved an individual the way we loved each other."

Today Shaw compares Cinque to Charles Manson and the SLA to a cult. "You can hardly have a hold on reality when you're all living in one room and staying up all night having self-criticism sessions. It was mass hypnosis. By the end they were all chanting, 'We won't live to see the end of the revolution.'"

SIGNIFICANCE

The Symbionese Liberation Army was a collection of radicals who had links to the California prison movement and who hoped to parallel the activities of the Black Panthers, a black revolutionary nationalist group that formed in the late 1960s.

For the most part, the SLA was efficient in publicizing their goals and philosophies to the media. The group distributed photographs, press releases, and taped interviews with the intention of explaining their activities to all who would listen. When the SLA staged violent actions, its members made sure those actions were recorded. Their ultimate goal was to gain support for their cause with the general public and other radical groups. Despite their concerted media campaign, the SLA never had more than thirteen members at any one time.

During the period from 1972–1974, the media showcased the SLA as some of its top newsworthy stories. The name, the Symbionese Liberation Army, became a household word, as did the members' names and nicknames, especially Patty Hearst and her alias Tania. The general public was interested in the escapades of the SLA when the group was vividly described on television and radio and in the newspaper, but otherwise, did not support the SLA philosophy and ideas by swelling its ranks.

FURTHER RESOURCES
Books

Boulton, David. *The Making of Tania Hearst*. London: New English Library, 1975.

Hearst, Patricia. *Every Secret Thing*. Garden City, NY: Doubleday, 1982.

Payne, Leslie. *The Life and Death of the SLA*. New York: Ballantine Books, 1976.

Web sites

Court TV's Crime Library. "The Claiming of Patty Hearst." <http://www.crimelibrary.com/terrorists_spies/terrorists/hearst/1.html?sect=22> (accessed June 19, 2005).

Court TV's Crime Library. "The Symbionese Liberation Army." <http://www.courttv.com/trials/soliah/slahistory_ctv.html> (accessed June 19, 2005).

PaperlessArchives.com. "The Symbionese Liberation Army, Patty Hearst Kidnapping, FBI Files." <http://www.paperlessarchives.com/sla.html> (accessed June 19, 2005).

Tania

Terrorists, Revolutionaries, or Criminals?

Photograph

By: Associated Press

Date: c. 1974

Source: This Associated Press photograph of Patricia Hearst posing before the Symbionese Liberation Army's (SLA) symbol was widely circulated during the months in which the SLA was active.

About the Photographer: The Associated Press is one of the leading international newswire services, providing articles and photographs to newspapers and broadcasting outlets around the world.

INTRODUCTION

On February 4, 1974, 19-year-old Patricia (Patty) Hearst was kidnapped from her apartment near the campus of the University of California at Berkeley, where she was a student. The kidnappers were a revolutionary group called the Symbionese Liberation Army (SLA). The kidnapping attracted widespread media attention because Hearst was the granddaughter of publishing giant William Randolph Hearst. Over the next year, the public grew fascinated with Patty Hearst's apparent conversion from kidnap victim to gun-toting member of the revolutionary group.

The SLA was founded in 1971 in the San Francisco Bay area by a group of Berkeley radicals led by Russell Little and Robyn Sue Steiner. Originally, the group, which adopted Marxist and South American revolutionary rhetoric, focused on problems of race, poverty, and prison reform. Its slogan was "Death to the fascist insect that preys on the life of the people."

By 1972, members of the SLA were attending meetings of a prison group called the Black Cultural Association. There they met Donald DeFreeze, who escaped from the prison later that year. In 1973, under the revolutionary name General Field Marshall Cinque Mtume (a name taken from the leader of the revolt on the slave ship *Amistad* in 1839), DeFreeze took over leadership of the SLA and pushed it in a new, more violent direction. Steiner fled to England when DeFreeze threatened to kill her.

Late that year, the group claimed responsibility for the assassination of Oakland, California, school superintendent Marcus Foster in the mistaken assumption that he advocated a "fascist" plan to require Oakland students to show identification on campus. In 1974, Little and Joseph Remiro were arrested and charged with the murder. Little was later acquitted at a retrial, but Remiro was sentenced to prison.

The SLA gained the media attention it craved on February 4, 1974, when eight of its members kidnapped Patty Hearst from her Berkeley apartment. The group described Hearst as a "prisoner of war" and called her family's Hearst Corporation a "corporate enemy of the people." The group offered to release her in exchange for a $2 million food giveaway to poor people, but in April it released a communiqué in which Hearst announced that she would "stay and fight" with the SLA under the name Tania. Days later, Hearst was photographed by a security camera as she apparently helped the SLA rob the Hibernia Bank in San Francisco, and in May, she sprayed a sporting goods store with bullets from a submachine gun as SLA members Emily and William Harris robbed the store.

By this time, American television viewers and newspaper readers were widely familiar with the following photo of Hearst, wielding a submachine gun and posing before the SLA's symbol, a seven-headed cobra.

■ PRIMARY SOURCE

TANIA

See primary source image.

SIGNIFICANCE

The SLA began to unravel in May 1974, when six of its members, including DeFreeze, were killed when the South Central Los Angeles house they were holed up in caught fire during a shootout—all shown live on television. Afterwards, surviving members Hearst and the Harrises joined Kathleen Soliah, her sister Josephine and brother Steven, and James Kilgore in relaunching the SLA. In April 1975, the group robbed

PRIMARY SOURCE

Tania Kidnapped heiress Patricia Hearst standing before a symbol of the organization whose members kidnapped her, The Symbionese Liberation Army, 1974. © BETTMANN/ CORBIS

the Crocker National Bank in Carmichael, California. During the robbery, Emily Harris shot and killed bank customer Myrna Lee Opsahl, who was in the bank to deposit her church's collection money. Harris told Hearst, "Oh, she's dead, but it doesn't really matter. She was a bourgeois pig anyway."

In September 1975, the Harrises, Hearst, and Wendy Yoshimura were arrested. When asked her occupation at her booking, Hearst replied "urban guerrilla." At trial, Hearst portrayed herself as an SLA victim, claiming that she was starved, tortured, and sexually abused while she was held captive. In March 1976, she was found guilty of bank robbery and sentenced to prison, but in February 1979, President Jimmy Carter granted her executive clemency and commuted her sentence. Meanwhile, the Harrises were convicted and sentenced to prison, but released in 1983.

The SLA story did not end with the Hearst trial. In 1999, Soliah was found living under the name Sara Jane Olson in Minnesota, where she was arrested as a fugitive. In 2001, she plead guilty to attempting to bomb Los Angeles Police Department patrol cars and was sentenced to 20 years in prison. Then in 2002, Soliah— along with the Harrises, Kilgore, and Michael Bortin— was charged with the murder of Opsahl. Kilgore fled,

but the former communist revolutionary was seized in his luxury apartment in South Africa on November 8, 2002. In May 2004, Kilgore was sentenced to six years in prison, finally closing the book on the SLA.

In January 2001, just before leaving office, President Bill Clinton granted Hearst an executive pardon.

FURTHER RESOURCES

Books

Holman, Virginia. *Rescuing Patty Hearst: Growing Up Sane in a Decade Gone Mad.* New York: Simon and Schuster, 2004.

McLellan, Vin, and Paul Avery. *The Voices of Guns: The Definitive and Dramatic Story of the Twenty-Two-Month Career of the Symbionese Liberation Army.* New York: Putnam, 1977.

Web sites

CourtTV.com. "'70s Radical Bombing Case." <http://www. courttv.com/trials/soliah> (accessed May 23, 2005).

Audio and Visual Media

Patty Hearst, directed by Paul Schrader (original release, 1988). Anchor Bay Entertainment, 1990 (VHS).

"Argentina: Boat Bomb"

Political Violence in Argentina as Opposition Groups Battle

News report

By: Latin American Newsletters

Date: November 8, 1974

Source: Intelligence Research, Ltd.

About the Author: This news report was originally published as part of the *Latin American News* series from Lettres, UK (now Intelligence Research, Ltd.), a London-based news agency. Established in 1967, the *Latin American Newsletters* were written by Latin American specialists in London, writing about political and social events throughout Latin America as they unfolded. Printed in both English and Spanish, the *Latin American Newsletters* were a compilation from a variety of sources, without author attribution.

INTRODUCTION

Argentina had been under the rule of military leader Juan Perón from 1946–1955, during which time the military leader developed economic and social policies that were populist in nature. Perón asserted that

Police officers taking the finger prints of Ricardo Palmera, a leader of the leftist Revolutionary Armed Forces of Colombia (FARC). AP/WIDE WORLD PHOTOS

nationalization and unionization empowered the working class, but those moves also alienated elites and foreign investors. In 1955, right-leaning military leaders forced Perón into exile. Leftists, union members, and the working poor were angered by the coup. By the early 1960s, Argentina faced the beginning of a long stretch of political violence from opposition groups.

Insurgent groups, such as the Montonero Peronist Movement, formed in support of exiled president Juan Perón. Perón's populist policies, and his economic protectionism, stood in stark contrast to the price freezes and nationwide strikes that plagued the country under the various military and civilian leaders. However, Perón and the Montoneros became increasingly at odds as Perón shifted his views to the right. By 1973, when Perón returned to Argentina and was permitted to run for office, the Montoneros were disenchanted with Perón. Political violence increased.

Assassinations and political violence swept through Argentina, including the assassination of labor leader José Alonso, in August 1970, the assassination of General Juan Carlos Sánchez, Commander of Army Corps II, on April 10, 1972, the murder of labor leader José Ignacio Rucci on September 25, 1973, the murder of a priest, Carlos Mugica, in May 1974, and the assassination of Arturo Mor Roig, former Minister of the Interior, on July 15, 1974.

Perón was elected to the presidency for the third time in October 1973. He died the following year, and his vice-president and third wife, Isabel, assumed the presidency. As the political violence had increased, Perón had resorted to emergency measures that stripped away the legal rights of detainees and suspected terrorists, in an attempt to stem political violence.

The violence reached a climax on November 1, 1974, when federal police chief Alberto Villar and his wife were murdered by a bomb that was planted on their boat.

PRIMARY SOURCE

The assassination of police chief Alberto Villar has rocked Argentina more than any other since the death of Peron, causing a fresh estimation of the Montoneros' strength, and speculation about the role of the armed forces.

The federal police chief went boating on the river Parana last Friday and his boat was blown up. Some 47,000 policemen were set to search for his assassins and President Isabel Peron ordered flags to be flown at half-mast. Within hours the Montoneros, the clandestine left-wing peronist movement, had claimed responsibility, threatening Jose Lopez Rega, minister of social security, and Ricardo Otero, minister of labour, with the same fate. *Cronica* published a full-page picture of Lopez Rega in his uniform as a commissioner general in the police force (he was promoted a few months ago, having ended his previous career in the police as a sergeant), prompting memories of the moment in January when General Peron put on his uniform to denounce the ERP attack on the garrison at Azul. Lopez Rega said that were it not for his other tasks, he would put on his uniform permanently to hunt out the police chief's assassins.

Next to Lopez Rega, Alberto Villar, head of the federal police since May, has been the left wing's most wanted man. He came to prominence during the military dictatorship as an expert in counter-insurgency. He was in charge of the investigations into the death of ex-President Aramburu, and was at one stage suspended after trying to hide evidence of police torture in Cordoba. He was retired on the accession of President Campora last year, but was brought back to active service in January to take charge of anti-guerrilla operations in the wake of the Azul attack. His return was interpreted at the time as an encouragement to police terrorism and prompted the resignation of a number of senior police officers. The government certainly hoped then that Villar and his deputy, Luis Margaride, would quickly clean up the guerrillas without it being necessary to call in the army. The two men set to work with enthusiasm, and between March and August (according to figures recently provided by Alberto Rocamora, minister of the interior) 32 suspected militants were shot and 827 detained. Nevertheless, although left-wing organisations were severely hit by the wave of police repression, they have not been rooted out. When a new right-wing group appeared a few weeks ago, called the Alianza Anticomunista Argentina, it was generally assumed to be the latest anti-terrorist weapon devised by the police. Indeed one of the leaders of the Montoneros, Roberto Quieto, claimed recently that the AAA was organised by Villar himself, and this claim was repeated in the Montonero communique claiming responsibility for Villar's death. If true, one would expect activity by the AAA to diminish, though the appointment of Villar's deputy and disciple, Luis Margaride, as the new police chief means that previous policies are unlikely to be changed.

The success of the Montoneros in assassinating one of their principal opponents suggests that they are still a significant force to be reckoned with, and the government must undoubtedly be wondering whether they will soon be forced to bring in the armed forces to join the police in the fight against the guerrillas. There is again talk of reviving the national security council and the security secretariat that had such a brief life in June. The original idea of the council, to be headed by General Alberto Caceres, federal police chief in the days of President Lanusse, was to involve the commanders of the three armed services in control of security operations. It was abandoned the week before Peron died—partly it seems because of the fear that the military, once unleashed against the guerrillas, would grow too powerful politically. This argument still holds good, though with the deteriorating security situation, the military must be growing restless.

Quite apart from the 25 deaths of leftists attributable to the AAA in recent weeks, the past week has seen a wave of bombings and murders. The police chief in Corrientes was shot and wounded, the police in Misiones have been on strike, the ERP took over a village in Tucuman, three Tupamaros were shot in San Antonio, two foreign journalists have been arrested, and Raimundo Ongaro has been detained. For the first time a prominent figure in the Frente de Izquierda Popular (FIP) of Jorge Abelardo Ramos has been shot, as have members of Juan Carlos Coral's Partido Socialista de los Trabajadores. The death of the FIP leader, Carlos Llorena Rosas, may have been due to the fact that he worked for the Instituto Nacional de Tecnologia Agropecuaria and was involved in the land reform proposals worked out by the agriculture secretary, Horacio Giberti.

SIGNIFICANCE

In 1974, the Montoneros initiated a full-scale assault on Isabel Perón's administration. Their targets included the Argentine government, United States companies, and United States government officials, in an effort to discourage foreign investment and the influence of the United States. As this document shows, the political violence from the left was reaching fever pitch in Argentina, as leftists targeted members of the military in successful bombings and assassinations.

By 1976, the military was increasingly frustrated by the political violence. Military forces kidnapped Isabel on March 24, 1976 and placed her under house arrest for the next five years.

In 1976, the military and security forces in Argentina began a "dirty war," officially called the National Reorganization Process, a seven-year campaign to rout out leftists and any opposition to the established government. Human rights observers claim that security forces used forced detention, torture, and murder in weeding out leftist elements throughout Argentina from 1976 to 1983. International observers estimate that, during this time, between 10,000 and 30,000 people were "disappeared" by government forces. These people, the *desaparecidos*, included academics (women as well as men), leftists, doctors and lawyers, and many union organizers.

In 1984, after Argentina's first democratic elections in decades, a shaky amnesty was granted to military and security forces for any perceived human rights abuses. However, in June 2005, the Argentine Supreme Court overturned this amnesty, opening the door to future charges and trials.

FURTHER RESOURCES
Books
Taylor, Diana. *Disappearing Acts: Spectacles of Gender and Nationalism in Argentina's "Dirty War"*. Durham, North Carolina: Duke University Press, 1997.

Web sites
University of Minnesota Human Rights Library. "Report on the Situation of Human Rights in Argentina, Inter-Am. C.H.R., OEA/Ser.L/V/II.49, Doc. 19 corr.1 (1980)." <http://www1.umn.edu/humanrts/iachr/country-reports/argentina1980-ch1.html> (accessed July 8, 2005).

Baader-Meinhof

"Terrorists Are Jailed for Life after Disrupted Trial Lasting 103 Weeks"

Newspaper article

By: Dan Van der Vat

Date: April 29, 1977

Source: The *Times*, a daily newspaper based in London.

About the Author: Dan Van der Vat, at the time the article was written, lived in Germany. He worked for six years as a journalist and foreign correspondent for the *Times* (London). He has also worked for the *Guardian*. In both positions, Van der Vat specialized in political and defense writing. During his journalistic career, Van der Vat, a historian and expert on modern warfare, has written such books as *Gentlemen of War: The Amazing Story of Captain Karl von Müller and the S.M.S. Emden* (1984), *Pacific Campaign: World War II, the U.S.-Japanese Naval War, 1941–1945* (1992), *Pearl Harbor: The Day of Infamy—An Illustrated History* (2001), and *D-Day: The Greatest Invasion—A People's History* (2004).

INTRODUCTION

On May 14, 1970, journalist Ulrike Meinhof led armed revolutionaries against a prison in West Berlin. The raid was staged to free Andreas Baader, a prisoner sentenced for politically motivated arson and seriously wounding a person. Due to the dramatic prison breakout, the *Springer Press* coined the name "Baader-Meinhof Gang." The German media adopted the popular name for the group that earlier had called itself the Red Army Faction.

The leftist revolutionary group carried out a number of shootings, bombings, robberies, and other violent crimes over the next two years while increasing numbers of police unsuccessfully hunted for them. Baader-Meinhof was known to have killed five people and injured fifty-four others during this time. Due to its sensationalistic crime spree, nearly all unsolved violent crimes were credited to the group's exploits. So many police were involved, the media compared the confrontations to warfare.

On June 1, 1972, however, a gunfight between Baader-Meinhof and the police resulted in the arrest of Baader-Meinhof leaders Baader, Holger Meins, and Jan-Carl Raspe. On June 7, Gudrun Ensslin, another leader, was arrested and, on June 16, Meinhof and Gerhard Müller were arrested when they were overwhelmed by police.

While jailed in Stammheim prison, but before their trial, Meins died (on November 8, 1974) while on a two-month hunger strike. The June 2 Movement, one successor organization to Baader-Meinhof, continued the terrorist movement, including the killing of the president of the West Berlin Supreme Court, the kidnapping of a leader of the West Berlin city parliament, and the killing of two diplomats in the West German embassy at Stockholm, Sweden.

Three years after the members of the Baader-Meinhof were arrested, on May 21, 1975, the trial began in Stuttgart, Germany. The trial would last nearly two years.

PRIMARY SOURCE

The three surviving leaders of the Baader-Meinhof urban terrorist gang were found guilty of four murders and 39 attempted murders here today and sentenced to life imprisonment.

Andreas Baader, aged 34, Gudrun Ensslin, aged 36, and Jan-Carl Raspe, aged 32, were also sentenced to a further 15 years each for other offences, including bombings, using firearms and founding a criminal organization. An appeal is being considered.

Although spectators have often disrupted the court during the 103 weeks of the trial, there was no visible or audible reaction as Judge Eberhard Foth, the court president, and his four colleagues handed down their judgment in the fortified temporary courtroom inside the maximum security block at Stammheim prison.

According to the German tradition, all present stood up as Judge Foth read out the verdict and sentences. He then took two hours and three-quarters to read a summary of the findings. The full text of the judgment, which is likely to be as long as a large book, will be sent to those concerned later.

The accused have one week in which to give notice of appeal and a further month to present their arguments. Under present penal policy, the sentences should mean a minimum of 20 years in prison.

For those who have followed this case from the beginning, the 192nd and last day in court was more notable for absences than for those present. The accused were not in court. They have been on hunger strike for a month in protest against the electronic bugging of conversations between them and their lawyers which the authorities admitted.

There should have been five defendants in the dock, but Holger Meins died after an earlier hunger strike before the trial began, and Ulrike Meinhof, the leader of the gang, committed suicide a year ago.

The defense lawyers chosen by the accused have been boycotting the proceedings since the bugging was disclosed and stayed away today.

Also absent was the original presiding judge, Dr. Theodor Prinzing, whose handling of the case aroused so much controversy that he was discharged in January.

The defendants, who had been declared unfit to endure more than three hours a day in court, were allowed to come and go as they pleased. They stayed away for months.

Thus ended the unhappiest episode in the history of West German justice.

Judge Foth rejected defense demands for the abandonment of the case, made last week by court-appointed defending lawyers. The accused were largely responsible for their own poor physical condition, he said.

SIGNIFICANCE

During the first three months of the Baader-Meinhof trial, both sides argued about various legal procedures. Four defense lawyers were present, but three others were expelled from the courtroom. Several legal procedures were eventually eliminated, while amendments to the criminal code and rules of procedure were enacted either specifically for use in the trial or in response to growing terrorism.

The indictment against the four alleged criminals was read to the accused on August 19, 1975. On January 13, 1976, after months of delays, the trial officially began.

Complicating the trial, Ulrike Meinhof committed suicide while in her prison cell in May 1976. An organization that had adopted her name then assassinated the West German attorney general, along with West Germany's chief prosecutor and two members of his department.

The judge, who had taken over for the original judge who had been dismissed, responded to past difficulties by deciding to rapidly end the trial. The defense lawyers claimed that wiretaps were the climax of a series of grievances that had destroyed their strategy—including questionable procedures, numerous illegalities, deficient laws, and biased and prejudiced judges, politicians, and media. Nevertheless, on April 28, 1977, the three surviving leaders of the Baader-Meinhof terrorist gang were found guilty and sentenced to life imprisonment. The trial became the longest trial (almost two years with 192 actual days of testimony) and the most expensive trial (over $15 million) in West Germany, up to that point.

On October 17, 1977, the remaining three Baader-Meinhof prisoners committed suicide after learning that Palestinian terrorists had failed in their attempt to free them after hijacking an airplane. Under new leadership, however, members of the Baader-Meinhof Gang continued to commit terrorist acts under the earlier-used name the Red Army Faction. Terrorist activities by Baader-Meinhof and its associated groups from 1970 to the time they disbanded in 1998 led to the death of over twenty-five people, many of them high-profile Germans, and the kidnapping and injury of numerous others.

The Baader-Meinhof Gang was so successful in carrying out its terrorist activities that the West German government assumed itself to be under a national political and societal crisis (called German Autumn) in the fall of 1977. Adding to the country's dilemma was the ineffectual nature of the country's lightly organized confederation of states. As a result of these two significant problems, the German government strengthened its confederation of states, approved new federal laws to provide widespread powers in countering terrorism, and created a national police force.

FURTHER RESOURCES

Books

Austs, Stefan. *The Baader-Meinhof Group: The Inside Story of a Phenomenon.* London: Bodley-Head, 1987.

Becker, Jillian. *Hitler's Children: The Story of the Baader-Meinhof Terrorist Gang.* Philadelphia: Lippincott, 1977.

Varon, Jeremy. *Bringing the War Home: The Weather Underground, the Red Army Faction, and Revolutionary Violence in the Sixties and Seventies.* Berkeley: University of California Press, 2004.

Wright, Joanne. *Terrorist Propaganda: The Red Army Faction and the Provisional IRA, 1968–86.* New York: St. Martin's Press, 1990.

Web sites

Huffman, Richard. "This Is Baader-Meinhof." <http://www.baader-meinhof.com> (accessed June 15, 2005).

"Rome Journal"

"Agony Lingers 20 Years after the Moro Killing"

Newspaper article

By: Alessandra Stanley

Date: May 9, 1998

Source: "Rome Journal; Agony Lingers, 20 Years After the Moro Killing," as published by the *New York Times.*

About the Author: Alessandra Stanley is a foreign bureau chief and high-ranking reporter for the New York Times.

INTRODUCTION

The body of former Italian Prime Minister Aldo Moro was found in Rome on May 9, 1978, fifty-five days after he was kidnapped by the Marxist-Leninist group, the Red Brigade (Brigate Rosse). The Red

Brigade was a leftist extremist group that used violence as a means to influence Italian politics.

At the time of his abduction, Moro was the leader of the ruling Christian Democratic Party. He had facilitated a compromise leading to the formation of the first Italian government to be actively supported by the Communist Party. On March 16th, Moro was to institute this new government, to be led by then Prime Minister Giulio Andreotti. That morning, while on his way to Parliament, Moro was seized from his car by gunmen. All five of his police escorts were killed.

A spokesman for the Red Brigade claimed the organization had taken Moro, and demanded the suspension of the trials of other suspected Red Brigade members in exchange for the release of Moro. While being held in a secret location in Rome, Moro sent letters to politicians and his friends and family, urging the Italian government to bargain for his release.

Prime Minister Andreotti refused to negotiate on Moro's behalf, claiming that the Red Brigade was a terrorist organization. The Italian police and secret services carried out hundreds of unsuccessful raids throughout Italy, searching for Moro. His bullet-filled body was eventually found in an automobile, in the center of Rome.

The Red Brigade was formed in 1969 from the student protest movements. The organization was an active political force in the 1970's and 1980's. Most of their attacks targeted people that they regarded as symbols of western capitalist society—unionists, politicians, and businessmen. The aim of the Red Brigade was to separate Italy from its Western allies.

PRIMARY SOURCE

"It has been 20 years, and still the deeper truth has not come out," said Marco Baliani, 47, an actor-playwright whose one-man show about the Moro case is to be shown live on Italy's second largest state network on Saturday night. "How can we found a new republic if we cannot tell the truth to ourselves?"

Like the Kennedy assassination in the United States, the killing of so powerful a political figure remains an obsession for Italians, who view it both as a national trauma that marked the end of innocence for an entire postwar generation, and as a dark conspiracy that remains veiled.

After hundreds of books, a parliamentary investigation that has dragged on for 10 years, five completed trials and a sixth that is about to begin, Italians are so bitterly consumed with the missing pieces that even on the 20th anniversary they overlook a larger irony that was unimaginable only five years ago.

Giulio Andreotti, 79, the wily, powerful politician who was Prime Minister seven times, including the period of the Moro crisis, is currently on trial in Perugia on charges that he conspired to order the killing of a journalist investigating, among other things, an alleged cover-up of the Moro case. Mr. Andreotti's refusal to negotiate with his colleague's captors is one of the more examined mysteries in the case.

And Italian society, so torn in the hate-filled 1970's that the Andreotti Government imposed special laws to combat terrorism and social unrest, is now serenely united on at least one point: The full story behind the crime has not yet been told.

Mr. Andreotti refused to make concessions to the terrorists to save Moro. The Italian police and secret services were unable to rescue him, and their stunning display of incompetence was quickly interpreted as deliberate. To this day, most Italians believe that Moro died because the powers-that-were had reasons not to keep him alive.

"On this anniversary I live the need to in some way understand what really happened," said Alberto Franceschini, 50, who, as one of the founders of the Red Brigades, should know. Arrested in 1974, he got out of prison in 1992 and now works at a foundation that distributes European grants to Italian unemployment programs.

Mr. Franceschini said that his comrades had definitely killed Moro, but that they might not have acted alone.

"I don't know whose hands were behind the scenes, Andreotti's or Nixon's," he said. "But I know we were part of a much larger game."

SIGNIFICANCE

Andreotti's refusal to negotiate with the Red Brigade on behalf of Moro is one of the most scrutinized aspects of the assassination. Andreotti did stand trial for his involvement in arranging the killing of a journalist who was investigating an alleged cover-up of the Moro case. Andreotti was convicted of this crime in a lower court, and sentenced to 24 years in prison. However, in 2003, Italy's highest court, cleared him of the charges.

Twenty-three Red Brigade members were convicted of participating in the killing of Moro and his five bodyguards. All twenty-three completed their sentences, or were given home-arrest or work-release punishments. One of the founders of the Red Brigade, Alberto Franceschini, who was in prison at the time of the Moro murder, said in 1998 that members of the Red Brigade did kill Moro, but that they were likely influenced by greater powers.

The kidnappings and killings carried out by the Red Brigade, particularly that of Moro, created fear in the 1970's and 1980's. This led to the enacting of laws to combat terrorism and social unrest in Italy, enhancing the powers of security forces, and encouraging defection from the Red Brigade. Beginning in the 1980's, the Red Brigade began to fall apart due to internal schisms, operational failures, and the arrests of many of its members. Eventually, in 1984, imprisoned leaders of the Red Brigade publicly described their armed struggle to break down Italy's links to capitalism as futile.

FURTHER RESOURCES

Web sites

30 Giorni (30 Days). "Remembering Moro." <http://www.30giorni.it/us/articolo.asp?id=8921> (accessed June 26, 2005).

Web sites

BBC News. On This Day 16 March: "1978: Aldo Moro snatched at gunpoint." <http://news.bbc.co.uk/onthisday/hi/dates/stories/march/16/newsid_4232000/4232691.stm> (accessed June 26, 2005).

BBC News. "Italy's Andreotti cleared of murder." <http://news.bbc.co.uk/1/hi/world/europe/3228917.stm> (accessed June 26, 2005).

International Policy Institute for Counter-Terrorism. "Red Brigades." <http://www.ict.org.il/inter_ter/orgdet.cfm?orgid=36> (accessed June 23, 2005).

Bernardine Dohrn, leader of the radical anti-Vietnam war movement Weather Underground, is shown in 1969. AP/WIDE WORLD PHOTOS

Weather Underground

"Cathy Wilkerson: The Evolution of a Revolutionary"

Newspaper article

By: Margot Hornblower (Roosevelt)

Date: July 15, 1980

Source: The *Washington Post*, a daily national newspaper based in Washington, D.C.

About the Author: Award-winning journalist Margot Hornblower was a staff reporter for the *Washington Post* for 13 years, and later, known as Margot Roosevelt, became a national correspondent for *Time* magazine.

INTRODUCTION

The Weather Underground, also known as the Weathermen, was a leftist terrorist group that grew out of the student radicalism of the late 1960s. Most of its members, including Cathy Wilkerson, were white, middle class, well educated, and formerly members of Students for a Democratic Society (SDS), the major student activist organization of the 1960s. Agreeing that traditional political protest had done little to end the civil rights problems of American society, Weather members advocated the violent destruction of the capitalist system. In the years between 1969 and 1975, the Weathermen bombed seventeen targets, mostly government buildings. Pursued by the Federal Bureau of Investigation (FBI), much of the group went underground in 1969. In the 1980s, the members began to reappear to face trial.

The Weathermen emerged in June 1969, during an SDS conference. Eleven SDS members had authored a June 18, 1969, *New Left Notes* statement entitled "You Don't Need a Weatherman to Know Which Way the Wind Blows," calling for a white fighting force to support the black liberation movement. The title of the statement came from folksinger Bob Dylan's lyrics. At a national SDS meeting a few days later, the group split between people who advocated violence and those who did not. The violent members became the Weathermen (later changed to the nonsexist Weather Underground).

The Weathermen saw themselves as the vanguard that would ignite a revolution. They proposed acts of armed propaganda aimed at pitting anti-Vietnam War protesters against the police. During the Days of Rage Vietnam protests in Chicago, they bombed a statue of a policeman on October 7, 1969. Arrested for disorderly conduct during a riot later that week, the Weathermen decided to go underground and failed to appear for their trials. They became fugitives, with several appearing on the FBI's Most Wanted list.

As terrorists, the group proved notoriously inept, though persistent. On March 6, 1970, three Weather members died when they blew up their own hideout in a Greenwich Village, New York City townhouse. On August 1, 1970, they bombed the exterior of the New York branch of the Bank of Brazil with a pipe bomb. On October 8, 1970, they bombed the ROTC building on the University of Washington campus, the Santa Barbara National Guard Armory, and a courthouse in San Rafael, California. On March 1, 1971, they bombed the U.S. Senate wing of the Capitol Building. Other targets included the Pentagon and the State Department.

■ PRIMARY SOURCE

The daughter of a wealthy advertising man and a graduate of a proper New England prep school, Cathlyn Platt Wilkerson traveled the well-worn path of many children of the '60s, through civil rights movement and the antiwar protests.

But perhaps because she was angrier, tougher or more desperate, she went one step further and became a leader of the Weather Underground, a group of several dozen youths who advocated armed struggle to overthrow the U.S. government.

A half-dozen Weathermen have turned themselves in the past few years, but Wilkerson is the first to face homicide charges. Three of her friends were killed in an explosion in her father's fashionable Greenwich Village townhouse in 1970. Police said the basement was being used as a bomb factory.

Wilkerson, who fled the scene of the accident, has pleaded not guilty to charges of criminally negligent homicide. For years, she and other Weathermen were sought by the FBI in one of the most massive manhunts in history.

The years underground were turbulent. *Osawatomie,* a magazine that Wilkerson and others published briefly in 1975, said, "We are . . . a revolutionary organization of communist women and men . . . responsible for over 25

armed actions against the enemy. Eight of these were bombings directed against imperialist war and in support of the people of Indochina. This includes the attack on the Capitol in 1971, on the Pentagon in 1972 and on the state Department in 1975."

The second of three daughters of James Platt Wilkerson, Cathy grew up in the placid suburbs of Connecticut and attended New Canaan Country School and Abbott Academy in Andover, Mass. Her parents divorced before she went to Swarthmore College, outside Philadelphia.

In her college freshman year, 1962, she went to a picket line in front of a Cambridge, Md., Woolworth's and heard a civil rights leader speak. "That was the beginning of realizing that there was a struggle going on that had deep importance for everybody's life, including mine," she said in the movie.

In 1964, she added, "I remember distinctly the day that I walked down a hall at school and there was a poster on the bulletin board. It was a leaflet that had been put out by a black community group in Chester [Pa.] that was fighting for integrating the schools. The word was around that people were going to be arrested and I remember standing and staring at that leaflet and knowing absolutely that this was the time when I had to make a decision. If I got arrested I knew what the consequences were. I knew in terms of everything I had been programmed to do for the rest of my life. One of the people arrested besides me was Kathy Boudin."

By 1966, Wilkerson was organizing against the Vietnam war as the regional Baltimore-Washington coordinator for the Students for a Democratic Society (SDS). Reporters who covered demonstrations here remember her as a commanding figure with penetrating eyes and a powerful, magnetic voice. She would frequently grab a bullhorn and shout exhortations to marchers. She was arrested at least once here, for occupying George Washington University's Sino-Soviet Institute in April 1969.

During those years, she lived in a commune at 1779 Lanier Pl. NW, and was friends with many of the radicals of the day, from Tom Hayden to Mark Rudd. Friends recall a young man who was in love with Wilkerson and followed her into the movement. But she had little time for personal life and the Weathermen adhered to a strict communal code in which monogamy was frowned upon and sexual freedom encouraged.

In a 1969 article in *New Left Notes,* Wilkerson wrote, "Within the movement it is crucial that men and women both begin to fight against the vestiges of bourgeois ideology within themselves, to break down existing forms of social relationships. Only by developing forms in which we can express love in nonexploitative and noncompetitive ways will men and women develop their full human and revolutionary potential for struggle."

One antiwar veteran remembers Wilkerson as militant and strong willed, but also thoughtful.

Another, a former SDS member, is less charitable. "She was driven by guilt about being born white and privileged," he said. "Any doubts about radical theory were thought to be signs of weakness, so she would draw herself further and further into a fantasy world about the way the world works. You could never have an intellectual discussion with her. She was mainly a tactics and strategy person."

This source remembered Wilkerson as "always trying to steel herself, to harden herself, as if it was in conflict with her nature. She was always trying to be tough. It was not easy to develop a close personal relationship with her."

At a demonstration outside Western High School in late '67 or '68, he recalled, "some greasers started fighting with the demonstrators. People were pushing and shoving and punching. I said, 'This is terrible.' Cathy looked at me, surprised, and said, 'Oh, no, this is terrific. People are communicating.'"

Wilkerson was among several dozen SDS leaders who splintered off in June 1969 to form Weathermen, taking their name from a line in a Bob Dylan song, "You don't need a weatherman to tell which way the wind blows."

The Weathermen demanded total commitment to revolution, with an almost religious fanaticism. They believed that if they proved, through violent acts, that they were not wimpy middle-class intellectuals, but "guerrillas fighting behind enemy lines," working-class youths would rise and join them.

"But it didn't work out so hot," recalled one Weatherman later. "We talked about racism and imperialism and the greasers talked about motorcycles and girls." Weathermen carrying Red flags into working-class neighborhoods were beaten up.

Barely a year passed before the townhouse explosion made national headlines and forced the Weathermen, already under surveillance by the FBI, to go underground. Wilkerson was one of 13 indicted by a federal grand jury in Detroit in July 1970 on charges of setting up a terrorist underground.

The indictment charged Wilkerson with making dynamite bombs on the day of the townhouse explosion.

The federal charges have since been dropped. (The current charges were brought by the Manhattan district attorney.) "The feds have dirty hands and they know it," said one of Wilkerson's attorneys, Elizabeth Fink. "They are afraid of what might be disclosed."

The Justice Department is prosecuting several top FBI officials who allegedly authorized an extensive illegal spying campaign on the Weathermen and on their friends and relatives.

Underground, the Weathermen, numbering perhaps two or three dozen, began by setting up several largely autonomous cells and according to one radical who kept in touch, "they assimilated themselves into the middle-class even to the point of forging IDs and using credit cards with false names . . . They were not hiding out. They were walking the streets, driving cars . . . They cut their hair, took off their jeans and started wearing double-knit suits and dresses."

Another friend said that since the Weathermen "came from well-heeled middle-class families . . . they had high-level contacts above ground. When they went underground, they used above-ground friends—you know, everything from 'Do you have a place for me to stay?' to 'Can you lend me a few dollars?'" Several held conventional above-ground jobs.

But the Weathermen spent as much time fighting among themselves as fighting the outside establishment. Revolutionary activity petered out after 1975, as they argued over feminism and "male supremacy," over whether to come above ground, or whether to limit violence to selected political targets without harming people or whether to venture into assassinations and kidnappings like the Red Brigade in Italy.

Some of the men reportedly felt the feminism was overbearing and bailed out, leaving a larger part of the leadership in the hands of the women, including Wilkerson, Boudin and Bernadine Dohrn. There were also arguments over whether the group was too rigid and elitist, or whether, as the "vanguard" of the coming revolution, it should be small, highly disciplined and exclusive.

All of these struggles must have taken their toll on Wilkerson. Moviemaker De Antonio, who spent two days with five Weathermen leaders in a house outside Los Angeles in 1975, remembers her as "a person of quiet intelligence. You thought more of Brook Farm than the Weather Underground. She was very intense and strong and extraordinarily attractive.

"If one were to say this person were accused of throwing bombs, I'd have laughed. Of course, I could be wrong."

In the slender, well-dressed, even demure figure of Cathy Wilkerson as she faced the judges in two court hearings last week and fended off dozens of reporters and television cameras, there was little to suggest a revolutionary. Her mother and sister have come to stay with her in New York and a bevy of lawyers is advising her.

Her statement, defiant by establishment standards, was mild in comparison with usual Weathermen rhetoric—no references to "armed struggle"—a concession perhaps to the belief that fighting words might not help her defense.

Attacking the FBI, the CIA, the police and the courts for "waging bitter battles" against Puerto Rican revolutionaries, blacks, native American radicals and Caribbean countries, Wilkerson said social conditions have not improved. "I have the same commitment to struggle . . . It is 1980, but the conditions still exist which caused colonized peoples to fight for liberation . . . "

But there was a hint of humility and a suggestion that a rejection of Weathermen machismo may have been what led her out from underground. "We've made many mistakes," she said. "Male supremacy undermined us, our arrogance led us to act as white supremacists even while we denounced it. However, national liberation struggles continue to teach us and inspire us and we must change and move forward . . . "

"Women's liberation has challenged the legitimacy of physical brutality, exploitation and oppression in all spheres of life."

In the end, Cathy Wilkerson was still struggling with the irony of being a well-bred revolutionary. "I am here today and able to talk to you because I am white, middle class and free on bail," she told reporters. "Others who are black and brown do not get this opportunity and therefore it is my responsibility to say these things. In the end, I must be judged by how I act and what I do during this, the next stage of my life."

SIGNIFICANCE

Despite being dedicated to working class and African-American rights, the Weather Underground never attracted significant numbers of workers and blacks into the organization. The organization remained small, overwhelmingly white, and predominantly middle class throughout its existence. Additionally, the decision to go underground in 1970 left the Weathermen isolated from society at large.

With the gradual withdrawal of the United States from the Vietnam War in the early 1970s amid increasing internal conflicts, the New Left split. Some leftists focused on racism and sexism, while others pursued a range of causes. The aboveground support network of the Weather Underground, known as the Prairie Fire Organizing Committee, faulted their hidden comrades for lagging behind in their commitment to combating sexism and racism. Weather Underground members then turned upon each other in internal ideological debates and purges of the members judged insufficiently committed.

The founding members of the Weather Underground who were forced out of the organization in the

mid-1970s eventually surrendered to law enforcement authorities. Mark Rudd gave up in 1977, while the married couple of Bernadine Dohrn and William Ayers surfaced in 1981. With the surrender of Jeffrey David Powell on January 6, 1994, the last of the six Weatherman wanted by the FBI had surfaced. Dohrn's life after surfacing is typical of the fate of the Weather Underground leaders. For her crimes, Dohrn received three years probation and a $1,500 fine. By 2000, she had become a noted advocate for children's rights and a professor of law at Northwestern University.

The ideological hardliners within the Weather Underground went on to create the May 19th Communist Coalition, which created the Revolutionary Armed Task Force (RATF) by merging the Weatherman remnants with the Black Liberation Army. May 19th established contacts and ties with other terrorist groups, such as the Puerto Rican FALN separatists and the Palestine Liberation Army. Members of May 19th attempted to recruit in prisons by presenting themselves to prison authorities and prisoners as providers of free legal services and counsel for indigent inmates. Once they gained access to potential recruits, they undertook consciousness-raising sessions to convert prisoners to the revolutionary cause. May 19th collapsed when the FBI arrested the leaders of RATF in 1985 and 1986 on charges stemming from their participation in criminal activities.

FURTHER RESOURCES
Books

Jacobs, Ron. *The Way the Wind Blew: A History of the Weather Underground.* London: Verso, 1997.

Audio and Visual Media

Green, Sam and Siegel, Bill. *The Weather Underground.* The Free History Project, Inc., 2003.

"Italy Marks One of Europe's Deadliest Bombings"

Bombing of the Central Train Station at Bologna, Italy

Magazine article

By: Thomas Sheehan

Date: January 22, 1981

Source: Feature Article from The *New York Review of Books.*

About the Author: Thomas Sheehan is Professor of Religious Studies at Stanford University.

Rescue workers attempt to look for remains and clear rubble from a 1980 Bologna blast site. AP/WIDE WORLD PHOTOS

INTRODUCTION

In 1980, Bologna was the center of the Italian Communist Party, making the city a target for anti-communist extremists.

On the morning of Saturday, August 2, 1980 at 10:25 A.M., an improvised explosive device (IED), packed with forty-four pounds of explosive materials detonated inside the central railroad station in Bologna, Italy. Eighty-five people were killed and an additional two hundred were injured.

Minutes after the attack, an accomplice called into the city's leading newspaper and claimed responsibility in the name of the Armed Revolutionary Nuclei, a Neo Fascist group. Neo Fascism and Neo-Nazism seek to re-introduce the fascist and nazi principles of government that ended with the conclusion of World War II (1939–1945). Neo-fascism usually reveres the 1922–1943 Italian fascist dictatorship of Benito Mussolini (1883–1945), especially his policy of nationalizing industry and business; neo-nazism is described as an attempt to reintroduce the racist policies of the Nazi regime.

On September 26, 1980, an attempted attack was also carried out by a neo-Nazi at the entrance to the Oktoberfest celebrations in Munich, Germany. The bomb, which exploded prematurely, killed the bomber and twelve other people and wounded an additional 215. A week later in Paris, another attack by neo-Fascist extremists outside a synagogue killed four people and injured thirteen.

These series of attacks, with the Bologna attack garnering the most attention and causing the greatest number of casualties, introduced Europeans to the danger of modern terrorism. Since the beginning of the 1970s, Europe had witnessed numerous attacks by various extremist groups. The neo-Fascist groups were also proven to have ties with Middle Eastern terrorist networks, receiving support and training from camps in Lebanon.

In recent years, the threats presented by neo-Fascist groups have reemerged. The Internet has been widely utilized by neo-Fascist and neo-Nazi groups, and despite being banned in several European nations, neo-fascist and neo-nazi groups have become increasingly vocal and visible in society, reinvigorating public concerns over the possible threats represented by these groups.

PRIMARY SOURCE

Bologna, August 2, 1980. It was a hot Saturday morning, the first weekend of Italy's traditional holiday month, and thousands of vacationers jostled their way to and from the trains in Bologna's central railroad station. In the midst of that noisy crowd someone stopped midway between the second-class waiting room and the coffee bar, put down a heavy suitcase, and quickly left the station. The suitcase contained over forty pounds of explosives, perhaps stable nitroglycerine, connected to a timer. At exactly 10:25 A.M. it exploded, ripping through the crowd, tearing apart the reinforced concrete walls, and bringing the roof crashing down on hundreds of bodies and parts of bodies.

In the bloody aftermath, rescue squads worked for over twelve hours to pull the dead and maimed from the rubble. As they labored, a young neofascist entered a telephone booth across town and dialed Bologna's leading newspaper. "This is the Armed Revolutionary Nuclei," he said. "We claim responsibility for the explosion in the railway station." The final toll: eighty-five dead—the eldest an eighty-six-year-old man, the youngest a three-year-old child—and more than two hundred wounded.

Eight weeks later, on the evening of September 26, a young man, Gundolf Koehler, tried to place six pounds of explosives in a refuse can at the entrance to Munich's Oktoberfest. The bomb went off, killing him and twelve others, wounding 215 people. On Koehler's body were found documents linking him to the illegal paramilitary Defense Sport Group of the neo-Nazi Karl-Heinz Hoffmann, who styles himself the "spiritual descendant" of Adolf Hitler and who has organized military maneuvers in southern Germany for his followers. Arrested along with twenty-four of his militants, Hoffmann was later released for lack of evidence.

A week later in Paris a twenty-six pound bomb exploded in front of the rue Copernic synagogue, where hundreds of Jews were gathered for sabbath services. The bomb killed four persons and wounded thirteen; if it had gone off twenty minutes later, when services would have ended, it would have killed scores of worshipers leaving the synagogue. The act was claimed by the European National Fasces (FNE), the same group that had machine-gunned five Jewish buildings in Paris a week earlier.

These latest of neofascist massacres have awakened Europeans to what many of them had managed not to see: the maturation over the last five years of what analysts now call Eurofascism—loosely associated but politically aligned neo-Nazi groups, many of them dedicated to terrorism, all of them intent on saving Europe from the twin evils of capitalism and Marxism. While their membership is relatively small, they are well funded and some have access to training camps in Lebanon. In an interview given eight days before the Munich explosion, the PLO leader Abu Ayad revealed that in late 1979 two members of Hoffmann's group were captured in Lebanon and confessed to him that they and some thirty other European fascists were training at the Falangist camp at Aquru, northeast of Beirut. The Germans told Ayad that their Italian comrades were about to "begin their operations with a major terrorist attack in the city of Bologna, because it is run by the Left."

The Eurofascist groups include the British Movement in England, New Force in Spain, the Flemish Militant Order in Belgium, Third Position and Armed Revolutionary Nuclei in Italy. In Germany there are sixty-nine extreme right groups (about 18,000 members in all), of which twenty-three are armed. In 1979, police raids on these German groups netted sixty-six pounds of explosives, 125 hand grenades, and more than 175 guns. On January 30, 1980, the day Hoffmann's Defense Sport Group was banded, police broke into his fortress headquarters at Ermreuth castle near Nuremberg and found everything from rifles and handbombs to a fully armed military vehicle.

In France, besides the two rival law-and-order organizations called New Forces Party and the National Front (which together polled some 200,000 votes in the 1978 legislative elections), the radical right is composed of two main "autonomist" groups: Marc Fredricksen's National European Action Federation (FANE)—one-third of whose membership is allegedly made up of policemen—and the Nationalist Revolutionary Movement (MNR) of Jean-Gilles Malliarakis, who seeks to prepare his followers for "the day of the great cleansing" in France. (Mr. Clean's group has a more nationalistic focus, Fredricksen's group a more European one.) FANE was dissolved by order of the French government last September, but it immediately reconstituted itself as the European National Fasces (FNE), with the same directorate and members. Fredricksen, who was recently sentenced to eighteen months (twelve suspended) for hate articles in his magazine *Notre Europe*, denies that FNE is responsible for the synagogue bombing. But he does admit that "the attack could have come from former FANE members who were shocked by the ban on their organization."

In Italy, the extreme right has long been active and well protected by the authorities, including the Italian Secret Services. A 1969 bomb explosion in Milan (sixteen dead) was at first blamed on anarchists, one of whom, under mysterious circumstances, fell to his death from the sixth-floor window of a police station. Later the massacre was traced to two neofascists, Franco Freda and Giovanni Ventura, and to an agent of the Secret Services (SID) named Guido Giannettini. Giannettini fled the country, but continued to receive checks from SID for a full year. He and three high SID officials were eventually jailed for conspiracy in the massacre, but the question of possible complicity on the part of high-ranking military and political figures has never been adequately clarified. . . .

Italy is living through its worst period since World War II. Inflation has passed 20 percent, young people can find no jobs, the political system is as unstable as the ground which recently shook under the impoverished villages of the south and took thousands of lives, many of which might have been spared if the Italian bureaucracy had simply taken the pains to enact a long-needed civil defense program. The country's fortieth government, just installed, has already been undermined by the biggest scandal in the history of the republic, a matter involving $2.2 billion of unpaid oil revenues and millions of dollars in kickbacks to government officials. . . .

In politics this sad and beautiful country seems more and more to resemble the *Andrea Doria:* faultily constructed at the beginning, its defects covered over for reasons of power and money, its potential for destroying innocent lives enormous. Italy is fertile soil for messianic terrorists who would right all its deep-seated wrongs by pulling a trigger or setting a timer. Could it be that Mussolini was right after all? "It's not impossible to govern the Italians," he once remarked. "It's simply useless."

SIGNIFICANCE

The attack on the Bologna train station represented the most costly acts of terror in the post-World War II period in Italy. Neo-fascist terrorism differentiates itself from other forms of politically driven terrorism in the fact that it acts as a reaction to what the terrorists view as a threat to their system of values. The principal threats to their beliefs come in the forms of capitalism and communism and attacks by neo-fascists have historically been directed at institutions which represent those systems.

The Bologna attack served as the largest international incident highlighting the dangers represented by neo-fascism, but attacks driven by similar political extremist motives have occurred around the world. For example, right-wing terrorists carried out high-profile attacks including the Oklahoma City bombing in 1995 and the bombing at Centennial Olympic Park, Atlanta, during the 1996 Summer Olympics. The majority of domestic terror attacks that occur in the United States are carried out by political extremist groups.

FURTHER RESOURCES

Books

Fraser, Nicholas. *The Voice of Modern Hatred: Tracing the Rise of Neo-Fascism in Europe.* New York: Overlook TP, 2002.

Web sites

BBC. "On This Day: 2 August; 1980: Bologna blast leaves dozens dead." <http://newssearch.bbc.co.uk/onthisday/hi/dates/stories/august/2/newsid_4532000/4532091.stm> (accessed July 8, 2005).

Lebanese President–Elect Slain

"Phalange Delivers 3 Gemayel Assassins to Lebanese Government"

News article

By: Mona Ziade

Date: April 26, 1983

Source: The Associated Press

About the Author: Mona Zaide was a journalist for United Press International before going to work at the Associated Press. She then joined the *Daily Star*, an English language newspaper in Lebanon where she worked as both national and managing editor. Zaide is the Communications Officer for the World Bank.

INTRODUCTION

The assassination of Lebanese President-elect Bashir Gemayel on September 14, 1982 became the spark that ignited two days of bloodshed in Sabra and Shatila, Palestinian refugee camps located in southern Lebanon. The assassination and subsequent violence followed years of civil war in Lebanon between political factions in competing alliances with neighboring states, namely Syria and Israel.

Once a bastion for ethnic cooperation, Lebanon's government was structured to reflect its population as identified in a 1932 census. The National Pact provided for representation of each of the parties in the country. By custom, the president would be a Maronite (Christian), the Prime Minister would be a Sunni Muslim, and the speaker of the Chamber of Deputies would be a Shia Muslim. By mid–1975, the government no longer accurately represented the population, creating political and cultural tensions that set the stage for civil war as sectarian militias and external regimes clamored for power.

The first events of the civil war occurred in 1975 with an assassination attempt on Bashir Gemayel's father, Pierre Gemayel. Pierre Gemayel had been the founder of the Phalange party, a Maronite paramilitary youth organization. The party gained support and power through the 1960's with its hope for a Lebanon distinctive from its Arab and Muslim neighbors.

Phalangists believed Palestinians were the would-be assassins of Pierre Gemayel and retaliated by killing twenty-six Palestinian passengers riding a bus across a Maronite Christian neighborhood. These were Palestinian refugees who had resided in the southern outskirts of west Beirut since the first Arab-Israeli War in 1949. Syria initially entered the civil war on the side of the Christians. By 1976, Syria had brokered a cease-fire at the Riyadh Conference that included a peace-keeping force called the Arab Deterrence Force (ADF) to quell unrest in Lebanon. By 1980 this force, which initially included members from several neighboring Arab nations, had been whittled down to include only Syrian forces. Internal struggles within Syria caused relaxed control in Lebanon. However, Phalangists exerted their power and the ADF took action against the party.

During this time, Bashir Gemayel began to gain power within the Phalange party. In 1970, prior to his rise as a political leader, Bashir was kidnapped by Palestinian militias. Although he was released, historians claim the experience dimmed his tolerance for Palestinians. Bashir obtained degrees in political science and law before being appointed in 1971 as inspector of the Kataeb (Lebanese for Phalange) Regular Forces, a paramilitary wing of the Phalange party. He served in several other militia leadership positions in the civil war until his election to president in 1982. During this time, Bashir's alliance with Israel provided the Lebanese Front with weapons, ammunition, supplies and training from Israeli forces. This angered many Muslim Arabs, who in turn boycotted the presidential election won by Bashir.

In response to the ADF action against the Phalangists, under the banner of striking Palestine Liberation Forces (PLO) using Lebanon as a base for action against it, and in retaliation for an assassination attempt on an Israeli ambassador in London, Israel invaded Lebanon in June of 1982 with 60,000 troops. Two months later, a U.S. led cease-fire called for international monitors to facilitate the withdrawal of PLO members from Lebanon, Israeli agreement not to advance further into Lebanon and to guarantee the safety of Palestinian refugees. With international observers watching, the PLO withdrew by September

1, 1982. The next day, and in violation of the agreement, Israel deployed forces around the refugee camps. The international forces intent on PLO compliance left the nation without forcing Israel to comply. Israeli Prime Minister Menachem Begin claimed PLO forces remained in Lebanon and pressured his ally Bashir Gemayel to keep an Israeli military presence. Bashir refused. On September 14, 1982, Bashir was assassinated.

■ PRIMARY SOURCE

President Amin Gemayel's Phalange Party turned over the alleged killer of his brother Bashir to Amin's government Tuesday after holding him for seven months.

The right-wing Christian party, which is headed by the Gemayel brothers' father, Pierre Gemayel, also turned over two other men it said confessed to killing Bashir's baby daughter in 1980 and three others accused of planting bombs in East Beirut, the capital's Christian sector.

The Phalange Party had said earlier it would keep them in custody until the government was once again in control after eight years of civil war, Syrian occupation, and the Israeli invasion last summer.

Party officials said the six men were Habib Shartouni, a 25-year-old leftist Christian accused of killing Gemayel; Joseph Kazazian and Nazih Shaya, accused of detonating the bomb that killed 18-month-old Maya Gemayel as she was being driven home in her father's limousine, and Faysal Hashem, Farouk Hashem and Khoren Vartanian, the other three alleged bombers.

They were transferred to government custody at the Phalangist-controlled port city of Jounieh, 10 miles north of Beirut.

The Phalange radio station Voice of Lebanon, reported all six said they had learned their lesson and would not commit atrocities again. But Shartouni said Gemayel's killing "was within the Lebanese war, although the problem cannot be solved by killing one person," the broadcast said.

Gemayel, Lebanon's president-elect and commander of the Christian Lebanese Forces militia dominated by the Phalangists, was killed along with 22 other members of the party on Sept. 14, nine days before his inauguration. He was speaking at a party headquarters in a house reportedly owned by Shartouni's grandfather when a bomb went off in a room above him.

Shartouni was arrested several days later. The Phalange radio said he was a member of the Syrian Social Nationalist Party which fought on the leftist side in the Lebanese civil war and advocated Syrian annexation of

Lebanon. It said the party decided on Gemayel's assassination and a senior party official talked Shartouni into planting the explosives.

The party radio also claimed Shartouni had formerly been involved with the intelligence organizations of the Syrian government and the Palestine Liberation Organization and with "international terrorist groups."

Shortly after his arrest, Beirut newspapers reported Shartouni told interrogators he did the killing on behalf of another man who was in contact with "foreign quarters."

The report said he did not identify the other man or the foreign quarters. But the *Washington Post* reported from Beirut in January that Phalange officials said Syrian intelligence was behind the assassination, and the chief plotter was Nabil Felaghi, alias Nabil Alam, another member of the pro-Syrian party who had ties to the Syrian and PLO intelligence services.

The Post said Felaghi was believed living in Syria.

SIGNIFICANCE

Israel blamed the Palestinians for the assassination of Bashir Gemayel. Phalange militia members sought retribution. On September 16, 1982, Israeli Defense Minister Ariel Sharon ordered the Israeli army to seal off the refugee camps at Sabra and Shatila and to provide logistical support for Phalangists to seek out PLO fighters, who Israel claimed remained in the camps. According to the International Committee of the Red Cross, over 2,750 people were killed in the camps within two days, including women and children. By December 16, 1982, the United Nations had declared the event an act of genocide.

Due in part to media attention, Israelis demanded an explanation as to the extent of Israeli involvement. Israel released the Kahan Commission, which absolved Israelis of guilt and blamed Phalangists for the massacre. Amin Gemayel, Bashir's brother, became president of Lebanon and served a six-year term until 1988.

FURTHER RESOURCES
Web sites

Campagna, Joel. "The Usual Suspects." *World Press Review.* 49 (4). <http://www.worldpress.org/Mideast/460.cfm> (accessed July 3, 2005).

General Assembly, United Nations Educational, Scientific, and Cultural Organization. "The Situation in the Middle East." <http://domino.un.org/UNISPAL.NSF/0/faabb796990cf95a852560d9005240cf?OpenDocument> (accessed July 6, 2005).

"Hezbollah Bombings in Europe"

News article

By: Stephen H. Miller

Date: July 22, 1985

Source: The Associated Press

About the Author: At the time this article was published, Stephen H. Miller was a reporter for the Associated Press, a world wide news agency.

INTRODUCTION

In 1982, Israel invaded southern Lebanon, asserting that the region was a base for Palestine Liberation Organization (PLO) terrorist operations against Israeli citizens. The invasion spurred resistance from Muslims in the region. Within Lebanon, extremist Muslims formed Hezbollah, or "Party of God." Conceived in Iran and funded by militant interests in both Iran and Syria, Hezbollah engaged in terrorist activities with the stated mission of ending Western and Israeli presence in the region. Hezbollah's preferred methods of terror included kidnappings, executions, paramilitary-style raids, and suicide bomb attacks.

Islamic Jihad, the most militant organization affiliated with Hezbollah, carried out some of the most deadly acts of terror in the 1980s. The group claimed responsibility for the April 18, 1983 attack on the U.S. embassy in Beirut. The embassy was the target of a suicide truck bomb that carried 400 pounds of explosives. The bomb killed sixty-three people, including seventeen Americans, decimating the Central Intelligence Agency's (CIA's) entire Middle East bureau. Later that year, on October 23, Hezbollah members drove a truck loaded with explosives into U.S. Marine barracks in Lebanon, killing 241 Marines. At the same time, a simultaneous suicide bomb attack occurred on French forces in Beirut, killing fifty-eight paratroopers. Finally, in December of 1983, a series of attacks were launched against U.S. and French interests in Kuwait. Six people died and eighty others were injured.

The wave of terror continued during the next several years. Between 1982 and 1992, many westerners were kidnapped by Hezbollah. Some were killed, others were held captive for several years. On April 12, 1984, a bomb planted by a Hezbollah-linked group exploded in a restaurant near a U.S. base in Torrejon, Spain, killing eighteen and injuring eighty-three. On

Shiite Muslim Sheikhs address supporters of the Hezbollah in a demonstration outside the bombed U.S. Embassy in West Beirut, Lebanon in 1986. AP/WIDE WORLD PHOTOS

September 20, 1984, a suicide bomber struck the U.S. embassy in Beirut, killing twenty people.

On June 14, 1985, Hezbollah took responsibility for hijacking TWA flight 847. One hundred and fifty-three passengers and crew were held for seventeen days. One passenger, U.S. sailor Robert Stethem, was killed during the ordeal. The hijackers demanded the release of the Kuwait 17, those arrested after the 1983 attacks in Kuwait, as well as seven hundred other Shia Muslim prisoners held by Israel.

PRIMARY SOURCE

Bombs tore open a U.S. airline office and damaged a synagogue and Jewish nursing home Monday in Copenhagen, a European capital that had previously escaped the recent international terrorist wave.

Twenty-seven people were injured, at least three seriously, authorities said. Three Americans were among those who suffered minor injuries, the U.S. Embassy reported.

Police later announced they had taken six foreigners into custody for questioning in the bombings, but they did not disclose the detainees' identities.

In Beirut, Lebanon, an anonymous telephone caller told The Associated Press the attacks were carried out by the Shiite Moslem terrorist organization Islamic Jihad to avenge an Israeli raid on a southern Lebanese village Sunday. The claim could not be verified.

One bomb gutted the quarters of Northwest Orient Airlines near Copenhagen's Tivoli amusement park. Northwest Orient is the only American airline with offices in the Danish capital.

Another attack, which some bystanders said involved two bombs, damaged the Copenhagen Synagogue and an adjacent Jewish home for the elderly, the Meyers Minne Nursing Home, on a narrow street near Copenhagen's 17th-century Round Tower.

J. H. Hasselriis, a deputy police director, said there was only one bomb at the synagogue and it apparently was planted in advance. The bomb at the airline office was either thrown at it or placed outside just before it exploded, he said.

He said each of the bombs was estimated to have contained 4.4 pounds of explosives.

Both attacks came within minutes of each other in mid-morning, as shoppers crowded nearby streets, taking advantage of late summer sales.

Harald Ruetz, a Northwest Orient manager, said one employee and two customers were in the office at the time of the explosion, which appeared to have been set off outside its plate-glass windows.

"Otherwise, she would have died," he said of the employee, who escaped with minor injuries. Ruetz said he did not know how badly injured the customers were.

An employee of the nursing home said about seven of its residents had been injured, none seriously. The other victims apparently were passers-by at the two sites.

Police said about half the injured were Danes and half foreigners. The most seriously injured victim was reported by police to have suffered burns over 85 percent of the body.

Hasselriis told reporters six foreigners were being questioned but had not been formally arrested. He declined to give their nationalities, but indicated they came from Mediterranean countries.

Hasselriis said none of the six were detained near the bombing sites. The Danish news agency Ritzau said at least some of them had been trying to leave Copenhagen on the 40-minute hydrofoil boat link to nearby Sweden.

Police were investigating a suspected bomb in a Northwest Orient flight bag pulled from Copenhagen's New Harbor, near the hydrofoil dock, Hasselriis said. News photographers said another suspected bomb was found in a courtyard of Christiansborg Palace, seat of Denmark's Parliament, but police said later it was not an explosive device.

Military bomb experts said the device fished out of the harbor appeared to be of the same type as those used at the airline office and synagogue, Danish television reported.

Prime Minister Poul Schlueter issued a statement expressing "sorrow that we now experience that Denmark too is hit by terrorist activity. We have escaped for many years, while unscrupulous men and organizations have spread death and destruction in other European countries."

The Beirut caller indicated Copenhagen was targeted precisely because Denmark had escaped terrorist activity until now.

"If certain countries believe they are free of our strikes, let them know that sooner or later we shall reach . . . the headquarters of all Western and Arab leaders who spin round the imperialist universe," the caller said.

"One of our cells in the Scandinavian countries" had retaliated for "the barbaric attack on the village of Qabrikha," the caller said.

Israeli troops raided the south Lebanon villages of Qabrikha and Sejoud on Sunday, and at least three local residents were reported killed.

Islamic Jihad, which translates as Islamic Holy War, is a shadowy group or network of terrorists that has claimed responsibility for many anti-Western attacks in Lebanon and abroad in recent years.

Some experts had theorized that terrorists used Scandinavia as a haven between actions elsewhere in Western Europe and would not endanger their refuge by attacks within Nordic territory.

SIGNIFICANCE

The 1982 Israeli invasion of Lebanon exacerbated the struggle for power within the country. Militant groups, such as Hezbollah, spread terror though the Middle East and Europe, through hijacking, suicide bombings, and assassinations. The Shia based organization, tactically and financially backed by both Syria and Iran, used the terror tactics to expel western and U.S. influences from the region. On some occasions, the strategy was effective, as both France and the U.S. withdrew their forces from Lebanon after the 1983 attacks. Terror activity by Hezbollah continued through the 1980s, usually in response to an Israeli action or to force the release of operatives.

Due in part to continuing casualties inflicted by Hezbollah, the Israeli Army withdrew from southern Lebanon in 2000 to a border approved by the United Nations. Hezbollah still considers the Israeli-occupied Shebaa Farms region of the Golan Heights near the Lebanon-Syria border to be part of Lebanon. The military wing of Hezbollah maintains a presence at this border and launches periodic attacks against Israeli forces in the area.

Many in the Arab world view Hezbollah as a legitimate political party seeking to establish an Islamic government in Lebanon, while most Western nations view Hezbollah as a terrorist organization.

FURTHER RESOURCES
Web sites

BBC News. "Timeline: Lebanon." <http://news.bbc.co.uk/1/hi/world/middle_east/country_profiles/819200.stm> (accessed July 10, 2005).

MIPT Terrorism Knowledgebase "Hezbollah." <http://www.tkb.org/Incident.jsp?incID=4272> (accessed July 10, 2005).

PBS. "Frontline: Battle for the Holy Land. The Combatants: Palestinians." <http://www.pbs.org/wgbh/pages/frontline/shows/holy/combatants/palestinians.html> (accessed July 10, 2005).

"Police Sure Drug Addict was Berlin Disco Bomber"

Libyan sponsored bombing of Berlin discotheque

Newspaper article

By: Tom Bower

Date: March 2, 1988

Source: The *Times*, a daily newspaper based in London.

About the Author: Tom Bower is an investigative journalist and author. His biographies include *Maxwell: The Outsider* (1992), *Fayed: The Unauthorised Biography* (1998), *Branson* (2000), and *Gordon Brown* (2004).

INTRODUCTION

A bomb exploded in a crowded Berlin disco on April 5, 1986. Two American soldiers and a Turkish woman died as a result of the blast. 229 others were wounded, many of them Americans. The disco, La Belle, was popular among U.S. servicemen. The bomb detonated around 1:45 A.M., Berlin time, with close to five hundred people in the building. The floor and ceiling of the disco collapsed, and the walls were blown in by the strength of the explosion.

Nine days after the incident, U.S. President Ronald Reagan announced that clear and indisputable evidence directly linked Colonel Gadaffi, the leader of Libya, to the bombing of the La Belle disco. Reagan used this information as the justification for bombing several sites in Libya, ten days after the disco explosion.

According to the *Times* article on March 2, 1988, the West Berlin police investigations were reaching different conclusions. The West Berlin investigations pointed towards a connection with Syria, not Libya. A Jordanian man, Ahmed Hazi, living in West Berlin, was the focus of the investigation. He admitted to receiving explosive materials made of Sentex, a chemical manufactured in Eastern Europe, from a Syrian diplomat. Forensic experts determined that the bomb used in the La Belle disco was also made of Sentex. Hazi also claimed responsibility for planting a Syntex bomb that exploded a week earlier at the German-Arab Friendship Society in Berlin.

Anti-Terrorist Squad officers at Scotland Yard contributed to the West Berlin investigation, as they had arrested Hazi's brother, Nezar Hindawi, for conspiring to place a Syntex bomb on an El Al jet at Heathrow airport. Hindawi admitted that the bomb he was to use at Heathrow was supplied by the Syrian

Lebanese police escort Yasser Mohammed Chreidi to a court in Beirut, Lebanon, in March 1994 on charges related to the 1986 Berlin disco bombing. AP/WIDE WORLD PHOTOS

embassy in London. Hindawi also admitted that his brother, Hazi, was a member of his small terrorist group living in West Berlin.

A contact book and a sketch identified as the plan of the La Belle disco found in Hazi's West Berlin flat, were further pieces of evidence that convinced investigators that Hazi was responsible for the disco bombing. A Berlin prostitute, for whom Hazi regularly supplied heroin, was first accused of working with Hazi in the bombing and of placing the bomb in the night club.

However, this line of investigation proved wrong as it was subsequently admitted by Libyan leader Gadaffi that Libya was behind the bombing.

■ PRIMARY SOURCE

. . . The West German discoveries contradict the announcement made by President Reagan nine days after the incident that Colonel Gadaffi of Libya was responsible for the 'monstrous brutality' in West Berlin. US evidence, the President said, "is direct, it is precise, it is irrefutable" and on that basis he announced his approval of the bombing of the Libyan capital, Tripoli. But the West Berlin police have never found evidence of a Libyan link.

Suspicion fell on Endrigkeit last autumn. It followed a complete review of the hitherto unsuccessful police investigation by the prosecutor in West Berlin, Herr Detlev Mehles. During his review, he visited Anti-Terrorist Squad officers at Scotland Yard, where he acknowledges that earlier British criticisms about the West German inquiry were justified.

The British connection with the West German inquiry is crucial. On April 18, 1986, Scotland Yard officers arrested Nezar Hindawi, a Jordanian who was responsible for conspiring to place a bomb on an El Al jet at Heathrow airport.

Hindawi told the police that his brother, Ahmed Hazi, was a member of his small terrorist network and lived in West Berlin. Acting on a tip from London, police burst into Hazi's flat to discover that the Arab, having heard the news of his brother's arrest, was burning documents.

Hazi soon confessed that he had planted the bomb which exploded on March 29, 1986, at the German-Arab Friendship Society in the city. Until then West Berlin police had been baffled both about the motive and identity of the perpetrators, and the type of the explosive, Sentex, manufactured in Eastern Europe and hitherto unseen in West Germany.

Significantly, the same explosives were used by Hindawi in London. Hazi said that the explosives were handed to him by a Syrian 'diplomat.' Hindawi also admitted that his Sentex bomb was supplied from the Syrian Embassy in London. By then, West German forensic experts had established that Sentex had been also used at La Belle discotheque.

Two incriminating documents were found by police in Hazi's flat—his contact book, and a vague sketch identified as a plan of the discotheque by the club's owner. The evidence was sufficient for Herr Mandred Ganshaw, the senior investigating police officer, to be convinced of Hazi's guilt.

SIGNIFICANCE

The bombing came at a time when tensions between the United States and Libya were boiling. The month prior to the disco attack, the U.S. carried out a naval strike against Libya in the Gulf of Sirte. U.S. and German officials claimed that Libya put a bomb in the La Belle disco to purposely target Americans in West Berlin, as the night club was known to be heavily frequented by off-duty American military personnel.

Firefighters search through debris after a bomb attack at the Berlin discotheque "La Belle." AP/WIDE WORLD PHOTOS

The U.S. government stated that intelligence information intercepted from the Libyan People's Bureau in East Berlin clearly linked Libya to the La Belle bombings. Washington said the U.S. military police knew an attack was coming, and had begun evacuating discos in West Berlin minutes before the La Belle incident took place. However, this claim was disputed by the U.S. deputy chief of the military police in Berlin.

In 1995, information files from the former East German secret police, the Stasi, led to arrests that did in fact link Libya to the bombing. The Stasi monitored many of what it called terrorist groups operating in East Berlin before the end of the Cold War. Telegrams sent from the Libyan embassy in East Berlin to Tripoli were used as evidence in the La Belle case. Fifteen years after the attack, in November of 2001, four people were convicted in Berlin. Despite the facts presented in the newspaper article, Hazi and the Berlin prostitute who was said to have helped him carry out the attacks, were not among the four.

Yassir Shraidi, a Palestinian who had been employed at the Libya embassy in East Berlin, was convicted of organizing the attack. He also assembled the bomb that was used. Libyan diplomat, Musbah Eter, the primary contact in the Libyan intelligence agency in East Berlin, was convicted as a co-conspirator. Another

Palestinian, Ali Chanaa, was also convicted, having scouted out appropriate targets where Americans would be gathered. The final conviction was of a 42-year-old German woman who actually planted the bomb near the dance floor of the disco.

In September 2004, Libya agreed to pay $35 million in compensation to the non-American victims of the disco attack. This settlement removed one of the last barriers to Libya's international rehabilitation, following years of being accused by Western governments of supporting terrorism. Libya stated it would not compensate American victims until Washington compensated victims of its retaliation bombings. Libya has also paid compensation to families of the victims of the Lockerbie Pan-Am bombing, and to families of victims who died in the 1989 bombing of a French UTA airliner.

The significance of the article lies in the fact that it demonstrates that investigators, working on reasonable assumptions, and with seemingly convincing evidence in hand, can come to the wrong conclusions. Such conclusions can be particularity perilous in the world of terrorism where groups, motives, and the devices used often overlap.

The article was one of many that cast doubt on then U.S. President Ronald Reagan's conclusion that Libya was involved in state-sponsored terrorism during the period and that Gadaffi knew and approved of the bombings. At the time, articles such as the example provided were used by political opponents of Reagan and of American foreign policy to criticize the U.S. for its policies and to discredit motives for the retaliatory attacks on Libya.

The revelation that Libya was behind the disco bombing and other terrorist acts, the subsequent acceptance of responsibility by Libya, and a public willingness to abandon attempts to gain weapons of mass destruction have paved the way for improved relations between Libya and Western countries. In September of 2004, Colin Powell became the first U.S. Secretary of State to meet with Libyan officials in over twenty years.

FURTHER RESOURCES
Periodicals

Weisman, Stephen R. "Powell Holds Brief Meeting With Minister From Libya." *New York Times.* September 24, 2004.

Web sites

BBC News. "On This Day 5 April 1986: Berlin Disco Bombed." <http://news.bbc.co.uk/onthisday/hi/dates/stories/april/5/newsid_4357000/4357255.stm> (Accessed July 4, 2005).

BBC News. "Libya inks $35m Berlin bomb deal." <http://news.bbc.co.uk/1/hi/world/europe/3625756.stm> (accessed July 4, 2005).

International Policy Institute for Counter-Terrorism. "Four Convicted for 1986 Disco Bombing." <http://www.ict.org.il/spotlight/det.cfm?id=706> (accessed July 4, 2005).

Lebanon Hostage Crisis

"President Calls for All Hostages to be Released"

News article

By: Rita Beamish

Date: July 31, 1989

Source: The Associated Press.

About the Author: Rita Beamish earned a degree in history before pursing a master's degree in journalism from Columbia Graduate School. Beamish served as a White House, political, and foreign affairs writer for the Associated Press for over ten years.

INTRODUCTION

In 1979, an Islamic revolution led by Shia Muslims ended the secular rule of the Shah of Iran and ushered in several decades of continued unrest in the region. Spurred on by western supported Israel and its occupation of the West Bank and Gaza, militants sought to rid the region of both Israel and all western influences. However, in the midst of civil war in Lebanon between Christian Maronites and Muslim fundamentalists, southern Lebanon was invaded by Israel, which added to the unrest. Multinational peacekeepers sent to enforce a cease-fire, journalists covering the conflict, and any other westerner in the region became a target for assassination or kidnapping.

The Shah of Iran, backed by the United States, lost popularity as the economic disparity in Iran increased. By 1979, the secular parties within the government could not compete with the power accumulated by the Islamic Republican Party, led by former students of the cleric Ayatollah Khomeini. In October 1979, a group of students entered the U.S. embassy in Tehran and took sixty-six Americans hostage. The hostage takers demanded that the Shah be returned to Iran so that he could stand trial for crimes. The captors also wanted the return of billions of dollars that they assumed the Shah had secretly funneled into his own accounts. Fifteen months later, a deal was brokered that allowed for the return of the hostages. These events, however, brought to an end the once close ties between the U.S. and Iran.

At the same time in Lebanon, Shia populations with familial ties to Shia Muslims in Iran facilitated the creation of militias. With Syrian approval, these militias, in the form of groups such as Hezbollah, entered Lebanon with the purpose to fight Israeli expansion. Within poor Shia communities, these groups began to promote the idea of an Islamic fundamentalist state in Lebanon, similar to Iran. The extremists promised to expel western influence and destroy Israel. After the 1982 Israeli invasion of southern Lebanon, these groups began to gain wide support. Their tactics included suicide bombings, hijackings, and kidnappings, harkening back to the 1979 hostage crisis.

The Phalange party of Maronite Christians, allies with Israel, supported the idea of modernizing Lebanon. Phalange policies before the civil war had expanded western influences in the country. The clash between the two camps fueled the nation's civil war. Peacekeeping became a multinational task, bringing western militaries into the war torn country. In addition, journalists also reported from the region. These people, by virtue of their U.S. and European citizenship, became targets for Islamic fundamentalist militias.

The first American kidnapped was William Buckley on March 16, 1984. Buckley was a political officer for the State Department and had been stationed in Beirut since 1983. Islamic Jihad claimed that he was the CIA station chief and killed him. Confirmation of his death did not occur until 1987. Also kidnapped in 1984 was Peter Kilburn, a librarian for American University. He disappeared on December 3, 1984 and was found shot to death on April 16, 1986. His death, along with two British hostages, was said to be in retaliation to the U.S. air strikes on Libya.

In 1985, Associated Press chief correspondent in Lebanon, Terry Anderson, was kidnapped by members of Hezbollah. (Anderson was the longest-held hostage, remaining in captivity for over six years before being released.) That same year, six foreign nationals were also kidnapped. Nicolas Kluiters, a Dutch Roman Catholic priest was abducted and killed. In May, British professor of English Denis Hill was also abducted and killed. Acting dean of agriculture for American University, Thomas Sutherland was kidnapped in June of 1985, and Italian businessman Alberto Molinari was also abducted later that year. Four Soviet officials were kidnapped in 1985; however, three were released immediately, while one was killed.

The kidnappings continued on through 1988. In 1986, Irish and British educators from American University and the Lebanese International School were abducted. On April 16, 1986, British professors Leigh Douglas and Philip Padfield were kidnapped and later found dead, along with Peter Kilburn. In 1987, three visiting professors at the Beirut University College were abducted. In addition, Terry Waite, a British envoy of the Anglican Church seeking the release of the hostages was taken. In 1988, abductions occurred with the accusation of espionage. In February, U.S. Marine Lt. Colonel William Higgins was abducted and accused of spying. Later that year, Belgian physician Jan Cools was also kidnapped and accused of collecting intelligence.

In all, thirteen hostages were taken by Lebanese terrorists from 1985–1992.

■ PRIMARY SOURCE

President Bush, condemning the reported hanging of Lt. Col. William Higgins by pro-Iranian kidnappers, Monday night called on "all parties" holding hostages in the Middle East to release them "to begin to reverse the cycle of violence."

In a statement telephoned to news organizations, Bush pointedly renewed his criticism of Israel, whose kidnapping on Friday of a Moslem Shiite cleric led Higgins' kidnappers to release a tape which they said showed his execution by hanging.

"On Friday, I said that the taking of any hostage was not helpful to the Middle East peace process. The brutal and tragic events of today have underscored the validity of that statement," Bush said.

"Tonight I wish to go beyond that statement with an urgent call to all, all parties, who hold hostages in the Middle East to release them forthwith, as an humanitarian gesture, to begin to reverse the cycle of violence in that region."

In his conference call to news agencies, presidential spokesman Marlin Fitzwater said it was "impossible to tell" what the reaction to the president's statement would be.

Asked if the U.S. government had contacted Israel in an attempt to persuade it to release its hostage, Fitzwater replied that "We have had contacts with Israel, but not in the past day." He did not elaborate on the nature of the contacts.

"We face a very difficult situation," Fitzwater said. "We have threats of two other possible deaths. We have hostages being held by a number of countries or factions or groups."

"The president feels his plea, with real attention focused on the situation, could give everyone a chance to release their hostages."

Fitzwater referred to threats made during the day by groups in the Middle East against two hostages, Joseph James Cicippio, an official of the American University of Beirut, and Anglican church envoy Terry Waite.

Earlier, referring to "this brutal murder" of the Marine officer, Bush said: "It is a most troubling and disturbing matter that has shocked the American people right to the core. There is no way that I can properly express the outrage that I feel."

While Bush cautioned publicly that he had no confirmation Higgins had in fact been hanged, Senate Republican Leader Bob Dole, R-Kan., said the president told congressional leaders Monday night that "it's about a 98 percent probability that it happened."

Bush monitored reports through the afternoon after returning from Chicago, then met into the evening in the Cabinet room with top advisers, including Defense Secretary Dick Cheney, Deputy Secretary of State Lawrence Eagleburger and other Cabinet members, before briefing the congressional leaders.

Senate Intelligence Committee Chairman David Boren, D-Okla., said after that meeting that Bush was considering several options but he declined to identify them.

"I don't think anything has been ruled out at this point," Boren said.

During his earlier meeting with advisers, Bush "received a briefing on the status of our knowledge of the situation. This was primarily an informational meeting at which all aspects of the case involving Col. Higgins and the other hostages were discussed," Press Secretary Marlin Fitzwater said in a statement.

Higgins' reported killing triggered an instant debate in Congress over Israel's role in the events. Israeli commandos kidnapped a Shiite Moslem cleric last week, and the announcement of Higgins' hanging said he was killed in retaliation.

"Perhaps a little more responsibility on behalf of the Israelis would be refreshing," Dole said. But Rep. Charles Schumer, D-N.Y., countered that blaming Israel would be "turning the world on its head."

At the White House, officials carefully avoided direct criticism of Israel, but Fitzwater said, "It is fair to say that many people do share the senator's concerns." He would not elaborate.

An Israeli official in Washington, speaking on condition of anonymity, said, "It's ridiculous to say that Israel is responsible for Higgins' death. We don't even know if it's him, and if it is, when he was killed."

A member of Congress who attended the leadership meeting with Bush, speaking on condition of no further identification, said the lawmakers were told repeatedly the United States was given no notice of Israeli's intent to kidnap the cleric, and "There was no consultation between Israel and the United States."

After meeting with Bush, Senate Majority Leader George Mitchell, D-Maine, said the president "strongly reaffirmed his belief in the appropriate policy of not negotiating with terrorists in any circumstances."

He, like others at the meeting, declined to discuss which possible responses, including military options, might be under consideration.

One administration official, asked about reports that Bush would not undertake military retaliation or rescue missions, said it would be premature to reach that conclusion.

The source, speaking on condition of anonymity, said administration officials planned more meetings to discuss the crisis, indicating a likelihood that no final decisions had been made.

Rep. William Dickinson, R-Ala., ranking Republican on the Armed Services Committee, said after the White House meeting: "The president made it very clear, until the facts are known, at least more facts than we have now, there's no way you can make a definitive decision" on what to do.

There are nine Americans in captivity in the Middle East, including Terry Anderson, Middle East correspondent for The Associated Press.

"Somehow there has got to be a return to decency and honor, even in matters of this nature," Bush said on the White House lawn after returning from Chicago, where he had addressed the National Governors' Association.

He also said he had spoken by telephone with Higgins' wife, "a wonderfully stoic individual who is going through sheer hell."

Bush had been scheduled to proceed from Chicago to Las Vegas for a speech to the Disabled American Veterans, and then on to Oklahoma City for a Tuesday address to the Fraternal Order of Police convention.

But he said in Chicago, "This matter is of such concern to me and to all of you and to the American people that I think it's appropriate that I go back to Washington."

He learned of reports of the execution as he landed in Chicago.

Higgins, 44, was serving as part of an international peacekeeping force in Lebanon when he was taken captive in February 1988. Pro-Iranian Shiite Moslem captors said they hanged him Monday in retaliation for Israel's kidnapping of a Moslem cleric. The group released a videotape purporting to show the execution.

Israel offered earlier in the day to swap the cleric, Sheik Abdul Karim Obeid, and other Shiite Moslem captives for all captured Israeli soldiers and foreign hostages held by Shiite groups in Lebanon.

Secretary of State James A. Baker, leaving Paris for Washington after a weekend of meetings focusing on U.S.-Soviet relations and the future of Cambodia, called the execution report "outrageous and uncivilized."

Dole said in Washington, "I would hope the Israelis would take another look at some of their actions that they must know in advance would endanger American lives."

But Rep. Schumer said, "Israel is among the few countries seeking to fight terrorism. The blame has to fall on the terrorists themselves."

Rep. Gary Ackerman, D-N.Y., was circulating a letter asking colleagues to support a resolution calling for the extradition of Sheik Obeid to stand trial in the United States for the kidnapping of Higgins.

SIGNIFICANCE

Several groups, including Islamic Jihad, the militant wing of Hezbollah, assumed responsibility for the hostage takings and for the killings. The group sought the release of seventeen of its members who had been convicted of terrorist activities against U.S. and French embassies in Kuwait in 1983. The groups used the hostage takings and assassinations as a terror tactic to dissuade foreign intervention in the Middle East.

The United States government maintained the public position that they would not negotiate with the terrorists holding American and European hostages. However, President Ronald Reagan (1911–2004) and his administration thought that they could influence Iran to persuade the pro-Iranian Hezbollah terrorists to free the hostages. In a series of secret dealings, the United States tried to establish an arms-for-hostages program where weapons were sold to Iran, who was then engaged in a war with Iraq. The money from the arms sales was used to help fund anti-communist Contra rebels in Nicaragua. When news of the program beame public, Congress urged President Reagan to convene an investigative Presidential Commission, which became known as the Tower Commission (named for former Sen. John Tower, head of the commission).

The Tower Commission implicated several top Reagan advisors in the scandal, but did not determine that Reagan himself had knowledge of the events. The Reagan administration weathered the scandal, despite widespread media coverage of the Iran-Contra Congressional hearings.

FURTHER RESOURCES

Books

Coughlin, Con. *Hostage: The Complete Story of the Lebanon Captives.* New York: Warner Books, 1993.

Web sites

BBC News. "On This Day, February 2, 1987: Negotiator Turned Hostage." <http://newssearch.bbc.co.uk/onthisday/hi/witness/february/2/newsid_2880000/2880753.stm> (accessed July 10, 2005)

BBC News. "Timeline: Lebanon." <http://news.bbc.co.uk/1/hi/world/middle_east/country_profiles/819200.stm> (accessed July 10, 2005).

"Higgins Ventured Into Southern Lebanon Alone"

Iranian-backed Hezbollah Kidnaps U.S. Marine Corps Lt. Col. W. Higgins

News article

By: Agence France Presse

Date: December 23, 1991

Source: Agence France Presse.

About the Author: Agence France Presse (AFP) is the third largest international news service, providing reporting for global media outlets. AFP reporting reaches subscribers via radio, television, and newspapers. The organization maintains a network of journalists in 165 countries.

INTRODUCTION

After one year of captivity and three years after his reported death, the body of U.S. Marine Corps Lt. Colonel William Higgins was finally returned to the United States. Higgins had been part of a United Nations (UN) peacekeeping contingency stationed in Lebanon in the late 1980s. His abduction and death was most likely organized by the militant group Hezbollah (also known as Hizballah, or Party of God) who had accused Higgins of espionage.

In early 1980, Lebanon was embroiled in a civil war that had been ravaging the country since 1975. Iranian and Syrian backed militias, intent on creating an Islamic-fundamentalist state in Lebanon, struggled for power against the Christian Maronites. Adding to the conflict, Israel invaded southern Lebanon in 1982, claiming that the military incursion was necessary to

Marine Lt. Col. William Higgins, assigned to temporary duty with the United Nations, was kidnapped in Lebanon and murdered in 1988. AP/WIDE WORLD PHOTOS

1980s through suicide bombings, kidnappings, and assassinations. Groups such as Islamic Jihad and the Organization of the Oppressed of the World fell under the umbrella of Hezbollah, whose goal is the expulsion of western influences from the region.

In 1983, Islamic Jihad launched simultaneous suicide attacks in Beirut against western multinational peacekeeping forces, killing 241 U.S. Marines and 58 French paratroopers. Throughout the decade, random kidnappings, and often murders, were also used as tools of Hezbollah.

The first American kidnapped was William Buckley on March 16, 1984. Although Buckley was serving as a political officer for the State Department, Islamic Jihad claimed that he was the Central Intelligence Agency (CIA) station chief and killed him. Confirmation of his death did not occur until 1987. Dozens more westerners were kidnapped; several were killed by their captors. One American, Terry Anderson, chief Middle East correspondent for the Associated Press, was held in Hezbollah captivity for almost seven years.

PRIMARY SOURCE

Colonel William Higgins, the slain U.N. officer whose body was handed over to the U.S. Embassy here Monday, was traveling alone in southern Lebanon, against U.N. advice, when he was abducted there three years ago.

U.S. press reports at the time of his abduction, February 17, 1988, said the 43-year-old Vietnam veteran had been on a mission to gather information on the pro-Iranian Hezbollah movement as part of efforts to free Western hostages held in Lebanon.

The White House denied the reports.

But U.N. spokesman in southern Lebanon Timur Goksel disclosed shortly after the kidnapping that Higgins, a U.S. Marine Corps colonel seconded to the U.N. Truce Supervision Organization, had not been obliged to respect U.N. regulations against travelling alone in southern Lebanon.

Higgins went off unaccompanied, according to Goksel, "because of his rank and the contacts he wanted to make with different groups."

The U.S. Defense Department a week after the kidnapping announced that just prior to his departure for Lebanon in 1987, Higgins had spent two years on the staff of then U.S. defense secretary Caspar Weinberger.

Married and the father of a daughter, Higgins was at the wheel of a U.N. vehicle in the southern Lebanese city

protect its borders from attacks by members of the Palestinian Liberation Organization (PLO) living in refugee camps. Two months later, a U.S. led cease-fire called for international monitors to facilitate the withdrawal of PLO members from Lebanon. The cease-fire also called for Israel to agree to halt further advancement into Lebanon and, according to international law, to ensure the safety of Palestinian refugees. The Israeli presence in Lebanon continued, and as the civil war between the Islamic fundamentalists and Southern Lebanon Army, armed and trained by Israel, escalated, a multinational force was called upon to make possible a new cease-fire and bring stability to the war-torn region.

Even with U.N. observers arbitrating between sides, conflict continued throughout the region. Militant groups tied to Hezbollah, a Shia Muslim extremist organization, began a wave of terror in the

of Tyre, controlled by the pro-Syrian Amal Shiite movement, when he was seized.

The abduction was not claimed until July 31, 1989, when a group identifying itself as the Organization of the Oppressed of the World released a videotape showing a man hanging from a rope and said Higgins had been executed for spying.

It said the execution had been carried out in retaliation for the kidnapping by Israeli troops two days earlier of a prominent southern Lebanese Shiite cleric, Sheikh Abdel Karim Obeid.

In a surprise development, Hezbollah, which had traditionally kept its official distance from hostage-taking, hailed both the kidnapping of Higgins, whom it accused of spying, and his execution.

A large man with thinning blond hair, Higgins was described by colleagues as an amiable officer. His kidnappers during his captivity released photographs showing him haggard and bearded.

SIGNIFICANCE

Operating as from the command of the U.N. Truce Supervision Organization, Marine Lt. Colonel William Higgins began his assignment in July of 1987. Prior to his position with the U.N., Lt. Colonel Higgins had served as the Military Assistant to the Secretary of Defense. His reported death and video of the slaying occurred in February 1988, and deeply disturbed the American people. In 1989, President George H.W. Bush called for an end to the violence that plagued the region and the release of all hostages being held. By December 1991, the last American hostages held by Islamic Jihad were released. Terry Anderson had been held since March 16, 1985. Joseph James Cicippio, the acting comptroller for American University, had been kidnapped on September 12, 1986, and Alann Steen, a communications instructor at Beirut University College had been abducted on January 24, 1987.

Hezbollah is still regarded by the United States as a foreign terrorist organization. In 1992, members of Hezbollah attacked the Israeli embassy in Buenos Aires, Argentina. The group is also suspected of involvement in the 1994 bombing of an Israeli Cultural Center in the same city. In 2000, Hezbollah captured 4 Israelis, three of them soldiers, whom they are suspected of luring to Lebanon under false pretenses. Hezbollah is suspected of maintaining cells in North and South America, Asia, Europe, and Africa.

FURTHER RESOURCES

Web sites

BBC News. "Who Are Hezbollah?" April 4, 2002. <http://news.bbc.co.uk/2/hi/middle_east/1908671.stm> (accessed July 8, 2005).

Thomas: Legislation Information on the Internet. "Profiles of Western Hostages of Lebanese Kidnappers." <http://thomas.loc.gov/cgi-bin/query/z?r101:S12MY9-551:> (accessed July 8, 2005).

United Nations. "Middle East: UNTSO: Background." <http://www.un.org/Depts/dpko/missions/untso/background.html> (accessed July 8, 2005).

Tupac Amaru Revolutionary Movement (MRTA)

"Peruvian Soldiers Storm Diplomatic Mansion"

News article

By: Lynn Monahan

Date: April 23, 1997

Source: The Associated Press

About the Author: Lynn Monahan is an Associated Press writer who covered Peruvian politics and society at the time of the Tupac Amaru hostage crisis. Her reports from Peru also included articles on Lori Berenson, an American accused of aiding Tupac Amaru Revolutionary Movement (MRTA) insurgents, as well as special interest articles on Peruvian society.

INTRODUCTION

Revolutionary movements developed in Latin American countries as a response to economic decline throughout the 1980s. As inflation reached rates as high as 10,000%, groups such as Shining Path in Peru, the Revolutionary Armed Forces of Colombia (FARC) and the National Liberation Army (ELN) in Colombia, and the Tupac Amaru Revolutionary Movement (MRTA) in Peru fought a guerilla war with established governments. These groups used tactics such as kidnappings, bombings, and power supply disruptions to gain attention for their cause. Tapping into the anger and frustration of the Native American population living in poverty, these movements often supported a leftist change that involved income and land redistribution.

When Alberto Fujimori, the son of Japanese immigrants, assumed the presidency of Peru on July 28, 1990, he ushered in a more authoritarian presidential style—one that harkened back to the militaristic,

A sign on the roof of the Japanese ambassador's residence in Lima, Peru reads "MRTA, surrender is not the way of Tupac Amaru." AP/WIDE WORLD PHOTOS

"strongman" rule of the nineteenth century *caudillo*— the strong military leader. Instituting dramatic free market reforms, he attempted to follow a Chilean path to end Peru's economic woes. Chile, Peru's neighbor to the south, had experienced the "Chilean Economic Miracle" of the 1980s, brought on by a combination of free market reforms, government program cuts, and massive privatization of government-held industries. Fujimori's "Fujishock" policies generated more than $9 billion from privatization and, in 1994, economic growth reached 12%, but with a detrimental effect on the poor. Coca (the leafy plant from which cocaine is made) farming became a path for economic prosperity in the countryside, but the United States pressured Peru to reduce coca exports as part of the United States' anti-drug trafficking policies.

By 1992, Fujimori's policies were in full force. As part of his authoritarian rule, Peruvian forces cracked down on both Shining Path and Tupac Amaru. Foreign investment was important for Peru's economy to recover, and Fujimori's relentless pursuit of the rebels was spurred by investors' fears that these groups represented instability in the country. When the leaders of both rebel groups were captured, it signaled to Peruvians and the world that Fujimori maintained control over Peru. Fujimori declared victory over the insurgents. By 1995, Japan invested more than $280 million in Peru's economy, surpassing the United States as Peru's largest foreign investor.

However, on December 17, 1996, the Tupac Amaru captured the Japanese ambassador's residence during a birthday party for the Japanese envoy. Fujimori faced a difficult balancing act. The Japanese Embassy was technically under Japanese control, and yet the crisis took place on Peruvian soil. Promising to take no action that might harm the hostages, Fujimori first negotiated the release of some or all of the 490 captives. Over the next two months, Tupac Amaru released all but 71 hostages. The group retained Fujimori's brother, the Japanese ambassador, Peruvian Supreme Court justices, members of the Peruvian Congress, and other high-ranking officials. Tupac Amaru demanded the release of all their imprisoned members, including the wife of current leader Nestor Cerpa Cartolini. Fujimori refused to release the imprisoned Tupac Amaru members, but maintained open negotiations while planning a possible military assault on the palace.

On April 22, 1997, Peruvian forces stormed the palace after receiving a tip that the rebels were playing a game of soccer, far from most of the hostages. The soldiers killed all 14 Tupac Amaru hostage-takers. One Peruvian Supreme Court justice and two soldiers died in the attack as well. The Japanese government was stunned, as Fujimori had given them no prior warning, and had not consulted legislators on the planned attack.

PRIMARY SOURCE

In a lightning assault, Peruvian troops stormed the Japanese ambassador's mansion Tuesday and rescued 71 hostages held for four months, killing all 14 rebel captors as the unsuspecting guerrillas played soccer.

One captive, Supreme Court Justice Carlos Giusti, and two soldiers also died, President Alberto Fujimori said. Some hostages were secretly warned just before the raid, one of the freed men said.

Fujimori said 25 other captives were injured in the gunfire and explosions that rocked the compound. Two were in serious condition, Peru's foreign minister, Francisco Tudela, and another Supreme Court justice, both suffering gunshot wounds.

"I didn't waver for a single minute in giving the order for this rescue operation," said the president, who throughout the crisis adamantly rejected the guerrillas' demand that jailed comrades be freed in exchange for the captive diplomats and businessmen.

The operation ended an international ordeal that had transfixed two nations and focused global attention on a little-known leftist rebel group, Tupac Amaru, which has waged guerrilla war here since 1984.

In Tokyo, Japan's prime minister called it a "splendid rescue," but also said it was "regrettable." that Peru had not forewarned his government of the surprise, broad-daylight attack.

Fujimori told reporters late Tuesday that intelligence information convinced him it was an ideal time to end the impasse by force.

He apparently was referring to word of the indoor soccer game. Bolivian Ambassador Jorge Gumucio, one of the freed hostages, said eight hostage-holders were playing soccer in the main hall of the diplomatic residence when the security forces struck, setting off an explosion in a tunnel directly under the hall about 3:30 P.M.

The 140-man military-police assault team then poured through the compound's front gate and blasted open the mansion's front door. Others attacked from the rear, and a third unit climbed to the rooftop and shepherded hostages down to the ground.

"I was playing mahjong with fellow hostages, and we suddenly heard the enormous blasts," said Tadashi Iwamoto, president of Lima Tomen, a Japanese trading house. "We grabbed blankets and covered our heads and lay flat on the floor."

Iwamoto said some hostages suffered burns, but one group kicked the iron fence and the door in until they broke and went outside and climbed down to the ground.

"When I heard the blast . . . I thought ah, this is the end of my life," Japanese ambassador Morihisa Aoki told the Japanese television NHK. "In order to have as many people survive as possible, I told everyone in my room again and again not to move, even an inch."

The assault ended quickly. As smoke billowed over the residence, triumphant soldiers hauled down the guerrillas' flag, and ex-hostages and rescuers cheered and jubilantly sang the Peruvian national anthem. A large pool of blood could be seen at the bottom of a stairway.

Fujimori said all 14 rebels were killed, including the group's leader, Nestor Cerpa, and at least two teen-age girls. Gumucio said Cerpa was one of those playing soccer.

Gumucio also said authorities managed to warn some of the captives 10 minutes before the raid. He declined to say how.

The hostages, all male, were mostly Peruvians and included Fujimori's brother. They also included 24 Japanese—12 businessmen and 12 diplomats, including Aoki, who suffered a slight elbow injury during the rescue. There were no Americans among the hostages.

Less than an hour after the raid, Fujimori strapped on a bulletproof vest and victoriously entered the compound. He shook ex-hostages' hands and joined with them and soldiers in singing the national anthem.

Smiling and carrying a large red-and-white Peruvian flag, Fujimori traveled with two busloads of hostages, apparently unharmed, to a military hospital.

Other hostages were rushed off in ambulances. Friends and family gathered at the nearby hospital to look for loved ones.

"We're here to applaud the hostages and police for their bravery," said one woman, Edith Gonzalez. "There was no other alternative but to attack."

But the sister of one hostage said she wasn't sure.

"I don't know if the attack was necessary," said Nancy Dominguez, 53. "All I know is it was a horrible shame."

At the White House, spokesman Eric Rubin said the United States believed the rebels bear "full responsibility for this crisis. We have stated that the Peruvian government was right not to make concessions to terrorists."

Japanese Prime Minister Ryutaro Hashimoto said Peru had not told him in advance of the raid, even though the compound is technically Japanese soil. Japan had repeatedly asked the Peruvians to avoid any actions that might endanger the hostages.

"Our country was not informed in advance and this is very regrettable," Hashimoto said. But he expressed support for Peru's leader, saying, "There should be nobody who could criticize Mr. Fujimori for his decision."

The two national leaders consulted closely during the crisis. At a meeting with Hashimoto in Canada, Fujimori agreed to talks with the guerrillas. He subsequently traveled to Cuba and won President Fidel Castro's agreement to grant asylum to the rebels if necessary to end the standoff.

But the negotiations broke down March 12 over the rebels' demand that Peru free their jailed comrades. Fujimori repeatedly ruled that out.

Fujimori had said he would use force to end the crisis only as a last resort, but Peruvian news media repeatedly reported military plans to raid the compound.

The heavily armed guerrillas stormed the residence on Dec. 17 during a cocktail party marking the Japanese emperor's birthday and took almost 500 hostages. They quickly released most of them.

Rebels had warned they had heavily mined the compound to prevent an assault, and staged drills earlier this month to prepare for raids.

The hostage crisis had sparked a political crisis in Peru, and Peru's interior minister and national police chief stepped down over the weekend to accept blame for security lapses that allowed the takeover.

The Tupac Amaru guerrillas took the group's name from a colonial-era Indian rebel. They espouse a vague leftist ideology, denouncing Fujimori's free-market reforms as a boost only for the rich, but don't call themselves communist or Marxist.

SIGNIFICANCE

Revolutionary insurgent groups such as the Shining Path rebels and Tupac Amaru affected Peruvian society at a critical point in Peru's economic modernization. Fujimori sought to stabilize Peru's economy and bring it in line with other stable economies in South America at the time, such as Chile and Argentina. Meanwhile, rebel groups tapped into the alienation and economic insecurity of the nation's poor.

Tupac Amaru's siege on the Japanese ambassador's house was a calculated national and international message. Japan had invested more then $280 million in Peru's economy in 1995. The hostage crisis was viewed as an attack on President Fujimori's strength as president and on his Japanese heritage as well.

As Monahan notes, "Japanese Prime Minister Ryutaro Hashimoto said Peru had not told him in advance of the raid, even though the compound is technically Japanese soil. Japan had repeatedly asked the Peruvians to avoid any actions that might endanger the hostages." In addition, "The two national leaders consulted closely during the crisis. At a meeting with Hashimoto in Canada, Fujimori agreed to talks with the guerrillas. He subsequently traveled to Cuba and won President Fidel Castro's agreement to grant asylum to the rebels if necessary to end the standoff." This trip to Cuba was viewed by the rebels as a minor victory. By forcing Fujimori to travel to Cuba and to ask the communist leader for his involvement in solving the crisis, Tupac Amaru was hailed by supporters as weakening Fujimori's anti-terrorist stance.

Japanese relations took an interesting turn. While the Japanese expressed shock that they had not been consulted, they nonetheless congratulated Fujimori for his actions and the operation's success. Political analysts speculated that Fujimori's reluctance to consult Japan stemmed in part from Japan's willingness to pay ransom for hostages, such as the 1977 hijacking of a Japan Airlines flight by the Japanese Red Army and the $6 million ransom paid by the Japanese government for the release of the captives.

The raid on the Tupac Amaru rebels was considered a success by Fujimori and international anti-terrorist analysts. Combined with the 1992 capture of Abimael Guzmán, the leader of Shining Path, Fujimori's granting the military broad powers to arrest suspected terrorists, military tribunals for suspected terrorists, and the arming of rural Peruvians called *rondas campesinas* (peasant patrols), the president had developed a series of steps that led to his declaration that he had achieved victory over revolutionary groups.

However, according to human rights agencies, the suppression of revolutionary movements came at a cost.

By some estimates from groups such as Amnesty International and Human Rights Watch, between 1980 and 2000, more than 30,000 Peruvians died or disappeared, many allegedly as a result of Fujimori's policies that permitted the military to round up suspected Shining Path rebels without granting formal legal protection. Incidents such as the May 14, 1988 killings of forty-seven peasants in Caymara, Ayacucho were brought to light. Fourteen members of the Peruvian military were tried and convicted of the killings, with sentences ranging from three months to one year. None of the convicted served any prison time. Before leaving office, Fujimori granted amnesty to any member of the Peruvian military or police force who was convicted or accused of crimes between the years 1980 and 1995.

On November 17, 2000, Fujimori arrived in Japan unexpectedly. Amid allegations of improper use of government funds, and with mounting pressure from human rights groups, Fujimori faxed his resignation to Peru from Japan on November 20, 2000. The Peruvian Congress rejected the resignation and instead deemed him "morally unfit to serve," barring him from holding office. On September 5, 2001, Peru's Attorney General filed homicide charges against ex-president Fujimori. In exile in Japan, which has no extradition treaty with Peru, Fujimori refuses to return to Peru voluntarily.

FURTHER RESOURCES

Books

Conaghan, Catherine M. *Fujimori's Peru: Deception In The Public Sphere*. Pittsburgh: University of Pittsburgh Press, 2005.

Web sites

PBS.org. "Hostage Crisis." <http://www.pbs.org/newshour/bb/latin_america/december96/peru_12–19.html> (accessed June 19, 2005).

"The Critics Multiply"

Political Terrorism in Brazil

Magazine interview

By: Tom Zé

Date: May 19, 1999

Source: Interview with Tom Zé, published in the *Minneapolis-St. Paul City Pages*.

About the Author: Brazilian musician Tom Zé was born in the Brazilian state of Bahia in 1936. Along with musicians such as Gilberto Gil and Caetano Veloso, Zé was at the forefront of Brazil's Tropicalista movement, a wide-ranging social and artistic phenomenon which gained momentum as an agent of protest against the Brazilian military dictatorship that seized power in 1964. Zé was discovered by North American audiences in the early 1990s, when his music was promoted by the musician David Byrne.

INTRODUCTION

"Every chord in a song had five bombs, ready to throw at the military headquarters." The words of Tom Zé reflect the mood of Brazilian artists and musicians who were critics of the Brazilian military government as the country entered 1970.

In the wake of the ouster of the democratically elected national government in 1964, the Brazilian military began to limit many personal freedoms. Under the leadership of General Costa e Silva, the government imposed Institutional Act No. 5. Known as AL-5 when proclaimed into law in December 1968, the act suspended the Brazilian constitution, closed the Congress, and broadened powers of search, arrest, and detention. AL-5 also censored the arts and the press in an effort to suppress public protest and opposition to the government.

The Tropicalia movement arose in the mid 1960s, as a form of Brazilian artistic nationalism, a fusion of older Brazilian forms with more modern influences. With the imposition of laws such as AL-5, "tropicalistas" such as Zé, Gil and Veloso, through music that was often harshly satirical in its form, became regarded as agents of protest and of change in the country. Their manner of conveying intensely critical images of the military rulers and the government made these musicians famous.

Tropicalia was not geared to violence; however, songs such as Veloso's *é Proibido Proibi* (It is Forbidden to Forbid) provoked stern government sanction. Veloso, Gil, and other musicians were exiled, often after being arrested and detained for period of time. Zé received similar treatment and left music altogether to work for what he thought would be the rest of his existence in a family gas station in Brazil, until his career was revived in North America in the late 1990's.

█ PRIMARY SOURCE

CP (City Pages): Given the relative freedom you grew up with, how did the government repression of the late '60s affect you?

Zé: Well, it was the I-5 [Institutional Act No. 5] that made the dictatorship more rigorous. We were like boxers who were close to being knocked out, but we couldn't really calculate how strong that hook would be. That law made our lives an absolute hell. The funny part,

which is always part of the tragic, is that I would go through the street in '69 and I would see the newspapers. You had to read them like an algebraic formula, which reminded me of my teachers in high school. We didn't know if we had to be worried about the censorship of our texts, or worried about our sisters involved in resistance who were incarcerated. I had two female friends who were jailed, then fled to Chile. Then, when Allende died, they fled to France. Everybody was saving up money to send them to safety.

It's as if the military was producing a show. One funny thing that doesn't come out in the papers is the way they extorted money. The phone would ring, and someone would say, "Tom Zé, this is Colonel So-and-so. I have a pair of knitting needles for you. But they're very special knitting needles. They're for you to use with French or English yarn. And you have to deposit so much money in such-and-such an account in a bank tomorrow so that you can have these needles, so they can knit the yarn of your life." This was the fear and the surrealism that we were going through. And sometimes we would actually deposit the money.

CP: What was your reaction to Gilberto Gil and Caetano Veloso being jailed?

Zé: With Gilberto Gil and Caetano, it was never explained—not when they were arrested, nor when they were set free—why this happened. When I was incarcerated for a few days in '71, they interrogated me on the day I was set free. And they asked me, like, if this or that star on TV in Brazil was actually nice in person. You were so scared that you didn't even ask them, "Why the heck was I in here?"

CP: What do you think the government feared about Tropicália?

Zé: Things worked in an organic manner. First they were afraid of ideas, then of youth, then of modernity. Then they were afraid of the Moon and the race to the Moon. We were making music that was a novelty in the aesthetic world, and it seemed that every chord in a song had five bombs ready to throw at the military headquarters.

CP: How did Tropicália change Brazil?

Zé: It had an effect on people, on business, on the whole concept of innovation. It influenced Brazilian engineering, which produced technology that had not been seen anywhere else in the world. Tropicália enabled them to build the bridge between Rio de Janeiro and the City of Niterói. And there was also simply a joy in knowing that this kind of music existed. It fed our resistance like some kind of protein or antibiotic.

SIGNIFICANCE

It is noteworthy that the opposition to the policies of the Brazilian military regime took a number of years to find a voice after the 1964 coup. When that voice was discovered, the loudest protests were initially those of artists and musicians. Violence, in the form of both political terrorism and of government counter-insurgency, came to Brazil in its most dramatic form in the period from mid-1970–1972.

Protests against government censorship and the suspension of civil liberties, as had been previously guaranteed in the suspended constitution, were unsuccessful both in the short term as well as in the succeeding period of years. Brazilian newspapers and television outlets continued to be the subject of rigorous government restrictions for over ten years after the imposition of AL-5. The first true democratic election was not held until 1989.

Paradoxically, as government restrictions on expression gained greater traction, the Brazilian economy began to grow at a record pace. Commencing in 1970, the Brazilian Gross National Product climbed at a rate of 12% per year for the next seven years.

Also, the focus of the criticism of the Brazilian artistic movement, the AL-5 legislation, was in some respects a touchstone for neighboring countries that also installed a form of military rule after 1970—Argentina, Chile, Bolivia, and Uruguay all imposed legislation similar in effect and in scope to the Institutional Act of Brazil.

FURTHER RESOURCES

Periodicals

Avelas, I. "The Muffled Cries: The Writer and Literature in Authoritarian Brazil, 1964–1985." *Hispanic American Review*. (2001): vol. 81, 82, p. 418.

Web sites

MIT Western Hemisphere Project. <http//:web.mit.edu/hemisphere> (accessed July 5, 2005).

Letter from Timothy McVeigh

Why I Bombed Oklahoma

Letter

By: Timothy McVeigh

Date: May 6, 2001

Source: The *Observer* (London).

About the Author: Timothy McVeigh was the perpetrator of the bombing of the Alfred P. Murrah federal office

Timothy McVeigh poses for his mugshot shortly after the bombing of the Alfred Murrah Federal Building in Oklahoma City. AP/WIDE WORLD PHOTOS

building in Oklahoma City, Oklahoma, on April 19, 1995.

INTRODUCTION

After Timothy McVeigh was convicted of the bombing and while he awaited execution in Terre Haute, Indiana, he wrote the following letter, justifying his act of political terrorism.

PRIMARY SOURCE

I explain herein why I bombed the Murrah Federal Building in Oklahoma City. I explain this not for publicity, nor seeking to win an argument of right or wrong. I explain so that the record is clear as to my thinking and motivations in bombing a government installation.

I chose to bomb a federal building because such an action served more purposes than other options. Foremost, the bombing was a retaliatory strike; a counter attack, for the cumulative raids (and subsequent violence and damage) that federal agents had participated in over the preceding years (including, but not limited to, Waco). From the formation of such units as the FBI's "Hostage

Rescue" and other assault teams amongst federal agencies during the '80s; culminating in the Waco incident, federal actions grew increasingly militaristic and violent, to the point where at Waco, our government, like the Chinese, was deploying tanks against its own citizens.

Knowledge of these multiple and ever-more aggressive raids across the country constituted an identifiable pattern of conduct within and by the federal government and amongst its various agencies. For all intents and purposes, federal agents had become "soldiers" (using military training, tactics, techniques, equipment, language, dress, organization, and mindset) and they were escalating their behavior. Therefore, this bombing was also meant as a pre-emptive (or pro-active) strike against these forces and their command and control centers within the federal building. When an aggressor force continually launches attacks from a particular base of operation, it is sound military strategy to take the fight to the enemy.

Additionally, borrowing a page from U.S. foreign policy, I decided to send a message to a government that was becoming increasingly hostile, by bombing a government building and the government employees within that building who represent that government. Bombing the Murrah Federal Building was morally and strategically equivalent to the U.S. hitting a government building in Serbia, Iraq, or other nations . . . Based on observations of the policies of my own government, I viewed this action as an acceptable option. From this perspective, what occurred in Oklahoma City was no different than what Americans rain on the heads of others all the time, and subsequently, my mindset was and is one of clinical detachment. (The bombing of the Murrah building was not personal, no more than when Air Force, Army, Navy, or Marine personnel bomb or launch cruise missiles against government installations and their personnel.)

SIGNIFICANCE

Until September 11, 2001, the largest terrorist attack on U.S. soil occurred in 1995. Shortly before 9:00 A.M. on the morning of April 19, 1995, McVeigh parked a yellow Ryder rental truck on the street in front of the Alfred P. Murrah Federal Building in Oklahoma City, Oklahoma, and walked away. Inside the truck was a powerful bomb made of 4,000–5,000 pounds of ammonium nitrate and nitromethane. At 9:02 A.M. the bomb detonated, destroying a third of the seven-story building, including a day-care center on the first floor. The final death toll was 168, including nineteen children and one rescue worker. Over 800 people, many of them blocks away, were injured by flying glass and other debris.

Shortly after the explosion, an Oklahoma highway patrolman pulled over Timothy McVeigh, a Gulf War veteran, for driving without a license plate. The patrol-

man discovered an illegally concealed handgun, so he arrested McVeigh and took him to the jail in the nearby town of Perry, where he awaited his bail hearing.

Meanwhile, Federal Bureau of Investigation (FBI) profilers working on the bombing investigation noted that it took place on the two-year anniversary of the Branch Davidian siege in Waco, Texas. During the siege in Waco, Federal agents acted on evidence that the religious cult's leader, David Koresh, had a cache of illegal weapons. As agents of the U.S. Bureau of Alcohol, Tobacco and Firearms (ATF) stormed Koresh's compound, the buildings erupted in flames and seventy-five people died. Because the Waco siege was portrayed as a day of infamy among right-wing militia and anti-government groups, FBI profilers concluded that the Oklahoma City bomber was most likely a white male in his twenties, a military veteran, and a member of a militia group.

As events turned out, the FBI profilers were correct. McVeigh had been fascinated with weaponry from an early age, and he put his skill to good use as a U.S. Army gunner, earning a Bronze Star in the first Gulf War in Iraq. After he left the army, he grew increasingly paranoid about the U.S. government, which he saw as bent on stripping its citizens of their constitutional rights, especially the "right to bear arms" guaranteed by the Second Amendment to the U.S. Constitution.

Holding the ATF responsible for the disaster in Waco, McVeigh decided to take action. McVeigh took his inspiration from *The Turner Diaries*, a novel written by American Nazi leader and white supremacist William L. Turner under the name Andrew MacDonald, in which the protagonist, Earl Turner, detonates a truck bomb outside a federal building.

Enlisting the aid of army companions Terry Nichols and Michael Fortier (both later convicted of aiding McVeigh), McVeigh planned a similar strike against the ATF. Ironically, the ATF did not have offices in the Murrah building in Oklahoma City.

The federal investigation of the bombing proceeded quickly. Investigators at the scene found remains of the truck, which they were able to trace to a rental agency in Junction City, Oklahoma, where employees helped an FBI artist create a sketch of the person who rented the truck. The manager of a local motel identified the man in the sketch as the same man who had stayed at the motel two nights earlier, registering under the name Timothy McVeigh. While still in jail on the traffic and gun charges, McVeigh was arrested for the bombing.

Following a change in venue to help assure a fair trial, McVeigh's trial began on April 24, 1997, in Denver, Colorado. He was found guilty and executed on June 11, 2001, in Terre Haute, Indiana. Nichols was later sentenced to life in prison, and Fortier was sentenced to twelve years for failing to warn authorities about the attack.

At the time of the bombing, terrorism for many Americans was defined by images of Islamic fundamentalism and Middle Eastern fanaticism. In fact, in the hours and days following the bombing, many people and news commentators assumed that the bombing was the work of Islamist terrorists.

McVeigh remained an enigma because, with his boyish looks and distinguished Gulf War record, he simply did not fit many people's idea of the profile of a terrorist. Particularly striking to many Americans was McVeigh's utter lack of remorse or expressions of regret, which he described as clinical detachment. From the time he was charged with the crime until the moment of his execution, he maintained the imperturbable demeanor of a man convinced of the rightness of his cause. Most Americans were especially horrified when, in a television interview for ABC's television program *PrimeTime Thursday*, McVeigh icily referred to the children who died in the bombing as "collateral damage." McVeigh considered the children as incidental civilian casualties unavoidable in his "war" against what he argued was a repressive U.S. government.

FURTHER RESOURCES
Books

Michel, Lou, and Dan Herbeck. *American Terrorist: Timothy McVeigh and the Oklahoma City Bombing*. New York: ReganBooks, 2001.

Oklahoma Today. The Official Record of the Oklahoma City Bombing. Norman: University of Oklahoma Press, 2005.

Philippine's New People's Army (NPA)

"In Philippines, a Threat Revives; Once Nearly Extinct, Communist Rebels Find New Converts"

Newspaper article

By: Carlos H. Conde

Date: December 29, 2003

Source: "In Philippines, a Threat Revives; Once Nearly Extinct, Communist Rebels Find New Converts" as published by *International Herald Tribune*, an English-language newspaper distributed in multiple locations throughout the world.

About the Author: Carlos H. Conde serves as Secretary-General of the National Union of Journalists of the Philippines, and writes from Manila for the *International Herald Tribune* and *New York Times*.

INTRODUCTION

In 2002, the Communist Party of the Philippines (CPP), and its military arm, the New People's Army (NPA) were formally classified as terrorist organizations by the United States and the European Union, with the agreement of the Philippines government of Gloria Macapagal Arroyo. When this newspaper article appeared the following year, the organization was gaining strength following a decline in its numbers in the 1990s, and was seen as the main security threat within the Philippines.

The group was founded in the late 1960s, when it broke away from the long-established Philippine Communist Party (PKP). Unlike the Moscow-orientated main party, the CPP splinter group followed the doctrines of Chinese communist leader Chairman Mao. They planned a people's revolution originating in rural areas. The group soon adopted armed struggle, and has consistently engaged in guerilla warfare, kidnappings, and killings ever since.

The NPA grew in strength during the 1970s and 1980s, drawing support from the many impoverished rural communities and those dissatisfied with the government, particularly during the years of dictatorship under Ferdinand E. Marcos from 1972 to 1986. It adopted the strategy of working closely with local residents in the Philippine countryside, and supporting those in dispute with central or local government over their loss of land to corporate interests. In many areas the party was able to establish control of local government, and generated finance for its activities through taxation of residents and extortion of payments from local businesses. Weapons were stolen from the Philippine armed forces. Anyone in a position of authority who was seen as a threat to the party, including government and military officials, police officers and community leaders, was targeted for assassination. The Philippine government estimated that 1,203 civilians and 144 officials were killed by the rebels in 1985.

At it's height in the mid-1980s, the CPP was reported to have a membership of 30,000 and the NPA from 10,000 to 15,000 active fighters. The guerrilla army was believed to be active in over two-thirds of the country's provinces, and the National Democratic Front (NDF), the party's political wing, was involved in running local government in up to a quarter of the barangays, the administrative units into which the Philippines is divided.

In response to the activities of the New People's Army, successive governments have retaliated with various counter-insurgency and anti-subversive policies, including the extensive use of military force. The Philippine army was expanded in number from 50,000 to 150,000 in the early 1970s to deal with the NPA as well as the Moslem separatists in the southern Philippines, and government troops have been responsible for many killings, not only of NPA fighters but of numerous civilians accused of collaborating with them. It has often been ordinary villagers who have borne the brunt of the military attacks after the guerrillas have retreated.

When Corazon Aquino became President in 1986, she negotiated a sixty-day ceasefire with the rebels, intended to provide the opportunity for both sides to explore the possibility of a longer-term settlement. However, the rebels and the military were unable to uphold the terms of the ceasefire. It broke down within two months. The negotiation period, when military force against the NPA was at a low level, is thought to have helped the party to expand its involvement in local government. However, there were already internal divisions, particularly regarding the decision to boycott the 1986 election that led to the downfall of Marcos, and active support for the party cause started to fall. By 1992, it was estimated that there were less than 10,000 NPA fighters compared with 25,000 in 1987. Throughout the 1990s, the party fragmented further into a number of competing groups.

Despite this decline, a significant core of active rebels have continued to present a security threat to the various governments which have held office in the Philippines, and in 2004, it was estimated that there were again more than 8,000 active fighters. The NPA themselves claimed to have a presence at this time in around seventy of the country's seventy-nine provinces.

Since the late 1990s, the United States has been conducting joint military exercises with the Philippine government within the country and, since 2002, these have focused on combating terrorism, particularly in the southern Philippines. The U.S. involvement is governed by a Visiting Forces Agreement.

▓ PRIMARY SOURCE

Christopher Suazo looked too fragile and innocent to be in the jungle. But there he was, wearing a pair of torn jogging pants and cradling an M-1 Garand rifle almost as tall as himself. He was only 18 and had managed only three years of schooling when he joined the communists three months ago.

Like many cadres of the New People's Army, the armed wing of the Communist Party of the Philippines, Suazo joined the rebellion because of a perceived injustice.

In March, his father and uncle, both farmers, were killed by the hired guns of a town mayor who is protected by the military, he said.

The mayor's men later hunted Suazo, thinking that he might seek revenge. Human rights groups have time and again cautioned the government that unless the state's security forces respect human rights and the laws of war, the ranks of the communist rebellion that started here 35 years ago will grow. The rebellion is considered by the Philippine military as the biggest threat to national security.

"They are our utmost security concern at present," said Colonel Daniel Lucero, a military spokesman. "We consider them a much bigger threat than the Abu Sayyaf, the Moro Islamic Liberation Front or the Jemaah Islamiyah," he said.

Since September, Suazo has been moving around in the mountains here, always alert for the enemies who lurk in the jungles below but, he says, happy about his decision to join the revolution. "I can only be safe here with the New People's Army. One day I and my family will have justice," he said.

In the foggy camp high up in the mountains of Compostela Valley Province, in the southern Philippines, the communists go about their business: training cadres in military tactics and martial arts, organizing the residents in the plains, helping peasants on their farms, and studying what some called the "evils of U.S. imperialism."

"The U.S. is a brutal enemy. It will not hesitate to use or kill its own people to justify its acts of aggressions all over the world," a guerrilla leader who uses the nom de guerre Richard told a dozen rebels during a class about the U.S.-led invasion of Iraq.

"The U.S. is in cahoots with the Arroyo regime in perpetuating poverty and injustice in this country," Richard added, referring to the Philippine president, Gloria Macapagal Arroyo.

Along with poverty and injustice here, what the rebels call U.S. imperialism is also fueling the revolution. In the party's "basic party course," the topic requires at least one and a half days of discussion.

"U.S. interventionism is even more blatant nowadays," said Rubi del Mundo, a guerrilla spokeswoman.

"It used to just influence the passing of Philippine laws to benefit the business interests of American companies here. Now, the U.S. is directly involved in counterrevolutionary activities," she said, referring to reports of U.S. military personnel going inside communist territory to gather intelligence.

During the administrations of Ferdinand Marcos and Corazon Aquino, the rebels' numbers grew, peaking at more than 25,000 in the mid-80's, according to military estimates.

Because of their growing number, the cadres became overconfident and lax with security and discipline. As a result, military spies penetrated the ranks of the New People's Army. Party officials purged the movement in the late 80's and early 90's, torturing and killing hundreds of their fellow guerrillas suspected of spying for the military.

The purges nearly destroyed the movement. The number of fighters plunged to only a few thousand. The group's guerrilla bases and zones disappeared one after the other. Its popularity among Filipinos plunged.

What saved the communists was a campaign begun by the central committee in 1992 to discipline those behind the purge, in some cases expelling them from the party.

The campaign's main thrust, however, was to bring back to the countryside the guerrillas who had been based in the urban areas.

It worked. The New People's Army, according to the party, now has 128 guerrilla fronts in 8,000 villages, or 20 percent of all villages in the country. The military estimates the rebels' strength at about 10,000.

In many parts of the country, the party functions as the government, providing services such as education, health and basic livelihood in areas the mainstream government cannot reach.

Although the government and the communists have been engaged in peace negotiations since the Aquino administration, little progress has been made. In the meantime, the fighting in the countryside continues. Hardly a week goes by without news of two or three firefights.

The government's response to the growth of the communist movement has mainly been force, often targeting civilians considered sympathetic to the rebels. Extrajudicial killings by the military have became common.

People are perplexed by the rebirth of the communists here in spite of the downfall of communist and socialist states in many parts of the world. But some say it would be a mistake to conclude that this revolution is fueled mainly by the communist ideology.

"There is so much injustice, so much despair in this country that people, particularly the poor and powerless, are naturally drawn to those who they think can protect them," said Representative Joel Virador, a member of Congress who formerly worked for a human rights group.

Lucero, the military spokesman, said checking the growth of the movement had become even more difficult because the rebels operate above ground, through legal organizations. The military had previously tagged some political parties led by former rebels, some of whom are now in Congress, as communist fronts. Two weeks ago, it said communists had infiltrated government agencies, including the Philippine Information Agency.

But the war is still confined to the countryside, fought by guerrillas such as Suazo and Jim, a 27-year-old former seminarian who has been in the mountains since 1996.

"I believe the movement has a clear direction, that its victory is inevitable, that the future is bright," Jim said. "The more I see the suffering of the people, the more I am convinced of the justness of this cause." Jim's wife, his mother, his four siblings and an uncle are also guerrillas. They joined the movement after Jim's father, a union activist, was abducted by the military during the Marcos years. He has never been found.

SIGNIFICANCE

The Philippines government has played a significant role in fighting terrorism in the region since the attacks on the U.S. World Trade Center in 2001. Following its election to power in 2001, Arroyo's government established an Inter-Agency Task Force Against International Terrorism, intended to coordinate intelligence operations and identify suspected terrorist cells based in the Philippines. In 2002, the government initiated a regional coalition in the fight against terrorism among fellow Association of Southeast Asia Nations (ASEAN) members to facilitate exchange of intelligence information. The Philippines' efforts in fighting terrorism have been rewarded by the U.S. in the form of $92.3 million in military equipment, specifically intended for use in fighting local insurgents as well as in fighting international terrorism.

In 2005, there were reported to be ongoing clashes between government troops and communist rebels. The Arroyo government, however, predicted that the NPA would be wiped out within six to ten years.

Some observers have questioned the classification of the New People's Army as a terrorist group. Although its activities over the years have been characteristic of terrorism, the Philippines government has allegedly retaliated with similar state-sponsored violence and killings.

Some observers have asserted that, over time, the CPP has increasingly moved towards involvement in the democratic political process to achieve its revolutionary aims, and many of the groups associated with the party contested the 2001 elections. However, the NDF pulled out of Norwegian-brokered peace talks scheduled to take place in Oslo in August 2004 in protest of the U.S. and E.U. renewing the classification of the CPP/NPA as terrorist organizations.

The U.S. collaboration with the Philippine government in the fight against terrorism enables it to retain a strong presence in Southeast Asia. This is seen as important by the U.S. due to reported al-Qaeda activities in the region, and particular concerns that the southern Philippines is one of al-Qaeda's operational hubs. The country has two known, significant, militant Isalmist groups that conduct terrorist activities and are thought to be linked with al-Qaeda: the Abu Sayyaf Group (ASG) and the Moro Islamic Liberation Front (MILF).

FURTHER RESOURCES

Journal articles

Banlaoi, Rommel C. "The role of Philippine-American relations in the global campaign against terrorism: implications for regional security." *Contemporary Southeast Asia*. August 1, 2002.

Rivera, Temario C. "Transition pathways and democratic consolidation in post-Marcos Philippines." *Contemporary Southeast Asia*. December 1, 2002.

3 | Insurgent Terrorism

Introduction to Insurgent Terrorism

Insurgent terrorism is violence perpetrated by those who seek to challenge or depose existing social or political structures. Insurgent terrorists may have diverse motives and goals, usually not as formal as those of separatist terrorists, but are unified to the extent that they oppose established authority, such as a government or occupation force.

The editors acknowledge that the terms insurgent and insurgency have political connotations, and the editors assert that the terms are used as neutrally as possible within this book. The Iraqi insurgency is addressed in this chapter of the book because coalition forces and the international media have adopted the term insurgency to describe terrorist activities in the nation since the declared end of major combat operations in 2003. Separatist terrorism, including anti-colonial terrorism, can fall into the category of insurgent terrorism, however, the editors have chosen to emphasize these groups in their own chapter.

Some may argue that the terms insurgent and insurgency imply illegitimacy of cause. No judgment is made here about the motivations of various insurgent groups. However, means of achieving insurgent aims that employ violence, are intended to instill fear, and are directed at unengaged civilian targets fit within the rubric of terrorism—acts unjustifiable by ideology. The editors leave history to judge the ends of insurgent and separatist groups, conceding that changes in politics, society, and morals influence the ultimate characterization of current events.

History often changes the light in which insurgent terrorist events are cast. For example, during the first half of the nineteenth century, the social and political status quo in many parts of the United States included the legality of slavery. Abolitionists, those who advocated that slavery be abolished, primarily relied on peaceful strategies to assert their cause. Militant abolitionists, however, asserted that the evils of slavery were so great that any means necessary should be taken to end the practice. The practice of slavery is now widely regarded as wholly wrong. However, at the time of John Brown and Nat Turner's raids from the 1830s to the early 1860s, the practice of slavery was still the subject of debate. In states where slavery was legal, and abolitionist sentiment weak, many viewed the raids as illegal acts of insurgent violence intended to scare slave owners and rouse slaves to revolt. Even in states where slavery was outlawed and abolitionist sentiment strong, many were critical of the violence against civilians employed by radical abolitionists. The question of how to best characterize these events remains complex. Slavery in the United States was unequivocally a despicable practice. Yet, if the means are divorced from the end, the murder of slave owners, the destruction of personal property such as the burning of homes and crops, and the execution of insurgents without trial can all be viewed as a cycle of terrorism.

"Disasters of War"

Spanish Insurgents Successfully Employ Terrorism Against Napoleonic Domination.

Etchings

By: Francisco José Goya y Lucientes

Date: Created 1810; first published 1863.

Source: Etchings entitled *Fatales consequencias de la sangrieta Guerra en España con Buonaparte. Y Otros Caprichos Enfáticos"* (*Fatal Consequences of the Bloody War in Spain with Bonaparte. And Other Caprices*). San Fernando: Royal Academy of Fine Arts, 1863. The series became popularly known as *Disasters of War*.

About the Author: Francisco José Goya y Lucientes was born in the village of Fuendetodos, near Saragossa, Spain, on March 30, 1746. He began his career as an artist in the

1770s when he completed a series of frescoes for the Royal Academy, created designs for the Madrid textile industry, and painted portraits of wealthy patrons. In 1789, he rose to the prestigious position of court painter to King Carlos IV. An illness that struck in 1792 left him completely deaf. From 1808 to 1813, Goya was the official court painter to Spanish King Joseph Bonaparte. Goya died on April 16, 1828, after pioneering the expression of uninhibited, realistic actions and emotions in his paintings, a style that was not to come to fruition until the late nineteenth century. Goya's works hang in major art museums throughout the world.

INTRODUCTION

By the early years of the nineteenth century, Emperor Napoleon Bonaparte had extended French dominance over much of Europe. He had absorbed Belgium, the Netherlands, and large portions of Italy into the French Empire, and satellite states included Spain, Switzerland, much of modern-day Germany,

PRIMARY SOURCE

Fatales Consequencias de la Sangrieta Guerra en España con Buonaparte. Y Otros Caprichos Enfáticos. (Fatal Consequences of the Bloody War in Spain with Bonaparte. And Other Caprices) #18 "Bury them and keep quiet."
© BURSTEIN COLLECTION/CORBIS

PRIMARY SOURCE

***Fatales Consequencias de la Sangrieta Guerra en España con Buonaparte. Y Otros Caprichos Enfáticos.* (Fatal Consequences of the Bloody War in Spain with Bonaparte. And Other Caprices)** #39 "Great deeds! Against the dead!"

© BURSTEIN COLLECTION/CORBIS

and Poland. Nominal allies included Norway, Denmark, Prussia, and the vast Austrian Empire.

Although a number of states—Russia, Sweden, and Portugal among them—remained hostile to Napoleon, it was Great Britain that posed the chief obstacle to Napoleonic hegemony (dominance of one state over another) over the entire European continent. Because a land invasion of the island nation would be next to impossible, the emperor concluded that the only way to bring Great Britain to heel was through economic warfare. His goal was to use his navy to close off the Continent, deny Great Britain access to markets, ruin its trade and credit, and cause economic unrest as the nation's economy collapsed.

Under the so-called Continental System, the emperor prohibited French allies from trading with Great Britain, which retaliated in 1807 with the

Orders of Council, requiring ships, even those from neutral nations, to put in at British ports and pay tariffs. In turn, Napoleon retaliated by seizing any ship that adhered to the Orders of Council. The leak in the system, however, was smuggling, and many of the major ports of entry for smuggled goods on the Continent were located in Spain.

Unrest had been rife in Spain since the 1795 alliance between Spain and France. Spain's corrupt and highly unpopular Prime Minister, Manuel de Godoy, had had an affair with the queen, and Crown Prince Ferdinand held Godoy in contempt. Napoleon concluded that the only way to put an end to the squabbling between Ferdinand and his royal parents and enforce the Continental System in Spain was through force of arms under the pretext of a planned invasion of hostile Portugal. To pave the way, in 1808 he persuaded

Fatales Consequencias de la Sangrieta Guerra en España con Buonaparte. Y Otros Caprichos Enfáticos. (Fatal Consequences of the Bloody War in Spain with Bonaparte. And Other Caprices) #12 "For this you were born." © BURSTEIN COLLECTION/CORBIS

King Carlos IV and Crown Prince Ferdinand to abdicate and installed his brother Joseph on the throne. Joseph naively believed that as Spain's monarch, and backed initially by 100,000 French troops, he could bring liberal enlightenment to the Iberian Peninsula.

Instead, large numbers of Spanish nationalist insurgents, angered by the loss of their royal family and the presence of a Frenchman on their throne, rose in rebellion. On May 2, 1808, a bloody riot, captured in Goya's painting *The Second of May, 1808*, erupted in Madrid. The French responded with brutal reprisals, also captured in one of Goya's most famous paintings, *The Third of May, 1808*, which depicts a squad of anonymous French soldiers executing a Spanish insurgent, his arms raised in a Christlike gesture.

Thus began a brutal six-year conflict that added the term *guerrilla war*, or "little war" to the lexicon. During this time about 30,000 Spanish insurgents, most of them peasants and Catholic monks led by local nobles and organized into *juntas*, or committees,

harassed and wore down the French troops, even though they were eventually outnumbered ten to one. The campaign was an escalating war of insurgent terrorism, as the insurgents brutally tortured and executed French troops and Spanish collaborators and the French launched equally brutal reprisals, often failing to distinguish combatants from civilians. Goya, as Joseph's official court painter, created an eyewitness account of the horror of the war, which Napoleon referred to as his "Spanish ulcer," in a series of eighty stark etchings known today by the title *Disasters of War*. Three of the etchings, which Goya never lived to see published, are reproduced here.

DISASTERS OF WAR

See primary source images.

SIGNIFICANCE

The Spanish ulcer marked the beginning of the end for Napoleon. Sensing for the first time that he was not invincible, the British seized the opportunity to land an army in Portugal, beginning what became known as the Peninsular War. Between the British army led by the Duke of Wellington and the Spanish insurgents, the French became trapped in a futile six-year war of attrition that, in late 1813, forced them back over the Pyrenees. In 1815 the crown prince assumed the throne of Spain as Ferdinand VII, restoring royalist rule. As the Peninsular War drained the French treasury, Napoleon inexplicably set his sights on Russia, a campaign that proved to be a disaster. In 1814 he was forced to abdicate and sent into exile.

A half century later, Goya's etchings were published for the first time. Rather than capturing the glory and heroism of warfare, they showed viewers the atrocities that were perpetrated on both sides as terrorist tactics ruled.

FURTHER RESOURCES

Books

Goya y Lucientes, Francisco. *The Disasters of War*, edited by Philip Hofer. New York: Dover, 1967.

Hughes, Robert. *Goya*. New York: Knopf, 2003.

Periodicals

Vega, Jesusa. "The Dating and Interpretation of Goya's *Disasters of War*." *Print Quarterly*. 11 (1994): 3–17.

Web sites

Bucksbaum Center for the Arts, Grinnell College. "I Saw It: The Invented Realities of Goya's *Disasters of War*." <http://web.grinnell.edu/faulconergallery/goya/index.htm> (accessed May 16, 2005).

"John Brown's Body"

John Brown and Nat Turner's Raids

Song

By: Anonymous

Date: circa 1860

Source: "John Brown's Body" as published on The *Civil War Music Site*, <http://www.civilwarmusic.net/display_song.php?song=johnbrown> (accessed July 5, 2005).

About the Author: The original author of the song "John Brown's Body" is unknown. During the Civil War, the song was sung primarily by Union supporters. It borrows its melody from the "Battle Hymn of the Republic."

INTRODUCTION

Opposition to slavery in the United States began with the importation of the first slaves to the American colonies. Slave insurrections occurred periodically, but were typically put down quickly and brutally. In the mid-nineteenth century, the debate over slavery became increasingly violent. Both sides engaged in terrorist activity, but Nat Turner and John Brown became the best known anti-slavery terrorists in American history because of the effects of their actions.

Nat Turner (1800–1831) was born into slavery in Virginia. Separated from his mother and then sold away from his wife, Turner turned to Scripture for guidance. In 1825, he had a vision in which white and black spirits engaged in battle as blood flowed in streams. Proclaiming himself a Baptist preacher, Turner described his vision to slave congregations and declared that he had been commissioned by Jesus Christ to act under his direction. In 1828, another vision told Turner to fight against the Serpent. Turner and six followers moved from house to house, killing whites in the early morning of August 22. Turner's group swelled to sixty men before being killed or dispersed by federal troops, militia, and armed landowners. Turner was hanged.

John Brown (1800–1859) grew up in an abolitionist family in Connecticut. In 1855, five of Brown's sons moved to "Bleeding" Kansas where they hoped to establish a free state. Brown joined them. After pro-slavery forces sacked Lawrence, Kansas, Brown and several of his sons murdered five pro-slavery settlers at Pottawatomie Creek. Brown then traveled to Massachusetts to raise support for a plan to liberate slaves. He planned to establish a free state in the southern mountains from where he could attack slave owners and liberate slaves. In 1859, Brown and his sons attacked the army arsenal at Harper's Ferry. The Brown forces killed five men, including an African American, while suffering ten deaths. Brown, found guilty of murder, treason, and conspiring with slaves to rebel, was hanged. His execution made him a martyr to the abolitionist cause.

PRIMARY SOURCE

John Brown's body lies a-mouldering in the grave,
John Brown's body lies a-mouldering in the grave,
John Brown's body lies a-mouldering in the grave,
But his soul goes marching on.

(Chorus)
Glory, glory, hallelujah,
Glory, glory, hallelujah,
Glory, glory, hallelujah,
His soul goes marching on.

He's gone to be a soldier in the Army of the Lord,
He's gone to be a soldier in the Army of the Lord,
He's gone to be a soldier in the Army of the Lord,
His soul goes marching on.
(Chorus)

John Brown's knapsack is strapped upon his back,
John Brown's knapsack is strapped upon his back,
John Brown's knapsack is strapped upon his back,
His soul goes marching on.
(Chorus)

John Brown died that the slaves might be free,
John Brown died that the slaves might be free,
John Brown died that the slaves might be free,
But his soul goes marching on.
(Chorus)

The stars above in Heaven now are looking kindly down,
The stars above in Heaven now are looking kindly down,
The stars above in Heaven now are looking kindly down,
On the grave of old John Brown.
(Chorus)

SIGNIFICANCE

Nat Turner's insurrection shocked and frightened slave owners, especially in the South. As a result of the fear generated by the violence, most Southern states eventually passed strict laws to police their slave populations and prevent insurrections. Slaves were forbidden to hold religious services unless such services were led by a white preacher, a man who would typically stress Biblical prohibitions against killing. Slaves were banned from learning to read and write and from using guns. In the years after 1831, Southern defenders of slavery became much more vocal and attacks against abolitionists rose dramatically. Assuming that abolitionism had somehow caused the uprising, most Southerners abandoned the cause of emancipation with Virginia holding its last serious debate on ending slavery in 1832.

Brown considered slavery so entrenched in the U.S. that only violent revolution could eradicate it. His raid emphasized that slavery was a key element in the sectional crisis that fueled the secession of southern states. Brown's attack on Harper's Ferry is often called the opening shot of the Civil War.

On September 22, 1862, President Abraham Lincoln drafted the Emancipation Proclamation, freeing all slaves in the United States (Union) and all territories held by Union forces. He signed the declaration on January 1, 1863. When the Civil War ended with the reunification of the states, the addition of the 13th and 14th amendments of the U.S. Constitution codified the abolition of slavery in the United States and granted rights of citizenship to former slaves.

FURTHER RESOURCES

Books

French, Scot. *The Rebellious Slave: Nat Turner in American Memory*. Boston: Houghton Mifflin, 2004.

Greenberg, Kenneth S. *Nat Turner: A Slave Rebellion in History and Memory*. New York: Oxford University Press, 2003.

Reynolds, David S. *John Brown, Abolitionist: The Man Who Killed Slavery, Sparked the Civil War, and Seeded Civil Rights*. New York: Alfred A. Knopf, 2005.

Rossbach, Jeffery S. *Ambivalent Conspirators: John Brown, the Secret Six, and a Theory of Black Political Violence*. New York: Brookings Institution Press, 2001.

Web sites

The Civil War Music Site. "John Brown's Body." <http://www.civilwarmusic.net/display_song.php?song=johnbrown> (accessed July 5, 2005).

Assassination of President Lincoln

Charge and Specification of the Co-conspirators

Indictment

By: Joseph Holt

Date: May 9, 1865

Source: Charge and Specification for the indictment of John Wilkes Booth's co-conspirators in the assassination of President Abraham Lincoln, printed in *Assassination of President Lincoln: And the Trial of the Conspirators David E. Herold, Mary E. Surratt, Lewis Payne, George A. Atzerodt, Edward Spangler, Samuel A. Mudd, Samuel Arnold, Michael O'Laughlin*, (Cincinnati, OH: Moore, Wilstach and Baldwin), 1865. The Charge and Specification was written by United States Army Brigadier General Joseph Holt.

About the Author: The judge advocate general for the trial of the co-conspirators in the assassination of Abraham Lincoln was U. S. Army Brigadier General Joseph Holt. Additionally, nine officers were appointed to the commission. Holt also appointed two special judge advocates.

INTRODUCTION

On the evening of April 14, 1865, Abraham Lincoln, the sixteenth president of the United States, was assassinated while attending a performance of *Our American Cousin* at Ford's Theatre in Washington, D.C. As he sat in his box, an actor named John Wilkes Booth crept into the theater, shot the president, then leaped to the stage and fled. The wounded president was carried to a house across the street, where he died the following morning. Meanwhile, Booth escaped to the Maryland and Virginia countryside, but Union troops shot him to death near Port Royal, Virginia, on the morning of April 26.

Some of Booth's alleged co-conspirators, named in the accompanying indictment, were tried for their part in a larger plot to kill other leaders, including the Vice-President and Secretary of War. Others were indicted and tried for simply rendering aid to the fleeing conspirators. Samuel Mudd, mentioned in the Charge and Specification as the Maryland doctor, subsequently treated the leg Booth broke when he jumped to the stage.

The following document is the "Charge and Specification"—that is, the indictment—in the military trial of John Wilkes Booth's co-conspirators for the assassination of President Abraham Lincoln. Benn Pittman served as chief stenographic reporter, and recorded the trial of the Lincoln assassination conspirators.

PRIMARY SOURCE

CHARGE AND SPECIFICATION
AGAINST
DAVID E. HEROLD, GEORGE A. ATZERODT,
LEWIS PAYNE,

An artist's interpretation of the scene in Ford's Theater immediately after the assassination of President Abraham Lincoln. AP/WIDE WORLD PHOTOS

MICHAEL O'LAUGHLIN, EDWARD SPANGLER,
SAMUEL ARNOLD, MARY E. SURRATT,
AND
SAMUEL A. MUDD

Charge: For maliciously, unlawfully, and traitorously, and in aid of the existing armed rebellion against the United States of America, on or before the 6th day of March, A.D. 1865, and on divers other days between that day and the 15th day of April, A.D. 1865, combining, confederating, and conspiring together with one John H. Surratt, John Wilkes Booth, Jefferson Davis, George N. Sanders, Beverly Tucker, Jacob Thompson, William C. Cleary, Clement C. Clay, George Harper, George Young, and others unknown, to kill and murder, within the Military Department of Washington, and within the fortified and intrenched lines thereof, Abraham Lincoln, late, and at the time of said combining, confederating, and conspiring, President of the United States of America, and Commander-in-Chief of the Army and Navy thereof; Andrew Johnson, now Vice-President of the United States aforesaid; William H. Seward, Secretary of State of the United States aforesaid; and Ulysses S. Grant, Lieutenant-General of the Army of the United States aforesaid, then in command of the Armies of the United States, under the direction of the said Abraham Lincoln; and in pursuance of in prosecuting said malicious, unlawful and traitorous conspiracy aforesaid, and in aid of the said rebellion, afterward, to wit, on the 14th day of April, A.D. 1865, within the Military Department of Washington, aforesaid, and within the fortified and intrenched lines of said Military Department, together with said John Wilkes Booth and John H. Surratt, maliciously, unlawfully, and traitorously murdering the said Abraham Lincoln, then President of the United States and Commander-in-Chief of the Army and Navies of the United States, as aforesaid; and maliciously, unlawfully, and traitorously assaulting, with intent to kill and murder, the said William H. Seward, then Secretary of State of the United States, as aforesaid; and lying in wait with intent maliciously, unlawfully, and traitorously to kill and murder the said Andrew Johnson, then being Vice-President of the United States; and the said Ulysses S. Grant, then being Lieutenant-General, and in command of the Armies of the United States, as aforesaid.

Specification: In this: that they, the said David E. Herold, Edward Spangler, Lewis Payne, Michael O'Laughlin, Samuel Arnold, Mary E. Surratt, George A. Atzerodt, and Samuel A. Mudd, together with the said John H. Surratt and John Wilkes Booth, incited and encouraged thereunto by Jefferson Davis, George N. Sanders, Beverly Tucker, Jacob Thompson, William C. Cleary, Clement C. Clay, George Harper, George Young, and others unknown, citizens of the United States aforesaid, and who were then engaged in armed rebellion against the United States of America, within the limits thereof, did, in aid of said rebellion, on or before the 6th day of March, A.D. 1865, and on divers other days and times between that day and the 15th day of April, A.D. 1865, combine, confederate, and conspire together, at Washington City, within the Military Department of Washington, and within the intrenched fortifications and military lines of the United States, there being, unlawfully, maliciously, and traitorously to kill and murder Abraham Lincoln, then President of the United States aforesaid, and Commander-in-Chief of the Army and Navy thereof; and unlawfully, maliciously, and traitorously to kill and murder Andrew Johnson, now Vice-President of the said United States, upon whom, on the death of said Abraham Lincoln, after the fourth day of March, A.D. 1865, the office of President of the said United States, and Commander-in-Chief of the Army and Navy thereof, would devolve; and to unlawfully, maliciously, and traitorously kill and murder Ulysses S. Grant, then Lieutenant-General, and, under the direction of the said Abraham Lincoln, in command of the Armies of the United States, aforesaid; and unlawfully, maliciously, and traitorously kill and murder William H. Seward, then Secretary of the United States aforesaid, whose duty it was, by law, upon the death of said President and Vice-President of the United States aforesaid, to cause an election to be held for electors of President of the United States: the conspirators aforesaid designing and intending, by the killing and murder of the said Abraham Lincoln, Andrew Johnson, Ulysses S. Grant, and William H. Seward, as aforesaid to deprive the Army and Navy of the said United States of a constitutional Commander-in-Chief; and to deprive the Armies of the United States of their lawful commander; and to prevent a lawful election of President and Vice-President of the United States aforesaid; and by the means aforesaid to aid and comfort the insurgents engaged in armed rebellion against the said United States, as aforesaid, and thereby to aid in the subversion and overthrow of the Constitution and laws of said United States.

And being so combined, confederated, and conspiring together in the prosecution of said unlawful and traitorous conspiracy, on the night of the 14th day of April, A.D. 1865, at the hour of about 10 o'clock and 15 minutes P.M., at Ford's Theater, on Tenth Street, in the City of Washington, and within the military department and military lines aforesaid, John Wilkes Booth, one of the conspirators aforesaid, in pursuance of said unlawful and traitorous conspiracy, did, then and there, unlawfully, maliciously, and traitorously, and with intent to kill and murder the said Abraham Lincoln, discharge a pistol then held in the hands of him, the said Booth, the same being then loaded with powder and a leaden ball, against and upon the left and posterior side of the head of said Abraham Lincoln; and did thereby, then and there, inflict upon him, the said Abraham Lincoln, then President of the said United States, and Commander-in-Chief of the Army and Navy thereof, a mortal wound, whereof, afterward, to-wit, on the 15th day of April, A.D. 1865, at Washington City aforesaid, the said Abraham Lincoln died; and thereby, then and there, and in pursuance of said conspiracy, the said defendants, and the said John Wilkes Booth and John H. Surratt did unlawfully, traitorously, and maliciously, and with the intent to aid the rebellion, as aforesaid, kill and murder the said Abraham Lincoln, President of the United States, as aforesaid.

And in further prosecution of the unlawful and traitorous conspiracy aforesaid, and of the murderous and traitorous intent of said conspiracy, the said Edward Spangler, on said 14th day of April, A.D. 1865, at about the same hour of that day, as aforesaid, within said military department and the military lines aforesaid, did aid and assist the said John Wilkes Booth to obtain entrance to the box in said theater, in which said Abraham Lincoln was sitting at the time he was assaulted and shot, as aforesaid, by John Wilkes Booth; and also did, then and there, aid said Booth in barring and obstructing the door of the box of said theater, so as to hinder and prevent any assistance to or rescue of the said Abraham Lincoln against the murderous assault of the said John Wilkes Booth; and did aid and abet him in making his escape after the said Abraham Lincoln had been murdered in manner aforesaid.

And in further prosecution of said unlawful, murderous and traitorous conspiracy, and in pursuance thereof, and with the intent as aforesaid, the said David E. Herold did, on the night of the 14th of April, A.D. 1865, within the military department and military lines aforesaid, aid, abet, and assist the said John Wilkes Booth in the killing and murder of the said Abraham Lincoln, and did, then and there, aid and abet and assist him, the said John Wilkes Booth, in attempting to escape through the military lines aforesaid, and did accompany and assist the said John Wilkes Booth in attempting to conceal himself and escape from justice, after killing and murdering said Abraham Lincoln as aforesaid.

And in further prosecution of said unlawful and traitorous conspiracy, and of the intent thereof, as aforesaid, the said Lewis Payne did, on the same night of the 14th day of April, A.D. 1865, about the same hour of 10 o'clock and 15 minutes P.M., at the City of Washington, and within the military department and the military lines aforesaid, unlawfully and maliciously make an assault upon the said William H. Seward, Secretary of State, as aforesaid, in the dwelling-house and bed-chamber of him, the said William H. Seward, and the said Payne did, then and there, with a large knife held in his hand, unlawfully, traitorously, and in pursuance of said conspiracy, strike, stab, cut, and attempt to kill and murder the said William H. Seward, and did thereby, then and there, with intent aforesaid, with said knife, inflict upon the face and throat of the said William H. Seward divers grievous wounds. And the said Lewis Payne, in further

prosecution of said conspiracy, at the same time and place last aforesaid, did attempt, with the knife aforesaid, and a pistol held in his hand, to kill and murder Frederick W. Seward, Augustus H. Seward, Emrick W. Hansell, and George F. Robinson, who were then striving to protect and rescue the said William H. Seward from murder by the said Lewis Payne, and did, then and there, with said knife and pistol held in his hands, inflict upon the head of said Frederick W. Seward, and upon the persons of said Augustus H. Seward, Emrick W. Hansell, and George F. Robinson, divers grievous and dangerous wounds, with intent, then and there, to kill and murder the said Frederick W. Seward, Augustus H. Seward, Emrick W. Hansell, and George F. Robinson.

And in further prosecution of said conspiracy and its traitorous and murderous designs, the said George A. Atzerodt did, on the night of the 14th of April, A.D. 1865, at about the same hour of the night aforesaid, within the military department and the military lines aforesaid, lie in wait for Andrew Johnson, then Vice-President of the United States aforesaid, with the intent unlawfully and maliciously to kill and murder him, the said Andrew Johnson.

And in the further prosecution of the conspiracy aforesaid, and of its murderous and treasonable purposes aforesaid, on the nights of the 13th and 14th of April, A.D. 1865, at Washington City, and within the military department and military lines aforesaid, the said Michael O'Laughlin did, then and there, lie in wait for Ulysses S. Grant, then Lieutenant-General and Commander of the Armies of the United States, as aforesaid, with intent, then and there, to kill and murder the said Ulysses S. Grant.

And in further prosecution of said conspiracy, the said Samuel Arnold did, within the military department and the military lines aforesaid, on or before the 6th day of March A.D. 1865, and on divers other days and times between that day and the 15th day of April, A.D. 1865, combine, conspire with, and aid, counsel, abet, comfort, and support, the said John Wilkes Booth, Lewis Payne, George A. Atzerodt, Michael O'Laughlin, and their confederates in said unlawful, murderous, and traitorous conspiracy, and in the execution thereof, as aforesaid.

And in further prosecution of said conspiracy, Mary E. Surratt did, at Washington City, and within the military department and military lines aforesaid, on or before the 6th day of March, A.D. 1865, and on divers other days and times between that day and the 20th day of April, A.D. 1865, receive, entertain, harbor, and conceal, aid and assist the said John Wilkes Booth, David E. Herold, Lewis Payne, John H. Surratt, Michael O'Laughlin, George A. Atzerodt, Samuel Arnold, and their confederates, with the knowledge of the murderous and traitorous conspiracy aforesaid, and with the intent to aid, abet, and assist them in execution thereof, and in escaping from justice after the murder of the said Abraham Lincoln, as aforesaid.

And in further prosecution of said conspiracy, the said Samuel A. Mudd did, at Washington City, and within the military department and military lines aforesaid, on or before the 6th day of March, A.D. 1865, and on divers other days and times between that day and the 20th day of April, A.D. 1865, advise, encourage, receive, entertain, harbor, and conceal, aid and assist the said John Wilkes Booth, David E. Herold, Lewis Payne, John H. Surratt, Michael O'Laughlin, George A. Atzerodt, Mary E. Surratt, and Samuel Arnold, and their confederates, with knowledge of the murderous and traitorous conspiracy aforesaid, and with the intent to aid, abet, and assist them in the execution thereof, and in escaping from justice after the murder of the said Abraham Lincoln, in pursuance of said conspiracy in manner aforesaid.

By order of the President of the United States.

J. Holt,
Judge Advocate General

SIGNIFICANCE

Charged with conspiracy before a special military court on May 9, 1865, that court tried and found guilty the named conspirators. The major conspirators—David E. Herold, George A. Atzerodt, Lewis Payne, and Mary E. Surratt—were hanged on July 7. The others were sentenced to prison, though Lincoln's successor, Andrew Johnson, pardoned them in 1869.

In addition to naming the conspirators who were directly involved with Booth, the indictment mentions the leaders of the Confederacy, including President Jefferson Davis. In the eyes of Northern authorities, the assassination of Lincoln was not the political terrorism of an isolated band of conspirators; it was an act of war for which the South was guilty. For this reason, the defendants were tried before a military tribunal as enemy agents rather than in a civilian court. Further, the trial was conducted in a highly irregular fashion. The defendants were never allowed to speak in their own defense. Defense objections were almost always overruled. Witnesses for the prosecution were coached. One defense attorney was accused of disloyalty to the Union. One member of the tribunal stated openly that he knew Mudd was guilty because of the shapes of the bumps on Mudd's head. Because of these actions, the major conspirators went to their deaths without telling any details of what they knew.

The question that has haunted historians is whether Booth simply manipulated his co-conspirators into an act of political terrorism or whether his act was directed by Confederate leaders in a last-ditch effort to win the Civil War by destabilizing the North.

Throughout the Civil War, Lincoln had been the target of numerous assassination and kidnapping attempts. Pro-slavery forces in the South, and even anti-Lincoln "Copperheads" in the North, vowed repeatedly to kill him. On one occasion, a woman dressed as a widow approached him and attempted to infect him with smallpox by kissing him. In 1864, a New York newspaper printed a letter that described an elaborate plot to kill Lincoln. Union spies turned up a Confederate agent named Thomas N. Conrad whose mission was to abduct the president. A year before Lincoln's death, a sniper took a shot at him near the Soldiers' Home in the capital, leaving a hole in the president's stovepipe hat. In December, 1864, a Selma, Alabama, newspaper printed a letter from "X" offering to kill the president for a million dollars. Booth had twice tried to kidnap the president, but in each case his effort was thwarted by the president's last-second change of plans.

In this context, some historians assert that Booth may have been a Confederate agent and saboteur. That he was a Southern sympathizer was well known, but as a prominent actor, he was able to travel freely in the North. Booth may have been involved with the so-called Gray Underground, the Confederate secret service based in Montreal, Canada, where the South's Canadian Cabinet directed espionage operations against the North from just over the border. In cities where Booth played onstage, he left behind a trail of sabotage. In late 1864, for example, he was playing in New York City when, on the night of November 25, Southern agents set fire to a number of large hotels, an act of terrorism directed by the Canadian Cabinet, whose members Booth had met with just days before.

Booth's death, coupled with the destruction of the Confederacy's records when its capital, Richmond, Virginia, fell, leaves gaps in the historical record that historians may never fill. What is proven, however, is that in the aftermath of the Lincoln assassination the North was out for vengeance and ill-disposed to the more moderate reconstruction policies toward the South once advocated by Lincoln.

FURTHER RESOURCES
Books

O'Neal, Michael. *The Assassination of Abraham Lincoln.* San Diego, CA: Greenhaven Press, 1991.

Web sites

Surratt House Museum. "Proceedings of the Conspiracy Trial." <http://www.surratt.org/su_docs.html> (accessed May 16, 2005).

Witnesses and Victims Recount Bombing

Bombing of U.S. Embassy in Beirut

News article

By: Terry A. Anderson

Date: April 23, 1983

Source: The Associated Press article "Witnesses and Victims Recount Bombing of U.S. Embassy in Beirut."

About the Author: Terry A. Anderson (1947–) was a chief Middle East correspondent for The Associated Press when, in 1983, he was kidnapped by a group of Hezbollah Shiite Muslims. He was eventually held for 2,454 days before being released. After being freed, Anderson actively publicized the right for freedom of the press, taught courses at Ohio University's E.W. Scripps School of Journalism and Columbia University's Graduate School of Journalism, appeared on various radio and television shows as guest and host, and wrote the best-selling book *Den of Lions* that was based on his experiences as a captive.

INTRODUCTION

The United States embassy in Beirut, Lebanon was established in 1952 due to increased U.S. military and economic interests in the region. Beginning in 1975, the functions of the U.S. embassy were reduced, however, due to security concerns from Lebanon's Civil War. By 1982, the Lebanese government asked the U.S. government to establish a military peace-keeping force in Beirut that would help control friction between Muslims and Christians after Israel's invasion into Lebanon. The Muslim side, however, regarded U.S. soldiers as their enemies and frequently attacked them.

One major incident occurred at about 1:00 P.M. on April 18, 1983. The Hezbollah Islamic terrorists, a part of the Islamic Jihad, drove a truck carrying explosives under the front entranceway of the seven-story U.S. embassy. The suicide terrorists then exploded the vehicle—killing sixty-three people and injuring hundreds of others. Among the dead were eighteen Americans including Corporal Robert V. McMaugh, an embassy guard; Janet Lee Stevens, a journalist; several U.S. State Department officials and Army trainers; and all of the Middle East members of the Central Intelligence Agency (CIA), including the CIA's Middle East director.

U.S. Marines are seen guarding the wrecked U.S. Embassy annex in East Beirut, Lebanon, on Sept. 22, 1984. AP/WIDE WORLD PHOTOS

The Hezbollah (or Party of God) is an Islamist terrorist organization that was formed by Lebanese Shiite Muslims in 1982 during the Lebanese Civil War in order to counter the Israeli invasion of Lebanon and to free the areas that were militarily occupied by Israel as a result of the war. The Hezbollah expanded its numbers, primarily with military support from Syria and Iran.

The terrorists reported that their attack on the embassy was in response to the intervention of the United States into the Lebanese Civil War. Specifically, their actions were inspired by the actions of the U.S. military in trying to restore peace and establish a governing body at the Shatilla and Sabra refugee camps after Lebanese and Israeli troops killed Palestinians.

PRIMARY SOURCE

Two Lebanese men were among the first to notice it—a black pickup truck driven by a man in a leather jacket. They watched it crash through a barricade and then erupt into a thunderous explosion. A normal, routine day at the U.S.

Embassy in Beirut became a nightmare of death and horror. Here is how it was before and after it happened.

The wide, pleasant promenade along the edge of the Mediterranean was quiet. A few dozen people idled along or sat on the concrete benches across from the U.S. Embassy in the grey, cool lunch hour.

Some of the Embassy's recently enlarged staff had gone to lunch in nearby coffee shops and restaurants. Others were in the basement cafeteria. But most were still in their offices, running late for lunch or eating at their desks.

As people recounted it later, Monday, April 18, seemed to be a quiet, routine day at the United States Embassy in Beirut, a city that has seen war and death almost constantly since 1976.

Two Lebanese men standing across the street, waiting for friends who were applying for U.S. visas, saw a black pickup truck and its driver in a leather jacket speeding up the Embassy driveway. It crashed through a barricade.

On the top floor of the Embassy, U.S. Ambassador Robert Dillon was busy on the telephone in his office, simultaneously trying to change into a T-shirt to take a lunch-hour jog.

Dundas McCullough, a consular officer, was behind in his schedule because of the crush of visa applicants in the first-floor visa section in the north wing. Five to ten people were still waiting.

The two men watching from across the street saw the black pickup truck careening around the arc of the Embassy driveway.

On the fifth floor, consular officer Lisa Piasik, 26, of Dover, Del., had just arrived from her first-floor office for her weekly Arabic lesson.

Political officer Ryan Crocker and his wife and secretary, Christine, of Spokane, Wash., were at their desks on the fourth floor. Ryan was editing a telegram; Christine was finishing a cheeseburger.

In the third-floor information office, press officer John Reid of Staunton, Va., was working on a report for Washington.

Marine Lance Cpl. Robert McMaugh, 21, of Manassas, Va., was on duty at the main entrance, standing in a bulletproof glass booth in the lobby, behind a waist-high counter. Armed with a pistol, he was checking people into and out of the building, logging their names in a book.

The pickup truck had reached the front overhang of the Embassy.

It was 1:05 P.M. The truck exploded in a thundering blast of fire and smoke.

The front half of the Embassy's center wing disintegrated, and parts of seven floors collapsing onto the main entrance and lobby, crushing Lance Cpl. McMaugh and others.

Front walls of the bottom offices in the east wing and some in the west wing were blown in. Windows and doors throughout the building exploded in showers of glass and shards and pieces of wood.

More than a dozen cars parked in front of the building, in a vacant lot across the street and on the boulevard were smashed and thrown aside. Some burst into flames.

The driver of a Lebanese army personnel carrier panicked or miscalculated, crashing the heavy vehicle through the guardrail along the boulevard. It fell upside down into the edge of the Mediterranean Sea.

At last count by the Embassy, 47 people were killed. Embassy officials listed 17 of them as Americans—three U.S. Army personnel, Marine Cpl. McMaugh, a visiting freelance journalist and the rest Embassy staffers. The remaining 30 were Lebanese who worked in the Embassy. The Embassy count, however, does not include pedestrians and motorists passing by. Lebanese police put the total number of dead at 52, and two more Lebanese victims' bodies were recovered Saturday.

Judging by the damage to the building, the U.S. Central Intelligence Agency suffered huge material losses in addition to a human toll that included at least one known CIA official.

While senior Embassy officials refused to comment on the exact location of CIA offices in the building, U.S. sources plus a general knowledge of the building indicate most if not all offices were in the grotesque tangle of concrete and plaster that broke off the front of the building and pan caked into the floors below.

CIA offices are said to have been on the Embassy's seventh floor, flanked by the communications room and the Defense Department offices, directly under the rooms housing the Marine guards and the ambassador's office.

In the Embassy itself, most survivors said they first heard a sound like thunder and rushing wind. Then came the blast.

"I realized my chin was on the counter and there was a big flash of light in front of me," said McCullough, the 25-year-old consular officer from Berkeley, Calif., whose office was just a few dozen yards from the explosion.

"Then the wall separating the file room from the waiting room fell on me and my interpreter.

"There was complete darkness, lots of dust. I struggled to stand erect. I thought what might kill me, aside from the explosion, was suffocation," he said a few days later, his voice trembling slightly.

When the air cleared, "there just wasn't much left," McCullough said.

The front part of the east wing, where his office was, had been blown open. "I had to make sure I didn't step off the edge."

A dead woman was buried in rubble. A badly wounded man was pinned down by a filing cabinet. As McCullough helped the man up, a Marine in a gas mask appeared in the hole where the stairs had been—part of the rescue crew that was gathering. What happened to the others in McCullough's office is unknown.

Stairs were still intact, all the way to the top floors. In smoke and dust so thick they could not see the people beside them, Embassy staffers made their way down, coughing, crying and helping the injured who could not walk. Marine guards helped them out a door on the back of the building.

Ambassador Dillon was pinned beneath rubble. His aide and his deputy used the staff of an American flag to pry him out and found him unhurt except for small cuts.

Both side wings in the front of the building were a mass of flames, spewing out greasy black smoke.

Students from the American University of Beirut, which is immediately behind the Embassy, were among the first to arrive. They and others began pulling people out of the carnage. Taxi drivers on the rubble-littered corniche stopped and the wounded were loaded into their vehicles and rushed to the university's hospital.

Most of the bodies were found in these areas, in the lobby and the basement cafeteria.

The grim search began. Most of the injured were found in minutes. The last live person was dragged out of the wreckage at 5 P.M., four hours after the blast.

"He was very glad to see us," commented one Red Cross worker.

Marines in the cordon around the building picked up the American flag from the ground and raised it on the flag pole, which survived the explosion.

The bodies continued to be found—for more than four days—as the tons of debris were slowly and carefully searched.

The Crockers, who had been on the fourth floor, and Miss Piasik, on the fifth for her Arabic lesson, were not injured, except for a few small cuts from flying debris.

Press officer Reid, pinned under a wall of his office before he managed to extricate himself, escaped with dozens of small cuts and bruises.

Four days after the bombing, the 43-year-old Reid looked up at the place where his office had been and marveled that he was still alive.

"You see where the searchlight has been put on the balcony? That's Maggie and Beth's office," he said, referring

to his administrative assistant, Beth Samuels, and his secretary, Maggie Tin, neither of whom was seriously injured.

"Then that next balcony, just behind that is the front of my office. And the next one that's gone is the back half of my office. That's where I was."

Cpl. McMaugh's body was recovered Thursday. Fellow Marines, refusing to allow Lebanese rescue workers near it, carefully draped it in an American flag and carried it away.

SIGNIFICANCE

The suicide bombing of the United States embassy in Beirut, Lebanon—thought to be the first suicide bombing experience of the United States—was considered, at the date of its occurrence, the most fatal attack of American personnel on a U.S. diplomatic facility. The U.S. government eventually moved the embassy to Awkar, which is located north of Beirut. However, in September 1984, a second bombing occurred at the new embassy site, killing eleven people. One month later—on October 23—a terrorist bombing occurred at a U.S. Marine barrack in Beirut, causing the death of 241 Americans. The embassy was closed that same month and all U.S. personnel were evacuated.

In the 1990s, the United States began to reestablish itself in Lebanon. After the embassy was reopened in 1990, American citizens were allowed to return to Lebanon in 1997, and services and positions within the embassy were steadily expanded in 1999.

In the post-September 11th era, United States government officials consider the two events—the Beirut embassy and Marine barrack bombings—the beginning of major, concerted attacks by Islamic groups against American facilities and personnel. In addition, because of these two events, the Inman Report, a report on overseas security, was performed by the U.S. Department of State to help clarify the terrorist situation in the Middle East.

By 2002, military analysts continued to debate the effects of the pullout of American troops from Beirut in 1983. Some terrorists today still claim that United States military troops will pull out of a country rather than fight back, if enough violence and death are inflicted upon them, and refer to the past conflicts in Beirut and Somalia to substantiate their claims. For instance, manuals found in al-Qaeda training camps in Afghanistan frequently referred to the 1983 experiences in Beirut.

Based in large part on the American experiences in Beirut, the U.S. military altered their philosophy in the 1980s when the Weinberger Doctrine stated that the United States would dedicate troops only when essential national interests were in jeopardy. Although

U.S. Marines and an Italian soldier dig through the debris at the Battalion headquarters in Beirut, Lebanon, in 1983. BILL FOLEY/AP WIDE WORLD PHOTOS

the doctrine was modified over the next two decades, its impact was deeply felt throughout the U.S. military.

FURTHER RESOURCES
Books
Anderson, Terry A. *Den of Lions*. New York: Crown, 1993.

Web sites
CNN.com. "20 Years Later, Lebanon Bombing Haunts America's First Encounter with a Suicide Bomb." <http:// www.cnn.com/2003/WORLD/meast/10/21/ lebanon.anniv.ap/> (accessed June 7, 2005).

Embassy of the United States: Beirut, Lebanon. "About the Embassy: U.S. Embassy Beirut Memorial." <http:// lebanon.usembassy.gov/lebanon/beirut_memorial.html> (accessed June 7, 2005).

Federation of American Scientists. "The Innman Report." <http://www.fas.org/irp/threat/inman/> (accessed June 7, 2005).

Reader's Companion to Military History, Houghton Mifflin. "Weinberger Doctrine." <http://college.hmco.com/ history/readerscomp/mil/html/ml_057800_weinbergerdo. htm> (accessed June 7, 2005).

"Double Blast Devastates Marines, French; Scores Dead"

Simultaneous Suicide Attacks Made by Islamic Jihad on American and French Compounds in Beirut, Lebanon

News article

By: Terry A. Anderson

Date: October 23, 1983

Source: The Associated Press.

About the Author: Terry A. Anderson (1947–) was the head of The Associated Press Beirut bureau when, in 1983, he was kidnapped by a group of Hezbollah Shiite Muslims. He was eventually held for 2,454 days (about seven years) before being released. After being freed, Anderson actively publicized the right for freedom of the press, taught courses at Ohio University's E.W. Scripps School of Journalism and Columbia University's Graduate School of Journalism, appeared on various

Rescue workers sift through the bombed-out rubble of a U.S. Marine base in Beirut, Lebanon on October 23, 1983. AP/WIDE WORLD PHOTOS

radio and television shows as guest and host, and wrote the best-selling book *Den of Lions* that was based on his experiences as a captive.

INTRODUCTION

Beginning on August 20, 1982, a multinational military force composed of United States Marines and French and Italian soldiers began overseeing the peaceful withdrawal of the Palestinian Liberation Army (PLO) from West Beirut during a civil war in Lebanon. However, from the start, the peacekeepers came in conflict with radical Islamists. In March 1983, U.S. Marines were attacked for the first time while on patrol. A month later, a suicide bomber drove a truck filled with 400 pounds of explosives into the U.S. embassy in Beirut, destroying the building, killing sixty-three people, and injuring 120 others. The suicide bombings prompted President Ronald Reagan, in September 1983, to add additional Marines in Beirut. However, the strengthened military presence only further angered the PLO.

In the early morning of October 23, 1983, near-simultaneous suicide truck-bomb attacks were made on American and French compounds in Beirut. In the first wave, Shiite Muslim fundamentalists drove a truck loaded with 12,000 pounds of dynamite through the outermost security perimeter of the U.S. Marine Corps headquarters near the airport. Then, the suicidal terrorists drove the truck into the military barrack and set off the explosives, which destroyed the building, killed 241 American military personnel as they slept, and seriously injured another eighty soldiers. At the time, the attack resulted in the largest loss of American lives due to a terrorist attack.

About 2 miles away and around two minutes later, a 400-pound bomb, driven by other members of the same terrorist group, destroyed a barrack within the French military base in West Beirut, causing the death of fifty-eight French paratroopers.

Islamic Jihad publicly claimed responsibility for both of these suicide-bombings. After the simultaneous bombings, United States intelligence analysts decided that Hezbollah, the secret terrorist organization within the Islamic Jihad, was behind the bombings. Analysts discovered that Hezbollah was first organized in 1982 by Lebanese clerics as a guerrilla group called the Islamic Resistance. It was financed by Iran and supplied with weapons by Syria. Its main focus was to reverse the 1982 Israeli invasion of Lebanon and its later occupation of southern Lebanon.

■ PRIMARY SOURCE

A suicide bomber rammed a pickup truck packed with explosives into an airport building full of sleeping Marines early Sunday and blew up the four-story structure. The U.S. Embassy said at least 76 Marines were killed and 115 wounded.

Moments later another terrorist drove a car loaded with explosives into a compound a mile away housing French members of the multinational force in Beirut, and Lebanon's state radio said as many as 100 French soldiers were killed.

The U.S. Embassy said the death toll probably would rise in the worst attacks against the Marines and multinational force since it arrived in Beirut more than a year ago at the Lebanese government's request to help keep peace in the war-ravaged capital.

Frantic survivors, some wearing only their underwear, grabbed shovels to dig for moaning survivors trapped in the rubble of the building that had housed a battalion of leathernecks and the Marine communication center. Blood oozed from the shattered glass and concrete into pools on the ground.

"I haven't seen carnage like that since Vietnam," said Marine spokesman Maj. Robert Jordan. He said most of the Marines had been sleeping on cots when the pickup truck-bomb exploded, raining tons of rubble down on them at 6:20 A.M. (12:20 A.M. EDT).

U.S. Embassy spokesman John Stewart said the latest official casualty toll in the explosion at the Marine base was 76 dead and 115 wounded but that an "unknown number" of Marines were still believed missing.

At the French position, soldiers said the bodies of 15 men and three seriously wounded French troops had been recovered. Up to 85 were still buried in the wreckage, they said.

No group claimed responsibility for the bombings and U.S. officials said they had no idea who was responsible.

Witnesses said the bomber drove into the airport parking lot outside the Marine fence, where a sentry spotted the pickup and radioed headquarters. The truck then speeded up, smashed through a gate and a sandbagged guardpost, roared around another barrier and vaulted through the sandbagged lobby of the building where it blew up. It was unclear whether Marine sentries fired at the vehicle.

Sirens wailing, Lebanese ambulances and U.S. rescue vehicles careened to the blast scene and medics evacuated the dead and maimed. Helicopters flew casualties to U.S. warships offshore.

The most seriously wounded were flown to a British Royal Air Force Hospital in Nicosia, Cyprus, British officials said. Britain and Italy also have contingents in the multinational force.

President Reagan cut short a golf weekend in Georgia and flew back to Washington, where he was expected to meet with national security advisers.

In Paris, French Defense Minister Charles Hernu called the attacks "odious and cowardly" and flew to Lebanon to inspect the damage, France government sources said.

The terrorist blasts came one day after a U.S. convoy with 2,000 Marines assigned to replace the Beirut contingent were diverted to the eastern Caribbean because of the unstable political situation in Grenada. Many of the Marines killed Sunday had been preparing to leave.

Before this explosion, six Marines had been killed by sniper fire or artillery explosions around their airport camp and a seventh died when a mine exploded.

Lebanese army explosive expert Staff Sgt. Youssef Bita estimated the force of the blast at the U.S. and French centers at 660 pounds each. Jordan estimated the Marine compound bomb contained 2,000 pounds of explosives.

The Marine bombing was worse than the April 18 bombing of the U.S. Embassy in west Beirut in which 17 Americans and 32 Lebanese were killed.

It bore a strong resemblance to the embassy bombing, which U.S. officials at the time blamed on pro-Iranian Lebanese extremists. In that explosion, a suicide terrorist drove a small truck loaded with explosives through a gate to the entrance of the building.

Col. Timothy Geraghty, commander of the 1,600-man U.S. peace contingent, rushed to the blast scene to direct rescue efforts. He told reporters that some of the trapped leathernecks were still alive hours after the blast.

"These kind of things just harden our resolve and we will continue to do what we came here to do, and that is to provide assistance for a free and independent Lebanon," Geraghty said.

■

SIGNIFICANCE

It can be fairly argued that the attacks were attacks of both religious and insurgent terrorism as they were

A U.S. Marine reaches for a body amid the rubble of the U.S. Marine base in Beirut, Lebanon on October 23, 1983. AP/WIDE WORLD PHOTOS

directed against a peacekeeping force that Islamic Jihad viewed as an occupying force.

Islamic Jihad, under the guise of Hezbollah, continued with its terrorist activities after the bombing of the American and French compounds. In January 1984, the organization directed the killing of Malcolm Kerr, the president of Beirut's American University. In March 1984, the terrorists kidnapped, tortured, and killed William Buckley, political officer for the Central Intelligence Agency (CIA) at the U.S. embassy.

On March 31, 1984, President Reagan ordered American military personnel out of Beirut. At about the same time, the Italian and French forces were also evacuated by their respective governments, which ended the multinational peacekeeping effort in Beirut.

The removal of foreign military personnel in Beirut did not stop terrorists actions against the United States

and its allies. Other Western officials and civilians were kidnapped including American and British professors from American University and journalist Terry Anderson, head of the Associated Press Beirut bureau. On June 19, 1985, TWA Flight 847 was hijacked while flying from Athens, Greece to Rome, Italy.

The United States intelligence network had a difficult time deciding how to confront these terrorist threats because of insufficient information as to which specific group was actually responsible. White House analysts alleged that the Iranian government supported and directed terrorist actions in Lebanon. In response, the Reagan Administration pursued a policy of secretly selling military weapons to Iran (in order for the country to fight a war with Iraq) in exchange for the release of U.S. and allied hostages. Money from the sales was diverted to anti-Communist forces in Nicaragua. The actions eventually turned into what became known as the Iran-Contra affair.

The United States, by 1991, was able to negotiate the release of all hostages held in Lebanon. The Lebanese Civil War ended in 1990, and the peace agreement allowed Hezbollah to maintain its position in Lebanon. Syria and Iran allegedly continued to supply Hezbollah with money, supplies, and personnel.

FURTHER RESOURCES

Books

Hamzeh, Ahmad Nizar. *In the Path of Hizbullah*. Syracuse, NY: Syracuse University Press, 2004.

Harik, Judith P. *Hezbollah: The Changing Face of Terrorism*. London, NY: I.B. Tauris, 2004.

Shai, Shaul. *The Axis of Evil: Iran, Hizballah, and Palestinian Terror*. New Brunswick, NJ: Transaction Publishers, 2005.

Web sites

Arlington National Cemetery. "Terrorist Bombing Of The Marine Barracks, Beirut, Lebanon." <http://www.arlingtoncemetery.net/terror.htm> (accessed June 14, 2005).

BBC News, British Broadcasting Corporation. "Country Profile: Lebanon." <http://news.bbc.co.uk/1/hi/world/middle_ east/country_profiles/791071.stm> (accessed June 14, 2005).

Biography.ms. "Hezbollah." <http://hezbollah.biography.ms/> (accessed June 14, 2005).

GlobalSecurity.org. "US Multinational Force [USMNF] Lebanon." <http://www.globalsecurity.org/military/ops/usmnf.htm> (accessed June 14, 2005).

LebaneseForces.com. "Historical Fact: Bombing of Marine Barracks, October 23, 1983." <http://www.lebaneseforces.com/bombingofmarinebarracks.asp> (accessed June 14, 2005).

"Are the Americans Going to Give Us a King?"

Journal of a Muslim U.S. Soldier in Iraq

Journal

By: Mohammed Omar Masry

Date: November 9, 2003

Source: "Are the Americans Going to Give Us a King?" as published on *Islam Online.*

About the Author: Sergeant Mohammed Omar Masry is a Muslim U.S. Army Civil Affairs Sergeant who served in Baghdad. He was assigned to the 354th Civil Affairs Brigade, a Civil Affairs Unit, out of Maryland. His unit was activated in March 2003 for Operation Iraqi Freedom. Born and raised in California, his mother was born in Makkah (Mecca), Saudi Arabia and his father, whose parents are Lebanese and Armenian, was born in Nigeria.

INTRODUCTION

The United States invaded Iraq with the stated purpose of eliminating the regime of Iraqi dictator Saddam Hussein. The United States, Britain, and several allied nations, later known as the coalition forces, alleged that Hussein's regime aided operations of the al-Qaeda terrorist network and maintained stockpiles of weapons of mass destruction. United States President George W. Bush had stated that Iraq was part of an "axis of evil," a cadre of nations that he asserted posed an imminent threat to global security requiring immediate intervention.

Ultimately, no stockpiles of weapons of mass destruction were located in Iraq, and the suspected strong and direct ties of the former Iraqi regime to al-Qaeda remained largely unsubstantiated. The United States then shifted its Iraq policy, stating a primary objective of bringing democracy to the nation.

After declaring an end to combat operations in Iraq on May 1, 2003, coalition nations did not immediately withdraw their forces. The United States-led coalition forces remained in Iraq to conduct policing

U.S. Army soldiers struggle to reach an injured woman caught in the crossfire from Iraqi troops and irregular forces. AP/WIDE WORLD PHOTOS

operations and train Iraqi security forces. Troops still deployed in the region met with increasing hostility; terrorist attacks on coalition interests and Iraqi civilians escalated.

Iraqi nationals, as well as the international community, are divided in their opinions of continuing coalition intervention in Iraq. Some see the presence of coalition troops as a peacekeeping force, aiding reconstruction of the war-torn national infrastructure such as roads, communication networks, utilities, and schools. Others view the presence of foreign troops as an unwarranted occupation of Iraq. The most militant elements in the region, including Islamist extremists, view the occupation of Iraq—especially by U.S. and British forces—as not only hostile, but also as justification for terrorist violence.

■ PRIMARY SOURCE

Yesterday was another chaotic day in Baghdad, but in the midst of it all there was one moment, one statement that gave me a little hope things might work for the better. In the Al-Shula district of Baghdad, I was talking to a big group of children outside a school. After the children finished asking me for the 30th time whether I was Kuwaiti or Egyptian (Apparently those are the only two other countries in the Arab world to some kids here), a few asked me if I was fasting. When I told them I was, they were somewhat shocked and, just like with any subject in Iraq, didn't believe me until I stated it three times and declared wallah (swore to Allah).

When I first got to Iraq I asked one of the interpreters assigned to us if maybe Iraqis would assume I was lying to them because I was a soldier. The interpreter told me, "No, Omar, they're used to being lied to all their life so they don't believe anything till you tell it to them over and over again."

While I was talking to the young boys, a little girl slowly made her way to the back of the group. One of the other soldiers pointed out how adorable she looked in her tracksuit and rose print hijab (veil). As soon as we looked at her, one of the boys holding a palm frond smacked her in the face with it; she began crying and ran to the other side of the street. I turned to the boy and said, "Are you a haywan (animal) or an Iraqi? If you are an Iraqi, you'll go and tell her sorry." Little Ali got mad and refused to. The other boys started chiding him and he then sat down, lowered his head and began sulking.

My attention got distracted though by another boy walking up towards me. He carried books in one hand and a full book bag, one of the school kits passed out by USAID, in the other. As I noticed how smartly dressed he was, even though his slippers were repaired with duct tape, I couldn't help but think that he exuded a lot of pride and class regardless of how poor his family may have been. Mustafa was 12 years old. He held up his notebook (adorned with a picture of the late Ayatollah Hakim) and asked me to write my name for him. After I handed the book to Mustafa he asked me, "Are the Americans going to give us a king?" I told him, "No, the Iraqis will write a constitution first with all the rules and ideas of Iraq Jadeed (a New Iraq)." This news made Mustafa so puzzled that he asked me three times if Iraqis would write it. Then I asked him what he wanted as the new rules. Mustafa, with the determination etched onto his face one would never expect from a child, said, "No more people missing." Mustafa's uncle had been in Dawa Party, a political party persecuted by Saddam, until he went missing one day. The moment he said the word Dawa, all the other children hushed.

By then it was time for my unit to leave. As we began to mount up and drive off in our humvees, the kids caught a glimpse of our Taiwanese driver and began yelling "Yabanee" (Japanese) and "Jackie Chan." The little boy stopped sulking, got up and said asif (sorry) to the little girl still hiding behind the man who I presume was her grandfather. I looked at him. We both said "ma'a salama" (peace be with you), and, as we drove off, the children kept running for a few blocks holding thumbs up and waving, with two little girls yelling "where's my backpack (the USAID school kits being given out to all the schoolchildren)?"

I can't help but wish, in sha' Allah (God Willing), that every child in every school in Iraq will learn about a constitution and speak up for what they want it to say.

Masry
09 Nov 2003
Baghdad, Iraq

SIGNIFICANCE

Before the invasion, the U.S.-led coalition forces underestimated the magnitude of insurgent resistance in post-war Iraq. President Bush and British Prime Minister Tony Blair assuaged skeptics by asserting that coalition troops would be welcomed as liberators as they entered Iraq. Even Iraqi citizens who applauded the ouster of Saddam Hussein's regime, however, were unsure of coalition intentions for the rebuilding of Iraq.

The Iraqi insurgency is comprised of many factions. All insurgent groups target coalition military forces, but some also target private contractors and Iraqi citizens of opposing religious and political sects. Former regime loyalists, extremist religious militants,

Soldiers of the Iraqi National Guard aim their guns as they participate in a raid at Sheikh Maroof neighborhood in Baghdad, Iraq in 2004. AP/WIDE WORLD PHOTOS

international Islamist groups, foreign jihadists, ethnic nationalists, and ordinary criminal groups all operate within the nebulous insurgency. Many insurgent groups fight each other, vying for power in the post-war state.

In January 2005, Iraq held its first post-war national elections. However, the insurgency continued in Iraq even after the establishment of an elected government. Many members of the international community also allege that global terrorist networks, such as al-Qaeda and Islamic Jihad, have proliferated in post-war Iraq.

FURTHER RESOURCES

Books

Tripp, Charles. *A History of Iraq*. London: Cambridge University Press, 2002.

Web sites

alt.Muslim.com. Masry, Mohammed Omar. "Opportunity as the Seas Recede" <http://www.altmuslim.com/perm.php?id=1376_0_25_60_C> (accessed July 12, 2005).

American Moslem Perspective "Ferial Masry is the Democratic Candidate for CA State Assembly." <http://www.ampolitics.ghazali.net/html/ferial_masry.html> (accessed July 12, 2005).

4 Separatist Terrorism

Introduction to Separatist Terrorism

Separatists seek nationalist aims, usually desiring to secure self-determination or home-rule for a certain faction or geographic community. Separatist terrorists (also called nationalist terrorists) use acts of terror to force the creation of a new state, or to join with another existing nation with which the separatist community is closely aligned.

Many groups who engage in separatist terrorism claim that they are neither extremists nor terrorists, but are rebels or freedom fighters. Separatist groups successfully garner international attention and sometimes even sympathy for their causes. Separatist actions that use violence against unarmed citizens who are not directly related to the conflict, however, constitutes terrorism.

The editors have chosen several articles that focus on separatist terrorism in Russia, Israel, Spain, and Ireland. Both the Basque Fatherland and Liberty (ETA) and the Irish Republican Army (IRA) have used terrorist violence to promote separatism. However, ETA supports the creation of a new, Basque state independent from Spain while the IRA wishes to dissolve British rule and unite Northern Ireland with the Irish Republic. The Basque conflict is driven by ethnic conflict; the conflict over Northern Ireland is fueled by religious tensions. The Russian-Chechen and Palestinian-Israeli conflicts are propelled by both ethnic and religious tensions.

The primary sources included deal with specific instances of terrorism committed by separatist groups. The editors acknowledge that the nature of nationalist-separatist groups is complex, and that such groups may cycle through stages of legitimacy as revolutionary forces and illegitimacy as terrorist networks. For example, this chapter features a series of articles on the IRA that charts its legacy from the Irish Revolution to the latest terrorist actions of its newest splinter groups. The chapter also covers separatist, anti-colonial violence in Africa and Asia during the 1940s–1960s. In all cases, the editors' primary goal is to provide primary sources that will allow the reader to form their own opinion about these complex issues.

Fenian Brotherhood

Illustration

By: Anonymous

Date: 1868

Source: Image from the cover of *Harper's Weekly* on January 18, 1868.

About the Artist: The artist of the cover illustration from the January 18, 1868 issue of *Harper's Weekly* is unknown.

INTRODUCTION

In 1858, in Dublin, Ireland, James Stephens (one of the leaders of an attempted armed insurrection against British rule in 1848) formed the Irish Revolutionary Brotherhood (IRB). In the same year in New York City, John O'Mahony formed a sister organization called the Fenian Brotherhood, named after the Fianna, a legendary band of third-century Irish warriors.

The IRB and the Fenian Brotherhood pursued parallel aims in the 1860s, and indeed the two organizations were indistinguishable. The goal of both was to create a network of Irish nationalists who would continue to oppose British rule in Ireland, by force and terrorism if necessary. A further goal of the Fenians was to raise United States money and manpower in support of the cause. By 1865, the organization had a quarter million followers, many of them Civil War veterans willing to put their military training to use in the cause of Irish independence.

The Fenian Brotherhood in the United States is best known for its plans to invade and seize Canada, particularly its rail lines. The Fenians assumed that England would trade Irish independence to regain its North American provinces. For its part, the U.S. government under President Andrew Johnson, still rankled by Britain's willingness to construct warships for the Confederacy during the Civil War, initially turned a blind eye to the raids. The first raid took place on April 12, 1866, but was speedily thwarted. A second took place on June 1, when a force of up to 1,500 Fenian raiders seized Fort Erie and actually turned back a company of Canadian militia. Later raids took place in 1870 and 1871, but by this time the U.S. government had become involved and the leader of the raids, John O'Neill, was arrested.

Meanwhile, in Ireland, Irish nationalists continued to advocate rebellion, their ardor fanned by Stephens's journal *Irish People*, which suggested using violence, until British authorities suppressed it. The Fenian Rising of 1867 targeted an armory in Chester, England. The plot unraveled when one of Stephens's lieutenants turned informer and exposed the plot to British authorities. The leaders were arrested and sentenced to hang, though no one was ever executed.

Unrest continued in September 1867, when two Irish nationalist leaders were arrested in Manchester, England. A week later, Fenians carried out a plot to release the prisoners as they were being transported in a prison van. The arrested leaders escaped, but those who executed the plot were arrested, and several, who came to be known among Irish nationalists as the Manchester Martyrs, were later hanged for murdering one of the prisoners' guards.

Then in November 1867, Richard Burke, one of the masterminds of the September prison-van incident, was in Birmingham, England, attempting to purchase arms for the Fenians when he was arrested and taken to London's Clerkenwell Prison. On December 13, Fenians attempted to rescue him by blowing a hole in the prison wall, but the explosion severely damaged a row of tenement houses across the street. Twelve people were killed, and another 126 were injured.

The following illustration depicts the scene of the Clerkenwell explosion.

■ PRIMARY SOURCE

FENIAN BROTHERHOOD
See primary source image.

SIGNIFICANCE

For weeks in late 1867, London had been the scene of demonstrations in support of the Fenians. The day before the bombing, England's Prime Minister Benjamin Disraeli had banned such demonstrations, though he feared the move would meet with opposition. The bombing at Clerkenwell, however, touched off a wave of support for Disraeli and his Tory government. The public was outraged by the explosion and demanded government action. Disraeli suspend the writ of *habeas corpus* (the right to be brought before a court before being imprisoned), introduced wide-ranging security measures, and formed a secret police branch to deal with the Fenian threat. Queen Victoria, herself the object of an unsuccessful Fenian assassination plot, said that Irish rebels should not be tried, but lynched on the spot.

A number of men were arrested and tried for the bombing, but only one, Michael Barrett, was condemned to death. On May 26, 1868, he was hanged outside the walls of Newgate Prison, the last person ever to be publicly executed in England. Barrett maintained his innocence, and many observers believed that he had been convicted on the basis of perjured testimony by an

HARPER'S WEEKLY.

JOURNAL OF CIVILIZATION.

VOL. XII.—No. 577.]   NEW YORK, SATURDAY, JANUARY 18, 1868.   [SINGLE COPIES, TEN CENTS.
[$4.00 PER YEAR IN ADVANCE.

Entered according to Act of Congress, in the Year 1868, by Harper & Brothers, in the Clerk's Office of the District Court of the United States, for the Southern District of New York.

THE FENIAN "GUNPOWDER TREASON."

ENGLAND continues to be terribly excited and frightened over her new and very much enlarged version of the GUY FAWKES gunpowder-plot, and the English press seems to think there is reason

"Why gunpowder treason
And Guy Fawkes plot
Should not be forgot."

England has not had for many years so thorough an excitement as has resulted from the explosions at the Clerkenwell prison, at Millbank, and at

Newcastle-upon-Tyne, and other places noticed in our former issues. Subsequently a powder mill at Faversham, near London, was blown up, and as the cause of the disaster, like that at Newcastle, was unknown it was at once attributed, like the other, to the Fenians. After using the general post-offices of the kingdom to distribute their destructive torpedoes, which however failed to kill any one, the Fenians are now reported as endeavoring to destroy the post-offices by means of Greek fire—another decided failure. No further explosions than those named have occurred; but a number of mysterious Fenians are reported to have attacked and carried a Martello

tower near Cork, and carried off a large supply of arms.

Our previous reports have been entirely by telegraph, and have been very unsatisfactory. We are now beginning to receive the illustrated accounts of the several explosions which occurred. We give on this page an illustration of the first of the explosions, that at Clerkenwell prison, in which RICHARD BURKE and JOSEPH CASEY were confined. Our illustration shows the ruin of the prison wall immediately after the occurrence of the explosion, with the police in possession engaged in guarding the breach in the wall and in removing the rubbish.

The effect of the explosion was to blow in a triangular section of the prison wall of about 20 feet at the base by 60 feet or 70 feet at the summit; to utterly destroy the house immediately opposite, burying all within it under the ruins; to demolish a great part of many other houses right and left and immediately in the rear, wounding fifty of the inhabitants; and to fill the whole lane with heaps of bricks from the prison wall.

DESMOND and ALLEN, who were arrested charged with placing and firing the barrel of gunpowder, were examined in London on January 3, and the evidence was by no means satisfactory or conclusive of their guilt. The examination

RUINS OF THE WALL OF CLERKENWELL PRISON, LONDON, IMMEDIATELY AFTER THE EXPLOSION.

PRIMARY SOURCE

"Fenian Brotherhood" Illustration from the cover of *Harper's Weekly* depicting the explosion at London's Clerkenwell prison in 1867 as a result of a bomb planted by the Fenian Brotherhood. The explosion was intended to free imprisoned Fenians, but instead injured over one hundred persons living in nearby tenement houses. © CORBIS

informant, himself a criminal, offered in exchange for a promise by the authorities of safe passage to Australia.

The Clerkenwell incident was a turning point in British-Irish relations, for it focused British attention on what was then known as the Irish question. Opposition leader William Gladstone, just days after the explosion, urged the government to at least consider granting the Irish home rule, saying that the explosion at Clerkenwell changed his mind.

FURTHER RESOURCES
Books
Campbell, Christy. *Fenian Fire*. New York: HarperCollins, 2002.

Rafferty, Oliver P. *The Church, the State and the Fenian Threat, 1861–1875*. New York: Palgrave Macmillan, 1999.

Web sites
American Catholic History Research Center and University Archives. "Fenian Brotherhood Collection." <http://www.aladin.wrlc.org/gsdl/collect/fenian/fenian.shtml> (accessed May 16, 2005).

Bylaws of the Organization: Union or Death

Black Hand

Excerpt of bylaws

By: Black Hand

Date: May 9, 1911

Source: Black Hand organization, 1911

About the Author: The Black Hand, known to its members as Unification or Death, was a secret Serbian terrorist society founded in 1911 to unite all ethnic Serbs within one nation. To do so, the society aimed to destroy the empire of Austria-Hungary. By 1914, the Black Hand had grown to about 2,500 members, most of whom were army officers and government officials. The organization's greatest success came when Black Hand member Gavrilo Princip assassinated Archduke Francis Ferdinand, heir to the throne of Austria-Hungary, in an act that led to the start of World War I (1914–1917). The Black Hand collapsed following the 1917 execution of several of its leaders and the imprisonment of over 200 members by the Serbian government.

INTRODUCTION
By 1903, nationalism in the Balkan countries began to rise. Serbia led the way with its dream of uniting

Lyrics from an Irish folk song or pub song are presented below that lament the fate of Michael Barrett, who was convicted for his part in the 1867 bombing of the Clerkenwell Prison in London. Designed to free fellow Fenian Brothers (members of the Irish Republican Brotherhood, a revolutionary organization against British rule in Ireland), the bombing instead killed twelve people and injured more than one hundred. Barrett was hanged in 1868, and was the last person to be executed in public in Britain.

The Ballad of Michael Barrett
Throughout the Kingdom, among high and low,
A great excitement has long been caused,
Of a dreadful crime—horrible to tell
The fatal explosion at Clerkenwell.
Out of the seven they for the crime did try,
One Michael Barrett was condemned to die.

Patrick Mullany was a witness made,
A military tailor, he was by trade;
To save himself, he evidence gave,
Which he his neck has saved.

The informers swore, and others beside,
When the prisoners, all at the bar was tried,
That by Michael Barrett the deed was done,
And from the spot did to Scotland run.

He was taken in Glasgow and to London brought,
He says of the crime he never thought,
He would not be guilty of such a deed,
But he was convicted, as we may read.

Though Michael Barrett is condemned to die,
The dreadful deed he strongly does deny,
There is one above who all secrets know,
He can tell whether Barrett is guilty or no.

We hope all men will a warning take,
And long remember poor Barrett's fate;
We find it difficult throughout the land,
For man to even trust his fellow man.

A dreadful tale we'll have long to tell,
The fatal explosion at Clerkenwell.

The assassination of Archduke Franz Ferdinand of Austria-Hungary and his wife on June 28, 1914, was commited by Gavrilo Princip, of the group Blank Hand. AP/WIDE WORLD PHOTOS

ethnic Serbs throughout the Balkan region into a Greater Serbia. In 1908, Austria-Hungary poured cold water on this dream by annexing the provinces of Bosnia and Herzegovina. Dominated by Germans and Hungarians, Austria-Hungary could not satisfy the grievances or contain the nationalist aims of its numerous minorities, especially the Serbs.

Officially a part of the Ottoman Empire, Bosnia and Herzegovina had been administered by Austria since 1878. The provinces had a large population of Serbians, Croatians, and Muslims, with annexation predictably outraging Serbia. The Serbian government threatened to invade Bosnia and Herzegovina to liberate the seven million or so South Slavs (Yugoslavs) from Austrian oppression, while the Serbian press proclaimed that Austria-Hungary had to be destroyed. The shrill appeals by Serbian nationalists made Austrian leaders fear that the South Slavs might press for secession. Seeing Serbia as a threat to the existence of Austria-Hungary, Austrian leaders vowed to destroy Serbia. They formed an alliance with Germany in the event of war.

Serbia, a small country, had the will but not the strength to take military action against Austria-Hungary. Instead, Serbia joined the Balkan states of Montenegro, Bulgaria, and Greece in attacking the weak Ottoman Empire. In the brief Balkan War of 1912, Serbia gained

the Albanian coast and a long-desired outlet to the sea. Austria, with Germany's support, did not want Serbia to get this prize. Unable to get Russian support, Serbia was forced to surrender the territory. Austria-Hungary had twice humiliated Serbia in just a few years. To Serbian nationalists, the empire formed the main obstacle to Slavic unity.

Formed in 1911 to unite Serbs, the Black Hand terrorist organization was led by Colonel Dragutin Dimitrijevi´c, chief of intelligence of the Serbian Army. Dimitrijevi´c used ritual to promote this secret society. The Black Hand initiation ceremony, designed to strengthen a new member's commitment to the cause and to foster obedience to the society's leaders, had the appearance of a sacred rite. The candidate entered a dark room in which a table stood covered with a black cloth. On the table lay a dagger, a revolver, and a crucifix. When the candidate declared his readiness to take the oath of allegiance, a masked member of the society's leadership entered the room and stood in silence. After the initiate pronounced the oath, the masked man shook his hand and departed without uttering a word.

Operating from Bulgaria, the Black Hand carried out propaganda campaigns and organized armed bands in Macedonia. It established revolutionary cells throughout Bosnia. Dominating the Serbian Army, the organization held enormous influence over the Serbian government, but it did so by terrorizing government officials.

◼ PRIMARY SOURCE

Article 1: This organization is created for the purpose of realizing the national ideal: the union of all Serbs. Membership is open to every Serb, without distinction of sex, religion, or place of birth, and to all those who are sincerely devoted to this cause.

Article 2: This organization prefers terrorist action to intellectual propaganda, and for this reason, it must remain absolutely secret.

Article 3: The organization bears the name *Ujedinjenje ili Smirt* (Union or Death).

Article 4: To fulfill its purpose, the organization will do the following: 1. Exercise influence on government circles, on the various social classes, and on the entire social life of the kingdom of Serbia, which is considered the Piedmont [the Italian state that served as the nucleus for the unification of Italy] of the Serbian nation; 2. Organize revolutionary action in all territories inhabited by Serbs; 3. Beyond the frontiers of Serbia, fight with all means the enemies of the Serbian national idea; 4. Maintain amicable relations with all states, peoples, organizations, and individuals who support Serbia and the Serbia element; 5. Assist those nations and organizations that are fighting for their own national liberation and unification. . . .

Article 24: Every member has a duty to recruit new members, but the member shall guarantee with his life those whom he introduces into the organization.

Article 25: Members of the organization are forbidden to know each other personally. Only members of the central committee are known to each other.

Article 26: In the organization itself, the members are designated by numbers. Only the central committee in Belgrade knows their names.

Article 27: Members of the organization must obey absolutely the commands given to them by their superiors.

Article 28: Each member has a duty to communicate to the central committee at Belgrade any information that may be of interest to the organization.

Article 29: The interests of the organization must stand above all other interests.

Article 30: On entering the organization, each member must know that he loses his own personality, that he can expect neither personal glory nor personal profit, material or moral. Consequently, any member who endeavors to exploit the organization for personal, social, or party motives, will be punished. If by his acts he harms the organization itself, his punishment will be death.

Article 31: Those who enter the organization may never leave it, and no one has the authority to accept a member's resignation.

Article 32: Each member must aid the organization, with weekly contribution. If need be, the organization may procure funds through coercion....

Article 33: When the central committee of Belgrade pronounces a death sentence the only thing that matters is that the execution is carried out unfailingly. The method of execution is of little importance.

Article 34: The organization's seal is composed as follows. On the center of the seal a powerful arm holds in its hand an unfurled flag. On the flag, as a coat of arms, are a skull and crossed bones; by the side of the flag are a knife, a bomb and poison. Around, in a circle, are inscribed the following words reading from left to right: "Unification or Death," and at the base "The Supreme Central Directorate."

Article 35: On joining the organization, the recruit takes the following oath: "I (name), in becoming a member of the organization, 'Unification or Death,' do swear by the sun that shines on me, by the earth that nourishes me, by God, by the blood of my ancestors, on my honor and my

life that from this moment until my death, I shall be faithful to the regulations of the organization and that I will be prepared to make any sacrifice for it. I swear before God, on my honor and on my life, that I shall carry with me to the grave the organization's secrets. May God condemn me and my comrades judge me if I violate or do not respect, consciously or not, my oath."

Belgrade, 9 May 1911

SIGNIFICANCE

Serbian government officials knew of a Black Hand plan to assassinate Archduke Franz Ferdinand of Austria-Hungary but, perhaps fearful of the terrorists, did little to stop the murder of the heir to the Austrian throne by Black Hand member Gavrilo Princip on June 28, 1914. Franz Ferdinand had been sympathetic to the grievances of the South Slavs and favored a policy that would place the Slavs on an equal footing with Hungarians and Germans within the empire of Austria-Hungary. If such a policy succeeded, it might have soothed the feelings of the Slavs and reduced the appeal of a Greater Serbia. The Black Hand would subsequently lose support and power.

The murder of the Archduke Ferdinand set in motion the events that led to the start of World War I. On July 28, 1914, Austria declared war against Serbia. The fighting did not go well for Serbia. In 1917, Prince Alexander, leader of the expatriate Serbian Army, took advantage of the Black Hand's weakening strength to bring Dimitrijeví c to trial. Dimitrijeví c and two other officers were executed, while over 200 Black Hand members were imprisoned. Alexander's actions effectively killed the Black Hand.

FURTHER RESOURCES

Books

Boghitchevitch, M.; edited by André Delpeuch; translated by Marvin Perry. *Le Procès de Salonique, Juin 1917.* Paris, 1927.

Web sites

Shackelford, Michael. "The Secret Serbian Terrorist Society." *Cooper Union for the Advancement of Science and Art.* <http://www.cooper.edu/humanities/core/hss3/m_shack elford.html> (accessed June 20, 2005).

"Easter, 1916"

Militants in the Irish Sinn Fein Party Form the Irish Republican Army (IRA)

Poem

By: William Butler Yeats

Date: September 25, 1916

Source: "Easter, 1916," a poem by William Butler Yeats

About the Poet: William Butler Yeats (1865–1939) was one of the twentieth century's most acclaimed English-language poets. Born in Dublin, Ireland, themes of Irish rebellion and independence from England often featured prominently in his poetry.

INTRODUCTION

On Easter Monday, April 24, 1916, as Padraig Pearse (Commander in Chief of Republican forces) read a "Proclamation of the Republic" declaring Ireland a nation separate from England, from the steps of Dublin's General Post Office, the silence of the surrounding crowd reflected the uncertainty of many Irish people. Such nationalist speeches of independence from Great Britain were not unfamiliar to Irish citizens. It would take action on behalf of the Irish Republican Brotherhood (IRB), the forerunner of the Irish Republican Army (IRA), and its political party Sinn Fein to convince the Irish people that freedom from the 750-year domination by the British was actually within their grasp.

The Proclamation's call for action was planned as the British were committing their troops to fight in Germany during World War I (1915–1918). Angered that the British were enlisting Irish men to fight in the war fueled a decision to rise up against the British. The IRB Military Council that was formed the previous year acted on the philosophy that "England's difficulty is Ireland's opportunity." The council included seven members: Padraig Pearse (1879–1916), James Conolly (1868–1916), Joseph Mary Plunkett (1887–1916), Thomas MacDonagh (1878–1916), Eamonn Ceannt (1881–1916), Thomas J. Clarke (1857–1916), and Sean MacDermott (1884–1916), all of whom were revolutionaries who signed the Proclamation.

Because of the secrecy and size of the Irish Republican Brotherhood, reinforcement was needed in order to execute the Uprising. The help of the Irish Volunteers and the Irish Citizens Army was beckoned. Any man willing to fight for independence was accepted. Weapons for the planned uprising were to be supplied by Germany. The ship carrying the weapons, however, was intercepted, thus, the volunteers arrived for the Uprising with an array of rifles, shotguns, and handguns.

One hundred and fifty armed men marched towards Dublin's General Post Office, awaiting James Connolly's command to charge. Other men were already positioned at different points throughout Dublin. As the uniformed and street-clothed men stormed the Post Office, townspeople and officers on duty were caught off guard. Inside, the British flag was torn down and replaced with two new flags: a green flag reading "Irish Republic," and another bearing the colors green, white, and orange, later to become the Republic of Ireland's national flag.

Under General W.H.M. Lowe, the British counter-attacked the next day, overwhelming the modest-numbered Irish. By the end of the day, only 100 Irish participants in the Uprising remained, offering little resistance against more than 5,000 British troops. Although the prospect of an immediate victory was impossible, the leaders of the uprising hoped the action of defiance would stimulate Irish Support for the cause of independence. The Irish militants surrendered, and were tried as traitors by the British.

■ PRIMARY SOURCE

Easter, 1916

I have met them at close of day
Coming with vivid faces
From counter or desk among grey
Eighteenth-century houses.
I have passed with a nod of the head
Or polite meaningless words,
Or have lingered awhile and said
Polite meaningless words,
And thought before I had done
Of a mocking tale or a gibe
To please a companion
Around the fire at the club,
Being certain that they and I
But lived where motley is worn:
All changed, changed utterly:
A terrible beauty is born.

That woman's days were spent
In ignorant good-will,
Her nights in argument
Until her voice grew shrill.
What voice more sweet than hers
When, young and beautiful,
She rode to harriers?
This man had kept a school
And rode our winged horse;
This other his helper and friend
Was coming into his force;
He might have won fame in the end,
So sensitive his nature seemed,
So daring and sweet his thought.
This other man I had dreamed
A drunken, vainglorious lout.
He had done most bitter wrong
To some who are near my heart,
Yet I number him in the song;
He, too, has resigned his part
In the casual comedy;

He, too, has been changed in his turn,
Transformed utterly:
A terrible beauty is born.

Hearts with one purpose alone
Through summer and winter seem
Enchanted to a stone
To trouble the living stream.
The horse that comes from the road.
The rider, the birds that range
From cloud to tumbling cloud,
Minute by minute they change;
A shadow of cloud on the stream
Changes minute by minute;
A horse-hoof slides on the brim,
And a horse plashes within it;
The long-legged moor-hens dive,
And hens to moor-cocks call;
Minute by minute they live:
The stone's in the midst of all.

Too long a sacrifice
Can make a stone of the heart.
O when may it suffice?
That is Heaven's part, our part
To murmur name upon name,
As a mother names her child
When sleep at last has come
On limbs that had run wild.
What is it but nightfall?
No, no, not night but death;
Was it needless death after all?
For England may keep faith
For all that is done and said.
We know their dream; enough
To know they dreamed and are dead;
And what if excess of love
Bewildered them till they died?
I write it out in a verse -
MacDonagh and MacBride
And Connolly and Pearse
Now and in time to be,
Wherever green is worn,
Are changed, changed utterly:
A terrible beauty is born.

SIGNIFICANCE

William Butler Yeats' description "A terrible beauty is born" illustrates the violence of Ireland's fight for independence as well as the "beauty" of the prospect of independence from Great Britain. "Easter 1916" captures the monumental change in the Irish collaboration towards home rule for what is now the Republic of Ireland.

Fifteen of the Uprising participants were sentenced to death by firing squad, and the harsh sentences roused the Irish people. Connolly was taken from his deathbed to be strapped in a chair and shot, fueling anti-British sentiment throughout the streets of Dublin and echoing throughout Ireland. The Sinn Fein ("we ourselves") Party that had no seats in Britain's parliament in 1910 would hold 70% of the seats allotted to Ireland in the British Parliament after the elections of 1918.

In 1919, Sinn Fein created an Irish Parliament based on the philosophy that Irish independence relied on the Irish vote. Rather than awaiting a change in British decision, the republicans decided they would be their own agents in the prospect of independent rule. A bloody war, including the infamous "Bloody Sunday" and the burning of Cork in 1920, waged until October 1921. At this time, the Anglo-Irish Treaty gave independence to Ireland's lower twenty-six counties, though six northeastern counties would remain British, while being allowed a government of their own based in Stormont.

France's Storming of the Bastille in 1789, the Boston Tea Party in 1773, and the Easter Uprising were all uprisings that triggered nationalism. However, the mood that Yeats captures of the Irish people on Easter Monday, 1916 is one of uncertainty and disheartenment, rather than vigorous, communal spirit. Though the leaders of both the French and American rebellions were backed by much support from fellow nationalists' enthusiasm, it was only after the Easter Uprising that the Irish leaders gained the status of heroes.

Yeats' interpretation of the Uprising is one example among many differing opinions regarding the acceptance of violent rebellions by the Irish. Militant members of the Irish Republican Brotherhood transitioned into the Irish Republican Army (IRA) about 1919, and began using guerrilla tactics in repelling the Black and Tans and the Auxiliaries, two of Britain's elite military units sent to repress the Irish bid for independence.

After the Anglo-Irish Treaty was negotiated in 1921, the IRA again split into factions for and against the provisions of the treaty that divided Ireland. During the civil war that ensued, these two divisions fought each other until mid–1923, when the anti-treaty IRA members were convinced to abandon their arms.

In the decades that followed, a succession of anti-British militia groups assumed the name of the Irish Republican Army. The IRA gained members, its factions periodically united and divided, and the organization carried out intermittent bombings, raids for arms, and attacks on British citizens, troops, and installations. During the 1970s, IRA violence escalated when it carried out multiple organized attacks against British troops in Northern Ireland, and launched a bombing campaign in London. It was during this period that many nations considered the IRA's status as freedom fighters as negated, and replaced by the status of terrorist organization. Some groups of the IRA were often financed through theft and the sale of drugs.

Several temporary cessations in the violence have occurred during official cease-fires announced by the IRA, and despite a general British governmental policy that discourages negotiations with terrorists, discreet methods of communication between the IRA and the government of Britain were kept open during the late 1970s and 1980s. In 1994, the IRA announced a formal cessation of operations.

As of 2005, four IRA splinter organizations, the Real IRA, The Provisional IRA, The Official IRA, and the Continuity IRA appear on the United Kingdom's list of foreign terrorist organizations. All four groups claim the title of IRA and legitimate historical precedent. The Irish Republican Army (IRA) denies legitimacy of all four of these splinter groups.

FURTHER RESOURCES

Web sites

About.com. "History of Terrorism in Ireland." <http://terrorism.about.com/od/historyofterrorism/a/ireland.htm> (accessed July 16, 2005).

Ireland's Own.net. "Irish History: Easter 1916." <http://irelandsown.net/easterrising.html> (accessed July 16, 2005).

Political Information Net. "Sinn Féin." <http://www.politicalinformation.net/encyclopedia/Sinn_Fein.htm> (accessed July 16, 2005).

Roots Web. "Easter Rising 1916." <http://www.rootsweb.com/~fianna/history/east1916.html> (accessed July 16, 2005).

Wellington College Belfast GCSE History. "Irish Political Developments From 1916–1972." <http://websites.ntl.com/~wellclge/depts/history/module1/ni20_72.htm> (accessed July 16, 2005).

Hebron Massacre

Palestine Disturbances of 1929

Commission Report

By: Sir Walter Sidney Shaw

Date: March 1930

Source: *Report of the British Commission on the Palestine Disturbances of August 1929.*

About the Author: Sir Walter Shaw, a retired chief justice of the British Straits settlements, headed a four-member

A Palestinian boy adjusts the headdress of a friend as another boy holds a Palestinian flag on a rooftop in Hebron. AP/WIDE WORLD PHOTOS

commission to inquire into the causes of unrest in Palestine in August 1929.

INTRODUCTION

The violence that erupted in Hebron, Palestine, in August 1929 had its roots in at least three developments—although Jewish-Muslim enmity in Palestine had predated these developments for centuries.

The first development occurred in 1917, when British foreign secretary Arthur James Balfour made a pledge (the Balfour Declaration) to the Zionist Federation that after World War I (1915–1918) the British government would provide a secure homeland for the Jewish people in Palestine, which Britain had occupied during the war. The second development was the Treaty of Versailles, which ended World War I and provided for the formation of the League of Nations. The league designated Palestine as a British mandate, leaving the region under Britain's administration. The third development occurred in June 1922, when the League of Nations passed the Palestinian mandate, a document that specified Britain's responsibilities in Palestine, particularly to "secure the establishment of the Jewish national home," but also to safeguard "the civil and religious rights of all the inhabitants of Palestine," including those of Muslims.

Although tensions simmered beneath the surface and rioting broke out in 1920 and 1921, Jews and Arab Muslims lived side by side in Palestine in relative peace through most of the 1920s. That changed in August 1929, when a longstanding dispute between Muslims and Jews over access to the Western Wall (also known as the Wailing Wall) in Jerusalem erupted in violence. On August 14, thousands of Jews in Tel Aviv staged a demonstration in which they chanted, "The Wall is ours." On August 15, hundreds of Betars, members of a Zionist youth movement, demonstrated at the wall. Rumors were rife within the Muslim community that Jewish activists were preparing to seize holy places in Palestine and that Muslims should prepare to defend them. Demonstrations and riots occurred on August 16 when inflamed Muslims burned Jewish prayer books and notes left in the Western Wall.

Meanwhile, in Hebron, the Haganah, a Zionist defense organization and the predecessor to today's Israeli army, offered to protect Jews in the city. Jewish leaders declined the offer, believing that the city's Arab leadership would protect them. Then on August 23, rumors circulated among the Arab community that Jews had murdered two Arabs. In Jerusalem, Jews were attacked and the violence quickly spread to other parts of Palestine. The British, who had fewer than 300 policemen and 100 soldiers in Palestine, were helpless to stop the violence. By the next day, 24 Jews had been killed.

The worst of the violence took place in Hebron, where the British had only one policeman. Sixty-seven Jews in Hebron were eventually massacred, many in horrific fashion or with their bodies mutilated. Many more Jews were wounded. Survivors hid with sympathetic Arab friends and neighbors and many were later evacuated, but only after the violence subsided. In all, 133 Jews and 116 Arabs lost their lives in the August violence. Hundreds more were wounded.

Although motivated by religious intolerance and hatred, the massacre occurred within the context of ongoing separatist terrorism. Jewish citizens banded together for tighter security. Following the massacre, Jews began leaving Hebron and by 1936, no Jews were left in the city.

In 1929, Great Britain appointed Sir Walter Shaw to head a commission to investigate the unrest. He and the other three members of the commission arrived in Palestine in October. They issued their report, generally referred to as the Shaw Commission report, in 1930, fixing the blame for the rioting and murders primarily on the Arab community. Excerpts from the report appear below.

PRIMARY SOURCE

- The outbreak in Jerusalem on the 23rd of August was from the beginning an attack by Arabs on Jews for which no excuse in the form of earlier murders by Jews has been established.

- The outbreak was not premeditated.

- [The outbreak] took the form, in the most part, of a vicious attack by Arabs on Jews accompanied by wanton destruction of Jewish property. A general massacre of the Jewish community at Hebron was narrowly averted. In a few instances, Jews attacked Arabs and destroyed Arab property. These attacks, though inexcusable, were in most cases in retaliation for wrongs already committed by Arabs in the neighbourhood in which the Jewish attacks occurred.

- . . . The Mufti was influenced by the twofold desire to annoy the Jews and to mobilize Moslem opinion on the issue of the Wailing Wall. He had no intention of utilizing this religious campaign as the means of inciting to disorder. . . . The Mufti, like many others who directly or indirectly played upon public feeling in Palestine, must accept a share in the responsibility. . . .

- . . . In the matter of innovations of practice [at the Western Wall] little blame can be attached to the Mufti in which some Jewish religious authorities also would not have to share. . . . No connection has been established between the Mufti and the work of those who either are known or are thought to have engaged in agitation or incitement. . . After the disturbances had broken out the Mufti co-operated with the Government in their efforts both to restore peace and to prevent the extension of disorder.

- The fundamental cause . . . is the Arab feeling of animosity and hostility towards the Jews consequent upon the disappointment of their political and national aspirations and fear for their economic future. . . The feeling as it exists today is based on the twofold fear of the Arabs that by Jewish immigration and land purchases they may be deprived of their livelihood and in time pass under the political domination of the Jews.

In our opinion the immediate causes of the outbreak were:

1. The long series of incidents connected with the Wailing Wall. . . . These must be regarded as a whole, but the incident among them which in our view contributed most to the outbreak was the Jewish demonstration at the Wailing Wall on the 15th of August. . . .

2. Excited and intemperate articles which appeared in some Arabic papers, in one Hebrew daily paper and in a Jewish weekly paper. . . .

3. Propaganda among the less-educated Arab people of a character calculated to incite them.

4. The enlargement of the Jewish Agency.

5. The inadequacy of the military forces and of the reliable police available.

6. The belief . . . that the decisions of the Palestine Government could be influenced by political considerations.

SIGNIFICANCE

In the aftermath of the violence, 195 Arabs and 34 Jews were convicted for crimes. Two Jews and 17 Arabs were sentenced to death, but the sentences of all but two Arabs were later commuted to life imprisonment. Further, fines were imposed on 25 Arab villages.

Although the Shaw Commission laid the blame for the unrest principally on the Arab community, its references to Jewish immigration to Palestine led to further action on the part of the British, much of it perceived as largely pro-Arab. Those actions were often cited as a spur to Zionist separatist terrorism over the next two decades. In 1930, the Hope-Simpson report, echoing the Shaw Commission report, recommended a halt to Jewish immigration and settlement in Palestine until the country's agricultural capabilities could be increased, primarily through a better irrigation system.

That same year, to the dismay of the Zionist separatist movement, the Passfield-White Paper asserted that the rights of Arabs in Palestine were coequal with those of the Jews. When Britain proposed division of Palestine into Jewish and Arab areas in 1936, militant Arabs, as well as Zionists, rejected the proposal and engaged in three years of terrorism against Jews (1936–1939) known as the Great Uprising. In 1939, the White Paper limited Jewish immigration to Palestine to 15,000 people a year for five years, effectively trapping many Jews in Europe during the Nazi Holocaust.

The British mandate in Palestine ended in 1948. Many observers in the twenty-first century regard the British mandate, with its shifting and inconsistent policies toward both Jews and Arabs, as a factor fostering separatist violence in both communities and furthering ongoing violence between Jewish settlers and Palestinians.

FURTHER RESOURCES

Books

Gavish, Dov. *A Survey of Palestine during the Period of the British Mandate, 1918–1948.* Routledgecurzon Studies in Middle Eastern History. London: Routledge, 2005.

Shepherd, Naomi. *Ploughing Sand: British Rule in Palestine, 1917–1948.* Piscataway, NJ: Rutgers University Press, 1999.

Web sites

MidEastWeb. "Middle East History and Resources: Middle East Historical and Peace Process Source Documents." <http://www.mideastweb.org/history.htm> (accessed May 16, 2005).

Ruins of Jerusalem's King David Hotel

Bombing of British Army Headquarters by Zionist Terrorist Group

Photograph

By: Mendelson Hugo

Date: July 22, 1946

Source: Photograph, part of the Israeli government National Photo Collection, item 003410, picture code D21-020, captioned "The Ruins of Jerusalem's King David Hotel, Blown Up by the Etzel, Causing the Death of 91 People."

About the Photographer: Mendelson Hugo was an Israeli photographer who took pictures for the Israeli government on state occasions in the 1940s.

INTRODUCTION

In the Balfour Declaration of 1917, Great Britain, which had occupied Palestine during World War I, pledged to support the creation of a secure Jewish homeland in Palestine. In the decades that followed, when Britain administered Palestine as a British mandate, tensions developed between Zionists—people who wanted to establish the Jewish state—and the British. At issue were Zionist perceptions of inconsistency and double-dealing by the British, who professed ongoing support for formation of a Jewish state while instituting policies that were perceived as pro-Arab. The last straw for Zionists was the 1939 White Paper that sharply limited Jewish immigration to and settlement in Palestine for five years, at the very time when many European Jews were attempting to flee Nazi oppression.

In response, Zionist insurgents launched a campaign of terror against the British in 1939, including bombings, kidnappings, and murders. This campaign was carried out by the Haganah, the Jewish defense force that had operated in Palestine since World War I (1914–1918) and the predecessor of today's Israel Defense Forces. With the outbreak of World War II (1939–1945), the Haganah saw Adolf Hitler as a greater enemy than the British, so

PRIMARY SOURCE

Ruins of Jerusalem's King David Hotel The scene at the King David Hotel, Jerusalem, Israel (British headquarters in Palestine) after bombing by Zionist terrorists. GETTY IMAGES. REPRODUCED BY PERMISSION

it suspended hostilities and vowed to remain loyal to the British until the Nazis were defeated.

A more radical splinter group of the Haganah called the Irgun honored the truce, but within the Irgun was a yet more radical splinter group, the Etzel, which continued the campaign of terror during the war. When the war ended in 1945, these groups united in common cause against the British, and the level of violence intensified. The goal of all three groups was to drive the British out of Palestine so that Zionists could establish an independent Jewish state with unfettered immigration.

Among the acts of violence was the "Night of the Trains" on November 1, 1945, when terrorist units blew up railroad tracks and stations throughout the country.

On December 27, they attacked British Intelligence offices. On February 25, 1946, they struck British air bases on the "Night of the Airfields." On March 6, terrorists disguised as British soldiers attacked an army base, and on April 2, they launched further attacks against the railway system. On June 17, the "Night of the Bridges," terrorists bombed 11 bridges linking Palestine with neighboring countries. In response to these and other attacks, British forces launched severe reprisals, seizing arms and arresting Zionist leaders; much of this activity took place on what became known as "Black Sabbath," June 29, 1946.

In response to the Black Sabbath, the leaders of Irgun decided to bomb the British Army headquarters in Jerusalem's King David Hotel. Leading the assault was Menachem Begin, who in 1977 would become Israel's prime minister. On the morning of July 22, 1946, terrorists assembled and received their weapons. Disguised as Arabs, they carried seven milk churns into the basement of the hotel, each holding 110 pounds (50 kg) of explosives. Thirty minutes later the explosives detonated, destroying the entire southern wing of the hotel and killing 91 persons (28 Britons, 41 Arabs, 17 Jews, and 5 others). The damage is shown in the official government photo.

PRIMARY SOURCE

RUINS OF JERUSALEM'S KING DAVID HOTEL
See primary source image.

SIGNIFICANCE
As the terrorists exited the hotel before the explosives detonated, they instructed two women accompanying them to carry out their piece of the mission. At a nearby telephone booth the women called the King David Hotel operator and the *Jerusalem Post* and gave them this message: "I am speaking on behalf of the Hebrew underground. We have placed an explosive device in the hotel. Evacuate it at once—you have been warned." British Army personnel in the hotel did not take the warning seriously and many remained at their desks, accounting for the high number of casualties.

The leaders of the Jewish Agency, the successor organization to the World Zionist Organization, expressed shock at the bombing and denounced it, as did the Hebrew press and the British public. Moderates within the Haganah were beginning to recoil from the violence and on August 5, 1946, ordered it to stop. After that, the Haganah focused its efforts on smuggling illegal Jewish immigrants into Palestine and, to appease its more radical members, occasionally sabotaging British ships used to deport those immigrants. The Irgun, however, continued its campaign of separatist terrorism. On October 30, 1946, it bombed the Jerusalem Railway Station; on March 1, 1947, it bombed the Jerusalem Officers Club; and on May 4, it launched an assault on a prison in Acre where Jewish prisoners were held.

On November 29, 1947, the United Nations partitioned Palestine into the state of Israel and a Palestinian-Arab state. British administration of its mandate in Palestine ended in 1948.

FURTHER RESOURCES
Books

Laqueur, Walter. *A History of Zionism: From the French Revolution to the Establishment of the State of Israel.* New York: Schocken, 2003.

Shepherd, Naomi. *Ploughing Sand: British Rule in Palestine, 1917–1948.* Piscataway, NJ: Rutgers University Press, 1999.

Web sites

Lapidot, Yahuda. "The Irgun Site." <http://www.etzel.org.il/english/index.html> (accessed May 16, 2005).

"President Resting: Awakened by Shots"

Puerto Rican nationalists attempt to assassinate President Truman

Newspaper article

By: Anthony Leviero

Date: November 2, 1950

Source: "President resting: Awakened by Shots, He Sees Battle in Which Three are Wounded", as published in the *New York Times.*

About the Author: Anthony Leviero, a reporter for the *New York Times*, won the Pulitzer Prize for national reporting in 1952.

INTRODUCTION
In order to protest American control over Puerto Rico, Oscar Collazo and Griselio Torresola attempted to assassinate United States President Harry S. Truman (1884–1972) on November 1, 1950, at Blair House in Washington, D.C. Both men belonged to the Puerto Rican Nationalist Party. They thought the assassination

Puerto Rican nationalist Oscar Collazo lies wounded at the base of the steps to Blair House after a failed attempt to assassinate President Truman. AP/WIDE WORLD PHOTOS

would call attention to Puerto Rico and advance the cause of Puerto Rican independence. Torresola and a Blair House guard died in the attack. Collazo, sentenced to death, had his sentence commuted to life by Truman. He left prison in 1979.

Puerto Rico is a 3,435-square-mile (8897 square-kilometer) island about 1,000 miles from the mainland of the United States. Long a colony of Spain, Puerto Rico became an American possession following the victory of the United States in the Spanish-American War of 1898. Congress made the island the first unincorporated territory in U.S. history. As a consequence, it was not eligible for American statehood, yet it remained part of the United States.

In the years after the American takeover, Puerto Rico experienced landlessness, chronic unemployment, and steady population growth. Puerto Rican politicians repeatedly declared, occasionally through the use of political violence and murder, that the island's problems could be solved by independence from the United States.

In the 1940s, the U.S. Congress permitted Puerto Rico to elect its own governor, Luis Muñoz Marín of the Popular Democratic Party. Muñoz assumed that the economic transformation of the Puerto Rican economy would result in political independence.

Puerto Rican nationalists did not want to wait. On the morning of November 1, 1950, Torresola and Collazo had just arrived from New York City. Part of the massive post-World War II Puerto Rican migration to New York City, Torresola and Collazo belonged to the Puerto Rican Nationalist Party. Torresola, a skilled gunman, taught Collazo how to load and handle a gun. They familiarized themselves with the area near Blair House, across the street from the White House, where they would stage the assault. (During the 1948–1952 renovation of the White House, the Truman family stayed in the Blair House.) In the ensuing gun battle, Collazo and Torresola traded gunfire with White House policemen and secret service agents. They wounded three White House policemen, but never reached the interior of the house. One of the wounded policemen, Leslie Coffelt, hit Torresola in the side of the head, killing him instantly. Coffelt died later that day at the hospital. Two other policemen, Donald Birdzell and Joseph Downs, were each hit more than once, but recovered from their wounds.

Collazo was sentenced to death for the attempt on President Truman's life. One week before his scheduled execution in 1952, Truman changed the sentence to life imprisonment. President Carter commuted Collazo's sentence in September 1979, and he was freed from prison. He died in Puerto Rico on February 20, 1994, at the age of 80.

■ PRIMARY SOURCE

Washington, Nov. 1—Quick-shooting White House guards cut down two assassins this afternoon when they attempted to invade Blair House in a Puerto Rico Nationalist plot to assassinate President Truman. . .

On the body of the dead assassin Secret Service agents found a letter and a "memorandum," both cryptic but indicative of conspiracy. The missives were in the same handwriting and on the same stationery. They bore in the form of a signature, the name of Pedro Albizu Campos, leader of the Puerto Rican Nationalist extremists who carried out the uprising in Puerto Rico Monday . . .

Taking his usual afternoon nap and roused by a fury of shooting, Mr. Truman looked down from an upstairs bedroom of Blair House. In the bright sun of Pennsylvania Avenue was terror and confusion. At the foot of the stoop leading into Blair House lay one of the assassins, alive, blood flowing from the middle of his chest and staining his blue shirt.

"A President has to expect those things," Mr. Truman said, later.

Serene, a man of good conscience, for he had told the people of Puerto Rico unequivocally that they were free to work out their own political destiny, Mr. Truman punctiliously kept his remaining appointments of the day.

The outrage, however, made the Federal police agencies increasingly alert, and new safeguards were put around the President and his family. Meanwhile, the Secret Service began to trace back the plot through New York, to its apparent source in the island possession in the Caribbean, which is burying the numerous dead of a violent uprising.

Tonight, Maj. Robert J. Barrett, superintendent of the Washington Police, said that Collazo had been booked on a murder charge . . . there was no previous record on the two gunmen. They began plotting to kill the President ten days ago in New York . . .

For two days the assassins had holed up in the Hotel Harris here at 17 Massachusetts Avenue, planning the deed. They were recklessly bold men, apparently fanatics. But they did not plan well enough.

If the two gunmen, armed with German pistols, had waited another half hour, Mr. Truman would have walked down the granite steps of Blair House in plain view. He was to go—and he did go despite the attempt on his life—to Arlington National Cemetery for a ceremony . . .

True, the gunmen like other onlookers would have been held off at a distance, but at least they could have drawn a bead on the President. They could have read of his appointment in the papers. Instead they made an attempted frontal invasion against a line of dead shots.

The story was pieced together at the scene. . . The time was between 2:15 and 2:20 P.M. Mr. Truman had left his office in the White House around 1 P.M. for lunch and his nap in the temporary official residence in Blair-Lee House, which is commonly known as Blair House.

After lunch, Mr. Truman went to a bedroom on an upper floor. For security reasons, the Secret Service would not say which floor, but the room faces on broad Pennsylvania Avenue. The day was unusually warm and Mr. Truman removed all but his underwear.

Elsewhere in the mansion were Mrs. Truman and her mother, Mrs. David Wallace . . .

Then came the burst of shout, a score of pistol shots . . . He was awakened by the shots. The window was open. He rushed to the window and saw a man lying on the steps of Blair House and great confusion all around.

A policeman looked up and saw the President and shouted, "Get back! Get back!" . . .

Collazo had come walking westward from the corner of Jackson Place. He passed a wooden guard booth at the western edge of Blair House . . . Private Birdzell was blocking the way, but he happened to be looking westward. Collazo did not get too close. At about ten paces he drew a German Walther P-38 pistol, a common war souvenir of G.I.s, and apparently slid back the barrel mechanism which cocks the hammer. Mr. Birdzell said afterward he heard the click of it, but not soon enough.

Collazo opened fire with ten rounds in the magazine. Private Birdzell then did a brave thing . . . He drew his 38-caliber revolver, but did not shoot. He ran into the middle of Pennsylvania Avenue, to draw the fire away from the occupants of Blair House and from his fellow guard.

On the way to the street, Mr. Birdzell received one or more of his wounds. He dropped to one knee and began shooting. Meanwhile, Torresola, within a few seconds of Collazo's first shot, opened fire in front of Lee House, which is adjacent to the Blair mansion on the westerly side . . . Birdzell fired many shots. One of them caught Collazo squarely in the chest.

Torresola toppled and he died on his back in the little lawn in front of Lee House, lined at the sidewalk by a boxwood hedge. Torresola's weapon was a German Lugar, another favorite weapon of the G.I.s. Both weapons were nine-millimeter caliber, about the same as the American .38 but they each load ten bullets while the police revolvers take only six. Torresola emptied his entire magazine and had another that was found on the sidewalk.

SIGNIFICANCE

The attempt on Truman's life did not change American attitudes toward Puerto Rico. Treated as a footnote to both the Truman presidency and the modern history of Puerto Rico, the attack failed to achieve any of its goals. Puerto Rico remained a possession of the United States into the twenty-first century, with the U.S. Congress continuing to establish major policy for the Puerto Ricans.

In the years following 1950, the nationalist movement waxed and waned, both in Puerto Rico and among Puerto Rican migrants to North America. Many men and women of Puerto Rican heritage wanted independence, but such a move did not seem practical because of economic changes. As Puerto Rico industrialized, it discovered that being an American possession had considerable economic value.

Since agricultural businesses could not provide the money needed to better living standards, Governor Muñoz had argued for industrialization. He instituted Operation Bootstrap to industrialize Puerto Rico. Unlike competing Latin American and Caribbean countries that also offered inexpensive work forces, Puerto Rico could boast of the stability of its government. It was essentially the United States, but Spanish-speaking and with lower labor costs. Major American corporations established branches in Puerto Rico because of its American links. As a result, Puerto Ricans began to enjoy increasing living standards.

The Puerto Rican economic boom began to fade in the 1970s. Even with massive migration to the United States mixing with industrial achievement, Puerto Rico failed to provide sufficient income or jobs to sustain continued heavy population growth. As the economy weakened, nationalism began to rise and new Puerto Rican terrorist movements developed.

FURTHER RESOURCES

Books

McCullough, David. *Truman*. New York: Simon & Schuster, 1992.

Maldonado, A. W. *Teodoro Moscoso and Puerto Rico's Operation Bootstrap*. Gainesville: University Press of Florida, 1997.

Capture of Viet Minh Guerrilla

Terrorism and Anticolonial Conflicts: Vietnam and France

Photograph

Date: November 18, 1950

Source: The Associated Press

About the Photographer: The Associated Press is an international wire service that provides news and photographs to media outlets around the world.

INTRODUCTION

For over a century, the Vietnamese resisted foreign domination of their country. In the mid-nineteenth century, after the French established a foothold in southern Vietnam (which they called Cochin China), they encountered resistance from local Vietnamese officials, who refused to submit. Later, after the French expanded into central Vietnam (which they called Annam) and northern Vietnam (called Tonkin) and established Vietnam as a protectorate in 1883, insurgent peasants joined the nation's educated elite in a guerrilla war fought in the name of Emperor Ham Nghi even after the French captured him and forced him into exile in Algeria in 1888.

By the early twentieth century, the French had subdued Vietnam and gained control of its resources. French nationals were in charge of the administration of the country, while the Vietnamese worked in low-level positions. Displacing large numbers of peasants, French settlers occupied large tracts of land primarily in southern Vietnam, which became a rice-exporting region. The French opened rubber plantations and mines, where they exploited local workers who faced fines and jail time if they refused to work. The French levied taxes on major commodities, including salt, alcohol, and rice, and established a monopoly on the opium trade, turning Vietnam into a lucrative colony.

Meanwhile, the Vietnamese enjoyed few political rights. They could not travel outside their district without authorization. Organized protest was brutally repressed. Fewer and fewer Vietnamese were able to pursue educational opportunities. The result of French colonial policies was to foster development of an underground resistance movement. Among the leaders of the resistance was Nguyen Tat Thanh, later known by the aliases Nguyen Ai Quoc and, more famously, Ho Chi Minh ("He Who Enlightens").

Ho Chi Minh began his organized opposition to French rule in 1941, when he formed the League for

Vietnamese Independence, abbreviated as Viet Minh. During World War II (1938–1941), the Vietnamese faced the problem of dealing with two foreign occupying powers, the Japanese and French who were loyal to the Vichy government, Nazi Germany's puppet government in France after it fell in 1940. During this period, Ho Chi Minh and other guerrillas received military and financial assistance from the United States and in turn, often helped downed American pilots escape. With the end of the war, the Vietnamese resistance was hopeful that the victorious Allies would prevent the French from reasserting control of Vietnam. On September 2, 1945, Ho Chi Minh declared Vietnam a free and independent nation.

The United States, concerned about the spread of communism in the early years of the Cold War—a concern that grew during and after the Korean War—supported France, its wartime ally, in its efforts against the Vietnamese resistance during the First Indochina War from 1946 until 1954. By 1954, the United States under President Dwight D. Eisenhower (1890–1969) was footing 75% of France's costs in the conflict, which were soaring because of successful guerrilla tactics used against French forces. While some Vietnamese leaders, including Vo Nguyen Giap advocated and led terrorist raids, the French were also brutal in their efforts to bring Vietnam into submission.

PRIMARY SOURCE

CAPTURE OF VIET MINH GUERRILLA

See primary source image.

SIGNIFICANCE

Eventually, Ho Chi Minh and the resistance movement emerged victorious. The climactic event was the defeat of the French at Dien Bien Phu, a military outpost in northwest Vietnam. The French had amassed 13,000 to 16,000 troops at the garrison, hoping to lure the Vietnamese into a pitched battle. Vietnamese forces began their assault in March 1954, but rather than conducting a full-scale frontal assault, they continued to employ guerrilla tactics. The French, under constant fire, unable to resupply, and battling monsoons as well as insurgent troops, fell on May 7, 1954, bringing an end to French Indochina. The dead included 2,200 French troops, with thousands more taken prisoner, and an estimated 8,000 of the 50,000 Vietnamese troops who took part in the battle.

In 1954, the Geneva Accords officially brought the fighting to an end. The accords divided Vietnam along

PRIMARY SOURCE

Capture of Viet Minh Guerrilla Two mercenaries of the French Foreign Legion hold a Communist Viet Minh fighter at gunpoint. AP/WIDE WORLD PHOTOS

the 17th parallel, with Ho Chi Minh in control of the area north of the line and Ngo Dinh Diem installed as president of the south. The division was regarded as temporary; the accords also called for elections in 1956 that would reunify the country.

Diem, however, did not hold the elections. Rather, he conducted a referendum that affirmed his position as president in the south. In the years that followed, Diem became increasingly authoritarian. His base of support consisted in large part of Catholic refugees from the north, so he faced intense opposition from Buddhists, some of whom protested his anti-Buddhist policies by setting themselves on fire with gasoline in public places. In response to Diem, insurgents formed the National Liberation Front, later called the Viet Cong. Diem was rapidly losing U.S. confidence and, with American support, was ousted in a military coup. He was assassinated by the Vietnamese military on November 1, 1963.

FURTHER RESOURCES

Books

Duiker, William. *Ho Chi Minh: A Life*. New York: Hyperion, 2000.

Rice-Maximin, Edward. *Accommodation and Resistance: The French Left, Indochina and the Cold War, 1944–1954*. Westport, Conn.: Greenwood Press, 1986.

Web sites

Asian Society: Education and Communications Department. "Vietnam: A Teacher's Guide." <http://www.askasia.org /frclasrm/readings/r000189.htm#p> (accessed July 12, 2005).

The Wars for Viet Nam. "The Final Declarations of the Geneva Conference July 21, 1954." Vassar College. <http:// vietnam.vassar.edu/doc2.html> (accessed July 12, 2005).

The Algerian Army (ALN)

Anticolonial conflicts: Algeria and France

Book excerpt

By: Joan Brace and Richard Brace

Date: May 1965

Source: "The Algerian Army" is a chapter in the book, *Algerian Voices*, published in 1965 by the Van Nostrand Company.

About the Author: Richard and Joan Brace were also the authors of another book dealing with the Algerian-French conflict entitled *Ordeal in Algeria*, published in 1960, and the first book in English that presented the conflict from an Algerian point of view. The Braces were later invited by the revolutionary government to spend a few days with the Army of National Liberation (ALN) on the Algerian-Tunisian border in 1961, and detailed the experience in *Algerian Voices*.

INTRODUCTION

In 1954, nine Algerian nationalists formed the Comité revolutionnaire d'unité et d'action (CRUA) [Revolutionary Committee for Unity and Action] to promote armed struggle against the longtime French rule of Algeria. Later that year, CRUA became the Front de liberation nationale (FLN) [National Liberation Front], which had an armed wing known as the Armée de liberation nationale (ALN) [Army of National Liberation]. In November 1954, the ALN began the Algerian revolution with terrorist attacks on police stations, garages, gas works, and post offices in the city of Algiers. ALN operations quickly spread to the countryside. After the signing of a ceasefire between the FLN and France on March 18, 1962, Algeria gained independence from France on July 3, 1962.

The Algerians never welcomed French governance. Following the French invasion of this predominantly Muslim North African country in 1830, the Algerians refused to be subdued. On May 8, 1945, when the French celebrated the Victory in Europe at end of World War II, Algerians displayed nationalist flags and began an uprising in Sétif that initially killed more than 80 French. Subsequent French reprisals killed either 1,500 Algerians, according to French estimates, 45,000 Algerians, according to Algerian estimates, or 10,000–15,000 Algerians, according to independent estimates.

In 1947, a faction of the nationalists formed the Organization armée secrete [Secret Organization] to advocate armed resistance. In March 1954, nine members of this group, including Ahmed Ben Bella, formed CRUA. As French authorities resorted to the use of torture to obtain information about the uprising, Algerian nationalists responded with terrorist attacks. When the FLN and ALN formed in 1954, they immediately began using terrorism as a tactic against French imperialism.

The number of terrorists in the field likely numbered about 9,000, but widespread Algerian support for the ALN helped the organization to thrive. By 1956, there were about 400,000 French troops in Algeria attempting to control the revolt. The number of French soldiers in North Africa would rise to 500,000 by 1961.

■ PRIMARY SOURCE

. . . The main tenor of Amar's conversation was to be echoed by every Algerian officer we met later. This was the importance of the ALN in the Algerian Revolution. The army was

A car burns after the bomb inside explodes in front of Saigon's Hotel De Ville in 1952. AP/WIDE WORLD PHOTOS

the heart of the Revolution: without its sacrifice no real progress toward independence could have been made, since everything else had been tried over the years. Neither could the army have been efficient or enduring without the support of the Algerian people. It would have been impossible for 150,000 men to stalemate French army forces of 500,000, particularly when these forces were reinforced by police, security guards, French militia, and naval personnel to bring the total to nearly 800,000. He pointed out a very interesting fact. In many cases army personnel had been first used in some other capacity by the FLN, which was the only political force behind the revolution until the Provisional Government of the Algerian Republic was formed in September 1958. Army men had acted as *fidayines* (Death Commandos) or *moussebelines* (in training for the army or *fidayines)* organizing men, money, and supplies, terror, liaison, etc., inside Algeria. Once the French knew of their identity or their work, they were passed through the lines into the army, where, in fact, mortality was much lower, food better, and a man was armed against his enemy. So also, in the Algerian Provisional Government, the men of the Interministerial Committee of National Defense, who served for twenty minutes after December, 1959, Abdel Hamid Boussouf, Lakhdar Ben Tobbal, Belkacem Krim, all former *wilaya* (military province) commanders, had passed into the government after ALN service. These are some of the reasons why one needed to understand and gauge the political feelings of the army in order to judge the possible drift of the Revolution . . .

. . . Amar believed that if it were true that there was no Algerian nation in 1954 on the eve of the rebellion, the Revolution, the great suffering under the French "pacification," and another batch of broken French promises, now signed by an illustrious name, had served to create it. The Revolution destroyed many old things and customs to build the brave new world. For example, the status of Algerian women had advanced more in seven years than in the previous thousand.

Girls who had not been out of their homes unchaperoned, girls who had worn the veil since the age of puberty even in front of their own fathers, adopted Western dress and Western mobility. They traveled all over the country alone, doing liaison work, delivering weapons. They went up into the mountains to care for the wounded and homeless children. Because they carried intelligence and were in continual contact with the rebels, they were often subject to the worst of the French torture apparatus.

When the French began singling out Western-dressed Algerian girls, such as that other Djamila, Bouhired, the wily females went back under the veil. It made a wonderful shelter for weapons small enough to be wrapped around the body. A *moudjahidine* or *fidayine* could show her hands shyly to a French paratrooper and continue on, a walking arsenal under her modest flowing robes. Young Algerian wives whose husbands and brothers were in the ALN hid *djounods* on the run, cared for the wounded, and harbored them until a safe moment for escape. This performance would have been unthinkable before 1954, when even a woman's nose was not for public contemplation. It would have brought violent protest from husbands and village elders. But the new Algerian woman is today approved of with pride by the young male community . . .

. . . No-nonsense of speech, as Turki had promised, the captain commenced our three-day interview by "falling on us" quite literally. So we were Americans, were we, he said, and why was it then, that Americans who pretended to love freedom and the cause of justice would permit the French to use their materials and equipment in this, the most unjust of colonial wars? Was NATO [North Atlantic Treaty Organization], then a hypocritical organism whose real purpose was to secure the power of the have nations against the have-not nations? Was NATO created to perpetuate the colonial regime? And many such uncomfortable questions, but all offered in the most perfect personal courtesy. We later learned that he had studied engineering before the war, and served in the French administration. After the experience of several faked elections for the Second College (the Algerian College), he joined the FLN. Later Ben Bella told us that at first he had tried to keep him out of the shooting war. When Ben Bella was hauled off the Moroccan plane and put in jail, Abdelghanid took off for the maquis . . .

. . . We were told that the men of the border lines kept nearly constant pressure—attacks every week or so—on the Challe-Morice Line. On May 5 and 6, for example, an attack by some 3,000 Freedom Fighters (*moudjahidines*) had taken place. The attacks were made for the purpose of passing men and supplies into Algeria and to capture weapons. Always they were made to gainsay French propaganda of a "pacified" Algeria, which no one believed anymore anyhow. The officers and men fighting on the Algerian lines knew that the war must be kept up until the conclusion of political agreements between the French and Algerians, or else the sacrifice of seven years would be meaningless . . .

SIGNIFICANCE

The Algerian uprising proved traumatic for the French, who were threatened by the loss of status that came with the loss of a colony. The Algerian conflict was a principal reason behind France's attack, along with Great Britain, upon Egypt in 1956 during the Suez Canal crisis. France sought to punish Egypt's leader, Gamal Abdel Nasser, for his support of the FLN. The failure of the Suez attack and the French government's inability to resolve the Algerian situation led to the collapse of the French Fourth Republic in 1958 and brought General Charles De Gaulle to power.

By 1958, the French people had grown tired of the troubles in Algeria. A French referendum approved a new constitution for Algeria in 1958, prompting new French President De Gaulle to propose a ceasefire. On September 16, 1959, De Gaulle promised that Algeria would have self-determination within four years. A provisional Algerian government formed in Algiers under President Abderrahman Farès on March 28, 1962. When Algerians voted for independence, De Gaulle granted it in on July 3, 1962.

The violence in Algeria was part of a straightforward independence struggle by indigenous people against their French rulers. It was the direct outgrowth of a wave of nationalism that swept through Africa after World War II. Part of an era that also saw anti-imperialist terrorism in the European colonies of Cameroon, Egypt, Ethiopia, Guinea-Bissau, Kenya, Mozambique, Tunisia, and Zimbabwe, the Algerian war left about 141,000 Algerians dead. The French costs of the conflict included 17,250 dead soldiers and 51,800 injured troops, with several thousand civilian casualties.

In the years following independence, Algeria has had a lukewarm relationship with France. It has since fully recovered from its war of independence. With large oil and gas deposits, Algeria is among the wealthiest and most advanced of African countries.

FURTHER RESOURCES
Books

O'Balance, Edgar. *The Algerian Insurrection, 1954–1962*. London: Faber & Faber, 1967.

Quandt, William B. *Revolution and Political Leadership: Algeria, 1954–1968*. Cambridge, MA: Massachusetts Institute of Technology, 1969.

"We Did Not Wish to Wage a Colonial War"

Anticolonial Conflicts: Belgium and the Congo

Speech

By: Louis M. Scheyven

Date: May 15, 1961

Source: *Vital Speeches of the Day.*

About the Author: Louis M. Scheyven served as the Belgian Ambassador to the United States during the early 1960s. *Vital Speeches of the Day* is a bi-weekly magazine that has archived speeches delivered by leaders since 1934.

INTRODUCTION

The independence of the Belgian Congo, later known as both Zaire and the Democratic Republic of the Congo, came unexpectedly in 1960 with no preliminary armed struggle. Influenced by independence movements in other parts of Africa, the Congolese began to press for an end to Belgian colonial rule. Belgium, hoping to avoid the same sort of conflicts experienced by the French in colonial Algeria and Indo-China, declared Congolese independence in July 1960. Fighting broke out almost immediately afterward throughout the Congo, however, as rival African tribal factions vied for control.

Congo was the second largest country in Africa with a population of about 40 million people in an area of over 900,000 square miles (2,331,000 sq. km) in Central Africa in 1960. In the European scramble for the wealth of Africa during the nineteenth century, Congo had first become the private project of Belgium's King Leopold II. When the Belgian government hesitated to become involved in colonization for fear of causing controversy, Leopold annexed the area in 1879. His rule over the Congo Free State is notable for its brutality, including slave labor on rubber plantations that cost the lives of millions of Congolese. In 1908, Belgium took control of the area, which became known as the Belgian Congo.

Belgium helped maintain control over their colony by providing little aid for African education and by restricting Congolese participation in the government to clerical work.

The Belgians had initially assumed that independence would be a lengthy process, perhaps hoping to maintain control over the region for as long as possible. However, independence movements in Africa in the late 1950s sparked an awakening of Congolese nationalism.

The Belgian government noted that French efforts to maintain control over its colonies in Algeria and Indo-China had become extremely costly and that the regions erupted in anti-colonial warfare. In contrast, quick British withdrawal from the Sudan and Ghana were conducted peacefully. Belgium adopted a policy of speedy withdrawal from the Congo. In December 1957, the Belgians permitted limited municipal elections. In 1958, the Belgian government created a commission to study constitutional reform. Meanwhile, secret Congolese political organizations were forming including the Mouvement National Congolais (MNC) led by Patrice Lumumba. The MNC, the first truly national Congolese movement, sought independence by peaceful means.

However, many Congolese were upset with the slow pace of Belgian-led independence reforms. In 1959, a mix of political frustration and anger over racial discrimination prompted Congolese rioters to attack Europeans in Leopoldville. In a conference held in response to the rioting, various Congolese political leaders demanded self-government by 1961. The Belgian government responded with a four-year plan for transition to independence that led to more Congolese rioting. Mid–1960 elections were held that enabled Lumumba to form a government. On July 1, 1960, the independent Republic of the Congo was established.

PRIMARY SOURCE

The purpose of my statement is mainly to answer two questions which are repeatedly raised against the Belgian policy in the Congo. 1) Why did Belgium grant independence to the Congo so quickly? 2) Why did Belgium not prepare the Congolese for self-government?

Of course, we knew in Brussels that the Congolese were not yet ready for independence, but we have been subjected to heavy internal and external pressure. I need only to remind you of the Bandung Conference in 1956, of the Accra Conference of December 1958. Furthermore, in 1960 alone, 17 new African states reached the status of independence. As far as internal pressure is concerned, riots broke out in Leopoldville in January 1959 and 47 people were killed. On October 30th 1959, riots broke out in Stanleyville, the strong-

hold of Patrice Lumumba: 70 people were killed and hundreds wounded. On the other hand, the General Assembly of the United Nations approved, last December, by 89 votes, a declaration on the granting of independence to colonial countries and peoples. It stated that (quote) "the lack of political, economic, social, or educational preparedness should never serve as a pretext for delaying independence . . . " (unquote).

The only way to prevent the Congolese from becoming independent was to wage a colonial war: as we Belgians have been fighting so long for our own independence, we were not ready to wage such a war, and of course, it was out of the question to get the support of anyone including the United States. So we took two important steps: First of all, on a proposal made by the Belgian Government, the Belgian Parliament agreed to earmark without strings $100,000,000 during the year 1960 alone for the Congo and the Trusteeship Territories of Ruanda-Urundi . . .

You are fully aware of what happened a few days after the independence of the Congo: the mutiny of the Force Publique, the raping of hundreds of Belgian women, the exodus of a large number of my countrymen, the appeal for help made by Lumumba to Moscow and Peking, the chaotic conditions which are now prevailing in some parts of the Congo, the dissention which has existed between some of their leaders and the intervention of the United Nations.

My Government is ready to recall the Belgians mentioned in the U.N. Security Council resolution of the 21st of February 1961. But in order to carry on, the Congolese need the help of foreign technicians and so far, the United Nations has only been able to recruit 196 foreigners for civilian operations in the Congo, while the need for technicians in the private as well as in the public field is much greater.

As Mr. Loridan, Belgian Ambassador to the United Nations, stated on the 6th of this month in the meeting of the General Assembly:

> The independence of the Congo was proclaimed by Belgium without any reservation, limitation, or afterthought. It is an accomplished fact.
> Belgium wishes to respect the sovereignty of the Congo and refuses to engage in any intervention in the internal affairs of that country.
> Belgium wishes to consolidate friendly relations with the Congo and to develop its cooperation with that country on a basis of esteem and complete equality. Belgium condemns any unilateral military aid or assistance furnished to the Congo in any form whatsoever.

As Mr. [Adlai] Stevenson stated in 1957, we have to meet the great challenge of emerging Africa. Your country, Gentlemen, is the leader of the Free World and you will, I feel convinced, meet that great challenge. You may rest assured that you will always find Belgium at your side.

SIGNIFICANCE

Congo has suffered from the legacy of colonialism. During the colonial era, police were used to quell disturbances, put down protests, and arrest political agitators. These practices were echoed after independence as rival politicians, political parties, and tribes clashed with each other over old and new differences. In July 1960, fighting in Leopoldville occurred between members of the Bakongo and Bayaka tribes. Later that month, Lumumba ordered the arrest of members of a rival provincial government led by Albert Kalonji. In Coquilhatville, several people were killed in riots that began when workers demanded a pay raise. On July 5, 1960, soldiers at a military garrison south of Leopoldville mutinied, killed Belgian officers (who were still in Congo at the request of Lumumba), and attacked resident Europeans. The mutiny spread, with many Europeans fleeing to the French Congo and Belgium sending additional troops to protect Belgian nationals.

The instability in the Congo prompted the United Nations (U.N.) to take action. On July 13, 1960, the UN Security Council approved a resolution condemning armed aggression by Belgium against Congo, calling for the withdrawal of all Belgian troops from Congo, and authorizing a U.N. intervention force of African troops to restore order. On July 29, Belgium withdrew its troops. Several Congolese politicians blamed Lumumba for the disorder and the Katanga province attempted to secede from Congo. Instability continued in Congo for the remainder of the twentieth century.

Congo, as a fledgling state, did not have the means to address major concerns such as creating employment opportunities and housing, or the development of adequate health care and educational systems. In January 1961, Lumumba was murdered by political opponents. In December 1961, the U.N. condemned the use of mercenaries in the continuing Congo bloodshed. In April 1967, the Congo became a one-party state under the dictatorship of Joseph Mobuto. In the early 1970s, Congo was renamed Zaire as part of an Africanization program that eliminated foreign-sounding words and place names. Foreigners were expelled from the country and tribal conflicts continued. In 1991, Belgian troops returned to the Congo to attempt to restore order. After several attempted coups, numerous uprisings, and violent ethnic clashes, Mobuto fled into exile in May 1997.

At the start of the twenty-first century, the Democratic Republic of the Congo was still attempting to establish a democratic form of government. The nation possesses considerable resources, especially uranium, diamonds, and copper, but political instability, ethnic partisanship, and brutal conflict have prevented the formation of a stable government and economy.

FURTHER RESOURCES

Books

Black, Jeremy. *War Since 1945*. London: Reaktion Books, 2004.

Lemarchand, René. *Political Awakening in the Belgian Congo*. Berkeley: University of California Press, 1964.

O'Balance, Edgar. *The Congo-Zaire Experience, 1960-98*. New York: St. Martin's Press, 2000.

"Bloody Friday—It Was the Worst Yet"

Provisional IRA Coordinated Bombings in Belfast, Northern Ireland

Newspaper article

By: Bernard Weinraub

Date: July 23, 1972

Source: *New York Times*.

About the Author: Bernard Weinraub was a veteran *New York Times* reporter, who served as a correspondent in a number of areas, from the UK to Hollywood. He retired in 2004.

INTRODUCTION

Northern Ireland's descent into political chaos and civil insurrection reached a bloody nadir in January 1972, when British paratroopers killed 13 unarmed civilians during a civil rights march in Derry. Ulster's "Bloody Sunday" provoked widespread outrage and worsened the already perilous security situation in the province.

As a consequence the British Prime Minister, Edward Heath, stripped the Unionist parliament at Stormont, which had governed Northern Ireland since the foundation of the state in 1921, of all of its powers at the end of March 1972. In its place he introduced direct rule from Westminster (the British Parliament in London). Unionists were outraged at the suspension of Parliament and set about leading a number of protest strikes; and while many Catholics welcomed the fall of Unionist-dominated Stormont, the Irish Republican Army (IRA) saw direct rule as further evidence of British intentions to remain in Northern Ireland. As a result, they stepped up their bombing campaign.

In the short term, this upsurge in violence had devastating consequences both for the victims and for republican support. A revenge attack on a British Army

The scene of a car bomb explosion that took place the previous day in the center of Dublin, Ireland. AP/WIDE WORLD PHOTOS

barracks in Aldershot had killed civilians rather than soldiers; and another attack in Derry had killed a Catholic soldier, attracting disastrous publicity for the IRA.

Sensing the changing mood of the nationalist community after these attacks, but also believing they were in a stronger negotiating position, the Provisional IRA called a press conference in Derry and proclaimed that they were ready to call a truce. In exchange for a ceasefire and talks, they announced, they wanted the British government to grant prisoner of war status to all of its operatives it held in detention. The government agreed, and the IRA announced a ceasefire at the end of June 1972.

IRA leaders, including Martin McGuinness and Gerry Adams, then traveled to London to meet the secretary of state for Northern Ireland, William Whitelaw, on July 7. At the meeting, they demanded that Britain withdraw from Ireland before January 1, 1975. Whitelaw invariably could not agree with the demand; the talks broke down almost immediately.

The ceasefire ended 48 hours later when the IRA opened fire on soldiers who had been preventing Catholics from moving into empty houses vacated by Protestants in west Belfast. That night, further clashes led to the deaths of nine people including a Catholic priest.

The IRA now set out to prove that the British were incapable of holding power in Northern Ireland. By bringing a reign of terror on the province, they sought to demonstrate that British forces had no control of events.

On Friday July 21, 1972, the IRA set off 21 bombs across Belfast. Nine deaths were caused by two of the bombs, including six people at Belfast's busiest bus station.

PRIMARY SOURCE

Belfast, Northern Ireland—Shopkeepers were preparing for the weekend. Office girls were returning to work. Children were strolling with their mothers. The time was 2:09 P.M. last Friday.

Suddenly a bomb blast rocked downtown Belfast. Then, one by one, other bombs were detonated at bus terminals, railroad stations, shopping centers, and cafeterias.

"The whole place exploded around us," said 20-year-old Robert McMaster, sitting with a friend in a downtown cafeteria. "People were screaming and moaning. Girls with blood all over them were staggering about. We got hold of them and helped them out."

At a railway station, John Hayes, a trainman, said: "The mutilation was terrible. I hope to God I never see another sight like this in all my life. What calloused killers can do this?"

In just over one horrific hour, Belfast was reduced to chaos. Eleven persons were killed and 130 injured. The city was—and remains—in panic.

"This was Bloody Friday," said an official close to William Whitelaw, the British Ambassador of Ulster. "It was a cold-blooded attempt by the "Provos" [the Irish Republican Army's Provisional wing] to maim and slaughter on an occasion when so many people in Belfast were shopping and travelling."

The reasons for the bombing remained unclear. There was some sense that the I.R.A. was trying to provoke the British Army into a new offensive in Roman Catholic areas, possibly even the rounding up of I.R.A. suspects and interning them without trial. Such a move by the army would be bitterly resented by Catholics and bolster support for the I.R.A.

A second possibility was that the I.R.A. was seeking to provoke the militant Ulster Defense Association into large-scale attacks on Catholic areas, thus plunging Northern Ireland into civil war.

There was some belief that the bombings had been staged as a massive show of force to set the stage for another cease-fire and that within a few days the Provisionals would ask for a bilateral truce.

Whatever the reason, the British are planning stiff counter measures against the I.R.A.—and the unrelenting nightmare in Northern Ireland seems likely to continue.

"You say things are terrible and you shake your head but that's all you can do," said a Protestant businessman in a Belfast surburb. "People's tempers are short. Everyone's on the bloody edge."

One ominous aspect of life in Belfast is the continuing "ghettoization" of both Catholic and Protestant communities—the gradual ending of mixed working-class neighborhoods through intimidation and fear and the cementing of sectarian divisions.

It was this intimidation that led, in effect, to the breakdown of the 13-day truce on July 9. On that Sunday afternoon, soldiers clashed with Roman Catholic demonstrators seeking to install 16 refugee families in homes left vacant by Protestants in the Lenadoon area. The Catholic families had left their own neighborhood in fear of Protestant violence, and they had been given permission to occupy the empty houses. But permission was revoked when militant Protestants objected. Negotiations continued until the clash—and the abrupt announcement by the "Provos" ending the truce.

The conflict over housing has continued—partly exploited by the "Provos." As the British Army sent 800 soldiers into the pleasant, leafy Lenadoon area—mostly to deny the I.R.A. positions in certain houses—other Catholics in the area angrily evacuated the area.

"We're going to stay away until the British get out," said Mrs. Shelia Boyle, sitting with other mothers at the La-Salle school, half a mile from their homes.

The problem of Lenadoon must be resolved before a cease-fire can be renegotiated. Associates of Mr. Whitelaw had conferred with members of the I.R.A. in both London and Belfast, and former Prime Minister Harold Wilson had met with I.R.A. leaders who secretly flew to London. But that was before Bloody Friday cast a pall over the prospects of another truce.

SIGNIFICANCE

The July bombings provoked widespread horror and the day soon became dubbed "Bloody Friday." Revulsion at the carnage was barely tempered by the IRA's insistence that the civilian deaths were the responsibility of the security forces, who, they claimed, had not passed on the warnings on time. Nor were further terrorist outrages ever far away.

Nevertheless, attempts by moderate republicans, such as the SDLP, to create a political solution to Northern Ireland's ongoing problems seemed to reach fruition in November 1973. Negotiations between Edward Heath and the Irish Taoiseach (head of the government), Liam Cosgrove, at Sunningdale in Berkshire, led to the creation of a power-sharing executive, which restored devolved government to Northern Ireland on January 1, 1974. This lasted just five months, however, after the assembly was repeatedly undermined by unionist politicians.

The IRA, however, after the collapse of talks with William Whitelaw two years earlier, would mark 1974 as the most notorious year of their campaign of mainland bombings. High profile attacks included the bombing of a bus filled with soldiers and their families, which killed twelve; attacks on pubs in Guilford and Birmingham, which left four and nineteen dead respectively; and the bombing of Harrods department store in London. In Ireland, car bombs in Dublin and Monaghan also killed thirty-three people.

Over the following twenty years, the IRA set upon a campaign of terror in mainland Britain and in

Northern Ireland. Despite claiming to only attack military and financial targets, civilians were frequently caught up in their actions.

Only in the mid–1990s would the stream of terrorist attacks start to ebb. Secret talks initiated by the British Prime Minister, John Major, led to a ceasefire in September 1994. This broke down seventeen months later, but a second ceasefire, called in July 1997, proved more enduring. The second ceasefire paved the way for talks on power sharing in Northern Ireland, which culminated in the Good Friday Agreement of 1998.

Devolved government in the province started later that year, and stuttered along through four years of disagreements between the republican-nationalist Sinn Fein, and the two main Unionist political parties. The Assembly was suspended in October 2002 because of the IRA's refusal to decommission its remaining arms and disband, but the ceasefire continued to hold.

FURTHER RESOURCES

Books

McKittrick, David and David McVeigh. *Making Sense of the Troubles*. London: Penguin 2003.

Audio and Visual Media

BBC News. <www.bbc.co.uk/history/war/troubles/ram/ocr09_a1.ram> (accessed July 5, 2005).

Munich Olympics and Black September

"Arab Commando Group Seizes Members of the Israeli Olympic Team at their Quarters at the Munich Olympic Village"

Photo

By: Kurt Strumpf

Date: September 5, 1972

Source: The Associated Press.

About the Photographer: Kurt Strumpf was a photographer for The Associated Press, an international wire service that provides news and photographs to news agencies around the world.

INTRODUCTION

When it occurred, the attack on the Israeli Olympic delegation to the 1972 Summer Olympics was one of the most shocking acts of terrorism ever carried out.

Blood stains and bullet holes mark the place where Israeli weightlifter, Moshe Romano, was killed by Arab commandos at the 1972 Olympics. AP/WIDE WORLD PHOTOS

The events began 4:30 A.M. on September 5, 1972 as the Israeli athletes were sleeping in their rooms in the Olympic village in Munich, Germany. Eight members of the Palestinian group Black September, a faction of the Palestinian Liberation Organization (PLO), broke into the village and took nine Israeli athletes hostage. The terrorists later killed the hostages during a series of dramatic events.

In the early moments of the attack, an Israeli weightlifter and a wrestling coach were immediately killed as two other Israelis escaped. The nine remaining athletes were taken hostage, and their captors demanded the release of 234 Palestinians being held in Israel as well as two other Palestinians being held in Germany. The Israelis immediately refused and asked the German government for permission to send a special-forces unit to Germany, but the German police chose to use their own forces to attempt to resolve the crisis.

After the terrorists were granted the right to move along with the hostages to a nearby airport, a German police team began a mission to rescue the hostages. With little or no special-forces training and poor communication and equipment, the German team fired on the terrorists, but failed to kill all of them. Three terrorists remained alive, along with the nine hostages who were still in the two helicopters that had flown them out of the Olympic village.

Just after midnight on September 6, one of the terrorists jumped out of one of the helicopters, threw a grenade onto the hostages, and shot at the four Israelis inside. The five other Israeli athletes in the second helicopter were killed when a gun battle broke out between the terrorists and the German police. By 12:30 A.M., all nine Israeli athletes were dead and three kidnappers were caught alive.

Despite the shock and tragedy of the attack, the decision was made that the 1972 Olympics would be completed after being suspended for the day of September 5, as the crisis unfolded.

On September 9, 1972, the Israeli Air Force bombed PLO facilities in Syria and Lebanon in retaliation for the Munich attack. Israeli Prime Minister Golda Meir (1898–1978) also agreed in secret meetings with the Israeli intelligence agency, the Mossad, that Black September members would be targeted wherever in the world they could be found. By 2005, only Mohammed Daoud Oudeh, who claimed to have masterminded the Munich attack, remained alive.

■ PRIMARY SOURCE

MUNICH OLYMPICS AND BLACK SEPTEMBER
See primary source image.

SIGNIFICANCE

The television images broadcast from the 1972 Olympics in Munich had a lasting impact on how terrorism would be covered by the international media. This image of the terrorist leaning over the balcony of the Olympic compound was to become one of the most widely known pictures of its day.

As the Olympic Games are typically one of the most watched events in television, the events in Munich in 1972 were recorded by cameras for almost the entire twenty-one hour ordeal—from the time the Israeli athletes were besieged until they were all dead early the next day. The 1972 games were, in fact, the first time that the Olympics were broadcast live.

The central media placement of the Munich terrorist attack has led many to ask the question of what role the media has to play in the minds of the terrorists themselves. Terrorist activity is often intended by its perpetrators to draw attention to a specific issue of interest by disrupting the daily life of intended victims by causing fear. Media attention does, in many ways, help the terrorists achieve their aims. The Black September group clearly understood that the Olympics would be a highly televised event. By choosing Munich as the site to launch the attack, they intended to reach the eyes and ears of millions across the globe. In the United States, the fact that the incident was recorded live directly exposed Americans to the extent of the violence that existed in the Middle East conflict. The Olympics massacre and the images which emerged

■ PRIMARY SOURCE

Munich Olympics and Black September A member of the Arab Commando group that seized members of the Israeli Olympic Team at the Munich Olympic Village. AP/WIDE WORLD PHOTOS

from it would have a lasting effect on how the West perceived the Arab-Israeli conflict.

In subsequent years, through technological innovation and expanded coverage, the media has been able to provide more extensive and live coverage of terrorist activity as it happens. The attack on the Munich Olympics was therefore perhaps most significant because, through the medium of television, the terrorists succeeded in terrorizing not just those directly affected but the general public watching around the world.

FURTHER RESOURCES
Books

Reeve, Simon. *One Day in September: The Full Story of the 1972 Munich Olympics Massacre and the Israeli Revenge Operation "Wrath of God."* New York: Arcade Publishing, 2001.

Periodicals

Web sites

ASEAN Mass Communications Studies and Research Center. "Television, Terrorism and the Making of Incomprehension." <http://www.utcc.ac.th/amsar/about/document3.html> (accessed July 4, 2005).

Council on Foreign Relations. "Terrorism and the Media." <http://cfrterrorism.org/terrorism/media.html> (accessed July 4, 2005).

U.S. Ambassador to Sudan Assassinated

"U.S. Ambassador to Sudan and His Aide Reported Seized by Guerrillas at Party"

Newspaper article

By: Richard D. Lyons

Date: March 2, 1973

Source: *New York Times.*

About the Author: At the time the primary source was written, Richard D. Lyons was a reporter for the *New York Times.*

INTRODUCTION

Early in the evening of March 1, 1979, United States Ambassador to the Sudan Cleo A. Noel, Jr., along with George Curtis Moore (Noel's *Chargé d'Affaires,* or deputy chief of mission) and Guy Eid (a Belgian diplomat), were kidnapped by eight masked gunmen while exiting a diplomatic reception at the Saudi Arabian embassy in Khartoum, the capital of the Sudan in north-central Africa.

After securing their prisoners, the terrorists sent out leaflets demanding the release of Sirhan Sirhan (the Palestinian assassin of Robert Kennedy) held in California, Palestinian women held in Israeli prisons, Palestinian terrorists (including Abu Daoud) held in Jordan and Israel, several members of the Baader-Meinhof gang held in Germany, and other hostages.

The terrorists were soon identified as members of the Black September Organization (BSO), a secret Palestinian terrorist group controlled by the intelligence organization, Jihaz al-Rasd, which is headed by Fatah, the main party of the Palestine Liberation Organization (PLO). Although U.S. President Richard Nixon publicly refused to negotiate directly with the terrorists, third parties conducted discrete negotiations.

Senator Robert F. Kennedy talks to campaign workers in Los Angeles minutes before his assassination at the hands of Sirhan Sirhan. AP/WIDE WORLD PHOTOS

On March 2, 1973, the Israeli government recorded radio conversations between leaders of the PLO in Beirut, Lebanon, and the BSO members in Khartoum.

According to transcripts of these conversations, at around 8:00 P.M. (local Khartoum time), Abu-Iyad called Abu-Ghassan, one of the terrorists, in order to give him the coded message: "Remember Nahr al-Bard 'Cold River.' The people's blood in the Narh al-Bard is screaming for revenge. These are our final orders. We and the world are watching you." (Cold River was the code to execute the prisoners.)

About an hour later, the eight terrorists lined up the three bound men against a basement wall and shot them. Thinking the executions had not taken place, PLO chairman Yasir Arafat then talked with Abu-Ghassan, asking him: "Why are you waiting? The people's blood in the Cold River cries for vengeance." Abu-Ghassan responded back to Arafat verifying that the order had been carried out.

Authorities assume that later in the month, the tape produced by Israel was given to the U.S. State Department and the White House. Its authenticity was verified by U.S. technical laboratories and its accuracy was later confirmed by Israeli General Ariel Sharon. In addition, at least one National Security Agency (NSA), employee subsequently claimed to have received transcripts of dialogue between Arafat and his subordinates.

PRIMARY SOURCE

Washington, March 1—The State Department received reports today that Palestinian guerrillas in the Sudan had captured five diplomats, including the United States Ambassador and outgoing charge d'affaires, and were seeking to exchange them for several hundred prisoners including Sirhan Sirhan, the murderer of Robert F. Kennedy.

Besides the Americans, according to the radio reports monitored here, members of the Black September terrorist movement in Khartoum captured the Saudi Arabian Ambassador and the charges d'affaires of Jordan and Belgium. [Japan's Foreign Ministry said its charge d'affaire was among the hostages, United Press International reported.]

[In Khartoum, Reuters reported, the Saudi Arabian Ambassador, Abdullah al-Malhouk, in whose embassy the capture took place, said by telephone that terrorists with submachine guns had invaded the embassy and had wounded the two American diplomats. A doctor was seen going into the embassy, and he later emerged and said that "everything is okay," the agency reported.]

The reports said that the terrorists had captured the diplomats at the Saudi Embassy during a reception given by the Ambassador in honor of George C. Moore, the counselor of embassy and charge d'affaires, who had been ordered back to Washington for reassignment.

Diplomatic relations between the United States and the Sudan, broken off after the Arab-Israeli war of 1967, were resumed last August.

Cleo A. Noel Jr., the United States Ambassador to the Sudan, was sent there in December to take over from Mr. Moore. Mr. Noel, a 54-year-old specialist on Arab affairs is serving his third tour of duty in Khartoum. He was first assigned there 15 years ago.

Reports monitored here said that the terrorists had entered the Saudi Arabian compound about 7 P.M. Khartoum time (noon, E.S.T.) when a large number of diplomats had gathered there.

During the confusion, according to the reports, the British, French, and Soviet Ambassadors escaped.

State Department officials said a task force had been assembled here to weigh the complexities of the situation and that Washington had been in contact with Khartoum, where an emergency session of the Cabinet was being held.

A spokesman for the State Department implied that the United States had not entered into negotiations for the release of Mr. Noel and Mr. Moore. "The reports are sketchy and we haven't had time to put it all together," he said.

But, reports from the Middle East said that President Gasfar al-Nimeiry of the Sudan had been in consultation with other Arab leaders on how best to deal with the situation.

The reported capture of Mr. Noel, Mr. Moore and the other diplomats was regarded by Arab specialists here with surprise because Arab extremist groups, especially Black September, had not been active in the Sudan.

The activities of the Black September movement have included aerial hijackings, bombings and assassinations and the murder of 11 Israelis who were participating in the Olympics in Munich last year.

In was unclear from the reports what the terrorists intended to do with the diplomatic hostages if Sirhan and the other prisoners were not released. Sirhan is imprisoned in California.

Sirhan was a Palestinian immigrant in Los Angeles who fatally shot Mr. Kennedy, then a Democratic Senator from New York, during the Presidential primary campaign in California five years ago.

Sirhan was sentenced to death in 1969, but his sentence was commuted to life imprisonment last year when the California Supreme Court outlawed the death penalty.

In addition to Sirhan, the radio reports stated that Black September was seeking the release from prisons in "the Zionist state of occupation," meaning Israel, of "all detained brothers and sisters and strugglers for the freedom of Palestine," While the number is uncertain, it is expected to be several hundred.

The radio reports said that the guerrillas had also demanded the release of 17 members of Al Fatah, the main Palestinian guerrilla group, and Maj. Rafeh Hindawi, a Jordanian officer serving a life sentence in Amman for complicity in a plot to kill King Hussein.

Abou Daoud, a member of Fatah's Revolutionary Council, is among the 17 in custody in Amman facing a court-martial on charges of subversive activity.

MOORE FLUENT IN ARABIC

Additionally, the demands monitored here, called for the release of 50 persons from Jordanian prisons and of two men held in West Germany. Most of the reports monitored here were broadcast by the state-controlled Omdurman radio.

Mr. Noel is a native of Oklahoma City who attended the University of Missouri and Harvard and joined the State department in 1949. He has served in various diplomatic posts in the Middle East and Europe. He and his wife, the former Lucille McHenry, have two children.

Mr. Moore, who is 47 years old, has degrees from the University of Southern California. He joined the State Department in 1950, is fluent in Arabic and has held diplomatic posts in six Middle Eastern cities. He is married to the former Sarah Stewart.

Charles W. Bray 3d, the State Department spokesman, said that he had been informed that some of those at the reception had been released by the guerrillas and allowed to leave the Saudi Embassy.

"I presume it is from them that we have the first word," Mr. Bray said.

The last major Black September operation in an Arab country occurred in November 1971, when four members of the group assassinated the former Premier of Jordan, Wasfi Tal, in Cairo. Mr. Tal had advocated a crackdown on terrorism.

The Black September is believed to be the secret arm of Fatah. Recent estimates have put the number of Palestinian guerrillas at 3,000, with several hundred belonging to Black September. The movement takes its name from the month in 1970 when King Hussein crushed guerrilla activity in Jordan and ousted most of the guerrillas.

For that reason, the movement has been seeking to overthrow the King and drum up support for its cause in other Arab nations.

Saudi Arabia's attitude toward the Black September movement is unclear. The Saudi Government said officially several years ago that it recognized Fatah but not some of the other guerrilla organizations. At that time, there apparently was no mention of Black September.

Black September itself is dedicated to the overthrow of Israel. In December, four members of the group entered the Israeli Embassy in Bangkok, seized six hostages and demanded the release of 36 Palestinians being held in Israeli jails. The four terrorists were permitted to leave Thailand on a plane bound for Cairo after the hostages were freed. The 36 prisoners were not released.

ENVOY TELLS OF INTRUSION

Khartoum, the Sudan, March 1 (Reuters)—The Saudi Arabian Ambassador, Abdullah al-Malhouk said by telephone from his besieged embassy today that Mr. Noel and Mr. Moore had been wounded by Black September terrorists who invaded the embassy carrying submachine guns.

He said they were urgently in need of a doctor. A doctor was later seen entering the embassy and there were some reports that an operation was being performed on the spot.

Mr. Malhouk said that "according to the fedayeen, the American ambassador is hurt and the charge d'affaires is even more seriously hurt." But the doctor later emerged and said, "everything is okay."

Diplomats who attended the reception said that the guerrillas rode up in Land Rovers, brandishing submachine guns. They shot their way into the building, but some of the guests, including the British Ambassador, managed to get out.

Reporters here were held back with a crowd of about 200 people 50 yards from the embassy. A police officer warned two advancing Sudanese press men, through a bullhorn, "If you approach any nearer you are liable to be shot at by the Black September activists."

The two newsmen said that a senior police officer had attempted to make contact with the guerrillas through a bullhorn but had achieved no response.

SIGNIFICANCE

After killing the three diplomats, the eight Palestinian terrorists voluntarily surrendered to Sudanese police authorities on March 3, 2005. Two of the Black September men were later released because of insufficient evidence to prosecute, while the other six were found guilty on June 24, 1974, and sentenced to life in prison. Within hours of the sentencing, however, the Sudanese president commuted their life sentence to seven years. Later, the six men were taken to Cairo, Egypt, and released to the PLO. Three of the prisoners escaped, while the other three men served out their sentences and were eventually released from prison.

The incident at Khartoum raised attention to Yassir Arafat's PLO involvement with attacks on U.S. citizens. A 1986 report by the Senate Judiciary Committee titled "The Availability of Civil and Criminal Actions Against Yassir Arafat's Palestine Liberation Organization" listed forty-two incidents between the years of 1968 and 1985 where American citizens were injured or killed from violent acts carried out by Arafat's organizations.

Increased tensions between Arafat, the PLO, and the U.S. made more difficult a peaceful resolution between the Palestinians and the Israelis with respect to the land disputes of the West Bank, the Gaza Strip, and Israel itself. Because many Arabs assume that the United States exerts strong influence over Israel, they also consider the United States their enemy. As a result, many Arab terrorist groups, such as the PLO, have perpetrated violent acts against U.S. citizens and U.S. property in the Middle East and around the world.

Incidents such as the murder of American diplomats Noel and Moore provide evidence of the violent means used by separatist terrorist groups against third parties.

FURTHER RESOURCES

Books

Gowers, Andrew. *Behind the Myth: Yasser Arafat and the Palestinian Revolution.* London: W.H. Allen, 1990.

Gowers, Andrew. *Inside the PLO: Covert Units, Secret Funds, and the War Against Israel and the United States.* New York: Morrow, 1990.

Korn, David A. *Assassination in Khartoum.* Bloomington, IN: University Press, 1993.

Web sites

USA Today.com. "U.S. had Stormy Relationship with Arafat." <http://www.usatoday.com/news/world/2004-11-11-stormy-arafat_x.htm> (accessed June 2, 2005).

Puerto Rican Nationalists

"Puerto Rican Terrorists Kill 4 in Wall Street Blast"

Newspaper article

By: The Associated Press

Date: January 25, 1975

Source: *The Associated Press*

About the Photographer: The Associated Press is an international wire service that provides news and photographs to news agencies around the world.

INTRODUCTION

At about 1:25 P.M. (New York local time) on January 24, 1975, Puerto Rican nationalists detonated a bomb in the inside hallway of the nineteenth-century annex to historic Fraunces Tavern and the adjacent Anglers Club. The blast—which occurred on the corner of Pearl and Water Streets in the Wall Street financial district of lower Manhattan in New York City (NYC)—caused extensive damage, while killing four people and injuring more than sixty others. At the time, the death toll in the explosion was the highest of any political bombings in New York City.

The Puerto Rican nationalist group Fuerzas Armadas de Liberación Nacional (FALN) [Armed Forces of National Liberation] claimed responsibility for the explosion via telephone calls to both United Press International and The Associated Press. The callers also led NYC police to their "Communique No. 3"; a note that stated the explosion was in response to the January 11, 1975 bombing allegedly ordered by the United States Central

Three persons were reported killed in an explosion, which occurred in the doorway of this Manhattan dining club in 1975.
AP/WIDE WORLD PHOTOS

Intelligence Agency (CIA), which killed two workers who supported Puerto Rican independence and injured eleven other people during a rally in the city of Mayaguez, Puerto Rico. The note also demanded the release of five Puerto Rican nationalists who were being held in prison for the 1950 attempted assassination of President Harry Truman, and the 1954 wounding of five U.S. Congress members at the House of Representatives.

The Puerto Rican nationalist-terrorist group FALN was founded in 1974 by Filiberto Inocencio Ojeda Rios, a Puerto Rican agent of Cuban intelligence who founded many of Puerto Rico's terrorist organizations. FALN, which advocates the complete independence for Puerto Rico (through liberation from the United States), had previously been linked to other bomb explosions in New York City. According to many counterterrorism experts, the group performed its terrorist acts with the help of Cuban intelligence agents. A U.S. Senate subcommittee dealing with terrorism warned of the Cuban connection in 1975 and a 1983 FBI investigation documented the day-to-day connection between FALN and the country of Cuba. Puerto Rican nationalists, including FALN, have consistently denied involvement with Cuba.

Investigation by detectives of the New York City police department and agents of the Federal Bureau of Investigation (FBI) decided that a quantity of high concentrated explosive material (with the explosive power of about ten sticks of dynamite) had been detonated with a short-fused timing device. They also found fragments of a propane tank that was similar to the ones used in two previous FALN explosions for which the group claimed responsibility.

PRIMARY SOURCE

New York (AP)—The explosion of a powerful fragmentation bomb that set a Wall street skyscraper quivering and damaged historic Fraunces Tavern killed four persons and injured at least 42 others.

A Puerto Rican nationalist group that has been linked with other terrorism here claimed responsibility for the blast that roared through the canyons of the crowded financial district.

The bomb had been planted in the Anglers and Tarpon Club adjacent to the tavern. The dead, including one man who was decapitated, apparently were lunchtime patrons at the club.

Built in 1719, Fraunces Tavern was the scene on Dec. 4, 1783, of George Washington's farewell address to the officers who served under him in the Revolutionary War. It is about 400 yards from the New York Stock Exchange.

The blast Friday afternoon sent glass shards flying into the street. Diners in the 60th floor cafeteria of the nearby Chase Manhattan Bank building said the structure shook.

"People were writhing on the sidewalk—we didn't know if they had been blown out of the building or if they were passersby," said Fire Lt. Thomas Regan, one of the first rescuers to arrive.

Fireman Charles Anderson described the blast scene as "utter havoc" with "people lying all over the place, many of them mumbling in shock . . . some buried under debris."

"It was like an earthquake," said the owner of a nearby grocery. Fifteen minutes after the explosion, an unidentified telephone caller told the Associated Press it was the work of FALN, a band of nationalist Puerto Rican terrorists. FALN stands for *Fuerzas Armadas de Liberation National Puertorrquena* (Armed Forces of the Puerto Rican Nation).

The group has claimed responsibility for other bomb explosions in the metropolitan area, but previous blasts caused no fatalities.

Later, police recovered a note in which the FALN claimed the latest bombing was in retaliation for the "CIA-ordered" murder of two young Puerto Ricans.

Authorities in Puerto Rico said a bomb went off Jan. 11 in a Mayaquez restaurant, killing two men and wounding 11 persons. The restaurant was in walking distance of a Puerto Rican Socialist party rally scheduled for later that evening.

Doctors said nails and other pieces of metal were found in the bodies of those who died in Friday's blast as well as in some of the injured.

One of the four dead, James Gezork, 32, of Wilmington, Del., died on an operating table at Beekman-Downtown Hospital Friday night.

The others killed were identified by police as Frank T. Conner, 30, of Fair Lawn, N.J.; Harold Sherbourne, 66, of Pine Orchard, Conn.; and Alejambro Berger of Philadelphia.

Mayor Abraham D. Beame rushed to the explosion scene from nearby City Hall and denounced the bombing as a "senseless act of terror which defies all reason and decency."

"It was a hell of a way to spend a Friday afternoon," said Richard Ross, 59, who was dining at the Anglers Club but escaped injury. "I'm afraid the fellow next to me was killed."

SIGNIFICANCE

Over a period from 1974 to 1983, members of FALN—with ties to Cuban intelligence networks—claimed responsibility for about 130 bombings in the United States that claimed six lives and injured numerous others. Some of these bombings included the January 1975 bombing of Fraunces Tavern; the four April 1975 bombings of the New York Life Insurance

Company, the Bankers Trust Company, the Metropolitan Life Insurance Company, and the Blimpie Base restaurant; the 1977 bombing of the Mobil Oil building; and the 1983 bombing of the headquarters of the New York Police Department (all in New York City); and the June 1979 bombing of the Shubert Theatre; the 1979 bombing of the Naval Armory; and the 1979 bombing of the Cook County building (all in Chicago or downstate Illinois).

The bombing of the Fraunces Tavern was the significant point for Puerto Rican terrorism because it indicated to U.S. authorities a beginning of a new wave of terrorism for Puerto Rican separatists. Authorities considered the previous wave of Puerto Rican terrorist attacks as not intended to kill people, since bombs were set off in vacant buildings and occupants of buildings were warned before an impending explosion. The new wave of terrorists, on the other hand, was seen by law enforcement officials as an aggressive attempt to kill people in order to publicize their political goals and philosophy.

In the Fraunces Tavern bombing, two Hispanic men were seen running from the annex moments before the explosion. Although the police suspected they were members of FALN—and the investigation centered on these two men—no one was ever prosecuted for the bombing of the Fraunces Tavern, the killing of four people, and the injuring of many others. During this time, however, many members of FALN were caught and convicted by U.S. authorities of various crimes within the United States. After serving their prison sentences, most returned to Puerto Rico.

Contemporary Puerto Rican terrorism began during the mid-1960s due to discontent with the widening economic divide among its citizens and strengthened by a desire for independence from the United States. By the 1980s, twenty years later, the country's economic stability had gone from good to poor, increasing the discontent amongst Puerto Rico's poor. This situation led to heightened terrorist activities on the island and in the United States.

During this time, Cuba remained a key player between Puerto Rico and the United States as it pursued its own agenda for Puerto Rico: the independence of Puerto Rico from the United States and increased influence over the strategically positioned island in the Caribbean. The United States remained equally interested in Puerto Rico—its associated commonwealth—realizing that (as of 1981) 60% of all imported oil to the United States was shipped through the Caribbean, and that large amounts of foreign military equipment and personnel often traveled by water near Puerto Rico on their way to Central and South America and other parts of the world.

As a result, the United States continued to counter extremist Puerto Rican terrorist activities in the United States and Puerto Rico, where many U.S. military facilities and personnel are located. By the early 1980s, many of the Puerto Rican terrorist groups, including FALN, had combined forces for a united opposition against the United States. Their combined experience and expertise gave them a greater level of precision and efficiency in carrying out their goals, although the bombing of the historic Fraunces Tavern in January, 1975, continues to be FALN's most notorious and deadly act of terrorism.

FURTHER RESOURCES

Books

Cuban-American National Foundation. *Castro's Puerto Rican Obsession*. Washington, D.C.: Cuban-American National Foundation, 1987.

Lidin, Harold J. *History of the Puerto Rican Independence Movement*. Puerto Rico: Hato Ray, 1981.

Zwickel, Jean Wiley. *Voices for Independence: In the Spirit of Valor and Sacrifice*. Pittsburg, CA: White Star Press, 1988.

Periodicals

McFadden, Robert D. "4 Killed, 44 Injured in Fraunces Tavern Explosion." *The New York Times*. January 25, 1975.

Prial, Frank J. "Bombers Called Intent on Killing." *The New York Times*. January 25, 1975.

Web sites

James, Daniel. *Latino Studies Resources, Indiana University*. "Puerto Rican Terrorists Also Threaten Reagan Assassination." <http://www.latinamericanstudies.org/puertorico/Daniel-james.htm> (accessed June 15, 2005).

"Magazine Says it Interviewed Top Terrorist"

Ilich Ramírez Sánchez, Alias Carlos the Jackal

Newspaper article

By: New York Times

Date: December 1, 1979

Source: *New York Times*

About the Author: *The New York Times*, a daily newspaper founded in 1851, has over one million subscribers and is distributed nationally.

Ilich Ramirez Sanchez (also known as "Carlos The Jackal").
AP/WIDE WORLD PHOTOS

INTRODUCTION

Ilich Ramírez Sánchez (1949–) was a terrorist, mercenary, and revolutionary between the 1970s and the 1990s. Ramírez Sánchez was known by the pseudonym "Carlos the Jackal," because he had taken the name Carlos while training with Soviet fighters and, later, because police allegedly found the Frederick Forsyth novel *The Day of the Jackal* while raiding Sánchez's hotel room. As a youth, Carlos joined the Communist party and was involved with Venezuelan revolutionary groups. After being expelled from universities in London and Moscow, Carlos joined a guerrilla training camp in Amman, Jordan run by the Popular Front for the Liberation of Palestine (PFLP)— with hopes of fighting in Venezuela.

Deciding against returning to Venezuela, Carlos joined the PFLP. He began his terrorism career in 1973 with a failed assassination attempt against Jewish businessman Edward Sieff, allegedly as revenge for the killing of a high-ranking PFLP member. Over the next several years, Carlos was responsible for carrying out attacks using such devices as car bombs, fragmentation grenades, and rocket propelled bombs. In September 1974, Carlos walked into a Paris cafe, threw a fragmentation grenade, and walked out. Carlos frequently used this method—casually walking into and out of his targets—during several subsequent bombings. The bomb detonation at the Paris cafe resulted in the deaths of two people along with numerous injuries. Carlos stated that his intention was to pressure French officials to negotiate the release of hostages associated with another terrorist group, the Japanese Red Army.

In 1976, PFLP leader Wadi Haddad expelled Carlos after he failed to kill two Organization of Petroleum Exporting Countries (OPEC) hostages, the oil ministers of Saudi Arabia and Iran. Both men became targets because PFLP leaders felt each country was not dedicated to the Palestinian cause. Carlos was also ejected because of his growing fame around the world and because he allegedly embezzled money paid for the release of the hostages—an amount estimated at between $20 and $50 million.

After being expelled, Carlos went to Aden, Yemen, to form his own rebel group composed of Lebanese, West German, Swiss, and Syrian terrorists under the name Organization of Arab Armed Struggle. Carlos set up the organization, critics contended, for monetary profit without real concern for the Arab struggle. He offered his organization's expertise to eastern European organizations such as Communist Romania's secret police and East Germany's Ministry for State Security, along with Cuba's Fidel Castro. However, the organization did not perform any terrorist acts until 1982, when it unsuccessfully attempted to destroy a French nuclear power station. The violent act resulted in two members of his group (including his wife, Magdalena Kopp) being arrested in Paris. To avenge their imprisonment, Carlos organized a series of bomb attacks on civilian French locations and overseas French diplomatic facilities in order to press for her release.

In 1983, Carlos attacked sites in Europe, his acts of political terrorism causing his expulsion from Europe. Subsequently refused entry into Iraq, Libya, and Cuba, Carlos eventually found a temporary home in Syria. When he angered Syrian officials, Carlos moved to Jordan, but eventually relocated to Khartoum, Sudan. The Sudanese, however, did not approve of Carlos' reported playboy lifestyle. Government officials forced him to France in August 1994 to stand trial for the killing of two French counter-intelligence agents and a Lebanese rebel/police informer. Found guilty, Carlos was sentenced to life imprisonment.

PRIMARY SOURCE

Beirut, Lebanon, Dec. 1—A Lebanese magazine published in Paris has printed an interview with a man who claimed he was the Venezuelan-born international terrorist known as Carlos.

In an issue sold on newsstands here yesterday, *Al Watan Al Arabi* also printed what it called the first genuine photograph of the 30-year-old man; who boasted about terrorist activity around the world.

He said his real name was Ilich Martinez Sánchez and that he was the son of a Venezuelan lawyer. He said he had been "born to a family dedicated to combating dictatorship." He said he embraced Marxism in high school in Caracas, studied for two years at a university in London, then moved to Moscow in 1968 to attend Patrice Lumumba University. The money for his studies was provided by the Venezuelan Communist Party, he said.

The magazine, which moved out of Beirut three years ago because of the Lebanese civil war, said the only other available picture of Carlos was an old one distributed by Interpol, the international law-enforcement agency. The Interpol picture, showing a clean-shaven young man with tinted glasses, bore little resemblance to *Al Watan's* photograph of a man with Hispanic features, a mustache dropping at the sides and no glasses.

The magazine's picture was signed Selim, which Carlos said was an alias. He said he had also been known as Martines and was often called The Jackal. His name has been connected with Palestinian guerrillas, the Japanese Red Army, and the Baader–Meinhof gang.

REPORT OF ESCAPE IN PARIS

In what *Al Watan* said was the first of two articles based on the interview, Carlos said that three years ago, as a special French squad closed in on his apartment in Paris, he fought his way out, killing a Lebanese informer who had been an associate and a French secret agent.

A few months later in Vienna, Carlos said, he led an attack against the headquarters of the Organization of Petroleum Exporting Countries. Sheik Ahmed Zaki Yamani, the Saudi Oil Minister, and Jamshid Amouzegar, then the Iranian Finance Minister, were kidnapped and flown to Libya, where they were freed.

Reports in the Arab press said the Saudi and Iranian Governments had paid $50 million each that went to the "foreign operations branch of the Popular Front for the Liberation of Palestine," one of the hard-line Palestinian groups. It was the last operation attributed to Carlos.

Analysts of Middle Eastern affairs believe Carlos may be abandoning terrorism after the decline of foreign operations by Palestinian guerrillas, the apparent inactivity of the Japanese Red Army and setbacks suffered by the Baader-Meinhof gang.

The publication did not say where Carlos was interviewed, but the writer of the story, Assem al-Jundi, lives in Paris.

SIGNIFICANCE

During his time in prison, Carlos published a book called *Revolutionary Islam* in which he described terrorism as a conflict between classes. He also stated that he converted to Islam, and expressed his support of Osama Bin Laden, labeling Bin Laden the appropriate leader to continue the fight against Western society.

The significance of Carlos' actions with regard to terrorism is cloudy at best. Many terrorist attacks were credited to him simply for the fact that no other likely suspects were found. For instance, Carlos was falsely linked for a time to the attack at the Munich Olympic Games in 1972 that killed eleven athletes from West Germany and Israel. Carlos also bragged of orchestrating terrorist activities that never occurred under his direction.

The majority of the terrorist attacks committed by Carlos were considered ineffective. For example, Carlos shot a prominent British businessman who supported Israel, but his victim survived; he later threw a bomb into an Israeli bank in London, but the bomb only partially exploded; he bombed several pro-Israeli newspaper offices in Paris without casualties; and he fired rocket-propelled grenades against Israeli El Al airplanes at Orly airport in France that failed to cause significant damage.

On the other hand, Carlos did carry out many atrocious crimes. He is credited with killing over eighty people, injuring thousands of others, and causing millions of dollars of property damage mostly motivated, analysts claim, out of his contempt for authority.

When Carlos rebelled against society, his violent actions were often cited by other terrorists as exciting and daring. Captured terrorists have claimed they received inspiration from Carlos' actions, especially with regards to his previous playboy lifestyle and violent activities. In 1994, Carlos the Jackal was apprehended and confined in a French prison.

The news article reporting the interview with Carlos was among the first English language accounts of the interview. The reports sparked controversy within the journalistic community as to how much protection journalists should offer wanted terrorists in order to secure interviews. That debate continues as news organizations are used by terrorist organizations to release statements and video to the public.

FURTHER RESOURCES

Books

Smith, Colin. *Carlos: Portrait of a Terrorist.* New York: Holt, Rinehart and Winston, 1977.

Follain, John. *Jackal: The Complete Story of the Legendary Terrorist, Carlos the Jackal.* New York: Arcade Publishing, 1998.

Yallop, David A. *To the Ends of the Earth: The Hunt for the Jackal.* London: Jonathan Cape, 1993.

Web sites

BBC Online News. "Carlos the Jackal: Trail of Terror." <http://news.bbc.co.uk/1/hi/world/42244.stm> (accessed June 3, 2005).

Court TV's Crime Library. Bellamy, Patrick. "Carlos the Jackal: Three Decades of Crime." <http://www.crimelibrary.com/terrorists/carlos/text/> (accessed June 3, 2005).

Weekly Standard. Taheri, Amir. Accessed on *Benador Associates.* "The Axis of Terror: Carlos the Jackal Pledges Alliance to Osama Bin Laden." <http://www.benadorassociates.com/article/700> (accessed June 3, 2005).

TWA Flight 847 Hijacking

Photograph

By: The photograph was taken by one of the hijackers.

Date: June 1985

Source: Available online from WorldHistory.com at <http://www.worldhistory.com/wiki/T/TWA-Flight-847.htm>.

About the Photographer: The photograph was taken by one of the hijackers.

INTRODUCTION

On June 14, 1985, Trans World Airlines (TWA) Flight 847, a Boeing 727 under the command of Captain John Testrake, was hijacked after departing from Athens, Greece, bound for Rome, Italy. The plane held 153 passengers and crew.

Two Shiite gunmen connected with the terrorist group Hezbollah (also known as Hizbollah) based in Beirut, Lebanon, seized command of the jetliner shortly after takeoff at 10:10 A.M., using guns and grenades they had smuggled aboard. A third hijacker, Ali Atwa, unable to board the plane because it was full, was arrested in Greece.

Thus began a seventeen-day ordeal for the crew and many of the passengers. The plane first stopped for refueling in Beirut, where nineteen of the passengers were released. The plane flew on to Algiers, where twenty more passengers were released. After the plane returned to Lebanon, the hijackers singled out one passenger, U.S. Navy diver Robert Dean Stethem, whom they beat and shot in the head before dumping his body onto the tarmac. At this point nearly a dozen armed terrorists joined the hijackers.

The odyssey continued when the plane next returned to Algiers. There, the hijackers released sixty-five passengers before returning again to Beirut, where the plane remained for the rest of the ordeal. The hijackers demanded that Israel release all of the Shiite Muslims it held in Lebanon. They also demanded that the international community condemn both Israel and the United States for their military activities in Lebanon. They insisted that the United States be specifically condemned for a car bombing in a Beirut suburb on March 8, 1985, which killed eighty people and which the hijackers considered to be the work of the U.S. Central Intelligence Agency (CIA). When the Greek government released Ali Atwa, the hijackers released eight Greek citizens.

On Monday, June 17, most of the remaining hostages were released to Nabih Berri, a moderate Shiite leader and a Lebanese government official. Berri protected the hostages at a secure location. By now forty hostages remained on the plane, although one was released when he developed heart trouble. The standoff lasted for two weeks, with the plane just sitting on the tarmac of Beirut International Airport. The crisis came to an end on June 30, when the remaining hostages, all Americans, were released and flown to West Germany.

During the hostage crisis, people around the world became familiar with the following dramatic photos. The first shows two of the hijackers in the cockpit of the plane with Captain Testrake. The second shows one of the hijackers threatening Testrake while holding his head out the plane's window.

PRIMARY SOURCE

TWA FLIGHT 847 HIJACKING
See primary source image.

SIGNIFICANCE

Beginning in the late 1970s and into the 1980s, Americans in the Middle East were the repeated targets of terrorist attacks and other forms of violence, usually at the hands of Islamic fundamentalists based in such countries as Lebanon and Iran.

PRIMARY SOURCE

TWA Flight 847 Hijacking Shiite terrorists in the cockpit with pilot John Testrake on board TWA flight 840 during its hijacking in 1985.

- On November 4, 1979, fifty-two Americans were taken hostage by radical militants at the U.S. embassy in Tehran, Iran. The ordeal dragged on for 444 days and likely contributed to President Jimmy Carter losing his bid for re-election.
- On April 18, 1983, the American embassy in Beirut was bombed, killing sixty-three people, including seventeen Americans.
- On October 23, 1983, a suicide bomber armed with a truck full of explosives killed 241 U.S. Marines at their barracks at the Beirut International Airport.
- On December 12, 1983, six people were killed when the U.S. embassy in Kuwait was bombed, part of a concerted series of attacks that included the French embassy, the country's major oil refinery, and a housing area for Americans.
- On March 16, 1984, CIA station chief William Buckley was kidnapped and tortured, one of thirty Westerners who were kidnapped in Lebanon from 1982 to 1992.
- On September 20, 1984, a U.S. embassy annex near Beirut was bombed.
- On December 3, 1984, Kuwait Airlines Flight 221 was hijacked, and when the hijackers' demands were not met, they killed two Americans from the U.S. Agency for International Development.

The United States had absorbed these blows, but the administration of President Ronald Reagan, along with the American public, was rapidly losing its patience. After the Italian cruise liner *Achille Lauro* was hijacked by Palestinian gunmen in October 1985, and elderly American Leon Klinghoffer was shot and his body dumped overboard, the United States took military action to force down the plane carrying the gunmen in Italy.

The hijackers of Flight 847 all escaped, although one, Mohammed Homadi, was captured two years later in West Germany. He was convicted of Stethem's murder and sentenced to life in prison. Three of the terrorists— Imad Fayez Mugniyah, Ali Atwa, and Hassan Izz-al-Din— were placed on the Federal Bureau of Investigation's list of most wanted terrorists in October 2001; a $25 million reward was offered for their capture.

Within a month of the end of the hijacking, Israel released its Lebanese prisoners. The Israelis have steadfastly denied that they struck a deal with the hijackers.

Flight 847 produced its share of heroes. One was Captain Testrake, who gave a dramatic interview to ABC News while the crisis was ongoing. Another was purser Uli Derickson, who spoke German and discovered that she could communicate with one of the hijackers in that language. During the ordeal, she was able to calm him and the others by singing a German ballad he requested. She frequently put herself in harm's way by confronting the hijackers when, for example, they were beating a passenger. In Algiers, when the ground crew refused to refuel the plane and the hijackers threatened to kill passengers, Derickson put a $5,500 charge for 6,000 gallons of fuel on her personal credit card.

FURTHER RESOURCES
Books

Snyder, Rodney A. *Negotiating with Terrorists: TWA Flight 847.* Pew Case Studies in International Affairs. Washington, DC: Institute for the Study of Diplomacy, School of Foreign Service, Georgetown University, 1994.

Testrake, John, and David J. Wimbish. *Triumph over Terror on Flight 847.* Old Tappan, NJ: Fleming H. Revell, 1987.

Audio and Visual Media

History Channel. "On the Hijacking of TWA Flight 847." Speech by President Ronald Reagan, June 18, 1985. Available from <http://www.historychannel.com/speeches/archive/speech_235.html> (with audio link; accessed June 27, 2005).

"Terror on Flight 847"

Magazine article

By: Ron Eschmann

Date: October, 2003

Source: "Terror on Flight 847," as published in *The Officer*, a publication providing news and analysis of military science.

A Shiite Moslem hijacker points his pistol toward an ABC news crew from the cockpit window of the Trans World Airlines jet. AP/WIDE WORLD PHOTOS

About the Author: Major Ron Eschmann is an Army staff officer assigned to the Office of the Chief Army Reserve.

INTRODUCTION

Since the overthrow of their biggest ally in the region, the Iranian Shah Mohammed Reza Pahlavi in January 1979, United States policy in the Middle East has lurched from one crisis to the next. The Iranian hostage crisis, the burning of the Tripoli Embassy, several skirmishes with Libyan forces, the assassination of the pro-American Egyptian President Anwar Sadat, and devastating terrorist attacks on U.S. peacekeepers in Lebanon each made disastrous reading for the Reagan administration and the American people in the 1980s. Unflinching support for Israel also bred deep resentment throughout the Arab World.

Another problem increasingly facing the United States in the early-1980s was the apparent sponsorship of terrorist groups by rogue governments, who were expected to do their bidding for them. Libya and Iran

were two states strongly considered to have sponsored terrorism and a third, Syria, was also often accused of involvement.

The two most notorious of these groups were both pro-Shi'ite: Hizbollah (also known as Hezbollah), which had gained notoriety during the Lebanese Civil War for its suicide bomb attacks; and Islamic Jihad, which had bombed the U.S. embassy in Beirut in April 1983, killing sixty-three people. The former was allegedly sponsored by Ayatollah Khomeni's Iranian government; the latter was based in Syria, but with alleged links to several regimes.

On Friday, June 14, 1985, TWA flight 847, a Boeing 727 flight from Cairo, landed at Athens to take on more passengers before heading on to Rome. Here it would be met by a connection that would take the flight's sizeable American contingent back home to San Diego via Boston and Los Angeles.

Twenty minutes into the flight to Rome, two terrorists brandishing grenades and a pistol and claiming to be from Islamic Jihad, seized control of the aircraft. They ordered the pilot, Captain John Testrake, to fly to Beirut. The Lebanese authorities, however, were not interested in a hostage situation on their soil and ordered Christian Druze militia men to block the runway (at the same time their Shi'ite Amal rivals battled with them to keep it clear). Eventually the plane was allowed to land after Testrake warned the Lebanese that the hostage-takers were ready to blow up the jet over Beirut.

There they refueled and released nineteen women and children. A request to speak to Shi'ite officials was turned down by the Amal leadership.

The hijacked aircraft then proceeded to Algiers, where twenty-one more hostages were released. It then crossed back to Beirut, where the Lebanese authorities again only allowed the plane to land at the very last minute, this time after the terrorists threatened to crash the fuel-depleted aircraft into the airport control tower.

On the tarmac, the hijackers dumped the body of a young U.S. Marine they had murdered (the Marines had made up the bulk of the U.S. peacekeeping operation, but had been accused by Shi'ite extremists of aiding their opponents). Demands that the airport lights be switched off were met and six Jewish passengers dispatched (the hijackers were apparently fearful of the involvement of Israeli special forces). A further twelve terrorist reinforcements then joined the flight, which again returned to Algiers.

Here negotiations stepped up. The principle demand of the hijackers was the release of Shi'ite prisoners from Israeli jails. A further sixty-five hostages were also released. The flight then returned to Lebanon for a third time, where it stayed.

On Monday, June 17, most of the remaining hostages were removed from the plane and placed in secure Shi'ite locations throughout Beirut. Negotiations carried on over the following fortnight until a breakthrough apparently came on June 30, when the hostages were driven to Syria. From there they were taken on a U.S. Air Force plane and flown to safety in West Germany.

PRIMARY SOURCE

On 14 June 1985, following a temporary tour of duty in Egypt, an Army Reserve civil engineering support planning officer boarded TWA Flight 847 bound from Athens, Greece to Rome. He was eager to get back to spend his first Father's Day with his wife and newborn child. On the same flight were two armed Hizbollah members with other plans. Soon after takeoff, the soldier wasn't sure if he would be alive the next day. Here is his story of extreme adversity, death, and redemption.

Filled mainly with American tourists, the TWA aircraft had 145 passengers and eight crewmembers. They finally took off midmorning on 14 June, about an hour and half late. As the aircraft gained altitude, all appeared normal as passengers settled in for the flight.

The sense of normalcy immediately changed when the flight engineer turned off the "fasten seatbelt" sign. Almost instantaneously, two well-dressed men in white suits with black shirts waving weapons rushed the cockpit door. One of them had a fragmentation grenade in his hand and was frantically pulling at the pin. They both screamed repeatedly, "Come to die! Americans die!"

One of the hijackers viciously kicked a flight attendant in the chest and held a chrome-plated 9mm pistol up to her ear. The hijackers were later identified as Mohammad Ali Hamadei and Hasan Izz Al Din, both members of a Lebanese Hizbollah faction. Hamadei, who was fluent in German, brandished the pistol and shouted at the attendant while pounding on the pilot's compartment door.

"They're on a suicide mission," thought Carlson. "My first reaction was to want to try to overpower them." He unfastened his seatbelt, stood up, but noticed that no other passenger contemplated the same action. Carlson did note that sheer terror filled their frozen faces. Realizing he couldn't take on two armed fanatics who could blow the aircraft out of the sky, he sat back down. There may even be others on the plane he reasoned. [Note: In fact there was a third hijacker, Ali Atwa, who was arrested by Greek police at the airport just before boarding. Later released by the Greek authorities, Atwa is still listed by the FBI as one of the most wanted terrorists for his role.]

By this time, Izz-Al-Din, who held the fragmentation grenade, had forced his way into the cockpit. Soon after, the pilot announced over the aircraft address system that their new destination was Beirut, Lebanon. Following the pistol-whipping of some of the flight crew, the hijackers went from row to row collecting passports.

Carlson hid his military ID in the airline seat cushion and worried about his passport and other official papers in his briefcase located in a different section of the aircraft. "I figured that if they searched me and found the ID card, I wouldn't have any opportunity to jump them at some future point because they would have either separated me from the rest of the passengers or killed me right there. I figured I would try to buy some time in order to help at any opportunity."

Hamadei kept waving his pistol and barking orders in German to the flight attendant, while Izz-Al-Din kept jumping up and down, making threatening gestures. The flight attendant spoke to the passengers, "Please no talking. Put your heads down and clasp your hands over your heads. We must do exactly as we are told." The aircraft became deathly quiet. As the hours went by, muscles in this contorted face-down position began to cramp and ache. Passengers who mistakenly made a noise or complained were severely beaten.

In what became a macabre game of musical chairs at gunpoint, men were placed in window seats and women and children were forced to sit in aisle seats to limit the threat to the hijackers. Passengers in the forward area of the aircraft were moved to the rear, armrests were removed from the rows and four people were crammed in the three seat row.

Major Carlson's luck ran out when the hijackers finally discovered his official passport, which he used on military travel. Maniacally screaming "CIA, FBI!" the pistol-carrying Hamadei pointed his weapon in the major's face. "Tell him I'm in the Army Reserve and am only on a one-week tour of duty," he told the flight attendant. Temporarily satisfied that he was not a CIA or FBI operative, the hijacker moved on to intimidate and bludgeon other passengers.

Beirut International Airport officials wanted no part of this escalating international incident, so with the assistance of local militia, they decided to block the runways with barricades. The control tower subsequently told the pilots that the airport was closed. As if matters couldn't get worse on the ground, a rival militia had engaged the militia putting up the runway obstacles in a firefight. The attacking militia, called the Muslim Amal, ultimately cleared the runway for the aircraft with no time to spare.

As the 727 was taking on fuel, the hijackers singled out a Navy diver, SW-2 Robert Stethem. They grabbed the sailor from his seat and pushed him to the forward compartment.

After refueling, Hamadei and Izz-Al-Din demanded to be flown to Algiers. The aircraft reeked at this point—nearly five hours from the initial takeover—and it became difficult to breathe. The stench became worse after landing in Algiers as the aircraft sat on the runway in sweltering heat. Some of the passengers—children and some of their mothers—were released. But Major Carlson's troubles hadn't started.

He felt a tap on his shoulder and turned around. He again faced the agitated Hamadei and his pistol. Carlson was forced to the forward compartment just inside the aircrew cabin area. He remembered that this was the same thing that had happened to the young Navy diver, who now remained unaccounted for.

Carlson was blindfolded with a bandana smelling of vomit, and his hands were bound tightly behind his back with a silk tie so firmly that it cut into his wrists and numbed his hands and arms. One of the hijackers pushed him just inside the pilot's compartment and then proceeded to severely beat him with a steel pipe. He heard the chief pilot talking to the Algiers control tower: "They're killing people and beating them." At the same time both Hamadei and Izz-Al-Din began kicking him, trying to make

him scream in order to get the aircraft refueled. Carlson, although badly injured, could not feel the kicks as his body was going numb.

The hijackers also started making demands to free Shi'ite prisoners in Kuwait and Israel. The situation got even worse when they began screaming over and over, "One American must die!"

In a surreal world of pain and peace, Carlson heard a strange sound. Click-click, click-click. It took him a moment to realize what it was—it was the aircraft pilot, keying his handheld mike nearby. He now realized his part in this brutal radio script. The pilot wanted to let the airport control tower hear Carlson's screams to let them know the hijackers were ruthlessly serious. The tower officials were just part of the audience.

"Where is the fuel," demanded the agitated pilot. "Your fuel is coming," said the non-committal voice in the tower. At this perceived delay, Hamadei and Izz-Al-Din began kicking Carlson in the head and spine. The ordeal continued for more than an hour and a half. The pistol was then put to the Reservist's head. "One American must die!" they repeatedly screamed and then gave a 10-minute deadline.

"I see the fuel truck," said the pilot. For the time being, the major was spared.

"Though I had been beaten very badly for over two hours, I had survived. It was a miracle that the fuel had come just before the hijacker was going to shoot me—an answer to a lot of prayer? He added that, "physically, several discs in my back were injured. I had broken ribs and fingers, internal and external bleeding and had lost a lot of blood. There was also head swelling and injuries, blurred vision, mouth and tooth damage, welts on my shoulders, and I had difficulty using my hands and arms."

The aircraft again headed late that night to Beirut Airport. The Beirut controllers had once again refused permission to land, but then gave in to the hijackers' demands and the pleading of the pilot, who matter-of-factly stated that they had only five minutes of fuel left. After a very rough landing, the hijackers made further demands. At this point, they dragged the Navy diver, Robert Stethem, to the door of the aircraft, shot him in the head and dumped his lifeless body on to the Beirut airport runway.

The pilot began screaming to the tower over his radio, "He just killed a passenger! He just killed a passenger!"

"There will be another in five minutes," exclaimed one of the hijackers. Beirut airport officials soon complied with their demands.

After some additional heated radio discussions with the tower, the tail door opened and on rushed a number of shouting and heavily armed militia members who ran up to and hugged Hamadei and Izz-Al-Din. With the militia

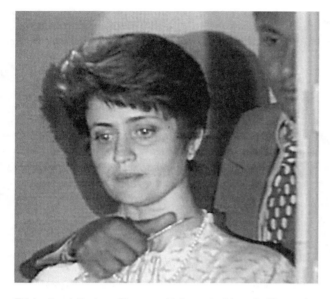

Ethiopian hijacker, Shamsu Kabret, holds a knife to the throat of a flight attendant while talking to TV crews from the plane. AP/WIDE WORLD PHOTOS

weapons pointing at them, Carlson and four of the other Navy divers were taken off the aircraft to an awaiting truck and sped off to face another nightmare. Following refueling, fresh water and food, the aircraft departed for Algiers.

The military hostages were taken into a battle-scarred building located near a Palestinian refugee camp and forced into a 12 by 20-ft. basement cell with a steel door and bars on the window.

SIGNIFICANCE

The hijacking of Flight 847 marked the third airline hijacking in as many days by Arab extremists. Although the other two had been carried out by Palestinians, the root cause was the same: protest at Israeli conduct in the region, and America's perceived support for it.

Israel released more than 700 Shi'ite prisoners within a month of the end of the hijacking of Flight 847. Most had been captured following Israel's intervention in Lebanon's Civil War in June 1982. Despite repeated promises that Israel would withdraw from South Lebanon, and despite the Lebanese Civil War effectively ending in 1990, Israel continued to occupy a 15km strip of South Lebanon until May 2000. From here it would launch sporadic attacks, and also launch sting operations to capture or assassinate militant leaders.

The United States Government was convinced of Islamic Jihad's links with both the regimes of Qaddafi's Libya and Ayatollah Khomeni's Iran. As part of its long-standing commitment against this state-sponsored terrorism, it continued to back Iraq's war against Iran and its antagonistic campaign towards Qaddaffi.

On April 14, 1986, U.S. jets attacked Tripoli, blowing up one of Qaddafi's Palaces and a number of other strategic targets. More than 100 Libyans were killed in the attacks and hundreds more were injured. These included two of Qaddafi's children, as well as an adopted baby daughter who died from her injuries.

The irony was that Qaddafi probably had nothing to do with the hijacking of Flight 847, but was so incensed by the death of his adopted child that he gave the green light to a further atrocity, the bombing of Pan Am flight 103 which exploded over Lockerbie, Scotland in December 1988, killing 259 people plus eleven on the ground.

The U.S., which already had sanctions in place against Qaddaffi, had no dealings with the Libyan regime until 2004, when rapprochement initiated by the European Union saw diplomatic links tentatively resumed.

On October 10, 2001, three of Flight 847's hijackers, Imad Mugniyah, Ali Atwa and Hassan Izz-Al-Din, were placed on the FBI's most wanted list. Despite rewards of $25 million being offered for information leading to their arrests, as of 2005 all three remain at large.

FURTHER RESOURCES

Books

Testrake, John, and David J. Wimbish, Triumph. *Over Terror on Flight 847*. New Jersey: Old Tappan, 1987.

Fisk, Robert. *Pity the Nation: Lebanon at War*. Oxford Paperbacks, 2001.

Sadar, Ziauddin, and Mervyn Wynn Davies. *Why Do People Hate America?* London: Icon Books, 2003.

Audio and Visual Media

Time Magazine.com. "Hijacked: TWA Flight 847." <http://www.time.com/time/covers/0,16641,1101850624,00.html> (accessed July 6, 2005).

"A Mediterranean Nightmare"

PLO terrorists seize the Italian cruise liner *Achille Lauro*

Magazine article

By: Mary Janigan

Date: October 21, 1985

Youssef Magied al-Molqi, the Palestinian terrorist, is shown behind bars at the time of his trial in Genoa, May 6, 1986.
AP/WIDE WORLD PHOTOS

Source: "A Mediterranean Nightmare," *Maclean's*, October 21, 1985, p. 40.

About the Author: Mary Janigan is a political writer for *Maclean's* magazine, which was founded in 1905 by journalist and entrepreneur John Bayne Maclean. The magazine is a leading newsweekly in Canada.

INTRODUCTION

On Monday, October 7, 1985, four armed Palestinian terrorists seized control of the *Achille Lauro*, an Italian passenger ship on a twelve-day cruise in the Mediterranean Sea. The ship had been carrying 680 passengers and 350 crew, but most of the passengers had disembarked in Alexandria, Egypt, for a sightseeing tour, leaving only about sixty-eight passengers still aboard to endure the fifty-two-hour ordeal.

The next day the gunmen sent a radio message threatening to begin killing passengers if Israel did not release fifty Palestinians held in Israeli jails. They identified themselves as members of the Palestinian Liberation Front, a name loosely applied to various breakaway factions of the Palestinian Liberation Organization (PLO). While some of these factions opposed PLO leader Yasser Arafat, the terrorists aboard the *Achille Lauro* were members of a pro-Arafat faction whose leader, Mohammed Abbas (also known as Abu Abbas) was the mastermind behind the hijacking.

On Wednesday, Egypt allowed the ship to dock at Port Said, where negotiations involving Egypt, the United States, Italy, and Arafat began. Arafat's representatives on the scene, including Abbas, wanted the hijackers turned over to the PLO for trial. The Egyptians, eager to get the hijackers off their hands, agreed. Accordingly, the smiling and waving hijackers were taken from the ship and placed aboard an EgyptAir jet bound for Tunis, Algiers.

Meanwhile, the United States was determined to bring the hijackers to justice, particularly after learning that they had murdered an American passenger, an elderly New Yorker named Leon Klinghoffer, and thrown his body and wheelchair overboard. As the EgyptAir flight was airborne, the United States dispatched four F-14 fighter jets that forced the plane down in Sicily, where a standoff ensued between 50 heavily armed U.S. Delta Force troops and an equal number of Italian troops. After diplomatic wrangling, the U.S. and Italian governments agreed that Italy would detain the men but that the United States would seek extradition.

That month, the Canadian newsweekly *Maclean's* ran the following article detailing the terror experienced by the hijackers' hostages onboard the ship.

PRIMARY SOURCE

. . . From the beginning, the four Palestinian hijackers singled out three categories of tourists for special abuse: Jews, Britons and Americans. Soon after they seized the 23,629-ton ship they forced the passengers from the dining room into a nearby salon. Then, methodically, the hijackers began sorting passports by nationality, isolating two Austrian Jews, 12 Americans, many of them also Jews, and six British women. "We expected to be shot," recounted Stanley Kubacki, a judge from Philadelphia. "They just hated Americans."

Meanwhile, Capt. Gerardo De Rosa and the remaining passengers and crew were left under the wary eye of erratic and gun-toting guards. The 51-year-old captain remained on the bridge while the terrorists screamed orders to guide the ship toward Syria and then to Libya. With most of the passengers huddled in the salon, their captors sprayed the walls and ceiling with bullets—and placed gasoline bombs on the stage and the showroom entrances. The hostages slept on chairs or on the floor. They watched their captors pull pins from grenades and toss them recklessly into the air. Above all, they learned to fear their captors' mercurial mood swings. "They looked like kids who were hopped up—dopeheads or schizophrenics," said Viola Meskin of Metuchen, N.J. "They kept saying things like 'Reagan no good. Arafat good.' Added her husband, Seymour: "They were constantly changing their minds. They would tell us to get in line to go to the toilet, then two minutes later they would tell us to sit down."

. . . The worst treatment was reserved for the 20 tourists whose nationality aroused their captors' ire. On Monday afternoon the Americans were herded to the top deck . . . The hijackers . . . positioned two barrels of flammable liquid next to them and threatened to set them on fire if anyone moved. Then, while the other hostages watched, three women were forced to hold live hand grenades. Said Kubacki: "We were forced to sit very close so that if one of these women fell asleep or fainted we would all be blown up."

. . . On Tuesday morning, the second day of their ordeal, the hijackers' mood grew uglier. The terrorists moved 19 of the 20 captives they had singled out to the deck above the ship's lounge and forced them to kneel. But one American, Leon Klinghoffer, a 69-year-old New Yorker and a stroke victim confined to a wheelchair, was left on the deck below. By early afternoon, as the 643-foot ship neared the Syrian port of Tartus, the hijackers told De Rosa to put them in contact with the Italian and American ambassadors in Damascus and to reiterate their demand that 50 Palestinians held in Israel be set free. When the answer did not arrive promptly the Palestinians shot Klinghoffer in the forehead, ordered other passengers to toss his body overboard and then announced that they would kill, in sequence, the Americans, the British and the elderly.

. . . About 12 hours after the terrorists finally left the ship, a ship cleaner discovered Austrian Anna Hoerangner, 53, concealed in a cabin toilet. Disabled by a foot amputation, Hoerangner had been walking along a gangway when the terrorists charged past her into the dining room. Apparently overlooked, she managed to hobble into a nearby cabin, where for more than two days she subsisted on two apples and water.

SIGNIFICANCE

The U.S. ability—and willingness—to force the plane carrying the hijackers down was perceived in the United States as an important victory over terrorism. Just a few months before, Palestinian terrorists had escaped after hijacking a TWA jetliner and holding the passengers hostage in Beirut, Lebanon, for two weeks. The administration of President Ronald Reagan was determined that the *Achille Lauro* hijackers would not elude justice. Meanwhile, Americans were elated. The *New York Daily News* ran a large headline exclaiming, "We Bagged the Bums!"

The incident, however, turned out to be more complicated. The ship was Italian, and the Egyptian airliner was forced down on Italian soil. Many Italians, both government officials and citizens, regarded the American response as heavy-handed and a violation of Italian sovereignty.

During the wrangling between Americans and Italian officials over who would take control of the hijackers, Abbas remained on the plane, claiming diplomatic immunity. Italian prime minister Bettino Craxi, eager to maintain good relations with both Egypt and the PLO, eventually concluded that he had no legal grounds to detain Abbas. Accordingly, Abbas was put on a plane and flown to Yugoslavia and from there to Baghdad, Iraq.

The U.S. government was infuriated. Abbas's escape led to a political crisis in Italy that eventually forced Craxi's resignation.

Three of the hijackers were prosecuted in Italy and given jail terms. In 1991, one was released for a short-term parole and disappeared; in 1996, the same happened with a second hijacker. In 2005, only one of the hijackers remained behind bars. For years, Abbas remained in hiding in Iraq, but in April 2003, U.S. forces arrested him outside of Baghdad. He died while in American custody in May 2004.

Klinghoffer's body was discovered when it washed ashore eight days after his death.

FURTHER RESOURCES

Books

Bohn, Michael K. *The Achille Lauro Hijacking: Lessons in the Politics and Prejudice of Terrorism.* Dulles, VA: Brassey's, 2004.

Web sites

"A Hijack on the High Seas." May 7, 2002. <http://www.bbc.co.uk/dna/h2g2/A730900> (accessed May 16, 2005).

Audio and Visual Media

Adams, John. *The Death of Klinghoffer.* Nonesuch, 1992 (audio CD of opera).

Adams, John. *The Death of Klinghoffer*, directed by Penny Woolcock. Universal Music, 2003 (DVD of opera performance).

Bomb Aboard TWA Flight 840

Italian Officials Say Arab Terrorist Was on TWA Plane

News article

By: Philip Dopoulos

Date: April 3, 1986

Source: The Associated Press.

About the Author: At the time the article was written, Philip Dopoulos was a writer for The Associated Press (AP). Since then, Dopoulos retired from AP but continues to write for such publications as the *Moscow Times*, an English-language newspaper in Russia.

INTRODUCTION

On April 2, 1986, at about 1:25 P.M. (local Athens time), Trans World Airlines (TWA) Flight 840 was on its descent to Ellinikon International Airport in Athens, Greece, having come from Leonardo Da Vinci International Airport (Rome, Italy). Suddenly, an explosion was heard throughout the cabin as the airplane flew over Peloponnesus, a peninsular region that forms southern Greece. Four American citizens, who were sitting around seat 10-F of the stricken Boeing 727 airplane were sucked out of a hole that formed by the blast under a passenger compartment window at floor level on the fuselage near the right wing.

The airplane with the remaining 111 passengers and seven crew members was able to land safely at the Athens airport. The formal investigation was conducted by Greece's Hellenic Civil Aviation Authority, with help from officials of the United States Federal Aviation Administration and Italian and Egyptian authorities.

On the day of the incident, an anonymous telephone caller declared to a news agency that the pro-Libyan Palestinian splinter group Izzeddin Al-Kassam, a part of the Arab Revolutionary Cells that is run by Palestinian terrorist Abu Nidal, was responsible for the explosion. The Arabic-speaking caller stated that the bombing was in response to American activities to defeat the Arab people; specifically, due to U.S. missile attacks on Libyan targets over the use of disputed waters from the Gulf of Sidra, located in the Mediterranean Sea off the northern coast of Libya.

The investigation centered around May (or Mai) Elias Mansur (or Monsour), a Lebanese-born Palestinian woman, who had flown from Beirut, Lebanon to Cairo on March 25th, and then had flown on the same TWA 840 airplane from Cairo to Athens on April 2nd. Seven hours after arriving at the Athens airport, the woman left

In December 1973, Palestinian guerrillas engaged in a gunfight with police before hijacking a jetliner at the Fiumicino Airport in Rome. AP/WIDE WORLD PHOTOS

on a Middle East flight for Beirut, shortly before the crippled TWA 840 airplane landed.

Mansur became the prime bombing suspect when it was determined from airline records that she sat in the same seat (10-F) during its route from Cairo to Athens, which later that day was the seat at the center of the explosion. Through the investigation, Mansur was found to have possible connections with several terrorist groups including the Lebanese Revolutionary Brigades, an organization with links to European Communist groups; Abu Nidal Organization; and Hawari Apparatus, a Palestinian terrorist group led by Colonel Hawari, which was operated secretly under Yasser Arafat.

After being interviewed by law enforcement authorities, Mansur denied any involvement in the crime.

During the multi-national investigation, explosive experts determined that the plastic explosive device weighed between 0.11 and 0.23 kilograms (0.25 and 0.50 pounds), and could have been as small as two bars of soap. The plastic material was likely made from (1) C-4, a high quality compound that is 91% RDX (Royal Demolition

Explosive) or (2) Semtex, a dark orange-colored compound that is 44.5% RDX, 44.5% PETN (penthrite), and 11% vegetable oil. The detonator was likely a simple plastic timer. During the 1980s, security screening devices were unable to detect such explosive devices.

■ PRIMARY SOURCE

Greek police sources said today they are hunting for a suspected woman terrorist they say was on a TWA jet hours before a bomb exploded on the aircraft, tearing open the cabin and killing four Americans.

Earlier, Italian officials said a known Arab terrorist occupied the seat of the TWA jet where the bomb exploded.

Italian Interior Minister Oscar Luigi Scalfaro told reporters in Rome, "It is certain that a suspect person, who is on file as a terrorist, got on in Cairo and got off in Athens occupying in the airplane the exact seat where the explosion occurred."

The Boeing 727 flew Wednesday from Cairo, Egypt, to Athens, Greece, and then to Rome. There it picked up 112 passengers and headed back to Athens as TWA Flight 840, ultimately bound for Cairo.

The bomb exploded as the jetliner approached Athens airport from Rome, and the four victims were sucked out of the plane, flying at about 15,000 feet.

Greek police sources identified the suspect as a woman, May Elias Mansur, who may have passed through Greece previously.

"We have launched a search around Athens and other cities and also put out a signal to trace this person through Interpol," one source said.

In Rome, the Italian news agency ANSA tonight quoted unidentified Italian investigators as saying the woman sought was believed to have boarded with a Lebanese passport.

ANSA said the woman may have boarded a Beirut-bound Middle East Airlines flight from Athens Airport shortly after arriving there.

An Egyptian security official at Cairo International Airport said that after the explosion, Egyptian authorities checked the names of passengers who boarded in Cairo and "we had no suspicion about anyone on the list." The official spoke on condition of anonymity.

The blast blew a 9-by-3-foot hole in the side of the plane in front of the right wing. TWA President Richard D. Pearson said in New York the explosion occurred on the cabin floor at row 10 or 11 of the passenger seats.

Officials at Rome's Leonardo da Vinci Airport said the terrorist was an Arab who sat in seat 10F on the Cairo-to-Athens flight.

ANSA said an Arab named Mansur or Monsour was sitting in the 10th row on that flight.

An anonymous caller to Western news agencies in Beirut claimed responsibility for the TWA attack on behalf of the Arab Revolutionary Cells. He said it was in response to last week's clash between U.S. and Libyan forces in the disputed Gulf of Sidra.

The Palestinian sources in Beirut, who spoke on condition of anonymity, said Abu Nidal had used the name Arab Revolutionary Cells in previous terrorist attacks.

Abu Nidal, whose real name is Sabry al-Banna, said in a statement issued in Damascus, Syria, last week that his group would strike at U.S. targets in retaliation for the U.S.-Libyan confrontation.

The Reagan administration also has accused Libya of backing Abu Nidal's group in the December airport attacks.

Libyan leader Col. Moammar Khadafy, however, distanced himself from the TWA attack, saying, "This is an act of terrorism against a civilian target, and I am totally against this," CBS News reported.

Reagan administration analysts believe Libya is not responsible for the explosion, a senior administration official in Washington said today. However, the undersecretary of state for political affairs, Michael Armacost, told a Washington news conference that possible involvement by Khadafy could not be ruled out until an investigation was completed.

After last week's confrontation in the Gulf of Sidra, during which the United States said at least two Libyan patrol boats were sunk and a missile site attacked, Khadafy threatened to attack U.S. interests worldwide.

The Greek government issued a statement saying it "condemns the barbarous terrorist action . . . and reiterates that terrorism undermines peace and democracy."

The statement said the blast was caused by an "explosive device," but it did not specify what kind. Greece's undersecretary for foreign affairs, Yiannis Kapsis, said the explosion was caused by a bomb in a piece of luggage.

Among the four Americans who died when they were sucked through the hole in the fuselage were a mother, daughter and baby granddaughter.

Reports from Greek officials, TWA, friends and relatives identified the victims as: Alberto Ospina, a Colombian-born American from Stratford, Conn.; Demetra Stylian, 52; her daughter, Maria Klug, 25, and 8-month-old granddaughter Demetra Klug, all from Annapolis, Md.

Seven other people, including four Americans, were injured aboard the plane, which landed safely in Athens 10 minutes after the explosion. Three of the injured were hospitalized overnight and released this morning, said the chief nurse at Voula Hospital near the Athens Airport.

Rome airport officials said 101 of the plane's passengers had transferred from a connecting flight from New York. A TWA official said they and their hand luggage had been checked in Rome but that their checked baggage, which was in sealed containers, was not.

The other 11 passengers began the flight in Rome. The airliner said besides the passengers, the plane carried seven crew members and three off-duty TWA employees.

SIGNIFICANCE

After the TWA 840 bombing, leaders of Greece and the United States realized that technical means to assure the safety of air travelers from terrorist attacks was lacking. In fact, leaders of a London pilots' organization suggested that all airports with a history of inadequate security procedures be banned. The U.S. Federal Aviation Administration considered that all airlines under their authority be forced to strengthen security measures. The International Airline Passengers Association issued a warning for all air travelers to avoid Mediterranean travel. After the attack, air travel around the Mediterranean dropped dramatically and the number of travelers going from North America to Europe declined. Tourism dropped for Italy, Greece, and other nearby countries. An economic crisis, which already affected Egypt, was lengthened by the attack.

Although the cities of Cairo, Athens, and Rome were well known terrorist areas in the 1980s, their international airports possessed some of the best security systems and trained personnel in the world. However, it was still possible for terrorists to sneak a primitive explosive device through these advanced security networks. In addition, only a small amount of explosive was necessary to damage the airplane. Thus, it could easily be carried and hidden anywhere onboard the airplane. Because either explosive could be set off with a small, inexpensive detonator and regulated by a simple timer, little technological knowledge was needed for the entire operation. The TWA 840 attack showed authorities that terrorists could effectively use low-technology devices against high-technology inspection systems.

Although investigators initially suspected that there was a link between Abu Nidal and TWA 840 due to similar terrorist activities in the past, in the end no connection was verified. Links to Libyan Leader Muammar Gaddafi were also initially suspected because he often dealt with subordinates, like Nidal, who were inexpensive to hire and difficult to link. However, no association between Gaddafi and TWA 840 were found.

May Elias Mansur was later arrested and admitted working for the May 15 Organization. However, after two years of investigation, little evidence was generated to prove Mansur had been directly involved in the crime or had been acting in conjunction with a terrorist organization.

In May 1988, Mohammed Rashid was captured and arrested at the Athens International Airport Greece for the bombing of several airplanes including TWA 840. Rashid was a veteran agent of May 15 Organization, having been involved in many attacks against American and Israeli airplanes. Rashid was also active in the Special Operations Group, one of the terrorist groups of Yassir Arafat's Fatah, under the command of Colonel Hawari. Rashid was later convicted in Greece, and served eight years of a fifteen-year sentence in prison.

In 2001, Rashid was indicted in a nine-count charge and tried before an American court for bombing, murder, sabotage, and other crimes involving the TWA bombings. He was convicted of conspiracy to kill American citizens, conspiracy to kill U.S. government personnel, first-degree murder, using weapons of mass destruction, and destroying U.S. government properties. He was sentenced to twelve years in prison.

TWA 840 was significant to anti-terrorist investigations because it showed the difficulty in proving which members of terrorist groups actually committed the crime. After years of intensive investigation, the principle planner of the TWA 840 bombing was finally convicted. However, the actual terrorist who planted the bomb was never convicted and the high-ranking terrorist leaders and organizations that authorized Rashid's plans were never held responsible.

FURTHER RESOURCES
Books
Davies, Barry. *Terrorism: Inside a World Phenomenon*. London: Virgin, 2003.

McDermott, Terry. *Perfect Soldiers, the Hijackers: Who They Were, Why They Did It*. New York: HarperCollins, 2005.

Sageman, Marc. *Understanding Terror Networks*. Philadelphia, PA: University of Pennsylvania Press, 2004.

Periodicals
TurcoWilliam E. Smith. "Terrorism Explosion on Flight 840." *Time*. April 14, 1986.

Web sites
BBC News. On This Day. "1986: Bomb Tears Hole in Airliner." <http://news.bbc.co.uk/onthisday/hi/dates/stories/april/2/newsid_4357000/4357159.stm> (June 13, 2005).

Yoram Schweitzer, International Policy Institute for Counter-Terrorism. "The Arrest of Mohammed Rashid—Another Point for the Americans." <http://www.ict.org.il/articles/articledet.cfm?articleid=35> (June 13, 2005).

The Stone Children

PLO's Terrorist Campaign (First Intifada)

Magazine article

By: Rod Nordland

Date: May 2, 1988

Source: "The Stone Children," as published in *Newsweek*.

About the Author: Rod Nordland is a Pulitzer Prize-winning journalist from Philadelphia. He began his work at Newsweek as bureau chief for the Middle East in 1984. He was first based in Beirut, Lebanon but later moved to Cairo, Egypt after he was the victim of a kidnapping attempt. He covered events in Bosnia, Kosovo, East Timor, and Afghanistan. Nordland serves as *Newsweek's* correspondent-at-large and reports from posts around the world.

INTRODUCTION

In December 1987, a spontaneous protest began among Palestinians living in Gaza and the West Bank territories controlled by Israel. This *Intifada*, or popular uprising, developed into six years of unrest in the region. The ongoing conflict did not abate until Palestinian leaders and Israeli government officials met at the negotiating table in Oslo, Norway, in 1993, to discuss the implementation of a long-term strategy for peace in the region.

On December 8, 1987, four Palestinians died in a car accident involving an Israeli army vehicle. As a result, a flood of Palestinians living in nearby refugee camps protested by throwing rocks at Israeli troops. The Israeli troops fired on the demonstrators and killed a teenage Palestinian boy. The event sparked the Intifada.

Palestinians protested at the beginning of the Intifada by throwing rocks, and those participating in these protests were not merely a disenfranchised few. Much of the general population took part in the activities, which were not all violent in nature. Palestinian protests took the form of organized strikes, closures, demonstrations, and boycotts of Israeli products. Violent protest escalated as rocks were replaced with Molotov cocktails, glass bottles filled with ignited flammable liquid. Over a twenty-seven day period in June of 1988, Palestinian militants set fire to Israeli interests in the region.

While the Israeli authorities demanded Palestinian leaders quell Arab resistance, they failed to prevent the expansion of Jewish settlements in the region (many established by fundamentalist or radical Jews) that

A Palestinian youth lies on the ground after being hit in the head by a rubber bullet fired by Israeli soldiers during clashes in Hebron. AP/WIDE WORLD PHOTOS

spurred on much of the conflict. In July of 1988, Jewish settlers began to dig a tunnel between the Islamic holy sites at al-Buraq and al-Aqsa in Jerusalem. Muslim clerics called on Muslim Arab Palestinians to defend the holy sites. Widespread fighting broke out with Israeli police. The bloody clashes led to the declaration of a state of emergency.

PRIMARY SOURCE

Educated and prosperous, the Abdulfattahs have a lot to lose. But every member of the West Bank Palestinian family supports the recent uprising, each in his own way. They know they may well go to jail for what they do, or even for what they say to reporters. "Please say nothing to harm my family," says Jaber Abdulfattah, 68, the eldest, a member of the generation that struggled with the Israelis for Palestine in 1948 and lost. Jaber is circumspect, but his sons and grandsons prevail. "For myself, I don't care," says his son Kamal, 45. "I want the whole world to know what it is to be a Palestinian." Kamal and his peers saw the West Bank occupied by Israelis in 1967 and despaired; the unrest has renewed his hopes. "I'll go to jail gladly," says Kamal's son Qays, 18. "I am not afraid." It is Qays's generation that picked up the Holy Land's plentiful stones and, by hurling them at the occupier's formidable Army, created the uprising, the *Intifada.*

The three generations have seen their land become someone else's. From the family's white stone house in the town of Jenin, they can see the lush Plain of Esdraelon, divided by the Green Line that separates the occupied West Bank from Israel. In the two decades of the occupation, that line had all but disappeared. Now Israeli roadblocks mark it again, keeping the Palestinians in. Off in the haze, some 10 miles away, it's possible to see the Israeli village of Umm al Fahm, the Abdulfattahs' original hometown. Jaber and his young family were caught on the Arab side of the Green Line in '48 and chose not to return. "I didn't want to go back and live among the Israelis," says his wife, Fawzyeh. "Little did I know that after 1967 the Israelis would come and live next to us."

Jaber's lands in Israel were confiscated; some of them were given to Jewish settlers, who built a community on it named Miami. Still, the Abdulfattahs were not a family of firebrands. Even after 1967, Jaber continued to work in the local school administration; his brother was the police chief. Detached from their land, they threw their energies into educating their children, a phenomenon that has given the Palestinians, a largely rural people before the birth of Israel, the highest rate of college education in the Arab world. Now nine of Jaber's 10 children have college educations, gained in five lands. Two are medical doctors, and eldest son Kamal has written three scholarly books. Even the grandsons, not yet in college, have learned to speak English. "They were always saving for our education," says Kamal. "I remember that for five years my mother wore the same dress." The older children worked, often in the wealthy gulf states, and financed the younger. Jaber and his wife lived in a small apartment rather than building a home.

The only one of Jaber's brood not to go to college was his second son, Kamel, 37, but of him Jaber seems the proudest. While his older brother studied during the first years of the occupation, Kamel met with fellow high-school students, plotting underground work for the Palestine Liberation Organization. "I was disappointed, frustrated and depressed by the Arab defeat," Kamel recalls. "Everything before me shattered like a broken vase." Sometimes small events move people more than grand, historic ones. In Kamel's case, the motivation was supplied by the sight of female Israeli soldiers insulting old Palestinian men. On March 18, 1971, Kamel threw a hand grenade at a passing patrol car, injuring two Arab policeman and 15 Palestinian bystanders. Kamel claimed he did not mean to hurt his own people, but he "believed in what Mao said: whenever you see your enemy, hit him."

An Israeli court sentenced Kamel to life in prison; he served 15 years before being freed in 1986 as the result of a PLO-Israeli prisoner exchange. "When I saw my brother go to jail, I was a baby," says Sura, 27. "When he came out I had graduated from college." The family was punished as well. Even the youngest of Jaber's children remember watching soldiers with axes and crowbars demolishing the Abdulfattahs' apartment. Jaber, a pious man, praised Allah that he had been too frugal to buy a house. Kamel went to prison a perpetrator of a quixotic PLO operation, but he emerged a local hero. Even strangers came from all over Jenin to meet him. Children called to him in the streets; storekeepers refused his money until finally he was too embarrassed to go shopping.

Kamel is not the only Abdulfattah to experience an Israeli jail. His sister Sura spent four months in administrative detention in 1986 for her role in demonstrations at Bir Zeit University, where she is a graduate student. When his nephew Qays was 13, he was arrested for throwing a stone at a car. "In this case I didn't do it," Qays said. "They handcuffed me to a wall, put a black sack on my head and kept me like that for two days and nights. Whenever anyone came by, they kicked me." Even his younger brother Usayd, now 14, was arrested at the age of 11 in a sweep of youth in Jenin. Kamal's sons are now *shebab*, activist youths; recently they were with one of their friends when he was shot dead; the group was throwing stones at soldiers.

At home they are obedient youngsters, jumping up to serve coffee on their father's orders. But when he urges caution, they can barely conceal their impatience. When their uncle Kamel is around, they hang on his every word. He seems to be the boys' hero, although their father insists that his sons' heroes are Yasir Arafat and Gamal Abdel Nasser, the late Egyptian leader. Who is Kamel's personal hero? He tries the names of Palestinian luminaries, but he sounds tentative, until finally he declares, *"Aftal al hejara,"* literally, "The children of the stones."

Now it is the children who lead their elders. "Before the uprising, our parents would say, 'Don't go out'," Usayd recalls. "Now they say, 'Don't throw a rock if you're in the line of fire,' or, 'Do it from a hiding place so the soldiers won't shoot you'." Parents strike, stockpile foodstuffs, sew the outlawed Palestinian flags, tend vegetable gardens in case of prolonged curfews. "Everyone is joining the Intifada, each in his own way," says Kamal.

Adults can also be *atfal al hejara.* In the neighboring village of Yabad, Qays's newlywed aunt Sura has gone to live with her husband, Yousef al Sheyleh, a dentist. When the West Bank erupted in protest over the assassination of the PLO's second-ranking military leader, Yousef the dentist was in the front row of the demonstration in Yabad, his fists full of stones. Sura was at home, pregnant with her "Intifada baby," as she calls it. She is a thoroughly modern woman who keeps her own name, rare in the Arab world, and asserts that it will be easier to defeat the Israelis than Arab male chauvinists. "Before the Intifada," says Yousef, "I only wanted two children. Now, many, many, 10 at least." Sura agrees. "We will have so many we will outnumber them in our land. And then, if they go to a demonstration and get killed, there will be others." Jaber is delighted by the couple's plans. Preoccupied with their own lives, his 10 children have given him only five grandchildren. "Be sure that 10 years from now I will have not less than 40 grandchildren. In so many ways has the Intifada changed our lives."

Most of those changes have made life harder for the family. Electricity and phone service are regularly cut off; stores are rarely open; schools and universities are closed by Israeli order. Grandfather Jaber's furniture shop has been closed for four months as a gesture of protest, and all but a handful of family members are out of work. (And those pay-checks that are coming in are hard to cash, the Israeli bank in Jenin is a favorite target for Molotov cocktails.) Israeli occupation authorities often deny permits for Palestinians to leave the West Bank, and on many days they also prohibit the Arabs from visiting neighboring communities. Ramadan, the month of fasting for Muslims, has just begun, and the family group that gathers at the Abdulfattah house is smaller than usual. Relatives abroad are afraid that, if they return, they won't be allowed to leave again. Grandson Qays will not be able to go to college in France next year as he had hoped.

Death or jail may wait, quite literally, around the corner. "The Army doesn't bother to gas us anymore," says Qays. "They only shoot to kill, immediately when they see you with a stone." The womenfolk grimly plan what they will do if one of the men is killed on the streets. They will wear white clothes, not black, and serve their guests sweet coffee rather than bitter, because one does not mourn a martyr.

What has the Abdulfattah family won for all this? Such a stupid question, says the old man, Jaber, shaking his head. All three generations know the answer. "The Intifada is the future and it's our life," says Qays. "Who writes of us?" asked Kamel. "We have been like ants." The Intifada has focused attention, even sympathy, on the Palestinians in a way that PLO exploits never did. "So you see," explains Jaber, "already we have gained so much," even more than the prospect of numerous grandchildren. "We know that only the great powers can return our land. [Secretary of State George] Shultz never cared to come here before. The Russians never wanted so much to make the peace process work." The old man shifts from the historical to the personal: "The very fact you have come to a small house in a small town like Jenin, a place they never heard of in America, shows what we have gained." Someplace else that would seem to be a victory of scant significance. To the Abdulfattahs, it repays the risks they take.

SIGNIFICANCE

The six years of violence leading to the Oslo Agreement electrified Palestinians and restructured their leadership. Yasir Arafat (1929–2004) and other members of the Palestine Liberation Organization (PLO) lived in exile. In an effort to provide Palestinians with alternatives to the PLO, Israel permitted Islamic groups to run their own schools, health clinics, mosques, and social institutions. This possibly allowed Islamic fundamentalism to grow and spread in Gaza and the West Bank. As a result, groups such as Hamas and Islamic Jihad began to gain power. Suicide bombings became a popular terrorist strategy in the region. Being exiled in Tunisia made it difficult for Yasir Arafat and the PLO to wrestle control of the Intifada away from increasingly violent Islamic fundamentalists who supported the Palestinian fight against Israel.

Within Israel, differences in dealing with the struggle affected the coalition between Likud and Labor parties in the 1990s. The public shift, due partly to media coverage, created a divide in the coalition government. The Likud party, under the leadership of Yitzhak Shamir, preferred a military solution to the Intifada. The Labor party, led by Yitzhak Rabin, concluded that the Intifada could not be suppressed and that Palestinian statehood must occur. In 1992, Yitzhak Rabin was elected prime minister in Israel. Rabin moved quickly toward secret talks with Arafat and the PLO.

Through the Oslo Agreement, Israel and the newly created Palestinian Authority officially recognized each other. A second round of Oslo Accords granted limited self-rule to Palestinians in Bethlehem, five other major towns, and over 450 small villages. In 1995, Rabin was assassinated by a right-wing extremist opposed to the ongoing peace process with Palestine. The assassination placed the Oslo Agreements in jeopardy and sparked a new wave of violence in the region. Violence reached a peak from 2000–2005, a period which became known as the Second Intifada.

FURTHER RESOURCES

Books

Lockman, Zachary and Joel Beinin, eds. *Intifada: The Palestinian Uprising Against Israeli Occupation.* Cambridge, MA: South End Press, 1989.

Periodicals

Shikaki, Khalil. "Palestinians Divided." *Foreign Affairs.* (2002): January/February.

Web sites

NPR. "The Mideast: A Century of Conflict Part 6: From the First Intifada to the Oslo Peace Agreement." <http://www.npr.org/news/specials/mideast/history/history6.html> (accessed July 8, 2005).

Real IRA

"Armed Opponents of Peace Accord Elude Pursuers"

Newspaper article

By: John Murray Brown

Date: August 6, 1998

Source: *Financial Times*.

About the Author: John Murray Brown is a staff writer for the *Financial Times*, a daily newspaper based in London.

INTRODUCTION

For the majority of Northern Ireland's population, the Good Friday Agreement—a peace treaty signed in April 1998 by all the main parties involved in Northern Ireland's thirty year-long troubles—had finally seemed to bring a political settlement to the province. It offered power-sharing between the main parties in a government that was devolved from Westminster (England). The hope of most Irish Republicans (Irish nationalists who advocate uniting Northern Ireland, currently part of Britain, with the independent Irish Republic) was that this agreement would eventually lead to a united Ireland.

For some, however, the Good Friday Agreement amounted to political treachery. The Republican move-

The destruction of a bomb blast near Britain's tallest high-rise, in 1996, just an hour after the IRA announced it was aborting a ceasefire held for more than a year. AP/WIDE WORLD PHOTOS

ment had a long tradition of refusing to recognize the British crown, and British rule in the province. Sections of the agreement also refused to even acknowledge the British government altogether (and also the Irish government, which was regarded as having betrayed Ulster when it signed over the Province to the British as part of independence negotiations in 1921), and would not countenance any negotiations. As early as the mid-1980s, the Continuity IRA had been formed in response to Sinn Fein (the political wing of the Irish Republican Army) ending its abstention from the Dail (Irish Parliament) and had begun carrying out violence in 1997 when the IRA announced a ceasefire ahead of the negotiations that preceded the Good Friday Agreement.

Around the same time, a second splinter group of dissident republicans, who became known as the Real IRA formed. Several senior IRA members joined in late 1997, including an IRA quartermaster. Its most high-profile and vociferous member was Bernadette Sands-McKevitt, sister of the late IRA terrorist, Bobby Sands, who in 1981 led a famous hunger strike among IRA members detained in Maze prison. (Sands and nine other prisoners died in 1981 during their protest.)

British intelligence was concerned by these developments. They asserted that members of the Real IRA were unrelenting hardliners who possessed the weaponry and know-how to perpetrate savage terrorist attacks. Moreover, their lack of a top-down leadership structure (as the IRA had always boasted) made them more difficult to infiltrate. Bombings on the towns of Moira and Portadown in early 1998 showed that Real IRA members worked in splinter cells and seemingly carried out attacks independent of a conventional command structure.

The first attacks by the Real IRA had been relatively minor, but on August 1, 1998, a large bomb was set off at peak shopping time in the center of the town of Banbridge. A warning had been received shortly before the explosion, but it did not provide sufficient time to prevent injuries to more than thirty people or prevent millions of dollars worth of damage.

PRIMARY SOURCE

Saturday's bomb attack in the small Northern Ireland market town of Banbridge was evidence of a new-found strength in the self-proclaimed "real IRA".

The attack, using a 240kg [529 lbs.] car bomb left in a busy shopping area, signalled a new operational capability within the group. The "real IRA" rejects the April peace agreement accepted by the mainstream Irish Republican Army and Sinn Fein, its political wing.

There had been signs that the Garda, the Republic of Ireland police force, was on top of the problem. There had been a significant bomb seizure in Howth, north of Dublin, and several bombing missions had been intercepted. Police had also had a shoot-out with raiders at a hotel south of Dublin, in which one gang member was shot. There were suggestions that the mainstream IRA might even be tipping off the Irish authorities.

The Garda remain confident they know the identity of the main organizer, a former IRA quartermaster linked with Bernadette McKevitt, sister of Bobby Sands, the IRA hunger striker. Sands died in prison in 1981 and became an IRA folk hero.

Ms. Sands denies her political group, the self-styled 32 County Sovereignty Committee, which demands immediate Irish unity and an end to British rule, has any links with the "real IRA". But she does not hide her contempt for the Sinn Fein peace strategy.

"I can't see what they are doing as being compatible with what Bobby died for," she says, tracing the history of the struggle from Bloody Sunday, when civil liberties protesters were shot dead by British soldiers, to the former policy of internment, to her brother's death, which inspired a generation of republicans.

But a bigger worry for the security forces is the growing evidence that the "real IRA", while recruiting disgruntled IRA members, may also be linking more formally with the Continuity IRA and the Irish National Liberation Army, both of which believe any settlement which implicitly accepts Irish partition and the re-establishment of a Northern Ireland parliament is a betrayal of republican principles.

The INLA is linked to the Irish Republican Socialist party.

The continuing threat means the UK government is likely to have to maintain a heavy security presence in the border area although some frontier checkpoints, which police say were never an effective intelligence tool, will continue to be dismantled.

But once the Northern Ireland assembly has opened, the UK government is expected to give the go-ahead for a more robust security response by the army and the police.

Any dissident action has the capacity to embarrass the Sinn Fein leadership and to provide encouragement to republicans who have misgivings about the accord. In addition, Sinn Fein's obstinate refusal to condemn the Banbridge attack has added to unionist unease.

Gerry Adams, the Sinn Fein president, said yesterday "the war will be over when all those engaged in war, and some are still engaging in war, stop". He was responding to calls to declare the war was over from David Ervine, a leading spokesman for the Progressive Unionist party, the small political wing of the outlawed Ulster Volunteer Force.

SIGNIFICANCE

The attack on Banbridge marked the arrival of the Real IRA, and a fortnight later they would carry out an attack that would secure their notoriety forever. In an almost identical bombing, a 500-pound car bomb was set off at the height of shopping time in the small County Tyrone town of Omagh, killing twenty-nine people (including a woman pregnant with twins) and injuring two hundred. This was the worst terrorist action in the province's history, and, barring the Lockerbie bombing, the worst act of terrorism ever carried out on British soil until the London transport bombings of 2005.

Revulsion across the political spectrum after Omagh led to a massive crack down on the nascent organization. Many of the Real IRA's most visible leaders were arrested, and a huge joint operation between MI5 (Britain's domestic intelligence service) and Irish Gardai (police) to infiltrate and track down Real IRA members was carried out. Throughout 1999 and much of 2000, further arrests were made, arms seized, and no further attacks followed. However, in September 2000, a missile attack on MI5's headquarters in London marked an end to the apparent cessation in hostilities. Three more attacks followed on mainland Britain over the next six months, but these were all low-tech attacks causing minimal injuries and disruption.

Not until August 2002 would the Real IRA again claim a life, when a booby trap at a Territorial Army (British Army Reserves) camp in County Londonderry killed a maintenance worker.

However, the organization has become increasingly marginalized. In October 2002, a message from Real IRA members in Portlaoise Prison in the Irish Republic, denounced the organization's leadership as corrupt, saying that it had "forfeited all moral authority", and called for its immediate disbandment. The group has since been virtually silent, although this may merely coincide with the current stalling in the peace process, after the Northern Ireland Assembly was suspended in October 2002 following the refusal of the IRA-proper to decommission its weapons.

FURTHER RESOURCES

Books

McKittrick, David and McVeigh, David. *Making Sense of the Troubles.* London: Penguin,

Mooney, John, and O'Toole, Michael. *Black Operations: The Secret War Against the Real IRA.* Dunshaughlin: Maverick House, 2003.

Web sites

Jane's Intelligence Review. "The Real IRA: after Omagh, what now?" August 24, 1998. <http://www.janes.com/regional _news/europe/news/jir/jir980824_1_n.shtml> (accessed July 8, 2005).

Omagh Bombing by Real IRA

"Omagh Massacre: Loyalists Signal Their Ceasefire is Secure"

Newspaper article

By: John Mullin and Ewen MacAskill

Date: August 17, 1998

Source: "Omagh Massacre: Loyalists Signal Their Ceasefire is Secure," as published by the *Guardian Unlimited* (London).

About the Author: Ewen MacAskill serves as the *Guardian's* chief political correspondent and diplomatic editor. John Mullin, the executive news editor of *The Independent* was a *Guardian* staff reporter in 1998.

INTRODUCTION

The Irish Republican Army (IRA) formed in 1916 to free Ireland from long-time British rule. Upon the division of Ireland in 1922, the IRA opposed the creation of Protestant-dominated Northern Ireland and sought to protect the civil rights of Catholics. In 1939, the IRA began a bombing campaign in Great Britain that prompted the Irish government to ban it in cooperation with the British government. In 1955, the IRA became active against the Protestant Royal Ulster Constabulary (RUC) in Northern Ireland but was again stifled by Anglo-Irish cooperation. In 1969, the IRA divided with the more nationalistic Provisional Irish Republican Army (PIRA) seeking unification of Ireland by force. The original IRA allegedly renounced armed struggle in 1972 and became the Worker's Party to compete openly in electoral politics. When the PIRA declared a ceasefire in

Victims are treated at the scene of a car bomb explosion in Omagh, Northern Ireland on August 15, 1998. AP/WIDE WORLD PHOTOS

Northern Ireland in 1997, over one hundred dissidents led by Michael "Mickey" McKevitt elected to continue the campaign of violence under the name of Real IRA.

The Real IRA (RIRA) is a small Catholic group that opposes British rule in predominantly-Protestant Northern Ireland. Allied with the 32 County Sovereignty Movement, the RIRA carried out a number of relatively minor bombings in Ireland prior to the 1998 Omagh attack. The explosion of a car bomb in the shopping center of Omagh killed twenty-nine people and injured 220 others. It was the single worst act of terrorism in the entire history of the "Troubles" in Northern Ireland.

The Omagh massacre aimed at derailing the Northern Ireland peace process. Since the 1960s, the IRA had been opposed in Northern Ireland by a Protestant terrorist organization, the Ulster Defense Association (UDA) and its military branch, the Ulster Freedom Fighters (UFF). The UDA sought Protestant domination. It opposed the British imposition of home rule in Northern Ireland as an attempt to undermine Protestant authority. The UDA and the UFF, who occasionally worked in conjunction with British security forces, are believed to be responsible for the killings of more than four hundred Catholics. In its heyday in the early 1970s, the UDA claimed 40,000 to 50,000 members but movements toward peace in Northern Ireland resulted in a loss of members. By the Omagh bombing, the UDA likely numbered less than 10,000 but it added to its strength by joining with another paramilitary organization, the Ulster Volunteer Force (UVF) in the 1990s. An equally violent Protestant terrorist organization, the UVF cooperated with UDA in the Combined Loyalist Military Command before the two groups had a violent falling-out in 2001.

PRIMARY SOURCE

Mainstream loyalist paramilitaries were last night ready to stick with their four-year-old ceasefires. Their position, signaled after a series of meetings, was some comfort on a savage weekend as Northern Ireland's leaders strove to keep the political process on course.

The move came as Tony Blair cut short his holiday in France to fly to Belfast. He was clearly affected by the tragedy, and stayed overnight. Mo Mowlam, the Northern Ireland Secretary, was due to return from Greece this morning.

The Ulster Defence Association and the paramilitary outfit to which it is linked, the Ulster Freedom Fighters, together with the Ulster Volunteer Force, were outraged at the bombing of Omagh. But they are prepared to withstand the Real IRA's attempts to goad them back into violence.

One senior loyalist source said that the groups realised it would be an error to retaliate when violent republicanism was so close to destroying itself over mass murder, which is thought to have killed more Catholics than Protestants.

But there could be rogue elements prepared to exact revenge, and the Loyalist Volunteer Force, on ceasefire only since May, is seen as the most likely to hit back. It has been responsible for 18 murders in two years.

There was a growing conviction in Northern Ireland last night that the Real IRA's support had dwindled to nothing, and that the Irish government was prepared to act against its leaders. Most live in the republic. Downing Street called it the group of last resistance.

The stand of the loyalist paramilitary groups, particularly the UDA and UFF, is an important boost. The UDA's political ally, the Ulster Democratic Party, failed to win a seat in the 108-seat assembly, sparking fears about the instability of the process. The UDP issued an appeal for no retaliation.

The UDA and UFF were engaged in a flurry of killings at the beginning of the year after the loyalist leader Billy Wright was shot dead. They restored the ceasefire after involvement in the killings of three Catholics.

A key factor in the loyalists' decision is thought to have been Gerry Adams's outright condemnation of Saturday's bombing. Although loyalists mistrust Mr Adams, it was the first time a Sinn Fein leader had used the term "condemnation" when commenting on an attack mounted by any republican organisation.

Mr. Adams was unequivocal. He said: "I reiterate my total condemnation of this action. There should now be an urgent meeting of all the political parties here to discuss a way out of the crisis. What we need to do is not to give up hope. People need to have the conviction that we are going to see peace in this country. We should keep going and not be deflected by anything from working towards that goal."

His colleague, Martin McGuinness, went further. He effectively accused the Real IRA of the bombing, a theme picked up on by Mitchel McLaughlin, the Sinn Fein chairman.

Mr McGuinness said: "I have no doubt over the course of the next 24 hours that we will have, I think, a very firm opinion as to who was responsible. I certainly have my own view that it could be this group, which describe themselves as the IRA, which I think most people within the republican community would not recognise as the IRA at all."

Ominously for the Real IRA, he predicted "a massive backlash within the republican nationalist community in the course of the next coming days and weeks". The voice of that community would be made "crystal clear" and he called on the Real IRA to cease its activities.

There is speculation in Belfast that Mr. Adams, praised by Mr. Blair for a genuine commitment to peace, could use the situation to marginalise the Real IRA further. That could signal some comfort for David Trimble, first minister and leader of the Ulster Unionists, ahead of next month's crucial meeting of the new assembly.

He has long been under pressure from Unionist colleagues over Sinn Fein's participation in the power-sharing executive. Sinn Fein is due two places in the 12-member executive under the proportionality rules.

Any small gesture on the part of the IRA to begin decommissioning of its terrorist arsenal, or a statement that the war is over, would give Mr Trimble room for manoeuvre. Some security sources believe that the IRA might hand over weapons to prevent them falling into the hands of the Real IRA.

Many Unionists remain unconvinced by the security forces' assertions that they do not believe that IRA members are involved with the Real IRA. These Unionists think that the Omagh massacre was the logical outcome of what they perceive as government concessions to Sinn Fein to prevent a return to IRA violence.

The bombing brought again calls for the re-introduction of selective internment without trial. Both the Dublin and London governments appeared to be flirting with the notion early yesterday. They believe it could work, but would be a high-risk strategy. Although intelligence is much better now and any arrests would be on a smaller scale, they are worried that internment could spark a resurgence in support for the paramilitaries, as it did a quarter of a century ago.

Ronnie Flanagan, chief constable of the RUC, and Pat Byrne, the Garda commissioner, will meet today. The identities of the prime suspects are known. One was at his home last night, advising reporters to talk to his solicitor if they wanted a comment.

Mr. Blair spoke to a range of politicians last night, including Mr. Trimble, Mr. Adams, and the political representatives of the loyalist paramilitaries. Most had broken their holidays to return to Northern Ireland.

He met Bertie Ahern, the Ireland prime minister, at Stormont House, and both men spelled out their determination to deal with the bombers. Mr. Ahern was scathing towards the Real IRA. He said: "Whatever has to be done will be done."

Mr. Blair described the explosion as "a blast of evil". Downing Street was anxious to draw a distinction between Omagh and other bombings down the years, such as Warrington. There was no political support for the Omagh bombers; the outlook had changed.

Mr. Blair, aware of the distaste for Baroness Thatcher's public appearances in the aftermath of bombings, initially stayed away. He left the Deputy Prime Minister, John Prescott, to make a highly visible visit to the scene of the devastation and to a nearby hospital. Mr. Blair later made a private visit to some of the victims.

Mr Blair said those behind the Omagh bombing had "no political organisation, no vote, no political voice." He added: "They stand for nothing other than the chance to wreck the future for the people of Northern Ireland."

He expressed his deep sympathy for the bereaved in Omagh. "How can we ever express what it must be like to lose a child or to lose your parents in such a way? But in the end I know that amongst all the emotions of grief and anger, people will want to know that we are carrying on working for peace. That is all we can do. Of course we feel a sense that this is a situation so appalling, but we have to carry on and take the measures that are necessary in terms of security. We will do that. I will never give up, we mustn't give up on the process of peace."

Atrocities in Northern Ireland used to beget retaliation. But government sources believe that recent experience has shown each to be a step away from enduring violence. While the Shankill bomb in 1993 provoked the Greysteel massacre and the Kennedy Way killings, with the loss of 19 lives in a week, the LVF's slaying of a Catholic and his Protestant friend in a bar in Poyntzpass, County Armagh, seemed to

Police officers and firefighters inspect the damage caused by a bomb explosion in Omagh on August 15, 1998. *AP/WIDE WORLD PHOTOS*

spur the politicians on to greater efforts. The Good Friday Agreement was the product a month later.

August, generally a month of drift for leaders, has this year, after the tumultuous year of rising to each ever more demanding challenge on the path of the political process, revealed even more than usual.

Omagh has concentrated minds once more. That may be scant consolation for the bereaved and injured, but the murders of 28 people may yet mark the end of poisonous violence in Northern Ireland.

SIGNIFICANCE

The IRA historically targeted British Army troops, Northern Ireland security forces, judicial officials, prison wardens and guards, and members of Ulster Protestant political parties and militias. The large number of civilian deaths and injuries at Omagh caused a widespread wave of revulsion toward the Real IRA. The bombing was condemned by Protestants and Catholics, both Irish and British. Sinn Fein, the political arm of the IRA and the major Catholic participant in the peace talks, condemned the attack. In response, the RIRA claimed that the killing of civilians had been accidental and it declared a ceasefire in September 1998. Two years later, the RIRA resumed attacks against British interests in Northern Ireland and on the English mainland. In 2001, the U.S. government formally declared the RIRA to be a foreign terrorist organization, a designation that permits the government to freeze the assets of anyone tied to the RIRA in the U.S. The designation attempted to block the RIRA from receiving funds from Irish-American supporters, historically among the largest financial backers of the IRA and related IRA organizations.

The Omagh bombing raised concerns that the UDA would retaliate against Catholics and set off another wave of violence. The UDA alternately participated and rejected ceasefires in the years since the Omagh massacre. In February 2003, it declared a unilateral ceasefire and apologized for fundraising through drug trafficking and racketeering.

In 2003, the Real IRA joined with the Continuity IRA (CIRA) in a promise of continuing attacks on Protestants and Northern Ireland security forces. The CIRA, rumored to be associated with a dissident offshoot of Sinn Fein known as Republican Sinn Fein, reportedly has fewer than fifty members.

The terror campaign conducted by the RIRA may have ultimately weakened the organization. The violence of Omagh, especially the numbers of dead and injured civilians, reduced public support for the group in Northern Ireland. The violence made RIRA appear to be less a true army and more of a collection of outlaws. It also hardened Irish Protestant attitudes toward militant Irish nationalists and may have strengthened the resolve of some British officials to not retreat from Northern Ireland.

FURTHER RESOURCES

Books

Cronin, Audrey. *Foreign Terrorist Organizations*. Washington, D.C.: CRS, 2004.

Dunnigan, John P. *Deep-Rooted Conflict and the IRA Cease-Fire*. Lanham, MD: University Press of America, 1995.

Geraghty, Tony. *The Irish War: The Hidden Conflict Between the IRA and British Intelligence*. Baltimore: Johns Hopkins, 2000.

Mooney, John and Michael O'Toole. *Black Operations: The Secret War Against the Real IRA*. Ashbourne, Ireland: Maverick House, 2003.

Suicide Bombers Target Israelis

"All Those Serving Food Are No Longer Among the Living"

Newspaper article

By: Ohad Gozani

Date: April 1, 2002

Source: *The Daily Telegraph* (London)

About the Author: Ohad Gozani is a native Israeli and a news reporter with the *Daily Telegraph*. He reports from Tel Aviv on events in Israel and also writes for the Associated Press.

INTRODUCTION

From the autumn of 2000 through the end of summer in 2002, more than four hundred people were killed in Israel as a direct result of political violence aimed at Israelis. The majority of deaths, and over one thousand injuries, occurred at the hands of suicide bombers, most of whom were Palestinian, and many were affiliated with Islamist extremist groups Hamas (the Arabic acronym for "The Islamic Resistance Movement") and Islamic Jihad, two terrorist organizations that advocate political violence as a means to establish a Palestinian state.

Yassir Arafat (1929–2004), then president of the Palestinian Authority (PA), which represents the interests of the Palestinian people and is treated as a putative government for the Palestinian people (although

Friends cry during the funeral ceremony for two sisters who died when a suicide bomber detonated explosives at a Tel Aviv disco. AP/WIDE WORLD PHOTOS

Palestine is not recognized by International law as a nation or country), allegedly condoned the bombings. Many nations asserted that the PA had lost control over more radical elements in the region. As the suicide bombings continued, and included the new occurrence of female suicide bombers, tension escalated.

Arafat was sharply criticized for not taking a firmer stance against the suicide bombings, and for not acting quickly to squelch the series of bombings and attacks. Both Hamas and Islamic Jihad opposed the Palestinian Authority, considering Arafat and his organization too moderate in fighting for the Palestinian state. The extremist groups also oppose peace process negotiations with Israel.

■ PRIMARY SOURCE

They spoke of a miracle in Haifa yesterday after a petrol station with tanks full of fuel was barely touched by the huge explosion that tore through a restaurant and shop 50 yards away.

At least 16 people were killed and 30 injured when a suicide bomber blew himself up among the lunchtime crowd at the Matza restaurant in the town centre.

A fire brigade commander said he believed "it was the hand of God" that prevented the bomb from igniting the fuel in the petrol tanks.

A passer-by, Shimon Sabag, described the scene after the explosion. "Pieces of flesh were all over the place,

people were burning," he said. "We pulled people out of the restaurant and store next door."

The roadside restaurant is owned by an Israeli Arab family and its Middle Eastern cuisine is popular with local people and travelers. It has long been a symbol of co-existence between Jews and Arabs.

"I am sure this was the reason why the bomber chose to hit this place," said Modi Sandberg, a former MP who lives in the locality.

Mickey Matza, whose family owns the complex, said: "Arabs and Israelis have worked and dined together here for many years. There was nothing unusual about it—and now such a great tragedy."

Shahar Azran, an Israeli news photographer on home leave from New York, said: "We ate at the restaurant and went home. Hardly two minutes later, I heard the explosion and rushed back. All the people who were serving food are no longer among the living."

The blast tore two holes in the asbestos roof. The windows were blown out and the mangled bodies were covered by upturned chairs, while tables were left standing in pools of blood.

A police spokesman said there was no security guard at the restaurant door.

Two militant Islamic groups, Hamas and Islamic Jihad, said they were responsible.

It was the fourth such bombing in Israel in five days, and the second in Haifa in four months. It came less than a day after another suicide bomber blew himself up in a cafe in the centre of Tel Aviv, killing himself and injuring 24 people.

The frequent bombings have discouraged outdoor activities during the Passover holiday. Many officials have urged Israelis to carry on with life as usual, but Amram Mitzna, the mayor of Haifa, broke ranks to urge people to stay indoors.

He cancelled several large functions, including a children's drama festival, and urged his citizens not to frequent places that had no security guards.

Mr Azran agreed. "I guess I won't be going out tonight at all," he said.

Ali, the restaurant manager, who was in hospital with concussion and shock, said from his bed: "I hope this was the last attack."

SIGNIFICANCE

The month of March, 2002, was one of the bloodiest in terms of terrorism on Israeli land. Between March 2 and March 31, twelve terrorist bombings occurred across the country, resulting in nearly eighty deaths and hundreds of injuries. In response to these bombings, Israeli Prime Minister Ariel Sharon ordered Operation "Defensive Shield," an extensive assault against groups such as Hamas and Islamic Jihad in the West Bank and Gaza. The Palestinian Authority head-quarters in Ramallah as well as Yassir Arafat's personal compound were seized.

During "Defensive Shield," which lasted from March 29, 2002 through May 10, 2002, the Israeli military called up more than 20,000 reservists, the largest number since the 1982 Lebanon War. Prime Minister Sharon declared the goal of the operation to be to "catch and arrest terrorists and, primarily, their dis-patchers and those who finance and support them; to confiscate weapons intended to be used against Israeli citizens; to expose and destroy terrorist facilities and explosives, laboratories, weapons production factories and secret installations."

The Israeli response included military action in four primary cities: Jenin, Nablus, Bethlehem, and Ramallah. Conflict in Jenin was particularly fierce, with twenty-three Israeli soldiers and fifty-two Palestinians dying during one day's fighting. The Israeli government imposed curfews on Palestinians and bulldozed houses that had been used by Palestinians during the armed conflict.

In a June 24, 2002 speech by United States President George W. Bush, the president called for "a new and dif-ferent Palestinian leadership," a direct reference to Yassir Arafat's perceived weakness as leader of the Palestinian Authority. Although violence decreased, and suicide bombings dropped to their lowest levels in years, in less than a year, Arafat was isolated in Ramallah and replaced as head of the Palestinian Authority by Mahmoud Abbas. Abbas resigned within four months, from lack of support from Arafat himself. After Arafat's death in 2004, Abbas ran for President of the PA in January 2005 and won with more than 60 percent of the vote.

FURTHER RESOURCES
Books
Oliver, Anne Marie and Steinberg, Paul. *The Road To Martyrs' Square: A Journey Into The World Of The Suicide Bomber*. Oxford University Press, 2004.

Web sites
Israel Ministry of Foreign Affairs. "Operation Defensive Shield: Special Update." <http://www.mfa.gov.il/MFA/MFA-Archive/2000_2009/2002/3/Operation%20Defensive%20Shield> (accessed July 14, 2005).

Yale Global Online. "Terrorists and Their Tools—Part I." <http://yaleglobal.yale.edu/display.article?id=3749> (accessed July 14, 2005).

PLO Leadership
"Psychological profile: Arafat moved by money, not might"

News article

By: *The World Tribune*

Date: June 14, 2002

Source: "Psychological Profile: Arafat moved by money, not might" as published by the *World Tribune.com*

About the Author: *The World Tribune* is an American Internet newspaper dedicated to covering world polit-ical, cultural, and economic events.

INTRODUCTION

Yassir (also spelled Yasser or Yasir) Arafat claimed to have been born in Jerusalem on August 4, 1929, although his registered birth certificate stated August 24, 1929 in Cairo, Egypt. His given name was Muhammad Abdel-Rahman Abdel-Raouf Arafat al-Qudwa al-Husseine. The nickname Yassir loosely translates to mean *easy-going*. He was the co-founder and Chairman of the Palestine Liberation Organization (PLO) from 1969 through his death in 2004, and the leader of the Palestine National Authority (PNA) from 1993 until 2004. In 1994, Arafat shared the Nobel Peace Prize with Israeli leaders Shimon Peres and Yitzhak Rabin.

Yassir Arafat's life and lengthy political career was controversial. His loyal supporters viewed him as a hero, a tireless freedom fighter, and a man who best symbolized the aspirations of the Palestinian nation. His vehement opponents declared Arafat a lifelong terrorist who advo-cated violence throughout his career, even while employ-ing the rhetoric of peace. Many others accused him of being apolitically corrupt, or of being a weak leader who made excessive concessions to the government of Israel during the era when efforts were being made to broker a peace settlement.

By the time he reached his teens, Arafat was aligned with the Palestinians. By 1946, he became a Palestinian nationalist who was engaged in the busi-ness of moving weapons procured in Egypt over the border to Palestine. Although he was not directly involved in the 1948 Arab-Israeli War, it was during this time that Arafat was developing the political net-work that would allow him to emerge as a leader in the Palestinian movement.

In the mid–1950s, Arafat joined the Muslim Brotherhood in Egypt; he became the leader of the

Palestinian demonstrators during the Palestinian uprising in Nablus, Occupied West Bank, on December 13, 1987.
AP/WIDE WORLD PHOTOS

Palestine Student Union at the University of Cairo shortly thereafter. He graduated with a degree in civil engineering. By the late 1950s, he had moved to Kuwait. In 1959, he founded a local sect of Al Fatah (the name Fatah is used interchangeably with Al Fatah) there. Al Fatah (loosely translated as *conquest*) was a pseudonym for the Palestine National Liberation Movement. Fatah was dedicated to the complete destruction of Israel and Jordan, and to the establishment of an independent Palestinian state in their stead. Arafat sough to ensure the financial security of Al Fatah by gaining ongoing and generous contributions from the highly paid Palestinian oil workers in Kuwait. Ultimately, Arafat's small, but well funded, splinter group would take control of the entire Palestinian liberation movement.

■ **PRIMARY SOURCE**

Palestinian leader Yasser Arafat, termed as not completely stable, appears unimpressed with Israeli military might or U.S. diplomatic pressure, a new study says.

A psychological profile prepared for the International Policy Institute for Counter-Terrorism says the Palestinian Authority chairman can be influenced by economic pressure, Middle East Newsline reported.

"Spectacular military operations—such as air strikes, massive fire directed at targets in the areas of the Palestinian Authority—have a limited effect on Arafat," the report said. "He knows the limitations of Israel's power and in situations of confrontation feels at his best, tends to take risks, and is willing to make sacrifices, more so than in normal circumstances."

The profile, authored by researchers Shaul Kimhi, Shmuel Even and Jerrold Post, said Arafat's behavior comprises limited emotional stability, rapid mood swings and a need to feel in complete control of his environment. The study said the PA chairman does not tolerate dissent or even constructive criticism.

"Arafat's interpersonal skills are characterized by problems with relationships, stemming from his need to manipulate people, bringing them closer or distancing them as needed," the report said. "He has neither intimate relationships nor any close friends, and apparently feels no need for them."

The profile said Arafat has no hobbies and does not engage in entertainment. The study dismisses reports in the 1970s that Arafat is a homosexual.

The profile recommended that Israel's military stage limited precision operations. The study said this would undermine Arafat's sense of control. Arafat, the study said, is also not affected by economic pressure on Palestinians. The report said measures such as cutting off water or electricity serve Arafat's aims of presenting Palestinian suffering to the international community.

In contrast, economic pressure on Arafat can reap gains. The report said withholding Israeli tax funds or ending international aid can be effective if it continues over a long period.

"Money is one of the means through which Arafat wields control," the report said. "These funds constitute the major bulk of the financial resources of the Palestinian Authority and are required to finance the work of administration and the security forces."

All three of the researchers have engaged in psychological profiles for either Israel or the United States. Kimhi, a member of the American Psychological Association and the International Society of Political Psychology, was an adviser to Israeli military intelligence.

Even is a reserve colonel who served in the intelligence corps. Post, a professor of psychiatry and political psychology, wrote psychological profiles of the late Israeli Prime Minister Menachem Begin and Egyptian President Anwar Sadat for U.S. President Jimmy Carter.

"It is very hard to predict his behavior, since it comes from a man whose manner of thought and behavior is completely different from that recognized and accepted in politics and business in the Western world, and, on the other hand, it is difficult to know what his intentions truly are," the report said.

SIGNIFICANCE

Fatah's ideology and philosophy were centered on financing terrorism and fomenting violence as the primary means of achieving political and ideological goals. Arafat promoted guerilla-style training in Syria and Algeria for Al Fatah members. In December of 1964, they unsuccessfully attempted their first major act of violence, blowing up a major Israeli water pump station. Fatah continually attacked Israeli public transportation, as well as villages and individual homes.

Also in 1964, the PLO was created by the Arab League, with the intent of establishing it as a central force in the continual efforts to destroy Israel. Arafat and the Al Fatah initially saw the PLO as a rival political faction; however, over the next several years, Al Fatah became a more and more focal part of the organization. When the Palestinian National Council held its annual meeting in 1968, it voted to change its charter in order to adopt the PLO/Fatah dogma of using violence and war as the primary means of achieving Palestinian independence.

The PLO was located in Jordan until 1970, when it was driven out—causing a bloody civil war—by the armies of Jordan's King Hussein. As a show of force and retaliation, Fatah hijacked several Western airliners and blew one up on a Cairo runway on September 12, 1970. On September 16, 1970, Yassir Arafat assumed command of the PLA, the traditional military arm of the PLO. Although the PLO/PLA engaged the military support of Syria during the battle with Jordan, the Jordanian army (with the active support of the United States and of Israel) defeated the insurgents, who were driven from the country and fled to Lebanon by way of Syria.

In Lebanon, Al Fatah and the PLO again incited civil war. The PLO achieved worldwide infamy when an extremist cell called Black September kidnapped and murdered eleven Israeli athletes at the Munich Olympic Games in 1972. In 1973, Arafat engaged the Khartoum faction of Al Fatah in a terrorist attack on the United States by abducting and murdering the United States Ambassador to Sudan, Cleo Noel, along with embassy aid, George Moore.

In the early 1990s, the PLO and Israel engaged in secret peace negotiations that formed the basis of the 1993 Oslo Accords, which called for the progressive development and implementation of Palestinian self-rule over the Gaza Strip and the West Bank, occurring over a five year time span. As a result of these groundbreaking efforts, Yassir Arafat, Shimon Peres, and Yitzhak Rabin were awarded the Nobel Peace Prize in 1994. The Oslo Accords held several conditions: Arafat signed two letters renouncing violence and terrorism and officially recognizing the state of Israel prior to signing the peace accords. Rabin, on behalf of Israel, officially recognized the PLO. A new entity, called the Palestinian Authority (PA), was created to preside over the territory to be controlled by Palestine. In 1994, Arafat moved the headquarters of the PLO from Tunisia to the West Bank and the Gaza Strip, in order to rule the new territories. This move enabled Arafat to continue to have virtually complete control over all Palestinian funds and political authority. In 1996, Yassir Arafat was duly elected president of the PA. His term of office was to end in 1999, with new elections. Arafat did not permit elections to be held and retained power until his death.

The first Oslo Accord failed amid escalating violence. PLO terrorism against Israeli civilian targets, characterized by more growing numbers of Palestinian suicide bombers and the inception of an Islamic martyrdom cult called Al-Aqsa Martyr's Brigade—were met with Israeli retaliatory strikes on suspected Palestinian extremist targets. Large sums of money were funneled by the PA into the Al-Aqsa, for the purposes of supporting escalating acts of terrorism against Israel, aimed at the destruction of the state in the service of a wholly Palestinian nation.

By 2002, the United States officially recognized the ongoing PA/Arafat financing and support of terrorism against Israel and called for Arafat's removal from political power. In order to achieve some degree of peace in the Middle East, the Israeli government, in 2003, acted to isolate Arafat in his Ramallah compound and to facilitate the election of a new Palestinian Prime Minister, Mahmoud Abbas. Arafat retained sufficient power as to be able to continuously undermine Abbas, who eventually resigned.

Throughout his career, Arafat achieved much of his political power by controlling the enormous financial resources funneled into Palestine by the PLO. His initial wealth came as a result of the financial backing achieved for the Fatah and early PLO; it was tremendously increased by the diversion of millions of dollars in international aid designed to ameliorate some of the destitution in war-ravaged Palestinian regions. In 2003, the PA's finance ministry retained a team of American accountants to assess Yassir Arafat's financial holdings. The results of the audit indicated that Arafat had created a personal investment portfolio estimated to be worth nearly one billion dollars. He had holdings in such diverse areas as a cell phone manufacturer in Tunisia, a Coca-Cola bottling plant in Ramallah, and venture capital funds in the Cayman Islands. It was determined that few of the funds intended for use by the Palestinian populace had reached them, and were, instead, controlled by Arafat and the PLO.

FURTHER RESOURCES

Books

Gowers, Andrew, and Walker, Tony. *Arafat: The Biography*. Virgin Books, 2005.

Rubin, Barry M., and Rubin, Judith Colp. *Yasir Arafat: A Political Biography*. Oxford University Press, 2003.

Web sites

CBSNews.com. "Arafat's Billions November 9, 2003." <http://www.cbsnews.com/stories/2003/11/07/60minutes/printable582487.shtml> (accessed July 11, 2005).

CNN.com. Profiles: Yasser Arafat. "Yasser Arafat: Homeland a Dream for Palestinian Authority Chief." <http://cnnstudentnews.cnn.com/fyi/school.tools/profiles/Yasser.Arafat/student.storypage.html> (accessed July 5, 2005).

The Electronic Intifada, Business and Economy. "IMF audit reveals Arafat diverted $900 million to account under his personal control. Report, IMF, 20 September 2003." <http://electronicintifada.net/cgi-bin/artman/exec/view.cgi/7/1958> (accessed July 2, 2005).

Forbes.com. "OutFront: Auditing Arafat." Nathan Vardi. 03.17.03. <http://www.forbes.com/forbes/2003/0317/049_print.html.> (accessed July 11, 2005)

Haaretz.com-Israel. "MI chief: terrorist groups trying hard to pull of mega attack." <http://www.haaretzdaily.com/hasen/pages/ShArt.jhtml?itemNo=197188&contrassID=1&subContrassID=0&sbSubContrassID=0> (accessed July 5, 2005).

Chechens Seize Moscow Theater

"The Shooting Began, We Covered Our Heads, But Then Everyone Fell Asleep"

Newspaper article

By: Julius Strauss, Ben Aris

Date: October 28, 2002

Source: "The Shooting Began, We Covered Our Heads, But Then Everyone Fell Asleep," published in the *Daily Telegraph*.

About the Author: The *Daily Telegraph* newspaper has been published in London since 1855.

INTRODUCTION

Just after 9:00 P.M. on October 23, 2002, the second act of *Nord-Ost (Northeast)*, a popular romantic musical play, was just beginning after an intermission at a theater in the Dubrovka area of Moscow, Russia. Suddenly, about forty to fifty heavily armed Chechen terrorists, more than a third of them women, stormed the theater and took some 800 audience members, actors, and staff hostage.

Hostages held by Chechen gunmen in the auditorium of a Moscow theater in 2002. AP/WIDE WORLD PHOTOS

Firing rifles into the air, the terrorists announced a single demand: that Russia immediately withdraw its forces from the largely Muslim republic of Chechnya in the Caucasus Mountain region.

The terrorists were clad in black with only their eyes exposed. Many, particularly the women, held pistols and had cables running to explosive packs attached to their belts. Most of the men bore Kalashnikov rifles as they worked their way through the building, attaching explosives to walls, pillars, and patrons' seats and threatening to blow the theater up if they met with resistance. The hostages later noted that the women, some of them likely widows of Chechen separatists who had been killed by Russian troops during years of warfare, seemed almost more determined than the men—and more willing to sacrifice their own lives.

The terrorists were led by Movsar Barayev, the nephew of a slain Chechen military leader. During the siege, Barayev released a videotaped statement announcing the terrorists' demands.

On October 24 and 25, the terrorists released about fifty-four hostages, including Muslims and preteen children. Some hostages were shot to death as they tried to escape through windows, but a few succeeded in getting away. The terrorists set a deadline of October 26 and threatened to begin killing hostages if their demands were not met.

Early in the morning of October 26, commandos from Russia's Federal Security Service launched a raid on the theater by pumping an aerosol anesthetic into the building to render the terrorists unconscious. The commandos then stormed the building. By the time the raid had ended, they had shot some forty of the terrorists, many of whom were already unconscious. Approximately 120 hostages lost their lives; some had been shot by the terrorists, but others died from a combination of dehydration, the aerosol, and inadequate medical treatment in part because the Russian government initially refused to disclose the nature of the anesthetic. The Russian health minister later revealed that the aerosol contained fentanyl, an opiate that is eighty times more powerful than morphine.

PRIMARY SOURCE

In the end it was a frightened little boy who triggered the end of the Moscow siege. "Mummy, I don't know what to do anymore," he shouted. Then he threw a bottle at a Chechen woman guarding him and fled towards the exit.

For the terrorists it was too much. One casually raised his Kalashnikov and fired, missing the boy and hitting a row of hostages.

Olga Chernyak, a journalist who had been among the hostages from the beginning, said: "They opened fire but they missed. Instead they hit the people sitting around him.

"One man was hit exactly in the eye and there was a lot of blood, bubbling blood."

For the Russian special forces monitoring the unfolding drama from the tunnels under the theatre, the killing was the signal to move.

Authorities had decided early in the siege that they would attack if hostages were executed and a plan had been readied.

For days they had been secretly practising at the Meridian Theatre on nearby Profsouznaya Street. Plainclothes policemen had been deployed to guard the perimeter and keep curious onlookers away.

Gas was pumped into the building's ventilation system and one hostage, Sergei Novikov, said: "I didn't know what was happening. We heard shouts and explosives and then we felt a tightening in our throats.

"The terrorists had warned us that if we tried to hide under the seats when an attack came they would blow up their bombs. So everybody just covered their faces with their arms. I was paralysed, I couldn't breathe. I thought the end had come."

Oleg Zyogonov said. "The rebels knew that an assault was coming. They forced the hostages to pray. At that time we really thought we were done for."

Then a light mist began to fall from the ceiling. The hostages smelt gas.

"A panic started among us and people were screaming, 'Gas, gas!' and, yes, there was shooting," said the theatre's technician, Georgi Vasilev.

"But then everyone quickly fell down. I was told later by a woman while we were in hospital together that she didn't fall asleep immediately because she covered her mouth and nose." She said it was very strange to look at everyone.

"When the shooting began, they told us to lean forward in the seats and cover our heads. But then everyone fell asleep. And the rebels were sitting there with their heads thrown back and their mouths wide open."

Another witness said: "After the first shots the gas came in. I saw a terrorist sitting at the scene jump up and try to get a gas mask. Then he convulsed, tried again to put the mask to his face and fell."

Olga Chernyak said: "We assumed that there would be an assault, when gas started to come in, and we were happy. After this I don't remember anything because I regained consciousness only in hospital."

By the time of the attack, many of the hostages were at their wits' end. Yesterday they painted a picture of increasing psychological terror as the siege progressed.

Throughout the three days they had been threatened by the Chechens with decapitation. Sometimes they were beaten or shouted at. Whispering conversations of encouragement amongst themselves was all they had to keep their moral up.

They had not been allowed to move out of their seats except to go to the lavatory in the orchestra pit under the stage. That became so loathsome that the hostages tried to drink as little water as possible to reduce the need. One man was beaten because he climbed out of the orchestra pit the wrong way. "He was beaten, kicked, it was awful," said a witness.

Day and night the rebels wandered among the hostages. Sometimes they said nothing, at other times they threatened or cajoled. As time went on the hostages were increasingly tormented.

"They wouldn't let us sleep and they harassed us with music and light. 'Don't sit like that, sit up straight,' the rebels shouted at us," said Olga Chernyak.

"Their music was Islamic music and they had tapes. The tough men slept a few hours, taking turns on mattresses that they brought from somewhere. The guards weren't worn down, but they were wearing us down, to break our will."

Many said that the 18 Chechen women were worse than the men. They talked constantly of becoming martyrs and taking all the hostages with them. Each had 4.5lbs of explosives around their bodies packed with nails and ball-bearings, designed to inflict maximum damage.

The Chechens marched among the hostages, threatening to kill 10 an hour if the authorities did not meet their demands. When they heard noises from outside, late on Friday evening, they dispersed themselves among the hostages, preparing to blow themselves up. In the event they didn't get the chance.

When the attack came, the gas appears to have confused the rebels. By the time they decided to act it was too late.

Another witness said that, crucially, the batteries to trigger the explosives and bring the building down were kept separately. The Chechens had no time to reach them. As the special forces poured into the theatre there was a series of explosions. Alpha special forces troops blew a hole in the side of the theatre to gain access at the back while others climbed out of the sewers in the basement.

Anya Andreyanova, a reporter for the Moskovskaya Pravda, was on a mobile phone and talking live to a radio station as the attack was launched.

"We are begging," she screamed into the phone as a stunned Moscow listened in. "Please guys, don't leave us." There were more shots and explosions. "Can you hear this?" she yelled. "We are about to be blown to the devil."

At the time of the attack, the terrorist leader, Movsar Barayev, was on the phone with Ali Asayev, a Chechen in the Azerbaijani capital of Baku who was trying to secure the release of three American hostages.

"I heard the shooting, and the American representative heard it too," said the negotiator. "Then the phone went dead."

The elite Alpha forces headed the storming of the theatre. In an interview given to a Russian newspaper one of the soldiers said: "The main thing was that we managed to eliminate the kamikaze women."

The Russians shot them, point blank, in the head. "I understand that this is cruel," he said. "But when there are two kilos of plastic explosive hanging on a person, we saw no other way of rendering them safe."

As the fumes cleared, experts rushed into the theatre to defuse the explosives in the building. Bodies and unexploded ordnance were strewn around, the floors stained red with blood.

Barayev lay dead, sprawled in a bloody mess. A Russian soldier placed an unopened bottle of brandy in his hand, apparently a crude attempt to discredit him in the eyes of Muslims.

Other rebels appeared to be sleeping. A female militant dressed in black was slumped forward on her hands. The head of another had fallen back, her mouth slightly open.

Rescue workers arriving in the main hall found it littered with bodies of dead and unconscious hostages. They began sorting through the crowd to find survivors.

"We had to step over bodies to get in," said Vadim Mikhailov, one of the first rescuers on the scene. "We were trying to figure out how hurt they were, who was alive, who was dead. We would run up to each one and take their pulse to see if they were alive."

They began smashing the windows in the foyer to let air in.

Mikhailov said that when he made it into the auditorium there was blood everywhere, but what shocked him most was the smell. "It was a horrible smell, excrement and urine."

He added: "Some could walk, barely. Others had to be carried. But even the ones who had to be carried couldn't talk. They just signaled with their hands."

By 6.30 A.M., as the first light came into the sky, a scene of mayhem was unfolding on the steps of the theatre. Special forces soldiers carried the lifeless bodies of the hostages into the open air and laid them out on the cold stone, one by one.

In the auditorium the toxic gas had failed to disperse as quickly as predicted and many of the hostages were in rapidly worsening conditions. Some were already dead.

The gas was taking its toll on some of the soldiers too. One was on hands and knees on the tarmac in pain while another washed his face in a dirty puddle to clear the vomit from his mouth.

In an attempt to vacate the theatre as soon as possible, the soldiers simply dumped the lifeless forms as they brought them out, right by the front door. Soon there was a sprawling mess of dozens of hostages, lying dead and dying.

Some had their heads thrown back and eyes wide open in a grimace of death. Others lay twitching. Two soldiers passed among the bodies, one slapping faces to try to bring them back to life. The other administered heart massages with one hand.

A few minutes later the ambulances began arriving. Within the next half an hour, more than 100 were loaded with the sick, but it was still not enough and buses had to be commandeered to help with the task.

A few hundred yards away, the ambulances stopped to separate the dead from the living. Doctors quickly checked pulses. The dead were zipped into black body bags, while the living continued their journey.

Witnesses described how one woman was thrown in with the dead. A doctor checked her again on a whim and found a weak pulse. She was transferred back to the ambulance.

Amid the mayhem, Russian authorities were quick to claim that the operation had been a success.

They briefed diplomats that only 10 to 20 hostages had died. Later the figured was upped to 36, then 90. By yesterday night it had topped 120 and was expected to climb higher still.

SIGNIFICANCE

The Moscow theater siege was the latest in a line of terrorist incidents involving Chechen separatists. The violence continued in 2004, when Chechens seized a school in Beslan, North Ossetia, and held up to a thousand hostages, most of them children, for three days before Russian special forces stormed the building.

In 2000, Russian prime minister Vladimir Putin had been elected in part based on a campaign promise to end the violence in Chechnya, which had been mounting a terror campaign for independence since 1991. By 2002, many Russians had come to regard the campaign in Chechnya as a quagmire, similar to the Soviet invasion of Afghanistan (1979–1989).

In the aftermath of the Moscow theater siege, many Russians, as well as other nations, alleged that Putin was using Chechen violence as a pretext for strengthening his personal power, as well as that of the Russian state. The government, for example, tightened media censorship because of its displeasure about coverage of the siege and the raid that ended it. The Russian parliament passed a law restricting press coverage of terrorist incidents and refused to appoint a commission to investigate the incident—and perhaps ask troubling questions about why so many of the hostages died and the government's decision to withhold information from medical personnel treating victims. Foreign governments also objected to initial Russian secrecy about the nature of the gas used in the raid.

In the months that followed, Putin took a hard-line stance in Chechnya. On October 28, 2002, Russian forces reported killing about thirty rebels in a battle outside Grozny. The government also tried to have Chechen envoy Akhmed Zakayev extradited from England, believing that he had a hand in the theater siege, though this effort proved unsuccessful and Zakayev was given political asylum in England. Meanwhile, Chechen rebel leader Shamil Basayev claimed responsibility for planning the siege and apologized to Chechen president Aslan Maskhadov for not informing him of the raid, although Russian authorities assert that they have evidence that Maskhadov knew that it was being planned.

FURTHER RESOURCES

Books

Meier, Andrew. *Chechnya: To the Heart of a Conflict.* New York: Norton, 2004.

Web sites

Donahoe, John J. "The Moscow Hostage Crisis: An Analysis of Chechen Terrorist Goals." *Strategic Insights* 2, no. 5 (May 2003). <http://www.ccc.nps.navy.mil/si/may03/russia.asp> (accessed July 2, 2005).

U.S. State Department. "Terrorist Designation Under Executive Order 13224 Islamic International Brigade, Special Purpose Islamic Regiment, and Riyadus-Salikhin Reconnaissance and Sabotage Battalion of Chechen Martyrs." Press release dated February 28, 2003. <http://www.state.gov/r/pa/prs/ps/2003/18067.htm> (accessed July 2, 2005).

Russia-Chechnya Conflict

"Declaration on the Hostage-Taking in Moscow"

Declaration

By: Society for Russian-Chechen Friendship

Date: October 25, 2002

Source: Available online from the International Society for Human Rights in Frankfurt, Germany, at <http://www.ishr.org/> (accessed June 30, 2005).

About the Author: The Society for Russian-Chechen Friendship was founded on April 17, 2000, by a branch of the International Society for Human Rights in Russia. Its main objectives are to monitor human rights in Chechnya, defend the rights of Chechen refugees, and search for kidnapped civilians and Russian soldiers.

INTRODUCTION

First recognized as a distinct ethnic group in the seventeenth century, the Chechens occupy the Caucasus Mountain region that divides southern Russia from Turkey to the southwest and Iran to the southeast.

Relations between Russia and Chechnya have long been troubled. The Chechens were forcibly annexed into the Russian empire in the early nineteenth century, but they resisted Russian rule. During the Russian Revolution in 1917, Chechnya declared its independence, but the Red Army put down the independence movement in 1920. During World War II, many Chechen units collaborated with German invaders in the Soviet Union.

After the collapse of the Soviet Union in 1991, Chechnya, under the leadership of former Soviet bomber pilot Dzhokar Dudayev, declared independence from the Russian Federation. The Russians, however, were not willing to let go of Chechnya. The area is of strategic importance to Russia because of its position on a narrow strip of land between the Black Sea to the west and the Caspian Sea to the east. Further, oil and gas pipelines between Russia and former Soviet republics Kazakhstan and Azerbaijan run through Chechnya.

Tensions between Chechnya and Russia grew until the First Chechnya War erupted in 1994. For two years, Russia backed armed opposition groups within Chechnya

A man carries the body of his child killed by a blast in the Chechen town of Znamenskoye in May, 2003. AP/WIDE WORLD PHOTOS

that attempted repeatedly to overthrow Dudayev's government. When these efforts failed, Russia responded with massive military force, including an air bombing campaign over the capital city of Grozny that produced thousands of casualties and refugees and destroyed much of the city.

Although the Russians installed a pro-Russian government, guerrilla warfare in Chechnya's rural regions continued into 1996 at a cost of some 25,000 civilian lives. While Russian troops were accused of the use of indiscriminant force, both sides in the conflict were guilty of torture, kidnapping, mistreatment of prisoners of war, and execution of prisoners. Chechen rebels carried out spectacular acts of terrorism in other parts of Russia, including seizure of a hospital in Budyenovsk in 1995. Russian public opinion turned against the war, and the Russians withdrew.

In the years that followed, Chechnya remained chaotic. Reports surfaced of numerous kidnappings, and Russia and Chechnya traded repeated charges that the other side was using chemical weapons. Then in March 1999, Russia's leading envoy to Chechnya, Gennady Shpigun, was kidnapped, and when Islamic militants invaded neighboring Dagestan, Russia again launched an air campaign over the Grozny to begin what has been called the Second Chechnya War.

In the new century, the Russia-Chechnya conflict remained an ongoing cycle of action and reaction, reprisal and counter reprisal. In 2002, Chechen terrorists seized a Moscow theater and, in 2004, they seized a school in Beslan, North Ossetia. These and other terrorist acts cost numerous civilian lives. In response, the Russian government launched new offensives against the rebels.

Attempting to break the cycle of violence is the Society for Russian-Chechen Friendship, which issued a statement in response to the Moscow theater crisis in 2002.

■ PRIMARY SOURCE

The interregional organisation "Society for Russian-Chechen Friendship." categorically condemns the action of the terrorists who took hostages in the Moscow theatre "Dubrovka" on 24 October 2002. The large-scale crimes of Russian soldiers against the peaceful population in the Republic of Chechnya must not serve as a justification for those who threaten the lives of innocent people and thus degenerate themselves to the level of their executioners.

Terror—regardless of its form—is a crime against humanity, for which there is no justification. This goes for both Russian state terrorism and the terrorism of individuals who fight against this state terrorism. Because the basis of terror is the principle of collective responsibility, it cannot be acceptable to a civilised individual and a civilised society. General Shamonov and Movsar Barayev abuse peaceful people as a human shield and are thus, both equally offensive.

The events in Moscow are another piece of evidence for the fact that the problems between Russia and Chechnya cannot be solved using violent methods. The so-called "anti-terror campaign" is not only inhuman, but also counter-productive. Violence begets violence, brutality begets retaliation. Negotiations are the only way to deliver both peoples from pain and grief. One may concede that the hostage-takers are driven by pain over the fate of their humiliated people, by desperation and grief over the murdered and tormented. But an act of terror is not a solution; it is a dead end. At a time when there were signs of possible negotiations between the Russian government and President Maskhadov, hostage-taking is a sheer provocation, and only serves to bury the chance of a peaceful resolution to the conflict for a long time.

A crime of this kind leads to an escalation of the tense situation in and national hatred by the Russian society, which is a consequence of the biased reporting on events in Chechnya. The ignorance of the Russian society about the real extent of the Chechen tragedy is one of the reasons why this conflict continues. A society which is force-fed the myth of a genetic inclination of the Chechen people towards banditry is easily convinced that it is necessary to lead a war "to the victorious end," that ethnic cleansings and forced deportations are necessary. The terrorists demand an end of the war; however, with their act, they play into the hands of those who are interested in a continuation of the war and their enrichment on the costs of the lives of others.

On the other hand, what happens now is a result of the indifference of the majority of the Russian society, above all the Russian intelligentsia, towards this monstrous war in the Caucasus. People who thought that this far-away war had nothing to do with them were caught by it on their own streets.

We plead to finally forget about our own political and ethnic prejudices, our own claims and ambitions. The lives of people are in our hands—in the hands of the Russian society. We appeal to all politicians and personalities of public life, who have not yet lost a feeling for compassion, responsibility and common sense, to do all they can to prevent the storming of the theatre and not to let human lives once more become the small change of political bargaining. A second Budyenovsk must not be allowed to happen.

We express our sympathy for those who wait for the return of their relatives and close friends. We pray to the Lord for their rescue.

We appeal to those who have taken responsibility for the lives of people who have nothing to do with what is happening in Chechnya today. Not only the bravery of the battlefield is required from you. Another kind of bravery is needed: The bravery to remain human under inhuman circumstances in a war against an inhuman opponent. Even, if you were not able to find another solution, do not forget that you are, just as your victims, human beings.

On behalf of the Society for Russian-Chechen Friendship and its regional sections.

Stanislav Dmitrievsky

Co-chairman of the Society of Russian-Chechen Friendship

Imran Eshiyev

Chairman of the regional section of the Society of Russian-Chechen Friendship in Chechnya and Ingushetia

SIGNIFICANCE

In 2003, voters in Chechnya elected a new president, Akhmad Kadyrov, and approved a new constitution. Some international observers, however, argued that the voting was not free and fair. The Russian government supported Kadyrov, but he was assassinated in 2004 and replaced by Alu Alkhanov. As of mid-2005, the conflict continues with no resolution in sight.

The story of Chechnya since 1991 can be told from two perspectives. From one point of view, the ongoing conflict is the story of a people fighting for self-determination, using the only weapons at their disposal to resist the heavy hand of Russia, which has used its military might to impose its will on a people who do not see themselves as Russians. In this scenario, Russia has been guilty of massive human rights violations and, under President Vladimir Putin, has seized on the crisis in Chechnya to bolster Russian power and influence in the Caucasus region, as well as to preserve its oil industry.

The opposing point of view characterizes Chechnya as a lawless region of organized crime, gun smuggling, drug smuggling, and, more recently, efforts by radical militants to impose Islamic fundamentalism not only in Chechnya, but in surrounding areas such as Dagestan. In 1999, Islamic law was established in Chechnya, and

Soldiers patrol the crumbling remains of a school in Beslan, Russia, after a hostage seizure by Chechen separatists ended with at least 335 people killed. © ANTOINE GYORI/AGP/CORBIS

reports began to surface that Al-Qaeda, the Islamic terrorist network controlled by Osama Bin Laden, operated training facilities in Chechnya and had been sending operatives to the region. The chief of operations under Basayev, for example, was an operative trained in Bin Laden's training camps, and numerous other links have been uncovered between Al-Qaeda and militant terrorists in Chechnya.

Meanwhile, most Chechens support some kind of rapprochement with Russia, but efforts in the fragmented nation to establish a stable government continue to be undermined by extremists.

FURTHER RESOURCES
Books
Meier, Andrew. *Chechnya: To the Heart of a Conflict*. New York: Norton, 2004.

Web sites
GlobalSecurity. "First Chechnya War: 1994–1996." <http://www.globalsecurity.org/military/world/war/> (accessed June 30, 2005).

Riebling, Mark, and E. P Eddy. *Jihad&Work*. National Review Online, October 24, 2002. Available at <http://www.nationalreview.com/comment/comment-riebling102402.asp> (accessed June 30, 2005).

"Crash Probe Turns to Bombs, 2 Women"

Female Terrorists: Black Widows

Newspaper article

By: Anatoly Medetsky

Date: August 30, 2004

Source: "Crash Probe Turns to Bombs, 2 Women," as published in the *Moscow Times*.

About the Author: Anatoly Medetsky is a staff writer for the *Moscow Times*, where his work appears regularly.

Bodies of blast victims are seen after a female suicide bomber set off an explosion in Moscow, December 9, 2003. AP/WIDE WORLD PHOTOS

INTRODUCTION

While the September, 2001 al-Qaeda attacks on targets in the United States were among the most graphic and shocking to date, numerous other terrorist assaults have been planned and executed, with varying degrees of success. While the vast majority of the perpetrators are young men, a growing number of terrorist foot soldiers are women. In one particular conflict, a corps of terrorist women have played an integral role in an ongoing political struggle.

The residents of the region known today as Chechnya trace their roots to the seventeenth century; the area was conquered by Russia during the nineteenth century and remained part of the Soviet Union, despite several attempts to break free, until its breakup in 1991 when the state's parliament declared independence. While Moscow never recognized the area's independence, this disagreement remained a source of intense conflict. Separatist tensions swelled until Russian troops were dispatched in 1994 to reign in the separatists. Following two years of bloody conflict and little progress, Russia withdrew in defeat, making the region essentially, though not formally, independent.

The coming of official Islamic law to the region, along with Russian President Vladimir Putin's newly announced get-tough policy, led to a new surge in violence beginning in 1999. Russian forces extensively bombed the region, forcing up to half the population to flee and leading to protests from the G-8 (an organization composed of eight industrialized nations) and the European Union. Chechen guerillas responded by repeatedly attacking Russian military units in and near Chechnya, while terrorists began striking civilian targets in Moscow and other Russian cities.

More than one dozen documented terrorist attacks have been carried out in Russia by Chechen rebels since 2002. Among the more deadly of these attacks was the 2002 seizure of a Moscow theater, in which eight hundred Russians were taken hostage. Three days into the siege, Russian forces pumped the building full of anesthetic gas, killing most of the rebels along with 112 hostages. Also, in late 2003, a suicide bomber detonated an explosive device on a crowded commuter train near Moscow, killing forty-one and injuring more than one hundred and fifty people.

While the tactics used by Chechen rebels fit the general pattern used by terrorists in other conflicts, the growing use of women as suicide attackers is somewhat unique. These so-called "black widows" first came to prominence during the 2002 theater siege, in which one-fourth of the terrorists were female. During a one month period in mid-2004, female Chechen terrorists participated in multiple attacks, including a bombing at a rock concert, another in a Moscow subway station, and the seizure of an elementary school, in which more than three hundred hostages, many of them children, eventually died. It was during this surge of terrorism that two Russian airliners crashed almost simultaneously. Given the high level of terrorist activity at the time and the coincidental timing of the two crashes, the investigation immediately turned to the possibility of terrorism.

PRIMARY SOURCE

Traces of the powerful explosive hexogen have been found in the debris of the two passenger jets that fell from the sky minutes apart last week, all but confirming fears that they were the targets of an organized terrorist attack, the Federal Security Service said. Investigators also said that two Chechen women bought tickets at the last minute for the flights at Moscow's Domodedovo Airport on Tuesday and that their bodies were the only ones unclaimed by relatives so far—raising suspicion that they may have been suicide bombers.

In its first official acknowledgment of terrorism, the Federal Security Service, or FSB, announced Friday that it had found traces of the explosive in the wreckage of the Sibir Tu-154 that crashed in the Rostov region. "A preliminary analysis showed that it was hexogen," FSB spokesman Sergei Ignatchenko said, Interfax reported. Ignatchenko also said the FSB has identified "a circle of people that may have been involved in the terrorist act on board the Tu-154 plane." His statement came hours after a group called the Islambouli Brigades claimed responsibility for both crashes.

On Saturday, the FSB announced that it had found traces of hexogen on the debris of the Volga-Aviaexpress Tu-134, which crashed in the Tula region. The Tu-154 was bound for Sochi, while the Tu-134 was headed for Volgograd. They crashed three minutes apart Tuesday night.

The death toll from both crashes rose to 90 on Friday after rescuers found the scattered remains of a 44th person on the Tu-134. The remains are believed to be of Amanta Nagayeva, one of the two Chechen women who took the flights, Kommersant reported. Izvestia gave her first name as Aminat. Chechen police on Friday opened an investigation into Nagayeva and the other Chechen woman, identified only as S. Dzhebirkhanova, whose remains were also scattered. Many of the other bodies at the crash sites were found relatively intact—suggesting the two women were in close proximity to the bombs, Kommersant and Izvestia reported. Both women bought their tickets shortly before the planes took off, investigators said.

Nagayeva's brother disappeared three years ago when unidentified armed men took him away from the family's home in the Chechen village of Kirov-Yurt, said the village's head, Dogman Akhmadova, Izvestia reported. Federal troops are often blamed for such disappearances in Chechnya, and rebels have in the past recruited the female relatives of killed and missing people to act as suicide bombers. Nagayeva was 27 and worked as a market vendor in Grozny, Chechen police told Kommersant. Dzhebirkhanova is only known to be from Chechnya's Shali district, Izvestia reported.

Details about the explosions—which tore off both planes' tails—emerged over the weekend. Only one body from the Tu-134 was burned, indicating that the explosion may have been triggered in a small space, such as the toilet at the rear of the plane, Kommersant said. Dzhebirkhanova was assigned to seat 19F, the fifth row from the back, Sibir said in a statement. She didn't have carry-on or check-in luggage, Sibir deputy director Mikhail Koshman said.

The group that claimed responsibility for the crashes, Islambouli Brigades, said five "holy warriors" were on board each plane but did not describe how they downed the planes. It published a statement Friday on an Arabic-language web site known to be a mouthpiece for Islamic militants, and the authenticity of the claim could not be independently confirmed. The group said the attacks aimed to help the rebels in Chechnya and threatened more attacks. "Our mujahedin, with God's grace, succeeded in directing the first blow,

which will be followed by a series of other operations in a wave to extend support and victory to our Muslim brothers in Chechnya and other Muslim areas that suffer from Russian faithlessness," the statement said, according to The Associated Press. The claim did not mention al-Qaeda, but a group with a similar name—the Islambouli Brigades of al-Qaida—claimed responsibility for an attempt to assassinate Pakistan's prime minister-designate in July. Moscow says al-Qaeda supports rebels in Chechnya.

The Islambouli Brigades did not say whether rebels carried out the plane attacks, but a rebel spokesman has denied any involvement. The group said the crashes did not go exactly as planned. The attackers "were crowned with success though they faced problems at the beginning," it said, without elaborating. The attackers may have initially wanted to board different planes. Dzhebirkhanova first bought a ticket for a larger Sibir plane, an Il-86 that seated about 350 passengers and was scheduled to take off for Sochi at 9:20 A.M. on Wednesday, Koshman said. She then changed the ticket for the Tuesday night flight to Sochi, he said. Vladimir Lutsenko, former head of the KGB's counterterrorism department, said that if the Chechen women were the attackers, they may have changed their plans after becoming scared or facing problems getting the explosives and detonators past airport security.

The attackers may have had an accomplice at the airport who bypassed security and handed them explosives and detonators, Izvestia reported, citing an unidentified bomb expert with the police. Another problem could have been a failure to send suicide bombers to more planes, said Peter Sederberg, a professor at the University of South Carolina who specializes in international terrorism. "Maybe they wanted more planes, three or four, and they got two," he said by telephone.

The masterminds behind the crashes also may have wanted to send the planes into prominent targets, rather than explode them in midair, but the plan failed for some reason, Sederberg said. "That is an important speculation—that it was supposed to be something imitating Sept. 11," he said. If the bomb on the Sibir Tu-154 had been connected to a timer and the flight had left Moscow on time, the plane would have blown up at about the time it was over Sochi, where President Vladimir Putin was vacationing at the time.

The FSB refused to comment on the claim by the Islambouli Brigades. "We don't comment on such statements, especially when their authenticity hasn't been established," a spokesman said, Interfax reported. Sederberg said the claim may be an attempt to misdirect the authorities, but added that it is not uncommon for previously unknown groups to claim responsibility for terrorist acts. The group is "more likely an offshoot of a more known phenomenon," he said. The Sibir Tu-154 sent two signals to air traffic controllers just minutes before exploding—an SOS call and a hijack alert, Interfax reported, citing an unidentified aviation official. Earlier reports differed on whether the plane had sent an SOS or hijack signal.

Putin has ordered the FSB to study how other countries combat hijackings, "including proposals to use the Israeli system of checking and monitoring air security, which today is recognized as the most effective in the world," FSB spokesman Ignatchenko said Saturday. Transportation Minister Igor Levitin, who is overseeing the investigation into the crashes, visited Domodedovo Airport on Sunday and said the country must develop unified standards for airport security. Finance Minister Alexei Kudrin said the government will set aside 2 billion rubles ($68.5 million) for a new counter-terrorism program next year. The program will include efforts to increase security measures in public places, including the Moscow metro, he said Thursday.

NATO, meanwhile, condemned the downing of the planes as an apparent terrorist attack Friday, saying NATO and Russia will be "relentless" in responding to the "scourge" of terrorism. Counterterrorism is one of the main areas where NATO is trying to work more closely with Russia under a 2002 cooperation agreement.

SIGNIFICANCE

While the U.S. received virtually universal sympathy and support in the wake of the 2001 attacks, Russian President Boris Yeltsin and his successor Vladimir Putin received lukewarm support from the international community in their handling of Chechnya, due in part to the perception that Russia has dealt brutally with the region. More recently, the U.S. and other nations have urged Putin to meet with Chechen leaders, a call which Putin has rejected, likening it to President Bush inviting Osama Bin Laden to the White House. The year 2005 marked a decade of conflict between Russia and Chechnya and attacks continued. Outside analysts see the nagging Chechnya situation as the largest of Putin's many ongoing problems.

For governments intent on preventing terrorist attacks, the use of women as suicide bombers complicates an already difficult task. In Russia, airline passenger screeners took on the task of increased searches among female passengers, including Muslim women who follow strict codes of dress. Just as the use of hijacked passenger jets as weapons expanded the arsenal of terrorist tools, the use of women as suicide bombers adds another option to the already versatile collection of tools at the disposal of terrorists.

While the black widows of Russia have frequently been portrayed as women seeking revenge for sons or husbands killed in Russian attacks, some analysts question their true motives, suggesting that outside organizations such as al-Qaeda are manipulating these women for their own benefit. Suicide bombings by Palestinian women are also on the rise despite the fact that many Muslim extremists see the task of jihad (holy war) as work appropriate only for male warriors.

FURTHER RESOURCES
Books

Orr, Michael. *Russia's Wars with Chechnya 1994–2003*. UK: Osprey Publishing, 2005.

Politkovskaya, Anna. *The Dirty War*. New York: Harvill Press, 2004.

Web sites

CNN.com. "Russia's 'black widows' wreak terror." <http://edition.cnn.com/2004/WORLD/europe/09/01/russia.widows/> (accessed June 14, 2005).

CNN.com. "Timeline: Russia Terror Attacks." <http://edition.cnn.com/2004/WORLD/europe/09/01/russia.timeline/> (accessed June 14, 2005).

Encyclopedia.com. "Chechnya." <http://www.encyclopedia.com/html/section/Chechnya_History.asp> (accessed June 14, 2005).

Global Issues. "Crisis in Chechnya." <http://www.globalissues.org/Geopolitics/Chechnya.asp> (accessed June 14, 2005).

Beslan School Massacre

"Carnage in Russian School Seige"

Photographs

By: Sergey Ponomarev and NTV-Russian Television Channel

Date: September, 2004

Source: Images taken by Sergey Ponomarev and NTV-Russian Television Channel.

About the Photographers: The photograph was taken by Sergey Ponomarev, a Russian photographer who has worked for The Associated Press, an international wire service. The video stills were broadcast by the NTV-Russian Television Channel, a satellite television channel.

INTRODUCTION

September 1, 2004, was the first day of the new term at Middle School Number One in the southern Russian town of Beslan, North Ossetia. That morning

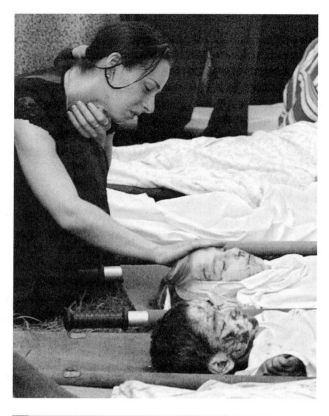

Beslan School Massacre A woman grieves over the bodies of children killed in a school seizure in Beslan, North Ossetia, on September 3, 2004. AP/WIDE WORLD PHOTOS

the school building was filled with hundreds of students, whose ages generally ranged from seven to eighteen. Also in the school were teachers and staff, as well as numerous parents, many with younger siblings of the schoolchildren.

At 9:30 A.M., a group of about thirty-two armed terrorists, including two women, stormed the school, beginning a sixty-two-hour hostage crisis. Most were wearing black ski masks and camouflage uniforms, and many wore belts with explosives attached.

The events surrounding the siege were chaotic, and reports vary about the exact number of terrorists, their identities and nationalities, the number of hostages, and what actually happened. Generally, it is known that the terrorists' first step was to shoot twenty adult men and dump their bodies out of the building. They then herded their hostages—numbering up to 1,000—into the school's gymnasium, where the heat grew stifling and food, water, and bathroom access were denied. The terrorists also mined the gym with explosives, hanging some of them above

the children's heads in bottles packed with pieces of metal, and set trip wires around the building to deter rescue operations. Meanwhile, Russian police and army troops surrounded the building and cordoned it off.

The Russian government tried to negotiate with the terrorists, primarily through the agency of the former president of neighboring Ingushetia, Ruslan Aushev, whom the terrorists requested by name. By the second day of the siege, negotiations were proving unsuccessful, although the terrorists did release twenty-six women and infants.

At about 1:00 in the afternoon of day three, the terrorists agreed to allow a medical team to remove the bodies of the dead, but as the team approached the building, the terrorists opened fire, killing two of the medical workers. When part of the gymnasium collapsed, about 30 hostages made a run for it, but several were shot and killed as they fled. Further gunfire was followed by explosions in the school. Russian special forces then stormed the school, supported by regular army troops, helicopter gunships, and a tank. Adding to the chaos was the presence of local civilians who had brought their own rifles and started shooting.

The assault lasted about two hours. During that time, the terrorists exploded more bombs, destroying the gym and setting much of the rest of the school building on fire. During the gun battle, eleven soldiers were killed and at least thirty others were wounded; many were shot in the back as they tried to rescue children. By about 3:00, Russian forces were in control of much of the school, but the chaos continued. Terrorists and hostages were discovered in the school's basement. A number of the terrorists managed to slip through the cordon and blend into the civilian crowd that had gathered or they pretended to be medical workers. Others escaped to a nearby house, which Russian forces destroyed with flamethrowers at about 11:00 that evening. One suspect was beaten to death by the father of one of the hostages. By the time the fighting had ended, 344 civilians were dead, at least 172 of them children. Hundreds more were injured. The Russian government stated that all but one of the terrorists were killed.

These photos capture some of the horror of the siege. Russian citizens watched televised video made by the terrorists during the crisis, showing them rigging explosives inside the gymnasium. The first video still image, while blurry, shows the children packed into the gym; an explosive can be seen hanging from the basketball rim. The second image shows a terrorist releasing a baby to a physician sent by Aushev, the

PRIMARY SOURCE

Beslan School Massacre Video still of hostages sitting below explosives strung from basketball hoops in the gymnasium of a school in Beslan. AP/WIDE WORLD PHOTOS

negotiator. The third image shows a photograph of the gym burning after an explosion 52 hours into the siege.

PRIMARY SOURCE

BESLAN SCHOOL MASSACRE

See primary source images

SIGNIFICANCE

Initially, there was confusion about the identity of the terrorists. It was assumed that they were Chechen separatists, especially because the attack bore many similarities to the Chechen hostage siege at a Moscow theater in 2002. An adviser to Russia's president Vladimir Putin, however, negotiated with the terrorists and claimed that they did not speak Chechen, and the government claimed that they were a mix of Arabs, Tatars, Kazakhs, and Chechens. Hostages, however, insisted that none of the terrorists seemed to be Arab or Middle Eastern and that while they spoke Russian, it was with a Chechen accent. Meanwhile, the leader of the Chechen separatist movement, Aslambek Aslakhanov, denied Chechen involvement. The government also suggested that the terrorists were linked to al-Qaeda, but this was never established.

On September 17, however, a Chechen separatist named Shamil Basayev released a statement claiming responsibility not only for the Beslan massacre but also for a number of other terrorist incidents, including the Moscow theater siege, a 1995 hospital hostage crisis, and two events during the preceding week: the bombing of a Moscow subway station in which ten people were killed and the downing of two Russian airliners, killing eighty-nine people. As of 2005, Basayev remained among the most wanted men in Russia.

The Putin government was sharply criticized for the Beslan siege. Critics pointed to the number of fatalities both at Beslan and at the Moscow movie theater and suggested that the military was out of control. The military was also sharply criticized for failing to

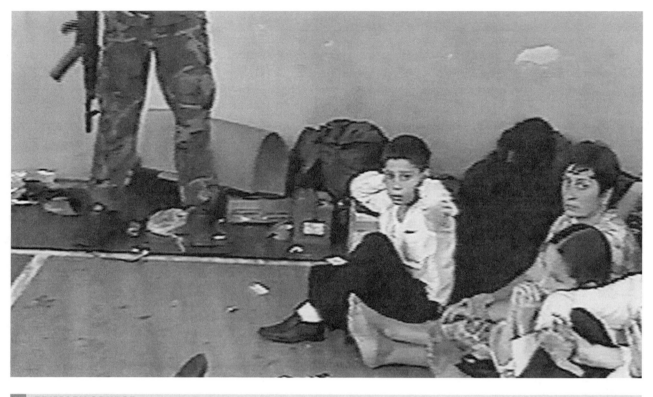

PRIMARY SOURCE

Beslan School Massacre Video still of hostages sitting on the floor in a Beslan school as a hostage-taker stands on a book with a device connected to explosives. AP/WIDE WORLD PHOTOS

control the scene of the crisis, and especially for failing to keep civilians away. One poll indicated that up to 83 percent of Russians considered that the government did not tell the full truth about the incident.

Meanwhile, Russia instituted severe security measures. Moscow police detained thousands of people lacking proper identification papers. Resident registration laws were tightened. The death penalty for terrorism was reintroduced. Both the United States and the European Union criticized Putin for abridgments of civil liberties. Putin's critics in Russia assert that Putin seized on the incident to consolidate power, especially over the nation's media.

FURTHER RESOURCES

Books

Meier, Andrew. *Chechnya: To the Heart of a Conflict*. New York: Norton, 2004.

Web sites

BBC News. "School Siege: Eyewitness Accounts." September 7, 2004. <http://news.bbc.co.uk/2/hi/europe/3627406.stm> (accessed May 23, 2005).

Observer. "When Hell Came Calling at Beslan's School No 1." September 5, 2004. <http://observer.guardian.co.uk/focus/story/0,6903,1297633,00.html> (accessed May 23, 2005).

Audio and Visual Media

BBC News. "Russian TV Shows School Siege Terror." September 8, 2004. Available from <http://news.bbc.co.uk/2/hi/europe/3636196.stm> (with video link).

"Orde says IRA offer 'was to Kill'"

IRA offers to kill own members

News article

By: BBC News Online

Date: March 9, 2005

Source: BBC News Online, <http://news.bbc.co.uk/1/hi/northern_ireland/4331819.stm> (accessed July 10, 2005).

About the Author: BBC News Online went "live" in November 1997. This article was written by a staff writer.

INTRODUCTION

When Northern Ireland's main political parties signed the Good Friday Agreement, the political settlement which brought an end to the province's 30-year-long troubles in April 1998, it closed one chapter of violence in Ulster's history, but seemingly opened up another. Even at the time, the treaty's critics, seeing through the frenzy of excitement that greeted peace, pointed out that while the Good Friday Agreement proscribed paramilitary activity, it made no mention of organized crime.

When the Good Friday Agreement came into place it had a twofold effect: it reduced the donations terrorist groups received (causing cash flow problems), and it also removed hundreds of men from frontline paramilitary activity. Activities more synonymous with organized crime such as money laundering, drug dealing, protection rackets, and counterfeiting had long been amongst the principal money-raising methods of groups like the Irish Republican Army (IRA) and the loyalist (pro-British) Ulster Defense Force (UDF). Short of money but rich in manpower, these illegal activities increased sharply in the months and years following the Good Friday Agreement.

Accompanying their transformation into criminal gangs came a shift in the rules of engagement. The previous politicization of paramilitary organizations tempered some of the excess in their own communities, but assassinations, punishment beatings, and kneecappings (where the knees or even elbows are shot or drilled) all rose exponentially. Extremist violence became more indiscriminate.

On January 30, 2005, Robert McCartney, a 33-year-old Catholic father of two, became involved in an altercation with Provisional IRA members in a Belfast city center bar. He was dragged outside, beaten, and stabbed. McCartney died of his injuries in hospital the following morning.

PRIMARY SOURCE

The IRA was prepared to kill those it claims were behind the murder of Belfast man Robert McCartney, the chief constable has said.

The IRA has offered to shoot the people who killed the 33-year-old after a row in a city centre bar on 30 January. His family have rejected the offer.

Hugh Orde said he had "no doubt" the IRA meant they would kill the men.

Mr. Orde said the police know who the suspects are, but could not make an arrest without evidence.

"We need people to give us the evidence that enables us to go and do our job properly," he told the BBC on Wednesday.

"This is an organisation theoretically on ceasefire. This is an organisation that is still prepared to kill people now from its own community."

Sinn Fein's Martin McGuinness said he was surprised by the IRA statement.

He said he thought it would have been "very unfortunate" if the organisation had shot the alleged killers.

"I think the difficulty about this particular sentence in the statement is it takes away from what I think is an awful lot of positive stuff," Mr. McGuinness said.

The U.S. Special Envoy to Northern Ireland, Mitchell Reiss, said it was "time for the IRA to go out of business."

Mr Reiss added: "It's time for Sinn Fein to be able to say explicitly, without ambiguity, without ambivalence, that criminality will not be tolerated."

In a statement on Tuesday, the IRA offered to shoot those directly involved in the murder and said it had given the family their names.

But Mr McCartney's cousin, Gerard Quinn, said: "I think the feeling is that to shoot and possibly kill these people is revenge and not justice. And revenge is not what the family is looking for."

A five-page statement from the IRA said the McCartney family had met the organisation twice and made it clear they did not want physical action taken against those involved.

The IRA said it had given the family the name of the man who allegedly stabbed Mr. McCartney and a second man who allegedly supplied, removed, and destroyed the murder weapon.

Both these men have been expelled by the IRA.

The republican organisation said it had also spoken directly to key eyewitnesses and told them they had nothing to fear from the IRA.

Former IRA hunger striker Tommy McKearney said the statement was extraordinary and showed an indecisiveness and lack of self-confidence within the IRA leadership.

Mr McKearney said he thought it was "inevitable" that Sinn Fein would have to break off from the IRA as the contradictions between them could not be reconciled.

"I think that's what we're seeing at the moment," he said.

Secretary of State Paul Murphy said he was appalled by the offer.

"There is no place for those who signed up to the Good Friday Agreement for the sort of arbitrary justice and murder that is being suggested here," he said.

DUP leader Ian Paisley called for the leaders of Sinn Fein to be arrested following the IRA statement.

"The offer to shoot those responsible for the murder of Robert McCartney confirms again that terrorism is the only stock and trade of Sinn Fein/IRA," he said.

Senior Ulster Unionist Sir Reg Empey said the statement proved the IRA had "clearly learnt nothing over recent weeks" and SDLP MP Eddie McGrady condemned the IRA proposal as "obscene."

The IRA expelled three members over the murder and Sinn Fein subsequently suspended seven of its members.

SIGNIFICANCE

McCartney's murder gained instant notoriety, not just for the savagery of the attack, but because it emerged that Provisional IRA members had threatened drinkers at the bar lest they report or discuss what they had seen and had undertaken a "forensic cleaning" of the bar to remove any traces of evidence. Moreover, no ambulance was ever called for the dying man.

The Police Service of Northern Ireland (PSNI) met a wall of silence when investigating the murder. Those that they could pin down as being present all claimed to be in the toilet at the time. When police attempted a forensic examination of the pub, they were attacked by a stone-throwing mob. Sinn Fein, the political wing of the IRA, waded into the argument, accusing the PSNI of heavy-handedness and using the investigation to disrupt Belfast's Catholic community.

Outraged not just at the murder of their brother, but at the apparent complicity of all levels of the Republican movement, McCartney's five sisters publicly accused the Provisional IRA of their brother's murder and the subsequent cover up.

The revelations about McCartney's death followed the suspension of the Northern Ireland Assembly because of the IRA's refusal to decommission its arms. A raid on the Northern Bank in December 2004, which had yielded 26.5 million pounds (approximately 50 million dollars) had been blamed on the IRA.

Representatives of Sinn Fein met with the McCartneys on several occasions during February and March 2005. As a result of those meetings, the IRA formulated their own unique solution that would bring Robert McCartney's murderers to justice: they offered to "shoot" his killers. Whether this was to be a punishment shooting (i.e., non-fatal) or an execution was not made clear. The McCartney sisters rejected the offer.

Revelations about the IRA's offer merely deepened the problems facing Sinn Fein leader Gerry Adams and increased the coverage of the McCartney sisters' bid for justice. They were invited by President Bush to Washington and to the White House's St. Patrick's Day celebrations; Adams was not. (Even at the height of the IRA's mainland bombing campaign in the 1980s, the Sinn Fein leader always visited senior U.S. politicians on St. Patrick's Day.)

Despite international press coverage, the McCartney sisters were apparently not beyond the threats of the IRA. The sisters claim that IRA militants threatened to burn their Belfast home unless they halted their crusade.

In April 2005, Sinn Fein suspended several of its members linked to the killing. However, the republicans alleged intimidation of potential witnesses and continual obstruction of the PSNI's investigation slowed the search for the killer. Finally, in June 2005, an arrest was made for the murder of Robert McCartney.

In July of 2005, Gerry Adams announced that the IRA was ending its armed campaign against British rule and would disarm. The announcement was met with praise from Tony Blair and from leaders in Ireland and the United States.

FURTHER RESOURCES

Books

McDowell, Jim. *Godfathers: Inside Northern Ireland's Drugs Racket*. Dublin, Gill & Macmillan, 2003.

McKittrick, David, and McVeigh, David. *Making Sense of the Troubles*. London: Penguin, 2003.

Web sites

Sinn Fein. <http://sinnfein.ie/> (accessed July 8, 2005).

Police Service of Northern Ireland. "Appeals for information: Murder of Robert McCartney." <http://www.psni.police.uk/index/appeals/appeals_for_information/mccartney-murder.htm> (accessed July 8, 2005).

Statement to Parliament on the London Bombings

Suicide Bombers Strike London City Transport

Speech

By: Tony Blair

Date: July 11, 2005

An anti-terrorism poster at London's Embankment tube station is part of a heightened awareness campaign, following the train bombings in Spain in 2004. AP/WIDE WORLD PHOTOS

Source: Speech delivered before British Parliament, available online at <http://www.number-10.gov.uk/output/Page7903.asp>.

About the Author: Leader of the Labour Party since 1994 following the death of John Smith, Tony Blair has been Britain's Prime Minister since 1997. Blair delivered this speech to Parliament in London four days after a series of suicide bombers struck London's Underground (subway) and bus transportation system.

INTRODUCTION

For much of the latter half of the twentieth century, of all the principle western powers, Britain perhaps held the most successful relationship with Arab countries and the Muslim world in general. For the most part, Britain had escaped the sort of postcolonial scars that characterized France and Russia's relationships with its former colonies. Britain also did not garner or excite the same contempt as U.S. intervention in the Middle East attracted. Britain's large native Muslim population was well integrated, and Britain had few of the race relations problems encountered by Germany with its large Turkish population, or France and its large Algerian community. Britain had long been the historical home of opposition clerics in exile, who indicated to intelligence sources that Britain was likely to escape Islamist extremist attacks.

Nevertheless, after September 11, 2001, British support for the United States and its War on Terror led many to suspect that Britain had become an increasingly likely target for Islamist terrorist attacks.

Reading between the lines of Al Qaeda's 1998 manifesto, it was perhaps surprising that Britain hadn't already suffered at the hands of its operatives. Osama Bin Laden's key demands—the removal of foreign troops from Saudi Arabia; the ending of sanctions against Iraq; and support of Israel—all implicated Britain to varying degrees.

During the twentieth century, with the exception of the anti-colonial movement in British Palestine and the Suez Crisis of 1956, Britain had largely avoided controversy in the Middle East. Britain had built close ties to a number of Arab regimes, was measured in its support of Israel, and tried to avoid controversial military intervention, such as the U.S. peacekeeping presence in Lebanon. For decades, simmering anti-Western sentiment in the region did not seem to afflict Britain in the same way as it did the United States.

In the months and years following the 9/11 attacks, however, British foreign policy in the Middle East began to more closely follow that of the United States. This shift in Mid-East policy was often controversial, both domestically and across the Middle East. Then, in

November 2003, a bomb attack on the British consulate in Istanbul, killing 27 people, made explicitly clear the possible threat facing British interests. Domestically, British security officials remained vigilant about potential attacks.

Sometimes they were accused of scare mongering. A high profile military presence at Heathrow airport in February 2003, for instance, which included tanks and armed soldiers was deemed an overreaction. Likewise, a highly publicized evacuation exercise, simulating a chemical weapons attack, at Bank tube station in the City of London was similarly derided.

The British government and police chiefs were nevertheless unrepentant and said that it was "inevitable" that Britain would be the subject of an Islamist terrorist attack. They also hinted that they had prevented earlier attacks.

On the morning of July 7, 2005, reports that London's Underground train system had broken down because of a power surge quickly led to a more complex emergency. Unconfirmed reports that three buses had exploded soon led to the realization that a terror attack had taken place. TV news broadcast images of a London double-decker bus with the roof ripped off.

By mid-afternoon, police had confirmed that four suicide bomb attacks had taken place: three on the London Underground; and one on a bus at Tavistock Square. Because of the nature of the attack, officials were unable to confirm a figure of dead for some days, but this was put at fifty-two (including the suicide bombers who had carried out the attacks) and eventually rose by another four, after victims died of their injuries in hospital.

■ PRIMARY SOURCE

With your permission, Mr. Speaker, I would like to make a statement on last Thursday's terrorist attacks in London. The number of confirmed dead currently stands at 52; the number still in hospital 56, some severely injured.

The whole House, I know, will want to state our feelings strongly. We express our revulsion at this murderous carnage of the innocent. We send our deep and abiding sympathy and prayers to the victims and their families. We are united in our determination that our country will not be defeated by such terror but will defeat it and emerge from this horror with our values, our way of life, our tolerance and respect for others, undiminished.

I would also like us to record our heartfelt thanks and admiration for our emergency services. Police, those working on our underground, buses and trains, paramedics, doctors and nurses, ambulance staff, firefighters and the disaster recover teams, all of them can be truly proud of the part they played in coming to the aid of London last Thursday and the part they continue to play. They are magnificent.

As for Londoners themselves, their stoicism, resilience, and sheer undaunted spirit were an inspiration and an example. At the moment of terror striking, when the eyes of the world were upon them, they responded and continue to respond with a defiance and a strength that are universally admired.

I will now try to give the House as much information as I can. Some of it is already well-known. There were four explosions. Three took place on underground trains—one between Aldgate East and Liverpool Street; one between Russell Square and Kings Cross; one in a train at Edgware Road station. All of these took place within 50 seconds of each other at 8.50 A.M.

The other explosion was on the No.30 bus at Upper Woburn Place at 9.47 A.M.

The timing of the Tube explosions was designed to be at the peak of the rush hour and thus to cause maximum death and injury.

It seems probable that the attack was carried out by Islamist extremist terrorists, of the kind who over recent years have been responsible for so many innocent deaths in Madrid, Bali, Saudi Arabia, Russia, Kenya, Tanzania, Pakistan, Yemen, Turkey, Egypt and Morocco, of course in New York on September 11th, but in many other countries too.

I cannot obviously give details of the police investigation now underway. I can say it is among the most vigorous and intensive this country has seen. We will pursue those responsible not just the perpetrators but the planners of this outrage, wherever they are and we will not rest until they are identified, and as far as is humanly possible, brought to justice.

I would also like to say this about our police and intelligence services. I know of no intelligence specific enough to have allowed them to prevent last Thursday's attacks. By their very nature, people callous enough to kill completely innocent civilians in this way, are hard to stop. But our services and police do a heroic job for our country day in day out and I can say that over the past years, as this particular type of new and awful terrorist threat has grown, they have done their utmost to keep this country and its people safe. As I saw again from the meeting of COBR this morning, their determination to get those responsible is total.

Besides the obvious imperative of tracking down those who carried out these acts of terrorism, our principal concern is the bereaved, the families of the victims. It is the most extraordinarily distressing time for them and all of us feel profoundly for them. Let me explain what we are trying to do.

The majority, though I stress not all, of the victims' families now have a very clear idea that they have lost their loved ones. For many, patterns of life and behaviour are well enough established that the numbers of potential victims can now be brought within reasonable range of the actual victims. Some 74 families now have police Family Liaison Officers with them. In addition, we have established, with Westminster City Council, the police and others the Family Assistance Centre. This is presently at The Queen Mother Sports Centre. Tomorrow it will move to a more suitable site at the Royal Horticultural Halls in Westminster. I would like to thank the many organisations involved including the Salvation Army, the Women's Royal Voluntary Service, the Red Cross, Westminster City Council and all those counsellors who are helping to staff the centre.

In this way we are doing our level best to look after the families. My RHF—the Culture Secretary—has taken charge of this aspect as she has done before.

More difficult is then the process of formal identification. The police are proceeding here with some caution. In previous terrorist attacks of a similar kind in other countries, mistakes have been made which are incredibly distressing. The effect of a bomb is to make identification sometimes very, very hard and harrowing. There is now a process in place, involving a group chaired by the Coroner which will, in each case, make a definitive pronouncement once the right procedures are gone through. I wish it could be quicker but I think the only wise course is to follow precisely the advice of Coroner and police and that is what we will do.

At some time and in consultation with the families, we will be ready to join in arrangements for a Memorial Service for the victims. Her Majesty The Queen has said she will attend. Two minutes silence will be held at noon on Thursday. This will be an opportunity for the nation to unite in remembrance.

There is then the issue of further anti-terrorist legislation. During the passage of the Prevention of Terrorism Act earlier this year we pledged to introduce a further counter-terrorism Bill later in this session. That remains our intention. It will give us an opportunity, in close consultation with the police and the agencies, to see whether there are additional powers which they might need to prevent further attacks.

As to timing, my Rt. Hon Friend, the Home Secretary, pledged to publish the Bill for pre-legislative scrutiny in the autumn with introduction in spring 2006, so that Parliament had time to digest the report on the operation of control orders produced by the independent reviewer, Lord Carlile. I do not currently see any reason to depart from that timetable.

However, that is subject to an important caveat. If, as the fuller picture about these incidents emerges and the investigation proceeds, it becomes clear that there are powers which the police and intelligence agencies need immediately to combat terrorism, it is plainly sensible to reserve the right to return to Parliament with an accelerated timetable.

Finally, I would like to record our deep appreciation of the huge outpouring of international support for London and for Britain over these past days. The G8 leaders demonstrated complete solidarity and also commented with an awe that gave me a lot of pride in Britain, on the courage of our capital city and its people.

The UN Security Council passed a unanimous resolution of condemnation of the terrorists and support for Britain.

The IOC kindly sent a resolution of support.

Messages have been received world-wide. There have been immediate offers of help from all the world's main intelligence agencies. An emergency meeting of the EU JHA Council will take place later this week.

Mr Speaker, the 7th of July will always be remembered as a day of terrible sadness for our country and for London. Yet it is true that just four days later, London's buses, trains and as much of its underground as is possible, are back on normal schedules; its businesses, shops and schools are open; its millions of people are coming to work with a steely determination that is genuinely remarkable.

The remnants of a bus that exploded near Tavistock Square, in central London, July 7, 2005. AP/WIDE WORLD PHOTOS

Yesterday we celebrated the heroism of World War II including the civilian heroes of London's blitz. Today what a different city London is—a city of many cultures, faiths and races, hardly recognisable from the London of 1945. So different and yet, in the face of this attack, there is something wonderfully familiar in the confident spirit which moves through the city, enabling it to take the blow, but still not flinch from re-asserting its will to triumph over adversity. Britain may be different today, but the coming together is the same.

And I say to our Muslim community. People know full well that the overwhelming majority of Muslims stand four square with every other community in Britain. We were proud of your contribution to Britain before last Thursday. We remain proud of it today. Fanaticism is not a state of religion but a state of mind. We will work with you to make the moderate and true voice of Islam heard as it should be.

Together, we will ensure that though terrorists can kill, they will never destroy the way of life we share and which we value, and which we will defend with the strength of belief and conviction so that it is to us and not to the terrorists, that victory will belong.

SIGNIFICANCE

The government of the United Kingdom remained adamant in its position that the war in Iraq was justified and used the bombing to rally the population behind its support of it actions against terrorists.

Many Britons, however, remained unconvinced, assuming that because of Blair's unconditional support of American intervention in Iraq and elsewhere, Britain had been the subject of an apparent Islamist terror attack. Blair counter-argued that 9/11 and the bombings of U.S. embassies in East Africa had occurred long before the invasion of Iraq; although at the same time he failed to acknowledge that the attacks in Africa were on American, not British, interests.

One of the most surprising elements of the attacks was the fact that they were carried out by British-born Muslims, mostly from mainstream and middle-class families. Amongst Britain's two million Muslims, it prompted a quick reflection and reaction. What had prompted these men to carry out the attacks? How had their militancy gone unchecked? Their communities, and even some of their families, were quick to denounce the suicide bomb attacks. In response, Britain's Muslim community began new efforts to steer Moslem youths away from Islamist activity.

A clear link with al-Qaeda was made apparent less than two weeks after the bombings. Police in Pakistan arrested a man who they claimed was the British al-Qaeda leader, Haroon Rashid Aswat, who had come from the same west Yorkshire town as one of the bombers and had apparently spoken to the suicide team on his mobile phone a few hours before the four men blew themselves up.

The specter of a large-scale al-Qaeda campaign against British targets raised itself a fortnight after the attacks on London's transport system. Four men, in a repeat of the earlier attack, attempted to set off bombs on London's transport system: three on the tube; one on a bus. This time, however, only the detonators exploded, and, leaving what appeared to be similar devices behind, all four men escaped from their targets and disappeared into the city. Police garnered key forensic evidence from the intended bomb sites that they anticipate (as of mid-July 2005) could lead them to perpetrators further up the organizational chain.

FURTHER RESOURCES

Books

Burke, Jason. *Al-Qa'eda: The Story of Radical Islam*. New York: Penguin, 2004.

Web sites

BBC News. "The London Bombs and the Iraq Connection." July 18, 2005. <http://news.bbc.co.uk/1/hi/uk_politics/4693437.stm> (accessed July 18, 2005).

BBC News. "Suicide Bombers' 'Ordinary' Lives." July 18, 2005. <http://news.bbc.co.uk/1/hi/uk/4678837.stm> (accessed July 18, 2005).

5 Religious Terrorism

Introduction to Religious Terrorism

Religious terrorism involves violence that is committed with the stated aim of fulfilling a divinely commanded purpose or that is argued to be sanctioned or demanded by religious belief. It is usually the product of fundamentalist fanaticism.

Religious terrorists often attempt to justify their actions by citing holy texts or receiving a command or blessing from a religious leader. Acts of religious terrorism are often carried out by those who accept that their death is a divinely mandated sacrifice or offering to a higher power or god. For example, suicide bombers are often recruited with assurances that their acts earn them martyrdom, a memorial reverence among the living, and an elite place in the afterlife. Religious terrorism can also involve non-traditional acts in the sense that they are not always affiliated with established religions. Indeed, religious terrorism is sometimes the product of groups or individuals who interpret the world through self-constructed systems of thought, such as millennial or doomsday extremist groups.

Most of the religious terrorist groups discussed in this chapter are Islamist (Muslim fundamentalist). Terrorism is perpetrated in the name of all of the world's great religions. At different times in history, every major religion has suffered cycles of violent discord that has resulted in terrorist acts. However, as the U.S. State Department has noted, since 1980 a majority of international terrorist networks assert Islamist ideals. Accordingly, the current historical cycle of religious terrorism focuses upon a complex web of global Islamist terror networks.

The Islamist groups featured here primarily operate in Afghanistan, Egypt, Iraq, Iran, Israel, Lebanon, Libya, Pakistan, and several other nations. Some are fundamentalist Shia Moslems, some are fundamentalist Sunni Moslems, and many uphold a different vision of the composition of the ideal Islamist state. In places such as Iraq, factions of various Islamist groups are engaged in armed conflict and terror campaigns against each other.

Terrorism committed by the Islamist Taliban government against the citizens of Afghanistan is also discussed in this chapter. The Taliban's terror campaign and sponsorship of al-Qaeda, the Islamist group responsible for the September 11, 2001 attacks in the United States, is more accurately described as state-sponsored terrorism. However, the editors have chosen to include the Taliban in this chapter because their terror campaign was instrumental in drawing international attention to the threat posed by a global surge in religious extremism. Other instances of terrorism perpetrated by state governments are discussed in the chapter on state-sponsored terrorism. Al-Qaeda is featured in the chapter on global terrorism.

Jewish, Christian, and other sectarian extremism acts are also presented. The assassination of Israeli leader Yitzak Rabin is included because his murder at the hands of Jewish extremists was intended to halt the Middle East peace process by instilling fear in those supporting diplomatic solutions to the Israeli-Palestinian conflict. Although also treated as an act of political terrorism the professed motivations of Timothy McVeigh (mastermind of the 1995 Oklahoma City bombing), were colored by Christian extremism. The Tokyo subway attacks by the Aum Shinri-kyu (Supreme Truth) cult, which became increasingly violent in the mid–1990s, demonstrate that religious terrorism is not the exclusive purview of the world's major, long-established religions.

Americans Held Hostage in Iran

Islamist Revolutionaries Seize American Embassy in Tehran, Iran

Photograph

By: The Associated Press

Date: November 9, 1979

Source: The Associated Press.

About the Photographer: Founded in 1848, the Associated Press claims to be the oldest and largest news organization in the world, serving as a news source for more than one billion people a day.

INTRODUCTION

Foreign intrigue had long been the rallying call for those unhappy with the regime of the Iranian Shah, Reza Mohammed Pahlavi, and even one that the Shah had himself used to invoke sympathy amongst his deeply unhappy people during his final days. His father, Reza Shah, owed both his installation as the first monarch of the Pahlavi dynasty in 1921, and his deposition in 1941 to the machinations of foreign powers. Likewise, Reza Mohammed's accession in 1953 came as part of a Central Intelligence Agency-backed coup and was merely seen by the Iranian people as a continuation of foreign intrigues.

Reza Mohammad Pahlavi was America's closest ally in the Middle East during the 1960s and 1970s. His goal was to build up Iran to be a Western-orientated regional superpower with the latest military technology and modern communications. The Shah positioned himself closely to Western leaders, in particular United States President Jimmy Carter. As recession and social unrest began to threaten his position from 1977 onwards, these ties increasingly became a liability and the Shah started to turn against his Western backers, accusing the CIA of plotting to overthrow him and the British Broadcasting Corporation (BBC) of spreading incendiary broadcasts via its World Service. Given his earlier allegiances, an increasingly enraged population began to grip the country with demonstrations throughout 1978. A social and religious opposition combined to topple the Shah's regime, and he fled Iran in January 1979.

This abandonment led to a power vacuum in Iran, with organizations from the political left to the far right beginning to contest for power. This was inflamed by a struggle between secular and religious forces. The only individual capable of providing any sort of national unity, and even that was tentative, was Ayatollah Khomeini, a senior cleric and long-standing opponent of the Shah's

regime who had been living in exile in France. Khomeini made a triumphant return to Iran in February 1979.

Even Khomeini, however, could not claim control of the revolutionary situation. Khomeini refused to recognize any officials or politicians who accepted an appointment from the Shah, regarding them as traitors to Islam. During 1979, state, army, and internal security forces all collapsed along with the economy. Khomeini installed his own Prime Minister, Medhi Bazargan, a moderate, but even his powers were limited by the authority invested in a parallel ruling organization known as the Council of the Islamic Republic, a body of clerics headed by Khomeini, which vetoed policies that it did not like.

This merely added to a prevailing sense of chaos, leaving Khomeini to rule by religious authority. He also advanced his support by blaming Iran's mess on American and Israeli interests. Khomeini denounced the American government as the "Great Satan" and caused chaos across the Moslem World in November and early December 1979 after (falsely) accusing the CIA of bombing the Grand Mosque in Mecca. This precipitated the destruction of the American embassies in Pakistan and Libya after widespread rioting.

The Shah, meanwhile, was terminally ill with lymphoma and living in Egypt. In October 1979, he was admitted to the United States for medical treatment. This merely enraged the revolutionary movement in Iran further, and on November 1, Ayatollah Khomeini urged the Iranian people to demonstrate against the United States. Thousands gathered around the U.S. embassy in Tehran in protest, a not uncommon occurrence. However, these demonstrations became increasingly violent and on November 4, a mob of around 500 Iranians students calling themselves the Imam's Disciples seized the main embassy building. A guard of Marines was completely outnumbered and of ninety occupants in the building, sixty-six were taken captive.

The revolutionaries justified their action as retaliation against years of American support for the Shah and for his admission into the United States for medical treatment. They demanded the Shah be returned to Iran for trial in exchange for the hostage's release. Khomeini's government gave backing to the hostage takers, and as news spread, the Arab world gloried in the act as a demonstration that the new Iranian government was capable of opposing the United States.

PRIMARY SOURCE

AMERICANS HELD HOSTAGE IN IRAN
See primary source image.

SIGNIFICANCE

President Carter retaliated by applying economic and diplomatic sanctions on Iran, freezing around $8 billion of Iranian assets on November 14, 1979.

Khomeini, however, was unrepentant and merely used the sanctions as the latest example of the United States acting against the interests of the Iranian people. Although thirteen hostages were released on November 19 and 20, fifty-three continued to be held, and, as Christmas passed, it became apparent that a solution to the crisis would be far more complicated than first anticipated.

In February 1980, Khomeini's government issued a set of demands in return for the hostages, which included the return of the Shah to Iran for trial, and an array of diplomatic gestures, including an apology for previous American actions in Iran, such as the 1953 coup, and a promise not to interfere in the future. Inevitably, Carter refused to meet these conditions, but he did try and seek a diplomatic solution to the crisis via neutral third-party governments, most notably Switzerland.

Carter also ordered a secret rescue mission code-named Operation Eagle Claw in April 1980. The mission ended in disaster when one of the rescue helicopters crashed, killing eight U.S. servicemen. Intelligence material was left behind for the Iranians to discover, and no hostages were rescued. In images broadcast world wide, the Iranians displayed the intelligence material along with the bodies of the dead servicemen, which were paraded through the streets of Tehran.

1980 was an election year in the United States, and Carter's presidential rival, Ronald Reagan, continually

PRIMARY SOURCE

Americans Held Hostage in Iran A bound and blindfolded American hostage is displayed to the crowd outside the U.S. Embassy in Tehran, November 9, 1979. AP/WIDE WORLD PHOTOS

exploited the fact that President Carter was unable to bring a satisfactory conclusion to the hostage crisis. Not even the death of the Shah on July 27, 1980, which removed one of Khomeini's main demands, seemed to ease matters. Only when Iraq invaded Iran in September was Khomeini's regime any more receptive to resolving the crisis. Negotiations continued behind the scenes, but no solution was forthcoming ahead of the November elections, which Ronald Reagan (1981–1989) won. In the final days of Carter's presidency and with the assistance of intermediaries, such as the Algerian government, successful negotiations were undertaken between the United States and Iran. In exchange for the unfreezing of $8 billion Iranian assets and immunity from lawsuits, the hostages were formally released into U.S. custody, minutes after President Reagan's inauguration on January 20, 1981.

Throughout his Presidency, Reagan railed against the Iranians, describing them as part of a "confederation of terrorist states." It was well established that Iran was a sponsor of the Shi'ite extremist group Hezbollah, which carried out a number of terrorist attacks against the U.S. in Lebanon. Iran was also linked to other Shi'ite extremists, most notably Islamic Jihad.

As a way of toppling Khomeini, Reagan began providing military aid to Iraq, who were engaged in a bloody war with Iran, passing on weaponry, intelligence, and military secrets. The Reagan administration also passed on arms to Iran—in what became known as the Iran Contra Affair—in 1985–1986 as part of their efforts to release U.S. hostages held by Hezbollah in Lebanon.

The Iran-Iraq war went on until 1988, before reaching an impasse. It is a matter of debate whether military aid from the Reagan administration unnecessarily prolonged that conflict. However, the war claimed more than a million lives and had devastating economic consequences for both countries. Ayatollah Khomeini died in June 1989. His death triggered mass outpourings of grief in Iran and marked the onset of a sustained period of political uncertainty within the country. Clerics and democratically elected politicians vied with each other for control of government; one side trying to rebuild bridges with the West, the other doing their utmost to pull them back down. In many ways, this situation extends to the present day.

In 2002, George W. Bush described Iran as being part of "an axis of evil" along with Iraq and North Korea, inferring that it was a rogue state that harbored terrorists and sponsored terrorism. In June 2005, the hard-liner Mahmoud Ahmadinejad defeated the moderate Akbar Rafsanjhani in Iran's presidential elections. Hopes that the détente which had passed between the European Union and Iran over previous years would be mirrored by an improvement in relations with the United States were seemingly dashed by the election of a man whose criticism of America was among the central tenets of his victorious campaign.

FURTHER RESOURCES

Books

Amuzegar, Jahangir. *The Dynamics of the Iranian Revolution.* NY: New York University Press, 1991.

Sullivan, William H. *Mission to Iran.* London: W. W. Norton & Co., London, 1981.

Web sites

Federal Bulletin Board. "Final Report of the Independent Counsel for Iran Contra Matters." <http://www.fas.org/irp/offdocs/walsh/> (accessed July 7, 2005).

Jimmy Carter Library and Museum. "The Hostage Crisis in Iran." <http://www.jimmycarterlibrary.org/documents/hostages.phtml> (accessed July 7, 2005)

U.S. Embassy in Pakistan Attacked

"Pakistani Troops Took Five Hours to Aid Embattled Embassy"

News article

By: Barry Shlachter

Date: November 22, 1979

Source: The *Associated Press*

About the Author: In November 1979, Barry Shlachter was a writer for the *Associated Press*. As of 2005, Shlachter is a columnist for the *Star-Telegram* in Fort Worth, Texas.

INTRODUCTION

The United States and Pakistan first established official diplomatic relations in 1947. At that time, the United States agreed to provide the country with military and economic assistance. However, beginning in 1965, the United States removed military aid to Pakistan and neighboring India at the beginning of the Indo-Pakistan war.

The United States later resumed military aid but stopped economic programs (except for food aid) as a result of anxiety over Pakistan' growing nuclear arms program. Thus, over the years, relations between the governments of the United States and Pakistan have been tense and has including several violent incidents against U.S. officials and employees in Pakistan.

A Pakistani soldier walks past a U.S. Embassy vehicle burned as militants raided the U.S. Embassy in Islamabad in 1979.
AP/WIDE WORLD PHOTOS

One such incident occurred on November 21, 1979, when thousands of radical students and angry Pakistanis attacked the thirty-two acre U.S. embassy compound in Islamabad, Pakistan. The attack was instigated when an inaccurate report by Iran's ruling Ayatollah Rohollah Khomeini went out over Pakistani airwaves stating that American and Israeli troops had attacked the holy city of Mecca and taken control of the Grand Mosque. (On that night, religious extremists from Saudi Arabia had forcibly subdued the Grand Mosque at Mecca.)

At this same time, other U.S.-controlled locations in Pakistan were also attacked, including the American Cultural Center in Lahore that was destroyed by fire.

As Pakistani protestors descended upon the embassy, Marine guards held back the crowds. Nearly 140 people retreated inside the embassy. U.S. diplomats,

Pakistani staff members, and visiting *Time* magazine reporter Marcia Gauger were among the people who locked themselves into a steel-encased communications room within a secure top-floor area known as The Vault. In the end, two Americans and two Pakistani employees were killed. Those hiding in the Vault eventually escaped the burning building through an opening on the embassy's roof.

One of the many media reports broadcast around the world that day was from the *CBS Evening News*, which stated: "The invaders ran shooting through the corridors, took over the roof and set fires, reportedly with Molotov cocktails . . . " [CBS News web citation] Because of the rumor that the United States had attacked Mecca, the embassy building was set on fire, and eventually burned down, and four people were killed (Army Warrant Officer Bryan Ellis, Corporal

Steven J. Crowley, and two Pakistani staff members). The alleged lack of immediate response on the part of the Pakistani government also contributed to the extent of the destruction.

▮ PRIMARY SOURCE

Witnesses said today it took about five hours for Pakistani troops to move against a violent mob that burned down the U.S. Embassy here, leaving two Americans and an estimated five Pakistanis dead.

A West European diplomat said the students who initiated Wednesday's riot were joined by thousands of "workers and layabouts" who arrived in state-owned Punjab Transport Corp. buses, which he claimed were provided without charge.

In Washington, Secretary of State Cyrus R. Vance ordered non-essential U.S. government personnel and about 300 dependents of government employees to leave Pakistan following the attacks on the Islamabad embassy and other U.S. facilities in the Moslem nation.

More than 2,000 angry Moslems, shouting "kill the American dogs," stormed the embassy with guns blazing about noon Wednesday and set it afire, witnesses said. They apparently were spurred by false reports of American involvement in Tuesday's takeover of the Grand Mosque in Mecca, Saudi Arabia.

"There is some concern about the inaction of the Pakistan army," U.S. Navy Cmdr. Chuck Monaghan said today. Monaghan, 43, is attached to the embassy's military assistance group.

"The only time they did something was when the (U.S.) Marines went on the roof"—about five hours after the disturbance began, said Monaghan, of Clinton, Iowa.

Cpl. Steven Crowley, 20, of Port Jefferson, N.Y., was killed when he was caught in a crossfire between Marines and Pakistani police on one side and the invading Moslems on the other, the Defense Department said.

The U.S. Defense Department today identified a body found in a charred apartment in the gutted embassy compound as that of 29-year-old Bryan Ellis, an Army chief warrant officer. Ellis' wife, Brenda, was away from their apartment at the time and was uninjured. The Pentagon said the dead man's mother and stepfather are Mr. and Mrs. Erwin B. Ellis of Mobile, Ala., and his father, Edmond Polinski of Spring Lake, N.C.

Some 37 other persons, including two unidentified Americans, were injured in the attack. The bodies of two fatally burned Pakistani employees of the embassy also were discovered, U.S. Ambassador Arthur W. Hummel Jr. said.

Pakistani news reports said three demonstrators died during the riot.

"I had not believed that there was any substantial anti-American feeling in this country," Hummel told reporters today at the U.S. Aid Office where the embassy staff has relocated.

"Whenever religion is concerned, and when Islam is concerned, this country has often shown violence," he said.

Hummel said police were dispatched quickly after being alerted by the embassy at about 1:30 P.M. local time (4:30 A.M. EST) but both this small contingent and later reinforcements were quickly overwhelmed by the mob.

He declined to say when army troops arrived, but reported the troops helped American and Pakistani staff members escape at about 6:45 P.M.

Hummel said the dependents and non-essential personnel would be evacuated to Washington on Friday on a chartered Pan American airways jetliner.

Thomas G. Putscher, 32, of Willingboro, N.J., told the Associated Press he suffered a concussion in a beating by rioters who called him an "imperialist pig."

Putscher, an auditor with the U.S. Aid Office in Karachi, said he was kidnapped by students from nearby Quaid-ia University, where he was held until "acquitted in a kangaroo court" five hours later.

"It was worse than Vietnam," said Monaghan, who was among 90 American and Pakistani staff members who locked themselves in a third floor, steel-encased communications area known as the "vault."

They were forced to leave the area, he said, after it filled with smoke and the floor began to buckle from the heat. Two marines climbed through a window and onto the roof to open an escape hatch. Only then, Monaghan said, did the Pakistan army move in to help them.

Feelings were running high in the diplomatic community over the failure of the Pakistani government to prevent the burning of the embassy.

One diplomat said darkness, not the presence of troops, sent rioters home.

"Obviously the feeling is that the military acted very slowly," said the diplomat, who asked not to be identified.

"The situation could have been handled by 2 P.M., an hour or so after it began," he went on. "But the Pakistan military took no effective action until a quarter-to-seven when the Americans already had released themselves from the strong room."

In Washington, The State Department blamed Ayatollah Ruhollah Khomeini's militant Islamic regime in Iran for "creating the climate" for the attack. Khomeini issued a statement that it was "not far-fetched to assume that this act (against the mosque) has been carried out by criminal American imperialism. . . . and international Zionism."

Gen. Zia ul-Haq, Pakistan's military dictator, spoke to President Carter by telephone and expressed "deep regret and apologies for the attack," White House spokesman Jody Powell said.

A leader of some 300 students who led the attack in Islamabad said the attackers believed rumors that American Jews were responsible for the mosque takeover. "We regret the lives lost and the destruction," the student said.

Hummel, who had gone home for lunch before the attack began, said all six buildings in the embassy compound—built at a cost of more than $20 million—were destroyed, as were 50 vehicles.

SIGNIFICANCE

At the time of the attack on the U.S. embassy in Islamabad, the Pakistani government and its citizens were angry at the United States for various reasons, including the U.S. government's decision to stop economic aid, false claims of U.S. military troops controlling the holy city of Mecca, human-rights' criticisms levied by U.S. officials against Pakistan dictator, General Mohammed Zia ul-'Haq, the takeover of the U.S. embassy in Tehran, and the removal by Shiite clerics of an Iranian dictator favored by the United States.

A false rumor was the catalyst for the 1979 fatal attack on the U.S. embassy in Islamabad. The instantaneous, around-the-clock news coverage that is present today was then only in its infancy. Today, rumor, propaganda, and terrorist communications can, in a matter of seconds, be seen and heard around the world via satellite broadcasts and the Internet. These technologies also afford the opportunity to rapidly disseminate accurate information and to correct false information.

FURTHER RESOURCES
Web sites

60 Minutes, CBS News. "The Big Lie." <http://www.cbsnews.com/stories/2002/09/04/60II/main520768.shtml> (accessed June 5, 2005).

Embassy of the United States: Islamabad, Pakistan. "Homepage of the Embassy of the United States: Islamabad, Pakistan." <http://islamabad.usembassy.gov/pakistan/index.html> (accessed June 7, 2005).

Washington Post. Barr, Cameron W. "A Day of Terror Recalled: 1979 Embassy Siege in Islamabad Still Haunts Survivors."

<http://www.washingtonpost.com/wp-dyn/articles/A15332–2004Nov26.html> (accessed June 5, 2005).

"Extremists Blamed for Sadat Killing"

Newspaper article

By: David B. Ottaway

Date: October 8, 1981

Source: "Extremist Blamed for Sadat Killing," as published by the *Washington Post.*

About the Author: David B. Ottaway joined the *Washington Post* in 1971. He served for over twenty years as a national security reporter and foreign correspondent in Africa, Europe, and the Middle East, before moving to the Post's investigative unit in 1994.

INTRODUCTION

Mohammad Anwar El-Sadat, born on December 25, 1918, joined Gamal Abdel Nasser in forming the Egyptian Association of Free Officers in 1938. The organization later helped bring down King Farouk and put Nasser into power. Upon Nasser's death, Sadat succeeded him as President of Egypt in October 1970. More moderate than Nasser and popular with the masses, Sadat became the first Arab leader to risk his political career by talking directly with Israeli officials. In 1977, Sadat participated in the Camp David accords that recognized the State of Israel. Two years later, Sadat angered much of the Arab world by signing a peace treaty with Israel. On October 6, 1981, he died along with ten others in an attack by Muslim religious fundamentalists.

Anwar Sadat and the other members of the Egyptian Association of Free Officers joined with the Muslim Brotherhood to overthrow King Farouk of Egypt in 1954. Conflict then broke out between the Brotherhood and the secular, modernizing military junta led by Nasser. When an October 23, 1954 assassination of Nasser by the Brotherhood failed, Nasser executed six Brotherhood leaders, jailed 4,000 followers, and banned the organization. Sadat, who held a number of posts in Nasser's government before succeeding him as President of Egypt, pardoned Brotherhood members upon taking office and allowed the organization to participate in elections.

A gunman wearing an Egyptian uniform fires into a military parade reviewing stand during an attack that took the life of Egypt's President Anwar Sadat and five others. AP/WIDE WORLD PHOTOS

By the late 1970s, the Muslim Brotherhood had become the largest legal source of opposition to Sadat's free trade and investment policies as well as to his policy of seeking peace with Israel. In 1977, Egypt had become the first Arab state to recognize Israel when Sadat signed the Camp David accords. For his efforts to establish peace in the Middle East, Sadat received the Nobel Peace Prize. In 1979, Sadat signed a peace treaty with Israel that called for the gradual return of the Sinai to Egypt. Instead of pacifying Muslim fundamentalists by acquiring the Sinai, Sadat angered them by negotiating with the Jews. Many in the Arab word condemned Sadat, especially after Israel delayed cooperating in a resolution of the Palestinian problem.

In the last month of his life, Sadat took sudden action against opposition elements in Egypt. He spoke publicly of a plot to undermine his government or take his life, planned by Muslim fundamentalists, and ordered the arrest of about 1,500 people.

On October 6, 1981, Anwar Sadat participated in a public review of the Egyptian armed forces on the anniversary of the Yom Kippur War. Suddenly, a vehicle veered out of the marching column and uniformed men stormed the platform where Sadat and his colleagues and guests stood. The soldiers threw hand grenades and fired machine guns into the audience. In the wake of the violence, there were thirty-eight wounded and eleven dead, including Sadat.

PRIMARY SOURCE

Egypt's defense minister said today that an "isolated" group of four men led by a Moslem extremist soldier carried out yesterday's bloody assassination of President Anwar Sadat at a suburban Cairo parade ground.

As the government moved swiftly to carry out an orderly transfer of power, Defense Minister Abdel Hamlim Abu Ghazala, wearing bandages on his right arm and left ear from the attack, told the National Assembly that the men who cut down Sadat with automatic weapons fire had acted on their own, without outside help.

"There was no coup," he told the National Assembly in a trembling voice. "It is an individual group and they are not even related to any other group or country."

Abu Ghazala said only four persons were involved in the shooting, but many eyewitnesses reported seeing at least eight, not including the driver of the truck carrying the men. The attackers, dressed as soldiers, were part of a military parade being viewed by Sadat and other dignitaries.

"One of the soldiers was a Moslem fanatic, and he did it. That's all," said Abu Ghazala.

Western diplomatic sources lent credence to reports circulating widely in the capital that the assailants were Moslem extremists belonging to the secret organization known as Takfir wa Hijra (Repentant and Holy Flight), which was involved in earlier terrorist activities against the Sadat regime.

"They the authorities are increasingly convinced, not just from guessing but interrogation that this is the group," one source said.

In addition to having a strong presence among Egyptian youth and on campuses here, Takfir wa Hijra is known to have some following within the Egyptian military, although the exact extent of its support has never been clear. Today, unofficial Egyptian sources and Western diplomats echoed the assertion of U.S. Secretary of State Alexander M. Haig Jr. that the group was "centered, not exclusively, in certain military units."

Ghazala, however, sought to downplay in his remarks to the assembly any implication that high-level elements within the Army were involved in the assassination. And though the assailants were clearly influential enough to gain access to the parade and ammunition for their weapons, the absence of additional movements toward a coup indicated that they did not have the power to direct the bulk of the Army.

Reuter quoted Abu Ghazala as telling Egyptian reporters 2nd Lt. Khaled Attallah led the assassins, having given his assigned men a vacation and recruited in their place two civilians with past military service plus another officer on inactive reserve.

While investigations of the assassins continued, National Assembly Speaker Sufi Abu Taleb was formally sworn in as interim president of the republic and the assembly overwhelmingly voted to endorse the ruling party's nomination of Vice President Hosni Mubarak as Sadat's permanent successor. An official statement said a national referendum would be held next Tuesday to approve the decision. Thus, if all goes according to schedule, Mubarak, 52, will take over by the middle of next week as the third president of Egypt's republic since the overthrow of the monarchy here in 1952.

At the same time, the government set the state funeral for the slain president at noon Saturday amid announcements that among those attending the ceremony will be Israeli Prime Minister Menachem Begin, former U.S. presidents Jimmy Carter, Gerald R. Ford, and Richard M. Nixon, and a delegation of the Reagan administration headed by Haig.

The plans of three former U.S. presidents to attend the funeral underlined Sadat's importance in the balance of power in the Middle East and the global implications of the quick barrage of grenades and gunfire that killed him.

Both Egyptian officials and Western diplomatic sources said the government's main objective in the present crisis was to carry out a calm transfer of authority and maintain the appearance of order, stability and continuity of policy in the face of widespread concern abroad about the nation's future direction.

Those same diplomatic sources said there was no evidence so far that the assassination team, which launched its attack from a military truck passing in front of the reviewing stand where Sadat and much of the rest of the Egyptian power elite was seated, intended to wipe out the entire leadership or overthrow the political system built by Sadat over the past 11 years.

However, many officials around Sadat were struck by the fire, and reports about the number of killed and injured continued to vary throughout the day. By late tonight, the government had still not provided an official list.

The number of those believed to be dead dropped from nine to eight or seven with the news that Fawzi Abdel Hafez, Sadat's private secretary, had not died as first reported and that the North Korean ambassador, one of a number of foreigners hit in the spray of bullets from the assailants' guns, was still alive.

The death toll may still rise, however, as a number of the roughly 30 wounded persons are still in critical condition.

Initial reports yesterday had indicated that another Islamic fundamentalist group, the Moslem Brotherhood, was probably connected to the assassination. Both the Brotherhood and Takfir wa Hijra were prime targets of Sadat's massive crackdown on religious extremists and opposition elements last month, in which more than 1,500 persons were arrested.

Egyptian and Western diplomatic sources ruled out the likelihood today that a third group, based abroad and led by dissident retired Army chief of staff Saadeddin Shazli, was responsible for the shooting. Yesterday, anonymous Arabs calling Western news agencies in Beirut claimed the assassination had been carried out by Shazli's group, which is backed by Libya and Syria and has been referred to by several names, including the Egyptian National Front and the Organization for the Liberation of Egypt.

Local press reports said security authorities have captured three or four of the assailants and had killed one or two others.

One report said three of the six were military officers and that one of them, a major, had had a brother arrested in the crackdown on Moslem extremists last month.

Western diplomats and analysts continued to puzzle today over the absence so far of any major public demonstration of grief over Sadat's assassination, in contrast to the dramatic displays that greeted the death of his predecessor, Gamal Abdel Nasser, in September 1970.

The day began at 5 A.M. with chanting from the Koran blaring through loudspeakers at the city's mosques, and incense sellers wandered from cafe to cafe, trailing thick fumes But the incense was meant to purify the air for an upcoming religious holiday, not commemorate Sadat's funeral, and Egyptians interviewed in the street, while expressing shock and dismay at what had happened, seemed too confused or uncertain to react more demonstratively.

Dassim Khatib, owner of a pharmacy in downtown Cairo, called the "accident" absolutely terrible. "The streets are calm," he said, "but everyone is listening and talking about what is going to happen next."

Everywhere today in this sprawling Nile Valley city of twelve million, people could be seen huddled around in small groups, looking at the often spectacular pictures of the assassination in the local press. Faces were somber and sometimes tense, but few tears were being shed.

In fact, only in the National Assembly, where deputies gave emotional eulogies to the slain president, was there any real sign of emotion over Sadat's death. Many deputies had tears in their eyes.

Elsewhere, business was very much as usual. The markets and butcher shops were filled with customers busy preparing for the four-day Moslem holiday of Id Al Adha. Banks were open, and there was no change in exchange rates, official or black-market, despite the jittery reaction on world currency markets.

At the fashionable Gezirah, a playground of the Egyptian middle class where Sadat had much support, there was an enormous crowd of people going about their business as usual.

Western diplomats were at a loss to explain the relative lack of reaction, but some ascribed it to general numbness, the upcoming holiday or simply uncertainty about what was going to happen next.

"Sadat was clearly out in front in a lot of things he was doing," said one diplomat, referring to Egypt's peace treaty with Israel and economic liberalization measures.

Lt. Col. Khaled al-Islambouli shouts, "The blood of a Muslim is not a sacrifice for Jews or Americans!" from the court cell at his trial for the assassination of President Anwar al-Sadat. AP/WIDE WORLD PHOTOS

SIGNIFICANCE

Although the Muslim Brotherhood received initial blame for the attack on Sadat, Islamic Jihad or Munazzamat al Jihad, carried out the assassination. This Sunni Muslim terrorist group, with several thousand dedicated members, has been active in Egypt since the 1970s and is an offshoot of Tahrir al Islami, which broke off from the Muslim Brotherhood. The Egyptian Islamic Jihad is not directly connected with the Shiite Muslim Islamic Jihad of Lebanon (Hezbollah) or the Islamic Jihad in the Hijaz that targets the Saudi Arabia monarchy, but it has cooperated with Islamic Jihad of Palestine. The Egyptian Jihad seeks the overthrow of the Egyptian government and the replacement of this government with an Islamic state. Based in Cairo, the group reportedly has sympathizers and possible cells in the United States, the United Kingdom, Iran, Sudan, and Afghanistan.

The assassination of Sadat by Islamic Jihad was intended to derail the Egyptian-Israeli peace process. To a large extent, Islamic Jihad succeeded. Sadat's death dramatically slowed momentum toward peace in the Middle East. The Sadat killing also demonstrated that secular states could not weaken Islamic fundamentalist groups by cooperating with them. Islamic fundamentalist organizations were subsequently seen as powerful and dangerous forces. The next significant steps toward peace in the region would not occur for another decade.

Through the 1980s and early 1990s, Islamic Jihad continued to concentrate its attacks on high-level, high-profile Egyptian government officials, including cabinet ministers. It claimed responsibility for the attempted assassination of Interior Minister Hassan al-Alfi in August 1993 and of Prime Minister Atef Sedky in November 1993. Islamic Jihad then shifted its focus to the United States, in retaliation for American assistance in the capture of Islamic Jihad members in Albania, Azerbaijan, and the United Kingdom.

FURTHER RESOURCES
Books

Finkelstone, Joseph. *Anwar Sadat: Visionary Who Dared.* Portland: Frank Cass 1996.

Guenena, Nemet. *The "Jihad": An Islamic Alternative in Egypt.* Cairo: American University in Cairo Press, 1986.

Heikal, Mohammed. *Autumn of Fury: The Assassination of Sadat.* London: André Deutsch, 1983.

Audio and Visual Media

ABC News. *The Assassination of Anwar Sadat.* MPI Home Video, 1989.

William Buckley Murdered

"Captive CIA Agent's Death Galvanized Hostage Search"

Newspaper article

By: Bob Woodward and Charles R. Babcock

Date: November 25, 1986

Source: "Captive CIA Agent's Death Galvanized Hostage Search," published by the *Washington Post.*

About the Author: At the time the article was written, Bob Woodward (1943–) was an investigative reporter for the *Washington Post.* Woodward is best known for the investigation, along with his partner Carl Bernstein, of the Watergate scandal involving the Nixon administration and President Richard Nixon, himself. During his professional career, Woodward has investigated and written on numerous topics, including terrorism. As of 2005, Woodward is an assistant managing editor at the *Washington Post,* responsible for special investigative projects. When the article was written, Charles R. Babcock was a staff writer for the *Washington Post.*

A picture of U.S. diplomat William Buckley was distributed by his kidnappers to newspapers throughout Lebabon in 1985. AP/WIDE WORLD PHOTOS

INTRODUCTION

In the early morning of March 16, 1984, William Francis Buckley, political officer/station chief for the Central Intelligence Agency (CIA) at the United States embassy in Beirut, Lebanon, was kidnapped outside his residence. As Buckley left for the U.S. embassy, armed men forced him into their car. The masked kidnappers would be later identified as fundamentalist terrorists from the Islamic Jihad, which is the parent organization of Hezbollah—its secret terrorist organization. Lieutenant Colonel Buckley—a decorated military veteran of the U.S. Special Forces—had been employed by the CIA since 1965, often in clandestine CIA assignments in foreign countries such as Syria and Pakistan.

Initially, Buckley was to be used by the Jihad for a prisoner exchange. However, the exchange failed to materialize and, instead, Buckley was airlifted to Iran.

At that time, several Islamic Jihad members allegedly drugged, and severely tortured and beat Buckley for more than a year. Two of the alleged interrogators and torturers, both high-ranking members of Hezbollah, were Imad Mughniyeh, and Dr. Aziz al-Abub (also known as Ibrahim al-Nadhir).

Mughniyeh was often considered by terrorist experts—before the September 11, 2001 attacks on the United States—to be more dangerous than Osama Bin Laden. The first terrorist attack planned by Mughniyeh is alleged to be the 1983 U.S. embassy bombing in Beirut, Lebanon. His involvement in the kidnapping, severe torturing, and eventual death of Buckley is one of a long list of terrorist events that Mughniyeh allegedly planned and successfully carried out.

Al-Abub is a psychiatrist who regularly in the 1980s used psychological/political persuasion methods such as drugs, brainwashing, and torture to convince hostages to divulge secrets. Al-Abub made graphic videos of Buckley and other hostages during and after torture events with the intent to antagonize foreign governments.

After about fifteen months in captivity, sometime in June 1985, Buckley died from injuries suffered from the brutal beatings of the Islamic Jihad and from medical neglect, specifically identified as untreated pneumonia. His body was returned to the United States on December 28, 1991. He was buried in Arlington National Cemetery, in Virginia, with full military honors.

■ PRIMARY SOURCE

For the Reagan administration and especially the Central Intelligence Agency, Iran and the Moslem extremists it supports in the Middle East took on urgent new significance on March 16, 1984, when a man named William Buckley—described at the time as a political officer in the U.S. Embassy in Lebanon—was snatched off the streets of Beirut by a group calling itself Islamic Jihad.

As his captors have since charged, Buckley was the chief of the CIA's Beirut station, U.S. sources have confirmed. He was one of the CIA's leading experts on terrorism, and his kidnapping initiated what one CIA official called the agency's "private hostage crisis." At agency headquarters in Langley, Buckley's colleagues watched helplessly as their expert on terrorism became a victim of terrorism, which the CIA believed led from Beirut to the revolutionary government in Tehran.

For at least a year, the CIA undertook extraordinary measures, spending what one source called a "small fortune" on informants, intercepting communications and enhancing satellite photographs in hopes of determining where Buckley and other U.S. hostages might be held.

The effort failed. After torture and a long period of medical neglect, Buckley died in Beirut, apparently in June 1985. His captors first declared him dead later in 1985. In a statement released in Beirut earlier this month, they reiterated that Buckley had been "executed" after having "confessed" to working for the CIA.

The Islamic Jihad statement said the group had "volumes written with 'Buckley's' own hand and recorded on videotapes." President Reagan indirectly confirmed that Buckley is dead in his news conference last week, when he spoke of five American hostages in Lebanon; Buckley would be the sixth.

Before Buckley died, the search for him became a crusade for the CIA and a preoccupation of William J. Casey, its director. Agency officials never felt confident that a rescue attempt would succeed. The agency did obtain "irrefutable" evidence that Buckley had been tortured and, after initially resisting, finally broke down and disclosed information about CIA operations, one source said. Some senior CIA officials wept when they heard details of the torture, which was prolonged and painful, the source said.

Buckley was assigned to Lebanon in mid-1983 to help the Lebanese develop methods for thwarting terrorism and to rebuild the U.S. intelligence presence after the bombing of the U.S. Embassy a few months earlier, the sources said. Seventeen Americans died in the attack, including Robert C. Ames, the CIA's chief Middle East analyst, and several other CIA officers.

On March 16, 1984, Buckley was seized on a Beirut street and spirited away—the first of what would become a string of kidnappings of Americans.

Buckley has been the least known among the group of Americans held by Moslem extremists in Lebanon. He had no wife or close family to speak for him. One source said Buckley was picked for the dangerous assignment because he did not have a family. Previously, one source said, Buckley was in Cairo, where he had helped train bodyguards for Egyptian President Anwar Sadat, later assassinated.

Terrorists might have suspected Buckley's true identity and targeted him for kidnapping, the sources said. Buckley often carried a walkie-talkie in Beirut and went nearly every day to the headquarters building of the Lebanese intelligence service—and could have been followed, the sources said.

For more than a year, CIA officials, including Casey, held out hope that Buckley was alive, deciding that reports on his whereabouts and condition were contradictory and did not support a definitive conclusion that Buckley had been killed.

At one point, the CIA received help from an FBI team trained in locating kidnap victims. The team went to Beirut but failed to locate Buckley after a month of careful and sophisticated detective work, according to a senior Reagan administration official. Officials now think that Buckley was in Lebanon during the entire period of his captivity, most of the time in Beirut.

At the time of Buckley's capture, the State Department released a brief biography, which said he was from Medford, Mass., and was a graduate of Boston University. It said he had worked as a librarian and as a civilian employee of the Army until joining the State Department shortly before he was assigned to Beirut.

SIGNIFICANCE

Buckley was the fourth person to be kidnapped by Islamic terrorists in Lebanon during an especially active hostage-taking period from 1982 to 1992. Eventually, thirty people were kidnapped during this ten-year period in Lebanon. While Buckley was a hostage in Iran, the Reagan administration, most especially CIA Director William J. Casey, began concerted actions to locate and free Buckley. A Federal Bureau of Investigation (FBI) team, which specialized in retrieving kidnap victims, was eventually recruited to rescue Buckley.

Upon the death of Buckley, the Reagan administration vowed to make the freedom of American hostages in Lebanon one of its primary policy objectives. As a result of covert operations involving the sale of high-technology weapons to Iran (which was needed for its war against Iraq) by way of Israel, the Reagan administration was able to secure the release of three American hostages. However, the Reagan administration diverted the arms deal money to U.S.-supported, anti-Communist Contra forces in Nicaragua, who were trying to overthrow the Sandinista regime. In the end, these secret actions turned into the Iran-Contra affair, which haunted the Reagan administration when it became publicly known in 1986.

The sources in the Woodward and Babcock article revealed the darkest aspects of Buckley's torture at the hands of psychiatrist al-Abub. It also provided insight into the powerful psychiatric drugging and conditioning techniques used by terrorists. Although such psycho-political terror techniques were known in the 1980s, their pervasiveness within the terrorist community has only recently been explained. Investigations conducted on terrorism with regards to the use of psychiatrists and psychologists provided important information on the ways and means in carrying out the violent goals of terrorist groups.

FURTHER RESOURCES
Books

Salem, Elie Adib. *Violence and Diplomacy in Lebanon: The Troubled Years, 1982–1988.* London and New York: I.B. Tauris, 1995.

Smit, Ferdinand. *The Battle for South Lebanon: The Radicalization of Lebanon's Shi'ites, 1982–1985.* Amsterdam: Bulaag, 2000.

Web sites

Arlington National Cemetery. "William Francis Buckley, Lieutenant Colonel, United States Army Assassinated CIA Station Chief." <http://www.arlingtoncemetery.net/wbuckley.htm> (accessed June 14, 2005).

Dairout Tourist Killing

"British Woman Slain in Attack on Egyptian Tourist Bus"

News article

By: Bahaa Elkoussy

Date: October 21, 1992

Source: United Press International.

About the Author: United Press International (UPI) is a global news and analysis provider headquartered in Washington, D.C., with offices in Beirut, Hong Kong, London, Santiago, Seoul, and Tokyo. At the time this article was written, Bahaa Elkoussy served as a news correspondent based in Cairo.

INTRODUCTION

In their attempts to overthrow the Egyptian government, which they view as corrupt, Islamic extremist groups have committed terrorist acts throughout Egypt—and other parts of the Middle East. Many of their targets have been tourists in the region, particularly those on tour buses. Tourism is a thriving industry in Egypt, one of the country's most lucrative forms of income.

In 1992, Islamic terrorists began violently voicing their opposition to Egyptian President Hosni Mubarak, in what many critics have called a reaction to the lack of opportunity for political participation in the region. Many of these Islamist groups are not permitted to voice their concerns within the dominant political parties of Egypt because their views are often considered dangerous and subversive. But, more importantly, the Muslim Brotherhood has its headquarters in Egypt. The Brotherhood is the largest and oldest Islamist group in the Arab world, and it is still the most influential force in Egyptian politics. Many observers view the rise of Islamist extremists to be the result of republican regimes in the region—particularly those of Gamal Abdel Nasser (president of Egypt, 1956–1970), who used governmental pressures and support to silence Islamist political groups. Islamic extremists have been labeled as such by the United Nations, the Egyptian government, U.S. intelligence agencies, and much of the international media.

These conflicting social forces have produced an intense political atmosphere that is most notably seen in the attacks against civilians and non-natives to the country. Particularly during the 1970s, with the release of many members of the Muslim Brotherhood from Egyptian prisons, fundamental shifts occurred in

Police look around a burned-out tourist bus after it was attacked in front of the Egyptian museum in Cairo AP/WIDE WORLD PHOTOS

Islamist philosophies. These ideologies labeled the state as infidel and asked supporters to plan for a revolution. These dramatic terms and intense calls for action further divided Islamist groups from mainstream politics. Finally, the belief that the state will turn Egypt into a secular society (similar to Turkey) adds to growing political tensions, and hostilities concerning Palestine and the perceived loss of Arab lands have continued to heighten already exasperated emotions.

The hostilities arising from the loss of Arab lands, and the Palestine movement, derives from the post–World War II creation of the Israeli state. The Brotherhood sent fighters to aid Palestinians in the fighting that led to the 1948 creation of Israel, and they protested in Cairo to draw attention to their opposition to the Jewish settler movement and the loss of traditionally Arab lands. As fighting progressed, and government officials became less and less tolerant toward groups aligning along lines of race, ethnicity, and religion, visible signs for resisting modernity erupted along militant lines. Coup attempts have been staged, assassinations have been carried out, and the level of fighting and insurrection has increased

throughout the decades. The 1990s finally brought the fighting to a new political level with the continued and deliberate attacks against tourists in the area. Tourists became marks for attacks because tour groups provide large targets, and the presence of Westerners against the backdrop of the fear of losing Arab lands and lifestyles provides platforms for expression.

PRIMARY SOURCE

Two suspected Muslim militants attacked an Egyptian tourist bus with automatic gunfire Wednesday, killing a British woman and wounding two British tourists and the Egyptian driver, security sources and news reports said.

Witnesses reported that two masked gunmen firing automatic weapons attacked a bus operated by South Sinai Travel Agency as it passed near the town of Dairout, located 175 miles south of Cairo near some of Egypt's Pharaonic antiquities along the Nile river.

The bus was carrying six British, two Australian and one Portuguese tourist. The gunfire critically wounded Sharon Hill, 28, who died after being rushed to the Dairout General Hospital.

Since March, Dairout and surrounding areas in the governorate of Assiut, have been the scene of frequent violence by Muslim extremists and a relentless campaign against them by the government security forces.

More than 70 people have been killed and many others wounded in violence involving Muslim fundamentalists. The militants want to create a theocracy in Egypt. They have targeted government security forces, Coptic Christians and fellow Muslims opposed to their goals.

More recently they have begun to attack tourists. Three weeks ago, masked militants fired automatic weapons at a Nile cruiser carrying 140 German tourists, wounding three of the vessel's Egyptian staff as the ship traveled 19 miles north of Cairo.

A few other largely ineffective attacks on tourists were mounted by militants in the past few months, including two on tourist buses in southern Egypt. The attack Wednesday was the first in which a foreigner was killed by suspected Muslim militants.

News reports last month said a spokesman for an Islamic group warned foreign embassies to keep their citizens out of the southern area near Luxor, site of some of the country's most famous Pharaonic temples and tombs.

The warning and other incidents created concerns among authorities and travel industry executives in a country where tourism represents one of four pillars of the economy and employs about 1 million citizens.

The concerns were all the more intense as they came at a time when Egypt was preparing to host the conference of the American Society of Travel Agents, with 54,000 delegates from around the world, making it among the largest travel fairs in the world.

Last month's ASTA conference made its slogan "Tourism, the Path to Peace," and both Egyptian President Hosni Mubarak and his minister of tourism opened the parley with messages emphasizing stability as necessary for thriving tourism industry.

SIGNIFICANCE

The terrorist attacks on October 21, 1992, coincided with a warning from Islamic extremists in September. A spokesman for Gama'a al-Islamiyyah aired a warning for tourists to stay away from the province of Qena—an area of Egypt holding some of the region's most visited temples and shrines. Then on October 1, masked gunmen opened fire on a Nile cruise ship, wounding three of the cruiser's Egyptian staff.

These terrorists attacks have occurred regularly since the 1990s, and the Egyptian government has taken numerous steps to obtain cease-fires from the Islamic groups, protect foreign tourists, and end the attacks. These attempts have not always been successful—as evidenced by the 1997 massacre of fifty-eight tourists at Luxor, Egypt. The Luxor massacre, along with the numerous other terrorist attacks on tourists, briefly curbed the Egyptian tourist industry. The industry remained in decline until 2002, but it has gradually recovered. The Egyptian government has continually refused to legally recognize the Muslim Brotherhood and many other Islamic groups as legitimate political parties for fear that their official emergence

Egyptian security policeman about to fire from a building at Luxor in 1997 as Islamic militant gunmen attacked tourists.
AP/WIDE WORLD PHOTOS

on the national scene will not stop the fighting. Rather, the government assumes that formal acknowledgment of these terrorist organizations will only give them a sense of justification for their actions.

In the wake of the terrorist attacks on the United States on September 11, 2001, and the ensuing war on terror, Egypt has increased its security and alert level. These actions derive from a need, and desire, to end the hostilities. They also stem from U.S. and Egyptian intelligence reports stating that some members of Islamic extremists groups have aligned with Osama Bin Laden, who is believed to be planning an attack on Egypt similar to the ones lodged against the United States.

FURTHER RESOURCES

Books

Hoffman, Bruce. *Inside Terrorism*. New York: Columbia University Press, 1999.

Web sites

CNN.com. "Egypt Seeks to Reassure Tourists after Terrorist Attacks." <http://www.cnn.com/TRAVEL/NEWS/9711/28/egypt.security/> (accessed June 21, 2005).

Organization) headed by Yassar Arafat and under Rabin, the Oslo Agreement was signed in September 1993. The agreement guaranteed Palestinians a five year period of self-rule while Israel withdrew from the Gaza Strip, Jericho, and later from territories in the West Bank. Rabin, Shimon Peres, and Arafat shared the 1994 Nobel Peace Prize for their agreement. Rabin's peace policy enraged some sectors of Israeli society who opposed compromise with the PLO and withdrawal from the territories. On November 4, 1995, a young Jewish student, Yigal Amir, shot and mortally wounded Rabin.

INTRODUCTION

The new global era ushered in by the end of the Cold War in 1989 and the subsequent collapse of the USSR and its empire of satellite states and strategic alliances transformed the two-nation geopolitical system—with the Soviet Union and United States constantly competing for preeminence—to a unipolar, American-led international system. In the Middle East, this quickly manifested itself with Arab states, previously supported by Soviet military and economic aid, realigning themselves with the United States and

Statement by Israeli Prime Minister Rabin on the 1994 Murders in Hebron

Speech

By: Yitzhak Rabin

Date: February 25, 1994

Source: Israeli Ministry of Foreign Affairs Archive available at: http://www.mfa.gov.il/MFA/.

About the Author: Yitzhak Rabin was born in Jerusalem on March 1, 1922. Elected as head of the Labor Party, Rabin served as Prime Minister from 1974 to 1977. As part of a national unity government, Rabin served as Minister of Defense from 1984 to 1990. In response to the First Palestinian Intifada (uprising) in 1987, Rabin directed Israeli Defense Forces (IDF) to respond "promptly and vigorously" to Palestinian assaults. In 1992 Rabin's Labour Party returned to power and he returned to act as Prime Minister. Rabin stated that reaching a peace accord with the Palestinians was a top priority of his government. Eventually Rabin entered negotiations with the PLO (Palestine Liberation

A Muslim woman walks through an Israeli checkpoint between Jerusalem and the Kalandiya refugee camp.
AP/WIDE WORLD PHOTOS

the West. So quick was this transformation that when Iraq invaded Kuwait in August 1990, former Soviet allies—such as Syria—were brought into an alliance with the West.

This realignment of U.S.-Arab relations was invariably followed by a reassessment of U.S.-Israeli relations. Previously the mainstay of U.S. strategic planning in the region, Israel had ceased to assume the same importance with the end of the Cold War—a fact heightened by the readiness of Arab states to align themselves with the West during the first Gulf War. From being a prized asset, Israel's occupation of the West Bank and Gaza proved problematic to U.S.-Arab diplomacy. This precipitated a renewed urgency for a diplomatic settlement to the seemingly unsolvable Arab-Israeli conflict.

Moves toward a solution were initiated at U.S.-Russian sponsored talks held in Madrid in October 1991 and heightened in the following year by the election of a Labor government in Israel. The new Israeli Prime Minister, Yitzhak Rabin, showed a greater readiness toward reconciliation than his hawkish predecessor, Itzhak Shamir. Talks were staged in Oslo, Norway, throughout 1993, where the Declaration of Principles (DOP) was agreed upon between the Israeli and Palestinian parties. The DOP—also known as the Oslo accords (later Oslo-A)—outlined arrangements for interim self-government, elections of a Palestinian council, and concessions in the West Bank, and was signed by Rabin and the Palestinian leader, Yasser Arafat, on the White House lawn on September 13, 1993.

The majority of Israelis were willing to give Rabin's vision for peace a chance, but the religious right was quick to frame the Oslo process in religious terms. The West Bank was presented as a sacred land and many religious leaders argued that Israeli withdrawal constituted the surrender of Jewish people's religious heritage.

For ultra-right Jewish sects, and extremist organizations, such as Kach, who favored the restoration of the biblical state of Israel, the Oslo accords were totally unacceptable. Between them, they staged a noisy campaign opposing the Oslo agreements, which sometimes teetered into violence.

Part of the Israeli right's campaign was to increase the number of Jewish settlements on occupied territory. The aims were twofold: in the short term it would bring biblical lands into Jewish hands; long term it promised to complicate any handover of territories to the Palestinians. Life in the settlements, however, was filled with danger. Most had few basic amenities, and they were often isolated from other Israeli urban communities. As such, they represented easy targets for Palestinian extremists, who attacked them regularly.

One man who apparently suffered at the hands of such attacks was the physician Baruch Kappel Goldstein. Born in Brooklyn, New York, in December 1956, Goldstein immigrated to Israel and served as a physician in the Israeli Defense Forces. He later became a member of Kach and was a West Bank settler. A friend of Goldstein's, as well as the man's son, were murdered by Palestinians in December 1993, which apparently served as a prompt for Goldstein to bring his beliefs into horrific action.

On Friday, February 25, 1994, Goldstein approached the Cave of Patriarchs, a site in the city of Hebron holy to both Muslims and Jews. Friday marked the Muslim day of prayer and around five hundred men were praying. Armed with a submachine gun, Goldstein opened fire, killing twenty-nine worshipers and injuring another hundred. He was eventually overcome by survivors and beaten to death.

A few hours after the massacre, Prime Minister Rabin issued the following statement which condemned Goldstein's act of religious terrorism.

■ PRIMARY SOURCE

STATEMENT BY PRIME MINISTER RABIN, 25 FEBRUARY 1994.

A loathsome, criminal act of murder was committed today at a site holy to both Jews and Arabs in Hebron.

The Prime Minister and Defence Minister, government ministers and citizens of the State of Israel severely condemn this terrible murder of innocent people, which occurred during Ramadan prayer services.

On behalf of the government and myself, I wish to express our sorrow over the incident and extend condolences to the families of those who were killed and to the Palestinian people, and wish a full and speedy recovery to the wounded.

We call on everyone, Arab and Jew alike, to act with restraint and to not be drawn into committing further acts which could worsen the situation.

The ministers of the political-security cabinet will be meeting this afternoon to discuss the situation in light of this terrible act.

This is a difficult day for all those, Jews and Arabs, who seek peace. However, the crazed actions of disturbed individuals will not prevent the reconciliation between the citizens of the State of Israel and the Palestinian people.

We will do everything necessary to advance the peace talks, to prevent misunderstandings, to remove obstacles in the way and to reach, together, the day of peace; the day on which extremists on both sides will lose all hope of damaging the peace process.

The IDF and security forces have been given instructions to do all they legally can to maintain public order and prevent further incidents and bloodshed.

SIGNIFICANCE

The Hebron massacre provoked repulsion on both sides of the Arab-Israeli divide. Rioting in the wake of the carnage led to the deaths of a further twenty-six Palestinians and two Israelis.

The Israeli government and most movements within Judaism publicly denounced Goldstein's actions as an act of terrorism. The Kach movement, however, though denying any knowledge of Goldstein's plans, gloried in his actions, claiming that he had prevented the mass murder of Jews by Arabs. The inscription on his tombstone reflects how his supporters regarded his actions:

"Here lies the Saint, Dr. Baruch Kappel Goldstein, blessed be the memory of this righteous and holy man, may the Lord avenge his blood, who devoted his soul to the Jews, Jewish religion, and Jewish land. His hands are innocent and his heart is pure. He was killed as a martyr of God."

Israel's government moved quickly to outlaw Kach and in 1998, the Knesset (the Israeli legislature) passed a bill forbidding the erection of monuments to terrorists. Two years later a small shrine surrounding Goldstein's tomb was demolished.

After Goldstein's murders, the Hamas movement (a group of Palestinian Islamic fundamentalists), which had previously focused its attacks against Palestinian collaborators and the Israeli army, radically switched tactics and began to copy the civilian-targeted suicide bomb attacks of Lebanon's Hezbollah. Invariably, this led to an upsurge in confrontation between the

Saja al-Jiaydi, 9, draws pictures of Israeli tanks and soldiers firing at Palestinians in 2002. AP/WIDE WORLD PHOTOS

Palestinians and Israelis, further polarizing the two camps and within them severely testing patience with the peace process.

Rabin pressed on with the Oslo process, although orthodox and nationalist organizations harshly criticized him, and each Hamas bombing made moderate sections of the Israeli population further question the value of the peace process.

The result of this conflict between the religious right and Rabin came on November 4, 1995. Leaving a peace rally in Tel Aviv, Rabin was assassinated by Yigal Amir, a devoutly religious student, acting on his conviction that Jewish law required the death of any Jew who turned over Jewish land to the enemy.

Rabin's assassination left negotiations between Israel and the Palestinians suspended. Not for another four years would serious efforts be made to resurrect them.

FURTHER RESOURCES
Books

Baram, Daphna. *Disenchantment: "The Guardian" and Israel.* London: Politico's Publishing, 2004.

Cleveland, William L. *A History of the Modern Middle East.* Boulder, CO: Westview Press, 2000.

Schulze, Kirsten E. *The Arab-Israeli Conflict.* London: Longman, 1999.

"Peres Takes Over"

"Rabin Slain after Peace Rally in Tel Aviv; Israeli Gunman Held; Says He Acted Alone"

Newspaper article

By: Serge Schmemann

Date: November 4, 1995

Source: The *New York Times*.

About the Author: Serge Schmemann began his career with the *New York Times* as a metropolitan reporter in 1980. He went on to make his mark as a Pulitzer Prize–winning foreign correspondent, serving as bureau chief in Moscow, Bonn, and Jerusalem. Returning to New York in 2001, he served as senior foreign affairs writer and chief of the United Nations bureau. In 2003, Schmemann was appointed to the editorial boards of both the *New York Times* and the *International Herald Tribune*.

INTRODUCTION

Soldier, statesman, war veteran, peacemaker— Yitzhak Rabin's life was as turbulent and storied as the land of Israel itself.

Rabin first rose to prominence in the Israeli military, commanding the Harel brigade in its defense of Jerusalem in the War for Independence. Later, as commander in chief of the Israel Defense Forces, he led Israel to victory in the 1967 Six-Day War.

In 1974, Rabin became the youngest and the first native-born prime minister in Israel's history. But it was nearly twenty years later, during his second term as prime minister, that he and Shimon Peres forged what their predecessors and the U.S. government had been unable to accomplish: a way forward through the Israeli-Palestinian conflict toward peace. In a series of secret meetings with representatives of the Palestine Liberation Organization (PLO) and Norwegian mediators, Foreign Minister Peres hammered out the key details of the agreements, concessions, and timetables that would form the basis of the Oslo Declaration of Principles.

With the signing of the Declaration of Principles in Washington, D.C., on September 13, 1993, the entire world became privy to the results of the secret negotiations. Millions of television viewers across the world were treated to the sight of Rabin shaking hands with Yasser Arafat, formally recognizing the PLO.

In the months after the agreement, extremists on both sides of the conflict did their best to halt the peace process. On February 25, 1994, an Israeli gunman opened fire inside the main mosque in Hebron, killing 29 worshipers. On April 6, a member of Hamas, a Palestinian Islamic fundamentalist organization, became the first suicide bomber to wreak destruction in Israel, killing eight Israelis. Seven days later another Hamas member followed suit, blowing himself up on a bus and killing six others.

Rabin's popularity at home plummeted as the impending concessions outlined in the Oslo Accords stirred fierce debate among the populace. The religious establishment and the Israeli right were vehemently opposed to Rabin's policies. In a series of emotional demonstrations attended by thousands, he was compared to an SS (Nazi) officer and branded a traitor. Opposition leaders Benjamin Netanyahu and Ariel Sharon used these demonstrations to their full advantage, denouncing the Rabin government's plan as absurd, characterizing them as entrusting Israeli security to Arafat.

Finally, Rabin's supporters responded by holding a mass rally in support of the government and the peace

Blood stains on lyrics of a song about peace carried by former Israeli Premier Yitzhak Rabin on the day he was assassinated in 1995. © REUVEN KASTRO/CORBIS SYGMA

process in Tel Aviv on November 4, 1995. After ending his speech and joining with the crowd to sing "The Song of Peace," Rabin left the platform and made his way to his car. As he approached the vehicle, he was shot dead by one of his own countrymen.

PRIMARY SOURCE

Jerusalem, Nov. 4 Prime Minister Yitzhak Rabin, who led Israel to victory in 1967 and began the march toward peace a generation later, was shot dead by a lone assassin this evening as he was leaving a vast rally in Tel Aviv.

Mr. Rabin, 73, was struck down by one or two bullets as he was entering his car. Police immediately seized a 27-year-old Israeli law student, Yigal Amir, who had been active in support of Israeli settlers but who told the police tonight that he had acted alone.

The police said Mr. Amir had also told them that he had tried twice before to attack the Prime Minister.

It was the first assassination of a prime minister in the 47-year history of the state of Israel, and it was certain to have extensive repercussions on Israeli politics and the future of the Arab-Israeli peace.

Mr. Rabin was to lead his Labor party in elections scheduled for November next year, and without him the prospects for a Labor victory, and of a continuation of his policies, were thrown into question.

In the immediate aftermath, Foreign Minister Shimon Peres, Mr. Rabin's partner in the peace negotiations, automatically became Acting Prime Minister. It was widely expected that he would be formally confirmed as Mr. Rabin's successor.

Mr. Rabin, who rose to national prominence as commander of the victorious Israeli army in the 1967 Six-Day War, became the second Middle Eastern leader, after President Anwar el-Sadat of Egypt, to be killed by extremists from his own side for seeking an Arab-Israeli peace. Mr. Sadat, the first Arab to make peace with Israel, was assassinated in 1984.

Mr. Rabin and his Labor Government have come under fierce attack from right-wing groups over the peace with the Palestinians, especially since the agreement transferring authority in the West Bank to the Palestine Liberation Organization was reached in September. Mr. Rabin has been heckled at many of his appearances in recent weeks and his security has been tight.

A gruff, chain-smoking career military man, Mr. Rabin led Israel both in its greatest military triumph and in one of its most dramatic bids for peace.

Shortly before his death, Mr. Rabin, obviously buoyed by the huge turnout of more than 100,000 supporters of the peace process, told the rally, "I always believed that most of the people want peace and are ready to take a risk for it."

He then joined other participants in singing the "Song of Peace," a popular paean. Unfamiliar with the words, the prime minister followed from a text he tucked into his pocket.

Hours after the shooting, Mr. Peres said the blood-soaked sheet of music was found in his pocket and stood as a symbol of Mr. Rabin's sacrifice.

Since achieving a historic peace agreement with the P.L.O. in 1993, and especially since the follow-up agreement two months ago on establishing Palestinian self-rule in much of the West Bank, Mr. Rabin had come under increasingly bitter attack from Jewish residents of West Bank settlements and right-wing opponents of the agreement.

As he walked to his car this evening, Mr. Rabin gave his last interview to a radio reporter, saying, "I always believed that the majority of the people are against violence, violence which in the recent period took a shape which damages the framework of fundamental values of Israeli democracy."

At 9:30 P.M., as he was preparing to enter his car, there were four shots. Two struck one of Mr. Rabin's bodyguards, who was reported in critical condition. One or two struck the prime minister. The Minister of Health, Ephraim Sneh, said Mr. Rabin had no heartbeat or blood pressure when he arrived at Ichilov Hospital. He was pronounced dead at 11:10 P.M.

At 11:15 P.M., the director of Mr. Rabin's office, Eytan Haber, came out before the waiting crowd at the hospital to read a brief statement: "The Government of Israel announces with shock and deep sorrow the death of the Prime Minister, Yitzhak Rabin, who was murdered by an assassin tonight in Tel Aviv."

The crowd, which only recently was singing and dancing in the streets, erupted in shouts of "No! No!"

The rally had been called by a coalition of left-wing political parties and peace groups as a response to increasingly strident street protests by the right-wing opponents of the peace agreement. More than 100,000 people turned out on Kings of Israel Square in front of Tel Aviv's city hall; organizers declared it the largest rally in the coastal city in at least a decade.

As word spread, seens [sic] of grief and fear spread through Israeli streets. In Jerusalem, women wept and stunned students gathered in groups, wondering what would happen to them and their future.

"I'm not crying for Rabin, I'm crying for Israel," one woman sobbed. About 1,000 mourners gathered outside Mr. Rabin's residence with candles, while devout Jews gathered at the Western Wall in the Old City to chant memorial prayers.

For all the passion of the debate over the peace, the notion of an assassination of an Israeli leader by an Israeli Jew was far from anybody's mind in a nation whose greatest bond has been the joint Jewish struggle for survival against hostile Arab neighbors.

Mr. Rabin's spokewoman [sic] and close aide, Aliza Goren, who was next to him when he was shot, said, "I never imagined that a Jew would murder a Jew. It's a horrible thing. If someone imagines that he can seize power through murder, then our state is simply finished."

In the immediate aftermath, the police gave no indication that the student, Mr. Amir, had any support, though some reporters received messages on their beepers from an unknown group that described itself as the "Jewish Avenging Organization" taking responsibility for the attack.

The police said that before entering the law school of Bar-Ilan University, Mr. Amir had studied in a yeshiva, a religious institution, and was a member of Eyal, an extreme right-wing group. Eyal leaders, however, denied any link to the killing.

Like many Israelis, Mr. Amir was licensed to carry a pistol. He lived in Herzliya, a northern suburb of Tel Aviv. The Israeli radio said he had confessed, and quoted him as saying: "I acted alone on God's orders and I have no regrets."

SIGNIFICANCE

Serge Schmemann, the author of the article, proved to be correct in his assessment of Labor's prospects for victory in 1996 and what that would mean for the peace process Rabin and Peres had begun. Peres would be defeated in 1996 by Benjamin Netanyahu, who ran on the slogan "Peace with Security," promising to slow down the peace process.

As prime minister, Netanyahu was true to his word. Not only was the peace process slowed, but gone also was the conciliatory attitude that Rabin and Peres had brought to the negotiations with Arafat. Instead, Netanyahu delayed the withdrawal from Hebron and the rural areas and took unilateral actions that enraged the Palestinians. Without consulting the Palestinian Authority, he opened a tunnel that ran adjacent to the

Temple Mount and emerged at the Muslim Quarter, which set off riots throughout the occupied territories in which seventy-one people were killed. He announced plans to build a new settlement in Har Homa in southern Jerusalem, a move that provoked the condemnation of the Palestinians and the Israeli left and resulted in a United Nations resolution against the construction.

Though Yigal Amir insisted that he acted alone on orders from God, conspiracy theories flourished in the aftermath of the assassination. His brother and two of his friends were ultimately convicted for failing to report his plan. Other people connected to Amir, including settlement activists and rabbis who had publicly called for the death of the prime minister, were questioned but never put on trial.

FURTHER RESOURCES

Books

Bickerton, Ian J., and Carla L. Klausner. *A Concise History of the Arab-Israeli Conflict*, 4th ed., updated. Upper Saddle River, NJ: Prentice Hall, 2005.

Gilbert, Martin. *Israel: A History*. New York: William Morrow, 1998.

Morris, Benny. *Righteous Victims: A History of the Zionist-Arab Conflict, 1881–1999*. New York: Alfred A. Knopf, 1999.

Web sites

Reuters.com. "Israeli Family of Rabin's Killer Opens Web Site." <http://www.reuters.com/newsArticle.jhtml?type=internet News&storyID=8744815> (accessed June 19, 2005).

Eulogy for Yitzhak Rabin

Israeli Prime Minister Yitzhak Rabin Assassinated

Eulogy

By: Noa Ben-Artzi Pelossof

Date: November 6, 1995

Source: Eulogy for Yitzhak Rabin, delivered by his granddaughter at his memorial service on November 6, 1995.

About the Author: Noa Ben Artzi-Pelossof delivered a passionate and heartfelt eulogy for her grandfather, Yitzhak Rabin, when she joined the world's dignitaries to speak at the funeral of the slain Israeli leader. She was not yet eighteen years old when her grandfather was assassinated. At age nineteen, she wrote the book *In the Name of Sorrow and Hope* that combined a biography of Yitzhak Rabin and an autobiography of his only granddaughter,

describing their lives in Israel, and making a strong plea for peace in the Middle East. Noa details life in war-torn Israel, including the constant fear of potential violence and the possibility of harm befalling friends and family. She writes of the horrors of random violence, political extremism, and of the long-lasting effects of wars in the Middle East (Lebanon, the Intifada, the Gulf War) and of the internal strife caused by terrorism both from outside and from within Israel.

INTRODUCTION

Yigal Amir, a law student and member of a right-wing Jewish extremist group, assassinated Israeli Prime Minister Yitzhak Rabin on the evening of November 5, 1994. The assassination occurred while Rabin was attending a peace rally intended to quell growing violence between factions of Israeli right-wing settlers and Palestinians. Rabin had intended the peace rally to affirm the dedication of the government and of the people to the creation of a lasting peace for Israel.

A blood stained barber's chair is evidence of bomb damage wrought in November 1968, in Israel. AP/WIDE WORLD PHOTOS

Although there had been many pledges by the Palestine Liberation Organization (PLO), a separatist Palestinian paramilitary group, to end acts of violence and terrorism in the months preceding the assassination, there had been increasing Palestinian aggression in the territories. This was met by agitation by Israeli right-wing and fundamentalist settlers who were opposed to the peace process. On the West Bank, some extremist Rabbis gave sermons in which they expressed the belief that Rabin was a traitor who persecuted the Jewish people. Some members of the Likud Party, political opponents to Rabin's Zionist Party, stated that Rabin's followers were traitors and terrorists. Extremist right-wing propaganda likened Rabin and his followers to Nazis.

Rabin refused to allow the threats to limit his public appearances or to diminish the energy with which he pursued the peace process. He was reported to have said that the Likud Party, which was vocally opposed to the peace process, was fomenting right-wing hatred that could lead to potential public acts of violence.

In confessing to the assassination of Yitzhak Rabin, Yigal Amir stated that he did so in order to put a halt to the Middle East peace efforts. He reported that he planned the attack on the Prime Minister well in advance and did so because Rabin wanted to "give our country to the Arabs. We need to be cold-hearted."

PRIMARY SOURCE

You will forgive me, for I do not want to talk about peace. I want to talk about my grandfather. One always wakes up from a nightmare. But since yesterday, I have only awakened to a nightmare—the nightmare of life without you, and this I cannot bear. The television does not stop showing your picture; you are so alive and tangible that I can almost touch you, but it is only "almost" because already I cannot.

Grandfather, you were the pillar of fire before the camp and now we are left as only the camp, alone, in the dark, and it is so cold and sad for us. I know we are talking in terms of a national tragedy, but how can you try to comfort an entire people or include it in your personal pain, when grandmother does not stop crying, and we are mute, feeling the enormous void that is left only by your absence.

Few truly knew you. They can still talk a lot about you, but I feel that they know nothing about the depth of the pain, the disaster and, yes, this holocaust, for—at least for us, the family and the friends, who are left only as the camp, without you—our pillar of fire.

Grandfather, you were, and still are, our hero. I want you to know that in all I have ever done, I have always

seen you before my eyes. Your esteem and love accompanied us in every step and on every path, and we lived in the light of your values. You never abandoned us, and now they have abandoned you—you, my eternal hero—cold and lonely, and I can do nothing to save you, you who are so wonderful.

People greater than I have already eulogized you, but none of them was fortunate like myself [to feel] the caress of your warm, soft hands and the warm embrace that was just for us, or your half-smiles which will always say so much, the same smile that is no more, and froze with you. I have no feelings of revenge because my pain and loss are so big, too big. The ground has slipped away from under our feet, and we are trying, somehow, to sit in this empty space that has been left behind, in the meantime, without any particular success. I am incapable of finishing, but it appears that a strange hand, a miserable person, has already finished for me. Having no choice, I part from you, a hero, and ask that you rest in peace, that you think about us and miss us, because we here—down below—love you so much. To the angels of heaven that are accompanying you now, I ask that they watch over you, that they guard you well, because you deserve such a guard. We will love you grandfather, always.

SIGNIFICANCE

Yitzhak Rabin was characterized by other world leaders as a man who died in an effort to bring peace to the nation of Israel. Rabin shared a Nobel Peace Prize with Shamon Peres and Yassir Arafat in 1994 for their joint efforts to achieve peace between the people of Israel and those of Palestine. He had pledged, as the goal of his political career, to bring an end to the religious and ethnic wars of the Middle East.

Rabin was in the process of leaving a peace rally in Tel Aviv, attended by an estimated 100,000 people, when he was killed. More than 4,000 invited dignitaries from around the world attended his memorial service. In recognition to Rabin's life mission to bring peace to the Middle East, the President of Egypt, Hosni Mubarek referred to him as "a fallen hero for peace." King Hussein of Jordan said of Rabin, "You lived as a soldier, you died as a soldier for peace." Shimon Peres, who became Acting Israeli Prime Minister upon Rabin's death, related a conversation with the former Prime Minister that took place at the peace rally immediately before the assassination: "You told me there are warnings of an assassination attempt at the large rally. We did not know who would strike. We did not imagine the harm would be so great. But we knew we must not fear death and we must not hesitate for peace."

Peres continued the peace process and attempted to negotiate a full peace accord with Syria. The talks broke down when the Arab extremist group Hamas began a wave of terrorist attacks in Israel. On April 17, 1996, Israel executed a 17-day attack on targets in Lebanon. During the bombardment, the Israeli military accidentally struck the UN base at Qana, killing over 100 civilians and UN personnel. The following day, members of the Lebanese terrorist group Hezbollah fired rockets into settlements in northern Israel.

The peace process begun by Rabin fully disintegrated as violence continued in the region. Israeli elections in 1996 ushered in the government of Prime Minister Binyamin Netanyahu, who made any further progress in the peace process contingent upon the Palestinian Authority's ability to control Arab extremist attacks in Israel. While suicide attacks were greatly reduced during Netanyahu's administration, the formal peace process stalled.

FURTHER RESOURCES

Books

Artzi-Pelossof, Noa Ben. *In The Name of Sorrow and Hope.* Schocken Trade Paperback, 1997.

Web sites

CNN World News. "Rabin's Alleged Killer Appears in Court." <http://www.cnn.com/WORLD/9511/rabin/amir/11-06/index.html> (accessed July 2, 2005).

MidEastWeb.Org. "The Last Speech of Israeli Prime Minister Yitzhak Rabin— Assassinated November 4, 1995." <http://www.mideastweb.org/rabin1995.htm> (accessed June 29, 2005).

Nobelprize.org. "Yitzhak Rabin—Biography." <http://nobelprize.org/peace/laureates/1994/rabin-bio.html> (June 29, 2005).

Spreading Good, Forbidding Evil

General Presidency of Amr Bil Marof

Government decree

By: Islamic State of Afghanistan

Date: The decree enitled "General Presidency of Amr Bil Marof, Kabul, December 1996" was part of a series of three decrees (or letters) issued by the religious police of Afghanistan's Taliban regime in December, 1996.

Source: Letter from the Cultural and Social Affairs Department of General Presidency of Islamic State of Afghanistan.

About the Author: This is an edict given by the Taliban government, which had come to power in Afghanistan in September 1996. Amr Bil Marof is a reference to Islamic fundamental Sha'ria law and roughly translates into English as "spreading good and forbidding evil."

INTRODUCTION

When the Taliban took control of Kabul at the end of September 1996, and with it Afghanistan's system of government, one of their first acts was to hang President Mohammed Najibullah and his brother in a public square. Their message to the watching world was as blunt as it was simple: no prisoners would be taken in the pursuit of the Taliban's fundamentalist beliefs.

Afghanistan's long-running war with the former Soviet Union (USSR) from 1979 to 1989 had bred a state of religious foment within the country. Comprised of a patchwork of ethnicities and minorities, a state of national unity had never really arrived in Afghanistan. Instead, the country's main unifying force was a common adherence to Islam. The resistance force, the Mujahideen, exploited this adherence, building up a patchwork of forces under local warlords to stage a highly effective guerilla war against the Soviets. These freedom fighters were trained, armed, and financed by successive U.S. administrations.

Following the withdrawal of Soviet forces in 1989, the Soviet-backed government soon lost ground to the Mujahideen, and, in April 1992, Kabul fell to its forces. Mujahideen rule soon slipped into anarchy as rival factions fell out with each other and Afghanistan moved into a state of civil war, with local warlords competing with each other on a regional basis.

This weakened state allowed the Taliban (whose name literally translates as "religious students") to step in. During both the Soviet occupation and civil war, the Taliban were organized as part of the Mujahideen but did not rise to pre-eminence until a group of well-trained Taliban members were chosen by Pakistan to protect convoys trying to open trade routes from Pakistan into Central Asia.

Under the leadership of Mullah Mohammed Omar, the Taliban promised order by adopting a strict interpretation of Sha'ria (Islamic law). Not only was this set of laws notoriously severe, but also were an incentive to others to conform. Enforcement was often carried out in public. Public executions and other punishments, such as floggings, became regular events at Afghan soccer stadiums. Sports and even

Taliban fighters greet each other in Kabul where the bodies of former Afghanistan President Najibullah and his brother Shahpur Ahmedzai hang. AP/WIDE WORLD PHOTOS

childrens' diversions, such as kite flying, were outlawed, as were television viewing and music listening. Men were not to shave or cut their beards, and women were to stay at home or to wear a burqa (a long, loose-fitting garment that covers the face and body) if they ventured outside.

The military gains made by the Taliban were considerable. Starting with the capture of Kandahar in November 1994, they went on to take Herat a year later and Jelalabad and Kabul in September 1996.

◼ PRIMARY SOURCE

[*Editor's note:* Wa Nai Az Munkir *refers to the Taliban religious "police."*]

Letter from the Cultural and Social Affairs Department of General Presidency of Islamic State of Afghanistan states that:

ISLAMIC STATE OF AFGHANISTAN

1. Notice of Department for enforcement of right Islamic way and prevention of evils: The Department for enforcement of right Islamic way and prevention of evils for the implementation of legal Islamic orders and prophet Mohammad tradition in order to prevent evils which cause serious dangers and problems for Islamic society requests from all pious sisters and brothers to seriously follow articles mentioned below to prevent occurrence of evils:

1a. No exit and traveling of sisters without escort of legal close relative.

1b. Those sisters are coming out of their homes with legal escort should use burqa or similar things to cover the face.

1c. Sitting of sisters in the front seat of cart and vehicle without legal relative is forbidden. In the case of appearance serious measures will be carried out against the vehicle and cart rider/driver.

1d. Shopkeepers do not have right to buy or sell things with those women without covered face, otherwise the shopkeeper is guilty and has no right to complain.

1e. Cars are strictly forbidden to be covered with flowers for wedding ceremony and also is not allowed to drive around the city.

1f. Women's invitations in hotels and wedding party in hotels are forbidden.

1g. Sisters without legal close relative with them cannot use taxis, otherwise the taxi driver is responsible.

1h. The person who is in charge of collecting fares (money) for sisters in buses, minibuses and jeeps should be under 10 years old.

The professional delegates of this department are in charge to punish violators according to Islamic principles.

2. Rules of work for the State hospitals and private clinics based on Sharia principles:

2a. Female patients should go to female physicians. In case a male physician is needed, the female patient should be accompanied by her close relatives.

2b. During examination, the female patients and male physicians both should be dressed with Islamic hejab.

2c. Male physicians should not touch or see the other parts of female patients except the affected part.

2d. Waiting rooms for female patients should be safely covered.

2e. The person who regulates turns for female patients should be a female.

2f. During night duty, in the rooms where female patients are hospitalized, a male doctor without the call of patient is not allowed to enter the room.

2g. Sitting and speaking between male and female doctors is not allowed. If there be need for discussion, it should be done with hejab.

2h. Female doctors should wear simple clothes, they are not allowed to wear stylish clothes or use cosmetics and makeup.

2i. Female doctors and nurses are not allowed to enter the rooms where male patients are hospitalized.

2j. Hospital staff should pray in the mosque on time. The director of hospital is bound to assign a place and appoint a priest (mullah) for prayer.

2k. Staff of *Amri Bel Maroof Wa Nai Az Munkar* are allowed to go for control at any time and nobody can prevent them. Anybody who violates the order will be punished as per Islamic regulations.

3. Letter from the Cultural and Social Affairs Department of General Presidency of Islamic State of Afghanistan No. 6240 dated 26.09.1375 states: The role and regulation of Amr Bil Marof Wa Nai Az Munkir is to be distributed via your office to all whom it may concern for implementation.

3a. To prevent sedition and uncovered females (be hejab): No drivers are allowed to pick up females who are using Iranian burqa. In the case of violation the driver will be imprisoned. If such kinds of female are observed in the street, their houses will be found and their husbands punished. If the women use stimulating and attractive cloth and there is no close male relative with them, the drivers should not pick them up.

3b. To prevent music: To be broadcasted by the public information resources. In shops, hotels, vehicles and rickshaws cassettes and music are prohibited. This matter should be monitored within five days. If any music cassette is found in a shop, the shopkeeper should be imprisoned and the shop locked. If five people guarantee, the shop could be opened and the criminal released later. If a cassette is found in a vehicle, the vehicle and the driver will be imprisoned. If five people guarantee, the vehicle will be released and the criminal released later.

3c. To prevent beard shaving and its cutting: To be broadcasted by the public information resources. After one and a half months if any one is observed who has shaved and/or cut his beard, he should be arrested and imprisoned until his beard gets bushy.

3d. To prevent not praying and order gathering prayer at the bazaar: To be broadcasted by the public information resources that the prayers should be done on their due times in all districts. The exact prayer time will be announced by the *Amr Bil Marof Wa Nai Az Munkir* department. Fifteen minutes prior to prayer time the front of the mosque, where the water facilities and possibilities are available, should be blocked and transportation should be strictly prohibited and all people are obliged to go to the mosque. At the prayer time this matter should be monitored. If young people are seen in the shops they will be immediately imprisoned. If five people guarantee, the person should be released, otherwise the criminal will be imprisoned for ten days.

3e. To prevent keeping pigeons and playing with birds: To be broadcasted by the public information resources that within ten days this habit/hobby should stop. After ten days this matter should be monitored and the pigeons and any other playing birds should be killed.

3f. To eradicate the use of addiction and its users: Addicts should be imprisoned and investigation made to find the supplier and the shop. The shop should be locked and both criminals (the owner and the user) should be imprisoned and punished.

3g. To prevent kite flying: First should be broadcasted by the public information resources advising the people of its useless consequences such as betting, death of children and their deprivation from education. The kite shops in the city should be abolished.

3h. To prevent idolatry: To be broadcasted by the public information resources that in vehicles, shops, room, hotels and any other places pictures/portraits should be abolished. The monitors should tear up all pictures in the above places. This matter should be announced to all transport representatives. The vehicle will be stopped if any idol is found in the vehicle.

3i. To prevent gambling: In collaboration with the security police the main centers should be found and the gamblers imprisoned for one month.

3j. To prevent British and American hairstyles: To be broadcasted by the public information resources that people with long hair should be arrested and taken to the *Amr Bil Marof Wa Nai Az Munkir* department to shave their hair. The criminal has to pay the barber.

3k. To prevent interest charges on loans, charges on changing small denomination notes and charges on money orders: All money exchangers should be informed that the above three types of exchanging money are prohibited in Islam. In the case of violation the criminal will be imprisoned for a long time.

3l. To prevent washing clothes by young ladies along the water streams in the city: It should be announced in all mosques and the matter should be monitored. Violator ladies should be picked up with respectful Islamic manner, taken to their houses and their husbands severely punished.

3m. To prevent music and dances in wedding parties: To be broadcasted by the public information resources that the above two things should be prevented. In the case of violation the head of the family will be arrested and punished.

3n. To prevent the playing of music drums: First the prohibition of this action to be announced to the people. If anybody does this then the religious elders can decide about it.

3o. To prevent sewing ladies' cloth and taking female body measures by tailors: If women or fashion magazines are seen in the shop the tailor should be imprisoned.

3p. To prevent sorcery: All the related books should be burnt and the magician should be imprisoned until his repentance.

The above issues are stated and you are requested, according to your job responsibilities, to implement and inform your related organizations and units.

[Editor's note: Letter (2) regarding public health carried the name and authority of Amirul-Mominin, Mullah; Mohammad Omer, Mujahed; and Mofti Mohammad Masoom, Afghani Acting Minister of Public Health. Letter (3) carried the name Mawlavi Enayatullah Baligh, Deputy Minister, General Presidency of Amr Bil Marof Wa Nai Az Munkir. The letter was dated 26.09.1375, a date according to the Hijri calendar (Muslim calendar) equivalent to 1996–1997. The Hijri is a strictly lunar calendar having twelve lunar months in a year of only 354 days (11.25 days short of the solar calendar year). For this reason Islamic holidays vary from year to year and exact equivalent dates to the Gregorian solar-based calendar are difficult and arrived at by algorithms that can vary even according to the Islamic authority issuing the date.]

SIGNIFICANCE

Even before the September 11, 2001, attacks, in which they were heavily implicated, the Taliban was officially recognized by only three countries. Two of them cut diplomatic links immediately after the 2001 attacks on the United States. Pakistan, the only country to initially keep diplomatic relations with Afghanistan, dropped them when it joined international efforts to defeat terrorism after the 2001 attacks on the World Trade Center in New York and the Pentagon in Washington, D.C.

The Taliban sheltered Osama Bin Laden and his al-Qaeda movement from 1998; they also harbored other extremist groups that struck out into Kashmir, the Fergana Valley (where Uzbekistan, Kurdistan, and Tajikistan meet), and parts of China. The Taliban destabilized their surrounding region by allowing their territory to become a base for the worldwide export of terrorism.

In the late 1990s and at the turn of the century, Afghanistan was best known in the West for the Taliban's fundamentalist ideology. The Taliban denied women the opportunity to pursue an education or receive health care. The international community also condemned the brutality of the Taliban's secret religious police forces and their actions against Afghan citizens.

Al-Qaeda's terrorist attacks on New York and Washington, D.C. in 2001 evoked an immediate response. The United States and its allies ordered the Taliban to hand over Osama Bin Laden, the al-Qaeda leader whom the Taliban had been harboring for three years, or face dire consequences.

Some 1,000 of Afghanistan's most senior clerics gathered in a conclave in the capital Kabul and ruled that America's most wanted man should be asked to leave the country. More ambiguously, however, they also added that any United States-led attack aimed at extracting him by force or punishing Afghanistan for harboring him would result in a declaration of holy war. Bin Laden remained in Afghanistan.

On October 7, 2001, the United States invaded Afghanistan. The war itself lasted barely two months, and Kabul fell within five weeks. President Hamid Karzai was installed, later overseeing democratic elections that saw his position confirmed. However, Osama Bin Laden remained free.

FURTHER RESOURCES

Books

Rashid, Ahmad. *Taliban. The Story of the Afghan Warlords.* Appendix l. London: Pan Books, 1971.

Marsden, Peter. *The Taliban: War, Religion and the New Order in Afghanistan.* Oxford: Oxford University Press, 1971.

Yasgur, Batya Swift. *Behind the Burqa: Our Life in Afghanistan and How We Escaped to Freedom.* Wiley, 2002.

"Aum Shinrikyo: Once and Future Threat?"

Cultists as terrorists: Aum Shinrikyo

Journal article

By: Kyle B. Olson

Date: July-August, 1999

Source: "Aum Shinrikyo: Once and Future Threat?", as published in the journal *Emerging Infectious Diseases*, (1999): Vol. 5, No. 4.

About the Author: Kyle B. Olson is adviser, consultant, and writer on high-technology terrorism, the threat of chemical and biological weapons, and the practical challenges of arms control. He is a member of the Central Intelligence Agency's Nonproliferation Advisory Panel, guest lecturer on chemical and biological weapons terrorism at the Defense Nuclear Weapons School, Air War College, Naval War College, and U.S. Air Force Special Operations School, and an adjunct faculty member at George Washington University.

INTRODUCTION

The offensive use of poisonous gas is historically rooted in warfare. However, in the latter half of the twentieth century, poisonous gas has also become a weapon of terrorists.

On March 20, 1995, a cult, then dubbed Aum Shinrikyo, released sarin gas in the Tokyo subway system. The cult still operates, but has been re-named Aleph. Twelve people died and approximately five thousand people were left with permanent health problems as a result of the attack.

The name Aum Shinrikyo was derived from the Buddhist meditative mantra "om" followed by the Japanese word that translates as "supreme truth." The cult believed that the prophesized millennial apocalyptic end of world was at hand and that Aum followers were among those who would be chosen to survive and experience the glorious post-apocalypse re-birth of mankind.

The cult's messages, and in particular its charismatic leader, Asahara Shoko, attracted many devotees, including some highly educated scientists. At the time of the sarin attack, the cult had over four thousand members.

Among the members were an inner cadre who, unknown to the general membership, were commissioned to plan and execute the sarin attacks. Five attack teams consisted of one person who released the gas and another who served as the get-away driver.

The cult's weapon of choice was sarin gas. The compound, which can also exist in liquid form, was developed by German scientists during the 1930s. Sarin is a highly potent nerve agent that blocks transmission of impulses between nerve cells. In liquid form, a drop of fluid adsorbed through the skin is sufficient to kill an adult. Inhalation of a small amount of sarin vapor can achieve the same lethal outcome.

On Monday, March 20, 1995, the teams were deployed to different stations along the Tokyo subway system. One team member entered a subway car carrying plastic bags that together contained approximately one liter of liquid sarin. At a pre-determined stop and at almost the same time, the bags were dropped and punctured with the sharpened tip of an umbrella carried by each person. The assailant then escaped from the subway cars and met the other team member who was in a vehicle parked on the surface. The liquid sarin volatized to a gas and dissipated throughout the subway cars.

The five attacks were carried out simultaneously at the height of the morning rush hour, when thousands of commuters were riding on the subway. Within forty-eight hours of the coordinated attacks, police raided various Aum Shinrikyo facilities throughout Japan. One raid discovered a chemical weapons production plant that was capable of producing thousands of kilograms of liquid sarin annually.

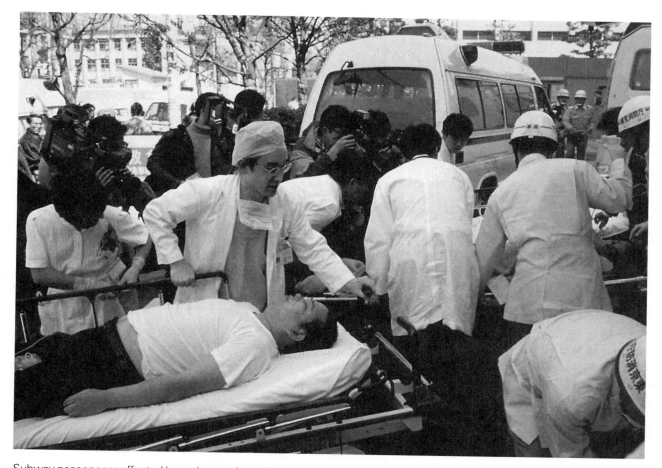

Subway passengers affected by sarin gas planted in central Tokyo subways are carried into St. Luke's International Hospital in Tokyo March 20, 1995. AP/WIDE WORLD PHOTOS

PRIMARY SOURCE

On March 20, 1995, members of the Aum Shinrikyo cult entered the Tokyo subway system and released sarin, a deadly nerve agent. The subway attack was the most deadly assault in an ongoing campaign of terror waged by this mysterious cult. Four years later, with Aum Shinrikyo attempting to rebuild itself, many in Japan and around the world are asking whether the "Supreme Truth Sect" poses a current or future threat. Answering this question may further our understanding, not only of the Aum but also of other extremist and terrorist groups.

Aum Shinrikyo began its public campaign of terror on June 27, 1994. On that Monday in Matsumoto, a city of 300,000 population, 322 kilometers northwest of Tokyo, a group of cult members drove a converted refrigerator truck into a nondescript residential neighborhood. Parking in a secluded parking lot behind a stand of trees, they activated a computer-controlled system to release a cloud of sarin. The nerve agent floated toward a cluster of private homes, a mid-rise apartment building, town homes, and a small dormitory.

This neighborhood was targeted for a specific reason. The dormitory was the residence of all three judges sitting on a panel hearing a lawsuit over a real-estate dispute in which Aum Shinrikyo was the defendant. Cult lawyers had advised the sect's leadership that the decision was likely to go against them. Unwilling to accept a costly reversal, Aum responded by sending a team to Matsumoto to guarantee that the judges did not hand down an adverse judgment. A light breeze (3 to 5 knots) gently pushed the deadly aerosol cloud of sarin into a courtyard formed by the buildings. The deadly agent affected the inhabitants of many of the buildings, entering through windows and doorways, left open to the warm night air. Within a short time, seven people were dead. Five hundred others were transported to local hospitals, where approximately 200 would require at least one night's hospitalization.

After successfully completing their mission, the cultists drove off to Kamakuishki, a rural community at the foot of Mount Fuji, home to golf courses, parks, dairy farms, small villages, and the headquarters of Aum Shinrikyo in

Japan. The cult's facilities consisted of a number of motley buildings, factories, and dormitories.

Aum Shinrikyo's next major act of violence would serve as a wake-up call to the world regarding the prospects of weapons of mass destruction and terrorism. On the morning of March 20, 1995, packages were placed on five different trains in the Tokyo subway system. The packages consisted of plastic bags filled with a chemical mix and wrapped inside newspapers. Once placed on the floor of the subway car, each bag was punctured with a sharpened umbrella tip, and the material was allowed to spill onto the floor of the subway car. As the liquid spread out and evaporated, vaporous agent spread throughout the car.

Tokyo was experiencing a coordinated, simultaneous, multi-point assault. The attack was carried out at virtually the same moment at five different locations in the world's largest city: five trains, many kilometers apart, all converging on the center of Tokyo. The resulting deaths and injuries were spread throughout central Tokyo. First reports came from the inner suburbs and then, very quickly, cries for help began to flow in from one station after another, forming a rapidly tightening ring around the station at Kasumagaseki. This station serves the buildings that house most of the key agencies of the Japanese government. Most of the major ministries, as well as the national police agency, have their headquarters at Kasumagaseki.

By the end of that day, 15 subway stations in the world's busiest subway system had been affected. Of these, stations along the Hbiya line were the most heavily affected, some with as many as 300 to 400 persons involved. The number injured in the attacks was just under 3,800. Of those, nearly 1,000 actually required hospitalization—some for no more than a few hours, some for many days. A very few are still hospitalized. And 12 people were dead.

Within 48 hours of the subway attack, police were carrying out raids against Aum Shinrikyo facilities throughout Japan. Police entered cult facilities carrying sophisticated detection systems and wearing military-issued chemical gear (which was issued to the Tokyo police the week before the subway attack).

The real target of the raids that began on March 17 was the building known as Satyan 7, a supposed shrine to the Hindu god Shiva, the most prominent figure in the Aum Shinrikyo religious pantheon. In reality, the building housed a moderately large-scale chemical weapons production facility, designed by cult engineers, with first-rate equipment purchased over-the-counter.

Although the facility's design was crude by industry standards, it was nonetheless very capable of producing the sarin used in the Matsumoto attack. At the time of the Tokyo attack, however, Satyan 7 was not in service, having been mothballed after an accident during the previous summer. In an effort to get the plant back into production, the cult had, during the fall of 1994, unsuccessfully attempted to recruit Russian chemical-weapons engineers. The cult was adept at recruiting educated professionals (scientists and engineers), but most were young and largely inexperienced. Satyan 7 was designed to produce sarin, not on a small terrorist scale, but in nearly battlefield quantities: thousands of kilograms a year.

Chemical weapons were not, however, the only option available to the Aum. The first cult laboratory for toxin production was actually in place by 1990 and was subsequently replaced with two new laboratories, one at Kamakuishki and the other in Tokyo. Aum dabbled in many different biological agents. They cultured and experimented with botulin toxin, anthrax, cholera, and Q fever. In 1993, Ashahara led a group of 16 cult doctors and nurses to Zaire, on a supposed medical mission. The actual purpose of the trip to Central Africa was to learn as much as possible about and, ideally, to bring back samples of Ebola virus. In early 1994, cult doctors were quoted on Russian radio as discussing the possibility of using Ebola as a biological weapon.

The cult's operations were worldwide, promoting a theology drawn from different sources, including Buddhism, Christianity, Shamanism, Hinduism, and New Age beliefs. Cult membership around the world was likely 20,000 to 40,000. One cult leader estimated the cult's net worth in March of 1995 at about $1.5 billion. The money was collected through donations, tithing, sales of religious paraphernalia, videotape and book sales, and other sources. The cult conducted seminars and hosted training courses for members, offering indoctrination in Aum's teachings, charging believers from hundreds to tens of thousands of dollars for attending these sessions. Aum Shinrikyo also had a number of commercial enterprises, even a company that manufactured computers.

Imported components from Taiwan were assembled in a cult factory at Kamakuishki and sold in Aum's computer store in downtown Tokyo. The cult also ran a chain of restaurants in Tokyo and several other Japanese cities.

Another source of income was the practice of green mail. Aum would threaten to establish a cult compound in a city and, if the city fathers did not bribe them to go away, the cult would set up shop. Several cities paid rather than have Aum establish operations there. The cult manufactured illegal drugs and had a marketing agreement with the Japanese Mafia (the Yakuza). In 1996, the Yakuza would be found responsible for the assassination of the cult's lead scientist, Hideo Murai, in the days following the Tokyo subway attack. Concerned at his frequent televised appearances, the Yakuza silenced him for fear that he would betray the linkage between the two shadowy groups. Extortion, theft, and murder were also part of the cult's fund-raising activities. Among the cult leaders,

"Doomsday guru" Shoko Ashahara is the undisputed head. Ashahara (born Chizuo Matsumoto) had numerous exalted titles, including venerated master, yogi, and holy pope. Highly charismatic, this partially blind, apparently very talented yoga instructor was very ambitious politically and financially. He and more than 20 of his followers ran for Parliament in 1989. They were defeated, which some Japanese analysts have suggested marks the moment when the cult's leader elected to pursue weapons of mass destruction and the violent overthrow of the established order.

Millennial visions and apocalyptic scenarios dominate the group's doctrine, evidenced by the prominent role of Nostradamus as a prophet in Aum Shinrikyo teaching. Ashahara has, on many occasions, claimed to be the reincarnated Jesus Christ, as well as the first "enlightened one" since the Buddha. He has frequently preached about a coming Armageddon, which he describes as a global conflict that would, among other things, destroy Japan with nuclear, biological, and chemical weapons. According to Ashahara, only the followers of Aum Shinrikyo will survive this conflagration.

Another cult leader, Fumihiro Joyu, now 35 years old, was a bright young engineer with the Japanese space program, specializing in artificial intelligence. He left that organization to go to work for Aum, where he very quickly rose through the ranks, ultimately to head the cult's operations in Russia. Joyu oversaw this important cult expansion, among other things "investing" as much as $12 million in the form of payoffs to well-placed officials. The cult's investment paid off with expedited access to office buildings, dormitories, and other facilities throughout Russia. At the time of the Tokyo subway attack, the cult's principle venture in Russia was the Moscow-Japan University, with headquarters in offices across the street from the Bolshoi Ballet. Their senior Russian partner in the university was a man by the name of Oleg Lobov, at that time also chairman of Russia's National Security Council and a close confidant of Boris Yeltsin.

Joyu was convicted of perjury after the subway investigation, but he received an extremely light sentence (3 years) for his involvement in the cult's activities. Joyu has apparently maintained close ties to the cult, and he is slated for release toward the end of this year. After leaving prison, he may make a play for leadership of the remaining cult elements. He is the most charismatic member of the cult, other than Ashahara. In the days right after the Tokyo subway attack, he was on Japanese television so frequently, and featured in magazines and newspapers so often, that he became a teen heartthrob.

In the days and weeks immediately following the gas attack, more than 200 key members of the cult were arrested. Approximately 120 are still in jail, on trial, or have been convicted. Ashahara himself has been on trial for 3 years. The trial may continue for 5 or 6 years, a judicial timetable that is aggressive by Japanese standards in cases where the defendant refuses to cooperate with the prosecution. Three cult members involved in the attack are still at large. Russian operations were ended by legal action and the assets seized by the government. The cult's legal status in Japan as a church has been revoked, but many of its assets are unaccounted for.

Today, Aum Shinrikyo is once again soliciting donations, collecting tithes, selling materials to members, holding seminars, conducting training, and selling computers. Active recruiting is under way. Aum Shinrikyo is holding 50 "educational" seminars a month for current and potential members. The cult has offices throughout Japan, around Tokyo and other cities, and, according to Japanese sources, they maintain 100 hide-outs throughout that country as "safe houses." These sources estimate that at least 700 members are live-in, fully committed devotees. Mind control is still a part of the cult's package. Cult members can be seen in Aum-owned houses wearing bizarre electric headsets, supposedly designed to synchronize their brain waves with those of the cult's leader.

What is the message that these events impart to policy-makers? The objective of the Tokyo subway attack was not irrational. The objective that day was to kill as many policemen as possible; Aum Shinrikyo had become aware of police plans to conduct raids against cult facilities, beginning on March 20. The cult's timetable could not permit that interruption.

Aum's actions were perfectly logical within the context of their value system. They were a self-legitimized group that had rejected and, ultimately, felt obliged to confront society. Outnumbered as they were by Japanese police and military might, one can argue that developing and even using an asymmetric capability was a logical consequence of their situation. Unable to achieve their objective—political power—through legitimate means, they determined that a preemptive strike was necessary.

Is Aum Shinrikyo a potential threat? Is Shoko Ashahara just the first of many, or has he been relegated to the scrap heap? These are open questions we will be forced to grapple with for many years to come.

SIGNIFICANCE

The Aum Shinrikyo sarin gas attack served as a wake-up call to governments, law enforcement agencies and the general public. The attack demonstrated how devastating an attack using commercially available materials could be. The attacks were well-organized and were carried out with precision.

The ease with which the gas attacks were carried also exposed the difficulty authorities experience in attempting to stop an individual or group with sufficient zeal for their cause. In contrast to conventional arms, which can be difficult to conceal, toxin gas can be hidden until the moment of deployment. Only minute quantities of a poison like sarin are needed to kill and a small amount is easy to carry to the scene of an attack.

In the years since the sarin gas attacks, thirteen cult members have been sentenced to death for their roles in the 1995 attack on the Tokyo subways.

FURTHER RESOURCES

Books

Kimura, Rei. *Aum Shinrikyo: Japan's Unholy Sect*. Charleston: Booksurge LLC, 2002.

Murakami, Haruki. *Underground: The Tokyo Gas Attack and the Japanese Psyche*. New York: Random House, 2000.

Web sites

BBC news. "Sarin attack remembered in Tokyo." <http://news.bbc.co.uk/2/hi/asia-pacific/4365417.stm> (accessed April 21, 2005).

Japan-101. "Sarin gas attack on the Tokyo subway." <http://www.japan-101.com/culture/sarin_gas_attack_on_the_tokyo_su.htm> (accessed April 21, 2005).

"Political Execution of a Woman"

Life under the Taliban

Video still

By: The Associated Press/Revolutionary Association of the Women of Afghanistan

Date: November 17, 1999

Source: Available from the Revolutionary Association of the Women of Afghanistan, <http://www.rawa.org/murder-w.htm>.

About the Author: The Revolutionary Association of the Women of Afghanistan (RAWA), was established in Kabul, Afghanistan, in 1977, as an independent political and social organization of Afghan women fighting for human rights and for social justice in Afghanistan.

INTRODUCTION

The Taliban (derived from the Pashtun/Persian word *talib*, meaning "student of Islam" or "student of the book," referring to the *Koran*) is the name of the Islamist regime that ruled most of Afghanistan from 1996 to 2001. The Taliban rose to power in the wake of the collapse of the Soviet Union–backed Democratic Republic of Afghanistan in 1992. In the resulting power vacuum, numerous mujahideen (Islamic guerrilla fighter) warlords competed for money, power, and influence, and the nation devolved into civil war. The Taliban, led by Mullah Mohammed Omar, emerged from the chaos as an effective fighting force, and many villages sought out Taliban fighters to protect them from competing warlords.

In 1994, Omar fled to neighboring Pakistan, but, later that year, he returned with a force of some 1,500 militia armed by the Pakistanis and with arms previously supplied to the mujahideen by the United States. Over the next two years, through both military and diplomatic victories, the Taliban gained control of most of the country, including the capital city, Kabul. In 1997, Saudi Arabia and Pakistan recognized the Taliban as the legitimate government of Afghanistan.

Life under the Taliban regime, which enforced strict adherence to Islamic law, was oppressive. The list of items or activities banned by the Taliban was extensive: cameras, televisions, radios, VCRs, movies, the Internet, all of which Taliban authorities assumed could be used to promote non-Muslim ideas. Even kite flying was banned because it was a Buddhist practice. In March 2001, the regime ordered the destruction of two massive Buddhist statues carved into the cliff sides at Bamiyan. These statues, one 1,800 and the other 1,500 years old, were part of the nation's cultural heritage, and their destruction was condemned internationally.

The position of women under the Taliban was particularly precarious. Women were required to be completely covered in public and were physically punished for exposing their faces or wearing see-through socks or sandals. Their shoes could not click when they walked, lest the sound excite men. They could have their fingertips amputated if they wore nail polish, and they could be whipped for wearing white shoes. They were not allowed to work outside the home (except in women's hospitals), attend school, or appear on television or in any kind of photograph. Women who lived in houses facing the street had to paint over the windows so that no one could see inside.

The Taliban regime was brutal in its exaction of justice. Men could be jailed for wearing beards that were not long enough. The hands of thieves were amputated. Many executions were conducted publicly, usually in sports stadiums; robbers had their throats slit, prostitutes and murderers were shot (the latter by the victim's family, sometimes by the victim's small children), and women adulterers were stoned to death.

The following still from a video shows the public execution of a woman, known only as Zarmeena, who was found guilty of killing her husband after enduring domestic violence. It was the first public execution in Afghanistan under the Taliban.

PRIMARY SOURCE

"POLITICAL EXECUTION OF A WOMAN"
See primary source image.

SIGNIFICANCE

Zarmeena was a 35-year-old woman, the mother of several children. At age 16, she entered an arranged marriage. Her husband was a police officer He allegedly subjected his wife to nightly beatings. She conspired with one of her daughters to kill him; the daughter actually delivered the fatal blow to her father. After Zarmeena's arrest, she was reportedly taken to an unsanitary jail cell where she was beaten with steel chains for two days before she confessed.

On November 16, 1999, Zarmeena was led into Kabul's Olympic Stadium. The Taliban had announced in advance that the execution would take place. Before up to 30,000 spectators, including Zarmeena's children, she was shot three times in the head. A video of the execution was taken with a camera smuggled into the stadium by the Revolutionary Association of the Women of Afghanistan (RAWA) and eventually broadcast in the United Kingdom as part of a documentary film titled *Beneath the Veil*.

After the August 7, 1998, bombings of U.S. embassies in East Africa, the international community more closely scrutinized Taliban rule in Afghanistan. United States intelligence services identified numerous terrorist training camps, including those run by

PRIMARY SOURCE

"Political Execution of a Woman" A woman, Zarmeena, is executed by the Taliban in front of a large crowd at a soccer stadium in Afghanistan for killing her husband. © RAWA/WPN

Osama Bin Laden and his al-Qaeda network, located within Afghanistan. On August 20, 1998, President Bill Clinton ordered cruise missile bombings of four of those training sites.

After the September 11, 2001, terrorist attacks, the United States, convinced that the Taliban was giving safe harbor to Bin Laden and al-Qaeda, led a coalition that invaded Afghanistan later that year. The Taliban was routed, and in October 2004, the nation elected a president. Parliamentary elections were scheduled for September 2005.

FURTHER RESOURCES

Books

Latifa. *My Forbidden Face: Growing Up under the Taliban: A Young Woman's Story*. New York: Miramax Books, 2003.

Audio and Visual Media

Rashid, Ahmed, and Nadia May. *Taliban: Library Edition* (MP3 CD). Blackstone Audiobooks, 2002 .

"Pak Floats Yet Another Militant Outfit"

Formation of Islamic Extremist Group
Jaish-e-Mohammed (JeM)

Newspaper article

By: Dwarika Prasad Sharma

Date: September 9, 2000

Source: *The Times of India*

About the Author: At the time the primary source article was written, Dwarika Prasad Sharma worked as a writer for *The Times of India*.

INTRODUCTION

The Jaish-e-Mohammed (JeM, or Army of Mohammed) was formed in Pakistan during January-February 2000 by Maulana Masood Azhar. The former leader of the extremist group, Harkat ul-Ansar (HuA), Azhar, was earlier released from prison by the Indian government on December 31, 1999, after hijackers demanded his exchange for 155 Indian Airlines hostages. Azhar is believed to have received assistance in setting up the JeM from the Inter-Services Intelligence (ISI) in Pakistan, the Taliban network in Afghanistan, and Osama Bin Laden.

Also known as Khuddam-ul-Islam and Tehrik ul-Furqaan, JeM is an Islamic extremist group whose

stated goals are to unite the disputed territory of Kashmir (located in the northern portion of the Indian subcontinent) with Pakistan, to unite the various Kashmiri extremist militant groups, and to fight and ultimately destroy India and the United States.

Most of the personnel and materials used by the JeM are supplied by the militant groups Harakat ul-Jihad-I-Islami (HuJi) and the Harakat ul-Majahidin (HuM). The JeM remains closely tied to Osama Bin Laden's al-Qaeda network, and is a member of Bin Laden's International Islamic Front for Jihad against Jews and Crusaders (IIF).

Some of the terrorist acts attributed to JeM include the suicide bombing at a local army headquarters at Badami Bagh in Srinagar, India, on April 23, 2000; the rocket-grenade attack into the office of the chief minister in Srinagar in July 2000, where four persons, but not the chief minister, were injured; the rifle-grenade attack on the Jammu and Kashmir Secretariat building in Srinagar on June 28, 2001; the car-bomb attack on the Jammu and Kashmir State Legislative Assembly complex at Srinagar on October 1, 2001, in which at least twenty-eight people were killed; and the attack on India's Parliament in New Delhi on December 12, 2001, in which nine employees were killed and eighteen others injured.

Other incidents that have gained international attention, to which members of the JEM were linked by authorities include the kidnapping (January 23, 2002) and later decapitation killing of *Wall Street Journal* reporter Daniel Pearl in Karachi, Pakistan, along with several assassination attempts against Pakistani President Pervez Musharraf in December 2003.

■ PRIMARY SOURCE

The Pakistani penchant for sponsoring new militant outfits so that any particular outfit does not get too big to be kept "under the thumb" was evident yet again when it recently floated the Jammu and Kashmir Liberation Army (JKLA) and helped infiltrate the first of its trained members into Poonch and Rajouri districts, to begin with.

The security agencies believe that the JKLA was formed after the Hizb, the major militant group in the state, declared a ceasefire on July 24 (which it, however, withdrew on August 8). The group was floated when there were also reports that the Pakistani Army, which is now directly controlling the ISI operations and consequently, of the militants, decided to give the blue-eyed treatment to Masood Azhar's Jaish-e-Mohammed to cut Hizb to size.

Last year, the ISI had gone about reviving the JKLA in Poonch and Rajouri districts in the belief that its local appeal would draw local youth to militancy. The move was to promote the Pakistani strategy to actively involve the two districts in militancy or at least attempt to project them as so by enacting violent incidents.

Though there were early reports of several youth missing from their villages, thought to have been motivated by JKLA members, the gambit did not seem to have made much progress as the Pakistanis increased the infiltration of foreign mercenaries, who now number 50 per cent of the militants operating in the two districts.

The new outfit, JKLA, considering the speed with which it was floated, has apparently been cobbled together with "floating" mercenaries and elements from other militant groups.

The Army drew its first blood on the JKLA on September 5, when it eliminated the outfit's commander for Surankot and Mendhar Tehsils of Poonch district. The card on him and the inscription on his rifle identified him as Sajjad Pakistani, from Pakistan's Gujranwala district.

It is not clear yet if JKLA members have infiltrated into other parts of the state as well, but the elimination of the commander indicates that they have started their operations in the two districts.

A security analyst said the floating of ever-new outfits did not only make for dispersal of centres of power, by which the Pakistanis presumably could maintain their stranglehold over the militants, but also served to create a crisscross pattern of militancy calculated to confuse the security forces, especially the police which attempted to keep tabs from local inputs. For example, he said, the creation of Jaish-e-Mohammed, which apart from its own cadre draws on "volunteers from other outfits, was posing an identification problem with regard to numbers and area of operation. The introduction of the JKLA is a bid for further confusion," he said and added, "By expanding the number of outfits, the Pakistanis also want to show that the insurgency is spreading."

SIGNIFICANCE

JeM is an integral part of the current struggle on the border region between India and Pakistan. It is a fight that originated when the state of Jammu and Kashmir was one of hundreds of semi-autonomous areas that in the 1930s were allowed to either join India, Pakistan, or become independent. The leader of Jammu and Kashmir, the Maharajah Hari Singh, preferred independence, but due to differences of opinion within its citizens on a course of action, nothing was decided on the day of independence. Throughout the next several decades, the people living in the region could not agree as to whether to be incorporated within

India or Pakistan, or to seek independence. When fighting broke out among factions within the region, the Maharajah asked the Indian government for help to resolve its internal strife. He eventually agreed to cede power to India in exchange for military aid.

However, the government of Pakistan continued to contest this arrangement between India and the Jammu and Kashmir. The government of India brought the issue before the United Nations Security Council initially in 1948 and several times thereafter. During the next few decades, conflicts and disputes continued over the fate of Jammu and Kashmir. Eventually, in 1972, a Line of Control was established so that India gained control of Kashmir to the east and south that included Jammu, Ladakh, and the Kashmir Valley, and Pakistan gained control of Kashmir to the north and west.

Wars over the still-disputed lands continued after 1972. Beginning in the 1980s, numerous discontented militant groups were organized, with some advocating the independence of Kashmir and others supporting its accession to Pakistan.

On January 19, 1990, the Indian government declared that it would begin ruling both areas of the Kashmir region. From then on, opposition militant groups swelled in numbers and new militant groups were formed to fight the common cause against India, and frequently, for their own particular causes. One of these major militant groups was the JeM. Under its leader Azhar, it rapidly gained membership and power.

Currently, both India and Pakistan do not favor the independence for Jammu and Kashmir. Both want the region under their own direct control. Tensions over Kashmir have mounted in recent years as India and Pakistan continue to assert their presence as nuclear powers. Both nations have conducted low-yield nuclear weapons tests in or near Kashmir.

About eighteen months after the formation of the JeM, the United States announced in October 2001 the addition of the group to the U.S. Treasury Department's Office of Foreign Asset Control (OFAC) list, primarily because of its ties with Osama Bin Laden's al-Qaeda network.

After a December 13, 2001, terrorist attack on the Indian Parliament in New Delhi, for which the JeM has been held responsible, the Indian government banned the group under the provisions of the Prevention of Terrorism Act.

FURTHER RESOURCES
Books

Ganguly, Sumit. *The Crisis in Kashmir: Portents of War, Hopes of Peace.* Cambridge: Cambridge University Press, 1999.

Hewitt, Vernon Marston. *Reclaiming the Past: The Search for Political and Cultural Unity in Contemporary Kashmir.* London: Portland Books, 1995.

Wirsing, Robert G. *India, Pakistan, and the Kashmir Dispute.* New York: St. Martin's Press, 1998.

Web sites

International Relations Center. Gershman, John. "Overview of Self-Determination Issues in Kashmir." <http://selfdetermine.irc-online.org/conflicts/kashmir_body.html> (accessed June 22, 2005).

South Asia Analysis Group. Ramon, B. "Jaishe-e-Mohammed (JeM)—A Backgrounder." <http://www.saag.org/papers4/paper332.html> (accessed June 22, 2005).

South Asia Intelligence Review. Gill, K.P.S. "Jaish-e-Mohammed Mujahideen E-Tanzeem (Army of the Prophet, Mohammed)." <http://www.satp.org/satporgtp/countries/india/states/jandk/terrorist_outfits/jaish_e_mohammad_mujahideen_e_tanzeem.htm> (accessed June 22, 2005).

6 State-Sponsored Terrorism

Introduction to State-Sponsored Terrorism

State-sponsored terrorism occurs when governments give weapons, equipment, safe harbor, training grounds, or financial support to terrorists. State-sponsorship of terrorism takes many forms. Some regimes actively recruit terrorists for certain actions, while others passively ignore the operation of terrorist networks within their borders. These regimes give aid to terrorist organizations as a means of committing covert, war-like actions against enemies. Many terror-sponsoring regimes are themselves extremist, often sponsoring terrorist groups that espouse similarly militant political or religious ideologies.

After the September 11 attacks in 2001, the United States Department of State considered eight nations—Afghanistan, Iran, Iraq, Syria, Libya, Cuba, North Korea, and Sudan—to be state sponsors of terrorism. Afghanistan was removed from the State Department list in 2002 after the fall of the Taliban. The Taliban's sponsorship of al-Qaeda—the international terrorist network who claim responsibility (either by direct or inspired action) for the attacks on New York, Washington, D.C., Madrid, and London—is addressed in the chapter on global terrorism. Iraq was removed from the list of state sponsors of terrorism in 2004 following the U.S. and U.K. led invasion to overthrow Iraqi Dictator Saddam Hussein. Terrorism related to the Iraqi insurgency is discussed in the chapter on insurgent terrorism.

In early 2005, the U.S. State Department and the Foreign Office in the U.K. acknowledged improved relations with Libya, but as of 2004, Libya remained on the U.S. list of state sponsors of terrorism. The decades-long problematic relationship between Muammar Qaddafi's regime in Libya and the United States is a central focus of this chapter. Primary sources track the Libyan regime's involvement in sponsoring attacks on U.S. interests in North Africa, the bombing of Pan Am flight 103, and Qaddafi's admission of his government's support of terrorism.

Some historians and political scientists distinguish terrorist acts perpetrated directly by a government (state terrorism) from those acts committed by an independent third-party supported by the government (state-sponsored terrorism). The editors have adopted the argument that state terrorism is the commission of violence by a government or its agents against a population with whom it is not engaged in armed conflict. State terrorism often targets ethnic, religious, and racial minority populations.

Torture, kidnapping, and murder are the most common acts of state terrorism. When such tactics are used with the aim of decimating an entire ethnic, religious, race, or cultural group, they constitute genocide. This volume reflects the argument that genocide falls within most accepted definitions of terrorism.

Two articles, both featuring primary sources from the Nazi era, illustrate the growth and escalating violence of a state terrorist regime. "Organized Will of the Nation" discusses the use of violence during the Nazi rise to power. The article "Testimony of gas-van driver Walter Burmeister" discusses the height of Nazi state terrorism during the Holocaust. Instances of genocide in Rwanda and Yugoslavia are also highlighted in the chapter.

The increasing concern in the international community about the use of weapons of mass destruction (such as chemical and biological weapons) as a means of perpetrating state terrorism is discussed further in the chapter on global terrorism.

On the Great Highway

Claims of Terrorism Spur the Spanish-American War.

Book excerpt

By: James Creelman

Date: 1901

Source: Excerpt from *On the Great Highway: The Wanderings and Adventures of a Special Correspondent*, by James Creelman (Boston: Lothrup, 1901), chapter 9, "Familiar Glimpses of Yellow Journalism."

About the Author: James Creelman was born on November 12, 1859, in Montreal, Canada, but moved to New York City in 1872. After studying both law and divinity, he decided to pursue a career in journalism and joined the staff of the *New York Herald* in 1876. He became one of the *Herald*'s most valued reporters, traveling widely, gaining interviews with elusive public figures, and often putting himself in personal danger to get adventuresome or controversial stories. In 1894, he went to work for Joseph Pulitzer at the *New York World*, then in 1897 William Randolph Hearst hired him as a special correspondent for the *New York Journal*. In this capacity he covered the Spanish-American War in 1898. He continued to write for various publications until his death on February 12, 1915.

INTRODUCTION

The Spanish-American War lasted from mid-April to mid-August in 1898 at a cost of 379 American combat deaths. Relations between the United States and Spain had been strained since mid-decade because of reports of Spanish brutality against Cuban insurgents fighting for independence and, from 1896 to 1898, the deaths of as many as 100,000 civilians among the many thousands more the Spanish had herded into fortified towns to prevent them from aiding the insurgents. The insurgents' base of operations, the so-called Cuban Junta, was the United States, and they received both material and moral support from American sympathizers.

President Grover Cleveland and his successor, William McKinley, tried to avoid war, and to that end McKinley dispatched the battleship *Maine* to Cuba on a friendly mission. The ship, however, blew up in the Havana harbor, killing 266 people, and while the explosion was accidental, many outraged Americans

Lifeboats rescue crewmen of the USS *Maine* after an explosion destroyed the battleship in 1898. AP/WIDE WORLD PHOTOS

believed that it was an act of Spanish terrorism. "Remember the *Maine!*" became the U.S. battle cry.

The Spanish-American War has often been termed "the Newspapers' War" because of the prominent role played by American journalists such as Richard Harding Davis and James Creelman, as well as by illustrators such as Frederic Remington. The war was a boon to William Randolph Hearst's *New York Journal* and Joseph Pulitzer's *New York World*, which for years had been carrying on a cutthroat war for circulation through a mixture of sex and scandal in their pages.

These and other papers gleefully reported on Spanish atrocities, real and imagined, as a way to attract readers. Some historians believe that the war was spurred on by the so-called yellow press as a way for the *Journal* and the *World*—as well as America's other 1,900 daily and 14,000 weekly newspapers—to boost circulation. An apocryphal story started by Creelman was that after Hearst dispatched Remington to Cuba, a bored Remington wired back: "Everything is quiet. There is no trouble. There will be no war. I wish to return"– to which Hearst replied, "Please remain. You furnish the pictures and I'll furnish the war."

Typical of the stories sent back from Cuba was one by Davis, published on February 12, 1897. Davis had been sent to Cuba to report on Spanish atrocities, and he found one in the story of a young woman who had allegedly been strip-searched on board an American vessel by Spanish authorities who believed that she was aiding the rebels by carrying documents and letters to Cuban sympathizers in the United States. The *Journal* headlines read: "Does Our Flag Shield Women? Indignities Practiced By Spanish Officials On Board American Vessels: Richard Harding Davis Describes Some Startling Phases of the Cuban Situation– Refined Young Woman Stripped and Searched by Brutal Spaniards While Under Our Flag on the *Ollivette*." This type of story about the "brutal" and rapacious Spaniards continued to whip up popular sentiment against Spain.

In August 1897, Hearst found another sensational story involving a young, pretty girl, Evangelina Cisneros, the daughter of the president of the Cuban Republic, who reportedly had been sentenced to twenty years in prison for aiding political prisoners who had come to her aid as she resisted the sexual advances of a Spanish colonel. In his 1901 book *On the Great Highway*, Creelman describes the incident, the popular American response, and the girl's dramatic rescue.

PRIMARY SOURCE

The incident which did more to arouse the sentimental opposition of the American people to Spain than anything which happened prior to the destruction of the *Maine,* was the rescue of the beautiful Evangelina Cisneros from a Havana prison by the *Journal's* gallant correspondent, Karl Decker. There is nothing in fiction more romantic than this feat of "yellow journalism." And the events which led up to it are worth telling.

One sultry day in August, 1897, the proprietor of the *Journal* was lolling in his editorial chair. Public interest in Cuba was weak. The Spanish minister at Washington had drugged the country with cunningly compounded statements. The government was indifferent. The weather was too hot for serious agitation. Every experienced editor will tell you that it is hard to arouse the popular conscience in August. Perspiring man refuses to allow himself to be worked into a moral rage. The proletariat of liberty was in a hole. The most tremendous headlines failed to stir the crowd.

An attendant entered the room with a telegram, which Mr. Hearst read languidly–

"HAVANA".

"Evangelina Cisneros, pretty girl of seventeen years, related to President of Cuban Republic, is to be imprisoned for twenty years on African coast, for having taken part in uprising Cuban political prisoners on Isle of Pines."

He read it over a second time and was about to cast it on his desk—but no! He stared at the little slip of paper and whistled softly. Then he slapped his knee and laughed.

"Sam!" he cried.

A tall, shaven, keen-eyed editor entered from the next room.

"We've got Spain, now!" exclaimed Mr. Hearst, displaying the message from Cuba. "Telegraph to our correspondent in Havana to wire every detail of this case. Get up a petition to the Queen Regent of Spain for this girl's pardon. Enlist the women of America. Have them sign the petition. Wake up our correspondents all over the country. Have distinguished women sign first. Cable the petitions and the names to the Queen Regent. Notify our minister in Madrid. We can make a national issue of this case. It will do more to open the eyes of the country than a thousand editorials or political speeches. The Spanish minister can attack our correspondents, but we'll see if he can face the women of America when they take up the fight. That girl must be saved if we have to take her out of prison by force or send a steamer to meet the vessel that carries her away– but that would be piracy, wouldn't it?"

Within an hour messages were flashing to Cuba, England, France, Spain, and to every part of the United States. The petition to the Queen Regent was telegraphed to more than two hundred correspondents in various American cities and towns. Each correspondent was instructed to hire a carriage and employ whatever assistance he needed, get the signatures of prominent women of the place, and telegraph them to New York as quickly as possible. Within twenty-four hours the vast agencies of "yellow journalism" were at work in two hemispheres for the sake of the helpless girl prisoner. Thousands of telegrams poured into the *Journal* office. Mrs. Jefferson Davis, the widow of the Confederate President, wrote this appeal, which the *Journal* promptly cabled to the summer home of the Queen Regent at San Sebastian:

"TO HER MAJESTY, MARIA CRISTINA, *Queen Regent of Spain*:

"*Dear Madam*: In common with many of my countrywomen I have been much moved by the accounts of the arrest and trial of Señorita Evangelina Cisneros. Of course, at this great distance, I am ignorant of the full particulars of her case. But I do know she is young, defenseless, and in sore straits. However, all the world is familiar with the shining deeds of the first lady of Spain, who has so splendidly illustrated the virtues which exalt wife and mother, and who has added to these the wisdom of a statesman and the patience and fortitude of a saint.

"To you I appeal to extend your powerful protection over this poor captive girl—a child almost in years— to save her from a fate worse than death. I am sure your kind heart does not prompt you to vengeance, even though the provocation has been great. I entreat you to give her to the women of America, to live among us in peace.

"We will become sureties that her life in future will be one long thank-offering for your clemency.

"Do not, dear Madam, refuse this boon to us, and we will always pray for the prosperity of the young King, your son, and for that of his wise and self-abnegating mother.

"Your admiring and respecting petitioner,
"VARINA JEFFERSON DAVIS."

Then Mrs. Julia Ward Howe, author of the "Battle Hymn of the Republic," wrote this appeal to the Pope, which the *Journal* cabled to the Vatican:

"TO HIS HOLINESS, LEO XIII:

"*Most Holy Father*: To you, as the head of Catholic Christendom, we appeal for aid in behalf of Evangelina Cisneros, a young lady of Cuba, one of whose near relatives is concerned in the present war, in which she herself has taken no part. She has been arrested, tried by court martial, and is in danger of suffering a sentence more cruel than death— that of twenty years of exile and imprisonment in the Spanish penal colony of Ceuta, in Africa, where no woman has ever been sent, and where, besides enduring every hardship and indignity, she would have for her companions the lowest criminals and outcasts.

"We implore you, Holy Father, to emulate the action of that Providence which interests itself in the fall of a sparrow. A single word from you will surely induce the Spanish government to abstain from this act of military vengeance, which would greatly discredit it in the eyes of the civilized world.

"We devoutly hope that your wisdom will see fit to utter this word, and to make not us alone, but humanity, your debtors.
"JULIA WARD HOWE."

The mother of President McKinley signed a petition to the Queen Regent. The wife of Secretary of State Sherman gave her name to the appeal, and soon the most representative women of the nation joined the movement. Fifteen thousand names were cabled by the *Journal* to the palace of San Sebastian. The country began to ring with the story of Evangelina Cisneros. Hundreds of public meetings were convened. The beautiful young prisoner became the protagonist of the Cuban struggle for liberty. Spain was denounced and the President was urged to lend his influence to the patriot cause of Cuba. The excitement grew day by day. It stirred up forces of sympathy that had lain dormant until then. The wily Spanish minister at Washington was in a trap. He did not dare to attack a movement supported by the wives and daughters of the great leaders of every political party in the United States.

How we worked and watched for poor Cuba in those days! How the tired writers stuck to the fight in those hot, breathless nights! And how the palace officials in Spain and the Captain-general in Cuba cursed us for our pains!

Presently there came a message from Cuba. Karl Decker had carried out his instructions. "Yellow journalism" had broken the bars of the Spanish prison. The beautiful young prisoner was safe on the ocean and would be in New York in a few days.

Not only had the girl been lifted out of the prison window through the shattered iron barriers and carried from rooftop to rooftop in the night over a teetering ladder, but she had been secreted in Havana in spite of the frantic search of the Spanish authorities and, disguised as a boy, had been smuggled on board of a departing steamer under the very noses of the keenest detectives in Havana.

"Now is the time to consolidate public sentiment," said Mr. Hearst. "Organize a great open-air reception in Madison Square. Have the two best military bands. Secure orators, have a procession, arrange for plenty of fireworks and searchlights. Announce that Miss Cisneros and her rescuer will appear side by side and thank the people. Send men to all the political leaders in the city, and ask them to work up the excitement. We must have a hundred thousand people together that night. It must be a whale of a demonstration— something that will make the President and Congress sit up and think."

SIGNIFICANCE

Hearst was successful in his petition drive. By August 23, 10,000 people had signed a petition demanding Cisneros's freedom; by the 26th the number had risen to 15,000, one of which was President McKinley's mother. Reports detailing the girl's escape began to appear in October under the byline Charles Duval, who turned out to be *Journal* correspondent Karl Decker. When she arrived in New York she was a sensation, and she later visited Washington, D.C., where she met President McKinley. The following year she married a Cuban dentist who had helped Decker engineer the escape.

The Spanish made some attempts to avoid war. In the same month that the Cisneros story broke, August 1897, the conservative prime minister of Spain, Antonio Cánovas del Castillo, was assassinated by an Italian anarchist and was replaced by the more liberal Práxedes Sagasta. The new government reviewed its Cuban policy and replaced the repressive military governor, Valeriano Weyler y Nicolau (nicknamed "the Butcher"), with General Ramón Blanco, who adopted more benign policies. In late 1897 Spain announced that it was granting Cuba autonomy, but the Cuban insurgency had taken on a life of its own, and the sensational reporting of Hearst and Pulitzer stoked war fever in the United States, which erupted in April 1898. The war boosted the reputation of future president Theodore Roosevelt, who led his Rough Riders, a force made up of a combination of cowboys and Ivy League students, up San Juan Hill outside Santiago.

When the war ended, the United States annexed Guam, Puerto Rico, and the Philippines. For the first time the United States, which for a century had heeded George Washington's warning against "entangling alliances," was something of an imperial power with interests across the globe. Many Americans decried the war, which they saw as naked imperialism; American steel magnate Andrew Carnegie offered to buy the Philippines for $20 million and return it. Many other Americans, though, believed that the war was one more step in the nation's Manifest Destiny.

FURTHER RESOURCES
Books

Goldstein, Donald M., et al. *Spanish-American War: The Story and Photographs.* Dulles, VA: Potomac, 2000.

Streitmatter, Rodger. *Mightier Than the Sword: How the News Media Have Shaped American History.* Boulder, CO: Westview Press, 1997.

Web sites

Creelman, James. *On the Great Highway: The Wanderings and Adventures of a Special Correspondent.* <http://www. cardinalbook.com/creelman/highway/iso8859/chap9. htm> (accessed May 16, 2005).

Giessel, Jess. "Black, White and Yellow: Journalism and Correspondents of the Spanish- American War." *The Spanish-American War Centennial Website.* September 12, 2004. <http://www.spanamwar.com/press.htm> (accessed May 16, 2005).

Terrorism in the Philippines

Filipinos Burned Bodies of Soldiers at Balangiga

Newspaper article

By: New York Times

Date: October 3, 1901

Source: *New York Times*

About the Author: *The New York Times*, a daily newspaper founded in 1851, has over one million subscribers and is distributed nationally.

INTRODUCTION

The Philippine-American War, an outgrowth of the Spanish-American War, began on February 4, 1899, and officially ended on July 4, 1902. When the United States government declared war on Spain in the spring of 1898, American forces quickly defeated the Spanish in the Philippines. Spain had ruled the Philippines for nearly three hundred years but, under the Treaty of Paris of December 10, 1898, agreed to turn over ownership of the nearly 7,000 islands to the victorious United States for $20 million.

The U.S. Senate approved annexation of the Philippines in February 1899. As American intentions became clear in the weeks preceding the Senate vote, Filipino revolutionary leader Emilio Aguinaldo declared the independence of his country and ordered his soldiers to fight American troops. In the spring of 1899, Aguinaldo switched from a formal style of fighting to guerilla warfare. In 1901, after enormous military efforts, prolonged guerilla warfare, and massive casualties on both sides, U.S. forces captured Aguinaldo and effectively smashed the Filipino insurrection. Aguinaldo issued a proclamation accepting the sovereignty of the United States on April 19, 1901.

A few Filipinos continued to fight after Aguinaldo's surrender. In the most famous case, supposedly loyal

Terrorist tactics have been employed for hundreds of years and have occurred throughout the world, from Tel Aviv in Israel (pictured above after a bus station explosion in 1968), to the United States, Nicaragua, and the Philippines. AP/WIDE WORLD PHOTOS

Filipinos on the island of Samar carried out a gruesome massacre of fifty-four American soldiers of Company C at Balangiga. Company C consisted of seventy-one men and three officers, most of whom had seen service in China, Cuba, and Northern Luzon in the Philippines. The company was led by Captain Thomas Connell, with Lieutenant E. C. Bumpus as second in command. In Balangiga, the outfit engaged in routine duties, including the cleanup of garbage by one hundred male conscripts. Later, eighty additional Filipinos from the nearby hills were added to the work force on recommendation of the town mayor. Unknown to the Americans, these eighty men were highly trained Filipino "bolomen," or soldiers, skilled in the use of cane cutting knives.

On the night of September 27, 1901, American sentries at Balangiga were surprised by the unusual number of women hurrying to church. They were all heavily clothed, which was unusual, and many carried small coffins. Inside all of the coffins were bolo knives. At 6:20 A.M. that morning, Pedro Sanchez, the Filipino chief of police, lined up the eighty laborers to start their daily cleanup of the town. Company C, already awake, was having breakfast at the mess tents. Sanchez walked behind an American sentry, grabbed the soldier's rifle, and brought the butt down on his head. Sanchez then fired the rifle and yelled out a signal. The church bell began to ring as conch shell whistles blew from the edge of the jungle. Bolomen then poured out of the church doors as the laborers suddenly turned on the soldiers and began chopping at them with bolos, picks, and shovels. A small group of American soldiers, a number of them wounded, were able to secure their rifles and fight back, killing some 250 Filipinos. Of the company's original complement, forty-eight were killed or unaccounted for, twenty-two were wounded, and only four were unharmed. The survivors managed to escape to the American garrison in Basey.

▇ PRIMARY SOURCE

Manila, Oct. 3.—The latest advices from the island of Samar give harrowing details of the slaughter of the members of

Company C, Ninth United States Infantry, last Saturday at Balangiga. It seems that the Presidente of the town, claiming to be friendly, led the assault in person.

On hearing of the slaughter Col. Isaac D. De Russy of the Eleventh Infantry started for the scene immediately with a battalion. The body of Capt. Connell was found tied at the heels, saturated with kerosene, and partly burned. Forty-five bodies had been burned in a trench. The charred remains of many were recovered. In numerous instances the bodies had been badly mutilated.

The American publishes a telegram giving an account of the fight. The fight was long premeditated and the Filipinos were called to commit the slaughter by the ringing of church bells at daylight. They got between the soldiers, who were breakfasting, and their quarters. The insurgents were mostly armed with bolos, but they had a few rifles with them.

As soon as a typhoon, now raging, subsides, the United States hospital ship Relief will leave with one battalion of the Seventh Regiment and at Legaspi will embark a battalion of the Twenty-sixth Regiment and 300 Macabebes to reinforce the troops in the island of Samar.

SIGNIFICANCE

The attack on Balangiga and its aftermath severely weakened American interest in overseas possessions. In the immediate days after the massacre, American soldiers in the Philippines sought revenge for the deaths of their comrades. Brigadier General Jacob Smith placed Major Littleton Waller in charge of pacifying Samar. Smith gave the instructions: "I wish you to kill and burn; the more you kill and burn the better it will please me." He directed that Samar be converted into a "howling wilderness." There were to be no prisoners and every male over the age of ten was to be killed because they were capable of carrying arms. Major Waller reported that in an eleven-day span, his men burned 255 dwellings, slaughtered thirteen carabaos, and killed thirty-nine people. Both Smith and Waller were later court-martialed. While Waller was acquitted, Smith was convicted of conduct to the prejudice of good order and discipline, among other counts. Sentenced to be admonished by a reviewing authority, he retired from active service.

Many Americans had initially opposed annexation of the Philippines because conquering a foreign territory seemed to be contrary to cherished American principles of freedom and liberty. The terrorism in the Philippines increased American resistance to the conquest of the Philippines and prompted the United States to lose interest in the future annexation of foreign lands.

In response to the violence in the Philippines, Americans reached the consensus that gains should be retained and protected, but not increased. Further overseas growth seemed unwise. While the United States would later intervene in countries such as Nicaragua and Haiti, it would make no attempt to turn those countries into American possessions.

FURTHER RESOURCES

Books

Miller, Stuart Creighton. *Benevolent Assimilation: The American Conquest of the Philippines, 1899–1903.* New Haven, CT: Yale University Press, 1982.

Wolff, Leon. *Little Brown Brother: How the United States Purchased and Pacified the Philippine Islands at the Century's Turn.* Garden City, NJ: Doubleday, 1961.

"Organized Will of the Nation"

Nazi Terrorism during Hitler's Rise to Power

Poster

By: Hans Schweitzer

Date: c. 1932

Source: Poster entitled "National Socialism: The Organized Will of the Nation," provided by Bridgeman Art Library.

About the Artist: Hans Schweitzer (1901–1980), who worked under the name Mjölnir at the time, was hired by Joseph Goebbels, Adolf Hitler's chief propagandist, to create numerous election posters for the Nazi Party. Schweitzer survived World War II and went on to a successful career as a graphic artist.

INTRODUCTION

In a presidential runoff election in Germany on April 19, 1932, the incumbent, Field Marshal Paul von Hindenburg, won with 53 percent of the vote. His chief opponent, Hitler, won 36.8 percent of the vote. On June 1 Hindenburg appointed Franz von Papen as chancellor. Papen immediately dissolved the Reichstag, the German parliament, and called for new legislative elections.

For over a decade Hitler's party, the National Socialists, or Nazis, had been a fringe political party. In the early 1920s they had risen to some prominence during the economic collapse following the Treaty of

Versailles that ended World War I. Hitler's manifesto, *Mein Kampf* (*My Struggle*), written while he was in prison after his attempt to seize power in Bavaria in the Beer Hall Putsch in 1924, had become something of a best-seller. With the return of relative prosperity in the late 1920s, the party returned to obscurity. But the worldwide economic collapse that began in 1929, the Great Depression, breathed new life into the party, which fixed the blame for all of Germany's troubles— unemployment, labor union agitation, political instability, military weakness, the humiliations of the Treaty of Versailles—on Jews and communists.

The Nazis exploited Germany's insecurity by creating unrest in the streets. The Nazi Party's muscle was the SA (*Sturmabteilung*), otherwise known as the storm troopers or Brownshirts, whose membership rose to between 2.5 million to 4 million by 1934. Functioning like an army, it carried out a campaign of terror against the party's political opponents and anyone who opposed the Nazis' desire to suspend the political liberties of the Weimar Republic in favor of a militarized, anticommunist dictatorship. Through beatings, murder, harassment, vandalism, robbery, and voter intimidation, they created chaos, causing martial law to be declared in Berlin.

The SA's tactics, though, proved to be effective. On July 31, 1932, the Nazis won 230 out of 608 seats in the Reichstag, making it the nation's largest political party. But because no one party held a clear majority, the Reichstag remained deadlocked, so new elections were called for November 6, 1932. The Nazi Party lost thirty-four seats in the new election, but that was a temporary setback. Hindenburg's appointee as chancellor, Kurt von Schleicher, also proved ineffective and resigned after just fifty-seven days. On January 30, 1933, Hindenburg, eager to put an end to the political instability, appointed Hitler chancellor; Hitler controlled a major voting bloc in the Reichstag.

Germans followed these events with rapt interest. Hitler was a gifted public speaker who was able to attract large crowds during the election campaigns. On a single day in July 1932, he spoke to an audience of 60,000 in Brandenburg, nearly 60,000 in Potsdam, and 120,000 in Berlin, while an additional 100,000 listened outside the stadium where he spoke on loudspeakers. He and his propagandist, Joseph Goebbels, seized every opportunity to manipulate the opinions of voters. The Nazi party produced brochures, pamphlets, and striking posters (such as the one shown) depicting determined-looking and vaguely threatening SA members. The caption identifies the SA and National Socialism as "The Organized Will of the Nation."

PRIMARY SOURCE

"ORGANIZED WILL OF THE NATION"

See primary source image.

SIGNIFICANCE

Hitler consolidated power through additional terrorist acts. The first such act attributed to Hitler's group was a fire at the Reichstag building on February 27, 1933. Hitler received a telephone call informing him of the fire, and when he arrived at the scene, Hermann Goering, who would later become Hitler's air minister, was shouting to onlookers: "This is the beginning of the Communist revolution! We must not wait a minute. We will show no mercy. Every Communist official must be shot, where he is found. Every Communist deputy must this very day be strung up."

Found cowering behind the building was a known Communist agitator, a Dutchman named Marinus van der Luube, who was arrested on the spot for starting the fire and later convicted and beheaded. The sense of crisis increased the following day, when authorities in Prussia announced that they had unearthed a Communist publication that said: "Government buildings, museums, mansions and essential plants were to be burned down. . . . Women and children were to be sent in front of terrorist groups. . . . The burning of the Reichstag was to be the signal for a bloody insurrection and civil war. . . . It has been ascertained that today was to have seen throughout Germany terrorist acts against individual persons, against private property, and against the life and limb of the peaceful population, and also the beginning of general civil war."

Historians widely debate whether Hitler or his allies actually started the Reichstag fire. However, Hitler certainly seized upon the event to manipulate media and public opinion. The next day, Hitler, fanning the fear of communism, persuaded Hindenburg to issue a decree called "For the Protection of the People and the State," suspending civil liberties. Two weeks later he persuaded the Reichstag to suspend the German constitution and grant him sweeping powers to deal with the crisis. In one final terrorist act designed to consolidate his power, the "Night of the Long Knives" on June 29–30, 1934, Hitler, eager to secure the loyalty of the regular German army, purged the SA, ordering the arrest and execution of up to 1,000 SA leaders.

On August 2, 1934, Hindenburg died. The office of president was abolished, and Hitler became Reich Chancellor and Führer of the Third Reich.

PRIMARY SOURCE

"Organized Will of the Nation" "National Socialism: The Organized Will of the Nation," Nazi Party election poster. BRIDGEMAN ART LIBRARY

FURTHER RESOURCES

Books

Bessell, Richard. *Political Violence and the Rise of Nazism: The Storm Troopers in Eastern Germany, 1925–1934.* New Haven, CT: Yale University Press, 1984.

Oberfohren, Ernst. *The Oberfohren Memorandum: What German Conservatives Thought about the Reichstag Fire; Full Text, with an Introduction and the Findings of the Legal Commission of Inquiry on Its Authenticity.* German Information Bureau, 1933.

Web sites

Bytwerk, Randall. Calvin College German Propaganda Archive. <http://www.calvin.edu/academic/cas/gpa> (accessed May 16, 2005).

The History Place. "World War II in Europe: The Night of the Long Knives." <http://www.historyplace.com/world-war2/timeline/roehm.htm> (accessed May 16, 2005).

"Testimony of Gas-Van Driver Walter Burmeister"

The Holocaust as Seen by its Perpetrators

Book excerpt

By: Willi Dressen and Volker Reiss

Date: 1988

Source: "Testimony of gas-van driver Walter Burmeister," from *The Good Old Days,* published by The Free Press in New York in 1988.

About the Author: Volker Reiss is a German historian, whose area of particular interest is the Holocaust. Willi Dressen is an attorney, a deputy director of the Central Bureau for the Judicial Authorities of the German Lander for the Investigation of National Socialist Crimes; Ernst Klee is a journalist, a teacher, award-winning filmmaker, and author of numerous books on the Holocaust.

INTRODUCTION

In their book, *The Good Old Days: The Holocaust as Seen by Its Perpetrators and Bystanders,* Germans Ernst Klee, Willi Dressen, and Volker Reiss have taken the position that many of the perpetrators in the mass exterminations of Jewish citizens and others deemed undesirable were far from reluctant victims who were forced, coerced and terrorized into carrying out orders against their will or better judgment. In this book, Klee, Dressen, and Riess have included photographs, photo albums,

An elderly Jew is harassed by Hitler's Brown Shirts in Berlin, Germany on April 4, 1933. AP/WIDE WORLD PHOTOS

personal diaries, official reports, and letters that attest to the willingness of some Germans to actively participate in the "Final Solution."

Holocaust deniers and Holocaust historical revisionists have suggested that either the extermination of Jews by the Nazi regime was grossly exaggerated or was carried out by individuals who were forced to do so. In this book, Klee and his co-authors provide original evidence that not only did the mass extermination of Jews and other marginalized groups occur, it was perpetrated, at least some of the time, by individuals who were willing and eager participants. "Of the annihilation of thousands of Jews in White Russia, one Nazi commander says, 'The action rid me of unnecessary mouths to feed.'"

Chelmno, also called Kulmhof, a small town not far from the city of Lodz (site of a large Jewish ghetto), was the location of the first mass extermination camp in Poland. The extermination camps were unique in that the people brought there were sent specifically to be killed; there were no work projects or experiments conducted at the camp. William Burmeister, a gas-van driver whose testimony is quoted below, was stationed at Chelmno. He was also responsible for oversight of the gold that had been removed from either the personal possessions or dental work of those killed. Chelmno was established in December of 1941, under the command of Herbert Lange. The first phase of operations took place between December 1942 and March 1943. After a brief hiatus, operations resumed in late June of 1944 and finally shut down on January 17, 1945. The cited death tolls for Chelmno have ranged from 150,000 to more than 350,000 individuals, the majority of whom were Jewish. The mass killings were carried out by means of gas-vans; groups of prisoners were taken into the castle at Chelmno, told to undress and hand over all valuables, and told that they were to be transferred to a work camp after showering and disinfection. They were then loaded into disguised freight vans. When the van was fully loaded, it was sealed and the exhaust pipe was connected to an opening in the freight area. The van's engine was started and the freight compartment's inhabitants were asphyxiated. After all prisoners were dead, the van was driven to another area, where the corpses were unloaded into mass graves. Eventually, cremation pyres replaced the mass graves.

■ PRIMARY SOURCE

. . . As soon as the ramp had been erected in the castle, people started arriving in Kulmhof from Lizmannstadt in lorries. . . The people were told that they had to take a bath, that their clothes had to be disinfected, and that they could hand in any valuable items beforehand to be registered. . .

When they had undressed they were sent to the cellar of the castle and then along a passageway on to the ramp and from there into the gas-van. In the castle there were signs marked "to the baths." The gas-vans were large vans, about 4–5 meters long, 2.2 meter wide and 2 meter high. The interior walls were lined with sheet metal. On the floor there was a wooden grille. The floor of the van had an opening, which could be connected to the exhaust by means of a removable metal pipe. When the lorries were full of people the double doors at the back were closed and the exhaust connected to the interior of the van. . .

The Kommando member detailed as driver would start the engine right away so that the people inside the lorry were suffocated by the exhaust gases. Once this had taken place, the union between the exhaust and the inside of the lorry was disconnected and the van was driven to the camp in the woods were the bodies were unloaded. In the early days they were initially burned in mass graves, later incinerated. . . I then drove the van back to the castle and parked it there. Here it would be cleaned of the excretions of the people that had died in it. Afterwards it would once again be used for gassing. . . I can no longer say what I thought at the time or whether I thought of anything at all. I can

also no longer say today whether I was too influenced by the propaganda of the time to have refused to have carried out the orders I had been given.

SIGNIFICANCE

In 1939, the Nazi government ordered several SS (*Schutzstaffel*, or specialized military) units to act as mobile killing squads. These killing squads, or *einsatzgruppen*, were highly efficient. Their mission was to murder the Jewish population of towns in Poland and Russia as the German army advanced eastward. The *einsatzgruppen* killed an estimated one million people during the Holocaust. *Einsatzgruppen* men were rewarded with extra rations, pay, and other incentives to continue their work. Concerned about the psychological toll direct executions could have on perpetrators, the Nazi government sought an alternative method of killing that would limit direct contact between perpetrators and victims. This lead to the creation of the death camps. Chelmno was reported to be the first operational extermination camp with the sole purpose of systematic killing of all individuals brought there

Chelmno was used expressly for exterminating large numbers of Jewish citizens who inhabited the western areas of Poland, particularly those who lived in Lodz (which was, at the time, the second largest city in Poland). In 1939, the Jewish population of Lodz was estimated at 202,000. Initially, the killings were carried out via the use of gas-vans equipped with special hoses carrying exhaust fumes from the idling van engines into the sealed freight areas.

The precursor to the gas vans was an experiment in Mogilev, in which a number of the inhabitants of a psychiatric facility were systematically killed through the use of automobile exhaust. Between twenty and thirty patients were brought into a room containing two pipes in one wall. The room was locked and sealed. The exhaust pipe of a car parked outside the facility had been connected to the pipe, and the room was filled with carbon monoxide. The experiment was initially unsuccessful, as all inhabitants were still alive after nearly ten minutes. An additional car's exhaust was connected to the second pipe, and both vehicles were operated simultaneously. Moments later, all in the room were dead, and the experiment was considered a success. This led to the development of a vehicle designed to be a portable execution chamber.

Extermination camps were considered a highly efficient means of eliminating Jewish citizens, as they were cost effective and required little feeding, housing, and supervision of prisoners. They were relatively secret and few prisoners escaped when arrivals were promptly killed. Efficiency dictated a streamlined process of arrival, removing of valuables, extermination, and burial.

The extermination camps were referred to by Hitler as the "Final Solution," and he was the high commander in direct charge of their operation, although Himmler was credited with the design of the extermination camps themselves.

Chelmno was the precursor to Operation Reinhard, which was a mass extermination effort located at Sobibor, Belzac, and Treblinka. The staff sent to operate the sites were not told the nature of their jobs in advance; instead, they were trained to consider their work as euthanasia. They were required to sign oaths of secrecy. Operation Reinhard took the technology developed at Chelmno and advanced it through the use of vast stationary gas chambers and massive crematoria. The killing centers were designed to be operational for brief periods of time, then completely destroyed in order to prevent identification of their intended, and successfully accomplished, missions.

FURTHER RESOURCES
Books

Browning, Christopher R. *Ordinary Men*. New York: Harper Perennial, 1993.

Wiesel, Eli. *Night*. New York: Bantam; Reissue edition, 1982.

Web sites

Jewish Gombin (Gabin, Poland, Jewish Genealogy) Chelm00. "Enquires on the Killing of the Gombin Jews." <http://dss.ucsd.edu/~lzamosc/chelm00.htm> (accessed July 18, 2005).

Jewish Gombin (Gabin, Poland, Jewish Genealogy) Chelm02. "Chelmno and Operation Reinhard." <http://dss.ucsd.edu/~lzamosc/chelm03.htm> (accessed July 18, 2005).

Jewish Gombin (Gabin, Poland, Jewish Genealogy) Chelm05. "Deposition of Theodor Malzmueller." <http://dss.ucsd.edu/~lzamosc/chelm05.htm> (accessed July 18, 2005).

Jewish Virtual Library. "Chelmno (Kulmhof)." <http://www.jewishvirtuallibrary.org/jsource/Holocaust/Chelmno.html> (accessed July 18, 2005).

"U.S. Embassy in Tripoli, Libya Attacked"

News article

By: The Associated Press

Date: December 3, 1979

Source: The Associated Press.

About the Author: Founded in 1848, the Associated Press (AP) is an international newswire service with offices and reporters stationed worldwide.

INTRODUCTION

The arrival of Colonel Muammar Qaddafi to the leadership of Libya by way of a *coup d'etat* in 1969 transformed the sparsely populated, oil-rich, desert state. Qaddafi's manifesto, the *Green Book*, extolled a cross between Egypt's charismatic leader from 1956–1970 Gamal Abd-Al Nasser's philosophy of pan-Arabism and Cuban Premier Fidel Castro's Leninist Marxism. It was also infused with a call against colonialism.

In practice, Qaddafi's rule initially manifested itself as a kind of political gangsterism, combined with an indifferent neutrality. In 1970, the property of Italians and non-resident Jews in Libya was appropriated, leading to the exodus of much of the 13,000-strong Italian community. A year later, Qaddafi nationalized foreign banks and imposed various regulations on other foreign companies operating within Libya, most notably when he nationalized the Libyan holdings of British Petroleum in December 1971.

Qaddafi did not only shun Western governments. He also broke diplomatic ties with Morocco and Jordan after disagreements with Morocco's King Hassan and Jordan's King Hussein (Qaddafi would allegedly later order an attempt to assassinate Hussein).

With the United States, Qaddafi held a deeply contradictory relationship. Successive administrations tolerated him as an anti-Communist bulwark, even tipping him off about stirrings of coup attempts. Qaddafi responded by reinforcing his non-alignment convictions and shrugging away U.S. attempts at friendship in the 1970s. He was also deeply against the concurrent U.S.-brokered peace negotiations between Israel and Egypt, and backed an attempt to assassinate the U.S. ambassador to Cairo who was acting as broker.

Yet at the same time, Qaddafi lobbied hard for U.S. concessions on other matters. He sought export licenses for American-made Boeing 727 passenger aircraft. In November 1979, the Libyan government also attempted to intercede in the U.S. hostage crisis in Iran. These efforts failed.

Rising anti-American feeling across the Middle East then received a further boost when Iran's leader, the Ayatollah Khomeini, blamed America for an attack on the Grand Mosque in Mecca in 1979. The allegations were unsubstantiated, but anti-American riots broke out across Pakistan (where the U.S. embassy was burned down), in India, Malaysia, and Turkey.

On December 2, 1979, 2,000 students gathered outside the U.S. embassy in Tripoli to protest these accusations.

PRIMARY SOURCE

Some 2,000 Libyans sacked the U.S. Embassy in Tripoli and set fire to the four-story building, but the embassy staff escaped unhurt.

The State Department filed a strong protest with the Libyan government and implied that it was responsible for the attack.

Charge d'Affaires William Eagleton's wife said about a dozen staff members were working in the Tripoli embassy at midmorning Sunday when a group of demonstrators arrived "quietly chanting." She said the staff "immediately locked up," and several male officials went to the Green Square, a central plaza several blocks away, where they "saw a large mob. They got back to the embassy and within five minutes the mobs arrived."

Consul Vincent Principe said the Libyans began "banging on the door and made it known to us they wanted to get inside. We just thought it prudent to leave."

The Americans fled through a back door and took refuge in their homes.

Only one Libyan policeman was on duty in front of the embassy at the time, and Libyan officials ignored appeals from the embassy for reinforcements, the State Department said in Washington. The embassy's Marine guard was withdrawn from Tripoli some time ago at the request of the Libyan government, the department said.

The State Department said the mob apparently used two-by-fours to break through the front door while some of the demonstrators climbed up to a second-floor balcony. JANA, the official Libyan news agency, said the mob burned an American flag and effigies of President Carter and the deposed Shah of Iran. U.S. officials said there was serious fire damage to the consular section on the first floor and damage also on the second floor.

State Department officials in Washington said the attack on the building set off an automatic tear-gas security system. JANA charged that the embassy staff "fired toxic gases believed to be used only by the military, confirming that the embassy's employees are military personnel." It claimed the gas seriously injured several students.

State Department spokesman Hodding Carter said the U.S. government protested the "inadequate and unresponsive" security protection.

Asked whether the attack had the backing of the Libyan government, he replied: "Libya is not a country in which demonstrations and other public manifestations happen in the same way in which they happen in this country."

JANA said the Libyan government protested the embassy's use of gas.

Mrs. Eagleton said police reinforcements arrived after the mob scattered. "But we have protection now at the embassy and our houses." The State Department said Libyan firemen extinguished the fires.

SIGNIFICANCE

The attack on the U.S. embassy in Tripoli exhausted American patience with Qaddafi. In 1980, President Jimmy Carter wrote: "There are few governments in the world with which we have more sharp and frequent policy differences than Libya. Libya has steadfastly opposed our efforts to reach and carry out the Camp David Accords between Israel, Egypt, and United States. . . We have strongly differing attitudes towards the PLO support of terrorism."

The expulsion of Libyan diplomats from Washington, D.C., in May of 1980, followed by Navy Sixth Fleet exercises in the Gulf of Sitre in August (which Libya claimed to be its sovereign waters, and led to skirmishes between U.S. naval fighter jets and Libyan fighter planes) soured relations still further.

When President Ronald Reagan took over the White House in January, 1981 he dubbed Libya "a base for Soviet subversion," with Qaddafi himself "the most dangerous man in the world." Further military exercises—creating further antagonism—were launched close to Libya; and in March 1982, Reagan declared a U.S. embargo on Libyan crude oil.

Plans to overthrow Qaddafi were hatched by the CIA and backing was even given to an Egyptian plan for an invasion of Libya, which were dropped after the assassination of Egyptian President Anwar Sadat in 1981. The United States also linked Libya to suspected plots to kill Reagan and then Vice President George H.W. Bush, as well as to Islamic Jihad, which hijacked flight 847 in June 1985. Libya was also implicated in terrorist attacks at the Rome and Vienna airports at Christmas 1985, and a bombing of a West Berlin disco in early April 1986, where two American servicemen were among the dead.

The disco bombing represented a "smoking gun" for U.S. intelligence services, who linked Libya to the attack. On April 15, 1986, the United States Air Force and Navy struck six targets in Tripoli and Benghazi, killing more than one hundred and injuring a further two hundred. Qaddafi escaped unharmed, but his wife and two children were seriously injured and his adopted daughter later died of her injuries.

The Tripoli bombings outraged Qaddafi. He then sanctioned the bombing of Pan Am flight 103, in

December 1988, which blew up over Lockerbie, Scotland, killing 259 people on board and an additional eleven on the ground. Until the September 11 attacks in 2001, this would be the worst terrorist act committed against the United States.

A period of rapprochement with the Libyan regime, initiated in the late 1990s by the European Union, and dependent on a compensation settlement for the Lockerbie bombing, along with a commitment from Qaddafi to improve his human rights record, brought an end to European sanctions of Libya. Taking the lead from Europe, in September 2004, the United States resumed relations with Libya after a gap of twenty-two years. The Libyan government has since admitted their involvement in several terrorist incidents over the past three decades, including the bombing of PanAm 103.

FURTHER RESOURCES

Books

Simons, Geoff. *Libya: The Struggle For Survival*. New York: Macmillan, 1993.

St John, Ronald B. *Qaddafi's World Design: Libyan Foreign Policy 1969–1987*. London: Saqi Books, 1987.

RPG-7 Russian grenades with a "Contra" pamphlet that reads "Commandos" held by soldiers of the Sandinista Army in Nicaragua. AP/WIDE WORLD PHOTOS

Iran-Contra Scandal

"Reagan Dumps 2 Top Officials Over Iran Cash Sent to Contras"

Newspaper article

By: Bob Hepburn

Date: November 26, 1986

Source: "Reagan Dumps 2 Top Officials Over Iran Cash Sent to Contras" as published by the *Toronto Star*.

About the Author: Hepburn is the editorial page editor of the *Toronto Star*.

INTRODUCTION

In 1986, President Ronald Reagan (1911–2004) authorized the sale of arms to Iran in exchange for Iran's influence in obtaining the release of four American hostages held by factions in Lebanon sympathetic to Iran's Ayatollah Khomeini. (The U.S. had ended diplomatic relations with Iran after the Iran hostage crisis in 1979.) The profits from the arms sales were used to fund the contra-revolutionaries in Nicaragua, who opposed the revolutionary Sandinistas. Although Congress had barred such assistance, administration officials and the Central Intelligence Agency (CIA) circumvented the ban by also applying pressure on friendly countries to provide aid to the contras.

The *Frente Sandinista de Liberación Nacional* or Sandinistas was a Marxist-Leninist political party that overthrew the dictatorship of Anastasio Somoza in 1979 and attempted to create a Marxist-Leninist state in Nicaragua from 1979 to 1990. The Sandinistas, named in honor of Nicaraguan General Augusto César Sandino who had fought the U.S. Marines in the 1920s, formed in 1960. Over the years, they engaged in a number of terrorist actions including the attempted kidnapping of a U.S. ambassador in 1974.

Before they rose to power, the Sandinistas established ties with the terrorist Popular Front for the Liberation of Palestine. After they were in power, the Sandinistas became friendly with Libya and Iran, both known as state sponsors of terror. The U.S initially offered financial aid to the Sandinistas, but this assistance stopped in 1981 when it became known that the Sandinistas were supporting a communist insurgency in

El Salvador. The Soviet Union and Cuba then became the major backers of the Sandinistas, with Libya lending military aid.

In 1985, members of the National Security Council became convinced that the release of American hostages (all private citizens) held in Lebanon could be achieved if the U.S. sold arms to Iran for Iran to use in its war against Iraq. National Security Advisor Robert McFarlane considered that moderates within the Iranian government would use their political influence to free the hostages. The actual shipment of weapons to Iran was carried out by Israel with the U.S. providing replacement munitions to the Israelis. The Iranians accepted the anti-tank and anti-aircraft missiles, but arranged for the release of only three hostages. However, the deal resulted in considerable profits. These monies were sent to Nicaragua to support the contras.

In November 1986, the American public learned that the U.S. had sold arms to the Islamist regime in Iran that had sponsored terrorist activities against the U.S. for most of the 1980s. Within a month, the revelation came that money obtained from the arms sales had been used to support the Nicaraguan contras in violation of the Boland Amendments. Named after Congressman Edward Boland of Massachusetts, these amendments were passed in 1982 to block funds from being used to oust the Sandinistas.

PRIMARY SOURCE

In a stunning twist to the secret American arms deal with Iran, President Ronald Reagan has dumped two top-ranking officials after learning money that Iran paid for the weapons was given to U.S-backed rebels in Nicaragua.

Reagan accepted the resignation yesterday of his national security adviser John Poindexter, and fired U.S. Marine Lt.-Col. Oliver North, one of Poindexter's key assistants and a key figure in both the covert sale of arms to Iran and U.S. support for the Nicaraguan Contra rebels.

U.S. Attorney-General Edwin Meese said the Justice Department will investigate how the Contras received "$10 million to $30 million" that Iran paid to Israeli agents for American weapons shipped to Tehran.

North was interrogated by Meese Sunday in the attorney-general's office, a knowledgeable source who asked not to be named told Associated Press.

The dramatic announcement came as Reagan struggles to retain credibility after admitting two weeks ago he approved arms shipments to Iran in an effort to improve relations between the two countries.

Rumors of a major shuffle in his cabinet, including the possible firing of Secretary of State George Shultz, White

House Chief of Staff Donald Regan and Poindexter, have circulated in Washington for days.

The disclosure shocked congressional leaders on Capitol Hill, where calls intensified for Reagan to shuffle his senior advisers and to make a full disclosure of all U.S. involvement in the Iranian arms deal.

New Senate majority leader Robert Byrd said he does not believe "one or two scapegoats are necessarily the answer to this whole matter. It is something that is eating away at the energy and time of the administration and the best thing to do would be for the president to lay it all out."

"What this says is that nobody seems to be really in charge of foreign policy. It says the White House is in a chaotic state of affairs."

Reagan, looking tense and irritated, said he was "not fully informed" about the arms agreement and will appoint a special commission to investigate U.S. conduct of the Iranian arms deal, which led to the release of three American hostages in Lebanon.

Meese said about $12 million worth of American arms to Iran were routed through Israel.

The Israeli agents dealing with Tehran then put the Iranian payments, which apparently far exceed the value of the weapons, into a Swiss bank account. Funds were then diverted to the Contras.

Meese said he needs more information to determine exactly how much money was involved, how it was transferred, and to identify who was involved in Israel, the United States and Nicaragua.

The funds were sent to the rebels during a period when Congress had passed a law banning U.S. government financial aid to the Contras.

Congress recently approved $100 million in military and other aid to the rebels, who are fighting to overthrow the leftist Sandinista government.

Meese acknowledged that Reagan was not told of a 1985 shipment of U.S. arms from Israel to Iran, saying the deal was approved by the president after it had been completed.

Anonymous White House sources said North gave Israeli officials the go-ahead for that shipment on his own authority, Associated Press reports.

Reagan refused to say he was wrong to authorize arms sales to Iran or whether he is planning a further shake-up of White House staff.

"As I have stated previously, I believe our policy goals toward Iran were well founded," he said.

Asked if the deal was a mistake, he snapped, "No, and I'm not taking any more questions."

Meese said he uncovered the Contra fund last weekend while investigating the role of the National Security

Council in the Iran deal. The council, which operates in the White House basement, reports directly to Reagan on foreign and domestic policy.

The agency, rather than Secretary of State George Shultz's department, was in charge of the Iranian operation.

"The only person in the U.S. government that knew precisely about this-the only person—was Lt.-Col.North,." said Meese, who briefed reporters after Reagan's terse announcement.

Poindexter "knew that something of this nature was occurring, but did not look into it further," he added.

Meese said Shultz, Vice-President George Bush and other senior Reagan advisers did not learn of the Contra connection until Monday when Meese informed the president of his findings.

The attorney-general said it is too early to tell if the money transfer was in breach of the law.

Reagan said the fact he was not told of the Nicaraguan connection "raises serious questions of propriety. I am deeply troubled that the implementation of a policy aimed at resolving a truly tragic situation in the Middle East has resulted in such controversy."

"As I have stated previously, I believe our policy goals toward Iran were well founded. However the information brought to my attention yesterday convinced me, that in one aspect, implementation of that policy was seriously flawed."

House Majority leader Jim Wright commented, "There is something profoundly wrong with U.S. foreign policy if the president was unaware of this aspect of the Iran dealings."

Wright said Reagan is "uniquely capable of psyching himself up into a frame of mind in which he can believe whatever he wants to believe and can just utterly reject factual information that does not fit comfortably with his preconceived predilection."

"It makes it very difficult for those who have information that is unpleasant to him to get through to him and to get him to accept it—that fact is fact and truth is truth."

SIGNIFICANCE

In nationally televised hearings, Congress explored the involvement of federal officials and a number of others in the Iran-Contra scandal. Subsequent investigations by Special Prosecutor Lawrence E. Walsh provided additional details of the illegal operations and the attempted cover-up. Several administration aides were forced out of their posts and some of these were indicted for violations of federal law. Robert C. McFarlane, the president's former national security adviser, pleaded guilty to withholding information from Congress about the Reagan administration's

efforts to help the contras. John M. Poindexter, one of Reagan's closest aides and a former national security advisor, was sentenced to prison for committing five felonies, including conspiracy to deceive Congress and lying to Congress. Oliver L. North, a former Marine lieutenant colonel who served as a staff member on the National Security Council, was convicted of aiding and abetting the obstruction of Congress, destroying confidential documents, and accepting an illegal gift. In videotaped testimony at the Poindexter trial, Reagan said that he had granted authority to supervise arms sales and contra-aid efforts, but he could recall few details of the operations and insisted that he had never advised disobedience of the law.

The scandal only temporarily affected President Reagan's popularity. Public interest in Iran-Contra faded quickly, with developments in the Soviet Union and a possible reduction of Cold War tensions capturing the attention of most Americans. The Sandinistas quietly disappeared from American notice. In 1990, after the U.S. finally abandoned armed efforts to depose the Sandinistas, they held free elections and stepped down from power when the conservatives under Violetta Chamorro won.

FURTHER RESOURCES
Books

_____. *The Iran-Contra Puzzle*. Washington, D.C.: Congressional Quarterly, 1987.

Marshall, Jonathan, Peter Dale Scott and Jane Hunter. *The Iran-Contra Connection: Secret Teams and Covert Operations in the Reagan Era*. Boston: South End Press, 1987.

Trager, Oliver, ed. *The Iran-Contra Arms Scandal: Foreign Policy Disaster*. New York: Facts on File, 1988.

Walsh, Lawrence E. *Final Report of the Independent Counsel for Iran/Contra Matters*. Washington, D.C.: U.S. Court of Appeals for the D.C. Circuit, 1993.

Walsh, Lawrence E. *Firewall: The Iran-Contra Conspiracy and Cover-Up*. New York: Norton, 1997.

"Suspects in Crash Take Suicide Pills"

KAL Flight 858 bombed by North Korea

Newspaper article

By: The Associated Press

Date: December 2, 1987

Russian sailors watch as crewmen of the Japanese Maritime Safety Agency haul a crate of wreckage from KAL Flight 858 to their vessel at Nevelsk. AP/WIDE WORLD PHOTOS

Source: The Associated Press.

About the Author: With reporters and photographers stationed throughout the world, the Associated Press is one of the world's largest news organizations.

INTRODUCTION

On November 29, 1987, the ground station tracking Korean Air Lines (KAL) Flight 858 lost radar contact with the commercial airliner. At the time of its disappearance, the airplane was over the Andaman Sea near Thailand and Burma (now known as Myanmar) while on its scheduled daily route from the Abu Dhabi International Airport in Abu Dhabi, United Arab Emirates, to the Don Muang Airport in Bangkok, Thailand. (It normally would have ended its regular Abu Dhabi-Bangkok-Seoul route at the Kimpo Airport in Seoul, South Korea). As information quickly came in about the disappearance, evidence mounted that the airplane had been destroyed by a terrorist bomb. It was eventually determined that the mid-air bombing completely destroyed the aircraft, killing everyone on board: four crew members and 104 passengers.

Two North Korean citizens were soon arrested in the country of Bahrain, located in western Asia, and became prime suspects in the terrorist bombing. At the time of bombing, KAL 858 was the deadliest terrorist attack against South Korea.

The two suspects, one male and one female, were traveling as tourists with forged Japanese passports that identified themselves as Shinichi Hachiya and Mayumi Hachiya, father and daughter, respectively. It was learned that the two suspects, who had boarded the airplane in Baghdad, Iraq, had left a radio and a glass bottle containing explosives in the airplane's overhead luggage compartment before exiting the aircraft in Abu Dhabi.

Upon being arrested, the male suspect (Shinichi Hachiya) committed suicide by swallowing poison. The woman (Mayumi Hachiya) also swallowed the same poison, but a lesser amount, and she survived.

The woman, whose real name was Kim Hyun-Hee, was turned over to South Korean officials who returned her to Seoul. She later confessed to the bombing on live Korean television. In 1990, Hyun-Hee was tried, convicted, and sentenced to death for the bombing crime. The court later granted her a pardon, ruling that Hyun-Hee was not the primary perpetrator in the bombing but an innocent victim of North Korean brainwashing. Hyun-Hee admitted during her interrogation that she had been tutored in Japanese language, mannerisms, and society by a Japanese national known as Lee Un Hae, who, unknown to Hyan-Hee, had been kidnapped by North Korea. Hyan-Hee was allowed to remain in South Korea.

PRIMARY SOURCE

SUSPECTS IN CRASH TAKE SUICIDE PILLS

Police Try to Question Couple Off Missing Korean Plane
Manama, Bahrain, Dec. 1—A man and woman who had been passengers aboard a South Korean jetliner before it left the Middle East and disappeared over Burma took suicide pills today as they waited for the police to question them, the authorities said.

The man died, but the woman was expected to live.

The plane, with 115 people aboard, vanished near the Burma-Thailand border, before a scheduled refueling stop in Bangkok. Officials in Seoul have said there are strong suspicions that a bomb destroyed the aircraft.

BOARDED AT BAGHDAD

Officials said the couple, whose identity was unclear, boarded Korean Air's Flight 858 at Baghdad, where it originated Sunday, and got off at Abu Dhabi before the Boeing 707 headed across Asia toward Seoul. From Abu Dhabi, they flew here.

The two, who were believed to be either Japanese or Korean, had been traveling on forged Japanese passports, apparently as father and daughter, Japanese officials here said.

The man, who appeared to be middle-aged, died four hours after biting into a suicide pill concealed in a cigarette, said Takao Natsume, Japan's acting Ambassador in Bahrain. He said the woman, who was younger, was unconscious in critical condition at a military hospital but added, "She will survive."

They had been waiting to be questioned by immigration officials who had stopped them from boarding a Rome-bound flight after Japanese officials told them the woman's passport was forged.

"Just after swallowing the pills they both fell on the floor and their bodies went very stiff," Mr. Natsume said.

The woman, he said, had apparently survived because she swallowed less of the poison, which was hidden in the cigarette filters. The type of poison was not known.

South Korea's Government broadcasting service said investigators were checking to see if there was a link between the woman and Chosen Soren, an organization of Koreans living in Japan that supports the Communist Government in North Korea.

Security officials in Bahrain said investigators also were checking on possible ties between the couple and the Japanese Red Army, which has been linked to several Middle East terrorist groups and to North Korea, but Mr. Natsume said he had no evidence of such a connection.

Thai police units searching for wreckage left by the plane reported today that there was a large swath of leveled trees in mountains along the border. An official of the airline said, "There is a high possibility that the missing plane crashed because of a bomb explosion" because no distress call was received from the aircraft.

Foreign Ministry officials in Seoul said the man and woman were "known to have arrived in Iraq from Yugoslavia," but did not indicate when.

In the passports they carried, the dead man was identified as Shinichi Hachiya, 69, and the woman as Mayumi Hachiya, 27, both from Okayama, Japan.

Mr. Natsume said the man's passport was believed to be authentic until Japanese authorities found the real Shinichi Hachiya in Tokyo.

North Korean Communist agent Kim Hyun-hee enters the court house in Seoul, Korea where she was sentenced to death. AP/WIDE WORLD PHOTOS

SIGNIFICANCE

Kim Hyun-Hee was born in North Korea to a father who was a senior government diplomat. Beginning late in her teenage years, at approximately 19, Hyun-Hee was trained in covert-operations for the North Korean government. Her career ended about seven years later when she was arrested for the 1987 bombing of KAL 858. At the time of the South Korean investigation, Hyun-Hee admitted that the bombing was ordered by Kin Jong Il, the son of North Korean leader Kim Il Sung. (Because South Korea was hosting the Olympic Games and North Korea had not been asked to do so, some experts argued that Kin Jong Il decided to plan a terrorist attack to scare tourists away from visiting the Summer Games.)

Hyun-Hee's testimony reinforced the evidence against North Korea as a country that supported terrorism and harbored terrorists.

In part due to the investigation of the bombing of KAL 858, it was learned that North Korea had been kidnapping innocent South Korean and Japanese citizens and using them as low-level agents for various espionage ventures. For example, in one kidnapping case relevant to Hyun-Hee, the National Police Agency in Japan identified in 1991 a young Japanese woman who had earlier disappeared. Using the name Yaeko Taguchi, the woman was identified as Lee Un Hae—the woman who had earlier tutored Hyun-Hee. Hae had been kidnapped earlier by operatives of North Korea.

South Korean's intelligence agency, by the late 1990s, had pieced together many of the stories and clues it had found about Japanese and South Korean citizens being kidnapped by people working for the North Korean government. At that point, under mounting pressure and evidence, North Korea's President Kin Jong Il, who had succeeded his father Kim Il Sung in 1994, confessed to his country's kidnappings of Japanese and South Korean citizens.

In the book *The Tears of my Soul*, author Hyun-Hee described the techniques used to train her as a spy for North Korea and, ultimately, the details of the KAL 858 bombing. Her account of North Korean brainwashing techniques described how people were forcibly coerced and controlled to perform violent acts of terrorism for North Korean leaders.

Although no specific person or organization was formally accused with the original authorization and resultant planning of KAL 858, many terrorist experts argue that the existing evidence indicates that the government of North Korea was behind the terrorist activity.

After the KAL 858 incident, the United States officially listed North Korea in 1988 as a terrorist state.

During the presidential State of the Union address in January 2002, President George W. Bush stated that North Korea was one of the countries included within regimes that sponsored terrorism—which was commonly called the Axis of Evil—along with the countries of Iraq and Iran.

FURTHER RESOURCES
Books
Hyun-Hee, Kim. *The Tears of My Soul: The True Story of a North Korean Spy*. New York: William Morrow and Company, 1993.

Web sites
Council on Foreign Relations. "Does North Korea Sponsor Terrorism?" <http://cfrterrorism.org/sponsors/northkorea.html> (accessed June 20, 2005).

Discovery Times. "Inside North Korea." <http://times.discovery.com/convergence/insidenorthkorea/timeline/timeline.html> (accessed June 20, 2005).

Pan Am 103 Bombing

Opinion of the Scottish High Court

Court Opinion

By: Lord Ranald Sutherland, Lord John Cameron Coulsfield, and Lord Ranald MacLean

Date: January 31, 2001

Source: Opinion of the Scottish High Court delivered by Lord Sutherland *in causa* Her Majesty's Advocate v. Abdelbaset Ali Mohmed al Megrahi and Al Amin Khalifa Fhimah, Prisoners in the Prison of Zeist, Camp Zeist (Kamp van Zeist), The Netherlands.

About the Author: Four judges of the Scottish High Court were appointed to preside over the trial of the defendants in the Pan Am Flight 103 bombing over Lockerbie, Scotland. Lord Ranald Sutherland, a judge since 1985, had worked primarily in appeals courts. Lord John Cameron Coulsfield, a judge for twelve years at the time, was editor of the journal *Scottish Law and Practice Quarterly*. Lord Ranald MacLean had been appointed to the bench in 1990. A fourth judge, Lord Alastair Cameron Abernethy, was an alternate who took part in deliberations but did not vote.

INTRODUCTION

At 6:25 P.M. on December 21, 1988, Pan Am Flight 103, originating in Frankfurt, Germany, took off from London's Heathrow Airport with 243 passengers and

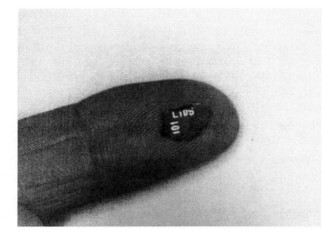

One of two fragments that proved crucial in tracking down the bombers of Pan AM Flight 103 that exploded over Lockerbie, Scotland in 1988. JUSTICE DEPARTMENT/AP WIDE WORLD PHOTOS

16 crew members aboard, including 189 American citizens. The flight path of the plane, a Boeing 747–121A, was to take it over the British Isles and the North Atlantic Ocean on its way to New York City and Detroit. Twenty-one minutes later, at 6:56, the plane leveled off at 31,000 feet. Seven minutes after that, air traffic control transmitted final oceanic clearance, but the plane did not acknowledge the transmission and dropped off the radar screen.

What controllers subsequently learned was that at 7:02 and 50 seconds, the plane had violently exploded over Lockerbie, Scotland. Most of the wreckage landed in Sherwood Crescent, a residential area on the southern edge of Lockerbie. The impact killed eleven people on the ground, gouged a crater measuring 155 by 196 feet, and demolished twenty-one residential buildings. The impact of the crash was so great that the British Geological Survey thought that it had recorded an earthquake measuring 1.6 on the Richter scale. Other parts of the wreckage landed in the countryside east of town, and bits of the plane were scattered up to eighty miles away.

Charged with investigating the crash was the United Kingdom's Air Accident Investigation Branch (AAIB). The AAIB sifted through mud and debris to find four million pieces of the plane's wreckage while forensic examiners dealt with the gruesome task of recovering bodies, many still strapped in their seats, hanging from trees and scattered in nearby gardens and yards. The AAIB determined that the explosion was caused by what investigators call an improvised explosive device (IED), a bomb. The investigation centered on a Toshiba radio and cassette recorder packed in a brown suitcase in the

plane's cargo hold. Inside the recorder were the remains of a timing device that detonated the bomb, which consisted of about 14 ounces of plastic explosive.

In November 1991, the Lord Advocate, Scotland's chief law-enforcement officer, issued a warrant for the arrest of two Libyan suspects in the crime. The men, Abdelbaset Ali Mohmed al Megrahi and Al Amin Khalifa Fhimah, had ties to the Libyan intelligence service and to Libyan Airlines. What followed was the diplomatic task of extraditing the two from Libya, a task made especially difficult given the virulent anti-Western sentiments of Libya's leader, Colonel Muammar al-Qaddafi, who argued for eight years that the men could not get a fair trial in a Scottish court.

The United Nations imposed economic sanctions against Libya, and it was not until United Nations secretary general Kofi Annan and South African leader Nelson Mandela intervened that Qaddafi agreed to extradite the men on the condition that the trial be held in a neutral third country. Accordingly, the Netherlands agreed to set aside a former air force base, Camp Zeist, as the site of the trial, and the men were handed over on April 5, 1999. Based on 10,000 pages of testimony from 235 witnesses, the court issued its verdict on January 31, 2001. A portion of the verdict, which lays out the chain of circumstances that led to the bombing, is reproduced below.

■ PRIMARY SOURCE

[82] From the evidence which we have discussed so far, we are satisfied that it has been proved that the primary suitcase containing the explosive device was dispatched from Malta, passed through Frankfurt and was loaded onto PA103 at Heathrow. It is, as we have said, clear that with one exception the clothing in the primary suitcase was the clothing purchased in Mr Gauci's shop on 7 December 1988. The purchaser was, on Mr Gauci's evidence, a Libyan. The trigger for the explosion was an MST-13 timer of the single solder mask variety. A substantial quantity of such timers had been supplied to Libya. We cannot say that it is impossible that the clothing might have been taken from Malta, united somewhere with a timer from some source other than Libya and introduced into the airline baggage system at Frankfurt or Heathrow. When, however, the evidence regarding the clothing, the purchaser and the timer is taken with the evidence that an unaccompanied bag was taken from KM180 to PA103A, the inference that that was the primary suitcase becomes, in our view, irresistible. As we have also said, the absence of an explanation as to how the suitcase was taken into the system at Luqa is a major difficulty for the Crown case but after taking full account of that difficulty, we remain of the view that the primary suitcase began its

journey at Luqa. The clear inference which we draw from this evidence is that the conception, planning and execution of the plot which led to the planting of the explosive device was of Libyan origin. While no doubt organisations such as the PFLP-GC [Popular Front for the Liberation of Palestine-General Command] and the PPSF [Palestinian Popular Struggle Front] were also engaged in terrorist activities during the same period, we are satisfied that there was no evidence from which we could infer that they were involved in this particular act of terrorism, and the evidence relating to their activities does not create a reasonable doubt in our minds about the Libyan origin of this crime.

[83] In that context we turn to consider the evidence which could be regarded as implicating either or both of the accused. . .

[84] We deal first with the second accused. The principal piece of evidence against him comes from two entries in his 1988 diary. This was recovered in April 1991 from the offices of Medtours, a company which had been set up by the second accused and Mr. Vassallo. At the back of the diary there were two pages of numbered notes. The fourteenth item on one page is translated as "Take/collect tags from the airport (Abdulbaset/Abdussalam)". The word 'tags' was written in English, the remainder in Arabic. On the diary page for 15 December there was an entry, preceded by an asterisk, "Take taggs from Air Malta", and at the end of that entry in a different coloured ink "OK." Again the word 'taggs' (sic) was in English. The Crown maintained that the inference to be drawn from these entries was that the second accused had obtained Air Malta interline tags for the first accused, and that as an airline employee he must have known that the only purpose for which they would be required was to enable an unaccompanied bag to be placed on an aircraft. From another entry on 15 December (translated as "Abdel-baset arriving from Zurich") it appears that the second accused expected the first accused to pass through Malta on that day. In fact the first accused passed through on 17 December and missed seeing the second accused. In his interview with Mr Salinger in November 1991, the second accused said that he had been informed by his partner Mr Vassallo that the first accused had spoken to him and asked him to tell the second accused that he wanted to commission him with something. On 18 December the second accused travelled to Tripoli. He returned on 20 December on the same flight as the first accused. The Crown maintained that the inference to be drawn from this was that on that date the first accused was bringing component parts of the explosive device into Malta, and required the company of the second accused to carry the suitcase through Customs as the second accused was well known to the customs officers who would be unlikely to stop him and search the case. This would be consistent with the evidence of Abdul Majid. Finally the Crown maintained that in order for the suitcase

to get past the security checks at Luqa on 21 December and find its way on board KM180, someone would have to organise this who was very well acquainted with the security controls at Luqa and would know how these controls could be circumvented. As someone who had been a station manager for some years, the second accused was ideally fitted for this role. Further, there was a telephone call recorded from the Holiday Inn, where the first accused was staying, to the number of the second accused's flat at 7.11 A.M. on 21 December. The Crown argued that this could be inferred to be a call arranging for the second accused to give the first accused a lift to the airport, and also it could be inferred that the second accused was at the airport from the fact that the first accused received special treatment both at check-in and at immigration control before departing on the LN147 flight to Tripoli.

[85] There is no doubt that the second accused did make the entries in the diary to which we have referred. In the context of the explosive device being placed on KM180 at Luqa in a suitcase which must have had attached to it an interline tag to enable it to pass eventually on to PA103, these entries can easily be seen to have a sinister connotation, particularly in the complete absence of any form of explanation. Counsel for the second accused argued that even if it be accepted that the second accused did obtain tags and did supply them to the first accused, it would be going too far to infer that he was necessarily aware that they were to be used for the purpose of blowing up an aircraft, bearing in mind that the Crown no longer suggest that the second accused was a member of the Libyan Intelligence Service. Had it been necessary to resolve this matter, we would have found it a difficult problem. For the reasons we are about to explain however we do not find it necessary to do so. The Crown attach significance to the visit by the second accused to Tripoli on 18 December 1988 and his return two days later in the company of the first accused. As we have indicated, we cannot accept the evidence of Abdul Majid that he saw the two accused arriving with a suitcase. It follows that there is no evidence that either of them had any luggage, let alone a brown Samsonite suitcase. Whatever else may have been the purpose of the second accused going to Tripoli, it is unlikely that his visit was to hand over tags, as this could easily have been done in Malta. We do not think it proper to draw the inference that the second accused went to Tripoli for the purpose, as the Crown suggested, of escorting the first accused through Customs at Luqa. There is no real foundation for this supposition, and we would regard it as speculation rather than inference. The position on this aspect therefore is that the purpose of the visit by the second accused to Tripoli is simply unknown, and while there may be a substantial element of suspicion, it cannot be elevated beyond the realm of suspicion. The Crown may be well founded in saying that the second accused would be aware

of the security arrangements at Luqa, and therefore might have been aware of some way in which these arrangements could be circumvented. The Crown however go further and say that it was the second accused "who was in a position to and did render the final assistance in terms of introduction of the bag by whatever means". There is no evidence in our opinion which can be used to justify this proposition and therefore at best it must be in the realm of speculation. Furthermore, there is the formidable objection that there is no evidence at all to suggest that the second accused was even at Luqa airport on 21 December. There were a number of witnesses who were there that day who knew the second accused well, such as Abdul Majid and Anna Attard, and they were not even asked about the second accused's presence. The Crown suggestion that the brief telephone call to the second accused's flat on the morning of 21 December can by a series of inferences lead to the conclusion that he was at the airport is in our opinion wholly speculative. While therefore there may well be a sinister inference to be drawn from the diary entries, we have come to the conclusion that there is insufficient other acceptable evidence to support or confirm such an inference, in particular an inference that the second accused was aware that any assistance he was giving to the first accused was in connection with a plan to destroy an aircraft by the planting of an explosive device. There is therefore in our opinion insufficient corroboration for any adverse inference that might be drawn from the diary entries. In these circumstances the second accused falls to be acquitted.

[86] We now turn to the case against the first accused. . .

[87] On 15 June 1987, the first accused was issued with a passport with an expiry date of 14 June 1991, by the Libyan passport authority at the request of the ESO who supplied the details to be included. The name on the passport was Ahmed Khalifa Abdusamad. Such a passport was known as a coded passport. There was no evidence as to why this passport was issued to him. It was used by the first accused on a visit to Nigeria in August 1987, returning to Tripoli via Zurich and Malta, travelling at least between Zurich and Tripoli on the same flights as Nassr Ashur who was also travelling on a coded passport. It was also used during 1987 for visits to Ethiopia, Saudi Arabia and Cyprus. The only use of this passport in 1988 was for an overnight visit to Malta on 20/21 December, and it was never used again. On that visit he arrived in Malta on flight KM231 about 5.30 P.M. He stayed overnight in the Holiday Inn, Sliema, using the name Abdusamad. He left on 21 December on flight LN147, scheduled to leave at 10.20 A.M. The first accused travelled on his own passport in his own name on a number of occasions in 1988, particularly to Malta on 7 December where he stayed until 9 December when he departed for Prague, returning to Tripoli via Zurich and Malta on 16/17 December.

[88] A major factor in the case against the first accused is the identification evidence of Mr Gauci. For the reasons we have already given, we accept the reliability of Mr Gauci on this matter, while recognising that this is not an unequivocal identification. From his evidence it could be inferred that the first accused was the person who bought the clothing which surrounded the explosive device. We have already accepted that the date of purchase of the clothing was 7 December 1988, and on that day the first accused arrived in Malta where he stayed until 9 December. He was staying at the Holiday Inn, Sliema, which is close to Mary's House. If he was the purchaser of this miscellaneous collection of garments, it is not difficult to infer that he must have been aware of the purpose for which they were being bought. We accept the evidence that he was a member of the JSO, occupying posts of fairly high rank. One of these posts was head of airline security, from which it could be inferred that he would be aware at least in general terms of the nature of security precautions at airports from or to which LAA operated. He also appears to have been involved in military procurement. He was involved with Mr Bollier, albeit not specifically in connection with MST timers, and had along with Badri Hassan formed a company which leased premises from MEBO and intended to do business with MEBO. In his interview with Mr Salinger he denied any connection with MEBO, but we do not accept his denial. On 20 December 1988, he entered Malta using his passport in the name of Abdusamad. There is no apparent reason for this visit, so far as the evidence discloses. All that was revealed by acceptable evidence was that the first accused and the second accused together paid a brief visit to the house of Mr Vassallo at some time in the evening, and that the first accused made or attempted to make a phone call to the second accused at 7.11A.M. the following morning. It is possible to infer that this visit under a false name the night before the explosive device was planted at Luqa, followed by his departure for Tripoli the following morning at or about the time the device must have been planted, was a visit connected with the planting of the device. Had there been any innocent explanation for this visit, obviously this inference could not be drawn. The only explanation that appeared in the evidence was contained in his interview with Mr Salinger, when he denied visiting Malta at that time and denied using the name Abdusamad or having had a passport in that name. Again, we do not accept his denial.

[89] We are. . . satisfied that the evidence as to the purchase of clothing in Malta, the presence of that clothing in the primary suitcase, the transmission of an item of baggage from Malta to London, the identification of the first accused (albeit not absolute), his movements under a false name at or around the material time, and the other background circumstances such as his association with Mr Bollier and with members of the JSO or Libyan military

who purchased MST-13 timers, does fit together to form a real and convincing pattern. There is nothing in the evidence which leaves us with any reasonable doubt as to the guilt of the first accused, and accordingly we find him guilty of the remaining charge in the Indictment as amended.

'90' The verdicts returned were by a unanimous decision of the three judges of the Court.

SIGNIFICANCE

The trial of Abdelbaset Ali Mohmed al Megrahi and Al Amin Khalifa Fhimah for the Lockerbie terrorist bombing attracted widespread international attention. The prosecution argued the terrorism was state-sponsored and that the men were acting under the direct orders of Colonel Qaddafi himself. Qaddafi's motive was vengeance for a 1986 U.S. bombing raid on Tripoli, Libya, conducted from British air bases. In that raid, Qaddafi's adopted daughter was killed.

The defense argued that the bombing was the handiwork of a militant terrorist faction of the Popular Front for the Liberation of Palestine with aid from Syria and Iran. In finding al Megrahi guilty and Fhimah not guilty, the court did not address these larger geopolitical issues, instead focusing entirely on the actions and movements of the two accused.

What remained outstanding was the issue of compensation. In October 2002, the Libyan government offered the victims' families $2.7 billion, about $10 million per family. On August 15, 2003, the Libyan government accepted formal responsibility for the bombing, and on September 12, 2003, the United Nations lifted its sanctions against the country, though the United States continued to refuse to do business with Libya, branding it a terrorist state.

Through the remainder of 2003 and 2004, Qaddafi tried to soften his image as a rogue leader. He received western European leaders; traveled to Brussels, Belgium; renounced efforts to develop weapons of mass destruction; and compensated victims of other terrorist attacks with Libyan connections. Al Megrahi is serving a twenty-seven-year sentence in Greenock prison near Glasgow, Scotland.

The crash of Pan Am 103 left wrecked houses and a deep gash in the ground in the village of Lockerbie, Scotland. AP/WIDE WORLD PHOTOS

FURTHER RESOURCES

Books

Gerson, Allan, and Jerry Adler. *The Price of Terror*. New York: HarperCollins, 2001.

Matar, Khalil R., and Robert W. Thabit. *Lockerbie and Libya: A Study in International Relations*. Jefferson, NC: McFarland, 2003.

Web sites

BBC News. "In Depth: Lockerbie Trial." <http://news.bbc.co.uk/1/hi/in_depth/scotland/2000/lockerbie_trial/default.stm> (accessed May 16, 2005).

"Former Yugoslavs" and "The Jewish Cemetery"

Ethnic terrorism: Serbian Murders of Bosnian Civilians

Poetry

By: Izet Sarajlic

Date: 1994

Source: Izet Sarajlic's *Sarajevo's War*, a collection of poems published in 1994.

About the Author: Izet Sarajlic was born in Bosnia in 1930 and studied Slavic philosophy in Sarajevo as a young man. He later became the editor of *Zivot* (*Life*) Magazine. Sarajlic was one of the most prolific and often translated poets of the former Yugoslavia, with more than thirty books of poems, several memoirs, and political writings to his credit. His first collection of poetry was published when he was only nineteen years old. He was a member of the Academy of Arts and Sciences of Bosnia and Herzegovina and an intellectuals association known as Krug 99. Sarajlic died in Sarajevo in February, 2002.

INTRODUCTION

The Geneva Conventions of 1949 and 1977 codified the protection and immunity of civilians during times of international conflict and civil war. Therefore, the hostilities directed at Muslim civilians in Bosnia-Herzegovina during the period of March 1992 through 1995 may be defined as a series of terrorist

A man looks at the wreckage of a Jewish shop in 1938 Berlin, the day after the "Kristallnacht" rampage that preceded Hitler's ethnic cleansing campaign against the Jews. AP/WIDE WORLD PHOTOS

acts perpetrated on the basis of ethnic and religious affiliation.

The complexities of the conflict are founded in the political and historical strife between Bosnian-Serbs and Bosnian-Muslims prior to the First World War (1915–1918). Most Baltic nations, including the former Yugoslavia, have traditionally been populated by diverse ethnic and religious groups that have clashed, sometimes violently, over the years. The region now known as Bosnia-Herzegovina is home to Serbs (mainly Orthodox Christian), Croats (mainly Roman Catholic) and Ethnic Albanians (Muslim).

Bosnia was a part of the Ottoman (Turkish) Empire until 1878 when it was annexed by the Austro-Hungarian Empire. Under the rule of Austria-Hungary, divisions between the three ethnic populations were cemented by a political system of proportional representation, divided by religious affiliation. Following WWI and the defeat of the Austrians, the victorious allies created the country of Yugoslavia. Once more invaded by Axis powers during World War II (1938–1945), Yugoslavia was divided into various regions as a means of gaining political control. Josip Tito lead a strong resistance movement against the German occupation and following the defeat of Germany and the end of the Second World War, Tito reunified Yugoslavia and became president.

Tito was a strong leader with a vision of a peaceful Yugoslavia, unified under a communist ideal that would surpass individual ethnic loyalties. He understood the problematic nature of the religious and ethnic divisions in Yugoslavia, and particularly the separatist leanings of the large Serbian population. To this end, he divided Serbia into two provinces, Kosovo and Vojvodina, to neutralise the threat of a Serbian uprising.

The death of Tito in 1980 coincided with the beginning of the end of communism in Eastern Europe. The ravages of the cold war had weakened the communist ideal and allowed the resurgence of ethnic nationalism. Without Tito's iron-grip method of leadership, Serbians began to dream of a reunified Serbian province and an independent Serbian nation. Serbian nationalist Slobodan Milosevic took charge of the Serbian cause in 1987 and under his leadership, the push for a separate nation began in earnest. Fuelled by allegations of Albanian cruelty toward Serbs in Kosovo (formerly part of the Serbian province) and a general sense of economic deprivation, Milosevic electrified the ethnic tension and pushed for decisive action throughout the region. In 1989, violent uprisings of the Serbian population in Kosovo and Vojvodina drove the elected leaders out of office and the situation in Yugoslavia quickly began to deteriorate. The increasingly poor economy and the resurgence of ethnic nationalism contributed to the eventual break-up of Yugoslavia, which commenced with the secession of Slovenia and Croatia in May of 1991.

Soon after, the leader of Bosnia-Herzegovina, Aliza Izetbegovic, proposed independence for Bosnia as well. Serbia originally attempted to keep Bosnia-Herzegovina from seceding by offering to redraw the territorial boundaries, but Izetbegovic refused and called for a referendum on Bosnian independence. While most Bosnian-Serbs boycotted the plebiscite, ninety per cent of those who voted were in favour of separation. On March 3, 1992, Bosnia-Herzegovina declared independence and soon after was recognised as such by both the European Union and the United Nations.

Bosnian-Serbs were not happy with the secession for they considered themselves to be a part of Milosevic's Serbian nation and in due course, rebelled against Bosnian-Muslims to wrest control of the territory. The struggle was violent and Serbs justified their cause by claiming that Aliza Izetbegovic planned to turn the Republic of Bosnia into a fundamentalist Islamic nation, even though Izetbegovic was considered a religious moderate by western diplomats. Although the Muslim forces within Bosnia were considerably larger than those of the Bosnian-Serbs, the latter of the two groups was supported by the Serbian army (The Yugoslav People's Army) under orders from Slobodan Milosevic and General Radovan Karadzic. Additionally, the Bosnian-Serbs established their own militia, under the command of General Ratko Mladic. Shortly after hostilities began the Serbian-led forces won control over two-thirds of Bosnia-Herzegovina and subsequently perpetrated a reign of terror against its Muslim inhabitants.

The Bosnian-Serbs wanted a "pure" Serbian territory and set out to enforce a policy of ethnic cleansing. Ethnic cleansing is generally defined as the elimination of particular ethnic or religious groups from a defined territory through forced removal, terror or genocide. Serbian military contingents forced Muslims to leave their homes, interned them in concentration camps and perpetrated rapes and mass killings. While under siege, the capital city of Sarajevo was razed of buildings and artifacts bearing cultural significance to Muslims in an effort to wipe all traces of Islamic culture and religion from the region. By the time the international community intervened and NATO ordered a ceasefire in 1994, the vast majority of Bosnian-Muslims had either fled as refugees or had been murdered. Only small pockets of Muslim citizens remained in villages throughout the countryside.

The eyewitness accounts and memoirs of those who lived through the regime of ethnic-cleansing in

Bosnia reveal stark differences between the indifferent international response to atrocities in Bosnia and the world-wide outrage over the Jewish Holocaust (or Shoah) during World War II.

■ PRIMARY SOURCE

Former Yugoslavs
(for Mustafa Cengicnek)

Some of us
former Yugoslavs
are marked for genocide
by a part of the late
Yugoslav People's Army.

The Jewish Cemetery

From the direction of Marindvor
the deadliest fire
comes out of the Jewish Cemetery.
Though he set up his machine-gun behind his grave,
Milosevic's mercenary had no way of knowing
who Isak Samokovlija was,
nor who were flattened by his out-going bullets.
He, simply, for every snuffed-out life,
be it a first-aid Doctor
or by chance a street car driver,
stuffs 100 German Marks into his pocket.

SIGNIFICANCE

These two poems by Bosnian poet Izet Sarajlic are reflective of the terrorism in Bosnia, perpetrated by agents of the Serbian state and military against Muslim civilians. The first poem, "Former Yugoslavs," alludes to the fact that the army that had been established to protect the citizens of Yugoslavia, The People's Army of Yugoslavia (PAY), now had turned against a group of those citizens. The PAY was comprised primarily of Serbian individuals. Under orders from Slobodan Milosevic, the army was sent into the newly independent Republic of Bosnia-Herzegovina to take back the territory for Serbians and to "cleanse" Bosnia of its Muslim population.

The second poem, "The Jewish Cemetery," provides a picture of the conflict from the perspective of its victims on the ground in Sarajevo, the capital of Bosnia. Marindvor is a square in the heart of the city of Sarajevo where the most violent attacks took place. Marindvor is also significant in Sarajevo because it is the location of the National Library, one of the vestiges of culture and history in Bosnia that was deliberately destroyed by Serbian bombs. A first attempt to bomb the National Library was miscalculated and destroyed a Holiday Inn across the street. When asked

why they bombed the hotel, Serbian military officials admitted their mistake and identified the library as their target, pointing to the calculated destruction, not only of Muslim lives, but of culture and history in Bosnia as well. Thus, it is seen that the war in Bosnia was not merely a political war, but a war against ethnicity and the Islamic religion.

The Jewish cemetery referred to in the poem is also a landmark in Marindvor and was at the heart of the siege of Sarajevo. The Jewish ceremony was described by American journalist Aernout Van Lynden during the trial of Slobodan Milosevic as "a sort of no-man's land between the warring parties, right on the front lines." The grave of Isak Samokovlija is located in that cemetery. Known as the "Poet of Sarajevo," Samokovlija was a Jewish doctor, born in Bosnia, who was exiled during World War II and then returned to Sarajevo to serve as a doctor in the refugee camps. Sarajlic makes reference to the targeting of civilians in Bosnia, pointing out that the soldiers did not know their victims, nor even their occupations, and that government officials, particularly Slobodan Milosevic sanctioned the targeting of Muslim civilians.

The reference to 100 German marks in the poem holds a double entendre. As a result of the economic recession in the former Yugoslavia, one hundred marks was the average yearly income of a working individual in Bosnia. At the time, it was also the going price to secure transportation to the border and flee the country.

The poetry of Izet Sarajilic and others like him is a living testimony of the horrors perpetrated on Bosnian Muslims. Poetry, memoirs, and eyewitness accounts have helped to preserve a record of the events in Sarajevo and throughout Bosnia in the absence of governmental and authoritative accounts. The international community has since recognized the atrocities and human rights violations committed in Bosnia, and former president Slobodan Milosevic and Generals Radovan Karadzic and Ratko Mladic were arrested and charged with war crimes in 2001. The trial of Slobodan Milosevic commenced in 2002.

FURTHER RESOURCES

Books

Sells, Michael. *The Bridge Betrayed: Religion and Genocide in Bosnia.* Berkley: University of California Press, 1996.

Cigar, Norman. *Genocide in Bosnia: The Policy of Ethnic Cleansing.* Texas: A&M University Press, 1995.

Web sites

CNN.Interactive. "The Balkan Crisis: A Brief History." <http://www.cnn.com/SPECIALS/1997/bosnia/history/> (accessed July 4, 2005).

"Gaddafi Has Admitted His Role in Lockerbie Bombing"

Libyan Leader Muammar Gaddafi Admits to Terrorism

Newspaper Article

By: Imre Karacs and Kim Sengupta

Date: May 16, 2001

Source: *The Independent* (London).

About the Author: In 2001, Imre Karacs was a Berlin-based correspondent for *The Independent*. Karacs has also written for *The Times* (London) and MSNBC online. Kim Sengupta writes for *The Independent*. Sengupta was *The Independent's* foreign correspondent in the Middle East in 2001, and later covered the wars in Afghanistan and Iraq.

INTRODUCTION

On September 1, 1969 a group of military officers led by Col. Muammar al-Qaddafi (also known as Gaddafi) staged a coup against the ruling King Idis and took control of the north African nation of Libya. While holding no official position, Qaddafi assumed the role of the leader of Libya.

Qaddafi's relationship with the West has been controversial, and stems from his support for a system he called Islamic Socialism, which encouraged government control of large businesses and extreme social conservative policies.

Qaddafi is a strong supporter of Pan-Arabism, calling for the unity of all Arab nations and inherited the role of leader of the Arab nationalist movement when Egyptian president Gamel Abdel Nasser died in 1970. Throughout the 1970s, Qaddafi became known internationally for his support of terrorist groups and was considered a principal financer of the Black September group which murdered eleven Israeli athletes at the 1972 Olympics in Munich.

The United States also claimed that Qaddafi was behind a 1986 bombing of a Berlin disco where three people were killed and more than two hundred injured—many of them U.S. Army soldiers. United States forces were involved in attacks on Libyan patrol boats, and in April 1986, President Ronald Reagan ordered the U.S. military to carry out major bombing attacks against Libya's large cities.

In the early 1990s, Libya faced economic sanctions following the involvement of two Libyan citizens in the bombing of Pan Am 103 over Lockerbie, Scotland, an attack that killed 270 people.

The nose section of the airliner *Maid of the Seas*, Pan Am Flight 103, lies in a field near Lockerbie, Scotland. AP/WIDE WORLD PHOTOS

■ PRIMARY SOURCE

Colonel Muammar Gaddafi has admitted involvement in two of the worst terrorist outrages of the 1980s: the bombing of the Pan Am airliner that crashed on Lockerbie and the assault on a Berlin discotheque, a leaked German government memo reveals.

The Libyan leader's alleged admission came during a secret meeting with Chancellor Gerhard Schroder's chief foreign policy adviser, who related it to Germany's allies in Washington. A confidential account of that briefing has been leaked to a German newspaper.

The admission is seen as important for attempts to reintegrate Libya into the international community and have UN [United Nations] sanctions lifted. Acceptance of responsibility for acts of terrorism is the key stipulation demanded by the UN for the lifting of the sanctions imposed after the Lockerbie bombing.

Sanctions were suspended after Tripoli agreed to hand over two suspects for the Lockerbie bombing. But Britain and America say the sanctions will not be officially lifted and could be reimposed unless the Libyan regime accepts the terrorist responsibility condition.

So far authorities in the West have had difficulty linking Colonel Gaddafi to the bombings. It has proved even more difficult to convict those suspected of the bombing of Berlin's La Belle discotheque in 1986, in which three people were killed. But Michael Steiner, the German official in whom the Libyan leader allegedly confided, faced a summons to give evidence after the revelation was made yesterday at the La Belle trial in Berlin.

According to Allgemeine Zeitung, which published the leaked memo, Mr. Steiner visited Colonel Gaddafi in February. When Mr. Schroder visited Washington a month later, Mr Steiner was there during a meeting with President Bush. Also present was the German ambassador, Jurgen Chrobog, who cabled an account to his bosses in Berlin. It is this memo that appears to have found its way to the newspaper and to La Belle victims' lawyers.

SIGNIFICANCE

In later years, there has been considerable evidence that Qaddafi's policies and attitudes towards the West have become far more moderate. In addition to admitting his past role in terrorism, he announced that his country had been harboring a weapons of mass destruction (WMD) program, which he invited foreign experts to analyze and dismantle.

Although Qaddafi's vision of unity among Arab nations has not been realized, he is now considered a moderate leader among Arab states. In August 2003, Qaddafi reached an agreement with the United States and the United Kingdom that included renouncing terrorism, paying restitution to the families of the Lockerbie bombing victims, and cooperating with international monitoring agencies to disarm any nuclear, chemical, and biochemical weapons.

In March 2004, Britain's Prime Minister Tony Blair became the first Western leader in over two decades to meet with Qaddafi. The destruction of thousands of pounds of Libya's chemical weapons has continued under the supervision of international monitoring groups. Libya was also found to have an active nuclear weapons program, and Qaddafi has cooperated with international efforts to dismantle it.

FURTHER RESOURCES

Naden, Corinne J. *Muammar Qaddafi (Heroes and Villains)*. San Diego: Lucent Books, 2004.

Web sites

The CIA World Fact Book. "Libya." <http://www.cia.gov/cia/publications/factbook/geos/ly.html> (accessed July 6, 2005).

Rwandan Genocide

"Priests, Doctors, and Teachers Turn Genocidal"

Book excerpt

By: Mahmood Mamdani

Date: 2003

Source: "Priests, Doctors, and Teachers Turn Genocidal" is an excerpt published in *Sources of the Western Tradition*, edited by Marvin Perry, et. al., and published by Houghton Mifflin in 2003. Originally published in *When Victims Become Killers: Colonialism, Nativism, and the Genocide in Rwanda*, Princeton University Press, 2001.

About the Author: Dr. Mahmood Mamdani, the Herbert Lehman Professor of Government at the Department of Anthropology at Columbia University in New York, was born in Uganda. He earned a Bachelor's degree from the University of Pittsburgh, an M.A. and an M.A.L.D. from Tufts University Fletcher School of Law, and a Ph.D. from Harvard University. He has been the A.C. Jordan Professor of African Studies and the Director for the Center for African Studies at the University of Cape Town in South Africa. He has also taught at the University of Dar-es-Salaam in Tanzania and at Makerere University in Uganda. Mamdani is the founding Director of the Centre for Basic Research in Kampala, Uganda and was the President of the Council for the Development of Social Research in Africa (CODESRIA), based in Senegal. His particular areas of interest are African history, politics, and international relations. He is the author of numerous scholarly works, including *Iraq: Collective Punishment in War and Peace*, and *Good Muslim, Bad Muslim: America, The Cold War, and the Roots of Terror*.

INTRODUCTION

Genocide is a crime unlike any other in that it has as an aim the destruction of an entire nation, race, or ethnic group. It requires a detailed and well-thought-out plan with the intent of complete annihilation of all individuals who are members of the target group, in an effort to cause the extinction of the undesired population. In 1944, Raphael Lemkin, then advisor to the United States War Ministry, first coined the term in an effort to describe the occurrences at the extermination and concentration camps under Hitler's regime during World War II. He endeavored to make a very clear distinction between war crimes and the crimes against humanity perpetrated during the Holocaust of World War II. Lemkin was the first to formalize the notion that genocide is not a war crime; its immorality renders genocide a crime against all humanity. War is amoral but characterized by religious dogma or political ideological differences—different goals, very different outcomes. If a group of persons, an entire race or culture of persons, is systematically exterminated simply because they exist, it is considered a crime of the greatest magnitude against humanity; it violates the fundamental belief that all humans have the right to exist and to develop within their particular social systems.

■ PRIMARY SOURCE

. . . [E]ven if we can never know the numbers of those who killed, there is no escaping the disturbing fact that many did enthusiastically join in the killing. The genocide was not simply a state project. Had the killing been the work of state functionaries and those bribed by them, it would have translated into no more than a string of massacres perpetrated by death squads. Without massacres by machete-wielding civilian mobs, in the hundreds and thousands, there would have been no genocide. We now turn to the social underbelly of the genocide: the participation of those who killed with a purpose, for whom the violence of the genocide and its target held meaning. . .

Like the middle class of which they were a prominent part, priests were also divided between those who were targeted in the killings and those who led or facilitated the killings. Here, too, there was hardly any middle ground. A Lutheran minister recalled what the gangs told him: "You can have religion afterwards." Explaining why he walked around with a club, the minister told a reporter: "Everyone had to participate. To prove that you weren't RPF 'Rwandan Patriotic front, the Tutsi army', you had to walk around with a club. Being a pastor was not an excuse." Priests who had condemned the government's use of ethnic quotas in education and the civil service were among the first victims of the massacres. In all, 105 priests and 120 nuns, *at least a quarter of the clergy,* are believed to have been killed. But priests were not only among those killed, they were among the killers. Investigators with the United Nations (UN) Center for Human Rights claimed "strong evidence" that "about a dozen priests were actually killed." Others were accused of "supervising gangs of young killers. . . "

How could it be that most major massacres of the genocide took place in churches? How could all those institutions that we associate with nurturing life—not only churches, but schools and even hospitals—be turned into places where life was taken with impunity and facility? Medicins sans Frontieres (Doctors Without Borders), a medical charity, pulled out of the University Hospital in Kigali after its patients kept disappearing. *The British Medical Journal* quote testimony of Dr. Claude-Emile Rwagasonza: "The extremist doctors were also asking patients for their identity cards before treating them. They refused to treat sick

Tutsis. Also, many people were coming to the hospital to hide. The extremist doctors prevented many of these people from hiding in the hospital." A medical doctor, a member of the hospital staff, directed the militia into the hospital at Kibeho and shut off the power supply so that the massacre may proceed in darkness. Some of "the most horrific massacres occurred in maternity clinics, where people gathered in the belief that no one would kill mothers and new-born babies." "The percentage of doctors who became killers 'par excellence' was very high," concluded African Rights on the basis of extensive investigations. They included persons as highly qualified as Dr. Sosthene Munyemana, a gynecologist at the University Hospital of Butare, Rwanda's principal teaching hospital. "A huge number of the most qualified and experienced doctors in the country, men as well as women—including surgeons, physicians, paeditricians, gynaecologists, anaesthetists, public health specialists and hospital administrators—participated in the murder of their own Tutsi colleagues, patients, the wounded, and terrified refugees who had sought shelter in their hospitals, as well as their neighbors and strangers." In a sector as small as Tumba, three doctors played a central part. Of these, one was a doctor at Groupe Scolaire Hospital, and the other, her husband, was the health director for Butare. "Two of the most active assassins in Tumba" were a medical assistant and his wife, a nurse.

Close on the heels of priests and doctors as prime enthusiasts of the genocide were teachers, and even some human rights activists. When I visited the National University at Butare in 1995, I was told of the Hutu staff and students who betrayed their Tutsi colleagues and joined in the physical elimination. Teachers commonly denounced students to the militia or killed students themselves. A Hutu teacher told a French journalist without any seeming compunction: "A lot of people got killed here. I myself killed some of the children . . . We had eighty kids in the first year. There are twenty–five left. All the others, we killed them or they have run away." African Rights compiled a fifty-nine-page dossier charging Innocent Mazimpaka, who was in April 1991 the chairman of the League for the Promotion and Defence of Human Rights in Rwanda (LIPRODHOR) and simultaneously an employee of a Dutch aid organization, SNV, with responsibility for the genocide. Along with his younger brother, the *burgomaster* of Gatare commune, he was charged with the slaughter of all but twenty–one of Gatare's Tutsi population of 12,263. Rakiya Omaar pointed out that "several members of human rights groups are now known to have participated" in the killings, refuting "the notion that an independent civil society—of which the educated and the political opposition were the backbone—resisted the project of genocide."

That victims looking for a sanctuary should seek out churches, schools, and hospitals as places for shelter is totally understandable. But that they should be killed without any let or hindrance—even lured to these places for that purpose—is not at all understandable. As places of shelter turned into slaughterhouses, those pledged to heal or nurture life set about extinguishing it methodically and deliberately.

That the professions most closely associated with valuing life—doctors and nurses, priests and teachers, human rights activists—got embroiled in taking it is probably the most troubling question of the Rwandan genocide.

SIGNIFICANCE

Rwandan president Juvenal Habyarimana (a Hutu) died on April 6, 1994, when members of the Tutsi extremist group the Rwandan Patriotic Front (RPF) shot down his plane. On the same day, the RPF assassinated the Hutu prime minister of Rwanda, Agathe Uwilingiyimana. In the ensuing four months, the Rwandan genocide of the Tutsi population claimed the lives of somewhere between 5,000 and 1.3 million individuals. Although there is lack of agreement on the exact death toll, there is universal consensus that the systematic extermination of the Tutsi population in Rwanda represented the single largest example of genocide in the era after the Cold War. As horrendous as the fact of the genocide's occurrence, in and of itself, what is even more incomprehensible is the fact that the genocide was perpetrated not just by the prevailing political regime, but was enthusiastically participated in by those commonly believed to preserve and protect life: clergy, medical practitioners, human rights activists, and teachers. Compounding the tragedy was the ennui of most of the "civilized world": the genocide was either watched from the comfort of living rooms across the globe, with little concerted public outcry, or remained undermentioned by the media or the national powers.

The development of the Hutu-Tutsi climate of strife and hatred, in many ways a metaphor for modern terrorist in-and-out group theories, had its origins in Rwanda in the thirteenth century. The Tutsi population, which make up about 15 percent of present-day Rwanda, migrated into the country from the Kenyan and Tanzanian grasslands of the north and progressively dominated the prevailing Hutu population (about 85 percent of present-day Rwanda). By the fifteenth century, Tutsi-dominated clans became chiefdoms. By the end of the nineteenth century, the sociopolitical and economic divisions between the Hutus and the Tutsis had reached a point where the pastoralist Tutsis held virtually complete domination over the agriculturally based Hutus. Tensions and strife escalated over time, and were significantly exacerbated with the arrival of the Belgians in Rwanda in the early part of the

twentieth century. The Belgian colonialists systematically "fed" the Hutus the propaganda (called the Hamitic Hypothesis) that the Tutsis were the cursed "Caucasian" descendents of Ham, who was considered to be the son of Noah. Throughout the first three decades of the twentieth century, the Belgians strove to institutionalize the belief that the Tutsis were superior (as they were considered Caucasians, rather than native Africans, which the Hutus were stated to be). To further emphasize their assertions, the Belgians gave preference to the Tutsis in the educational and public sectors.

In 1959, Rwanda experienced a "Social Revolution," wherein the economically powerful Hutus, led by Gregore Kayibanda, proposed the segregation of the Hutu and Tutsi populations. This occurred just after Rwanda became independent of Belgian colonial rule. The growing cultural tensions between the Hutu and the Tutsis, worsened by the impositions of colonial rule, effectively set the stage for the genocide that would take place in 1994. Although there was a period of stability during the 1970s and 1980s, largely as a result of a robust economy in Rwanda, tensions began to simmer began Hutus and Tutsis at the start of the 1990s when the economy of Rwanda collapsed. When the Tutsi extremist group called the RPF (Rwandan Political Front) attempted a coup during their 1993 uprising, the Hutus, driven by both fear and small group psychology, became so fearful of a shift in political power (from Hutu domination to a return to Tutsi domination) that the governmental powers were easily able to create the massive backlash that became the Rwandan Tutsi genocide of 1994.

In a manner analogous to the Nazi genocide of World War II, the well-organized leaders were able to create an atmosphere of fear and hatred that had the result of mobilizing the common people, as well as members of the educated elite—doctors, priests, teachers, human rights activists—to enthusiastically, willingly, or even reluctantly, commit atrocities against friends, colleagues, and neighbors, as well as strangers.

FURTHER RESOURCES
Books

Mamdani, Mahmood. *When Victims Become Killers: Colonialism, Nativism, and the Genocide in Rwanda.* Princeton University Press, 2002.

Perry, M., Peden, J.R., and T.H. Von Laue. *Sources of the Western Tradition. Volume II. 5th ed.*. Houghton Mifflin, 2003.

Mamdani, Mahmood. *Good Muslim, Bad Muslim: America, the Cold War, and the Roots of Terror.* Academic Literature, Pantheon Books, 2004.

Perry, M., Peden, J.R., and T.H. Von Laue. *Sources of the Western Tradition. Volume II. 5th ed.* Houghton Mifflin, 2003.

Web sites

Frontline: Who Were The Organizers. "Special Reports: The Rwanda Crisis." <http://www.pbs.org/wgbh/pages/frontline/shows/rwanda/reports/prunierexcerpt.html> (accessed July 2, 2005).

Frontline: The World's Most Wanted Man: Genocide and War Crimes. "Special Reports: The Crime of Genocide." <http://www.pbs.org/wgbh/pages/frontline/shows/rwanda/reports/dsetexhe.html> (accessed July 2, 2005).

Frontline: The Crime of Genocide. "Never Again: The World's Most Unfulfilled Promise." <http://www.pbs.org/wgbh/pages/frontline/shows/karadzic/genocide/neveragain.html> (accessed July 2, 2005).

7 Global Terrorist Movements

Introduction to Global Terrorist Movements

Global terrorist groups are a relatively new terrorist phenomenon, at least in terms of their structure and organization. Until the last decades of the twentieth century, actions of terrorist groups were localized and mostly confined to the regions where the disputes between peoples and ideologies inflamed passions. Separatist groups in particular sometimes traveled vast distances to strike at the heart of a colonial empire, although terrorist acts could usually be traced to a group or dispute most commonly associated with a particular geographic area.

As the world has drawn closer in terms of communication and ease of travel, ideas and disputes increasingly transcend old political or geographic boundaries. Not surprisingly, this same closeness has fostered the rise of terrorist groups capable of operating on a global scale.

Terrorist organizations have embraced many of the concepts of asymmetric warfare, particularly when planning operations against Western power forces. Because of the superpower status of the United States, terrorist groups utilize asymmetric warfare techniques to bolster hopes of achieving limited victories. For example, terrorist organizations seek to exploit the vulnerabilities of free and open societies, such as those in the United States and Europe. By attacking infrastructure and civilian populations, terrorist groups aim to cause political turmoil, dissent, and ultimately bring change to United States and European foreign policy without exposing themselves directly to the might of Western military forces.

The escalation of the range of terrorist groups, and their ability to draw on multiple sources of personnel and materials, however, raises real concern in the international community that the next evolution in global terrorism could involve the acquisition and use of weapons of mass destruction (nuclear, chemical, or biological weapons).

The interdependence and integration of the world's economies also make financial markets attractive targets for international terrorism. The selection of the World Trade Center Towers, as targets of international terrorism, demonstrated that global terrorists often seek to damage both physical and economic infrastructure.

Global terrorist groups often do not rely on the same structure and lines of command communication as localized terrorist cells. Small groups or cells of terrorists may be effectively isolated from each other so that counterterrorism measures that root out one cell may leave others intact and operational. Support for individual cells by a command structure may be tangible in terms of personnel, training, and money, such as the support given by al-Qaeda to the September 11th hijackers, or cells may be "home grown" or otherwise act independently of a global command structure. Such "copycat" cells, inspired rather than directed, are argued to have been responsible for bombings in Madrid and London.

Facets of organized crime, certainly not new phenomena, may also now be characterized as terrorist groups or terrorist cells. In particular, narcoterrorists and weapons smugglers have adopted terrorist tactics that range the globe as part of their efforts to sway political opinion, strike out at enemies, or extend power.

"What Went Wrong in Somalia?"

U.S. Army Rangers Killed in Downed Helicopter

Magazine article

By: Louise Leif, et al.

Date: October 18, 1993

Source: *U.S. News & World Report.*

About the Author: Louise Leif is a former journalist, with extensive experience in both print and television media. Leif is fluent in Arabic and has coordinated seminars dealing with women's rights, diplomacy, and Arab television. She is currently employed by the Pew Charitable Trusts.

INTRODUCTION

By the fall of 1992, the nation of Somalia was war-torn and ravaged by famine. An estimated half million Somalis were already dead, and hundreds of thousands more were facing possible starvation. Despite extensive efforts by the United Nations (UN) and other international aid organizations, a long history of ongoing clan violence within the nation created a major obstacle to achieving famine relief. In response to this situation, U.S. President George H. W. Bush deployed U.S. troops to Somalia in order to protect international relief workers. This effort, dubbed "Operation Restore Hope," accompanied a UN mandate both to protect humanitarian workers and to secure a stable environment for eventual political self-rule, employing military force as necessary.

Over the following year, almost 30,000 U.S. troops, along with 10,000 soldiers from other nations, entered Somalia, and by mid-1993, mass starvation had been largely eliminated. The peacekeepers then faced the task of overcoming the decades-long intertribal conflicts within the war-torn nation. Among the most notorious of the warlords was former army general Mohamed Farrah Aidid, leader of the Habr Gidr clan.

Aidid had risen to the top of the UN's wanted list following a bloody battle with UN forces in June 1993 in which 24 Pakistani soldiers were killed and several were skinned. In response, the UN called for his arrest. The UN relied on specially trained U.S. Army units to conduct surgical strikes in which Aidid and his close associates would be extracted from their hideouts to stand trial. The Army Rangers arrived in August, with plans to locate and apprehend Aidid that fall. On

October 3, the Rangers got their opportunity, when reliable intelligence placed Aidid and his top lieutenants in the town of Mogadishu, at the Olympic Hotel.

■ PRIMARY SOURCE

At first the raid went like clockwork. "The intelligence was very good, it was very timely," says a U.S. military official. At 3:30 P.M. about 100 Rangers of Task Force 160 "fast roped" down from Blackhawk helicopters, descending on the hotel and quickly capturing 19 of Aidid's aides. Unable to climb back up to their helicopters with their prisoners, the soldiers waited for another Ranger detachment to make its way to the hotel through Mogadishu's shattered streets in trucks and humvees. Then disaster struck. One Blackhawk was hit by 23-mm cannon fire from the hotel and crashed. Minutes later a second helicopter was hit and went down about 1/14 miles from where the first Blackhawk had crashed. A third helicopter arrived; it was hit and limped back to the relative safety of the city's seaport.

Aidid's men opened up on the trapped Americans from rooftops, buildings and even trees. The Rangers, armed only with machine guns and grenade launchers, were cut off and outgunned. "Those guys were flat playing Custer's last stand," says one senior officer. A rescue convoy finally broke through from the airport some nine hours later, but at least 15 Americans were killed, 77 others were wounded, four were missing in action and at least one, Chief Warrant Officer Michael Durant, was Aidid's captive.

What went wrong? How had American soldiers who had gone to Somalia for the noblest of purposes—feeding a starving nation—come to be seen by many Somalis as just another militia, and by no means an invincible one? . . . The mistakes that were made cover the waterfront, from political to tactical: . . .

False premises. Both the U.N. and the United States have based their policies on fundamental misunderstandings about Somali society, chiefly the idea that General Aidid personally was the problem and removing him from the equation was the solution. While U.N. investigators found persuasive evidence that Aidid's forces did ambush the Pakistanis, no one looked deeper to understand the interclan politics that led up to the attack. . . . "Aidid is his clan," says Mohammad Sahnoun, a former U.N. envoy to Somalia who was dismissed . . . last October for criticizing U.N. operations there. "In Somali culture, the worst thing you can do is humiliate them, to do something to them you are not doing to another clan. . . . It's the kind of psychology the U.N. doesn't understand. . . . "

Abandoning negotiations. On June 6, the day after the Pakistani ambush and 11 weeks before the U.N.'s inquiry into it was completed, the U.N. Security Council, with strong backing from the United States and U.N. Secretary General Boutros Boutros-Ghali, passed a resolution calling for the detention and arrest of "those responsible," and the hunt for Aidid began. From that point, negotiations among the Somali factions came to a halt. [Tom] Farer and many diplomats, including members of the secretary general's own staff, thought the U.N. should have instead negotiated a cease-fire in place while it arranged a trial for Aidid by an impartial tribunal. But the U.N.'s attitude, says Farer, was "punish and convict Aidid. . . . "

Reports by the Army and the Joint Chiefs' intelligence directorate, produced within two days of last week's raid, catalog a host of other mistakes committed by U.S. forces in the October 3 raid. The Rangers chose to launch their raid in midafternoon rather than take advantage of U.S. night-fighting capabilities, and the Americans were surprised by Aidid's coordinated counterattack. "We send a rescue force that's not adequate to the job," says one officer. "How many times do we have to let that happen before we catch on?"

The final and most tragic mistake, however, may be allowing the Somali debacle to discourage any U.S. involvement in post–Cold War peacekeeping operations. "We're learning terrible lessons," says a State Department official.

SIGNIFICANCE

Michael Durant, the captured U.S. soldier, was released after eleven days of captivity; his release was cited by President Bill Clinton as proof that the administration's Somalia policy was a success. While plans continued for withdrawal of U.S. troops, the administration dispatched heavy armor to protect U.S. forces in Somalia, including 30 M1-A1 tanks and Bradley armored fighting vehicles. Ironically, this type of heavy armament was urgently requested by commanders in Somalia more than two weeks before the Mogadishu debacle, and would have provided the level of firepower necessary to rescue the downed troops. On March 25, 1994, with Aidid still at large, the final U.S. troops left Somalia.

After the conflict in Somalia, Defense Secretary Les Aspin resigned, and the incident put a damper on Clinton's ongoing efforts at nation-building. In the U.S. political arena, the conflict in Somalia may have created greater reluctance to commit troops to such missions.

In 1997, Mark Bowden, a reporter for the *Philadelphia Enquirer*, published an extensively researched, month-long series of stories on the battle at Mogadishu titled "Black Hawk Down." The series was expanded

and published as a hardcover book in 1999, and was made into a feature film directed by Ridley Scott in 2001.

FURTHER RESOURCES
Books

Bowden, Mark. *Black Hawk Down: A Story of Modern War*. New York: Atlantic Monthly Press, 1999.

Durant, Michael J. *In the Company of Heroes*. New York: G.P. Putnam's Sons, 2003.

Web sites

Carnegie Reporter. "The International Reporting Project: Giving Journalists a New Perspective on the News." <http://www.carnegie.org/reporter/09/news/index2.html> (accessed June 13, 2005).

Philly Online. "Black Hawk Down." <http://inquirer.philly.com/packages/somalia/sitemap.asp> (accessed June 13, 2005).

World Trade Center Bombing, 1993

World Trade Center Bombing Suspect Apprehended in Pakistan

Press release

By: U.S. Department of Justice, Office of Public Affairs

Date: February 8, 1995

Source: U.S. Department of Justice, Office of Public Affairs

About the Author: The Office of Public Affairs (OPA) serves to keep the public informed of the Department of Justice's activities to the best extent possible without jeopardizing ongoing investigations, violating individual rights, or compromising U.S. security interests. To this end, the OPA issues hundreds of press releases each year, responds to queries from news organizations, and arranges interviews and news conferences.

INTRODUCTION

In the early morning hours of February 16, 1993, a rental van loaded with more than 1500 pounds of explosives was detonated in the parking garage beneath Tower One of the World Trade Center in New York City.

FBI agents view the damage caused by the 1993 terrorist bombing of the parking garage at the World Trade Center towers in New York. © REUTERS NEWMEDIA INC./CORBIS

The bomb blew a hole 150 feet wide and several stories deep in the parking garage, killing six and injuring more than a thousand people. The explosion caused more than $300 million in property damage, but the towers did not fall, as the men who set the bomb had hoped.

The idea of a terrorist attack on U.S. soil was so unthinkable in 1993 that at first the explosion was assumed to be an accident. The detection of nitrates at the bomb crater, however, soon alerted FBI bomb experts to the nature of the bomb.

The investigation of the attack was thorough and yielded quick arrests. The first to be apprehended was Mohammad Salameh, caught when he tried to retrieve his security deposit for the van used in the attack. Within days, the other conspirators were identified from a small community of Arab radicals living in New Jersey. Within a few weeks, a second conspirator, Mahmud Abouhalima was apprehended in Egypt and extradited to the United States. In the process of the

investigation, the agents even found another cell of extremists who were planning to blow up a series of New York City landmarks. By 1995, many of the bombers, and many of those involved in the landmark plot, had been arrested, tried and convicted.

Ramzi Yousef, known to his co-conspirators only as Rashid the Iraqi, was the undisputed leader and mastermind of the 1993 attack on the World Trade Center. Within hours of the bombing, he boarded a plane to Pakistan. After spending some time traveling around the Middle East and Asia, Yousef and some associates moved to the Philippines and began hatching a bold plot to blow up as many as twelve airliners en route to the United States from Asia. In December of 1994, Yousef and his associates bombed the Greenbelt Theater in Manila. Less than a week later, he placed a small bomb on Philippine Airlines Flight 434 to Tokyo, killing one Japanese businessman.

On January 6, 1995, Yousef and two accomplices were mixing chemicals in his apartment when a fire broke out, forcing them to flee into the streets of Manila. Remembering he had left his laptop computer behind, he sent one of his accomplices back to retrieve it. Philippine police, responding to the fire, captured the accomplice and the laptop, which contained detailed plans for the airliner plot. Yousef fled to Pakistan, where neighbors ultimately turned him in to the Pakistani authorities. After being tried and convicted for the Manila bombing, he was extradited to the United States to stand trial for the World Trade Center attack.

PRIMARY SOURCE

Attorney General Janet Reno said today that Ramzi Ahmed Yousef, a fugitive indicted for the 1993 World Trade Center bombing in New York City, has been arrested abroad and returned to the United States by the Federal Bureau of Investigation to be tried on the bombing charges.

Reno said "Yousef was apprehended in Pakistan and turned over to American authorities to face charges of taking part in a bombing that killed six persons and injured more than 1,000 others."

Reno said Yousef was taken into custody Tuesday in Pakistan, turned over to FBI agents there, and then flown aboard a U.S. aircraft to New York last night.

FBI Director Louis J. Freeh said "The FBI has conducted a world-wide search for Yousef since he was charged shortly after the bombing on February 26, 1993." Yousef was first indicted on March 11, 1993, and named in a fifth superseding indictment on September 1.

Freeh said "Other parts of the federal government that made invaluable contributions to the investigation were the Department of State, including its Diplomatic Security Service, and the Drug Enforcement Administration. "

United States Attorney Mary Jo White of the Southern District of New York said "Yousef is expected to be arraigned in Manhattan Federal Court on Thursday."

White said "The message that this sends is that we will pursue accused terrorists wherever they seek to hide and bring them to justice."

Four of Yousef's co-defendants were convicted of federal charges on March 4, 1994, in the World Trade Center bombing: Mohammad Salameh, Nidal Ayyad, Mahmud Abouhalima, and Ahmad Mohammad Ajaj. They have each been sentenced to 240 years of imprisonment without the possibility of parole.

The indictment charged Yousef, 27, who was born in the Middle East, with 11 counts relating to the World Trade Center bombing. The most serious charges carry a maximum penalty upon conviction of life in prison without parole.

FBI and ATF agents entering the World Trade Center parking garage in New York after the 1993 bombing. © REUTERS/CORBIS

The indictment said Yousef, using a false name, flew to New York from Pakistan in September 1992, and later purchased chemicals. In January and February 1993, the indictment said, Yousef and other co-conspirators mixed chemicals in a Jersey City, New Jersey, apartment to produce explosive materials.

The co-conspirators caused an explosive device to detonate in a van in a garage area beneath the World Trade Center complex on February 26, 1993, the indictment said. On the same day, Yousef again used a false name when he boarded a flight in New York City for Pakistan, the indictment said.

SIGNIFICANCE

Despite the tone of this press release, terrorism experts view the U.S. government's response to the 1993 World Trade Center bombing as flawed, especially in the failure of intelligence agencies to coordinate, collect, and analyze valuable information about the attack and attackers.

Of special note is the paragraph in which Freeh acknowledges the contributions of other governmental agencies to the case. Conspicuous by its absence is any mention of the Central Intelligence Agency (CIA). At the time, federal statute actually prevented information sharing among federal agencies in criminal cases, in order to preserve the government's ability to prosecute without being forced to provide critical information to the defendants' legal counsel. Consequently, the CIA did not learn the full details of the attack until the FBI made its case public at the end of the first trial.

As a result, several important connections were missed by both agencies. Yousef had trained in Osama Bin Laden's camps in Afghanistan and had stayed in Bin Ladin's guesthouse, the so-called house of martyrs, both before and after the 1993 bombing. At the time of Yousef's arrest, several pictures of Bin Laden were found in his luggage.

Among the information gathered from Yousef's captured laptop and the subsequent interrogations of his Manila accomplice was the fact that several Middle Eastern pilots were in the process of training in U.S. flight schools. At least one of the pilots had already proposed flying hijacked planes into federal buildings, a strategy that would be used a mere six years later to devastating effect against the very same target chosen by Yousef.

FURTHER RESOURCES

Books

Reeve, Simon. *The New Jackals: Ramzi Yousef, Osama Bin Laden, and the Future of Terrorism*. Boston: Northeastern University Press, 1999.

Coll, Steve. *Ghost Wars: The Secret History of the CIA, Afghanistan, and Bin Laden, from the Soviet Invasion to September 10, 2001*. New York: The Penguin Group, 2004.

Web sites

Musarium.com. "WTC Bombings: 1993." <http://www.musarium.com/stories/america-attacked/wtc/index.lasso> (accessed July 5, 2005).

Television image of Osama Bin Laden released by Qatar's Al-Jazeera television broadcast on October 5, 2001. AP/WIDE WORLD PHOTOS

"Osama Bin Laden: Islamic Extremist Financier"

CIA Assessment

Analyst report

By: Central Intelligence Agency (CIA)

Date: August 14, 1996

Source: The Central Intelligence Agency

About the Author: Established by the National Security Act of 1947, the Central Intelligence Agency is charged with providing intelligence on matters of national security to top decision makers in the United States government. The director and the deputy director are appointed by the president with the advice and consent of the Senate. In 1986, President Reagan established the CIA's Counter Terrorism Center (CTC) amid growing concern about international terrorism. The CTC is specifically charged with coordinating the efforts of the national intelligence community to "preempt, disrupt, and defeat terrorists."

INTRODUCTION

In 1996, Osama Bin Laden was known to the CIA primarily as an Islamic extremist wanted by the government of Saudi Arabia, who had been trying to kidnap and/or kill him since 1991. Today, it is known that the United States had earned Bin Laden's permanent enmity even before that, in 1990, by using Saudi Arabia as a staging ground for the first Gulf War.

The following 1996 assessment by an unknown CIA analyst offers a fascinating snapshot into what little we did know of Bin Laden before he ever declared a fatwa against the United States.

PRIMARY SOURCE

Osama bin Muhammad bin Awad Bin Laden is one of the most significant financial sponsors of Islamic extremist activities in the world today. One of some 20 sons of wealthy Saudi construction magnate Muhammad Bin Laden, founder of the Kingdom's Bin Laden Group business empire, Osama joined the Afghan resistance movement following the 26 December 1979 Soviet invasion of Afghanistan. "I was enraged and went there at once, " he claimed in a 1993 interview. "I arrived within days, before the end of 1979."

Bin Laden gained prominence during the Afghan war for his role in financing the recruitment, transportation, and training of Arab nationals who volunteered to fight alongside the Afghan mujahedin. By 1985, Bin Laden had drawn on his family's wealth plus donations received from sympathetic merchant families in the Gulf region, to organize the Islamic Salvation Foundation, or al-Qaeda, for this purpose.

- A network of al-Qaeda recruitment centers and guesthouses in Egypt, Saudi Arabia, and Pakistan has enlisted and sheltered thousands of Arab recruits. This network remains active.
- Working in conjunction with extremist groups like the Egyptian al-Gama'at al-Islamiyyah, also know as the Islamic Group, al-Qaeda organized and funded camps in Afghanistan and Pakistan that provided new recruits paramilitary training in preparation for the fighting in Afghanistan.
- Under al-Qaeda auspices, Bin Laden imported bulldozers and other heavy equipment to cut roads, tunnels, hospitals, and storage depots through Afghanistan's mountainous terrain to move and shelter fighters and supplies.

After the Soviets withdrew from Afghanistan in 1989, Bin Laden returned to work in the family's Jeddah-based construction business. However, he continued to support militant Islamic groups that had begun targeting moderate Islamic governments in the region. Saudi officials held Bin Laden's passport during 1989–1991 in a bid to prevent him from solidifying contacts with extremists whom he had befriended during the Afghan war.

Bin Laden relocated to Sudan in 1991, where he was welcomed by National Islamic Front (NIF) leader Hasan al-Turabi. In a 1994 interview, Bin Laden claimed to have surveyed business and agricultural investment opportunities in Sudan as early as 1983. He embarked on several business ventures in Sudan in 1990, which began to thrive following his move to Khartoum. Bin Laden also formed symbiotic business relationships with wealthy NIF members by undertaking civil infrastructure development projects on the regime's behalf:

- Bin Laden's company, Al-Hijrah for Construction and Development, Ltd., built the Tahaddi (challenge) road linking Khartoum with Port Sudan, as well as a modern international airport near Port Sudan.
- Bin Laden's import-export firm, Wadi al-Aqiq Company, Ltd., in conjunction with his Taba Investment Company, Ltd., secured a near monopoly over Sudan's major agricultural exports of gum, corn, sunflower, and sesame products in cooperation with prominent NIF members. At the same time, Bin Laden's Al-Themar al-Mubarak-ah Agriculture Company, Ltd. grew to encompass large tracts of land near Khartoum and in eastern Sudan.
- Bin Laden and wealthy NIF members capitalized Al-Shamal Islamic Bank in Khartoum. Bin Laden invested $50 million in the bank.

Bin Laden's work force grew to include militant Afghan war veterans seeking to avoid a return to their own countries, where many stood accused of subversive and terrorist activities. In May 1993, for example, Bin Laden financed the travel of 300 to 480 Afghan war veterans to Sudan after Islamabad launched a crackdown against extremists lingering in Pakistan. In addition to safehaven in Sudan, Bin Laden has provided financial support to militants actively opposed to moderate Islamic governments and the West:

- Islamic extremists who perpetrated the December 1992 attempted bombings against some 100 U.S. servicemen in Aden (billeted there to support U.N. relief operations in Somalia) claimed that Bin Laden financed their group.
- A joint Egyptian-Saudi investigation revealed in May 1993 that Bin Laden's business interests helped funnel money to Egyptian extremists, who used the cash to buy unspecified equipment, printing presses, and weapons.
- By January 1994, Bin Laden had begun financing at least three terrorist training camps in northern Sudan (camp residents included Egyptian, Algerian, Tunisian and Palestinian extremists) in cooperation with the NIF. Bin Laden's Al-Hijrah for Construction and Development works directly with Sudanese military officials to transport and provision terrorists training in such camps.
- Pakistani investigators have said that Ramzi Ahmed Yousef, the alleged mastermind of the February 1993 World Trade Center bombing, resided at the Bin Laden-funded Bayt Ashuhada (house of martyrs) guesthouse in Peshawar during most of the three years before his apprehension in February 1995.
- A leading member of the Egyptian extremist group al-Jihad claimed in a July 1995 interview that Bin Laden helped fund the group and was at times witting of

specific terrorist operations mounted by the group against Egyptian interests.

- Bin Laden remains the key financier behind the Kunar camp in Afghanistan, which provides terrorist training to al-Jihad and al-Gama'at al-Islamiyyah members, according to suspect terrorists captured recently by Egyptian authorities.

Bin Laden's support for extremist causes continues despite criticisms from regional governments and his family. Algeria, Egypt, and Yemen have accused Bin Laden of financing militant Islamic groups on their soil (Yemen reportedly sought INTERPOL's assistance to apprehend Bin Laden during 1994). In February 1994, Riyadh revoked Bin Laden's Saudi citizenship for behavior that "contradicts the Kingdom's interests and risks harming its relations with fraternal countries." The move prompted Bin Laden to form the Advisory and Reformation Committee, a London-based dissident organization that by July 1995 had issued over 350 pamphlets critical of the Saudi Government. Bin Laden has not responded to condemnation leveled against him in March 1994 by his eldest brother, Bakr Bin Laden, who expressed, through the Saudi media, his family's "regret, denunciation, and condemnation" of Bin Laden's extremist activities.

SIGNIFICANCE

History and hindsight cast a sober light on this assessment. Nine days after its issuance, Bin Laden removed all doubt about his intentions by publishing his own Declaration of War against the United States. Clearly Bin Laden saw his own role as more than that of financier; his enmity was focused squarely on the United States.

While the author is aware of most of Bin Laden's activities during the period in question, there are some significant gaps. In October 1993, for example, eighteen U.S. servicemen involved in a humanitarian relief effort were ambushed and killed in Somalia. Bin Laden claimed responsibility in a 1997 interview with CNN.

Bin Laden's connection to the 1993 World Trade Center bombing was not completely understood in 1996. Ramzi Yousef, mastermind of the 1993 attack, had been in contact with Bin Laden's organization since 1988, had stayed in the house of martyrs before as well as after the bombing, and had acquired his bomb-making skills in one of Bin Laden's training camps.

Also notably absent is any mention of Bin Laden's combat experience during the war against the USSR in Afghanistan. Here, Bin Laden is cast in the role of financier, but beginning in 1986, he had occupied his own front, commanding his own fighters in hundreds of small operations and at least five major battles. Bin Laden has said that these experiences on the battlefield and later events in Somalia convinced him that terrorism was an effective weapon. Through his al-Qaeda terrorist network, he coordinated several attacks on United States and allied interests, including the September 11, 2001 terrorist attacks in the United States and the March 11, 2004 attacks in Madrid, Spain.

FURTHER RESOURCES

Books

Moore, Robin. *The Hunt for Bin Laden*. New York: Random House, Inc., 2003.

Jacquard, Roland. *In the Name of Osama Bin Laden: Global Terrorism and the Bin Laden Brotherhood, Revised and Updated Edition*. Durham: Duke University Press, 2002.

Web sites

CNN.com. "Special Report, War Against Terror: Osama Bin Laden." <http://www.cnn.com/SPECIALS/2001/trade.center/binladen.section.html> (accessed June 26, 2005).

Fatwa Issued by Osama Bin Laden

"Declaration of War against the Americans Occupying the Land of the Two Holy Places"

Book excerpt

By: Osama Bin Laden

Date: August 23, 1996

Source: "Declaration of War . . . ," as published in Rubin, Barry, and Judith Colp Rubin's *Anti-American Terrorism and the Middle East: Defense of Legitimate Rights*, Oxford: Oxford University Press, 2002.

About the Author: Born in Riyadh, Saudi Arabia in 1957, Osama Bin Laden was the youngest son of a multimillionaire construction mogul and his fourth and youngest wife. From an early age, Bin Laden embraced his father's conservative view of Islam. Most biographers trace Bin Laden's radicalism to his university days at King Abdul-Aziz University in Jeddah, where he was exposed to the teachings of his professor and spiritual leader Shaykh Abdullah Azzam. In 1979, Bin Laden traveled to Afghanistan to support the resistance to the Soviet invasion, using his family's money and connections to provide logistical support and aid to the Afghani fighters. As the years of conflict wore on, Bin Laden's participation intensified, his role evolving from financier to combat engineer, to finally commander of his own Arab forces fighting his own front against the Soviet invaders. By this time, Bin Laden had formed al-Qaeda, which began as an organization to channel money and supplies from international supporters to the resistance. In 1989, Bin Laden returned to Saudi Arabia for what he thought would be a short visit. Two surprises awaited him there. The first was that he had become famous as a leader of the resistance in Afghanistan. The Saudi public had strongly supported the resistance and followed the events of the conflict closely. The second was that his passport had been restricted, preventing him from leaving Saudi Arabia again. The Saudi government had become increasingly worried about his popularity and radicalism during the mid-eighties, and were concerned that he would use his connections to open another front for jihad (holy war), perhaps in Yemen. Bin Laden's conflict with Saudi authorities came to a head with the Iraqi invasion of Kuwait in 1990. The final straw came when Saudi

Arabian King Fahd allowed the United States and its allies to occupy the Saudi kingdom as a staging ground for operations in the first Gulf War. Claiming later that his religious sensibilities were offended by the presence of United States troops (especially women), Bin Laden was transformed by that event into an implacable foe of both the Saudi government and the United States. Today, Bin Laden is considered by governments on three continents to be the most dangerous terrorist in the world. The U.S. government holds Bin Laden responsible for the 1998 bombings of U.S. embassies in Kenya and Tanzania, the attack on the USS *Cole* in October 2000, and the September 11, 2001 attacks on the World Trade Center and the Pentagon.

INTRODUCTION

In the months leading up to the first Gulf War, the Saudi Arabian government was aware that its decision to allow American troops on the Arabian Peninsula would not be a popular one. Afraid of what Bin Laden

U.S. Ambassador Prudence Bushnell, being evacuated from the U.S. Embassy following an explosion in Nairobi, August 7, 1998. AP/WIDE WORLD PHOTOS

بسم الله الرحمن الرحيم

الأحد ٦ رجب ١٤٢٢هـ

(والشهداء عند ربهم لهم أجرهم ونورهم)

إلى إخواننا المسلمين في باكستان...

السلام عليكم ورحمة الله وبركاته، وبعد:

A copy of Osama Bin Laden's statement that aired on Al-Jazeera, September 24, 2001. AP/WIDE WORLD PHOTOS

might do, and mindful of his considerable ability to incite like-minded Islamists among the populace, the Saudis placed him under house arrest as the first U.S. forces were arriving. In 1991, he managed to convince his elder brothers to use their influence with the government to obtain permission for him to take a brief visit to Pakistan. Departing in April of that year, he never returned to Saudi Arabia.

After an interlude in Afghanistan, Bin Laden went to Sudan, where he resided until May of 1996. In Khartoum, he reconnected with his old allies from the Afghan resistance, now members of Sudan's ruling National Islamic Front (NIF). He built a number of construction, agriculture, and trading businesses which turned a handsome profit. He brought in his old fighters from Afghanistan and employed them in his businesses. At that time, Bin Laden began to sponsor attacks on U.S. interests in Yemen and Somalia.

The first of these operations seems to have failed because of faulty intelligence. Although the attacks on two hotels in Yemen killed two tourists, no U.S. soldiers were occupying them at the time of the explosions. Citing the fact that the U.S. troops left Yemen

for Somalia within days after the attacks, Bin Laden would later claim the bombing as the first al-Qaeda victory against the United States.

He was more successful in Somalia. In 1993, eighteen U.S. soldiers were ambushed and killed in Mogadishu. Bin Laden later claimed responsibility for the action, though some have disputed his assertion that his fighters were personally involved.

Returning to Afghanistan in 1996, he issued his first public declaration of war against the United States. With this declaration, published in a London newspaper, Bin Laden begins an extended dialogue with Arab and Western journalists that will span the next few years. The following excerpt reveals both the depth of his enmity and his rationale for declaring the international jihad against America that persists to this day.

■ **PRIMARY SOURCE**

The people of Islam had suffered from aggression, inquiry, and injustice imposed on them by the Zionist-crusaders alliance and their collaborators, to the extent that the Muslims' blood became the cheapest and their wealth as loot in the hands of the enemies. Their blood was spilled in Palestine and Iraq. The horrifying pictures of the massacre of Qana, Lebanon, are fresh in our memory. Massacres in Tajikistan, Burma, Kashmir, Assam [in India], the Philippines, Fatani, Ogadin, Somalia, Eritrea, Chechnya, and Bosnia-Herzegovina took place, massacres that send shivers in the body and shake the conscience. All of this the world watches and hears, and not only didn't respond to these atrocities, but also, with a clear conspiracy between the United States and its allies and under the cover of the iniquitous United Nations, the dispossessed people were even prevented from obtaining arms to defend themselves.

The people of Islam awakened and realized that they are the main target for the aggression of the Zionist-crusaders alliance. All false claims and propaganda about "human rights" were hammered down and exposed by the massacres that took place against the Muslims in every part of the world.

The latest and greatest of these aggressions, incurred by the Muslims since the death of the prophet . . . is the occupation of the Land of the Two Holy Places—the foundation of the house of Islam, the place of the revelation, the source of the message, and the place of the noble Kaba [the central Islamic holy site], the *qibla* [direction of prayer] of all Muslims—by the armies of the American crusaders and their allies. (We bemoan this and can only say: "No power and power acquiring except through Allah.")

From here, today we begin the work, talking and discussing the ways of correcting what happened to the

Islamic world in general, and the land of the two holy places in particular. We wish to study the means that we could follow to return the situation to its normal path. And to return to the people their own rights, particularly after the large damages and the great aggression on the life and the religion of the people. An injustice that had affected every section and group of the people: civilians, military and security men, government officials and merchants, [and both] the young and old people, as well as schools and university students. Hundreds of thousands of unemployed graduates, who became the widest section of the society, were also affected.

To push the enemy—the greatest *kufr*—out of the country is a prime duty. No other duty after Belief is more important than [this] duty. Utmost effort should be made to prepare and instigate the *umma* against the enemy, the American-Israeli alliance—occupying the country of the two Holy Places . . . to the [al-Aqsa mosque in Jerusalem] . . .

The regime is fully responsible for what has been incurred by the country and the nation. However, the occupying American enemy is the principal and the main cause of the situation. Therefore efforts should be concentrated on destroying, fighting, and killing the enemy until, the grace of Allah, it is completely defeated . . .

SIGNIFICANCE

Although the target of the fatwa (an official order from an Islamic leader) is very specific (U.S. troops stationed in Saudi Arabia), the scope of the charge against the United States is a great deal broader.

Bin Laden casts the occupation by U.S. troops as the latest and greatest insult suffered by the Muslim world in their ancient struggle with the Zionist-crusader forces. In invoking the crusades, he places the conflict in a religious context, appeals to centuries-old resentments, and provides a theological imperative for jihad against the United States and Israel.

The jihad was widened in February 1998 to include civilian targets. In a joint statement with his associates in the name of the World Islamic Front, Bin Laden charged faithful Muslims across the world with killing Americans wherever they could be found. On August 7 of that year, the eighth anniversary of the ordering of U.S. troops into the Gulf region, bombs exploded simultaneously at the U.S. embassies in Kenya and Tanzania, killing 224 people and injuring thousands.

FURTHER RESOURCES
Books

Cook, David. *Understanding Jihad.* Berkley: University of California Press, 2005.

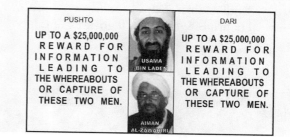

Leaflets dropped over Afganistan by the U.S. military advertising rewards of up to $25 million for information leading to the capture of Osama bin Laden or Aiman al-Zawahiri. AP/WIDE WORLD PHOTOS

Jacquard, Roland. *In the Name of Osama Bin Laden: Global Terrorism and the Bin Laden Brotherhood, Revised and Updated Edition.* Durham: Duke University Press, 2002.

Web sites

pbs.org. "Hunting Bin Laden" <http://www.pbs.org/wgbh/pages/frontline/shows/binladen/> (accessed June 26, 2005).

Indictment of Osama Bin Laden

Bombings of U.S. Embassies in Tanzania and Kenya

Indictment

By: Mary Jo White

Date: November 4, 1998

Source: *United States of America v Osama bin Laden.*

About the Author: Mary Jo White is a U.S. Attorney.

INTRODUCTION

In November 1998, the United States Federal Court issued an indictment of Osama Bin Laden and four of his associates for their involvement in the bombings of the U.S. embassies in Kenya and Tanzania on August 7, 1998. Two truck bombs had exploded outside the embassies, killing a total of more than 200 people and injuring more than 4,500, many of them African civilians. The Islamic terrorist organization al-Qaeda (ahl-KY-duh), which is led by Bin Laden, claimed responsibility for the bombings.

Al-Qaeda was formed in 1989 from Islamist volunteers including Bin Laden, who had gone to Afghanistan to fight against the Soviet Union's invasion and occupation of the country. When the Soviet army withdrew from Afghanistan, Bin Laden, a wealthy Saudi Arabian national, returned to his own country. He protested the Saudi government's policy of allowing U.S. troops into the country during the Gulf War with Iraq in 1990, objecting to the presence of "infidel" armies in Arab lands. As a result, he was expelled from the country and fled to Sudan. There he established the first al-Qaeda training camps and made alliances with Islamic militant groups around the world, until he was removed by the Government for his alleged involvement in terrorist activities.

Bin Laden then fled to Afghanistan, where he lived under the protection of the Taliban, an extremist fundamentalist Islamic group that took over the country in 1996. Bin Laden provided the Taliban with funds and fighters, and was in return allowed to establish a number of camps for the terrorist training of al-Qaeda members from around the world. In February 1998, Bin Laden and other Islamist extremist leaders issued a *fatwa*, or religious edict, stating that "to kill the Americans and their allies—civilians and military—is

Lewis Schiliro of the FBI's New York office in 1998 announcing the indictments of Osama Bin Laden and Muhammad Atef for the 1998 U.S. Embassy bombings. AP/WIDE WORLD PHOTOS

an individual duty for every Muslim who can do it in any country in which it is possible to do it." The bombing of the U.S. embassies in Nairobi and Dar es Salaam was the first major terrorist attack against the U.S. following the announcement of the *fatwa*.

As a response to the bombings, U.S. President Bill Clinton ordered Operation Infinite Reach, a series of military strikes against targets associated with Bin Laden. On August 20, 1998, terrorist training camps in Afghanistan and an alleged chemical-weapons factory in Sudan were hit by U.S. cruise missiles.

Investigations into the embassy bombings were conducted by the FBI and by Kenyan and Tanzanian authorities and a number of suspects were identified. In November 1998, Bin Laden and co-defendants Wadih el Hage, Fazul Abdullah Mohammed, Mohamed Sadeek Odeh, and Mohamed Rashed Daoud al-Owhali were indicted by a U.S. grand jury in New York court for the bombings of the United States embassies in Kenya and Tanzania.

The indictment accused Bin Laden of heading a terrorist conspiracy to kill members of U.S. armed forces in Saudi Arabia and Somalia and U.S. nationals employed at the Embassies in Nairobi, Kenya, and Dar es Salaam, Tanzania. It was alleged that the conspiracy had been concealed by the establishment of front companies, the provision of false identity and travel documents, the use of coded correspondence and the provision of false information to the authorities. According to the indictment, al-Qaeda was assumed to be functioning both on its own and in collaboration with other terrorist organizations including Al Jihad group and the Islamic Group (Gamaa Islamia). It was held to have established cells and recruited members in a number of countries including in Kenya, Tanzania, the United Kingdom and the United States to further its activities, and to have made alliances with the National Islamic Front in the Sudan and with representatives of the government of Iran and its associated terrorist group Hezballah.

Bin Laden and the co-conspirators were specifically accused of establishing al-Qaeda training camps, recruiting U.S. citizens to al-Qaeda, purchasing weapons and explosives and establishing headquarters and businesses in the Sudan. The indictment also alleged that *fatwahs* were issued that ordered the killing of Americans, and that the bombings of the U.S. embassies in Kenya and Tanzania were conducted as part of the conspiracy to kill American nationals.

In May 2001, following a four-month trial in a U.S. Federal Court in New York City, the four co-defendants named in the Indictment were charged with bombing the two embassies, causing the deaths of

more than 200 people and injuring more than 4,500. Each received a life sentence and was ordered to pay $7 million to the victims' families and $26 million to the U.S. government.

Two former al-Qaeda members, Jamal Ahmed Al-Fadl and L'Houssaine Kherchtou, testified as key witnesses in the trial, and provided detailed information about the international al-Qaeda network. Another former member, Ali Mohamed, did not testify but provided additional information about the organization. He had been the first person to plead guilty to charges of involvement in the embassy bombings and admitted conducting surveillance of U.S., British, and French targets in Nairobi, including the U.S. embassy, and delivering pictures and reports to Bin Laden.

Al-Qaeda has continued to carry out major terrorist attacks against the United States and its allies. These have included the attacks on the World Trade Center and the Pentagon on September 11, 2001, the Madrid train bombings on March 11, 2004, and the attacks on the public transport network in London on July 7, 2005.

PRIMARY SOURCE

UNITED STATES OF AMERICA
V
USAMA BIN LADEN

At all relevant times from in or about 1989 until the date of the filing of this Indictment, an international terrorist group existed which was dedicated to opposing non-Islamic governments with force and violence. This organization grew out of the "mekhtab al khidemat" (the "Services Office") organization which had maintained offices in various parts of the world, including Afghanistan, Pakistan (particularly in Peshawar) and the United States, particularly at the Alkifah Refugee Center in Brooklyn, New York. The group was founded by defendants USAMA BIN LADEN and MUHAMMAD ATEF, a/k/a "Abu Hafs al Masry," together with "Abu Ubaidah al Banshiri" and others. From in or about 1989 until the present, the group called itself "al Qaeda" ("the Base"). From 1989 until in or about 1991, the group (hereafter referred to as "al Qaeda") was headquartered in Afghanistan and Peshawar, Pakistan. In or about 1991, the leadership of al Qaeda, including its "emir" (or prince) defendant USAMA BIN LADEN, relocated to the Sudan. Al Qaeda was headquartered in the Sudan from approximately 1991 until approximately 1996 but still maintained offices in various parts of the world. In 1996, defendants USAMA BIN LADEN and MUHAMMAD ATEF and other members of al Qaeda relocated to Afghanistan. At all relevant times, al Qaeda was led by its emir, defendant USAMA BIN LADEN. Members of al Qaeda pledged an oath of allegiance (called a "bayat") to defendant USAMA BIN LADEN and al Qaeda. Those who were suspected of collaborating against al Qaeda were to be identified and killed.

Al Qaeda opposed the United States for several reasons. First, the United States was regarded as an "infidel" because it was not governed in a manner consistent with the group's extremist interpretation of Islam. Second, the United States was viewed as providing essential support for other "infidel" governments and institutions, particularly the governments of Saudi Arabia and Egypt, the nation of Israel and the United Nations organization, which were regarded as enemies of the group. Third, al Qaeda opposed the involvement of the United States armed forces in the Gulf War in 1991 and in Operation Restore Hope in Somalia in 1992 and 1993, which were viewed by al Qaeda as pretextual preparations for an American occupation of Islamic countries. In particular, al Qaeda opposed the continued presence of American military forces in Saudi Arabia (and elsewhere on the Saudi Arabian peninsula) following the Gulf War. Fourth, al Qaeda opposed the United States Government because of the arrest, conviction and imprisonment of persons belonging to al Qaeda or its affiliated terrorist groups or with whom it worked, including Sheik Omar Abdel Rahman.

One of the principal goals of al Qaeda was to drive the United States armed forces out of Saudi Arabia (and elsewhere on the Saudi Arabian peninsula) and Somalia by violence. Members of al Qaeda issued *fatwahs* (rulings on Islamic law) indicating that such attacks were both proper and necessary.

Counts One Through Six: Conspiracies To Murder, Bomb And Maim

Count One

Conspiracy To Kill United States Nationals It was a part and an object of said conspiracy that the defendants, and others known and unknown, would and did: (i) murder United States nationals anywhere in the world, including in the United States, (ii) kill United States nationals employed by the United States military who were serving in their official capacity in Somalia and on the Saudi Arabian peninsula; (iii) kill United States nationals employed at the United States Embassies in Nairobi, Kenya, and Dar es Salaam, Tanzania, including internationally protected persons, as that term is defined in Title 18, United States Code, Section 1116(b)(4); and (iv) engage in conduct to conceal the activities and means and methods of the co-conspirators by, among other things, establishing front companies, providing false identity and travel documents, engaging in coded correspondence, providing false information to the authorities in various countries and seeking to detect and kill informants.

SIGNIFICANCE

The bombing of the U.S. embassies in Kenya and Tanzania was one of the major anti-American terrorist incidents that preceded the attacks of September 11, 2001. It was also one of the first significant demonstrations of transnational terrorism. U.S. citizens were attacked on foreign soil in Kenya and Tanzania by a terrorist organization which was becoming increasingly global in its presence.

Before the formation of al-Qaeda, most terrorist movements had been tightly knit and linked to specific geographical locations. In contrast, al-Qaeda has developed into a loosely knit organization linking numerous groups or "cells" in at least 50 countries, not only in the Middle East and Asia, but also in Africa, North America and Europe. These cells are considered to have a high degree of independence from the center both in their activities and their administration. Many experts now regard al-Qaeda more as a sharing of ideology, aims, and methods than a specific organization. The ideology is Islamist and anti-western: Bin Laden and his followers call for driving the United States and Israel out of the Muslim world, and to replace moderate Islamic governments with fundamentalist rule.

The original al-Qaeda structure that was developed in Afghanistan has now been destroyed and many of its members have been captured, killed, or dispersed around the world. Yet, support organizations continue to form and become identified, due to their diffuse structure and the presence of active cells in so many countries.

The embassy bombings were also one of the first demonstrations of the use of suicide bombers and everyday means of transport as weapons to inflict thousands of casualties in a coordinated attack on more than one target. This foreshadowed the major attacks on Western countries that would follow in the years to come, particularly the September 11, 2001. In these attacks, 19 young men, mostly Saudi Arabian nationals, hijacked four passenger airliners and crashed them into the World Trade Center in New York and the Pentagon in Washington, killing some 3,000 people. The scale of the September 11 attacks, in particular, gave international terrorism a new political and strategic significance in global politics, and has raised security concerns worldwide.

The U.S. military response to the Embassy bombings also foreshadowed an increasing emphasis on armed retaliation against major terrorist attacks. When the Taliban refused to hand over Bin Laden to the USA for trial following the September 11 attacks, President George W. Bush declared a war against terrorism and invaded Afghanistan, fully supported by the United Nations. The Taliban was subsequently defeated, but as of mid-July 2005, Osama Bin Laden has not been captured.

FURTHER RESOURCES
Web sites

BBC News. "US embassies hit in African blast." (August 7, 1998) <http://news.bbc.co.uk/1/hi/world/africa/147065.stm> (accessed July 10, 2005).

Hearings, 107th Senate. "The Global Reach of al-Qaeda." *Joyner Library* <http://frwebgate.access.gpo.gov/cgi-bin/getdoc.cgi?dbname=107_senate_hearings&docid=f:77601.wais> (accessed July 10, 2005).

PBS. "Frontline: Hunting Bin Laden." <http://www.pbs.org/wgbh/pages/frontline/shows/binladen> (accessed July 10, 2005).

U.S. Department of State. "Bombings in Nairobi, Kenya and Dar es Salaam, Tanzania: August 7, 1998." <http://www.state.gov/www/regions/africa/kenya_tanzania.html> (accessed July 10, 2005).

Department of Defense USS *Cole* Commission Report

Attack on the USS *Cole*

Government Report

By: United States Department of Defense

Date: January 9, 2001

Source: USS *Cole* Commission Report, as released by the United States Department of Defense.

About the Author: On October 19, 2000, then Secretary of Defense William Cohen assigned retired Army Gen. William W. Crouch and retired Navy Adm. Harold W. Gehman Jr. as co-chairs to head up a commission to carry out an investigation from the perspective of the Department of Defense into the circumstances surrounding the attack on the USS *Cole*. Separate investigations were also carried out by the Federal Bureau of

U.S. Navy and Marine Corps personnel patrol the damaged destroyer USS *Cole* following the October 12, 2000 terrorist bombing attack on the ship in Aden, Yemen. © AFP/CORBIS

Investigation (FBI) and the U.S. Navy. The purpose of the Defense Department investigation was to discover ways to avoid future similar attacks. The FBI was charged with discovering and apprehending those responsible for the attack and the Navy investigation focused on analyzing the standards of procedure before, during, and following the attack.

INTRODUCTION

On October 12, 2000, a boat laden with explosives pulled up alongside the USS *Cole*, a United States Navy destroyer, and detonated while the *Cole* was refueling in the Middle Eastern port of Aden, Yemen. The explosion, which was set off by two suicide terrorists, blasted a hole in the side of the vessel 40 feet wide and killed 17 members of the U.S. Navy. An additional 40 people were injured in the attack.

The bombing was soon proven to have been carried out by a cell operating within the al-Qaeda network and who had ties with the Islamic Army of Yemen, an extremist group opposed to the government of Yemen as well as Western influence in Yemen.

The bombing of the USS *Cole* was the first major international terrorist attack on a United States facility since the bombings of the embassies in Kenya and Tanzania in the summer of 1998.

In the wake of the attack, the Federal Bureau of Investigation (FBI) was sent to Yemen where they developed a close working relationship with the local government and opened up one of the largest ever FBI investigations for a crime occurring outside of the United States. It was later revealed that the successful attack on the USS *Cole* had been preceded by an earlier attempt by an al-Qaeda cell to carry out a similar bombing against the USS *The Sullivans*, which had been planned for January 3, 2000. Prior to reaching that destination, the boat carrying the explosives had sunk. The terrorists had salvaged the boat and the explosives, which were then used in the attack on the *Cole*.

The legal definition of an act of terrorism, as defined by the U.S. Code, establishes that terrorism is an act perpetrated against "non-combatants." Though some claim that this definition possibly precludes the USS *Cole* bombing as an international terrorist incident, the U.S. government and military both asserted that the ship was not engaged in combat and that the bombing was intended as terrorism. In the immediate hours following the attack, President Bill Clinton said, "If, as it now appears, this was an act of terrorism, it was a despicable and cowardly act."

By the end of 2000, eight suspects had been arrested by Yemeni authorities in connection with the attack on the USS *Cole*. On November 3, 2002, Abu Ali al-Harithi, the suspected mastermind behind the attack was killed in a missle attack in Yemen fired by an unmanned drone operated by the CIA.

PRIMARY SOURCE

Since the attack on Khobar Towers in June 1996, the Department of Defense (DoD) has made significant improvements in protecting its service members, mainly in deterring, disrupting and mitigating terrorist attacks on installations. The attack on USS *COLE (DDG 67)*, in the port of Aden, Yemen, on 12 October 2000, demonstrated a seam in the fabric of efforts to protect our forces, namely in-transit forces. Our review was focused on finding ways to improve the U.S. policies and practices for deterring, disrupting and mitigating terrorist attack on U.S. forces in transit. . . .

UNCLASSIFIED FINDINGS AND RECOMMENDATIONS SUMMARY

Organizational

Finding: Combating terrorism is so important that it demands complete unity of effort at the level of the Office of the Secretary of Defense.

Recommendation: Secretary of Defense develop an organization that more cohesively aligns policy and resources within DoD to combat terrorism and designate an Assistant Secretary of Defense (ASD) to oversee these functions.

Finding: The execution of the engagement element of the National Security Strategy lacks an effective, coordinated interagency process, which results in a fragmented engagement program that may not provide optimal support to in-transit units.

Recommendation: Secretary of Defense support an interagency process to provide overall coordination of U.S. engagement.

Finding: DoD needs to spearhead an interagency, coordinated approach to developing non-military host nation security efforts in order to enhance force protection for transiting US forces.

Recommendation: Secretary of Defense coordinate with Secretary of State to develop an approach with shared responsibility to enhance host nation security capabilities that result in increased security for transiting US forces.

Antiterrorism/Force Protection (AT/FP)

Finding: Service manning policies and procedures that establish requirements for full-time Force Protection Officers and staff billets at the Service

Component level and above will reduce the vulnerability of in-transit forces to terrorist attacks.

Recommendation: Secretary of Defense direct the Services to provide Component Commanders with full-time force protection officers and staffs that are capable of supporting the force protection requirements of transiting units.

Finding: Component Commanders need the resources to provide in-transit units with temporary security augmentation of various kinds.

Recommendation: Secretary of Defense direct the Services to resource Component Commanders to adequately augment units transiting through higher-threat areas.

Finding: More responsive application of currently available military equipment, commercial technologies, and aggressive research and development can enhance the AT/FP and deterrence posture of transiting forces.

Recommendation: Secretary of Defense direct the Services to initiate a major unified effort to identify near-term AT/FP equipment and technology requirements, field existing solutions from either military or commercial sources, and develop new technologies for remaining requirements.

Finding: The Geographic Commander in Chief should have the sole authority for assigning the threat level for a country within his area of responsibility.

Recommendations: Secretary of Defense direct that the Geographic CINCs be solely responsible for establishing the threat level within the appropriate area of responsibility with input from DIA. Secretary of Defense coordinate with Secretary of State, where possible, to minimize conflicting threat levels between the Department of Defense and the Department of State. Secretary of Defense designate an office or agency responsible for setting the threat level for Canada, Mexico, Russia, and the United States.

Finding: Using operational risk management standards as a tool to measure engagement activities against risk to in-transit forces will enable commanders to determine whether to suspend or continue engagement activities.

Recommendation: Secretary of Defense direct the CINCs to adopt and institutionalize a discrete operational risk management model to be used in AT/FP planning and execution.

Finding: Incident response must be an integral element of AT/FP planning.

Recommendation: Secretary of Defense direct the Geographic CINCs to identify theater rapid incident response team requirements and integrate their utilization

in contingency planning for in-transit units, and the Services to organize, train, and equip such forces.

Intelligence

Finding: In-transit units require intelligence support tailored to the terrorist threat in their immediate area of operations. This support must be dedicated from a higher echelon (tailored production and analysis).

Recommendation: Secretary of Defense reprioritize intelligence production to ensure that in-transit units are given tailored, focused intelligence support for independent missions.

Finding: If the Department of Defense is to execute engagement activities related to the National Security Strategy with the least possible level of risk, then Services must reprioritize time, emphasis, and to prepare the transiting units to perform intelligence preparation of the battlespace—like processes and formulate intelligence requests for information to support operational decision points.

Recommendation: Secretary of Defense direct the Services to ensure forces are adequately resourced and trained to make maximum use of intelligence processes and procedures, including priority information requests and requests for information to support intelligence preparation of the battlespace for in-transit unit antiterrorism/force protection.

Finding: DoD does not allocate sufficient resources or all-source intelligence analysis and collection in support of combating terrorism.

Recommendations: Secretary of Defense reprioritize all-source intelligence collection and analysis personnel and resources so that sufficient emphasis is applied to combating terrorism. Analytical expertise must be imbedded, from the national, CINC, and Component Command levels, to the joint task force level. Secretary of Defense reprioritize terrorism-related human intelligence and signals intelligence resources. Secretary of Defense reprioritize resources for the development of language skills that support combating terrorism analysis and collection.

Finding: Service counterintelligence programs are integral to force protection and must be adequately manned and funded to meet the dynamic demands of supporting in-transit forces.

Recommendation: Secretary of Defense ensure DoD counterintelligence organizations are adequately staffed and funded to meet counterintelligence force protection requirements.

Finding: Clearer DoD standards for threat and vulnerability assessments, must be developed at the joint level and be common across Services and commands.

The USS *Cole* being pulled out of Aden port by Yemeni tugboats to deep water. AP/WIDE WORLD PHOTOS

Recommendations: Secretary of Defense standardize counterintelligence assessments and increase counterintelligence resources. Secretary of Defense direct DoD-standard requirements for the conduct of threat and vulnerability assessments for combating terrorism. Secretary of Defense direct the production of a DoD-standard Counterintelligence Collection Manual for combating terrorism.

Training

Finding: Better force protection is achieved if forces in transit are trained to demonstrate preparedness to deter acts of terrorism.

Recommendations: Secretary of Defense direct the Services to develop and resource credible deterrence standards, deterrence-specific tactics, techniques, and procedures and defensive equipment packages for all forms of transiting forces. Secretary of Defense direct the Services to ensure that pre-deployment training regimes include

deterrence tactics, techniques, and procedures and AT/FP measures specific to the area of operation and equipment rehearsals.

SIGNIFICANCE

With the attack on the USS *Cole* in October 2000, the United States was reminded of the threats posed by international terrorist networks such as al-Qaeda.

This report was issued before the attacks of 9/11, but it marks the seriousness with which the United States regarded the threat of terrorism. This report specifically recommends that the job of counterterrorism become a central focus of the Secretary of Defense and that an Assistant Secretary be named to specifically oversee this process. The report calls for the Defense Department to provide a strategy that would allow the various governmental agencies to better coordinate with each other to prevent future strikes. Some of the recommendations made in this report

A hooded Palestinian member of Islamic Jihad holds up a Holy Koran and a grenade, during a rally held by Islamic Jihad in 2003. AP/WIDE WORLD PHOTOS

were later adopted in response to the September 11, 2001 terrorist attacks.

Critics of the handling of intelligence and the counterterrorism effort prior to 9/11 point to this report issued in January of 2001 as a possible indicator that the United States government understood the threat posed by al-Qaeda and similar international terrorist groups, but failed to expeditiously implement new counterterrorism measures. The 9/11 Commission, the body appointed to investigate government handling of the 9/11 attacks, noted that the brief span of months between the attack on the USS *Cole* and the 9/11 attacks did not leave enough time to significantly overhaul U.S. counterterrorism efforts.

FURTHER RESOURCES
Web sites

FindLaw.com. "Congressional Research Service: Terrorist Attack on *USS Cole*; Background and Issues for Congress." <http://news.findlaw.com/cnn/docs/crs/coleterrattck13001.pdf> (accessed July 1, 2005).

Navy.com. "USS Cole (DDG 67)." <http://www.cole.navy.mil/> (accessed July 1, 2005).

The Meaning of Jihad

Testimony of Al-Fadl regarding discussion with Osama Bin Laden

Court transcript

By: Jamal Ahmed Al-Fadl

Date: February 6, 2001

Source: Testimony of Jamal Ahmed Al-Fadl provided in the case of The United States of America v. Usama (Osama) Bin Laden, et., al., 2001.

About the Author: Testimony provided by former al-Qaeda member Jamal Ahmed Al-Fadl.

INTRODUCTION

In 2001, a United States court in New York conducted the trial of four men accused of murdering 224 people in the bombing of two American embassies in Africa in 1998. They were found guilty and sentenced to lifetime imprisonment.

The case was based on the testimony of two key witnesses, Jamal Ahmed Al-Fadl and L'Houssaine Kherchtou. These men had both been long-term members of the al-Qaeda network and had intimate knowledge of the way in which the organization operated. A third man, Ali Mohamed, a former member of the U.S. Armed Forces, also testified after pleading guilty to similar charges relating to the bombings.

Ali Mohamed provided evidence of Osama Bin Laden's role in the terrorist attacks, testifying that he had conducted surveillance of Western embassies in Africa under Osama Bin Laden's instructions, providing the al-Qaeda leader with photographs, diagrams, and reports of the embassies' security arrangements. He also reported that he had even witnessed Osama Bin Laden use one of the photographs to pinpoint the exact location of a future bombing.

The trial testimony provided an insightful picture of the operations of al-Qaeda. It documented the group's early movement from Afghanistan to Sudan and highlighted their plans to use violence against Islamic governments, such as Saudi Arabia, that failed to follow extreme Islamic principles.

▮ PRIMARY SOURCE

UNITED STATES OF AMERICA
V
USAMA BIN LADEN, ET AL.,

New York, N.Y.

February 6, 2001

10:00 A.M.

MR. FITZGERALD: Yes, your Honor. The government calls as its first witness, Jamal Ahmed al-Fadl.

Q: Can you tell us what happened, the circumstance under which you met Abu Hajer al Iraqi and Usama Bin Laden at this guesthouse?

A: I met them during the prayer, after prayer and usually they talk with new people and they tell them about jihad and what's going on with that.

Q: If you can identify what you recall that Usama Bin Laden told you about jihad after the prayer during that meeting.

A: He talk about the Soviet Union army come to Afghanistan and kill people and we have to help them,

we have to make jihad out of them and you have to be patient, you have to follow the rule of the emir.

Q: And do you recall anything in particular that Abu Hajer al Iraqi said that day during the meeting after the prayer?

A: He say similar what Bin Laden talk about, but he make lecture for all new people about Jihad Fardh al Ein.

Q: Can you explain your understanding of what Jihad Fardh al Ein is?

A: Jihad Fardh al Ein mean when the enemy come to Muslim war or Muslim country and the people live in that country, they cannot push the enemy back and they ask for other brother or other Muslim to come and join them. That means any Muslim in the war, he should go over there and push the enemy out of the country.

Q: And during the time when there's a Jihad Fardh al Ein, if a person is busy in personal matters with their family, with school, are they allowed not to go to the Jihad Fardh al Ein?

A: If it's Jihad Fardh al Ein means your family, your kids, your money, your business, you have to forget everything, just focus on jihad.

Q: And is there a time of Jihad where it's optional if you actually go to do the fighting? Do you have a choice other than jihad, something different than Jihad Fardh al Ein, where a person has the option not to go and fight but instead to take care of their other business?

A: Yeah, we have another kind, it's called Jihad Fardh al Khafiya.

Q: Can you tell us what Usama Bin Laden said he was going to do after the Russians left Afghanistan?

A: He thinking about making group.

Q: Can you explain to us anything else you recall about what he wanted this group to do?

A: To be ready for another step because in Afghanistan everything is over.

Q: And did he explain at that time what that other step was?

A: They say we have to make Khalifa.

Q: Can you explain to the jury what a khalifa is?

A: Khalifa mean we need one Muslim leader for the whole Muslim in the war.

Q: Continue with what else you recall Usama Bin Laden stated he wished to do after the Russians left Afghanistan.

A: He say also we want to change the Arab government because there's no Muslim government in the war, so we have to make Muslim government.

Q: Can you tell us what Abu Ayoub al Iraqi said?

A: He said we going to make group and this is group that under Farook, and it's going to be one man for the group and it's going to be focused in jihad and we going to use the group to do another thing out of Afghanistan.

Q: And did Abu Ayoub al Iraqi tell you what the name of this group was?

A: Yes.

Q: Can you tell the jury what the name of the group was?

A: Al Qaeda.

Q: During the time you were in the Sudan and attending the lectures at the guesthouse in the Riyadh section and the Thursday meeting at Soba farm, did you ever learn of the al Qaeda position towards the United States?

A: Yes.

Q: Can you tell the jury how you learned what al Qaeda's view or position towards the United States was?

A: Well, I was in the guesthouse and they talk after Iraq government took Kuwait. After few months, they say American army now, they should leave the Gulf area.

They say the fatwah, it say we cannot let the American army stay in the Gulf area and take our oil, take our money, and we have to do something to take them out. We have to fight them.

Q: Who actually said this after the fatwah was formed that you heard?

A: Bin Laden by himself and Abu Hajer al Iraqi and Saad al Sharif.

Q: And can you tell us how you heard about the next fatwah?

A: I was in the guesthouse and in a Thursday meeting and they say it's new fatwah because we proved more about the American army in Gulf area.

Q: Tell us as best you can recall what they said about America at that time.

A: They say they got another proof for the fatwah and they say Prophet Mohamed say don't allow true religion in our islands.

Yes. After that, also, we got another fatwah because they say the American army come to the home of Africa in Somalia.

Q: Can you tell us how you learned of that fatwah?

A: Also I was in the guesthouse and Abu Ubaidah al Banshiri, he talk about that. He says the American army in home of Africa in Somalia and now they already took off Gulf area and now they go to Somalia, and if they successful in Somalia, the next thing it could be south of Sudan and that's going—they going to take the Islamic countries.

Q: Did you ever hear of a discussion within al Qaeda of whether or not innocent people could be killed?

A: I remember in, yes, I hear that.

Q: When did you hear it?

A: During the Somalia fatwah.

Q: Can you tell the jury what discussion was had about whether or not innocent civilians could be killed?

A: I remember Ibn al Tamiyeh, he said—

Q: Let's stop. Would you just briefly explain to the jury who Ibn al Tamiyeh is?

A: He's a scholar for Islamic history 1700 or 1800 years ago.

Q: Can you tell us now what Abu Hajer al Iraqi said about Ibn al Tamiyeh?

A: He said that our time now is similar like in that time, and he say Ibn al Tamiyeh, when a tartar come to Arabic war, Arabic countries that time, he say some Muslims, they help them. And he says Ibn al Tamiyeh, he make a fatwah. He said anybody around the tartar, he buy something from them and he sell them something, you should kill him. And also, if when you attack the tartar, if anybody around them, anything, or he's not military or that—if you kill him, you don't have to worry about that. If he's a good person, he go to paradise and if he's a bad person, he go to hell.

Q: Was there any further discussion at a later time about whether it was appropriate to kill, to allow innocent civilians to be killed?

A: Also, I remember they say if you—if the people want to make explosives for building and it's military building and sometimes it could be civilian around the building and you don't have any choice other than that, you should do it and you don't have to worry about that.

SIGNIFICANCE

Jamal Ahmed Al-Fadl's testimony provides a unique insight into the religious dogma of the al-Qaeda group. Al-Qaeda represents an extremist faction of the religion in which the concept of jihad is fundamental.

Al-Fadl's close relation with Islamic fundamentalist movements, and his links with Osama Bin Laden, allowed him to provide an unusual narrative of the moments in which al-Qaeda was born. He detailed that after the Russians left Afghanistan in 1989, Osama Bin Laden was "thinking about making group," which was "to be ready for another step because in Afghanistan everything is over." However, Al-Fadl indicated the groups higher aim, that of making a Khalifa, which would mean "one Muslim leader for the whole Muslim in the war." Even at these early stages, al-Qaeda was preparing to operate in a global theatre.

Al-Fadl's testimony painted a picture of an organization run by Osama Bin Laden, which was "focused in jihad." He was also able to document the group's disintegrating attitudes towards America. He explained that after the Americans occupied Kuwait in 1992, Osama Bin Laden expressed outrage at their presence in the region. Al Qaeda's views towards the U.S. became even more aggressive after American military action in Somalia.

Al-Fadl's testimony documents the development of al-Qaeda's strategy for terrorism. Al-Fadl relates that in conversations with Al Qaeda group leaders, it was explained that the group's plans included attacks on civilians.

FURTHER RESOURCES

Books

Bergen, Peter. *Holy War, Inc.: Inside the Secret World of Osama Bin Laden*. Free Press, 2002.

Web sites

Frontline. "The U.S. Embassy bombing trial." <http://www.pbs.org/wgbh/pages/frontline/shows/binladen/bombings/bombings.html> (accessed July 7, 2005).

Transcript of Flight Attendant Betty Ong

Terrorist attacks on the U.S., September 11, 2001

Telephone call transcript

By: Betty Ong

Date: Recorded September 11, 2001; entered as testimony before the National Commission on the Terrorist Attacks upon the United States (9–11 Commission) on January 27, 2004.

Source: Available online at American Radioworks, "Witness to Terror: The 9/11 Hearings, " <http://americanradioworks.publicradio.org/features/911/ong.html> (with audio).

About the Author: Betty Ong (1956–2001) was a flight attendant aboard American Airlines Flight 11, the first plane to strike the World Trade Center in New York City in the terrorist attacks of September 11, 2001. Nydia Gonzalez was an American Airlines Operations employee who took Ong's cell phone call that morning. Gonzalez testified before the 9–11 Commission investigating the attacks.

INTRODUCTION

At 7:59 A.M. on September 11, 2001, American Airlines Flight 11, a Boeing 767 took off fourteen minutes late from Boston's Logan Airport. The plane, under the command of Captain John Ogonowski, was bound for Los Angeles with 81 passengers and 11 crew members aboard. Among the passengers were five Islamist terrorists, including Mohammad Atta, the terrorists' leader. As the plane was sitting on the runway waiting for clearance to depart, Atta placed a cell-phone call to Marwan Alshehhi, a terrorist aboard United Airlines Flight 175, to confirm that the coordinated hijacking plot planned for that day was under way.

At 8:13 A.M., the last routine communication took place between the aircraft and ground control. Over the next several minutes, as ground control operators could get no response from the pilot and the plane's IFF ("identify friend or foe") beacon was turned off, they began to consider that the plane had been hijacked. By 8:20, the plane was dramatically off course, and at 8:24 any doubts ground control had were dissipated when the plane made a 100-degree turn to the south. Also at 8:24, ground controllers heard the voice of one of the hijackers, who said simply "We have some planes." At 8:33, ground controllers again heard the voice of a hijacker telling the passengers, "Nobody move, please, we are going back to the airport. Don't try to make any stupid moves."

At 8:37 A.M., the plane entered New York airspace. At about 8:38, Mohammad Atta likely replaced the captain at the controls of the plane, although the time when this occurred is uncertain. Meanwhile, ground controllers had contacted the U.S. military, which scrambled fighter jets to pursue the plane.

At 8:46:26 A.M., Flight 11, traveling at a speed of about 470 miles per hour, slammed into the north tower of New York City's World Trade Center between the 94th and 98th floors. At 10:28, the tower collapsed, structurally weakened by 10,000 gallons of burning jet fuel. It was later speculated that the terrorists deliberately targeted a transcontinental flight because its large complement of fuel would maximize the damage it would cause.

At 8:20 A.M., flight attendant Betty Ong placed an Airfone call to an American Airlines reservation desk, where she spoke to Vanessa Minter (the "female voice" below). About two minutes later, Minter patched her supervisor, Nydia Gonzalez, into the call. In turn, Gonzalez later patched in American Airlines manager Craig Marquis (the "male voice" in the second portion of the transcript below).

Ong remained on the phone until it crashed into the World Trade Center. Her call, which was recorded,

An aircraft, at right, is seen as it is about to fly into the World Trade Center in New York, 2001. AP/WIDE WORLD PHOTOS

provided the National Commission on the Terrorist Attacks upon the United States, popularly called the 9–11 Commission, with important information about the events that transpired aboard the plane. Gonzalez testified before the 9–11 Commission on January 27, 2004, when the tape of Ong's call was played.

PRIMARY SOURCE

Betty Ong: [I'm] Number 3 in the back. The cockpit's not answering. Somebody's stabbed in business class and— I think there's mace— that we can't breathe. I don't know, I think we're getting hijacked.

Male Voice: Which flight are you on?

Betty Ong: Flight 12. [Note: This is incorrect. The correct number is Flight 11.]

Operator: And what seat are you in? Ma'am, are you there?

Betty Ong: Yes.

Male Voice: What seat are you in?

Female Voice: Ma'am, what seat are you in?

Betty Ong: We're— just left Boston, we're up in the air.

Female Voice: I know, what—

Betty Ong: We're supposed to go to LA and the cockpit's not answering their phone.

Female Voice: Okay, but what seat are you sitting in? What's the number of your seat?

Betty Ong: Okay, I'm in my jump seat right now.

Female Voice: Okay.

Betty Ong: At 3R.

Female Voice: Okay.

Male Voice: Okay, you're the flight attendant? I'm sorry, did you say you're the flight attendant?

Betty Ong: Hello?

Female Voice: Yes, hello.

Male Voice: What is your name?

Betty Ong: Hi, you're going to have to speak up, I can't hear you.

Male Voice: Sure. What is your name?

Betty Ong: Okay, my name is Betty Ong. I'm number 3 on Flight 11.

Male Voice: Okay.

Betty Ong: And the cockpit is not answering their phone, and there's somebody stabbed in business class, and there's— we can't breathe in business class. Somebody's got mace or something.

Male Voice: Can you describe the person that you said— someone is what in business class?

Betty Ong: I'm sitting in the back. Somebody's coming back from business. If you can hold on for one second, they're coming back.

Betty Ong: Okay. Our number 1 got stabbed. Our purser is stabbed. Nobody knows who stabbed who, and we can't even get up to business class right now 'cause nobody can breathe. Our number 1 is stabbed right now. And who else is?

Male Voice: Okay, and do we—

Betty Ong: And our number 5— our first class passengers are— galley flight attendant and our purser has been stabbed. And we can't get into the cockpit, the door won't open. Hello?

Male Voice: Yeah, I'm taking it down. All the information. We're also, you know, of course, recording this. At this point—

Nydia Gonzalez: This is Operations. What flight number are we talking about?

Male Voice: Flight 12.

Female Voice: Flight 12? Okay. I'm getting—

Betty Ong: No. We're on Flight 11 right now. This is Flight 11.

Male Voice: It's Flight 11, I'm sorry Nydia.

Betty Ong: Boston to Los Angeles.

Male Voice: Yes.

Betty Ong: Our number 1 has been stabbed and our 5 has been stabbed. Can anybody get up to the cockpit? Can anybody get up to the cockpit? Okay. We can't even get into the cockpit. We don't know who's up there.

Male Voice: Well, if they were shrewd they would keep the door closed and—

Betty Ong: I'm sorry?

Male Voice: Would they not maintain a sterile cockpit?

Betty Ong: I think the guys are up there. They might have gone there— jammed the way up there, or something. Nobody can call the cockpit. We can't even get inside. Is anybody still there?

Male Voice: Yes, we're still here.

Female Voice: Okay.

Betty Ong: I'm staying on the line as well.

Male Voice: Okay.

Nydia Gonzalez: Hi, who is calling reservations? Is this one of the flight attendants, or who? Who are you, hon?

Male Voice: She gave her name as Betty Ong.

Betty Ong: Yeah, I'm number 3. I'm number 3 on this flight, and we're the first—

Nydia Gonzalez: You're number 3 on this flight?

Betty Ong: Yes and I have—

Nydia Gonzalez: And this is Flight 11? From where to where?

Betty Ong: Flight 11.

Nydia Gonzalez: Have you guys called anyone else?

Betty Ong: No. Somebody's calling medical and we can't get a doc—

With that, the portion of the tape played at the commission hearing ended. Then, the commission heard a recording of a second phone call, the call Nydia Gonzales placed to American Airlines' emergency line. Gonzales was still on the phone with Betty Ong as well. She relayed what Ong was telling her to the emergency operator.

Male Voice: American Airlines emergency line, please state your emergency.

Nydia Gonzalez: Hey, this is Nydia at American Airlines calling. I am monitoring a call in which Flight 11— the flight attendant is advising our reps that the pilot, everyone's been stabbed.

Male Voice: Flight 11?

Nydia Gonzalez: Yep. They can't get into the cockpit is what I'm hearing.

Male Voice: Okay. Who is this I'm talking to?

Nydia Gonzalez: Excuse me. This is Nydia, American Airlines at the Raleigh Reservation Center. I'm the operations specialist on duty.

Male Voice: And I'm sorry, what was your name again?

Nydia Gonzalez: Nydia.

Male Voice: Nydia. And what's your last name?

Nydia Gonzalez: Gonzalez— G-o-n-z-a-l-e-z.

Male Voice: (Inaudible)—Raleigh Reservations. Okay, now when you—

Nydia Gonzalez: I've got the flight attendant on the line with one of our agents.

Male Voice: Okay. And she's calling how?

Nydia Gonzalez: Through reservations. I can go in on the line and ask the flight attendant questions.

Male Voice: Okay. I'm assuming they've declared an emergency. Let me get ATC on here. Stand by.

Nydia Gonzalez: Have you guys gotten any contact with anybody? Okay, I'm still on with security, okay, Betty? You're doing a great job, just stay calm. Okay? We are, absolutely.

Male Voice: Okay, we're contacting the flight crew now and we're, we're also contacting ATC.

Nydia Gonzalez: Okay. It seems like the passengers in coach might not be aware of what's going on right now.

Male Voice: These two passengers were from first class?

Nydia Gonzalez: Okay, hold on. Hey Betty, do you know any information as far as the gents— the men that are in the cockpit with the pilots, were they from first class? They were sitting in 2A and B.

Male Voice: Okay.

Nydia Gonzalez: They are in the cockpit with the pilots.

Male Voice: Who's helping them, is there a doctor on board?

Nydia Gonzalez: Is there a doctor on board, Betty, that's assisting you guys? You don't have any doctors on board. Okay. So you've gotten all the first class passengers out of first class?

Male Voice: Have they taken anyone out of first class?

Nydia Gonzalez: Yeah, she's just saying that they have. They're in coach. What's going on, honey? Okay, the aircraft is erratic again. Flying very erratically. She did say that all the first class passengers have been moved back to coach, so the first class cabin is empty. What's going on your end?

Male Voice: We contacted Air Traffic Control, they are going to handle this as a confirmed hijacking, so they're moving all the traffic out of this aircraft's way.

Nydia Gonzalez: Okay.

Male Voice: He turned his transponder off, so we don't have a definitive altitude for him. We're just going by— they seem to think that they have him on a primary radar. They seem to think that he is descending.

Nydia Gonzalez: Okay.

Male Voice: Okay, Nydia?

Nydia Gonzalez: Yes dear, I'm here.

Male Voice: Okay, I have a dispatcher currently taking the current fuel on board.

Nydia Gonzalez: Uh, huh.

Male Voice: And we're going to run some profiles.

Nydia Gonzalez: Okay.

Male Voice: To see exactly what his endurance is.

Nydia Gonzalez: Okay.

Male Voice: Did she—

Nydia Gonzalez: She doesn't have any idea who the other passenger might be in first. Apparently they might have spread something so it's— they're having a hard time breathing or getting in that area.

What's going on, Betty? Betty, talk to me. Betty, are you there? Betty? (Inaudible.)

Okay, so we'll like— we'll stay open. We— I think we might have lost her.

SIGNIFICANCE

Betty Ong provided the authorities with crucial information about the hijacking. By providing the numbers of the seats occupied by the hijackers, she enabled the authorities to determine their identities. By maintaining her resolve, the information she relayed to ground control over a 25-minute period confirmed that a hijacking was under way. Authorities assumed that other planes might have been hijacked that day, but that their plans were thwarted as the scope of the attacks rapidly became clear and flights were grounded.

Betty Ong was not the only flight attendant who placed a call to the ground that morning. Also on an Airfone was Madeline "Amy" Sweeney, who at 8:20 A.M., placed a call to Logan's flight services manager Michael Woodward. "Listen, and listen to me very carefully," she told Woodward. "I'm on Flight 11. The airplane has been hijacked."

Over the next 25 minutes Sweeney, too, remained on the phone and provided details about the hijacking (her call was not recorded, but reconstructed from Woodward's notes). At one point she said that the hijackers had stabbed the two first-class flight attendants. She also noted, "A hijacker cut the throat of a business-class passenger, and he appears to be dead." At another point she said that the hijackers had shown her a bomb. Still on the phone at 8:45, with the plane flying very low and ground controllers attempting to determine its location, she told them chillingly, "I see the water. I see the buildings. I see buildings." After a pause, she said quietly, "Oh, my God." At about the same time, Betty Ong was repeatedly saying, "Pray for us. Pray for us."

On September 21, 2001, a memorial service for Betty Ong was held in San Francisco's Chinatown, where she was born and her family still lived. In declaring the day Betty Ong Day, San Francisco mayor Willie Brown said "It is with pride and sadness that I join in paying tribute to Betty's courage and her heroism. I hope it is a comfort to her family that so many people remember and honor her heroic acts."

FURTHER RESOURCES

Books

National Commission on Terrorist Attacks. *The 9/11 Commission Report: Final Report of the National Commission on Terrorist Attacks Upon the United States.* New York: W.W. Norton, 2004.

Web sites

National Commission on the Terrorist Attacks upon the United States (9–11 Commission) website. <http://www.9-11commission.gov/> (accessed June 28, 2005).

Thompson, Paul. "Complete 9-11 Timeline: American Airlines Flight 11." *Center for Cooperative Research.* <http://www.cooperativeresearch.org/timeline.jsp?timeline=complete_911_timeline&day_of_911=aa11> (accessed June 28, 2005).

Audio and Visual Materials

American Radioworks. *Witness to Terror: The 9/11 Hearings: A Voice from the Sky.* <http://americanradioworks.publicradio.org/features/911/ong.html> (with audio link).

"Subj: Escape from New York on 9/11"

September 11, 2001 attacks on the United States

E-mail

By: Kenneth Travis LaPensee

Date: September 21, 2001

Source: An e-mail note sent from KlaPensee@aol.com to family and friends ten days after the September 11, 2001 terrorist attacks on New York's World Trade Center.

About the Author: Ken LaPensee holds advanced degrees in health services research and epidemiology. He was working in Lower Manhattan a few blocks from the World Trade Center towers as they were struck by the terrorist attack on September 11, 2001.

INTRODUCTION

In the immediate aftermath of the terrorist attacks on the World Trade Center in 2001, Ken LaPensee, along with hundreds of thousands of others that had witnessed the attacks firsthand, wrestled with symptoms of post-traumatic stress, including flashbacks of the explosive impacts, an overwhelming sense of dread and unnatural alertness, constantly monitoring the skies for aircraft, and frequently waking with a start in the predawn hours whenever aircraft passed overhead. One of the things that helped him regain a more composed perspective was to respond to requests from family and friends to write a brief account of his experiences on September 11. The source document included here is an e-mail letter that he wrote to address their questions and their need for information to help them with their own efforts to come to terms with the terrorist attacks.

■ PRIMARY SOURCE

Subj: Escape from New York on 9/11

Date: 21-9–2001 13:06:31 Eastern Daylight Time

From: KlaPensee

To: PatSLP

I have been asked to provide an account to family and friends regarding my experiences on the day of the World Trade Center attack.

I commuted into New York Tuesday morning by bus from Annandale, N.J. and arrived at my stop in the city at the Trinity Church in Lower Manhattan at about 8:00 AM. My bus route passed right under the World Trade Center, and the stop is only about 100 yards from 1 Liberty Plaza, the building that houses the NASDAQ [stock exchange] and is currently deemed by some as being in danger of collapse. From there I walked one short block east to Broad Street, and 1/12 blocks south past the NYSE to 80 Broad Street and took the elevator up to our offices on the 35th floor. I set up my computer on the company network, got a cup of coffee and prepared for an ordinary workday.

At about 8:50, the first jet hit Tower 1 of the WTC. We went to our north side windows to see an immense plume of smoke rising straight up into the sky. We could not see the hole from our perspective, but soon learned that an airplane had crashed into the tower. We all thought that this was a horrible accident similar to that when an airplane crashed into the Empire State Building years ago. None of us was particularly alarmed, but some of the people who arrived late and had seen the fire from the subway entrance just under the burning tower were very upset. One woman, a junior consultant, was sobbing uncontrollably. She has subsequently fled New York to move in with her parents.

From time to time over the next few minutes I went to the window to monitor the fire. About 20 minutes later as I was watching the tower, I heard a thunderous roar overhead, and then saw a large jet slam into Tower 2, of which we had an unobstructed view. At that point I said aloud, "These are terrorist attacks!" I sent an e-mail to all company members globally saying that the World Trade Center was under attack and that a normal workday should not be expected! That turned out to be the understatement

People run from the collapse of the World Trade Center in New York on September 11, 2001. AP/WIDE WORLD PHOTOS

of the century! Over the next few minutes we turned on a speakerphone and dialed into broadcast news, and we heard the first reports of hijacked airplanes. I wondered how the second plane had been allowed to get close to New York after the first attack. The only explanation that I could think of was that the hijackers had duped everyone in our air control system and security establishments into believing it was an accident . . .

. . . The smoke from the first tower had been rising straight up, so there had not yet been any consequences on the street except for a blizzard of floating pieces of office paper descending to the earth from the huge smoke plume. However, with the second impact, the streets began to fill with smoke. Shortly afterwards, our office began to fill with smoke 35 floors up, and we received an order to evacuate the building. Tom, a friend of mine and I made sure all of the staff were out of the

office, then headed for the exit, where one of the construction workers that had been working on our uncompleted offices on the top, 36th floor came down to our floor and handed us both paper masks, for which we were very grateful since the fumes and smoke had begun to get very heavy.

We walked down 35 floors in what seemed no time at all. We were wearing business suits, ties, etc., clothing totally inappropriate for any kind of action. When I reached the bottom floor I stuffed my jacket and tie into my nylon computer case and went out onto the street. By that time, the sky was darkening and I felt that breathing was dangerous. Fortunately, the main lobby of our building was open, lit up and air conditioned, and we ducked through the revolving doors into relative safety and filtered air. We stayed in there about an hour and experienced only faint fumes. Some people opened the swing doors to try to make their way out of the area instead of using the revolving doors, so I shouted at them to use only the revolving doors.

After about forty minutes, the smoke over our building and to the South toward the East River had begun to clear due to favorable winds lifting the smoke high overhead, so Tom and I decided to make our way toward the river in hopes of finding a ferry off Manhattan. Just as I walked outside I heard another roar that sounded like another jet coming in for a suicide attack. A huge cloud of smoke and debris came rushing around the corner of the block, so we ducked back into the lobby. The roar turned out to be the collapse of Tower 2, followed soon after by the collapse of Tower 1. The sky grew pitch black and street lights came on outside since the power to buildings only a few blocks away from the WTC was not interrupted.

We remained in the lobby for another hour until the sky began to brighten again in our area. Only once did I feel any physical effect—my heart was racing and I felt a bit dizzy for about a minute, then it passed. Finally we could see blue sky over the river, so Tom and I bade the others good-bye and headed south toward the water with our paper masks on. There was still a lot of grit, dust and microscopic glass particles in the air . . .

We walked south about 1/4 mile to the river and saw a sea of humanity walking slowly and sadly across the Brooklyn Bridge. Traffic was blocked and only pedestrians were walking across. It turns out that bridges from Manhattan to the North such as the 59th Street Bridge were closed to pedestrians as well as cars. Nobody has explained the logic of this to me yet and I find it difficult to understand. Suffice to say that people were forced to walk south to the Brooklyn Bridge to cross the river there. Perhaps a million people trying to get out of Manhattan were forced to walk 6 miles or more to Brooklyn where they presumably could catch buses to their destinations.

We were about to follow the crowd over to Brooklyn when we heard megaphones from the ferries announcing that they were headed to Hoboken and Jersey City. We walked down off the bridge and down under to the ferry piers where we got on a ferry bound for Hoboken, which we knew to be a big transportation hub for New Jersey.

As we crossed the river at high speed, we could see the devastation of lower Manhattan. The scene resembled my imagination of an atomic bomb hit on the city of New York. There was not a trace of the two 1/4 mile high towers that I have known since the 1960s. There was a gaping hole in the skyline of New York as people say, and I felt a gaping hole in my heart as I looked back over the river. It was the saddest feeling I have ever felt other than grieving for a loved one, because I knew that many thousands of people so much like me had died, just ordinary, hard working people trying to make a living . . .

I had just come back from China with our new daughter Aimee the week before, and I recall going into work in Lower Manhattan all that week with a feeling that this bastion of capitalism was vulnerable and had enemies. I thought this feeling was just a natural adjustment reaction after two intense weeks in China and some sort of appreciation of the freedom and prosperity that many of us enjoy and take for granted . . .

Most of the people on the ferry crowded over to the port side to look at the awesome fire. The ferry started to list. Tom and I hung back, fearing that if we joined them, the ferry would capsize, which would be a bitterly ironic exclamation mark on the morning's events.

Although our ferry was originally headed for Hoboken, it was diverted to Jersey City. We were all told to get off because the ferry was needed to evacuate the injured from Lower Manhattan. Later it turned out that not enough people survived to make a massive med-evac necessary. As we departed the pier at Jersey City, rescue crews gave us bottled water, which I gargled because my throat was sore from breathing the grit and fumes. My eyes were also sore. I had contact lens rewetting drops in my computer case that I used to bathe my eyes (I had thrown away my contacts back in the building lobby because I felt they might trap grit).

We walked a few blocks to a place where people with megaphones told us we could catch buses to Hoboken and Newark. Tom and I got in the Newark line, and a free New Jersey Transit bus picked us up about 20 minutes later.

New Jersey Transit was generally very good to us and helped with free evacuation transportation out of the metropolitan area. However, when I got to Penn Station in Newark and said good-bye to Tom, who was going to Princeton, I was ordered off the train to Annandale (Clinton) by conductors who told me I would expose my family to asbestos if I didn't get "decontaminated." It turns out that a whole bunch of people were told to stay off the trains, but nobody gave us any instruction as to how we could get cleaned off. I saw a big rain puddle in front of Penn Station, so I stepped into it to wash off my shoes, then started heading back into the station. However, a policeman tapped me on the shoulder and told me I should head over toward the South side of the station toward a bunch of ambulances to get cleaned off. I and about 50 other people went over there, but when we got to the ambulances, they loudly yelled at us to stay away and said they could do nothing for us. Finally somebody who had a good head on his shoulders said, "Let these people out of here." So we went back to the station and I caught a later train. By this time it was about 2:00 P.M.

The train ride out was free, and the conductors on the second train were very nice and empathetic. I had purchased a ticket using a station vending machine. The conductor told me to save it for another day. I still have the ticket as a memento, with the date September 11, 2001 printed across the bottom.

One older man in a business suit . . . was grinning foolishly, twitching, and talking to himself. A conductor radioed ahead to the next stop where an ambulance was waiting for this guy.

Even though the train was only scheduled to go out to Raritan, the conductors took a survey, found that many of the passengers lived west of there, and announced that the train was going to take us all the way out to our home destinations. When I finally got to Annandale, police and rescue squad workers met us. We were briefly detained and asked whether we wanted to get a ride to the hospital. I had them check my pulse and blood pressure, and then waived the ambulance ride. I walked about a half mile to the Annandale bus stop where I had parked my car. As I walked through the pretty, peaceful streets of Annandale, when parents were just welcoming their children getting off school buses, again I felt a heavy sadness just thinking about how delicate and vulnerable our daily lives in this country really are.

I reached my car and drove home. When I arrived there, I took off my suit, covered with white soot, and threw it into the trash barrel. I also threw away my shirt and tie. Then I went into the house and showered. I had been trying to contact my wife all day long by cell phone but it wouldn't work. I called using landlines from phone booths, but only got the answering machine. She did not learn I was safe until she reached home and found me there. When we saw each other we cried.

Now I am trying to resume ordinary life. Our company has been incapacitated because our offices (and all of Lower Manhattan) are off limits. Telephone communication to staff members' homes has been almost impossible due to overloaded circuits and technical difficulties. It has been hard to get business rolling again and I had to cancel important client presentations because we were not ready. When I visit clients in offices even as close as Princeton I am amazed at how we can devote barely a minute to talking about the attack before the client wants to move on and jump into business, as though the attack had never happened. This coming Monday we will meet at a prearranged site somewhere either in Midtown or at somebody's home in New Jersey near NYC. Our firm is relatively lucky. Hundreds of small companies have been wiped off the face of the Earth by the attack.

Several times over the past week I have sat bolt upright in bed, roused from sleep by the sound of an airplane over our house 50 miles west of Manhattan in the hills of Hunterdon County. My daughter, fresh from China, tracks planes flying overhead. Because she is just beginning to learn English, her understanding of what has happened is dim and confused.

This is my story . . . Please feel free to forward it to whomever you feel might be interested.

Ken

SIGNIFICANCE

The attacks on the World Trade Center were unique among acts of terrorism in the comprehensiveness of their effects on the target society, which were at once sociocultural, epidemiological, psychological, and economic.

From his greatly circumscribed vantage point on Broad Street in the canyon-like surroundings near the New York Stock Exchange, it was impossible for LaPensee to apprehend the complex reaction of the city government and the populace to the attacks. What he witnessed was actually an extremely narrow slice of the event that in New York local terms began at 8:47A.M. when American Airlines flight 11, carrying 20,000 gallons of fuel, crashed into the North Tower, killing the 92 passengers and crew, and within minutes turning the upper ten floors of the building into an inferno.

The city's response was quick: by 8:59, a nearby television studio lot at Chelsea Piers was turned into an emergency trauma unit and by 9:00, two-hundred firefighters were at the World Trade Center, many of them already climbing the stairwells to rescue occupants. While they were on their way up, the South Tower was hit by a second jet at 9:02. Because news was initially fragmented, neither the firefighters climbing the stairs nor the occupants walking down in the extreme heat, some slipping on the sweat of those that had gone before them, realized that the second tower had been attacked until someone in the stairwell received the news on his pager. Complicating matters, the building sprinkler system activated, and the water flowed down the stairs, making the descent even more dangerous. By the time people reached the escalators to the mall underneath the trade center, the flowing water had created noisy waterfalls that the disoriented survivors had to shout over to communicate directions to safety.

By 9:09, New York Mayor Rudy Giuliani checked in at a fire department command post right in the trade center that soon had to be abandoned because of cascading debris. The mayor and senior firefighters first relocated one block north, but that also was much too close, and the command post had to be established elsewhere. The determination of city officials, police and firefighters to be as close as possible to the center of the catastrophe was admirable in the extreme, but in view of the unanticipated events that ensued, it compounded the tragedy.

At 9:21, the New York-New Jersey Port Authority closed all bridges and tunnels into Manhattan. Only foot and emergency traffic were allowed. Closer to LaPensee in the financial district, the New York Stock Exchange delayed all trading at 9:25. At 9:30, the Stock exchange was evacuated and all trading was suspended.

At about this time, the first report of casualties (6 dead and 1000 injured) was broadcast. Estimates would swell to as many as 40,000 dead before they were revised down to several thousand in the days immediately following September 11.

Twenty minutes later at 9:50, the South Tower collapsed unexpectedly. This event completely changed the character of the scene by bringing the fire and the enormous cloud of debris down to ground level. It was at this point, when the whole area was darkened and filled with fumes, that further normal business or residential activity anywhere in Lower Manhattan became impossible. Videotape captured the flight north on Church Street of crowds of people who had been spectators up to that moment, running to escape the rapidly expanding cloud of debris.

The nature of the catastrophe was such that most of the immediate casualties were killed rather than injured. Only a few hundred were physically injured, and the anticipated numbers of trauma victims never materialized. The extensive preparations for enormous numbers of injured at the makeshift trauma center at Chelsea Piers proved unnecessary. The Weil-Cornell Burn Center received only 25 patients. There was far greater need for temporary morgues than for trauma centers.

FURTHER RESOURCES

Books

Friedman, Thomas L. *Longitudes and Attitudes: Exploring the World after September 11.* New York: Farrar, Straus and Giroux 2002.

One Nation: America Remembers September 11, 2001. Boston: Little, Brown and Co., 2001.

Web sites

The Wall Street Journal. "The War on Terror series." <http://www.wsj.com> (2001–2003).

Speech to Labor Party Conference

British Prime Minister Tony Blair announces: "I say to the Taliban, surrender the terrorists or surrender power."

Speech

By: Tony Blair

Date: October 2, 2001

Source: Speech

About the Author: Tony Blair, as the head of the British Labor Party, assumed the role of English Prime Minister in 1997. Blair was reelected to the post in 2001 and again in 2005. From the early days of his premiership, Blair had proven himself committed to working closely alongside the United States on foreign affairs issues. Blair aligned himself with the United States-led offensive in Kosovo in the late 1990s, and enjoyed a positive working relationship with President Bill Clinton, which carried over to the Bush administration. Blair's foreign policy vision was outlined in an address—which has since become known as his "Doctrine of the International Community"—to the Chicago Economic Club. In that address, Blair made clear his position that the world has changed to the point where, "isolationism has ceased to have a reason to exist. By necessity, we have to cooperate with each other across nations."

INTRODUCTION

In the weeks following the attacks of September 11, 2001, Britain reaffirmed its position as a strong and vocal ally of the United States. Sixty-seven British citizens died in the attacks at the World Trade Center in New York, and the attacks led to several displays of solidarity by Britons towards the United States, including a performance of the Star Spangled Banner at Buckingham Palace. Prime Minister Tony Blair committed Britain to standing "shoulder to shoulder" with the United States in the war on terror.

On October 2, 2001, after returning from a diplomatic tour to Germany and France and visiting the attack site in New York, Blair addressed his Labor Party Conference in Brighton, England, with a speech Blair drafted himself. The speech, which has been described as one of the most powerful of his career, combined his emotions after visiting New York with his vision for the British government's response to September 11.

PRIMARY SOURCE

. . . What happened on 11 September was without parallel in the bloody history of terrorism.

Within a few hours, up to 7000 people were annihilated, the commercial centre of New York was reduced to rubble and in Washington and Pennsylvania, further death and horror on an unimaginable scale. Let no one say this was a blow for Islam when the blood of innocent Muslims was shed along with those of the Christian, Jewish and other faiths around the world.

We know those responsible. In Afghanistan are scores of training camps for the export of terror. Chief amongst the sponsors and organizers is Osama Bin Laden.

He is supported, shielded, and given succour by the Taliban regime.

Two days before the 11 September attacks, Masood, the leader of the opposition Northern Alliance, was assassinated by two suicide bombers. Both were linked to Bin Laden. Some may call that coincidence. I call it payment—payment in the currency these people deal in: blood.

Be in no doubt; Bin Laden and his people organized this atrocity. The Taliban aid and abet him. He will not desist from further acts of terror. They will not stop helping him.

Whatever the dangers of the action we take, the dangers of inaction are far, far greater.

Look for a moment at the Taliban regime. It is undemocratic. That goes without saying.

There is now no contact permitted with western agencies, even those delivering food. The people live in abject poverty. It is a regime founded on fear and funded on the drugs trade. The biggest drugs hoard in the world is in Afghanistan, controlled by the Taliban. Ninety per cent of the heroin on British streets originates in Afghanistan.

So what do we do?

Don't overreact some say. We aren't.

We haven't lashed out. No missiles on the first night just for effect.

Don't kill innocent people. We are not the ones who waged war on the innocent. We seek the guilty.

Look for a diplomatic solution. There is no diplomacy with Bin Laden or the Taliban regime.

State an ultimatum and get their response. We stated the ultimatum; they haven't responded.

Understand the causes of terror. Yes, we should try, but let there be no moral ambiguity about this; nothing could ever justify the events of 11 September, and it is to turn justice on its head to pretend it could.

The action we take will be proportionate, targeted, we will do all we humanly can to avoid civilian casualties. But

understand what we are dealing with. Listen to the calls of those passengers on the planes. Think of the children on them, told they were going to die.

Think of the cruelty beyond our comprehension as amongst the screams and the anguish of the innocent, those hijackers drove at full throttle planes laden with fuel into buildings where tens of thousands worked.

They have no moral inhibition on the slaughter of the innocent. If they could have murdered not 7,000 but 70,000 does anyone doubt they would have done so and rejoiced in it?

There is no compromise possible with such people, no meeting of minds, no point of understanding with such terror.

Just a choice; defeat it or be defeated by it. And defeat it we must.

Any action taken will be against the terrorist network of Bin Laden.

As for the Taliban, they can surrender the terrorists, or face the consequences and again, in any action, the aim will be to eliminate their military hardware, cut off their finances, disrupt their supplies, target their troops, not civilians. We will put a trap around the regime.

I say to the Taliban: surrender the terrorists; or surrender power. It's your choice.

We will take action at every level, national and international, in the UN, in G8, in the EU, in NATO, in every regional grouping in the world, to strike at international terrorism wherever it exists.

For the first time, the UN security council has imposed mandatory obligations on all UN members to cut off terrorist financing and end safe havens for terrorists.

Those that finance terror, those who launder their money, those that cover their tracks are every bit as guilty as the fanatic who commits the final act.

Here in this country and in other nations round the world, laws will be changed, not to deny basic liberties but to prevent their abuse and protect the most basic liberty of all: freedom from terror. New extradition laws will be introduced; new rules to ensure asylum is not a front for terrorist entry. This country is proud of its tradition in giving asylum to those fleeing tyranny. We will always do so. But we have a duty to protect the system from abuse.

It must be overhauled radically so that from now on, those who abide by the rules get help, and those that don't can no longer play the system to gain unfair advantage over others.

Round the world, 11 September is bringing governments and people to reflect, consider, and change. And in this process, amidst all the talk of war and action, there is another dimension appearing.

There is a coming together. The power of community is asserting itself. We are realizing how fragile are our frontiers in the face of the world's new challenges.

Today conflicts rarely stay within national boundaries.

Today a tremor in one financial market is repeated in the markets of the world.

Today confidence is global, either its presence or its absence.

Today the threat is chaos, because for people with work to do, family life to balance, mortgages to pay, careers to further, pensions to provide, the yearning is for order and stability and if it doesn't exist elsewhere, it is unlikely to exist here.

I have long believed this interdependence defines the new world we live in.

SIGNIFICANCE

Prime Minister Blair's address stated Britain' plan to join the allied offensive against the Taliban and terrorist networks in Afghanistan. This speech publicly established the alliance between the United States and Britain that continued during Operation Iraqi Freedom.

Blair used this speech to anticipate criticism that would be directed towards him. He stated unequivocally that there would never be diplomacy with terrorists and that negotiation would be impossible with the Taliban regime. The speech also proposed that the British government adopt a policy to strike at international terrorism wherever it could be found. Prime Minister Blair contended that the events of 9/11 would present a new security environment that would lead to changes in British law. He asserted that rather than deny British citizens their basic liberties, these new laws were designed to help prevent terrorism. Despite this contention, such legislation has been met in subsequent years with considerable criticism from civil libertarians.

FURTHER RESOURCES
Periodicals

"Britain's prime minister gives Taliban ultimatum." *Baltimore Sun*. October 3, 2001.

Web sites

CNN.com. McCaleb, Ian C. "U.S. talks diplomacy, Blair talks action." <http://cnnstudentnews.cnn.com/2001/US/10/02/ret.diplomacy/> (accessed June 25, 2005).

Guardian Unlimited. "Full Text: Tony Blair's Speech." <http://politics.guardian.co.uk/print/0,3858,4268838-108975,00.html> (accessed June 28, 2005).

"I Am at War with Your Country"

Shoe Bomber Attempts Suicide Bombing of American Airlines Paris-to-Miami Flight

Court transcript

By: Richard Reid and Judge William Young

Date: January 30, 2003

Source: Court hearing transcript, January 30, 2003; excerpts published January 31, 2003. Available from CNN.com/Law Center at <http://www.cnn.com/2003/LAW/01/31/reid.transcript/> (accessed July 8, 2005).

About the Author: Richard Reid, widely known as the shoe bomber, was born August 12, 1973, in England. After his conviction in 2003, he began serving a life sentence in prison in Florence, Colorado. William Young, the chief justice of the United States District Court for the District of Massachusetts, imposed the sentence.

INTRODUCTION

On December 22, 2001, American Airlines Flight 63, a Boeing 767, was en route from Paris to Miami, Florida, with 185 passengers and twelve crew members aboard. At about 11:00 A.M. EST, when the plane was about ninety minutes away from Boston, a flight attendant noticed the smell of sulfur in the cabin. She approached an unkempt passenger who had lit a match and appeared to be attempting to set fire to wires protruding from the tongue of his shoe. She leapt at the passenger and wrestled with him while crying out, "Oh, my God! Somebody help me!"

A brief struggle followed. The man pushed the flight attendant to the floor. When another flight attendant tried to restrain him, he wrestled with her and bit her thumb. By this time, surrounding passengers had joined the struggle. After the man was subdued, he was secured with belts provided by other passengers, and two doctors on board administered a sedative from the aircraft's medical kit. The pilot, concerned that the man had accomplices on board, alerted the North American Aerospace Defense Command (NORAD), which dispatched two F-14 fighter jets to accompany the aircraft to Boston's Logan Airport. The plane landed at 12:50 and was secured on a remote section of the runway.

The passenger, Richard Reid, was traveling without luggage on a false British passport issued in Belgium three weeks earlier. Just the day before, he had paid for a ticket for a Paris-to-Miami flight with cash and carried no baggage, prompting airport security personnel to question him for so long that he missed the flight.

In Boston, he was taken into custody, and when the FBI examined his high-top basketball sneakers, they discovered a foreign substance in the lining, as well as wires. The substance turned out to be C-4, a powerful explosive used not only by military forces but also by terrorists; C-4, for example, was the explosive that severely damaged the *U.S.S. Cole* in Yemen in October 2000. The wires led to a detonator made of triacetone triperoxide. An air disaster had been diverted.

On January 16, 2002, a federal grand jury indicted Richard Reid on nine counts, including attempted murder and use of a weapon of mass destruction. Reid pled not guilty. After trial, he was found guilty in January 2003. At his sentencing hearing on January 30, he had the following exchange with presiding judge William Young.

■ PRIMARY SOURCE

Richard Reid: I start by praising Allah because life today is no good. I bear witness to this and he alone is right to be worshiped. And I bear witness that Muhammad Sa'laat Alayhi as-Salaam is his last prophet and messenger who is sent to all of mankind for guidance, with the sound guidance for everyone.

Judge William Young: I didn't hear the last. I admit my actions and then what did you say?

Reid: I further admit my allegiance to Osama bin Laden, to Islam, and to the religion of Allah. With regards to what you said about killing innocent people, I will say one thing. Your government has killed 2 million children in Iraq. If you want to think about something, against 2 million, I don't see no (*sic*) comparison.

Your government has sponsored the rape and torture of Muslims in the prisons of Egypt and Turkey and Syria and Jordan with their money and with their weapons. I don't know, see what I done (*sic*) as being equal to rape and to torture, or to the deaths of the two million children in Iraq.

So, for this reason, I think I ought not apologize for my actions. I am at war with your country. I'm at war with them not for personal reasons, but because they have murdered more than, so many children and they have oppressed my religion and they have oppressed people for no reason except that they say we believe in Allah.

This is the only reason that America sponsors Egypt. It's the only reason they sponsor Turkey. It's the only reason they back Israel.

As far as the sentence is concerned, it's in your hand. Only really, it is not even in your hand. It's in Allah's hand. I put my trust in Allah totally and I know that he will give victory to his religion. And he will give victory to those who believe and he will destroy those who wish to oppress the people because they believe in Allah.

So you can judge and I leave you to judge. And I don't mind. This is all I have to say. And I bear witness to Muhammad this is Allah's message.

Young: Mr. Richard C. Reid, hearken now to the sentence the Court imposes upon you.

On counts 1, 5 and 6 the Court sentences you to life in prison in the custody of the United States Attorney General. On counts 2, 3, 4 and 7, the Court sentences you to 20 years in prison on each count, the sentence on each count to run consecutive one with the other. That's 80 years.

On Count 8 the Court sentences you to the mandatory 30 years consecutive to the 80 years just imposed. The Court imposes upon you on each of the eight counts a fine of $250,000 for the aggregate fine of $2 million.

The Court accepts the government's recommendation with respect to restitution and orders restitution in the amount of $298.17 to Andre Bousquet and $5,784 to American Airlines.

The Court imposes upon you the $800 special assessment.

The Court imposes upon you five years supervised release simply because the law requires it. But the life sentences are real life sentences so I need not go any further.

This is the sentence that is provided for by our statutes. It is a fair and a just sentence. It is a righteous sentence. Let me explain this to you.

We are not afraid of any of your terrorist co-conspirators, Mr. Reid. We are Americans. We have been through the fire before. There is all too much war talk here. And I say that to everyone with the utmost respect.

Here in this court where we deal with individuals as individuals, and care for individuals as individuals, as human beings we reach out for justice.

You are not an enemy combatant. You are a terrorist. You are not a soldier in any war. You are a terrorist. To give you that reference, to call you a soldier gives you far too much stature. Whether it is the officers of government who do it or your attorney who does it, or that happens to be your view, you are a terrorist.

And we do not negotiate with terrorists. We do not treat with terrorists. We do not sign documents with terrorists.

We hunt them down one by one and bring them to justice.

So war talk is way out of line in this court. You're a big fellow. But you're not that big. You're no warrior. I know warriors. You are a terrorist. A species of criminal guilty of multiple attempted murders.

In a very real sense Trooper Santiago had it right when first you were taken off that plane and into custody and you wondered where the press and where the TV crews were and you said you're no big deal. You're no big deal.

What your counsel, what your able counsel and what the equally able United States attorneys have grappled with and what I have as honestly as I know how tried to grapple with, is why you did something so horrific. What was it that led you here to this courtroom today? I have listened respectfully to what you have to say. And I ask you to search your heart and ask yourself what sort of unfathomable hate led you to do what you are guilty of and admit you are guilty of doing.

And I have an answer for you. It may not satisfy you. But as I search this entire record it comes as close to understanding as I know.

It seems to me you hate the one thing that to us is most precious. You hate our freedom. Our individual freedom. Our individual freedom to live as we choose, to come and go as we choose, to believe or not believe as we individually choose.

Here, in this society, the very winds carry freedom. They carry it everywhere from sea to shining sea. It is because we prize individual freedom so much that you are here in this beautiful courtroom. So that everyone can see, truly see that justice is administered fairly, individually, and discretely.

It is for freedom's seek that your lawyers are striving so vigorously on your behalf and have filed appeals, will go on in their, their representation of you before other judges. We care about it. Because we all know that the way we treat you, Mr. Reid, is the measure of our own liberties.

Make no mistake though. It is yet true that we will bear any burden; pay any price, to preserve our freedoms.

Look around this courtroom. Mark it well. The world is not going to long remember what you or I say here. Day after tomorrow it will be forgotten. But this, however, will long endure. Here, in this courtroom, and courtrooms all across America, the American people will gather to see that justice, individual justice, justice, not war, individual justice is in fact being done.

The very President of the United States through his officers will have to come into courtrooms and lay out evidence on which specific matters can be judged, and juries of citizens will gather to sit and judge that evidence democratically, to mold and shape and refine our sense of justice.

See that flag, Mr. Reid? That's the flag of the United States of America. That flag will fly there long after this is all forgotten. That flag still stands for freedom. You know it always will. Custody, Mr. Officer. Stand him down.

Reid: That flag will be brought down on the Day of Judgment and you will see in front of your Lord and my Lord and then we will know. (Whereupon the defendant was removed from the courtroom.)

SIGNIFICANCE

Initially, authorities considered that Reid was an eccentric, perhaps mentally unbalanced man who was acting alone. The indictment, however, painted an entirely different picture. It alleged that he had received training in al-Qaeda terrorist camps in Afghanistan and that the shoe bomb, which Reid claimed he built himself from a design he had found on the Internet, was too sophisticated to have been his sole work.

Further, investigation of Reid's movements in the days and weeks before his aborted attack showed that he regularly had contact with known terrorists in the Middle East and in Europe, particularly in the Netherlands, where other terrorists networked (among them was Zacarias Moussaoui, who was implicated in the September 11, 2001, terrorist attacks on the United States). Additionally, the FBI found on the shoe bomb palm prints and a hair from another person, suggesting that Reid had help building it. Later, in April 2005, a British court sentenced Saajid Mohammed Badat, to thirteen years in prison for his part in the conspiracy.

In the early 1990s, Reid was in and out of British jails, where Muslim imams were allowed to distribute Islamist literature, including calls to *jihad* (holy war). During his last stint in jail in 1994, Reid converted to Islam. Reid turned to extremism under the name Abdel Rahim (also Abdul Raheem) in 1998 and over the next three years, moved freely back and forth between London and Paris, Amsterdam, Brussels, Turkey, Egypt, Pakistan, and Afghanistan, learning the craft of terror.

Largely because of the shoe bomber, airplane passengers must now remove their shoes and have them inspected for explosive residue before boarding.

FURTHER RESOURCES
Web sites
CNN.com. "Timeline: The Shoe Bomber Case." January 7, 2002. <http://archives.cnn.com/2002/US/01/07/reid. timeline/index.html> (accessed July 8, 2005).

Time. Elliott, Michael. "The Shoe Bomber's World." February 16, 2002. <http://www.time.com/time/world/article/0,8599,203478,00.html> (accessed July 8, 2005).

United States of American v. Richard Colvin Reid. Indictment, January 16, 2002. <http://news.findlaw.com/hdocs/docs/reid/usreid011602ind.pdf> (accessed July 8, 2005).

Periodicals

Stephen, Andrew. "America's Very Own Muslims: Top Basketball Players, Heroes to Millions, Are Converting to Islam. So Does the U.S. Shelter an Army of Home-Grown Richard Reids?" *New Statesman*. (January 7, 2002): pp. 12 ff.

Shoe Bomber Attempts Airliner Explosion

District of Massachusetts, United States of America against Richard Colvin Reid

Indictment

By: United States District Court

Date: January 16, 2002

Source: Indictment, United States District Court, District of Massachusetts, United States of America against Richard Colvin Reid.

About the Author: The United States District Courts hear federal, civil, and criminal cases. There are ninety-four judicial districts in the United States District Court system, with courts in all fifty states, the District of Columbia, Puerto Rico, and three United States territories.

The shoe-bomber suspect of American Airlines Flight 63, who boarded the flight using a British passport under the name Richard Reid. AP/WIDE WORLD PHOTOS

INTRODUCTION

British-born Richard Colvin Reid (1973–), more widely known as the "Shoe Bomber," first gained notoriety on December 22, 2001, for attempting to bomb American Airlines Flight 63 as it flew over the Atlantic Ocean from Charles De Gaulle International Airport in Paris to Miami International Airport. Reid was noticed by other passengers acting suspicious when he attempted to light a match to his high-top basketball sneakers. Eventually, he was restrained with the help of flight attendants and several passengers. No damage occurred to the airplane and two flight attendants were slightly injured. Under escort by U.S. Air Force F-15

fighter jets, the airplane was diverted to Boston's Logan Airport.

Reid was indicted on January 16, 2002, on nine criminal counts including attempted murder, the use of a weapon of mass destruction, and attempted destruction of an airliner.

After pleading guilty, Reid was convicted at a Boston federal court on January 30, 2003. During his sentencing hearing, Reid publicly declared himself to be an Islamic fundamentalist and an enemy of the United States. In other public statements, Reid confirmed he was a member of al Qaeda and a supporter of Osama Bin Laden. Later at the hearing, he was sentenced to life in prison.

Reid was sent to the Administrative Maximum (ADX) Security Florence prison in Florence, Colorado. The prison, operated by the U.S. federal government, holds some of the country's most dangerous prisoners.

PRIMARY SOURCE

UNITED STATES OF AMERICA
V
RICHARD COLVIN REID

Count One:

(18 U.S.C. §2332a(a)(1)—Attempted Use of Weapon of Mass Destruction)

The Grand Jury charges that:

1. At all times relevant to th[ese] count[s] brought under Title 18, United States Code, Chapter 113B—Terrorism, Al-Qaeda was a designated foreign terrorist organization pursuant to 8 U.S.C. §1189.

2. At various times relevant to this count, Richard Colvin Reid received training from Al-Qaeda in Afghanistan.

3. On or about December 22, 2001, at Paris, France, and on board American Airlines Flight 63 en-route from Paris, France to Miami, Florida, but landing at East Boston, Massachusetts, in the District of Massachusetts,

RICHARD COLVIN REID,
a/k/a ABDUL-RAHEEM,
a/k/a ABDUL RAHEEM, ABU IBRAHIM,

defendant herein, did, without lawful authority, attempt to use a weapon of mass destruction, to wit: a destructive device, consisting of an explosive bomb placed in each of his shoes, against one and more than one national of the United States while such nationals were outside of the United States.

All in violation of Title 18, United States Code, Section 2332a(a)(1).

Count Two:

(18 U.S.C. §2332—Attempted Homicide)

The Grand Jury further charges that:

RICHARD COLVIN REID,

defendant herein, did, outside the United States, attempt to kill and to commit a killing that is a murder of one and more than one national of the United States, while such nationals were outside the United States.

All in violation of Title 18, United States Code, Section 2332(b)(1).

Count Three:

(49 U.S.C. §§46505(b)(3) and (c)—Placing Explosive Device on Aircraft)

The Grand Jury further charges that:

RICHARD COLVIN REID,

defendant herein, did knowingly have on and about his person when on American Airlines Flight 63, an aircraft in and intended for operation in air transportation, and did place on that aircraft, explosive devices contained in the footwear he was then wearing; and did so willfully and without regard for the safety of human life, and with reckless disregard for the safety of human life.

All in violation of Title 49, United States Code, Sections 46505(b)(3) and (c).

Count Four:

(49 U.S.C. §§46506(1) and 18 U.S.C. §1113—Attempted Murder)

The Grand Jury further charges that:

RICHARD COLVIN REID,

defendant herein, did, on an aircraft in the special aircraft jurisdiction of the United States, attempt to commit murder of one and more than one of the 183 other passengers and 14 crew members on board American Airlines Flight 63.

All in violation of Title 49, United States Code, Section 46506(1) and Title 18, United States Code, Section 1113.

Count Five:

(49 U.S.C. §46504—Interference with Flight Crew and Attendants)

The Grand Jury further charges that:

RICHARD COLVIN REID,

defendant herein, did, on an aircraft in the special aircraft jurisdiction of the United States, by assaulting and intimidating Hermis Moutardier, a flight attendant of the aircraft, interfere with the performance of the duties of said flight attendant, and did lessen the ability of said flight attendant to perform those duties; and did use a dangerous weapon in assaulting and intimidating said flight attendant.

All in violation of Title 49, United States Code, Section 46504.

Count Six:

(49 U.S.C. §46504—Interference with Flight Crew and Attendants)

The Grand Jury further charges that:

RICHARD COLVIN REID,

defendant herein, did, on an aircraft in the special aircraft jurisdiction of the United States, by assaulting and intimidating Cristina Jones, a flight attendant of the aircraft, interfere with the performance of the duties of said flight attendant, and did lessen the ability of said flight attendant to perform those duties; and did use a dangerous weapon in assaulting and intimidating said flight attendant.

All in violation of Title 49, United States Code, Section 46504.

Count Seven:

(18 U.S.C. §§32(a)(1) and (7)—Attempted Destruction of Aircraft)

The Grand Jury further charges that:

RICHARD COLVIN REID,

defendant herein, did willfully attempt to set fire to, damage, destroy, disable, and wreck American Airlines Flight 63, an aircraft in the special aircraft jurisdiction of the United States and a civil aircraft used, operated, and employed in interstate, overseas and foreign air commerce.

All in violation of Title 18, United States Code, Sections 32(a)(1) and (7).

Count Eight:

(18 U.S.C. §924(c)—Using a Destructive Device During and in Relation to a Crime of Violence)

The Grand Jury further charges that:

RICHARD COLVIN REID,

defendant herein, during and in relation to a crime of violence for which he could be prosecuted in a court of the United States, to wit: (1) attempted use of a weapon of mass destruction against a national of the United States while such national is outside of the United States, as charged in Count One of this Indictment; (2) attempted homicide of a national of the United States outside the United States, as charged in Count Two of this Indictment; (3) attempted murder on an aircraft in the special aircraft jurisdiction of the United States, as charged in Count Four of this Indictment; (4) interference with flight crew and attendants, as charged in Counts Five and Six of the Indictment; (5) attempted destruction of an aircraft in the special aircraft jurisdiction of the United States, the aircraft also being a civil aircraft used, operated, and employed in interstate, overseas, and foreign air commerce, as charged in Count Seven of this Indictment; and (6) attempted wrecking of a mass transportation vehicle, as charged in Count Nine of the Indictment; did use and carry a firearm, to wit, two destructive devices each consisting of an explosive bomb, and did, in furtherance of such charged crimes, possess those same destructive devices.

All in violation of Title 18, United States Code, Section 924(c).

Count Nine:

(18 U.S.C. §§1993(a)(1) and (8)—Attempted Wrecking of a Mass Transportation Vehicle)

The Grand Jury further charges that:

RICHARD COLVIN REID,

defendant herein, did willfully attempt to wreck, set fire to, and disable a mass transportation vehicle, American Airlines Flight 63, a Boeing 767–300 International airliner operated by American Airlines, a mass transportation provider engaged in and affecting interstate and foreign commerce, at a time when American Airlines Flight 63 was carrying passengers.

All in violation of Title 18, United States Code, Section 1993(a)(1) and (8).

SIGNIFICANCE

About three months after the September 11, 2001 attacks in New York City, Washington, D.C., and Pennsylvania, Reid attempted to blow up the commercial airplane. Although law enforcement authorities initially found no connection between Reid and terrorist groups, this opinion dramatically changed. After investigations by the Federal Bureau of Investigation, the Federal Aviation Administration (FAA), the Justice Department, various foreign governments, and many other investigative organizations, it was later confirmed that Reid, along with British-born Saajid Badat, were part of a second terrorism wave planned against the United States by al-Qaeda. (Badat, who would have blown up his airplane at about the same time as Reid, backed down from his suicide mission.)

A large amount of evidence was collected over the next few months that substantiated that Reid did not act alone, and in fact was actively assisted and directed by the al-Qaeda organization.

Some of this collected evidence includes: (1) the bomb used contained palm prints and hair strands that did not belong to Reid, implying that at least one other person handled it; (2) the sophistication of the bomb indicated that Reid did not design nor assemble it; (3) all the active ingredients used within the bomb eventually linked Reid to Islamic fundamentalist groups who were further linked to Osama Bin Laden's al-Qaeda; (4) *Wall Street Journal* reporters stated they had acquired a used computer that held thousands of files written by al-Qaeda members, with one file detailing a trip made by Abdul Ra'uff, which corresponded to locations traveled by Reid; (5) European investigators directly linked Reid with many well-known terrorist cells operating in Europe; and (6) terrorist training performed by Reid at al-Qaeda camps in Afghanistan.

Contrary to early reports of a crude attempt to detonate explosives in his shoes, subsequent analysis of the boots worn by Reid showed a detonation device deliberately designed to thwart airport security. The soles of each boot contained pentarythritol tetranitrate (PETN), a type of plastic explosive, and each had a detonator made of triacetone triperoxide (TATP). Such explosive devices have been used by other groups and suicide bombers in the Middle East. The lack of metal parts made the bomb virtually undetectable to airport security screening used at the time.

One aspect highlighted by the Shoe Bomber case is that terrorism is not only headquartered in well-known countries such as Afghanistan, Iraq, Indonesia, Yemen, the Philippines, and Somalia, but active cells also exist in some countries of western Europe. Reid and Zacarias Moussaoui, a French citizen accused of participating in the planning of the September 11 terrorist attacks on the United States, both attended the Brixton mosque in London for a period in the late 1990s before traveling to Afghanistan to join and train with al-Qaeda.

Reid's case also highlighted the trend for extremist Islamist sects to attract people who feel oppressed by the society in which they live. Psychologists often assert that religious sects and other "life disciplines" can be attractive to individuals with low self-esteem. Reid was often scorned in England for his Jamaican background. Once drawn into fanatical religious systems—not only those associated with Islam—impressionable converts, such as Reid, can be led into a process of recruitment, indoctrination, and training, and ultimately to a life of terrorism.

Because of Reid's actions, the FAA, on December 11, 2001, announced a civil aviation security warning that terrorists may try to sneak weapons onto aircraft in their shoes. They ordered airlines to add random shoe inspections to the already-random security checks being performed. Shoe inspections are now a routine part of the security process at U.S. airports.

Terrorism security experts and the public are also more cognizant that al-Qaeda operatives and terrorists are not solely of Middle Eastern descent. Because of this, ethnic profiling, which was criticized for targeting particular groups, is no longer a major criterion for identifying terrorists.

The incident also highlighted the continuing vulnerability of civil aviation and public transportation to the potential for terrorist acts, especially at the hands of Osama Bin Laden, and illustrated how well organized the terrorists are at planning and carrying out their violent activities.

FURTHER RESOURCES
Web sites

Clough, Sue. *News Telegraph*. "British Muslim Planned Second Shoe Bombing." <http://www.telegraph.co.uk/news/main.jhtml?xml=/news/2005/03/01/nshoe01.xml> (accessed June 17, 2005).

CNN.com/Law Center. "Reid: 'I Am at War With Your Country'." <http://www.cnn.com/2003/LAW/01/31/reid.transcript/> (accessed June 17, 2005).

FindLaw's Legal Commentary. Kayyem, Juliette. "The Sentencing of 'Shoe Bomber' Richard Reid: Its Larger Significance for Terrorism Cases and The 'War on Terrorism' In General." <http://writ.news.findlaw.com/commentary/20030203_kayyem.html> (accessed June 17, 2005).

McCarthy, Andrew C. *National Review Online*. "Shoe Bomber 2.0." <http://www.nationalreview.com/mccarthy/mccarthy200410050818.asp> (accessed June 17, 2005).

Terrorist Hiding Places

"U.S. Forces Find Troubling Items in Afghan Caves"

News article

By: The Associated Press

Date: January 27, 2002

Source: The Associated Press is an international news organization with offices and reporters located worldwide.

About the Author: Founded in 1848, the Associated Press claims to be the oldest and largest news organization in the world, serving as a news source for more than one billion people a day.

INTRODUCTION

The nation of Afghanistan has a long history of conflict and invasion. In the second half of the twentieth century, the Soviet Union spent more than a decade in an unsuccessful attempt to prop up the Soviet-sponsored government there. The results for the Soviets were disastrous by almost any measure: 60,000 casualties and costs of more than $20 billion per year. Yet the results for the Afghan people were far worse: six million refugees driven into neighboring countries, 70% of the nation's paved roads destroyed, and 1.5 million people dead. Economically, the war reduced the country's net worth by as much as one-half and left it few resources with which to rebuild.

Following the September 2001 terrorist attacks, U.S. attention quickly turned to this impoverished nation, where Osama Bin Laden and his advisers had been guests of the ruling Taliban since 1996. United States President George W. Bush promptly gave the Taliban an ultimatum requiring the handover of Bin Laden and full access to the terrorist training camps. A similar demand for Bin Laden's surrender was adopted by the United Nations. When the Taliban refused to

Hermes the robot exits an empty cave after searching for mines and traps hidden by Taliban or al-Qaida fugitives in the eastern border town of Qiqay, Afghanistan. AP/WIDE WORLD PHOTOS

comply with the demands, the United States and its allies launched an invasion on October 7, 2001.

In a few days, the allied air campaign destroyed most air defenses and terrorist training camps. Pinpoint air attacks and carpet bombing (the dropping of many bombs in a particular area) against Taliban troops were also employed and significant land attacks began as well. The capital city of Kabul fell on November 13, just over a month after the invasion began.

While the capture of Kabul was a moral victory in the invasion, the conflict continued throughout the rest of the nation. With few valuable fixed assets, the Afghan fighters were highly mobile, and coalition forces found the rugged terrain difficult, just as the Soviets had two decades before. In particular, a network of caves in the rugged Tora Bora region became a focal point of much of the ongoing conflict, including the search for Bin Laden.

Tora Bora is located in eastern Afghanistan, near the Taliban stronghold of Kandahar and the Pakistani border. While few details are known about the area, it is generally acknowledged to include an extensive network of facilities concealed in interconnected caves. While the term "cave" may be technically correct, the rugged image it conjures up is not; some reports from the Soviet era suggested that the facilities might include elaborate underground structures complete with hydroelectric power, although these reports were unverified.

Despite enormous progress toward self-rule by the Afghan people, fighting remains widespread in the outlying regions of the country. The region around Kandahar has remained particularly volatile.

PRIMARY SOURCE

Kandahar, Afghanistan (AP)—The guns and ammunition were expected. The poster of New York's Twin Towers set against Afghan mountains was not.

Marines who joined elite Navy SEALS in searching al-Qaeda caves said yesterday they made some unsettling discoveries: a photo of President George W. Bush with blood running down his face and another of Osama bin Laden holding a Kalashnikov rifle and marked with the words "Leader of Peace."

The Marines' accounts, given during interviews at the U.S. military base here in southern Afghanistan, provided a rare glimpse into the cave-by-cave war being waged by U.S. forces hunting for elusive al-Qaeda and Taliban fighters and any tidbits of information about bin Laden's worldwide terrorist network.

With the Taliban ousted from power and hiding out in Afghanistan's rugged mountains and valleys, U.S. bombing is winding down.

Instead, the battle against terrorism has shifted to the painstaking search of caves and other remote locations for al-Qaeda and Taliban renegades as well as intelligence information to prevent further terrorist attacks.

It's dangerous, daunting work.

Marines described the cave complex they searched this month as elaborately constructed. Reinforced with concrete and tall enough to walk freely around, the caves had an irrigation system to water trees and flowers outside.

"It didn't look like a cave. Someone put some time into this place," said Sgt. Charles Calfee, 28, of Dublin, Va. "It reminded me of the Flintstones."

Originally, the 50 Marines from Lima Company, Battalion Landing Team 3/6 of the 26th Marine Expeditionary Unit were flown to the caves in the area between Khost and Gardez in eastern Afghanistan to guard the SEALS while they searched.

The SEALS, along with special forces from the Army and Air Force and CIA operatives, are taking a lead in the current phase of the Afghan conflict, which began after the U.S.-backed northern alliance routed the Taliban in last year's fighting.

The mission was meant to last 10 hours. Instead, it took several days, and the SEALS—overwhelmed with the amount of intelligence information they found—had to enlist the Marines in their search.

"Every day we found more," said 1st Sgt. Joseph Bolton, of Gillette, Wyo.

The Marines, stationed at Camp Lejeune, N.C., refused to reveal the exact locations of or give details about the caves. They also would not say what type of information or how many weapons and rounds of ammunition were found.

Marines spokesman 1st Lt. James Jarvis said the information is being analyzed and could help American forces find suspected Taliban and al-Qaeda fighters.

"Obviously it's still early in the campaign," Jarvis said. "There are still Taliban and al-Qaeda forces in the region."

The caves have proved a headache even for the high-tech U.S. military. U.S. aircraft targeted some caves with "bunker-busting" bombs that pierce concrete and with 15,000-pound "daisy cutters"—the most powerful conventional bombs in the U.S. arsenal—to kill al-Qaeda and Taliban forces thought to be hiding inside.

U.S. forces chasing leads on the whereabouts of terror mastermind Osama bin Laden and Taliban leader Mullah Mohammed Omar have also come up empty-handed.

Gen. Tommy Franks, commander of the Afghan campaign, said yesterday he did not know the whereabouts of either man. But he said they get fresh leads daily.

"Some of it turns out to be good information, and some of it not," he said.

The Marines said it is clear that those who hid in the caves left in a hurry. They found flour, sugar, corn meal and eggs, which the U.S. soldiers baked into bread because they were short of rations for the first few days of their search.

In nearby mud-walled huts, where the Marines used to sleep, they also found a chilling reminder of what brought them to Afghanistan in the first place: the date Sept. 11, written in Arabic-style writing on the wall.

"There was no doubt we were in bad guy country," said Capt. Lloyd Freeman, 34, of Bells, Texas.

"It felt good to be part of the force, like we came out here to do what we came to do, fix what started the whole thing in the first place."

SIGNIFICANCE

Prior to September 2001, the U.S. military was designed and deployed to counter the threats found in a Cold War-style conflict, in which the enemy consists of well-organized, well-financed nations offering numerous high-value fixed targets. In such a conflict, the primary consideration is generally how best to attack a heavily defended, but clearly identified target.

The war on terror has forced a radical rethinking of U.S. military doctrine, specifically in terms of the hardware used to fight wars. While showpieces of the U.S. arsenal such as the B-2 bomber have seen relatively little use, tiny flyweight unmanned aircraft such as the Predator have been used with devastating impact. And while heavy bombing with so-called bunker buster bombs had limited success in rooting out cave-hiding insurgents, smaller automated search devices now being developed and deployed will allow ground troops to search caves more efficiently and with more safety.

As U.S. military planners look to the future, they anticipate few large threats such as the old Soviet Union. Instead, they expect the United States to find itself in a series of asynchronous (not following an expected pattern or timeline) conflicts in which the enemy is difficult to find and destroy. Because asynchronous conflicts are fought in a fundamentally different way than traditional wars, U.S. spending and planning is already shifting in preparation for this new type of conflict.

Another change brought about by this new type of warfare has been felt by U.S. reservists called up for active duty. While past deployments of reserve units have been rare and generally short-lived, this new type of warfare has required some reservists to spend extensive tours of duty away from home.

FURTHER RESOURCES

Books

Lindroth, David. *First In: An Insider's Account of How the CIA Spearheaded the War on Terror in Afghanistan.* New York: Presidio Press, 2005.

Micheletti, Eric. *Special Forces in Afghanistan 2001–2003: War against Terrorism.* Paris: Historie and Collections, 2003.

Web sites

CNN.com. "US Bombers Pound Afghan Caves." <http://www.cnn.com/2003/WORLD/asiapcf/central/02/13/afghan.bombing.ap> (accessed June 23, 2005).

American soldiers rest during their inspection of a cave complex where they found arms, ammunition, and personal effects of the former inhabitants. AP/WIDE WORLD PHOTOS

"Axis of Evil"

The President's State of the Union Address

Speech

By: George W. Bush

Date: January 29, 2002

Source: The President of the United States is required by the Constitution to deliver a periodic assessment of the state of the nation to Congress, and to make recommendations to Congress regarding the nation's welfare. Traditionally, the State of the Union speech is delivered annually in January by the president before a joint session of Congress. The following excerpt is taken from the State of the Union speech delivered by President George W. Bush on January 29, 2002.

About the Author: George W. Bush was elected President of the United States in November 2000, and re-elected

in 2004. The son of former President George H.W. Bush, he was previously Governor of Texas.

INTRODUCTION

The State of the Union address, once known as the President's Annual Message to Congress, is an annual speech given before a joint-session of Congress (U.S. House of Representatives and Senate). It is intended to report on the status of the nation, including important events of the previous year, and outline the President's policy agenda for the next year. The address may be given by a written message read by a clerk or delivered as a speech. Modern tradition dictates that the speech is delivered by the President on the last Tuesday in January, in the evening.

On January 29, 2002, President George W. Bush delivered his second State of the Union address. Coming just four months after the September 11, 2001, terrorist attacks on the United States, much of the speech focused on the effects of the attacks and

During his State of the Union address in 2002, President Bush discussed his vision for the war on terrorism and mentioned "an axis of evil." AP/WIDE WORLD PHOTOS

subsequent war in Afghanistan. However, President Bush stated that terrorism was not a problem confined to Afghanistan. He proceeded to outline what would become a new foreign policy agenda and military strategy for the United States. He identified three nations that he declared possessed dangerous arsenals of chemical and biological weapons, were pursuing development of nuclear weapons, or were state sponsors of terrorism. He dubbed three nations—North Korea, Iran, and Iraq (and later, Syria)—an "axis of evil," further asserted that immediate intervention was necessary to combat both the spread of global terrorism networks and the proliferation of weapons of mass destruction (WMDs).

The phrase "axis of evil" was created by senior White House speechwriter, David Frum. Frum later claimed that he had actually penned the words "axis of hatred," but that the phrase was refined by the speechwriting team or the President in a subsequent draft of the State of Union address.

PRIMARY SOURCE

January 29, 2002 . . . Our cause is just, and it continues. Our discoveries in Afghanistan confirmed our worst fears, and showed us the true scope of the task ahead. We have seen the depth of our enemies' hatred in videos, where they laugh about the loss of innocent life. And the depth of their hatred is equaled by the madness of the destruction they design. We have found diagrams of American nuclear power plants and public water facilities, detailed instructions for making chemical weapons, surveillance maps of American cities, and thorough descriptions of landmarks in America and throughout the world.

What we have found in Afghanistan confirms that, far from ending there, our war against terror is only beginning. Most of the 19 men who hijacked planes on September the 11th were trained in Afghanistan's camps, and so were tens of thousands of others. Thousands of dangerous killers, schooled in the methods of murder, often supported by outlaw regimes, are now spread throughout the world like ticking time bombs, set to go off without warning.

Thanks to the work of our law enforcement officials and coalition partners, hundreds of terrorists have been arrested. Yet, tens of thousands of trained terrorists are still at large. These enemies view the entire world as a battlefield, and we must pursue them wherever they are. (Applause.) So long as training camps operate, so long as nations harbor terrorists, freedom is at risk. And America and our allies must not, and will not, allow it. (Applause.)

Our nation will continue to be steadfast and patient and persistent in the pursuit of two great objectives. First, we will shut down terrorist camps, disrupt terrorist plans, and bring terrorists to justice. And, second, we must prevent the terrorists and regimes who seek chemical, biological, or nuclear weapons from threatening the United States and the world. (Applause.)

Our military has put the terror training camps of Afghanistan out of business, yet camps still exist in at least a dozen countries. A terrorist underworld, including groups like Hamas, Hezbollah, Islamic Jihad, Jaish-i-Mohammed, operates in remote jungles and deserts, and hides in the centers of large cities.

While the most visible military action is in Afghanistan, America is acting elsewhere. We now have troops in the Philippines, helping to train that country's armed forces to go after terrorist cells that have executed an American, and still hold hostages. Our soldiers, working with the Bosnian government, seized terrorists who were plotting to bomb our embassy. Our Navy is patrolling the coast of Africa to block the shipment of weapons and the establishment of terrorist camps in Somalia.

My hope is that all nations will heed our call, and eliminate the terrorist parasites who threaten their countries and our own. Many nations are acting forcefully. Pakistan is now cracking down on terror, and I admire the strong leadership of President Musharraf. (Applause.)

But some governments will be timid in the face of terror. And make no mistake about it: If they do not act, America will. (Applause.)

Our second goal is to prevent regimes that sponsor terror from threatening America or our friends and allies with weapons of mass destruction. Some of these regimes have been pretty quiet since September the 11th. But we know their true nature. North Korea is a regime arming with missiles and weapons of mass destruction, while starving its citizens.

Iran aggressively pursues these weapons and exports terror, while an unelected few repress the Iranian people's hope for freedom.

Iraq continues to flaunt its hostility toward America and to support terror. The Iraqi regime has plotted to develop anthrax, and nerve gas, and nuclear weapons for over a decade. This is a regime that has already used poison gas to murder thousands of its own citizens, leaving the bodies of mothers huddled over their dead children. This is a regime that agreed to international inspections, then kicked out the inspectors. This is a regime that has something to hide from the civilized world.

States like these, and their terrorist allies, constitute an axis of evil, arming to threaten the peace of the world. By seeking weapons of mass destruction, these regimes pose a grave and growing danger. They could provide these arms to terrorists, giving them the means to match their hatred. They could attack our allies or attempt to blackmail the United States. In any of these cases, the price of indifference would be catastrophic.

We will work closely with our coalition to deny terrorists and their state sponsors the materials, technology, and expertise to make and deliver weapons of mass destruction. We will develop and deploy effective missile defenses to protect America and our allies from sudden attack. (Applause.) And all nations should know: America will do what is necessary to ensure our nation's security.

We'll be deliberate, yet time is not on our side. I will not wait on events, while dangers gather. I will not stand by, as peril draws closer and closer. The United States of America will not permit the world's most dangerous regimes to threaten us with the world's most destructive weapons. (Applause.)

Our war on terror is well begun, but it is only begun. This campaign may not be finished on our watch, yet it must be and it will be waged on our watch.

We can't stop short. If we stop now, leaving terror camps intact and terror states unchecked, our sense of security would be false and temporary. History has called America and our allies to action, and it is both our responsibility and our privilege to fight freedom's fight. (Applause.)

Our first priority must always be the security of our nation, and that will be reflected in the budget I send to Congress. My budget supports three great goals for America: We will win this war; we'll protect our homeland; and we will revive our economy.

September the 11th brought out the best in America, and the best in this Congress. And I join the American people in applauding your unity and resolve. (Applause.) Now Americans deserve to have this same spirit directed toward addressing problems here at home. I'm a proud member of my party, yet as we act to win the war, protect our people, and create jobs in America, we must act, first and foremost, not as Republicans, not as Democrats, but as Americans. (Applause.)

It costs a lot to fight this war. We have spent more than a billion dollars a month, over $30 million a day, and we must be prepared for future operations. Afghanistan proved that expensive precision weapons defeat the enemy and spare innocent lives, and we need more of them. We need to replace aging aircraft and make our military more agile, to put our troops anywhere in the world quickly and safely. Our men and women in uniform deserve the best weapons, the best equipment, the best training, and they also deserve another pay raise. (Applause.)

My budget includes the largest increase in defense spending in two decades, because while the price of freedom and security is high, it is never too high. Whatever it costs to defend our country, we will pay. (Applause.)

The next priority of my budget is to do everything possible to protect our citizens and strengthen our nation against the ongoing threat of another attack. Time and distance from the events of September the 11th will not make us safer unless we act on its lessons. America is no longer protected by vast oceans. We are protected from attack only by vigorous action abroad, and increased vigilance at home.

My budget nearly doubles funding for a sustained strategy of homeland security, focused on four key areas: bioterrorism, emergency response, airport and border security, and improved intelligence. We will develop vaccines to fight anthrax and other deadly diseases. We'll increase funding to help states and communities train and equip our heroic police and firefighters. (Applause.) We will improve intelligence collection and sharing, expand patrols at our borders, strengthen the security of air travel, and use technology to track the arrivals and departures of visitors to the United States. (Applause.)

Homeland security will make America not only stronger, but, in many ways, better. Knowledge gained from bioterrorism research will improve public health. Stronger police and fire departments will mean safer neighborhoods. Stricter border enforcement will help combat illegal drugs. (Applause.) And as government works to better secure our homeland, America will continue to depend on the eyes and ears of alert citizens. . .

SIGNIFICANCE

The term "axis of evil" proved controversial. Critics claimed that the President chose the words in an attempt to characterize the nebulous threat of global terrorism as parallel to the threat posed by the Axis powers of Germany and Japan during World War II in order to garner public support for any future military action. They further claimed that despite the chosen rhetoric, the extent and immediacy of the threat to global security posed by the new axis was not fully known. Some claimed that rhetoric would further flame anti-American passions, especially throughout

Khalid Shaikh Mohammed, top terrorist organizer for the 9/11 terrorist attacks, was one of the FBI's most-wanted terrorists and a lieutenant of Osama Bin Laden. AP/WIDE WORLD PHOTOS

the Islamic world. Supporters of the shift in policy cite successes in the war in Afghanistan, including the ousting of the Islamist Taliban government who had supported the al-Qaeda terrorist network responsible for the September 11 attacks.

The speech declared that North Korea and Iran were developing nuclear capability. North Korea broke a string of international treaties banning its further development of nuclear weapons technology. Iran's militant, fundamentalist Islamic government also fed regional anti-American sentiment that influenced Islamist terrorism. In the 1980s and early 1990s, Iraq had used an array of chemical weapons against its Kurdish population. Bush asserted that Iraq maintained a stockpile of these WMDs. The inference in the "axis of evil" speech was that three countries could use, and potentially desired to use, these weapons of mass destruction against the United States or its allies. The phrase conflated problems with the three nations into one operational policy.

Soon after the State of the Union address, the Bush administration declared that Iraq posed the most immediate threat to global security. Iraq's military dictatorship under Saddam Hussein had a problematic relationship with the United States. During the Iran-Iraq War (1980–1988), the United States armed Iraqi troops. However, during the 1991 Gulf War, the United States fought Iraqi troops after they invaded Kuwait.

The U.S. and British governments presented to the international community intelligence reports and information that allegedly linked Iraqi leader Saddam Hussein to both al-Qaeda terrorism and illegal stockpiles of weapons of mass destruction. Saddam Hussein refuted allegations that his regime sponsored al-Qaeda actions and claimed to have destroyed WMDs following the 1991 Gulf War. United Nations (UN) inspectors were called in to Iraq, but the investigations proved inconclusive—teams reported finding no weapons but also claimed to be obstructed in their work. The United States and Britain lobbied for a UN mandate (a resolution of support) to invade Iraq, but after failing to secure a resolution, proceeded with military action against Iraq on March 20, 2003.

The United States declared an end to the war in Iraq on May 1, 2003, though fighting continued against insurgent forces. As of 2005, United States and coalition troops remained in Iraq. Coalition security forces and UN weapons inspectors did not find Iraqi stockpiles of weapons of mass destruction, and ended the official hunt for WMDs in Iraq in October 2003. Allegations of the ties between the former-Iraqi regime and al-Qaeda have also proven tenuous.

North Korea declared itself a nuclear power on February 10, 2005. Since the nation has refused all UN weapons inspections, the current extent and capabilities of North Korea's nuclear program remains unknown. Several rounds of multi-national talks with North Korea have failed.

The United States continues to allege that Iran is developing nuclear weapons technologies and harboring al-Qaeda operatives. In June 2005, hardliner Mahmoud Ahmadinejad defeated the more-moderate Akbar Rafsanjhani in Iran's presidential elections. Anti-Americanism was one of the central tenets of Ahmadinejad's campaign.

FURTHER RESOURCES
Books

Tripp, Charles. *A History of Iraq*. Cambridge: Cambridge University Press, 2002.

A photograph of "The 9/11 Commission Report" cover.
AP/WIDE WORLD PHOTOS

Web sites

The White House. "President Delivers State of the Union Address." <http://www.whitehouse.gov/news/releases/2002/01/20020129-11.html> (accessed July 10, 2005).

9/11 Commission Report

Outline of the 9/11 Plot

Government document

By: National Commission on Terrorist Attacks Upon the United States

Date: July 22, 2004

Source: The 9/11 Commission Report: "Final Report of the National Commission on Terrorist Attacks Upon the United States."

Salt Lake City police watch practice at the ice center during the 2002 Winter Olympics. AP/WIDE WORLD PHOTOS

Al-Qaeda (literally translated "the Base"), led by Saudi Arabia's Osama Bin Laden operating from the then Islamist-controlled nation of Afghanistan, aimed to rid the Middle East of Western influence. Also known as the International Front for Jihad Against Jews, Islamic Salvation Foundation, and the Islamic Army for the Liberation of the Holy Places, al-Qaeda first came to public notice when it killed six people by bombing the World Trade Center on February 26, 1993. Like other Islamist extremists, al-Qaeda members resent the spread of Western goods, culture, and values into the Muslim world and blame the U.S. for its support of Israel. The organization is global, recruiting terrorists from Islamist ranks throughout the world.

PRIMARY SOURCE

According to KSM, [Khalid Sheikh Mohammed, called the mastermind of the attacks by the 9/11 Commission and captured in March 2003] the 1998 East Africa embassy bombings demonstrated to him that Bin Ladin was willing to attack the United States. In early 1999, Bin Ladin summoned KSM to Kandahar to tell him that his proposal to use aircraft as weapons now had al Qaeda's full support. KSM met again with Bin Ladin and Atef at Kandahar in the spring of 1999 to develop an initial list of targets. The list included the White House and the Pentagon, which Bin Ladin wanted; the U.S. Capitol; and the World Trade Center, a target favored by KSM.

Bin Ladin quickly provided KSM with four potential suicide operatives: Nawaf al Hazmi, Khalid al Mihdhar, Walid Muhammad Salih bin Attash, also known as Khallad, and Abu Bara al Taizi. Hazmi and Mihdhar were both Saudi nationals—although Mihdhar was actually of Yemeni origin—and experienced mujahidin, having fought in Bosnia together. They were so eager to participate in attacks against the United States that they already held U.S. visas. Khallad and Abu Bara, being Yemeni nationals, would have trouble getting U.S. visas compared to Saudis. Therefore, KSM decided to split the operation into two parts. Hazmi and Mihdhar would go to the United States, and the Yemeni operatives would go to Southeast Asia to carry out a smaller version of the Bojinka plot.

In the fall of 1999, training for the attacks began. Hazmi, Mihdhar, Khallad, and Abu Bara participated in an elite training course at the Mes Aynak camp in Afghanistan. Afterward, KSM taught three of these operatives basic English words and phrases and showed them how to read a phone book, make travel reservations, use the Internet, and encode communications. They also used flight simulator computer games and analyzed airline schedules to figure out flights that would be in the air at the same time. . .

About the Author: The 9/11 Commission, formally known as The National Commission on Terrorist Attacks Upon the United States, was an independent, bipartisan commission created to prepare a full account of the September 11, 2001, terrorist attacks. The commission examined the roots of the attacks, American preparation for terrorist attacks, and the specific events of September 11. As mandated by Congress and President George W. Bush, the commission provided recommendations designed to guard against future attacks. On July 22, 2004, the commission released its public report before disbanding on August 21, 2004.

INTRODUCTION

In the deadliest terrorist attack on U.S. soil, more than 3,000 people died on the morning of September 11, 2001, when U.S. civilian airliners crashed into the twin towers of the World Trade Center in lower Manhattan and the Pentagon in Washington, D.C. Nineteen members of Osama Bin Laden's (Usama Bin Ladin) al-Qaeda terrorist organization launched the attack. The al-Qaeda members had hijacked four planes and flown three of them into the buildings. The fourth plane crashed into a field in Pennsylvania. The dead included Americans as well as citizens from sixty other nations.

A Navy patrolman and his dog search seats at the Utah Olympic Oval in Salt Lake City during the 2002 Winter Olympics. AP/WIDE WORLD PHOTOS

While KSM was deploying his initial operatives for the 9/11 attacks to Kuala Lumpur, a group of four Western-educated men who would prove ideal for the attacks were making their way to the al Qaeda camps in Afghanistan. The four were Mohamed Atta, Marwan al Shehhi, Ziad Jarrah, and Ramzi Binalshibh. Atta, Shehhi, and Jarrah would become pilots for the 9/11 attacks, while Binalshibh would act as a key coordinator for the plot. Atta, the oldest of the group, was born in Egypt in 1968 and moved to Germany to study in 1992 after graduating from Cairo University. Shehhi was from the United Arab Emirates (UAE) and entered Germany in 1996 through a UAE military scholarship program. Jarrah was from a wealthy family in Lebanon and went to Germany after high school to study at the University of Greifswald. Finally, Binalshibh, a Yemeni, arrived in Germany in 1995. . .

By the time Atta, Shehhi, and Binalshibh were living together in Hamburg, they and Jarrah were well known among Muslims in Hamburg and, with a few other like-minded students, were holding extremely anti-American discussions. Atta, the leader of the group, denounced what he described as a global Jewish movement centered in New York City, which, he claimed, controlled the financial world and the media. As time passed, the group became more extreme and secretive. According to Binalshibh, by sometime in 1999, the four had decided to act on their beliefs . . .

When Binalshibh reached the camps in Kandahar, he found that Atta and Jarrah had already pledged *bayat,* or allegiance, to Bin Ladin, and that Shehhi had already left for the UAE to prepare for the anti-U.S. mission the group had been assigned. Binalshibh followed suit, pledging *bayat* to Bin Ladin in a private meeting. Binalshibh, Atta, and Jarrah met with Bin Ladin's deputy, Mohamed Atef, who directed them to return to Germany and enroll in flight training. Atta was chosen as the emir, or leader, of the mission. He met with Bin Ladin to discuss the targets: the World Trade Center, which represented the U.S. economy; the Pentagon, a symbol of the U.S. military; and the U.S. Capitol, the perceived source of U.S. policy in support of Israel. The White House was also on the list, as Bin Ladin considered it a political symbol and wanted to attack it as well. KSM and Binalshibh have both stated that, in early 2000, Shehhi, Atta, and Binalshibh met with KSM in Karachi for training that included learning about life in the United States and how to read airline schedules. . .

While the pilots trained in the United States, Bin Ladin and al Qaeda leaders in Afghanistan started selecting the muscle hijackers—those operatives who would storm the cockpit and control the passengers on the four hijacked planes. (The term "muscle" hijacker appears in the interrogation reports of 9/11 conspirators KSM and Binalshibh, and has been widely used to refer to the non-pilot hijackers.) The so-called muscle hijackers actually were not physically imposing, as the majority of them were between 5'5" and 5'7" in height and slender in build. In addition to Hazmi and Mihdhar, the first pair to enter the United States, there were 13 other muscle hijackers, all but one from Saudi Arabia. They were Satam al Suqami, Wail and Waleed al Shehri (two brothers), Abdul Aziz al Omari, Fayez Banihammad (from the UAE), Ahmed al Ghamdi, Hamza al Ghamdi, Mohand al Shehri, Saeed al Ghamdi, Ahmad al Haznawi, Ahmed al Nami, Majed Moqed, and Salem al Hazmi (the brother of Nawaf al Hazmi).

The muscle hijackers were between 20 and 28 years of age and had differing backgrounds. Many were unemployed and lacked higher education, while a few had begun university studies. Although some were known to attend prayer services regularly, others reportedly even consumed alcohol and abused drugs. It has not been determined exactly how each of them was recruited into al Qaeda, but most of them apparently were swayed to join the jihad in Chechnya by contacts at local universities and mosques in Saudi Arabia.

By late 1999 and early 2000, the young men who would become the muscle hijackers began to break off contact with their families and pursue jihad. They made their way to the camps in Afghanistan, where they volunteered to be suicide operatives for al Qaeda. After being picked by Bin Ladin himself for what would become the 9/11 operation, most of them returned to Saudi Arabia to obtain U.S. visas. They then returned to Afghanistan for special training on how to conduct hijackings, disarm air marshals, and handle explosives and knives . . .

In late April 2001, the muscle hijackers started arriving in the United States, specifically in Florida, Washington, DC, and New York. They traveled mostly in pairs and were assisted upon arrival by Atta and Shehhi in Florida or Hazmi and Hanjour in DC and New York. The final pair, Salem al Hazmi and Abdulaziz al Omari, arrived New York on June 29 and likely were picked up the following day by Salem's brother, Nawaf, as evidenced by Nawaf's minor traffic accident while heading east on the George Washington Bridge. Finally, on July 4, Khalid al Mihdhar, who had abandoned Nawaf al Hazmi back in San Diego 13 months earlier, re-entered the United States. Mihdhar promptly joined the group in Paterson, New Jersey.

In addition to assisting the newly-arrived muscle hijackers, the pilots busied themselves during the summer of 2001 with cross-country surveillance flights and additional flight training. Shehhi took the first cross-country flight, from New York to San Francisco and on to Las Vegas on May 24. Jarrah was next, traveling from Baltimore to Los Angeles and on to Las Vegas on June 7. Then, on June 28, Atta flew from Boston to San Francisco and on to Las Vegas. Each flew first class, in the same type of aircraft he would pilot on September 11. . . .

The next step for Atta was a mid-July status meeting with Binalshibh at a small resort town in Spain. According to Binalshibh, the two discussed the progress of the plot, and Atta disclosed that he would still need about five or six weeks before he would be able to provide the date for the attacks. Atta also reported that he, Shehhi, and Jarrah had been able to carry box cutters onto their test flights; they had determined that the best time to storm the cockpit would be about 10–15 minutes after takeoff, when they noticed that cockpit doors were typically opened for the first time. Atta also said that the conspirators planned to crash their planes into the ground if they could not strike their targets. Atta himself planned to crash his aircraft into the streets of New York if he could not hit the World Trade Center. After the meeting, Binalshibh left to report the progress to the al Qaeda leadership in Afghanistan, and Atta returned to Florida on July 19.

Just over two weeks before the attacks, the conspirators purchased their flight tickets. Between August 26 and September 5, they bought tickets on the Internet, by phone, and in person. Once the ticket purchases were made, the conspirators returned excess funds to al Qaeda. During the first week in September, they made a series of wire transfers to Mustafa al Hawsawi in the UAE, totaling about $26,000. Nawaf al Hazmi attempted to send Hawsawi the debit card for Mihdhar's bank account, which

still contained approximately $10,000. (The package containing the card would be intercepted after the FBI found the Express Mail receipt for it in Hazmi's car at Dulles Airport on 9/11.) The last step was to travel to the departure points for the attacks. The operatives for American Airlines Flight 77, which would depart from Dulles and crash into the Pentagon, gathered in Laurel, Maryland, about 20 miles from Washington, DC. The Flight 77 team stayed at a motel in Laurel during the first week of September and spent time working out at a nearby gym. On the final night before the attacks, they stayed at a hotel in Herndon, Virginia, close to Dulles Airport. Further north, the operatives for United Airlines Flight 93, which would depart from Newark and crash in Stony Creek Township, Pennsylvania, gathered in Newark. Just after midnight on September 9, Jarrah received this speeding ticket as he headed north through Maryland along Interstate 95, towards his team's staging point in New Jersey.

Atta continued to coordinate the teams until the very end. On September 7, he flew from Fort Lauderdale to Baltimore, presumably to meet with the Flight 77 team in Laurel, Maryland. On September 9, he flew from Baltimore to Boston. By this time, Marwan al Shehhi and his team for Flight 175 had arrived in Boston, and Atta was seen with Shehhi at his hotel. The next day, Atta picked up Abdul Aziz al Omari, one of the Flight 11 muscle hijackers, from his Boston hotel and drove to Portland, Maine. For reasons that remain unknown, Atta and Omari took a commuter flight to Boston during the early hours of September 11 to connect to Flight 11. As shown here, they cleared security at the airport in Portland and boarded the flight that would allow them to join the rest of their team at Logan Airport.

SIGNIFICANCE

In the wake of the September 11 attacks, President George W. Bush sought a global alliance against terrorism, garnering at least verbal support from many nations. On October 11, the United States and Great Britain began bombing Afghanistan. By December, Afghanistan's Islamist Taliban government had collapsed, but Bin Laden could not be found. Some al-Qaeda forces remain in hiding around the globe. As of 2005, American forces remain in Afghanistan. The U.S. government continues to pursue Bin Laden and al-Qaeda cells around the world through both overt and covert actions.

In the United States, the USA Patriot Act, approved by Congress by large margins in October 2001, gave the federal government new powers to monitor suspected terrorists and their associates, including the ability to obtain personal information from libraries, universities, and businesses. When the

A search canine for the Federal Emergency Management Agency (FEMA) stands atop a pile of rubble at the World Trade Center site in New York. AP/WIDE WORLD PHOTOS

FURTHER RESOURCES

Books

Flynn, Stephen. *America the Vulnerable: How the U.S. Has Failed to Secure the Homeland and Protect Its People from Terrorism.* New York: HarperCollins, 2004.

National Commission on Terrorist Attacks Upon the United States. *The 9/11 Commission Report: Final Report of the National Commission on Terrorist Attacks Upon the United States.* New York: W.W. Norton, 2004.

Pillar, Paul R. *Terrorism and U.S. Foreign Policy.* New York: Brookings Institution Press, 2001.

Web sites

National Commission on Terrorist Attacks Upon the United States. "The 9/11 Commission Report." <http://www.9-11commission.gov/report/index.htm> (accessed July 5, 2005).

shock of September 11 faded, both conservatives and liberals called for reform of the legislation in light of Constitutional guarantees of free speech, free assembly, right to counsel, and proper search, seizure, and detainment procedures. Privacy and civil liberties advocates argued that the Patriot Act violated basic Constitutional principles and overextended government powers while offering little protection from terrorist activity. Proponents of the legislation asserted that national security issues outweighed civil liberties concerns and that Patriot Act reforms would significantly aid counterterrorism operations.

The 9/11 Commission made 41 specific recommendations to protect the U.S. from another terrorist attack resulting in mass casualties. Many of the key recommendations have not yet been put in place as of 2005, particularly recommendations relating to the prevention of nuclear terrorism, the allotment of funds at the state and local levels for anti-terrorism measures, and the creation of a reliable radio system for first responders. The commission considered a nuclear attack at the hands of terrorists as not likely to occur. Yet the human toll and the quality of living consequences of such an attack would be extremely high. Accordingly, the commission called for a maximum effort to prevent nuclear terrorism by securing the world's limited supply of weapons-grade nuclear material.

Commissioners also recommended allocating homeland security grants solely on the basis of risks and vulnerabilities, not as political pork. Since 9/11, the federal government allocated more than $6 billion in federal funding for terrorism preparedness.

"IRA Suspects on Foreign Land"

Narcoterrorism

News article

By: Mervyn Jess

Date: October 4, 2002

Source: "IRA Suspects on Foreign Land," as written for the British Broadcasting Corporation (BBC).

About the Author: Mervyn Jess is a Northern Ireland correspondent for the BBC.

INTRODUCTION

Founded in 1964 as the military wing of the Columbian Communist Party, the Fuerzas Armadas Revolucionarias de Colombia-Ejército del Pueblo ("Revolutionary Armed Forces of Colombia- People's Army", or FARC) is Colombia's largest, most powerful, and best equipped paramilitary group. Although claiming to stand for an array of apparently legitimate causes including the rights of the country's rural poor and opposition to right-wing paramilitary violence, the organization funds itself through a variety of illegal activity, including kidnapping, extortion, and participation in the drug trade.

Controlling vast swathes of Colombian territory—up to two fifths of Colombia lies in FARC hands—and opposing a succession of governments and rival

Colombian activists protested in front of a Bogota hotel where Irish lawmakers and rights activists were asking for release of three IRA-linked men. AP/WIDE WORLD PHOTOS

drug-trade interests, has brought FARC into perpetual conflict. A rising tide of violence in the mid-1990s culminated on September 4, 1996 with a FARC attack on a military base in Guaviare. This precipitated three weeks of guerrilla warfare that claimed the lives of at least 130 Colombians and prompted further violence over following months.

With a view to negotiate a peace settlement, in November 1998 President Andrés Pastrana Arango granted FARC a vast safe haven, centered around the San Vicente del Caguan settlement. This was the FARC condition for beginning peace talks, discussions which subsequently lasted for three years.

FARC, however, used the safe haven to import arms, export drugs, and build their military operations. A series of high-profile actions, which included the kidnapping of a presidential candidate traveling in guerrilla territory, led to Arango calling a halt to the peace talks in February 2002. Arango also ordered the Colombian Army to retake the FARC safe haven.

In August 2001, with peace talks faltering and FARC apparently regrouping and rearming, three men with links to the Irish Republican Army (IRA), an Irish nationalist terrorist group, were captured in Colombia. The men vigorously denied the claims, saying they were eco-tourists (albeit travelling on fake passports).

British officials disclosed that two of the three men had well-documented IRA pasts, while the third was a senior member of Sinn Fein, the IRA's political wing. Jim 'Mortar' Monaghan is credited with inventing the IRA's first homemade mortars and, according to the Police Service of Northern Ireland, was the IRA's head of engineering. Martin McAuley was assumed to be his deputy; and the third man, Niall Connolly, has served as Sinn Fein's official representative in Cuba since 1996.

The notion that the Irish Republican Army would be involved with South American guerillas was less surprising than it first seemed. The IRA has historically traded knowledge, weaponry, and money for laundering with an array of rogue states and extremist groups. During the First World War (1914–1918), it received arms shipments from Germany, with whom Britain (who at that time ruled Ireland) was at war. More recently, the IRA has had alleged links with regimes and terrorist groups in Libya, Cuba, and several Balkan states.

■ PRIMARY SOURCE

Friday, 4 October, 2002, 16:18 GMT 17:18 UK

BBC Northern Ireland reporter in Bogota

The teeming Latin American capital of Bogota is the last place on earth you would expect three Irishmen to appear in court accused of being IRA members who were training left-wing rebels.

In a unique hearing on Friday, the three men were scheduled to go before a judge for the first time since their arrest in Colombia in August of last year.

But in a surprise move the three refused to leave their cells when their armed escort arrived and the hearing was postponed until later in the month.

In court on Friday, the prosecution outlined the case against the three men.

Martin McCauley from Lurgan in County Armagh, James Monaghan from County Donegal and Niall Connolly from Dublin were detained at Bogota's El Dorado airport as they were about to board a flight out of the country.

They were found to have false passports and the Colombian security services accused them of having been to Farclandia—an area controlled by the left wing rebels, the FARC (Revolutionary Armed Forces of Colombia).

The Irishmen strenuously deny this, claiming they were in the area to monitor the fledgling peace process as well as being eco-tourists.

Their arrests made world headlines and sent a shock wave through the corridors of power in Washington.

The US had been ploughing millions of dollars in military aid into Colombia to back up the government's ongoing war against the drugs barons.

Narco-terrorism is the tag given to those groups who control and protect the remote jungle areas where the cocaine is manufactured.

The FARC is "numero uno" on the narco-terrorist list. For their trouble, it is estimated the FARC rakes in about $600m a year.

This enables the group to be one of the best-equipped terror organizations in the world.

The prosecutors allege this is where the IRA comes in.

Military commanders claim up to 15 Irish republicans have been to Colombia to help to train the rebels in the use of improvised urban weaponry such as mortar bombs and car bombs.

For its part, the IRA issued a statement saying its "army council sent no-one to Colombia to train or engage in any military co-operation with any group".

The three suspects have been held in a number of custody centers over the past 13 months.

Concerns for their safety while in jails housing right wing paramilitary prisoners were raised with the authorities and they are currently behind bars in La Picota prison.

It sits on the southernmost limits of Bogota, sandwiched between a military base, a school and breeze block homes for displaced people.

When the three men face their accusers for the first time in a court of law, a legal process will begin which is likely to last several months.

Already, the defense lawyers have been highlighting what they say is "a violation of their rights" after statements made by both Colombian and US politicians.

In the wake of 11 September, the American crackdown on world terrorism put the three IRA suspects right in the spotlight.

The Prosecutor General, Luis Osorio, has stated confidently that "there is sufficient evidence to put them on trial".

The defense lawyers stress that their clients have already been condemned guilty even before the trial gets under way.

In a news conference in Bogota on Thursday, they said the men were being used as "guinea pigs in a political experiment".

SIGNIFICANCE

Colombia's long-running civil war had largely been played out away from its main cities, with left-wing guerillas and their right-wing paramilitary foes battling for control of territory and drug trafficking routes in the countryside.

When three years of peace talks broke down in February 2002, however, FARC started to bring its terrorist war into the cities with a wave of bombings and political kidnappings. This coincided with a Presidential election for which the favorite (and eventual winner), Alvaro Uribe, had promised tougher military action against the violence. The FARC response was intended to demonstrate to urban Colombians that their armed forces were unable to protect them. Indeed, while campaigning that April, Uribe was himself almost the victim of a FARC attack when a bomb damaged his armored jeep and killed three passers by.

After a single week of violence at the start of August claimed more than 100 lives, the country's senior prosecutor, General Luis Camilo Osorio, claimed that recent mortar bomb attacks had used technology developed by the Provisional IRA, a radical splinter group of the IRA. He also claimed that the Provisional IRA tested weapons while visiting rebels in the jungle. "The techniques that the FARC has developed in recent years show that it has had technical assistance and used technology similar to that used by the IRA," General Osorio said in an article with the British newspaper *Guardian* in 2002.

The revelation of the FARC links came as a deep embarrassment to the IRA's political wing, Sinn Fein, and particularly its leader Gerry Adams. Despite vigorously denying any links, the incident further tainted his organization's reputation among supporters in the United States, from where it received much of its funding and political support.

Connolly, Monaghan, and McAuley maintained their innocence, but were found guilty of training Marxist guerillas in December 2004 and sentenced to 17 years in jail. The sentence, however, was given in absentia, as the three men had absconded six months earlier.

FURTHER RESOURCES

Books

Kline, Harvey F. *Colombia: Democracy Under Assault.* Boulder: Westview, 1995.

McKittrick, David., McVeigh, David. *Making Sense of the Troubles.* London: Penguin, 2003.

"Death Toll in Bali Attack Rises to 188"

Newspaper article

By: Alan Sipress and Ellen Nakashima

Date: October 14, 2002

Source: "Death Toll in Bali Attack Rises to 188," as published by the *Washington Post.*

About the Author: Alan Sipress and Ellen Nakashima are foreign correspondents in Southeast Asia for the *Washington Post.* Alan Sipress was one of five *Washington Post* journalists to receive the 2005 Jesse Laventhol Prize for Deadline News Reporting from the American

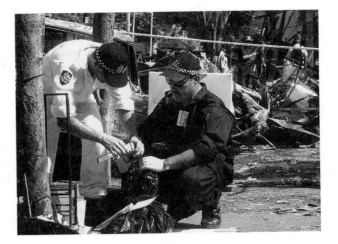

An Australian forensic team collects evidence at the bombing site of a nightclub in Kuta, Bali, that killed nearly 200 people. AP/WIDE WORLD PHOTOS

Society of Newspaper Editors for his coverage of the 2004 tsunami disaster.

INTRODUCTION

Indonesia is the world's largest predominantly Muslim country with more than 17,000 islands and a population of over 200 million people. With over 300 different ethnic groups and hundreds of languages, it has an extremely diverse culture. The long-time stability of the government and the beauty of the Indonesian islands has made Indonesia into a major East Asian travel destination, especially for tourists from neighboring Australia. Bali, a predominantly Hindu island, has long been the center of Indonesia's tourism industry.

On October 12, 2002, two near-simultaneous explosions in the Kuta Beach nightclub district of Bali killed 202 people and injured more than 300 in the worst terrorist attack in Indonesia's history. The first blast, which killed eight people outside one nightclub, came from a suicide bomber's backpack. Hundreds of people fleeing the initial explosion headed towards another nightclub, outside which a vehicle was parked containing a car bomb, which exploded several seconds after the suicide bombing. This explosion blew in roofs and smashed in windows in other buildings around the targeted nightclubs.

About 20,000 Australians were thought to be in Bali at the time of the bombing, and the majority of the Bali casualties came from Australia. Most of the other victims hailed from Britain, Canada, the Netherlands, France, Germany, and Ecuador. Many Indonesians were also among the dead. In the immediate wake of the attack, frightened vacationers camped overnight on beaches, shunning built-up areas incase more attacks occured. Many stayed in their hotels or headed to Bali's airport to look for flights out of the region.

No one initially claimed responsibility for the bombing, but suspicion immediately focused on Jemaah Islamiyah (JI). The United States had been urging the Indonesian government of President Megawati Sukarnoputri to investigate earlier JI attacks more vigorously, partly because of JI's reputed links to al-Qaeda. JI had already been implicated in a plot at the beginning of 2002 to bomb foreign embassies in the region. Foreign observers had worried that conflict was imminent, but Megawati hesitated to antagonize the many Muslims in Indonesia by closely examining the activities of Muslim militants.

Based in Malaysia, with rumored links to al-Qaeda, JI aims to establish an Islamic pan-Asian state that would include parts of Indonesia, Malaysia, and the Philippines. The group was inspired by the Darul Islam uprising in the 1940s that unsuccessfully tried to force Indonesia to adopt Islamic law when it gained independence from the Dutch. Abu Bakar Bashir, an ex-Darul Islam member, founded JI at an unknown date. Initially targeting Christians in Indonesia, JI is blamed for a series of terrorist attacks on Westerners including the 2002 Bali bombing that killed 202 people. Both the U.S. and British governments as well as the United Nations have officially declared JI to be a terrorist organization.

▮ PRIMARY SOURCE

The death toll rose to 188 today in the aftermath of a devastating car bomb attack Saturday that turned several teeming Bali nightclubs into deadly infernos. The attack brought new demands for Indonesia, the world's most populous Muslim nation, to crack down on Islamic militants.

No one asserted responsibility for the attack. A top Indonesian official said the government had a suspicion about who was behind the bombing but declined to provide details. Several foreign diplomats said they suspected it was the work of the Jemaah Islamiah, an Islamic militant network in Southeast Asia that intelligence officials say is linked to al-Qaeda.

At least three-quarters of the victims were foreigners, packed into crowded bars in the entertainment district of Kuta Beach. The buildings burned and collapsed in a series of fires and explosions set off by a bomb hidden in a sport-utility vehicle.

Among the dead were tourists celebrating after the opening of a rugby tournament. They included at least 14 from Australia; others were from Canada, Britain, Germany, and Sweden. The State Department said two Americans were known dead and three were among the nearly 300 injured.

The State Department tonight ordered the departure of all non-emergency U.S. government officials and their families from Indonesia, and is advising all American citizens in the country to consider leaving, a department spokeswoman said.

In Washington, President Bush condemned the attack as "a cowardly act designed to create terror and chaos." Indonesia's national police chief, Da'l Bachtiar, called it "the worst act of terrorism in Indonesia's history." Australian Prime Minister John Howard declared, "The war against terrorism must go on with unrelenting vigor and an unconditional commitment."

Australia dispatched passenger jets and Hercules C-130 military transport planes to evacuate frightened tourists and the injured, and Australian Embassy officials said an estimated 120 injured people had been evacuated to Australia on military and commercial flights. Bali hospitals reported shortages of some medicines to treat the wounded.

The attack seemed to signal a shift in tactics by militant groups, diplomats said. They noted that earlier attacks were aimed at embassies and U.S. Navy vessels, including a threat that prompted the closing of the U.S. Embassy for six days last month.

But the Bali attack was aimed at civilians. "It's clear that whoever's behind these attacks is branching out to softer targets," a U.S. Embassy official said. "That's why we're concerned about it."

"The fact of the matter is, groups are targeting Westerners and using the most outrageous [means] to target foreigners," U.S. Ambassador Ralph L. Boyce said.

The attack came on the second anniversary of the bombing of the destroyer USS *Cole* off the coast of Yemen, in which 17 sailors died. In other attacks Saturday, police reported bombings near the U.S. Consulate in Bali and at the Philippine Consulate in the Indonesian city of Manado. No injuries were reported in either incident.

After an emergency cabinet meeting, Indonesian President Megawati Sukarnoputri flew here to see the devastation, which was centered at a popular nightspot, the Sari Club.

According to police, the attack came at about 11:30 P.M. Saturday, when a small, homemade bomb went off in front of a disco, Paddy's. That was followed by a huge blast across the street in front of the Sari Club. The second bomb, hidden in a Toyota Kijang, ripped into the open-air bar, triggering a massive burst of flames caused by gas cylinders used for cooking. Subsequent fires and explosions flattened about 20 buildings and much of the block, trapping victims under flaming debris.

"This bombing is a warning to all of us that terrorism is a real danger and potential threat to national security," Megawati said. "The Indonesian government will continue cooperation with the international community to overcome terrorism."

Indonesia has been under growing pressure to deal with Islamic militancy, and the attack Saturday brought new demands from abroad for action. Although Indonesia's Muslim population is overwhelmingly moderate, U.S. officials have said that the country's geography—17,000 islands offering myriad ports of entry that are difficult to control—makes it easy for militants to penetrate and operate away from official scrutiny. Bali, a largely Hindu enclave, had been considered immune to political violence.

Megawati's chief security minister vowed that the attack in Bali would force the Indonesian government to strengthen its efforts against terrorism. "This incident has created a turning point, and from now on, the government will not be able to entertain doubts about harsh action," the minister, Susilo Bambang Yudhoyono, told Indonesian reporters, adding that the government had suspicions about who was responsible but would not provide details.

Boyce, the U.S. ambassador, told the Associated Press that although it was not possible to pin the attack on al-Qaeda, there has been growing evidence that the network of Osama Bin Laden has been reaching out to local militants.

"In recent weeks, we have been able to put to an end a year of speculation as to whether al-Qaeda might be in Indonesia, or relocating to Indonesia, or using Indonesia as a base of operations, after the fall of Afghanistan," Boyce said.

Howard, the Australian prime minister, said: "We would like to see a maximum effort on the part of the Indonesian government to deal with the terrorist problem within their own borders. It's been a problem for a long time."

Jusuf Wanandi, founder of the Center for Strategic and International Studies in Jakarta, said Megawati's government must now act "for their own survival and for the republic's survival." Failure to do so "will damage the credibility of Indonesia." He added, "If she does not make a real effort to combat terrorism, the number one backlash will be from the international community. "

Australia said it was sending an investigative team, including forensic specialists, to assist the Indonesians. The United States dispatched a regional security officer from the embassy in Jakarta and an FBI agent from Singapore to help, officials said.

[On Monday, Indonesian government officials said they welcome foreign investigative assistance if it is coordinated by the Indonesians. Gen. Endriartono Sutarto, the armed forces chief, said government officials would discuss how to coordinate their intelligence efforts, now run independently by the military, the police and the state intelligence agency.]

Before the Bali bombing, the United States had been urging Indonesia to investigate some earlier attacks more vigorously. In particular, U.S. officials want to see police actively pursue a Sept. 23 grenade explosion outside a U.S. Embassy house in central Jakarta. Indonesian and Western officials said the blast was a bungled attempt by Islamic militants to attack a U.S. target. The police have dismissed the grenade explosion as a debt-collection effort gone awry, unrelated to terrorism.

After the blast in Bali, the State Department said it was recalling nonessential diplomatic personnel. "These measures reflect our assessment of increased security concerns in Indonesia arising as a result of the most recent bombings," spokeswoman Jo-Anne Prokopowicz said.

The United States has also issued a travel warning advising Americans to defer travel to Indonesia, she said. The embassy in Jakarta and consulate in Surabaya will remain open, though they may close occasionally for security reasons, she added.

The last time the embassy sent staff members home was during the 1998 riots that led to President Suharto's downfall.

The withdrawal of U.S. diplomats could further sour the confidence of investors and enthusiasm of tourists for Indonesia, economists said. The Indonesian economy is already struggling to recover from the 1997 Asian financial crisis, and tourism, a crucial component of the economy, was dealt a major setback by the Saturday attack on an island that offers tropical beaches, lush forests and a mystical aura.

SIGNIFICANCE

Bali's tourism-dependent economy collapsed after the attack. Travelers began to slowly return, but as of 2005, the Indonesian tourist industry has not fully recovered. The bombing also prompted security concerns. Sites that attract great numbers of tourists such as hotels, nightclubs, and restaurants are so-called "soft targets" and are easier to attack than government buildings and military installations. Thailand and Malaysia, among others, reviewed security measures and pushed Indonesia's government to crack down on JI.

Indonesia's neighbors considered that JI had joined with other al-Qaeda linked groups, including the Philippines's Abu Sayyaf, to develop a network of extremists able to carry out attacks across the region. These countries joined with the U.S. in urging Indonesia

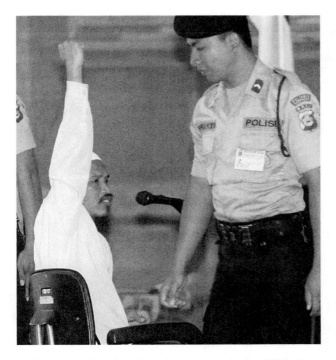

Ali Guhfron, alias Mukhlas, a key suspect in the 2003 nightclub bombing in Bali shouts "Greats of God" during his trial. AP/WIDE WORLD PHOTOS

FURTHER RESOURCES

Books

Downing, David. *The War on Terrorism: The First Year.* Chicago: Raintree, 2004.

Millard, Mike. *Jihad in Paradise: Islam and Politics in Southeast Asia.* Armonk, NY: M.E. Sharpe, 2004.

Smith, Paul J. *Terrorism and Violence in Southeast Asia: Transnational Challenges to States and Regional Stability.* Armonk, NY: M.E. Sharpe, 2005.

Soesastro, Hadi, Anthony Smith, and Han Mui Ling, eds. *Governance in Indonesia: Challenges Facing the Megawati Presidency.* Singapore: Institute of Southeast Asian Studies, 2003.

Vaugh, Bruce, et al. *Terrorism in Southeast Asia.* Washington, D.C. CRS, 2005.

Khalid Sheikh Mohammed Captured

"Elusive Sept. 11 Suspect Finally Caught Sleeping"

Newspaper article

By: Erik Eckholm and David Johnston

Date: March 5, 2003

Source: *International Herald Tribune.*

About the Author: Erik Eckholm has held a variety of reporting and editing positions at the *New York Times*, including five years as Beijing bureau chief. David Johnston is a *New York Times* investigative reporter and winner of the Pulitzer Prize in 2001.

to take strong measures against JI. However, Indonesia refused to list the group as a terrorist organization fearing a political backlash from Muslims. Banning JI would likely lead to a counter-response from organizations such as the Majelis Mujahidin Indonesia (Council of Islamic Holy Warriors), who may attack Indonesia for cooperating with western nations. Meanwhile, JI has continued its terrorist actions, including an attack on Jakarta's JW Marriot hotel in 2003 that killed 12 people, and a car bombing at the Australian embassy in 2004 that left eleven dead.

Indonesia did arrest and convict the key suspects in the Bali bombing but the relatively light sentences received by the suspects angered the victims. Abu Bakar Bashir received thirty months in jail for conspiracy in the bombing. Abu Bakar Bashir, head of JI, received two and half years in prison. Imam Samudra, the mastermind of the attack, and Amzozi bin Nurhasyim, supplier of the bombs, were both sentenced to die. Muklas, a financier, also received a death sentence. Ali Imron, the operations chief, received life in prison. Abdu Rauf and Andri Oktavia, who stole money to pay for the attacks, each received sixteen years in prison. The remaining 27 bombing conspirators received sentences ranging from three years to fifteen years.

INTRODUCTION

Khalid Sheikh Mohammed (widely known by the acronym KSM) was described by the Commission investigating the 9/11 attacks as the "model of the terrorist entrepreneur" and the "principal architect" of the atrocities. A career terrorist, KSM was born in Kuwait in 1964 and educated in the United States, graduating from the North Carolina and Technical State University with a degree in mechanical engineering in 1986. A year later, he went to Afghanistan to join the Mujahadeen's guerrilla war against the Soviet Union.

In 1993, KSM played a small role in the World Trade Center Bombing, an act carried out by his nephew Ramzi Yousef. Impressed by the respect and attention Yousef gained as a result of the attack, KSM

CONSPIRACY TO KILL NATIONALS OF THE UNITED STATES

KHALID SHAIKH MOHAMMED

Aliases: Ashraf Refaat Nabith Henin, Khalid Adbul Wadood, Salem Ali, Fahd Bin Adballah Bin Khalid

DESCRIPTION

Dates of Birth Used:	April 14, 1965; March 1, 1964	**Hair:**	Black
Place of Birth:	Kuwait	**Eyes:**	Brown
Height:	Medium	**Sex:**	Male
Weight:	Slightly Overweight	**Complexion:**	Olive
Build:	Unknown		
Language:	Unknown		
Scars and Marks:	None known		
Remarks:	Mohammed is known to wear either a full beard or a trimmed beard, or he may be clean shaven. He has been known to wear glasses.		

Khalid Shaikh Mohammed on a page from the Federal Bureau of Investigation's Website. AP/WIDE WORLD PHOTOS

also decided to engage in anti-U.S. activities. He travelled to the Philippines in 1994 to work with Yousef on Operation Bojinka, a plot to blow up a dozen passenger jets flying between the U.S. and Asia. This marked the onset of his professional terrorist career, which would encompass a plot to kill President Clinton in Manila in 1994 and a long list of other conspiracies. According to the 9/11 Commission Report, "These ideas included conventional car bombing, political assassination, aircraft bombing, hijacking, reservoir poisoning, and, ultimately, the use of aircraft as missiles guided by suicide operatives."

In January 1996, KSM went into hiding, and from around 1998 onwards was with Osama Bin Laden in Afghanistan and Pakistan. There he supervised the planning and preparations for the 9/11 operation and also worked with and eventually led al-Qaeda's media committee.

Following the September 11, 2001 attacks, the U.S. immediately identified KSM as one of their principle targets. On the first anniversary of the 9/11 attacks, reports surfaced that he had either been killed or escaped during a raid in Karachi, Pakistan by the Pakistani Secret Service. Six months later, in March 2003, muddled reports again surfaced that he had been captured in the Pakistani city of Rawalpindi.

■ PRIMARY SOURCE

The broken door of the spacious, two-story villa in an upper-middle-class district of this city is the only outward sign that it was a hideout for suspected terrorists where the authorities say they captured a major leader of al-Qaeda, Khalid Sheikh Mohammed.

It was here in the city's affluent Westridge district that the Pakistani authorities triumphantly announced the arrest of Mohammed, along with an unidentified Middle Eastern man and a Pakistani man, Ahmed Qadoos. The home belongs to Qadoos's elderly parents, but the son, 42, also lived there with his wife and two children.

Mohammed, who is on the FBI's list of most-wanted terror suspects and is believed to have been the operational planner of the Sept. 11 attacks against the United States, was quickly handed over to the Americans for questioning at an undisclosed location outside Pakistan. Unlike the violent shoot-out last fall that resulted in the arrest of another top Qaeda member, Ramzi Binalshibh, Mohammed's arrest came without incident.

Early Saturday morning, Mohammed's pursuers finally found the suspect who had long eluded them. He was pulled from his sleep to be photographed by the police, beardless, seemingly dazed, wearing a loose-fitting white T-shirt against the backdrop of an apartment with paint peeling from the walls.

Mohammed had been hiding in the Rawalpindi house "for quite some time," Pakistan's interior minister, Syed Faisal Saleh Hayat, said in a telephone interview Sunday afternoon. His capture ended one of the most intense manhunts since Sept. 11, 2001, delivering the man believed to have the most detailed knowledge of the plot for the attacks on that date and others in the last 18 months.

Although U.S. officials had been frustrated in earlier attempts to seize the operations chieftain of al-Qaeda, intelligence and law enforcement officials said they had

continued to receive solid leads about his whereabouts after Sept. 11, in large part because Mohammed remained in active communication with Qaeda members, using couriers, e-mail, and coded telephone messages.

In the past year, according to interviews with officials and intelligence reports, he gave instructions and provided funding to Qaeda lieutenants around the world.

Counterterrorism officials said that Mohammed was in part responsible for the U.S. government's decision last month to raise the terror alert level from yellow to orange, a heightened alert that has since been rescinded.

"Some of the information did lead back to him and anything that leads back to him in the past is stuff that causes you to take it seriously," an official said. "There were indications that he was involved in near-term planning."

Details of Mohammed's arrest were still somewhat murky, according to interviews with American and Pakistani authorities. Qadoos, one of the men arrested with Mohammed, is the son of Mah Laqa, a neighborhood leader of Jamaat-e-Islami, the largest of the country's Islamic political parties.

In interviews, Qadoos's family denied he was involved with al-Qaeda and his relatives disputed that Mohammed had been arrested in Qadoos's parents' house. Hayat, the interior minister, said Mohammed had been apprehended there, adding, "In such cases, the families always proclaim innocence."

Qadoos's sister, Qudsia Khanum, 44, said her brother still lived with his parents because he was "slow, of below-average intelligence," did not pass junior high school and was unable to hold a job.

She said that more than 20 agents had entered the family home at 3:30 A.M., held her brother's wife and children in a room at gunpoint and taken away her brother with no warrant or subsequent notice of any charges. Khanum said the raiding agents had ransacked the house, seizing what she said were tapes of the Koran and a new computer that she said was filled with children's electronic games.

Some American law enforcement officials said cellular telephones and other items seized in the arrest contained valuable intelligence about Mohammed's travels and al-Qaeda. Before moving to Rawalpindi earlier in the winter, Mohammed had been spotted in different cities in Pakistan.

Intelligence officials said they had penetrated his circle deeply enough in recent weeks to conclude that Mohammed was actively planning for terror operations inside the United States in the "near term," as one official described it.

One target was again New York City, the officials said, possibly involving the revival of a discarded plan that was first discussed in the months before the World Trade Center attacks in September 2001. Before that, Mohammed had considered attacks on the city's gas stations, bridges, hotels and power plants, the officials said, confirming a report in this week's *Newsweek* magazine.

A renewed effort by Mohammed set off alarms because of another intelligence finding about him. According to intelligence officials, he had grown increasingly interested in radiological devices, expressed keen interest in obtaining toxins, and urged others in al-Qaeda to develop weapons of mass destruction.

In recent weeks, the heightened concern about the threat posed by Mohammed increased as intelligence officials focused more closely on his suspected presence in Pakistan and began to collect highly reliable information about his activities and operational planning.

Since the mid-1990s, U.S. intelligence repeatedly had trailed Mohammed to specific hideouts only to lose him in the vastness of Central Asia and the Middle East. He slipped away with the help of confederates, sometimes in disguise and often carrying as many as 20 different passports.

The closest "near miss," as intelligence officials referred to their unsuccessful efforts to catch Mohammed, occurred in September 2002, a few days after Al Jazeera, the Arabic-language television network, broadcast in an interview with Mohammed and Binalshibh, another important figure in the Sept. 11 attacks on the World Trade Center.

The interview was said to have occurred at an apartment in Karachi and within days, the Pakistani authorities arrested Binalshibh in a shoot-out in Karachi. Officials have said that they hoped to capture Mohammed in the raid, but netted only two of his sons, ages 7 and 9.

Mohammed barely escaped from Qatar in 1996 after U.S. intelligence and law enforcement agencies had received specific information about his whereabouts; living with a member of the Qatari royal family. During intense discussions between the United States and the government in Doha, Mohammed dropped out of sight and fled the country.

The Pakistani authorities were alerted to the possibility that Mohammed was in Pakistan last summer, Pakistani officials said. That was when terror suspects began to identify him in connection with other acts of violence like the January 2002 kidnapping and subsequent murder of Daniel Pearl, the *Wall Street Journal* reporter.

Captured terror suspects told the Pakistani authorities that Mohammed had acted as a link between al-Qaeda and Pakistani extremist groups. The suspects said that Mohammed had moved frequently between several cities in Pakistan, among them Faisalabad, Peshawar and Karachi.

Within the last two weeks, a tip from an informant for the Pakistani security service led to a raid in Quetta in hopes of finding Mohammed, Pakistani officials said. But he had disappeared again.

Early Saturday, Mohammed's pursuers struck again.

"It's still a little early to tell what he's going to say," an official said. "But he was the guy that gave the go signal, so he could give us an awful lot."

SIGNIFICANCE

Khalid Sheikh Mohammed's capture represented a coup in the United States' War on Terror. Since waging its campaign against global terror, the United States faced difficulty capturing senior al-Qaeda operatives. KSM's arrest was seen as a breakthrough. Not only was he part of the senior command of al-Qaeda, but he was the suspected mastermind behind the attacks on the World Trade Center and Pentagon. Of particular interest to investigators were KSM's attempts to procure radiological material and ingredients for chemical weapons.

It appears that no efforts have been made to bring Khalid Sheikh Mohammed to the United States for trial. Moreover, prosecutors in Germany were frustrated when they saw the fifteen-year sentence handed out to suspected 9/11 plotter Mounir el Motassadeq overturned because they had no access to testimony from KSM.

Indeed, KSM's whereabouts remain a mystery. A report by Human Rights Watch in October 2004, more than eighteen months after his capture, suggested that he had been transferred to a Jordanian prison. However, no confirmation or denial of these allegations has been forthcoming from U.S. authorities.

FURTHER RESOURCES

Web sites

Shannon, Elaine, and Weisskopf, Michael. "Kalid Shiekh Mohammed Names Names." *Time* (online) March 24, 2003. <http://www.time.com/time/nation/article/0,8599,436061,00.html> (accessed July 1, 2005).

BBC News. "Profile: Al-Qaeda 'kingpin'." <http://news.bbc.co.uk/2/hi/south_asia/2811855.stm> (accessed July 1, 2005).

"Inferno and Panic at Tropical Retreat; Volunteers Offer Aid as Bombing Casualties Overwhelm Hospitals"

Bali Bombing

Newspaper article

By: Alan Sipress

Date: October 13, 2002

Source: "Inferno and Panic at Tropical Retreat; Volunteers Offer Aid as Bombing Casualties Overwhelm Hospitals," as published by the *Washington Post* foreign service.

About the Author: Alan Sipress is a reporter for the *Washington Post* foreign service.

INTRODUCTION

On October 12, 2002, a terrorist bombing on the Indonesian island of Bali killed 194 people and wounded over 300. The bombing had the highest death toll of any single terrorist action since the terrorist attacks of September 11, 2001.

The terrorist action was later attributed to the militant Islamic separatist group Jemaah Islamiyah, also known as Jamaa Islamiyya, or JI. The investigation into the bombing found that the attack was planned as part of a JI strategy to target cafés and nightclubs in the Asia Pacific region where Westerners would be present.

The bombings took place at two nightclubs in the resort area of the town of Kuta. As a popular holiday destination, the nightclubs were filled mainly with tourists. Bali is particularly popular with Australian visitors and 88 of the casualties were Australian. The casualties also included 38 Indonesians, 26 Britons, 9 Swedes, 7 Americans, and 6 Germans. There were also casualties from other nations.

The bombing involved three separate devices. A small bomb hidden in a backpack was triggered in Paddy's Bar by a suicide bomber. A larger car bomb was detonated by remote control in front of the Sari Club. Another bomb was detonated near the American consulate in Bali, but did not cause any injuries. The explosion and resulting fires caused extensive injuries, with many people trapped inside the burning nightclubs. Bali's hospitals were overwhelmed by the number of burn victims, and many patients were flown to Australia for treatment.

The initial death toll for the bombings was 194, with an additional eight people dying in overseas hospitals as a result of the injuries they sustained. The final death toll was 202.

◼ PRIMARY SOURCE

This resort's main drag, known as Jalan Legian, is a strip of open-air restaurants, sunglass shops, and tattoo parlors. It is the place where surfers, sailors, and sunburned hippies head to tame the tropical heat, downing potent concoctions with names like Jungle Juice when they retire at sunset from the island's famed Indian Ocean beaches.

Bali's most loyal visitors, the Australians, often head to a pair of bars that face each other across Jalan Legian in the heart of Kuta's entertainment district, the Sari Club and Paddy's. Late Saturday the nightclubs were crowded with rugby players and fans from Australia and several other countries in the region, visiting Bali for a tournament.

At the height of the rush, police say, a large Toyota packed with explosives erupted on the street out front, engulfing both clubs in flames. Described by witnesses as a pair of blasts a second apart, the attack devastated the two bars, caving in the roof of the Sari Club with scores of patrons trapped inside. At Paddy's, those who had been drinking upstairs were set afire by burning thatch from the walls and ceiling. Some tried to escape by leaping to the street from the second floor, witnesses said.

"It was just major panic," said Richard Hananeia, 29, an Australian bartender vacationing in Bali. "There was fire on both sides of the street."

At least 188 people were killed. Hospital officials in Bali reported treating almost 300 other victims, including visitors from more than 20 countries on six continents as well as Indonesians. But the largest share by far were Australians, at least 14 of whom were killed.

The casualties overwhelmed Bali's hospitals and clinics. On the sprawling campus of Sanglah hospital in Denpasar, the capital of Bali, the morgue could not accommodate all the dead. About 20 corpses were lined up on a covered outdoor walkway, charred limbs protruding from under sheets. Police pushed back a gawking crowd.

In the steamy, spartan wards inside, the injured, bloody and burned, were arrayed on dozens of paint-chipped metal-frame cots as relatives and volunteers stood beside them, fanning them with pieces of scrap paper, ripped sheets of cardboard and clipboards. Blood supplies appeared to be lacking.

Indonesians and foreigners, some shuffling in a daze and others scrambling breathlessly, crowded through the corridors looking for missing friends and relatives. They thronged around lists of several hundred names posted at the entrance. The names of some were complete and accompanied by nationality. For others, there was only a first name.

While the explosion shattered windows hundreds of yards away and rocked hotel rooms even farther afield, it was only after daybreak today that the Balinese and their guests discovered the extent of the carnage as the death toll soared toward 200.

"It's staggering. It's beyond belief," said Jan Lovett, an Australian who has lived in Bali for 21 years and was volunteering at Sanglah hospital. "The burns are the worst. I don't know how they're ever going to identify people."

At the blast scene, shards of glass crunched under the shoes of investigators as they picked through the smoldering remains of the Sari Club, razed by the explosion and fire. The bar's three-story red sign, once a neighborhood landmark, was reduced to a tower of mangled metal. Nearly 20 buildings nearby were gutted, including the Ticket to the Moon hammock shop and the Aloha swimsuit store. Electrical wires dangled perilously over pools of water.

Some tourists continued their rounds elsewhere in Kuta as if it were any other holiday weekend. They browsed through shops selling traditional wood carvings and batik, attracted by the burning incense that Bali's Hindu shop owners leave out front on the sidewalk. They lingered in the cafes to have coffee and to spread on sunscreen.

But others, such as Mark Tolley, 28, a British computer programmer, headed to the hospitals to volunteer. On Saturday night, he was enjoying the first leg of his round-the-world tour, reading a book in his hotel room down the block from the Sari Club. He heard a blast and then a second, louder one. The windows came crashing in.

"There were people in the street, Australians and Japanese, running, yelling, 'Is everyone alright?'" Tolley said. He said he headed down the street and discovered a young German woman who had been blown out of the club. He took her to the hospital and said he has not left her side since.

Skyler Grant, 15, a Californian, had been having a typical Bali day on Saturday. He had intended to meet some friends at Paddy's but ended up dallying on the beach for several hours after dark. "It was just luck," Grant said. As he stepped out of a van down the block from the bar, he saw the lights suddenly go dark and heard a whirring sound, followed by two blasts. He paused and then ran to the scene to help the victims.

"We were lifting out bodies and chucking them into cars," said Grant, who has lived with his family in Bali for five years. "Our hands were covered with blood."

SIGNIFICANCE

The bombings were carried out by members of JI, a militant Islamic separatist group whose stated goal is to remove the governments of Southeast Asia and replace them with Islamic states. JI is also considered responsible for various terrorist bombings in Southeast Asia, including a string of bombings of Christian churches in 2000, the bombing of the Marriott Hotel in Jakarta in August 2003, and the bombing of the Australian embassy in Jakarta in 2004. After the Bali bombings, the U.S. State Department officially classified JI as a foreign terrorist organization. The U.S. State Department also recognized JI as having links with the terrorist group al-Qaeda.

The investigation into the bombings found that it was organized at an initial meeting in Bangkok, Thailand, in February 2002. At this meeting, the terrorist group decided to plan actions against soft targets such as cafés and restaurants in Southeast Asia. This decision was reportedly based on the increased security on other targets such as consulates and embassies. Nightclubs and cafés were selected as targets because of the number of Westerners that would be present.

Mukhlas, who is also known as Ali Gufron, was found guilty of masterminding the attack and sentenced to death on October 2, 2003. Mukhlas is recognized as being the head of JI. Mukhlas was found guilty of both organizing the attack and helping to fund it. His lawyer stated that Mukhlas considered the bombing a form of jihad or holy war. The lawyer also stated that Mukhlas considered the bombing an act of revenge against America's treatment of Muslims in the Middle East.

Abu Bakar Bashir was found guilty of conspiracy relating to the Bali bombings and was sentenced on March 3, 2005, to two and a half years in prison. Bashir is a Muslim cleric with links to al-Qaeda and is reportedly the spiritual leader of JI. The court case of Bashir found that he had no direct involvement in the Bali bombings, except that he had given his approval for the attacks. The lack of direct involvement was the reason for the light sentence. The governments of Australia and the United States both expressed concern that the sentence was too short.

Amrozi bin Haji Nurhasyim was found guilty of planning and carrying out the bombings. The court case found that Amrozi owned the vehicle used in the attack and purchased the explosives. Amrozi was sentenced to death on August 7, 2003.

Imam Samudra was found guilty of organizing the Bali bombings and was sentenced to death on September 10, 2003. The court case described Samudra as the field commander of the attack, including stating that he selected the targets and led the planning meetings.

Ali Imron was found guilty of planning the Bali attacks and sentenced to life imprisonment on September 18, 2003. Imron was found guilty of helping to build the car bomb that was detonated outside the Sari Club. The lighter sentence was based on the court's observation that Imron showed remorse for his actions.

The Bali bombings had a significant impact on antiterrorism laws in Indonesia. Before the Bali bombings, an antiterrorism bill that would allow terrorism suspects to be held without being charged was delayed in parliament based on human rights concerns. Under international pressure due to the Bali bombings, Indonesian President Megawati Sukarnoputri approved the new law. The Bali bombings also increased international pressure on Indonesia to take action on threats from terrorist groups operating within the country.

FURTHER RESOURCES

Books

Gunaratna, Rohan. *Terrorism in the Asia-Pacific: Threat and Response.* Singapore: Eastern Universities Press, 2003.

The Jemaah Islamiyah Arrests and the Threat of Terrorism: White Paper. Singapore: Ministry of Home Affairs, 2003.

Web sites

Sherlock, Stephen. *The Bali Bombing: What It Means for Indonesia.* <http://www.aph.gov.au/library/pubs/CIB/2002-03/03cib04.htm> (accessed June 22, 2005).

Madrid Bombing

"Investigators See ETA, not al-Qaeda, behind Madrid Blasts"

News article

By: Matthew Schofield and Alejandro Bopido-Memba

Date: March 12, 2004

Source: Knight Ridder newspapers.

About the Author: Knight Ridder is the second-largest newspaper publisher in the United States, with thirty-one dailies and numerous nondaily papers. The company also maintains a network of news Web sites.

INTRODUCTION

On March 11, 2004, ten homemade bombs hidden in backpacks and triggered by cell phones exploded in Madrid, Spain, at the height of the morning rush hour. The target was a busy commuter rail line just to the south of the city's downtown. Four bombs exploded at 7:39 A.M. on a train at the Atocha rail station; three more exploded at the same time on another train near Téllez Street, just outside the Atocha station. Two minutes later, two bombs exploded on a train at the El Pozo del Tio Raimundo station, and one minute after that, a tenth bomb exploded on a train at the Santa Eugenia station. Three other bombs did not detonate and were found later. The attacks were the deadliest terrorist attacks in modern Spanish history; 177 people

An Italian policeman holds a photo of Egyptian suspect Rabie Osman Ahmed, who was arrested in Milan in connection to train bombings in Madrid, Spain. AP/WIDE WORLD PHOTOS

were killed at the scene, 13 more died later in hospitals, and over 1,800 were wounded. The attacks have been called "Spain's 9/11."

The Spanish government immediately cast blame for the bombings on the Basque terrorist group Euskadi Ta Askatasuna (Basque Fatherland and Liberty), commonly referred to as the ETA. The ETA was formed in 1959 to promote the culture and traditions of the Basque people, an ethnic group that lives in the mountainous regions along the border between France and Spain. In time, the organization came to advocate establishment of a separate Basque nation. By the 1970s, the organization, one of several Basque separatist groups, was resorting to terrorism directed primarily against the Spanish government. Over the years, the ETA claimed responsibility for numerous car bombings, assassinations, murders, and kidnappings. It also used threats to extract a "revolutionary tax" from the Basque population to fund its operations. By the end of 2003, the ETA had claimed over eight hundred victims. While most were police and public officials, more than three hundred were civilians, including children.

The Madrid bombings occurred in the wake of the September 11, 2001, terrorist attacks in the United States, and Spain's decision to contribute some 1,300 troops to the U.S.-led war in Iraq. For this reason, other officials assumed that the bombings were more likely the work of al-Qaeda, the terrorist network led by 9/11 mastermind Osama Bin Laden. The following article, published the day after the bombings, outlines the Spanish government's initial assumption that the ETA was responsible, as well as the skepticism expressed in some quarters.

PRIMARY SOURCE

Madrid, Spain—Armed with what they said was new evidence, Spanish officials remained adamant Friday that they believe that the Basque separatist group ETA, not the al-Qaeda terrorist network, was behind the morning rush-hour train bombings that rocked this capital city Thursday.

With the death toll nearing 200 and dozens of the wounded still in critical condition, Interior Minister Angel Acebes announced Friday evening that he was more convinced than ever that ETA was to blame for the 10 explosions that ripped through three Madrid commuter rail stations just as people were disembarking on their way to work.

Acebes said the bombs consisted of satchels filled with 20 to 30 pounds of dynamite, set off by a cell phone. He said the dynamite chemically matched 1,100 pounds of explosives seized in February from an ETA van heading toward Madrid, and that the satchel and cell phone setup matched that found on two ETA members when they were arrested at a northern Madrid commuter rail station on Christmas Eve.

"This explosion had a very similar modus operandi used by the terrorist group ETA," he said.

Millions of Spaniards filled the streets of Madrid and other major cities Friday in tribute to the dead and injured and to protest the attacks. Spanish Prime Minister Jose Maria Aznar marched in front of one group in Madrid, and columns of demonstrators stretched for miles.

Spanish flags with black banners hung from light poles and balconies throughout the capital.

The outpouring of grief and anger was unprecedented. Some reports said nearly a quarter of Spain's 50 million people had participated in the marches, including an estimated 2.5 million in Madrid.

The crowds were so densely packed in Madrid that it was impossible to move against the tide. Anger was palpable.

"Snakes," "assassins" and "murderers" were among the insults hurled in unison by hundreds of demonstrators at a time. Placards proclaimed that "A people united will never be defeated" and "ETA No." If the crowd seemed united in its denunciation of ETA, there was still much discussion from Washington to Madrid about responsibility for the attacks.

A caller claiming to represent ETA denied that the group had been involved in the attack. Journalists here said ETA never had rejected responsibility for an attack before.

In Washington, the FBI said it hadn't dispatched any agents to Spain and wouldn't do so unless the Spanish government requested them. No Americans died in the blasts, though the dead included citizens of at least 11 countries.

Aznar offered citizenship to all illegal residents of Spain whose relatives were killed in the blasts. He said the government thought they would be essential to identify the final 70 bodies at the city's makeshift morgue. The dead are thought to be illegal immigrants whose relatives are afraid of being deported if they come to claim the bodies.

U.S. Senate Majority Leader Bill Frist, R-Tenn., said he'd been briefed on the attacks and that American officials were interested in any similarities to the Sept. 11, 2001, attacks in the United States.

"The patterns—multiple sites, multiple stations," Frist said. "Very much like having multiple places here in this country." U.S. officials said the evidence cut both ways. Asa Hutchinson, the Homeland Security Department's undersecretary of borders and transportation, said American intelligence agencies had detected no spike in "chatter" among al-Qaeda-related groups before the attacks. Other U.S. officials stressed that the group that claimed responsibility for the bombings, the Abu Hafs al Masri Brigades, is thought to exist in name only and has made implausible claims of responsibility before.

Hutchinson also said, however, that the pattern of the attacks required considering al-Qaeda's involvement.

"One of the things that gives you cause for concern is the level of complexity in the attack and the coordination and the simultaneous nature of it, which all is a characteristic of the capability and style of al-Qaeda," he said. "That's not to say that means it's them, but that certainly gives you concern." Even in Madrid, there were open doubts about the government's insistence that ETA was behind the attacks.

Many Spaniards, particularly those who support the Socialist Party in Sunday's elections, suggested that Aznar's government might not be willing to disclose an al-Qaida link until after the vote, for fear of hurting the chances of Aznar's Populist Party holding on to power.

"Listen, ETA has never done a bombing like this without calling and warning the government beforehand," said Olga Gonzalez, a 32-year-old secretary. "Ninety percent of Spaniards were against the war in Iraq. If al-Qaida is involved and not ETA, this changes everything for the elections. It will only help to elect the Socialist Party." Interior Minister Acebes was adamant that the evidence pointed to ETA. He noted that ETA has a history of creating havoc in the days before a national election.

He also said the explosives used—Goma II Eco—were made in Spain and that ETA had used the same brand in previous attacks.

"Of course we will continue to investigate any and all information we get on who may be responsible," he said. "But at this point there is mounting evidence that this was not the work of al-Qaida."

SIGNIFICANCE

From the beginning, many investigators questioned the Spanish government's position that the ETA was responsible for the bombings, as the ETA had never demonstrated the resources and organizational capability to mount such coordinated attacks. Further, the ETA normally issued warnings about impending attacks, relying on the threat of violence to have as much of a disruptive effect as the impending violence itself. Also, the ETA had consistently taken responsibility for its attacks, but the organization vehemently denied that it had a hand in the Madrid bombings.

Just two days after the bombings, an audiotape was found near a Madrid mosque. The tape made it clear that a group called the Moroccan Islamic Combatant Group, part of the al-Qaeda network, was responsible for the blasts. On April 3, 2004, police raided the group's holdout in Leganes, a suburb of Madrid, where seven suspects blew themselves up as the police closed in. Within weeks, fifteen members of this group had been arrested and several more detained. By April 2005, twenty-four suspects were in jail and another sixty-five suspects had been charged with lesser crimes in connection with the bombings. Investigators concluded that the ETA had no role in the bombings.

The Madrid bombings had profound effects in Spain. They took place three days before national elections. The bombings provoked public debate on Spain's involvement in the Iraq war. In a surprise outcome to the elections, Socialist Party candidate Jose Luis Rodriguez Zapatero came to power. Zapatero immediately announced that Spain would withdraw its troops from Iraq.

The bombings had profound effects throughout Europe as well. The bombings prompted discussion of Europe's relationship with Islam—a troubled relationship that dates back to the eighth century, when Muslims seized large portions of the Iberian Peninsula and invaded what is now France; the ninth century, when Muslims invaded Italy and conquered the Mediterranean islands; the twelfth and thirteenth centuries, the era of the Crusades; and the Reconquista in the fifteenth century, when Spain drove the Muslims out of their last Iberian stronghold in Grenada.

In modern times, Europe has become home to some approximately twenty million Muslims, many from North Africa and Turkey. The Madrid bombings heightened anti-Muslim sentiment throughout Europe and fueled opposition for plans to admit predominantly Muslim Turkey into the European Union.

FURTHER RESOURCES

Periodicals

Gee, John. "The Bombings in Spain: Implications for Islam and the West; Islam vs. Al-Qaeda." *Washington Report on Middle East Affairs.* 23 (May 1, 2004): 16ff.

Web sites

Gardiner, Nile, and John Hulsman. "The Madrid Bombings: Staying the Course in the War on Terror." Heritage Foundation. March 12, 2004. <http://www.heritage.org/Research/Europe/wm445.cfm> (accessed May 23, 2005).

Audio and Visual Media

Democracy Now! "Remembering March 11: The Madrid Bombings and Their Effect on Spanish Government, Society and the Antiwar Movement." November 23, 2004. Available from <http://www.democracynow.org/article.pl?sid=04/11/23/1457202> (accessed May 23, 2005).

PBS. "Frontline: Al-Qaeda's New Front." Available from <http://www.pbs.org/wgbh/pages/frontline/shows/front/view> (accessed May 23, 2005).

Madrid Bombing

"Bishop Urges Lucidity as Basques Pay Homage to Madrid Bomb Victims"

News article

By: Gillian Handyside

Date: March 13, 2004

Source: "Bishop Urges Lucidity as Basques Pay Homage to Madrid Bomb Victims", Reuters news report.

Rescue workers by a bomb-damaged passenger train following a number of explosions on trains in Madrid, Spain, 2004. AP/WIDE WORLD PHOTOS

About the Author: Gillian Handyside is a journalist for Reuters, a world-wide news agency based in London.

INTRODUCTION

On March 11th, 2004, in the run up to the Spanish general election, 191 people were killed and more than 1,800 injured when bombs exploded on four morning rush-hour trains in Madrid.

Responsibility for the bombings was initially attributed by the Spanish Government to the Basque national liberation movement (ETA), a separatist group that has a long history of terrorist activities in Spain.

Immediately after the March 11th train bombings, Prime Minister José María Aznar, and Interior Minister ángel Acebes, stated publicly that ETA was definitely responsible for the terrorist attack. Foreign correspondents, newspaper offices, and Spanish embassies were all contacted by the government and assured that the bombings were the work of ETA. In response to these accusations, a spokesman for Batasuna, the political arm of ETA, denied that ETA had been involved. A TV station and newspaper in the Basque region were also contacted by ETA representatives, who denied responsibility for the bombing.

Evidence soon emerged that Islamic militants may have carried out the attacks, when police found a stolen van containing detonators and an Arabic language tape close to a Madrid station. A number of Islamic groups came forward to claim responsibility although their claims were not authenticated. These included Abu Nayaf al-Afgani, linked to an alleged terrorist cell based in Madrid, and the Abu Hafs al-Masri Brigades, a group that aligns itself to Osama Bin Laden's al-Qaeda network. The Moroccan Islamic Combatant Group soon became the main focus of investigations by the police.

The Norwegian Defense Research Establishment (FFI) revealed shortly after the bombings that intelligence had been available for two months about a terrorist attack that was being planned for a country during an election period. The FFI claimed that the country where the attack was planned had been misinterpreted as Iraq.

In the Spanish general election held just three days after the bombings, Aznar's Popular Party was defeated by the PSOE (socialist party) led by José Luis Rodríguez Zapatero. Many political experts assert that the government's handling of the March 11th attacks influenced the outcome of the election. The election outcome was unexpected; Aznar's party had been leading in the opinion polls throughout the election campaign.

Several weeks later, more explosives were found and detonated by police on a high-speed train line between Seville and Madrid. Police identified an apartment in Leganés, south of Madrid, as the likely base for the terrorists responsible for planting these explosives and the Madrid train bombs. On April 3, as the police closed in, the terrorists blew up the Leganés apartment, killing themselves and one police officer. A video was found in the rubble containing a recording of three men demanding the immediate withdrawal of Spanish troops from "Muslim lands." The men claimed to be members of a group called the "al Mufti and Ansar al-Qaeda brigades". Experts hold that the video was made by the terrorists shortly before they committed suicide. Because the explosives used to blow up the apartment were of the same type used in the train bombings, investigators consider the terrorists killed at Leganés were those responsible for the March 11th attacks.

By early April, fifteen people, many of them Moroccan nationals, had been arrested in connection with the train bombings and others were being detained. A year later, a total of twenty-two suspects were in Spanish custody awaiting trial.

During the election campaign, Zapatero had made a commitment to withdraw Spanish troops from Iraq by June if responsibility for Iraq was not handed over to the United Nations when the United States' occupation of Iraq formally ended. Zapatero withdrew Spanish troops shortly after becoming Prime Minister.

■ **PRIMARY SOURCE**

The vast, sobre cathedral in the Basque city of San Sebastian was packed on Saturday evening for the last in

Spain's series of memorial service for the victims of this week's devastating bomb attacks in Madrid.

There were few tears among the estimated 1,000 to 1,500 attendants who came to hear Bishop Juan-Maria Uriarte deliver his message of consolation in Basque and Spanish. Just an occasional nose pinching, a sea of grave faces, a need for comfort and a desire "to be with the victims and their families."

As they passed the font in the form of a huge oyster shell, many stooped to add their names to a black-bordered book marked in Basque: "Zuen atsekabean laguntzen zaituztegu," We offer our deepest condolences.

Uriarte— who in 1998 and 1999 mediated between the right-wing government and their sworn enemies, armed Basque separatist group ETA, while the latter was on ceasefire—offered soothing words of consolation.

Noting that Easter was just a few weeks away, he talked of resurrection after death, and urged the faithful not to react to Thursday's "immense tragedy" in Madrid by "dividing the world into good and evil, us and them."

"In the current emotional climate we have to remain lucid. The story of good and evil is not outside us, it's inside our own hearts," he told the silent throng.

The bishop, the Catholic church's most senior official in the Basque province of which San Sebastian is the capital, left long moments of silence during the hour-long ceremony so mourners could simply reflect and draw solace from the ancient building.

Humans were capable of fanaticism and acts of barbarity like the commuter train bombings that killed 200 people in the capital, 500 kilometers away, he said. But they were also capable of marvellous deeds and that was what they should seek to sustain.

Standing arms outstretched behind a purple-covered altar marked: "Oh Lord, give us new hearts", he urged both the authorities and the public to root out all forms of violence, a significant theme in a region that has been plagued by it for decades.

When one of the 20 priests flanking him stepped forward to read a passage from the *Bible*, it was from the Book of Apocalypse. But rather than speaking of fire and brimstone, the passage promised a new world where there would be no death, no mourning, no tears and no pain.

After the service, as they stood on the cathedral square among the teenagers playing football and the beggars seeking change, service-goers said Uriarte's words had helped, but not much.

"It can't really console you. We came for the victims and to find some peace but this is going to take a long, long time to get over," said 47-year-old Maria-Teresa.

Her husband, Angel, was even more grim. "This is a problem that's not going to go away easily. And on top of that the government is trying to trick us," he said, referring to the latter's insistence that the Madrid attacks were the work of ETA rather than of Islamic extremists linked to Al-Qaeda.

"They're playing with the victims' lives for political ends. It's scandalous. And even if they do get a majority (in Sunday's general election), what's this government going to be able to do after that?"

SIGNIFICANCE

This press article reports on a Catholic memorial service for the victims of the Madrid train bombings, held in the Basque region which is home of the terrorist group ETA (Euskadi Ta Askatasuma, or 'Basque Homeland and Freedom'). The ETA had been accused by the government of carrying out the bombings before evidence emerged to suggest they had been the work of Islamic extremists.

ETA was established in 1959, when the language and culture of the Basque region of northern Spain and southern France were suppressed by the Spanish dictator General Francisco Franco (1892–1975). The group wants independence from Spain for the Basque region. From the 1970s onwards the ETA has employed terrorist methods in pursuit of this aim, including car bombings, snipings, and kidnappings. These are usually targeted at policemen, government officials, members of security forces, and businessmen, although the group has also attacked foreign tourists. Its members are thought to have received terrorist training in Libya, Lebanon, and Nicaragua, and the group allegedly maintains close links with the Provisional IRA (Irish Republican Army).

Although the post-Franco democratic government established an autonomous Basque region, with self-government, a police force, tax-raising powers, and an educational system, some extremist separatists continue to employ terrorism in pursuit of full independence from Spain. There was a brief ceasefire in 1998–1999, when the moderate nationalists agreed to commit themselves to a peaceful campaign for full independence and the radicals agreed to abandon armed struggle in return for their support. However, ETA militants soon became impatient with the lack of movement towards sovereignty, and attacks resumed.

Popular support for ETA has declined over time, and there have increasingly been public demonstrations within the Basque region in protest of terrorism. Aznar's government consistently refused to renegotiate the Basque region's constitutional relationship with Spain, and tackled the Basque problem as a security and policing issue, using anti-terror laws to ban its political wing,

Firefighters examine the damage after three suspected terrorists blew themselves up in a building that was surrounded by police in Leganes, Spain. AP/WIDE WORLD PHOTOS

Batasuna. Shortly before the 2004 elections, the government had announced that the ETA was nearly defeated.

Indeed, the government's success in weakening ETA, along with its reputation for openness and the strong recent performance of the Spanish economy, were factors underlying the expected success of the ruling party in the March 2004 election, despite widespread opposition to Spain's involvement in the war with Iraq. The government's response to the Madrid train bombings are considered a major factor in its surprise election defeat, especially after leading Spanish newspapers accused the government of attempting to use the attacks for political gain.

The Spanish government released information showing that law enforcement agencies were convinced that the ETA was responsible for the attacks, until the stolen van was found with its evidence suggesting Islamic involvement. It has also been argued that ETA was a natural suspect as the group had previously tried to bomb a train and had a large consignment of explosives recently intercepted en route to Madrid, where they had bombed Madrid many times before.

However, the attacks were not characteristic of ETA's usual methods, which have never been on such a large scale or targeted against such large numbers of civilians. Moreover, the group was believed to have been weakened considerably and was not likely to have had the infrastructure to carry out attacks of this scale.

Before the Madrid bombings, al-Qaeda had already issued threats to Spain to revenge the government's backing of the U.S.-led invasion of Iraq and the involvement of Spanish troops.

FURTHER RESOURCES

Journal articles

Woodworth, Paddy. "Spain changes course: Aznar's legacy, Zapatero's prospects." *World Policy Journal.* June 22, 2004.

Web sites

BBC. "In depth: Madrid Train attacks." <http://news.bbc.co.uk/1/hi/in_depth/europe/2004/madrid_train_attacks/default.stm> (accessed June 29, 2005).

CNN.com. "Special Report: Massacre in Madrid." <http://www.cnn.com/SPECIALS/2004/madrid.bombing/inde.html.htm> (accessed June 29, 2005).

8 Special-Interest Terrorism

Introduction to Special-Interest Terrorism

This chapter on Special-interest terrorism covers events that highlight a spectrum of issues within the socio-political landscape: immigration, racism, industrialism, labor, political and religious extremism, and environmentalism. The chapter primarily focuses on the exploits of domestic American terrorists and extremist groups—such as the Unabomber, Eric Rudolph, and the Ku Klux Klan (KKK)—but some international subjects also receive attention.

Whether domestic or foreign, special interest terrorists usually focus on a single issue. That single issue is usually rooted in the predominant social concerns of the time. At the turn of the last century, anti-immigrant sentiment, racism and segregation, and labor and wage issues spurred terrorists. In the 1960s, some terrorists seized on Cold War tensions between communism and capitalism, others acted in opposition to the Civil Rights movement. Today, issues may range from militant opposition to abortion to radical environmentalism; from anti-industrialism to anti-globalism.

The editors have chosen to include in this chapter a primary source that advocates the use of arson for ecological preservation and an entry on the shooting of a doctor by an extremist anti-abortion activist. Many people hold anti-abortion or environmentalist convictions. Both are controversial topics on which opinions transcend the boundaries of politics, religion, gender, and class. However, the terrorist acts and groups featured here favor the use of violence to manipulate public opinion. Most people who are opposed to abortion abhor the murder of abortion providers by extremists; most people who espouse environmentalism do not condone the destruction of property.

As with many complex issues, it is often too easy to conflate the terrorist actions featured here with the mainstream movements from which these extremist-terrorists often depart. The editors assert that a careful reading of the following selected primary sources will enable readers to distinguish and contrast the motives and thought processes of those willing to use terror to further their cause as opposed to the vast majority of citizens who oppose policies within the confines of civil debate and the law.

An entry on the antrax letter sent to a U.S. senator is included in the chapter because the motive and identity of the perpetrator remains unknown. However, law enforcement officials assert that the anthrax attacks were most likely carried out by a domestic "special interest" terrorist or terrorist group.

"The Chinese, The Chinese, You Know"

Terrorist Attacks on Chinese Immigrants in the United States

Song

By: John E. Donnelly, W. S. Mullally

Date: 1885

Source: "The Chinese, The Chinese, You Know", a song.

About the Author: In 1885, a well-known minstrel leader, W. S. Mullally, teamed with John E. Donnelly to produce a local song, "The Chinese, The Chinese, You Know." The song proved popular enough to be picked up by the National Music Company of Chicago for national distribution.

INTRODUCTION

The Chinese were the first group of Asians to migrate to the United States in significant numbers, and they became the first Asians to suffer racially motivated attacks by white Americans. The Chinese came to the United States in the 1850s at the invitation of business owners to work in the mines and on the railroads. The Chinese, typically single males, worked for less money than white laborers and frequently took the dangerous and unpleasant jobs that whites did not want. About one-twelfth of the population of California consisted of people of Chinese descent by 1870.

The end of the Civil War dramatically changed the employment situation in the West. Demobilized whites competed with the Chinese for work in an economy suffering from a postwar recession. Additionally, the completion of the transcontinental railroad in 1869 made it much easier for white laborers to move to California. White unemployment rose in the state.

As a direct result of job fears by white laborers, agitation against the Chinese grew rapidly. By 1867, an increasing campaign of moral, political, and economic pressure by white workers against the employment of Chinese proved moderately successful. Despite persuading many employers to dismiss Chinese laborers, white workers became steadily more hostile toward the Asians. The Chinese who worked in mines were often subject to taxes by white miners. Assaults against Chinese men were common. In the winter of 1867, 400 white workingmen attacked a group of Chinese who were excavating for a street railway in Eureka, California. The crowd stoned the Chinese, maimed several people, and burned their shanties.

Afterward, the leaders of the riot were jailed and the Chinese resumed work under armed guard. In 1871, a Los Angeles mob lynched twenty-one Chinese workers.

When a depression struck in 1873 and continued through the 1870s, Chinese labor was blamed. Denis Kearney founded the Workingman's Party of California in 1877 and mounted a massive drive in support of a new state constitution to severely restrict Chinese residence, employment, and education.

PRIMARY SOURCE

I'll sing of a subject, but your ears you must lend,
And listen to what I've to say.
We'll have to do something with this curse in our land,
For our business has gone to decay.
The merchants are idle, their goods on their hands,
And the cause of this terrible woe
I'll tell you my friends, and you'll say I am right
It's the Chinese, the Chinese, you know.
Let labor and capital go hand in hand
And crush out this terrible foe
For a crying disgrace is this abominable race,
The Chinese, the Chinese, you know.

SIGNIFICANCE

Workers in the West convinced Congress to pass the Chinese Exclusion Act in 1882. The legislation applied to Chinese laborers, skilled or unskilled, who intended to immigrate to the United States from any foreign port. Ship captains who accepted Chinese workers as passengers were subject to fines, imprisonment, and the forfeiture of their vessels. In addition, state and federal courts were forbidden to naturalize Chinese, thereby preventing Chinese immigrants from becoming American citizens. The freedom to become a citizen was granted only to native-born Chinese.

The Chinese Exclusion Act was the first national law ever passed banning a group of people based on race or nationality. It was reenacted in 1892 and again in 1902 before being made permanent in 1904. In that year, Chinese laborers already living in U.S. possessions, such as Hawaii and the Philippines, were barred from coming to the mainland. As a result of federal legislation, the Asian immigrant populations in the United States stagnated.

Most Americans saw the act as solving the problem of scarcity by eliminating a triple threat: a competitor for jobs, a people they considered racially inferior, and an emissary of a competing empire. The false issue of Chinese exclusion deflected the workers from the real problems of employment and capital. The situation for workers would not improve because of the anti-Chinese legislation. Workers would continue to struggle for better pay, better hours, and better working conditions into the twentieth century.

The anti-Chinese legislation set a pattern of discrimination that would be applied to other Asian groups. Over the years, other Asians were also excluded from the United States. The Chinese Exclusion Act remained a law until World War II. By this time, the legislation had become an embarrassment to the government of the United States. In 1943, eager to demonstrate interest in joining with the Chinese against the common enemy of Japan, the government removed the Chinese from exclusion. People of Chinese heritage were granted the right to become citizens regardless of where they were born.

FURTHER RESOURCES

Books

Saxton, Alexander. *The Indispensable Enemy: Labor and the Anti-Chinese Movement in California*. Berkeley: University of California Press, 1971.

Southern Horrors

The Ku Klux Klan (KKK)

Pamphlet

By: Ida B. Wells

Date: 1892

Source: *Southern Horrors* is a pamphlet published in 1892 by Ida B. Wells.

About the Author: Journalist and speaker Ida B. Wells-Barnett (1862–1931) is best known for leading the fight against the lynching of African Americans in the late nineteenth and early twentieth centuries. Already established as a respected voice within the African American community in Memphis, Wells published *Southern Horrors* in 1892 after a close friend died along with two other black men at the hands of a lynch mob. The book's title mocked Southern honor as the commonly cited justification for lynching. Forced out of the South because of her activism, Wells moved to Chicago. She spent the remainder of her life speaking and writing on behalf of African Americans.

INTRODUCTION

In the decades following the end of the Civil War, lynching (killing by a mob) became a popular terrorist weapon against African Americans. These ritualized killings were public displays designed to terrorize black people from claiming economic or political power. Lynchings were frequently announced in newspapers and treated as social events by some white people, who would take home souvenirs such as bits of bone and flesh of the victim. While most common in the Deep South, lynching was a nationwide problem, occurring as far north as Duluth, Minnesota, and often drawing thousands of white spectators.

Lynching generally required the support of local law enforcement agents that allowed white vigilante groups to remove blacks, often falsely accused of crimes, from jail cells. In the overwhelming majority of the cases, the victims were male. The white perpetrators were almost never punished for these murders, even when photographs illustrating their involvement in such acts circulated as postcards or novelty items. Despite the efforts of activists such as Wells, the U.S. Congress never passed an anti-lynching bill. Blacks were effectively left on their own to deal with a form of terrorism that claimed thousands of lives.

Members of the Ku Klux Klan (KKK), the nation's oldest right-wing extremist group, organized many lynchings. Founded in 1866 in Tennessee by Confederate veterans as a fraternal organization, the KKK became a terrorist group within a year. Groups of a few to more than 100 Klansmen would visit their victims late at night, on the pretense of a suspected crime. Their chosen victims were usually black men, who would be whipped, stabbed, beaten, shot, or sometimes hanged.

■ PRIMARY SOURCE

Lynch law has spread its insidious influence till men in New York State, Pennsylvania and on the free Western plains feel they can take the law in their own hands with impunity, especially where an Afro-American is concerned. The South is brutalized to a degree not realized by its own inhabitants, and the very foundation of government, law and order, are imperiled. . . .

Col. A.S. Colyar of Nashville, Tenn. is so overcome with the horrible state of affairs that he addressed the following earnest letter to the *Nashville American*.

Nothing since I have been a reading man has so impressed me with the decay of manhood among the people of Tennessee as the dastardly submission to the mob reign. We have reached the unprecedented low level; the awful criminal depravity of substituting the mob for the court and jury, of giving up the jail keys to the mob whenever they are demanded. We do it in the largest cities and in the country towns; we do it in midday; we do it after full, not to say formal, notice, and so thoroughly and generally is it acquiesced in that the murderers have discarded the formula of masks. They go into the town where everybody knows them, sometimes under the gaze of the governor, in the presence of the courts, in the presence of the sheriff and his deputies, in the presence of the entire police force, take out the prisoner, take his life, often with fiendish glee, and often with acts of cruelty and barbarism which impress the reader with a degeneracy rapidly approaching savage life. . . .

To palliate this record . . . and excuse some of the most heinous crimes that ever stained the history of a country, the South is shielding itself behind the plausible screen of defending the honor of its women. This, too, in the face of the fact that only *one-third* of the 728 victims to mobs have been *charged* with rape, to say nothing of those of that one-third who were innocent of the charge. A white correspondent of the *Baltimore Sun* declares that the Afro-American who was lynched in Chestertown, Md., in May for assault on a white girl was innocent; that the deed was done by a white man who had since disappeared. The girl herself maintained that her assailant was a white man. When that poor Afro-American was murdered, the whites excused their refusal of a trial on the ground that they wished to spare the white girl the mortification of having to testify in court.

This cry has had its effect. It has closed the heart, stifled the conscience, warped the judgment and hushed the voice of press and pulpit on the subject of lynch law throughout this "land of liberty." Men who stand high in the esteem of the public for Christian character, for moral and physical courage, for devotion to the principles of equal and exact justice to all, and for great sagacity, stand as cowards who fear to open their mouths before this great outrage. They do not see that by their tacit encouragement, their silent acquiescence, the black shadow of lawlessness in the form of lynch law is spreading its wings over the whole country.

Men who, like Governor Tillman, start the ball of lynch law rolling for a certain crime, are powerless to stop it when drunken or criminal white toughs feel like hanging an Afro-American on any pretext.

Even to the better class of Afro-Americans the crime of rape is so revolting they have too often taken the white

man's word and given lynch law neither the investigation or condemnation it deserved.

SIGNIFICANCE

With the end of the Civil War and the passage of federal legislation giving political rights to black men, whites felt threatened by blacks. The changes in race relations were so dramatic that a backlash resulted. The broader purpose of lynching was to turn back the clock to the days of slavery and to put fear into the hearts of black men. It was a way of setting limits not only upon the behavior of African Americans, but also on black hopes for social and political advancements.

To a great extent, lynching succeeded. The activities of the KKK helped to overturn radical Republican rule in the South and to end Reconstruction. After Ulysses S. Grant assumed the presidency in 1869, the federal government began to take action against the KKK. The organization faded by 1872, only to revive in the 1920s, collapse, and then appeared for a third time following the 1954 *Brown* decision desegregating public schools. Every incarnation of the KKK employed violence to intimidate and kill blacks.

During Wells's lifetime, lynchings did not stop, but they did become a national embarrassment, partially as the result of her reporting. Anti-lynching bills were periodically introduced in Congress, but never passed. The Dyer Anti-Lynching Bill, approved by the House of Representatives in 1922, was typical. The Dyer Bill would have tried culpable state officials and mob participants in federal courts if state courts refused to take action. The Senate never approved the Dyer Bill or any other anti-lynching legislation. By 1922, more than 3,500 African Americans had been lynched by mobs. The number of dead continued to rise until the 1960s, when cultural changes made violence against African Americans socially unacceptable to most Americans. In 2005, the U.S. Congress issued a formal apology for failing to enact anti-lynching legislation.

FURTHER RESOURCES
Books

Chalmers, David M. *Hooded Americanism: The History of the Ku Klux Klan.* Durham, NC: Duke University Press, 1981.

Royster, Jacqueline Jones, ed. *Southern Horrors and Other Writings: The Anti-Lynching Campaign of Ida B. Wells, 1892–1900.* Boston: Bedford Books, 1997.

Trelease, Allen W. *White Terror: The Ku Klux Klan Conspiracy and Southern Reconstruction.* Baton Rouge: Louisiana State University, 1999.

"Make Way for the Molly Maguires"

Song

By: Anonymous

Date: Unknown

Source: Available from King Laoghaire: The Home of Irish Ballads and Tunes, <http://www.kinglaoghaire.com/site/home>.

About the Author: "Molly Maguires" is an example of the traditional ballads that emerged spontaneously from the Irish community, both in Ireland and in the United States, often to comment on political events and social conditions of the time.

INTRODUCTION

The Molly Maguires were a highly secretive organization of Irish Catholic miners who, for at least a decade beginning in the mid-1860s and probably for some ten years before that, employed the tools of arson, riot, murder, and beatings in an effort to improve working conditions in the anthracite coal country of eastern Pennsylvania. All belonged to a fraternal organization called the Ancient Order of Hibernians.

Little is known about the origins of the Mollies. The organization was thought to have originated in Ireland, where Catholic land tenants frequently rebelled against absentee English landlords and the Protestant estate managers they put in place. Legend has it that they took their name from a Catholic woman who had refused to be intimidated by Protestants who wanted to drive her out of her home because of her religion. Prior to administering a beating to an enemy, members of the group were reputed to have said, "Take that from a son of Molly Maguire!"

Many Mollies arrived in the United States as part of the wave of immigration that followed the Irish potato famine of the 1840s. In 1851, more than 221,000 Irish immigrated to the United States, and between 1820 and 1880, the total number was about 3.5 million. While most Irish were fleeing harsh conditions at home, they often found conditions in the United States little better. Help wanted signs in businesses were often positioned above signs that said "Irish need not apply." The *Chicago Post* wrote, "The Irish fill our prisons, our poor houses. . . . Scratch a convict or a pauper, and the chances are that you tickle the skin of an Irish Catholic. Putting them on a boat and sending them home would end crime in this country."

Irish immigrants were often forced to take the worst kind of manual labor, such as coal mining. But in the mid-nineteenth century, no child labor laws, minimum wages, or standards to protect the miners were in place. The only union was the General Council of the Workingmen's Associations of the Anthracite Coal Fields, but this union was poorly organized and generally ineffective. Accordingly, the Molly Maguires took matters into their own hands. Operating outside the law, they blew up railroad cars full of coal, organized riots, and beat, crippled, or murdered police, mine owners, mine supervisors, and anyone else who opposed them.

Like modern-day terrorist organizations, the Mollies employed a cell organization. The Ancient Order of Hibernians in each town formed a tiny group called a body, each with its own master, secretary, treasurer, and brethren. The "King of the Mollies" was John "Black Jack" Kehoe, the master of the body in Schuylkill County, Pennsylvania. Each body met regularly and functioned much like a star chamber—a secret court that may make arbitrary decisions—listening to cases and deciding on a course of action.

Thus, for example, if a miner was fired for coming to work drunk, the body would discuss the case and vote on what, if any, form of reprisal to take, which could range from a beating to murder. The body would contact another body elsewhere in the state and one or more of its members would carry out the "sentence," then disappear into the countryside or on a train while the members of the local body ensured that they had alibis for the time of the crime. In turn, the first body might later be called on to execute a sentence for the second. In this way, members of the organization were able to operate with relative impunity.

The following ballad is one of several that attempts to capture a sense of the working conditions the Mollies—and other miners—faced.

PRIMARY SOURCE

Make way for the Molly Maguires
They're drinkers, they're liars but they're men
Make way for the Molly Maguires
You'll never see the likes of them again

Down the mines no sunlight shines
Those pits they're black as hell
In modest style they do their time
It's Paddy's prison cell
And they curse the day they've traveled far
Then drown their tears with a jar

So make way for the Molly Maguires
They're drinkers, they're liars but they're men

Make way for the Molly Maguires
You'll never see the likes of them again

Backs will break and muscles ache
Down there there's no time to dream
Of fields and farms, of woman's arms
Just dig that bloody seam
Though they drain their bodies underground
Who'll dare to push them around

So make way for the Molly Maguires
They're drinkers, they're liars but they're men
Make way for the Molly Maguires
You'll never see the likes of them again

So make way for the Molly Maguires
They're drinkers, they're liars but they're men
Make way for the Molly Maguires
You'll never see the likes of them again

SIGNIFICANCE

In 1877, twenty members of the Molly Maguires, including Black Jack Kehoe, were hanged. In 1873, Allan Pinkerton of the Pinkerton National Detective Agency hired one James McParlan to infiltrate the organization. Pinkerton did so on behalf of Franklin B. Gowen, an Irish Protestant coal baron who owned the Reading railroad—that had a virtual monopoly on the transport of coal out of Schuylkill mines—and who wanted to control the coal industry in part by crushing organized labor.

Accordingly, McParlan, under the name of James McKenna, spent nearly five years working his way up as a member of the Molly Maguires. After he had accumulated enough evidence—often by taking part in decisions that led to murder—twenty members of the organization were prosecuted in a biased trial conducted by Judge Cyrus L. Pershing. All twenty were later hanged. To many observers, the Mollies were martyrs to the labor movement; to others, they were terrorists.

Nevertheless, the end of the Molly Maguires did not signal the end of the labor movement in the mines. Just thirteen years later, in 1890, the United Mine Workers union was formed.

FURTHER RESOURCES

Books

Kenny, Kevin. *Making Sense of the Molly Maguires*. New York: Oxford University Press, 1998.

Web sites

Philips, James. "The Molly Maguires." <http://www.geecoders.com/MollyMaguires> (accessed May 16, 2005).

Audio and Visual Media

The Molly Maguires, directed by Martin Ritt. Paramount Home Video, 2004 (release of 1970 film).

KKK in the Civil Rights Era

"Organized Resistance to Racial Laws Grows"

Newspaper article

By: John N. Popham

Date: December 2, 1956

Source: The *New York Times*.

About the Author: John N. Popham was hired by the *New York Times* in 1947 to work in Chattanooga, Tennessee, near the offices of the *Chattanooga Times*. Popham reported on the important social changes that were occurring in the region during the late 1940s and 1950s. Popham quickly established himself as a reliable and unbiased journalist, with an expertise concerning political and social events brewing in the southern states. Popham continued to work at the *New York Times* until 1958, when he left to become the executive editor of the *Chattanooga Times*.

INTRODUCTION

The Ku Klux Klan (KKK, or the Klan) is a secret white supremacist, terrorist organization that was created in the winter of 1865–1866 during the beginning of Reconstruction following the United States Civil War. Its goal was to terrorize Southern blacks and white Northerners who replaced white Southerners in powerful positions of business and government.

The KKK was dissolved in 1944 after the country's entry into World War II, when it was unable to pay its federal taxes to the government. Its power increased again later in the twentieth century as a result of southern civil-rights activities, and ultimately to the Civil Rights movement, of the 1950s and 1960s.

On May 17, 1954, the U.S. Supreme Court ruled in the federal decision of *Brown v. Board of Education* (of Topeka, Kansas). The ruling stated that racial segregation in the public school system was unconstitutional because it denied black children equal rights and protection under the law. Unwilling to accept such a decision, the KKK organization was revived to counter integration throughout the country, especially in the southern states.

The establishment of the U.S. Commission on Civil Rights and the authorization of the U.S. Attorney General to enforce voting rights was enacted into law in 1957. The Klan began to terrorize anyone who favored, or was suspected of favoring, desegregation or black civil rights. The group began to use more violent methods such as threats, intimidations, and murder to oppose civil rights programs. The Klan especially used lynchings, bombings, and the burning of churches to illustrate their opposition to civil rights.

Membership within the Klan increased as the Civil Rights movement gained momentum. As the result of the U.S. Civil Rights Act of 1964—a comprehensive bill that made racial discrimination illegal in public buildings and other facilities, and by unions, employers, and voting assemblies—membership of the KKK dramatically increased to around 40,000 members in 1965.

PRIMARY SOURCE

Chattanooga, Tenn., Dec. 1—Organizations to resist racial integration in the Southern states have become an important factor in the region's reaction to Federal court decisions dismantling the scaffolding of local Jim Crow laws and customs.

The influence and effectiveness of the resistance groups varies from state to state. But in general they now represent a considerable and growing force backed in many instances by persons of wealth, political power and community status.

About twenty–five states, border, Southern and what the pro-segregationists term "sympathetic areas," have some form of resistance organizations.

In any meaningful sense, however, sixteen of these states have only "fringe" operations, while activity that really impinges on community affairs occurs in the nine-state area of Arkansas, Alabama, Georgia, Louisiana, Mississippi, North and South Carolina, Tennessee, and Texas.

Virginia and Florida have several small but relatively ineffective resistance groups, none of which has attained a position of community importance. But the hardening of segregation attitudes in both states leads some to believe that a resistance movement, particularly of the "respectable" type, could catch on in either state.

In the nine states the central resistance organization uses the designation "citizens' councils," sometimes with the world "white" or the name of the state. In Georgia the key group is the States Rights Council, Inc., and in North Carolina it is North Carolina Patriots, Inc.

NATIONAL UNIT SET UP

In many of the states there are organizations of similar design closely associated with the citizen's councils. To coordinate the activities of all chapters in any part of the country there is now a "Citizens' Councils of America" with offices in Greenwood, Miss.

Altogether, these resistance groups claim a membership of more than 500,000. A recent survey by the Southern Regional Council, the South's foremost interracial improvement organization, credits the resistance groups with at least 200,000 members in the key nine-state area as well as Virginia and Florida.

Moreover, the survey reports that these groups probably have at their disposal funds estimated in excess of $2,000,000, which would include about $1,000,000 in contributions, fund drives and memberships where no fee evaluation has been made.

This accounting of the citizen's council type of resistance organization is distinct from the activity of the Ku Klux Klan, which has been on the increase in recent months, notably with impressive meetings in North and South Carolina, Georgia, Tennessee, Florida, Alabama, Louisiana, and Texas.

ORGANIZE UNDER COVER

Klansmen, while unmasked by state laws in recent years, are still furtive in their organizational work and give no public announcements on membership and treasury standings. Some klaverns, or units, reportedly have initiation fees of $10.

It is this resurgence of the Klan that has underscored what appears to be the twin dilemmas of the citizen's council movement. In a related sense, these two problems which concern the potential for violence and the political overtones, pose equally sharp dilemmas for the Southern commonwealth.

The citizen's council movement was touched off two years ago in response to the Federal Supreme Court decision of May 17, 1954, that held public school racial segregation statutes were unconstitutional. It got started in Mississippi, which remains the fountainhead of the region-wide movement.

Initially, the councils received their strongest leadership from the black belt sections, which have a plantation-economy heritage and where Negroes generally far outnumber whites. This pattern was very true of Mississippi, South Carolina, and Alabama.

In this formative stage, there were scattered instances of reprisals, against Negroes, mainly economic and night-riding threats. At the same time, there were many who sincerely strove to create what they regarded as "respectable" organizations that publicly deplored violence in any form.

Many of them had no personal ill will toward Negroes, but held to the belief that segregation was in the best interests of both races, and that "we've got to maintain our kind of society because of the disparate numbers."

APPEAL TO MASSES

To be effective and to raise sufficient operational funds, the councils had to bid for a broad grass-roots membership. This brought the no violence theme up against a rank-and-file that mirrored almost every conceivable attitude on race relations and a lot of other intergroup cultural conflicts. In effect, it introduced the ancient cry for bread and circuses.

It was here that a leadership cleavage took place. The north Alabama Citizens' Council, led by Asa (Ace) Carter, was expelled from the state association because of its extremist approach. The Carter faction has little influence in the state now. But he has been active throughout the South speaking to crowds of angry faced men, women and teenagers who sometimes have rioted publicly in protest of school integration developments.

Others have fanned out across the South, spellbinding crowds of rednecks, sharecroppers, town loafers and social malcontents with a message of hatemongering and denunciation of the Supreme Court justices as "brainwashed stooges for communism"

John Kasper of Washington, D.C., executive secretary of the Seaboard White Citizens Council, is a principal council chapter organizer of this ilk, operating effectively in the mountain sections of the South.

The Georgia States Rights Council, for instance, maintains a downtown Atlanta office that distributes pro-segregation publications.

A "visiting school teacher" recently requested some literature there and received a statement of alms and purposes, a listing of purported pro-segregation statements by Abraham Lincoln and Thomas Jefferson, a booklet entitled *The Supreme Court, the Broken Constitution and the Shattered Bill of Rights*, Georgia Attorney General Eugene Cook's pamphlet "The Ugly Truth About the N.A.A.C.P.," a copy of a third-party movement newspaper and a copy of "Williams Intelligence Summary," a largely anti-Semitic tract.

ANTI-SEMITISM APPEARS

Anti-Semitism is one of the principal threads woven through the talks and literature of the extremist council leaders and followers. It was strongly manifested by pro-segregationists during school integration developments at Clinton, Tenn. Speakers at Klan rallies have been stepping up their attacks against Jews and Roman Catholics.

Some of the council chapters in South Carolina, Mississippi, and Alabama still keep a "respectable." operation as they view their aims, and many of the leaders are openly distressed about the introduction elsewhere of violence and broad-scale bigotry.

In the Clinton disturbances, several leaders of Tennessee pro-segregation groups appealed to the rioters to be calm "because you are hurting our cause this way."

There are many Southerners who warned from the start, however, that white citizens' councils would release a hornet's nest of ills because of a basic communications problem: sincerely posed challenges about unconstitutional impositions of Federal authority would often be translated generally as a call to rebellious action.

In the main, evidence of late points to an upsurge by the frustrated elements that want more boldness and action. In this contest, the Klan affords the drama of cross burnings, night riding, robes and rituals, and appeals to the know-nothingism that is generations old in this area.

The political problem came to the front in the recent election campaign, when philosophical divisions found many council leaders and supporters fishing in different waters.

Some topflight Democratic officeholders who had been outspokenly sympathetic to the council aims and who had sometimes added fuel to fire by denouncing Federal Government institutions as inimical to Southern philosophies, backed their national party nominees for the sake of party regularity. But many council officers plumped for third-party movements and accused the national Democrats of "betraying" the region.

The net result was that some of the political leaders lost a measure of control over council following and the embittered rank and file struck out for bolder paths. This is essentially a political wrangle, however, and does not tend to weaken the overriding pro-segregation sentiment of the white South.

The importance of the political overtones is evinced by the fact that Alabama's council leaders include three state senators. Georgia's has the backing of Gov. Marvin Griffin and 200 influential business leaders. Louisiana's has a state senator, state university board supervisor, farm bureau president, former state medical association president and a number of wealthy business men.

IMPORTANT LEADERS

Mississippi's has the vast majority of the leaders of the powerful delta section. North Carolina's "patriots" is headed by a University of North Carolina medical school professor and includes three former Speakers of the state Assembly, a university trustee, several leading industrialists and clergymen and a former United States Attorney.

South Carolina's includes a cross-section of leaders in all fields, and Tennessee's Federation for Constitutional Government includes many business executives in the Nashville area.

What all this means for the South is that certain areas have a climate in which public leaders and communications media are subject to a "watchdog" element that jumps on anyone who would suggest a different approach on the segregation-integration controversy.

To many of the region's liberals and moderates, the growing power of the resistance organizations, with pipelines into state legislatures, has created an issue of the basic freedoms of speech, thought and association. Many feel their right to dissent has been abridged by covert pressures.

[WATCHDOG] ALLIANCES

In many ways the resistance groups have formed alliances with factions disgruntled with certain phases of complex modern society, such as income taxes and labor unions. Consequently, many of the "watchdog" climates embrace a sort of search for "heresies" that have slipped into local mores and presumably altered an old way of life that also kept the Negro in his place.

Illustrative of this is the Louisiana council's attitude that one cannot trust anyone who has access to the secret ballot. The council's chairman has warned that "we are going through a familiar pattern set by registration of Negroes in the early days of Reconstruction and our forefathers knew well the disastrous consequences of that pattern in the South."

It is manifest that the resistance organizations have been a big factor in slowing down any process toward desegregation in the public schools. At this stage, even with extremist upsurges by Klan and council, there is no official proposal to deal with the resistance group problem.

SIGNIFICANCE

During the Civil Rights movement, the Klan was responsible for violent attacks against African Americans and civil-rights workers in cities throughout the South, including major incidents in Jacksonville and St. Augustine (Florida), Birmingham and Montgomery (Alabama), and Meridian (Mississippi). The efforts of Klan members were not particularly effective. By the end of the 1960s, its power and membership had declined.

KKK violence during the Civil Rights era was directly used to restrain and deny the rights of African-Americans just as it had been doing during Reconstruction. The Klan did slow down the Civil Rights movement with its violence, but the public, for the most part, did not support Klan activities. As a result, public sentiment helped to eventually mobilize additional support for the passage of Civil Rights legislation.

In the end, the Klan was unsuccessful in its efforts to block the Civil Rights movement that eventually provided formal equality for black Americans.

The Klan sill exists today, in a reduced state. Small, scattered cells of the Klan are still prevalent in various areas of the country (primarily in the southern and midwestern states) with a membership of no more than 6,000 within about 150 chapters. In addition, other racist groups and movements (such as the skinheads and Neo-Nazi groups) have diverted interest away from the Klan. In recent years, the Klan has tended to stay away from a central organization due to problems with lawsuits. Instead, it has sprung up as various subgroups such as the American Knights of the Ku Klux Klan, the Knights of the White Kamelia, and the Imperial Klans of America.

FURTHER RESOURCES

Books

Randel, William Peirce. *The Ku Klux Klan: A Century of Infamy*. Radnor, PA: Chilton Book Company, 1965.

Tourgée, Albion Winegar. *The Invisible Empire*. Baton Rouge, LA: Louisiana State University Press, 1989.

Web sites

National School Boards Association. "The Ruling That Changed America." <http://www.asbj.com/BrownvBoard/> (accessed June 22, 2005).

Public Broadcasting Corporation. "The Rise and Fall of Jim Crow: Ku Klux Klan." <http://www.pbs.org/wnet/jimcrow/stories_org_kkk.html> (accessed June 22, 2005).

"U.S. Plane Seized, Flown to Havana"

The Hijacking of National Airlines Flight 337

Newspaper article

By: Milt Sosin

Date: May 1, 1961

Source: The *New York Times*.

About the Author: Milt Sosin was a newspaper reporter who worked for both the Miami News and the Associated Press. Sosin remained an active journalist until his death at age ninety-two in 2000. His 1975 article regarding the May 1, 1961 hijacking of National Flight NA 337 to Havana is the only known press report to quote hijacker Antulio Ramirez Ortiz, regarding both his role in the execution of the hijacking, and his subsequent

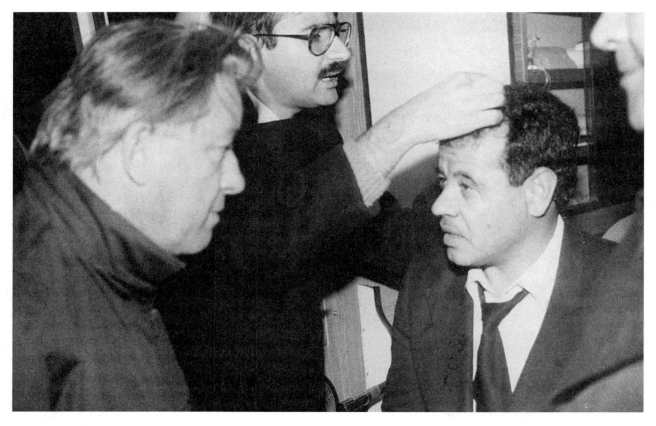

Captain Hani Galal, pilot of the hijacked Egypt Air Flight 648, receives medical attention after Egyptian commandos stormed the hijacked jetliner in Valletta, Malta. AP/WIDE WORLD PHOTOS

attempts to flee Cuba, where he had been granted asylum.

INTRODUCTION

On May 1, 1961, Puerto Rican born Antulio Ramirez Ortiz, a 35-year-old American citizen, locked himself in a forward bathroom compartment of National Airlines Flight 337, bound for Key West from Miami, Florida. He passed a note under the compartment door, claiming that he had a bomb sufficient to destroy the aircraft. Ortiz demanded that the plane be flown to Havana, Cuba.

The National Airlines pilot and crew complied with the threat. The plane was diverted to Havana where Ortiz disembarked without incident. The aircraft then returned to Key West. No one was physically injured and Ortiz was granted immediate asylum by the Cuban government.

Ortiz would ultimately be the subject of prosecution both in Cuba, when he attempted to leave that country in 1962, as well as in the United States, when he returned in 1975.

History's first hijacker of a plane to Cuba told a U.S. magistrate today he became disillusioned with Fidel Castro but it took him 14 years to get back home.

Antulio Ramirez Ortiz said he served two prison terms in Cuba's notorious Morro Castle and La Cabana prisons for a total of six years during his long stay on the island.

Ramirez Ortiz pleaded for release on his own recognizance so he could look for a job. But Magistrate Peter Palermo said his story would have to be checked out first. Meantime, his $25,000 bail was reduced to $10,000.

Now 49, Ramirez Ortiz testified he went to the Swiss Embassy in Havana to seek his return to the United States and even tried to escape the island by raft, getting more prison time after he was picked up by a Cuban vessel.

Finally, after he was released from his second prison term last August, he was permitted to leave. He took a flight to Kingston, Jamaica on Nov. 11, but he spent 10 days there before he could talk to a U.S. embassy official who permitted him to fly to Miami. The official also tipped off the FBI which was waiting to arrest him when he arrived here Nov. 21.

Ramirez Ortiz hijacked a National Airlines two-engine plane to Cuba in 1961—the first such midair piracy. There was not even a federal charge to cover that specific act at the time. He was charged with assault and transporting a stolen aircraft across state lines.

The NAL flight was en route from Key West to Miami with a stop at Marathon, a trip the airline no longer makes.

When the Cuban missile crisis developed in October of 1962, Ramirez Ortiz said, he "could no longer be in sympathy with Castro."

He went to the Swiss embassy and paid for a plane ticket to Mexico, he said, but then was arrested, and charged with espionage. He was sentenced to three years in Morro Castle.

"After I got out, I tried to figure out a way to leave Cuba," he testified. With another man, whom he did not identify, he built a sailing raft and got to sea for two days. They, spotted a merchant ship—but it turned out to be Russian, he said. His companion went aboard but Ramirez Ortiz stayed on the raft. The Russian ship left the area and the companion was never heard from again.

A Cuban fishing boat picked up Ramirez Ortiz the next day and returned him to Cuba, where he was sentenced to three more years for attempting to escape.

Ramirez Ortiz said that from a New York Times account of the hijacking, which he read in Cuba, he realized he was in trouble back home. He told the embassy in Jamaica, he said, that he would probably face charges.

While in Cuba he worked as a general laborer. He had divorced his second wife before he left the United States and married a woman in Cuba in 1969, he said. His wife left on a Freedom Flight to the United States and is now in California, he said.

His attorney, Michael Osman, told the court that a Miami woman, Marta Ibarra, of 525 NE 63rd St., has offered to let the returned hijacker stay in her house until he could get established here.

U.S. Attorney Don Ferguson objected either to rejection of Ramirez Ortiz' bond or his release, even if his story checked out. He said the man had been indicted on charges of a serious crime which carried a substantial prison penalty if convinced. Ferguson also said the prisoner had "no roots" in this community.

But Palermo said, "If this man's story checks out . . . I would he inclined to grant the defendant's release on his own recognizance."

Palermo told government officials to check out the story with the FBI and advise the court on Monday, when another hearing will be held.

SIGNIFICANCE

Ortiz was not the first international aircraft hijacker, a distinction belonging to a group of rebel soldiers who took charge of an aircraft at Arequipa, Peru in 1933, intending to drop propaganda leaflets on Lima. However, this was the first hijacking of an American aircraft. There were four more hijackings in 1961 alone, and 177 hijackings committed worldwide between 1961 and 1969. Over 70 percent of these either originated in Cuba or involved an attempt to divert a flight to Cuba. The expressions "Take me to Havana" and "skyjacking" became a part of the North American lexicon.

Further, the hijacking occurred in the immediate aftermath of the attempted invasion of Cuba by American backed Cuban exiles at the Bay of Pigs, on April 15, 1961. The actions of Ortiz and the immediate grant of his asylum by Cuba took place at a time of extreme political tension between the United States and Cuba.

When Ortiz subsequently had a change of heart regarding his view of both Cuba and Castro, he was jailed for several years for attempting to leave the country.

The events of the Flight 337 hijacking precipitated significant changes to the manner in which the American legal system would regard such acts. As of May 1, 1961, the United States did not have a specific law designed to address an act of air piracy, nor was there any security structure in place to deter such activity. In September 1961, in response to concerns in the United States regarding the safety of air travel and the apparent vulnerability of aircraft to hijackers, President John F. Kennedy implemented the first Sky Marshall program, a policing program that returned to prominence in the wake of the 9/11 terrorist attacks forty years later. President Kennedy also signed into federal law several criminal sanctions for aircraft hijackings, ranging from a minimum of twenty years imprisonment to the death penalty.

FURTHER RESOURCES
Books

Ortiz, Antulio R. *Castro's Red Hot Hell*. 1963; (unpublished), stored at National Archives and Records Administration, Washington, D.C. Kennedy Assassination, Doc. 005134.

Highjacker Leila Khaled totes a submachine gun at a Palestinian refugee camp in Lebanon on Nov. 29, 1970. AP/WIDE WORLD PHOTOS

Web sites

Aviation Safety Network. "Hijackings." <http://aviation-safety. net/database/record> (accessed July 4, 2005).

Unites States Department of State. "Significant Terrorist Incidents, 1961–2003." <http://www.state.gov/r/pa/ho/pubs/fs/5902> (accessed July 4, 2005).

"Industrial Society and Its Future"

Unabomber initiates a series of attacks that extends almost 17 years

Essay

By: Theodore Kaczynski

Date: September 19, 1995

Source: "Industrial Society and Its Future," sometimes referred to as the "Unabomber Manifesto," published by the *Washington Post*.

About the Author: Theodore (Ted) Kaczynski began his career as a promising mathematician on the faculty of the University of California at Berkeley. In the early 1970s, he left his job and eventually moved to the woods of Montana, where he launched a series of mail bomb attacks from 1978 to 1995, earning him the designation "Unabomber." In 1998, Kaczynski pleaded guilty to the terrorist bombings and began serving a life sentence in a Colorado prison.

INTRODUCTION

The longest and most expensive manhunt in American law enforcement history began on May 25, 1978, when a security officer at Northwestern University in Evanston, Illinois, was injured when a suspicious parcel he opened exploded. The United States Postal Service had returned the parcel to a university professor, but the professor had never mailed it. The university contacted the U.S. Bureau of Alcohol, Tobacco, and Firearms (ATF), which determined that the explosion was caused by a crude pipe bomb. The authorities could not know it, but the bomb was the first of 15 bombs that would become increasingly sophisticated, and lethal, over the next 17 years.

A second bomb detonated at Northwestern on May 9, 1979. On November 15, 1979, the bomber's target appeared to have shifted when an explosive device began to smolder in the cargo hold of an American Airlines flight. Then on June 10, 1980, the president of United Airlines received a similar bomb in the mail. It was at this point that the Federal Bureau of Investigation (FBI) coined the term *UnAbom*, referring to *U*niversities and *A*irlines *bomb*ings.

After a period of 16 months with no incidents, the bombings resumed. Bombs were found on October 8, 1981, at the University of Utah; in May 1982 at Vanderbilt University in Nashville, Tennessee; and on July 2, 1982, at the University of California at Berkeley. After a three-year hiatus, bombings began again on May 15, 1985, at Berkeley; on June 13, 1985, at a Boeing aircraft plant in Washington State; and on June 15, 1985, at the University of Michigan.

The first death occurred on December 11, 1985, in the parking lot of a computer store in Sacramento, California. After another hiatus, the bombings resumed with renewed force at the University of California at San Francisco on June 22, 1993, and the following day at Yale University in New Haven, Connecticut. At this point the UNABOM task force, consisting of the FBI, the ATF, and the U.S. Postal Service, was created, but it could not prevent two more fatal bombings, on December 10, 1994, when an advertising executive was

Masked protesters, some supporting the Earth Liberation Front, hold signs during a demonstation in Portland, Oregon, in 2002. AP/WIDE WORLD PHOTOS

killed, and on April 24, 1995, when the president of the California Forestry Association was killed.

Although in 1987, investigators had found a witness who was able to help artists create a now famous sketch of a suspect with sunglasses and a hood, by early 1995, investigators were seemingly no closer to identifying the Unabomber than they had been in 1978.

The case finally broke in 1995, only when the Unabomber began to communicate with the world. That year in June, in a letter to the *New York Times*, he threatened further violence, but promised to stop if the *Times* or another major newspaper would publish his manifesto, a 35,000-word essay that decried the Industrial Revolution and modern technology.

After consulting with the FBI—and agonizing over whether to give in to the request of an alleged murderer to publish his views—in September the *Washington Post* published the Unabomber manifesto, under Kaczynski's title "Industrial Society and Its Future." The *New York Times* shared the cost of publishing the Unabomber manifesto.

Although both the *Times* and *Post* editors expressed deep reservations regarding the journalistic ethics and implications of agreeing to a terrorist's demand to publish his views, the FBI was convinced that publication might provide clues about the Unabomber's identity. The FBI hoped that a reader somewhere would recognize the Unabomber's writing style, words, or ideas.

PRIMARY SOURCE

1. The Industrial Revolution and its consequences have been a disaster for the human race. They have greatly increased the life-expectancy of those of us who live in "advanced" countries, but they have destabilized society, have made life unfulfilling, have subjected human beings to indignities, have led to widespread psychological suffering (in the Third World to physical suffering as well) and have inflicted severe damage on the natural world. The continued development of technology will worsen the situation. It will certainly subject human beings to greater indignities and inflict greater damage on the natural world, it will probably lead to greater social disruption and psychological suffering, and it may lead to increased physical suffering even in "advanced" countries.

2. The industrial-technological system may survive or it may break down. If it survives, it MAY eventually achieve a low level of physical and psychological suffering, but only after passing through a long and very painful period of adjustment and only at the cost of permanently reducing human beings and many other living organisms to engineered products and mere cogs in the social machine. Furthermore, if the system survives, the consequences will be inevitable: There is no way of reforming or modifying the system so as to prevent it from depriving people of dignity and autonomy.

3. If the system breaks down the consequences will still be very painful. But the bigger the system grows the more disastrous the results of its breakdown will be, so if it is to break down it had best break down sooner rather than later.

4. We therefore advocate a revolution against the industrial system. This revolution may or may not make use of violence: it may be sudden or it may be a relatively gradual process spanning a few decades. We can't predict any of that. But we do outline in a very general way the measures that those who hate the industrial system should take in order to prepare the way for a revolution against that form of society. This is not to be a POLITICAL revolution. Its object will be to overthrow not governments but the economic and technological basis of the present society.

5. In this article we give attention to only some of the negative developments that have grown out of the industrial-technological system. Other such developments we mention only briefly or ignore altogether. This does not mean that we regard these other developments as unimportant. For practical reasons we have to confine our discussion to areas that have received insufficient public attention or in which we have something new to say. For example, since there are well-developed environmental and wilderness movements, we have written very little about environmental degradation or the destruction of wild nature, even though we consider these to be highly important . . .

STRATEGY

180. The technophiles are taking us all on an utterly reckless ride into the unknown. Many people understand something of what technological progress is doing to us yet take a passive attitude toward it because they think it is inevitable. But we (FC) [Note: FC refers to Freedom Club; forensic investigators found these initials stamped in the metal of some of the Unabomber's bombs] don't think it is inevitable. We think it can be stopped, and we will give here some indications of how to go about stopping it.

181 . . . The two main tasks for the present are to promote social stress and instability in industrial society and to develop and propagate an ideology that opposes technology and the industrial system. When the system becomes sufficiently stressed and unstable, a revolution against technology may be possible. The pattern would be similar to that of the French and Russian Revolutions. French society and Russian society, for several decades prior to their respective revolutions, showed increasing signs of stress and weakness. Meanwhile, ideologies were being developed that offered a new world view that was quite different from the old one. In the Russian case, revolutionaries were actively working to undermine the old order. Then, when the old system was put under sufficient additional stress (by financial crisis in France, by military defeat in Russia) it was swept away by revolution. What we propose in something along the same lines . . .

183. But an ideology, in order to gain enthusiastic support, must have a positive ideals well [sic] as a negative one; it must be FOR something as well as AGAINST something. The positive ideal that we propose is Nature. That is, WILD nature; those aspects of the functioning of the Earth and its living things that are independent of human management and free of human interference and control. And with wild nature we include human nature, by which we mean those aspects of the functioning of the human individual that are not subject to regulation by organized society but are products of chance, or free will, or God (depending on your religious or philosophical opinions) . . .

185. As for the negative consequences of eliminating industrial society—well, you can't eat your cake and have it too. To gain one thing you have to sacrifice another.

186. Most people hate psychological conflict. For this reason they avoid doing any serious thinking about difficult social issues, and they like to have such issues presented to them in simple, black-and-white terms: THIS is all good and THAT is all bad. The revolutionary ideology should therefore be developed on two levels . . .

190. Any kind of social conflict helps to destabilize the system, but one should be careful about what kind of conflict one encourages. The line of conflict should be drawn between the mass of the people and the power-holding elite of industrial society (politicians, scientists, upper-level business executives, government officials, etc.). It should NOT be drawn between the revolutionaries and the mass of the people. For example, it would be bad strategy for the revolutionaries to condemn Americans for their habits of consumption. Instead, the average American should be portrayed as a victim of the advertising and marketing industry, which has suckered him into buying a lot of junk that he doesn't need and that is very poor compensation for his lost freedom. Either approach is consistent with the facts. It is merely a matter of attitude whether you blame the advertising industry for manipulating the public or blame the public for allowing itself to be manipulated. As a matter of strategy one should generally avoid blaming the public . . .

193. The kind of revolution we have in mind will not necessarily involve an armed uprising against any government. It may or may not involve physical violence, but it will not be a POLITICAL revolution. Its focus will be on technology and economics, not politics . . .

197. Some people take the line that modern man has too much power, too much control over nature; they argue for a more passive attitude on the part of the human race. At best these people are expressing themselves unclearly, because they fail to distinguish between power for LARGE ORGANIZATIONS and power for INDIVIDUALS and SMALL GROUPS. It is a mistake to argue for powerlessness and passivity, because people NEED power. Modern man as a collective entity—that is, the industrial system—has immense power over nature, and we (FC) regard this as evil. But modern INDIVIDUALS and SMALL GROUPS OF INDIVIDUALS have far less power than primitive man ever did. Generally speaking, the vast power of "modern man" over nature is exercised not by individuals or small groups but by large organizations. To the extent that the average modern INDIVIDUAL can wield the power of technology, he is permitted to do so only within narrow limits and only under the supervision and control of the system. (You need a license for everything and with the license come rules and regulations). The individual has only those technological powers with which the system chooses to provide him. His PERSONAL power over nature is slight.

198. Primitive INDIVIDUALS and SMALL GROUPS actually had considerable power over nature; or maybe it would be better to say power WITHIN nature. When primitive man needed food he knew how to find and prepare edible roots, how to track game and take it with homemade weapons. He knew how to protect himself from heat, cold, rain, dangerous animals, etc. But primitive man did relatively little damage to nature because the COLLECTIVE power of primitive society was negligible compared to the COLLECTIVE power of industrial society.

199. Instead of arguing for powerlessness and passivity, one should argue that the power of the INDUSTRIAL SYSTEM should be broken, and that this will greatly

INCREASE the power and freedom of INDIVIDUALS and SMALL GROUPS.

200. Until the industrial system has been thoroughly wrecked, the destruction of that system must be the revolutionaries' ONLY goal. Other goals would distract attention and energy from the main goal. More importantly, if the revolutionaries permit themselves to have any other goal than the destruction of technology, they will be tempted to use technology as a tool for reaching that other goal. If they give in to that temptation, they will fall right back into the technological trap, because modern technology is a unified, tightly organized system, so that, in order to retain SOME technology, one finds oneself obliged to retain MOST technology, hence one ends up sacrificing only token amounts of technology.

SIGNIFICANCE

After a series of bombings that left three dead and twenty-nine injured over the span of seventeen years, the *New York Times* and *Washington Post*'s publication of the Unabomber's manifesto, "Industrial Society and Its Future," was the critical factor in breaking the case.

FBI hopes were realized when Kaczynski's brother, David Kaczynski, read the manifesto and concluded that it had to be the work of his brother, Ted. One detail in particular stood out for David: In paragraph 185, the author used the phrase "you can't eat your cake and have it too," a variation on the expression "you can't have your cake and eat it too" that David and Ted's mother had frequently used.

Six weeks after David Kaczynski came forward, on April 3, 1996, a dirty and disheveled Ted Kaczynski was arrested at his tiny cabin in the woods outside Lincoln, Montana. After two years of legal wrangling, during which Kaczynski refused to enter an insanity plea, he pleaded guilty to the charges on January 22, 1998, and was sentenced to life in a Colorado prison. Evidence introduced in court by a forensic psychiatrist indicated that Kaczynski has a long-term, episodic mental disorder known as paranoid schizophrenia, which has as its characteristics abnormal thoughts, distorted perceptions, social withdrawal, and feelings of persecution. The psychiatrist who examined Kaczynski concluded that he was competent to stand trial despite his mental illness because he clearly understood the nature and consequences of the charges and proceedings against him, and could participate in his defense. The case of Theodore Kaczynski sparked debate about the insanity plea, criminal behavior, and terrorism that appears to have a social or political agenda attached, but is actually the work and philosophy of one mentally ill person.

Some extremist environmental groups have since adopted some of the Unabomber's rhetoric.

FURTHER RESOURCES

Books

Chase, Alston. *Harvard and the Unabomber: The Education of an American Terrorist.* New York: Norton, 2003.

Web sites

WashingtonPost.com. "The Unabomber Case: The Manifesto." <http://www.washingtonpost.com/wp-srv/national/longterm/unabomber/manifesto.htm> (accessed May 16, 2005).

"Soldier in the Army of God"

Anti-abortion Activist Shooting of Dr. Gunn

Magazine article

By: Anne Bower

Date: February 18, 1996

Source: "Soldier in the Army of God." *Albion Monitor.* Originally published in the magazine the *Body Politic.*

About the Author: Anne Bower was educated as an anthropologist but in 1991 turned to journalism and the publication of the *Body Politic,* a pro-choice magazine in Binghamton, New York, to oppose the radical anti-abortion group Operation Rescue, also based in Binghamton.

INTRODUCTION

On March 11, 1993, the anti-abortion movement took a new, more violent direction when Michael Griffin shot and killed David Gunn, a doctor who performed abortions at a local clinic near Pensacola, Florida. Gunn was the first known health-care worker to be killed by radical opponents of abortion.

Gunn, forty-seven at the time of his death, was a graduate of the University of Kentucky medical school. He originally planned to be an obstetrician/gynecologist, and he took a job at a hospital in Brewton, Alabama, specifically because, according to him, it had the highest infant mortality rate in the nation. When a local clinic that was unable to find willing doctors asked him to, he began to perform abortions–surprisingly to some, for he was raised in a fundamentalist Christian home. His parents did not learn that he was an abortion provider until his death.

Soon, Gunn was crisscrossing Alabama, Florida, and Georgia full time to perform abortions at six

An armed search team enters the forest in North Carolina as authorities continue their search for abortion clinic bombing suspect Eric Rudolph. AP/WIDE WORLD PHOTOS

different clinics, many for women no other doctor would help. He stayed in motels and often logged 1,000 miles of travel a week. Aware of threats from abortion protestors, he carried three guns in his car.

Meanwhile, Griffin, a navy veteran, remained largely to himself; he and his wife occasionally associated with other members of their Christian fundamentalist community. Before shooting Gunn, he had participated in only a few anti-abortion protests.

The facts of the crime were simple. On the day in question, Griffin, dressed in a gray suit, positioned himself near the back door of the Women's Medical Services clinic where Gunn worked. The clinic, located in a complex of professional offices, had no signs that identified it; a notice inside the entrance to suite 46 simply instructed patients to proceed upstairs to sign in. When Gunn arrived at the clinic and was getting out of his car, Griffin stepped forward, allegedly said to him "Don't kill any more babies," and shot him three times in the back with a .38-caliber revolver. Gunn died in surgery two hours later.

Meanwhile, the police had been called to monitor an anti-abortion protest that was taking place at the front of the building. Moments after the shooting, Griffin walked around the building and informed the police that he had just shot Gunn.

Griffin was part of an anti-abortion movement that was adopting increasingly bold and terrorist-like tactics. Not content with protests, groups such as Rescue America and Operation Rescue had graduated to harassing doctors, nurses, and patients; then to vandalism, attacks with butyric acid (a noxious compound that left an odor that was almost impossible to eradicate), and arson. One tactic that outraged health-care providers and pro-choice advocates was the distribution in print and on the Internet of Wild West–type "Wanted" posters with the names, pictures, addresses, and phone numbers of abortion providers. Gunn was known to Griffin and the protesters outside Gunn's clinic because Operation Rescue had recently put his picture and phone number on such a poster distributed at a rally in Alabama.

Emboldened by Griffin's actions, pro-life advocate Shelley Shannon, who had taken part in violent protest since 1988, armed herself with a .25-caliber pistol and wounded Dr. George Tiller of Wichita, Kansas, continuing a string of at least ten shootings in the United States and Canada during the 1990s. Anne Bower, publisher of the pro-choice magazine *Body Politic*, interviewed Shannon and wrote a profile of her titled "Soldier in the Army of God." The article details Shannon's evolution from abortion protester to anti-abortion terrorist (a form of special-interest terrorism) and would-be murderer, as well as her reaction to the shooting of Gunn.

■ PRIMARY SOURCE

At first, Shelley Shannon was content to perform civil disobedience with Operation Rescue. According to her own notes, she engaged in 35 different actions, beginning in 1988. She kept track of her "rescues" and her jail time in a computer file, titled "Mom's Jail Time Total." By her count, the total was 98 days.

But during 1991, according to her sentencing report, Shannon underwent a transformation from civil disobedience to violence. She wrote about it in a document entitled "Join the Army:"

> The biggest hurdle was being willing to even consider that God could indeed require this work of anyone. Christians don't do that kind of thing, do they? But prayer and God cleared that up. Then I realized that I needed to stop the killing too.

She also began to correspond with men and women named in the "Prisoner's of Christ" list. This dialogue convinced her that most rescuers were not willing to put their convictions into action because they were unwilling to pay the price. Taking inspiration from these arsonists, bombers, and kidnappers, Shannon decided to risk her freedom. She was especially encouraged by arsonist Marjorie Reed who wrote:

> If you are going to get a year for just blocking the doors, you might as well do much more drastic measures. . . . It is going to get a whole lot worse. Blood will be shed, not just the babies blood either.

Shelley Shannon recorded her last blockade as November 17, 1992. By then, this wife and mother of two teenage children, had committed herself to violence and engaged in a year-long arson and butyric acid bombing spree across three states . . .

Her transformation manifested in January of 1993 when Shannon wrote a letter to *Life Advocate* magazine, a publication that has condoned violence to end abortion. In the letter Shannon, referring to the recent spate of attacks on clinics (some of her own making) said,

> I'm sure the bombers are acting in the will of God, and doubt they would or should stop if a guilty bystander or innocent person is hurt. If they don't act, a lot of people will be killed. Let's pray no one gets hurt, but this is war and we have to be realistic.

Two months after this letter appeared, Dr. David Gunn was shot in the back as he attempted to enter Pensacola Medical Services. The murderer, Michael Griffin, was immediately taken into custody. In "Next Advent" her computer file diary, Shannon said of the murder,

> He didn't shoot Mother Teresa, he shot a mass murderer such as Saddam Hussien [*sic*] or Hitler. I don't even think it is accurately termed 'murder.' God is the only one who knows whether Gunn would ever have repented or if he would have killed another 5,000 babies and probably 3 or 4 more women who probably weren't Christians either.

With these chilling words, the quiet housewife embarked on her own path to murder.

The murder of David Gunn shocked the pro-choice community and was the beginning of the awakening of the public and law enforcement that things were getting serious in the trenches. Many in the Right-to-Life community were astonished that their years of calling abortion "murder" and doctors "baby killers" had resulted in such action. Some in the "rescue" community, who had been willing to blockade clinics and hassle women with "sidewalk counseling," were not prepared to condone cold-blooded murder. Michael Griffin was roundly condemned in many circles.

But not by Shelley Shannon. She wrote in "Christ Advent,"

> I'm not convinced that God didn't require it of Michael to do this. It is possible. I'm praying God will push more of us 'off the deep end' . . .

Before his trial, Shannon began corresponding with Griffin and eventually spoke with him by telephone. In her diary she noted that Michael called her and said of him, "He is definitely a Christian." She was very upset by the apparent lack of support for Griffin in the pro-life community.

In her diary, Shannon expressed the belief that God could not lead her to do anything sinful, even if it seemed so to the outside world—a place that was fast receding from Shannon's consciousness. Just as Michael had been called to d.r. [direct rescue], she believed her path had become clear. God asked her to kill, and after praying on it and reading the Bible, she finally had no doubt. Her only prayer now was, "please help me do it right."

Shannon's target was Dr. George Tiller, a physician who practiced in Wichita, Kansas and was a major target of the anti-abortion movement. Dr. Tiller was especially hated because he performed late term abortions for which he was nicknamed "Tiller the Killer." In a letter to her daughter Angie written in prison after her arrest, Shannon tells the story of her quest to emulate Michael.

She obtained a .25 caliber pistol from an unnamed friend and practiced shooting at her home. A bus took her to Oklahoma City where she rented a car and drove to Wichita. Posing as a patient, she was unable to kill the doctor inside the clinic. Eventually she left the building and hung around outside with the protesters, where she says she got the idea to shoot the doctor when he drove out. Around 7:00 P.M. the doctor and another woman left. Shannon explained to her daughter how she made her move.

> Finally they both came out, and fortunately her car was right in from of him, so if he lost control, his vehicle would only smash into hers. So I kept praying, shot, and took off. It never occurred to me that people would come after me, but they did!

Both the woman and Doctor Tiller—who was not seriously wounded—chased Shannon, but she got away and headed for Oklahoma City. Enroute she ditched the gun, which was never recovered. But before she could get on a plane home, Shannon was taken into custody.

That was August 19, 1993. Shannon has not been a free woman since. She was easily convicted and sentenced to 11 years for attempted murder. In her prison letters to Angie, Shannon showed no remorse for her actions. A few days after the shooting she wrote,

> I'm not denying I shot Tiller. But I deny that it was wrong. It was the most holy, most righteous thing I've ever done. I have no regrets. I hope he's not killing babies today. If he is, at least I tried.

Some in the anti-abortion community supported her actions, especially Rev. Paul Hill who came to her trial. Rev. Hill had emerged on the anti-choice scene a few days after the murder of Dr. Gunn. He was first seen on the

"Donahue Show" arguing that Dr. Gunn's murder was justifiable homicide, a theme he continued until July 28, 1994 when he gunned down Dr. John Britton and his volunteer escort, Colonel James Barrett . . .

But 1995 was not a good year for Shannon. She was found guilty of arson and sentenced to 20 more years to be served consecutively with the previous 11 . . .

Today, back in Kansas prison, Shannon is seldom visited by family or old friends. Her daughter has recently been arrested for a 1993 death threat on a California doctor. But she still remains a good little soldier in the Army of God.

SIGNIFICANCE

Griffin's attorney tried to enter a temporary insanity plea, but the trial judge would not accept it because Griffin refused to undergo psychiatric examination. Nonetheless, at trial the defense tried to show that Griffin was the victim of brainwashing on the part of John Burt, head of Rescue America, alleging that Burt subjected Griffin to relentless anti-abortion rhetoric and graphic images, including a "funeral" for a pair of aborted fetuses. The jury, however, after deliberating for less than three hours, found Griffin guilty of first-degree murder. The judge sentenced him to life in prison, with the possibility of parole after twenty-five years.

Meanwhile, the violence continued. In addition to the wounding of Tiller by Shannon, further shootings and bombings occurred in British Columbia, Ontario, Manitoba, Massachusetts, Florida, Alabama, and New York. In 2003, the Reverend Paul J. Hill was executed for the murder of an abortion provider in Florida in July 1994. Suspected in much of the violence was James Kopp, who was finally arrested, tried, and convicted for the 1998 killing of an abortion provider while he slept in his Amherst, New York, home.

Largely in response to the killing of Gunn, and the increasingly violent sentiments and views expressed by Shannon, Congress passed the Freedom of Access to Clinical Entrances Act, which President Bill Clinton signed into law on May 26, 1994. The law provides stiff civil and criminal penalties for intentionally using force, the threat of force, or obstruction to "injure," "intimidate," or "interfere with" a person attempting to obtain reproductive health-care services.

The law applies equally to abortion clinics and pro-life counseling centers. It does not prohibit protests, prayers, singing, or distribution of literature.

In the years that followed, anti-abortion groups mounted numerous legal challenges to the act, arguing that it was vague and that it infringed on the right of free speech. While these challenges led to modification of details (for example, the distance at which protestors had to remain from patients and entrances, and the allowable level of noise from amplified microphones), the law has survived.

FURTHER RESOURCES

Books

Baird-Windle, Patricia, and Eleanor J. Bader. *Targets of Hatred: Anti-Abortion Terrorism*. New York: Palgrave Macmillan, 2001.

Mason, Carol. *Killing for Life: The Apocalyptic Narrative of Pro-Life Politics*. Ithaca, NY: Cornell University Press, 2002.

Web sites

Rutherford Institute. "Abortion Protests." <http://www.rutherford.org/documents/pdf/H01-Abortion%20Protests%20_1_.pdf> (accessed May 16, 2005).

Olympic Park Bombing

"FBI Takes Lead in Developing Counterterrorism Effort"

Magazine article

By: Lois R. Ember

Date: November 4, 1996

Source: *Chemical & Engineering News*, November 4, 1996.

About the Author: Lois R. Ember, a senior correspondent for *Chemical & Engineering News*, regularly writes about issues involving chemical and biological warfare and U.S. national security.

INTRODUCTION

In 1996, the Summer Olympic Games were held at the Centennial Olympic Park near downtown Atlanta, Georgia. At 12:30 on the morning of July 27, the tenth day of the games, security guard Richard Jewell noticed a green military-style backpack beneath a sound tower used for a rock concert that was just winding down from the evening before. Suspicious that the unattended backpack may have contained a bomb, Jewell pointed it out to a Georgia Bureau of Investigation agent. Federal explosives experts rushed to the scene and observed that wires protruded from the backpack. They in turn called in a bomb disposal crew.

At 12:58 A.M., an anonymous 911 caller was warned that a bomb would explode in Centennial Olympic Park in a half hour. As the authorities attempted to clear the area and Jewell evacuated the sound tower, they met

The body of an explosion victim lies on the commemorative bricks in Atlanta's Olympic Centennial Park after a blast early July 27, 1996. AP/WIDE WORLD PHOTOS

with resistance from many people in the area who had been drinking, so the evacuation efforts were only partially successful.

Any doubts about what was inside the backpack were dispelled at 1:20 when it exploded. The pipe bomb sent nails, screws, and metal shrapnel flying in all directions. One woman, Alice Hawthorne, was killed by the blast, a Turkish television cameraman named Melih Uzunyol died of a heart attack as he ran to cover the explosion, and 111 people were wounded, including Uzunyol's young daughter.

Initially, Jewell was regarded as a hero for his prompt action. Just three days later, however, an Atlanta newspaper ran a story revealing that he was a suspect in the bombing and that the Federal Bureau of Investigation (FBI) considered that he may have planted the bomb just so he could win acclaim by finding it. Jewell vigorously denied the allegations, but for nearly three months he lived under a cloud of suspicion. In 1997, U.S. Attorney General Janet Reno issued a public apology to Jewell for the FBI leak that led to the news story, and Jewell was cleared of any suspicion.

Initially, the authorities believed that the bomb may have been the work of foreign or domestic terrorists intent on disrupting the Olympic Games. Of particular concern was the possibility that the bomb dispersed some type of chemical or biological agent. Accordingly, the FBI sent samples from the blast debris to the Science and Technology (SciTech) Center Laboratory, part of the Centers for Disease Control and Prevention (CDC). The following article, excerpted from *Chemical & Engineering News*, outlines the activities of the lab and the reasons for its formation.

PRIMARY SOURCE

In the early-morning hours of July 27, an exploding pipe bomb shattered the jubilation of the large, boisterous crowd attending an open-air concert in Atlanta's Centennial Olympic Park. Within minutes of the explosion, the park was swarming with hundreds of firefighters and law enforcement and medical personnel.

A few hours after the blast, two special Federal Bureau of Investigation (FBI) agents crawled around the site, collecting samples from or near the bomb crater. One agent then carried the samples to an analytical laboratory at the Centers for Disease Control & Prevention (CDC) where they were screened for chemical and biological warfare agents.

Within five hours of receiving the samples, the laboratory could confidently say that no biological or chemical warfare agents were present in the soil, shrapnel, or textile samples tested. This probably marked the first time a domestic bomb had ever been screened for these agents of mass destruction.

Though largely unknown to the public, the laboratory—called the Science & Technology (SciTech) Center—was part of the massive security arrangements for the summer Olympic games (C&EN, July 15, page 11). It was specifically—and swiftly—created to fill a void, a weakness in the initial plans for a response to a chemical or biological terrorism event: rapid and accurate agent identification.

That the analytical lab could be put together and, by all accounts, function successfully was, like many things, serendipitous: All of the key players knew each other from their earlier involvement in investigating the 1995 sarin nerve gas attack in the Tokyo subway system.

The SciTech Center, together with the so-called Chem/Bio Response Team, formed a broad multiagency partnership, an FBI-led federal response capability to counter chemical or biological terrorism at the Olympic games. About 400 professionals were involved at a cost of several million dollars, estimates Randall S. Murch, chief of the scientific analysis section of the FBI's Laboratory Division.

This multiagency partnership also serves as a prototype for combating future chemical and biological terrorist acts. "It really has become the model upon which we are building a national response" to nuclear, biological, or chemical terrorism, explains Murch.

With the collapse of the Soviet Union, the rise of state-sponsored and independent terrorist groups, the expanding global communications network, and the ease with which raw materials and the data on how to use them in weapons can be acquired, countering domestic terrorism—not deterring warfare against the U.S.—has become the top national security priority.

Although nuclear weapons would cause more damage, the intelligence, defense, and scientific communities recognize that terrorists are more likely to use chemical or biological warfare agents. As Sen. Sam Nunn (D-Ga.) says: "The threat over the next decade may come by missile, but it is more likely to arrive by suitcase."

So the response model, with its strong analytical component, fills a national need. And as Murch explains, "the package of capabilities will be drawn together and deployed quickly" when required. In fact, a slightly different and smaller mix of agencies than those assembled in Atlanta was deployed to the national political conventions in San Diego and Chicago in August.

The nascent model is in the throes of being refined, formalized and, maybe eventually, codified. In the meantime, Presidential Decision Directive 39 (PDD 39) signed by President Clinton on June 21, 1995, lays out in general terms U.S. policy on counterterrorism. Although it doesn't directly address the model, it does give the FBI lead responsibility for managing the crisis posed by a credible threat of deployment of a weapon of mass destruction, and the Federal Emergency Management Agency (FEMA) the lead in managing the consequences of actual use.

PDD 39 is short on particulars, lacking details on precise missions for the approximately 40 federal agencies with some responsibility to respond to a terrorist threat. The directive also fails to lay out a mechanism for coordination among agencies and especially between the FBI and FEMA. For example, when during a terrorist event is the baton to pass from the FBI to FEMA? The National Security Council, charged as the oversight and coordinating body, is now addressing these details.

The presidential directive also is silent on the types of future events that will trigger the deployment of capabilities similar to those fielded at the Olympics. Drew C. Richardson, acting chief of the hazardous materials response unit in the FBI's scientific analysis section and one of the agents who collected the bombing samples, says major "political and sporting events" are likely to be candidates. But it's not a decision to be made by a scientist like himself, he says. "It's a political decision, a threat assessment decision, an intelligence decision." And within the FBI, the National Security Division will give the scientific analysis section its marching orders.

PDD 39 was, in part, issued to enable the U.S. to respond to an event like the nerve gas attack in the Tokyo subway system. And it was, in part, a response to salient deficiencies in the nation's ability to manage a similar event in the U.S.

Nunn, an acknowledged Senate expert on defense issues, is a leading proponent of enhancing the nation's ability to counter a terrorist incident. He is especially concerned about the lack of coordination among federal, state, and local governments. And he frets about the absence of training and equipment for such local first responders as police and firefighters. During several hearings of the Governmental Affairs Permanent Subcommittee on Investigations, Nunn, its ranking minority member, has cited full-scale field and tabletop exercises that have revealed how disjointed responses translate to woefully inadequate defenses to a random terrorist act.

But for discrete events—like the Olympics, political conventions, visits of foreign dignitaries—the nation has shown it is able to marshal its vast resources and, through cooperation and coordination, take necessary precautions to adequately defend against terrorism.

Nunn was given a tour of the SciTech Center and, according to those present, was pleased by what he saw. A Senate staffer familiar with the center but who asks not to be identified says, "The FBI seems to have done a pretty good job of coordinating the various federal assets. Turf battles were resolved before [the games]." And he commends the effort as "a very good prototype for special events."

Security planning for the Olympics was an effort of several years. But only three months before the games were to begin did planners realize that, without agent identification, nothing that followed the use of a chemical or biological warfare agent—not the medical response, hazardous materials cleanup, a law enforcement investigation, or evidence collection—would be meaningful.

That realization set in motion a cascade of events that led to the formation of the SciTech Center—the brainchild of Murch and Richardson. During the Olympics, Richardson served as the center's coordinator and supervised, at any one time, from 50 to 75 chemists and biologists from various federal agencies. Richardson reported to Murch, who acted as science adviser to the FBI Command Center.

The SciTech Center brought together under one roof the best chemical and biological warfare agent analytical capability to be found within the federal government. The Army contributed its Army Materiel Command Treaty Laboratory for chemical warfare agent identification; the Navy provided its Biological Defense Research Program for biological warfare agent verification.

SIGNIFICANCE

The investigation by the SciTech Center was a first step in the investigation of the crime. The center discovered no chemical or biological agents, but the fact that the lab was called on to participate in the investigation suggests the extent to which fears of terrorism have come to influence criminal investigations.

Further, it suggests that the ongoing threat of terrorism has affected the nature and extent of security procedures at public events: major sporting events such as the Super Bowl and the Olympic Games, New Year's Eve on New York City's Times Square, political conventions—any venue at which large numbers of people gather and that would provide a high-profile target for a terrorist bent on making a dramatic statement.

The investigation of the Centennial Olympic Park bombing eventually produced results, but only after the crime was linked with others. On January 16, 1997, two bombs exploded at the Northside Family Planning Clinic in Sandy Springs, a suburb of Atlanta. On February 21, 1997, a bomb exploded on the patio area of a lesbian nightclub in Atlanta; police defused a second bomb outside. Like the bomb at Centennial Olympic Park, each of these bombs was contained in a backpack and nails were used as shrapnel.

Then on January 29, 1998, a bomb exploded at an abortion clinic in Birmingham, Alabama—and investigators obtained their first real break when a witness saw a man drive away in a pickup truck. Investigators eventually traced the truck to Eric Robert Rudolph, a domestic terrorist, anti-government extremist, and member of the loosely knit anti-abortion group the Army of God. After eluding law enforcement officials for five years, he was arrested on March 31, 2003. On April 13, 2005, Rudolph, to avoid the death penalty, pled guilty to the two-year string of bombings.

FURTHER RESOURCES

Books

CSIS Homeland Defense Project. *Combating Chemical, Biological, Radiological, and Nuclear Terrorism: A Comprehensive Strategy: A Report of the Crisis Homeland Defense Project*. Washington, D.C.: Center for Strategic and International Studies, 2001.

Web sites

CNN.com. "Atlanta Olympic Bombing Suspect Arrested." March 31, 2003. <http://www.cnn.com/2003/US/05/31/rudolph.main/> (accessed June 17, 2005).

TKB.org. "Terrorism Knowledge Base: Terrorist Group Profile: Army of God." Available from <http://www.tkb.org/Group.jsp?groupID=28> (accessed on June 17, 2005).

Ecoterrorism

"2000: Acts of Ecoterrorism by Radical Environmental Organizations."

Testimony before Congress

By: Testimony before the Subcommittee on Crime, Committee on the Judiciary, U.S. House of Representatives.

Date: June 9, 1998

Source: Testimony included in "2000: Acts of Ecoterrorism by Radical Environmental Organizations," a report of the hearing before the Subcommittee on Crime of the Committee on the Judiciary, House of Representatives, 105th Congress, Second Session, Serial No. 142.

About the Author: The Committee on the Judiciary, often called "the lawyer for the House of Representatives," has jurisdiction over matters relating to the administration of justice in federal courts, administrative bodies, and law enforcement agencies. It was formed in 1813. The Subcommittee on Crime, now called the Subcommittee on Crime, Terrorism, and Homeland Security, was chaired at the time by Illinois representative Henry Hyde. Bruce Vincent, a citizen of Montana, presented testimony to the Subcommittee on Crime, relaying his personal experience with ecoterrorism.

INTRODUCTION

Since the 1970s, a number of radical environmental groups and numerous individuals acting on their behalf have resorted to violence in the name of protecting animals and the environment. These organizations, including the Animal Liberation Front (ALF), the Earth Liberation Front (ELF), Stop Huntington Animal Cruelty (SHAC), and Green Anarchy, have used arson, bombings, harassment, and vandalism to promote their agenda. They gain support and membership through numerous Web sites and publications such as *No Compromise, Green Anarchy,* and *Bite Back Magazine.*

The targets of ecoterrorism have included car dealerships, fast-food restaurants, logging companies, construction companies, fur farms, housing developments, and corporate- and university- based research facilities that employ animal testing. Estimates are that ecoterrorists have caused more than $100 million in property damage, and from 1996 to 2002, authorities investigated at least 600 criminal acts of ecoterrorism.

In the following prepared statement before the Subcommittee on Crime of the U.S. House of Representatives Committee on the Judiciary in 1998, Montanan Bruce Vincent details the terror he and his family were subjected to at the hands of ecoterrorists.

Emergency personnel walk past an automobile destroyed by ELF members in a pre-dawn arson fire at a California auto dealership in 2003. REUTERS/CORBIS

PRIMARY SOURCE

Dear Committee Members,

Thank you for the opportunity to comment to you on the issue of eco-terrorism. My name is Bruce Vincent. I am from Libby, Montana, a small timber and mining town. I am currently the President of Alliance for America, an umbrella group for several hundred farming, ranching, mining, logging, fishing and private property grassroots groups throughout America. My day job is business manager for our small family company that is involved in the practical application of academic forest management theory, Vincent Logging . . .

I am from an area that does not expect easy solutions to our forest management problems—and is ready, willing, and able to work hard on the difficult choices we feel can and must be made if we are to achieve our vision. I am here today to share with you one of the tragic consequences of this involvement that is as painful as anything I have had to deal with in my life.

I have been, my family has been, subjected to ecoterrorism.

When I first started speaking out about my personal belief that the existing environmental legislative and regulatory regime was in need of reform I was completely unaware of the dark side of the debate I naively thought of as based upon simple disagreement of fact. At first, the consequences were fairly innocuous. I began receiving letters and phone calls from unknown individuals that were extremely upset with my views.

The calls, at first, were nothing more than irrational ramblings of persons who would not give their names but with whom my views disagreed. A few unsigned letters with vicious statements of disapproval were sent that echoed the sentiments of the phone callers. No threats were made—just statements of disagreements with requests for me to "shut up." During the summer of 1989, however, the nature of the calls began to change. The dialogue of the perpetrators began to get more and more vicious and the disagreements and request to have me "shut up" began to be coupled with threats about "getting me" if I didn't "shut up."

In the summer of 1989, the threats became more than just "idle." While working on a job in the Kootenai National Forest our companies [sic] equipment was sabotaged. Dirt was put into the engine of one of our dozers. When the dozer engine failed my Father was, thankfully, operating the dozer on flat ground. Since the hydraulics on this particular 100,000 pound machine are directly connected to the engine and since the hydraulics make the brakes of this machine work, had the failure occurred on the steep ground my Father would have been the jockey of an out of control, 50 ton, deadly, projectile. Further, the brake lines

on one of our dump trucks were cut and the hydraulic lines on one of our excavators were cut. Since laborers worked under the excavator boom and the boom was controlled by its hydraulic system, we were fortunate to discover the imminent failure of the boom before anyone was physically injured. During this same time period, other local logging contractors had equipment sabotaged but, unfortunately, no one was ever caught.

While the approach to the equipment sabotage was exactly as outlined in Dave Foreman's Earth First! book *Ecodefense: A Field Guide to Monkey Wrenching*, the terrorists did not leave a calling card and slipped away. Although no one ever stepped forward to take credit for the actions against our company and other companies attacked that summer, it is worth noting that the newsletter *Wild Rockies Review* issued a call to actions in the inland northwest two summers later. The advertisement for ecoterrorists included a drawing of a burning dozer situated on a map of northwestern Montana with the caption of "Burn That Dozer." Posted on campuses throughout the area, the advertisement's plea went to students looking for summer work and promised room and board for those wanting to spend the summer terrorizing resource workers and managers.

Shortly after our equipment was sabotaged, the phone calls and the viciousness of those calls escalated. I phoned the authorities and asked for help. I was told that unless I could prove that I had been harmed, there was nothing that could be done.

During this same period, a group of extremists in Missoula, Montana, developed a short skit in which I was portrayed as a hunter of animals along with then U.S. Representative Ron Marlenee. At the end of the skit, as performed and videotaped on the steps of the federal building in Missoula, I was shot and killed to protect the animals. The fear that this caused within myself and my family was understandable.

In the fall of 1989 the CBS news magazine, "60 Minutes," called and asked if I would be available for an interview on eco-terrorism. I participated in the show and it aired in the spring of 1990. Shortly after the "60 Minutes" show aired, the producer of the news magazine called to tell me that the CBS studio had received an inordinate number of phone calls from persons who were asking for the address of Earth First!. The producer was concerned that by airing the show CBS may have inadvertently focused unwanted attention on me and my family since the callers seemed to be happy to learn that there was an avenue for expressing the hatred that they felt. The producer's warning proved prophetic.

Soon, the threatening phone calls turned from focusing on harm to be done to myself to harm to be done to my children. Callers threatened, in graphic detail, to do acts of sexual and physical torture to my children before killing them. I was told that I would be forced to watch. One caller played a recorded version of a song written about my children, another was a recording of children screaming in pain and terror for their mother to "help me, help me, help me." Finally, my local sheriff installed phone traps on my phone line—but because of the antiquated system of phones in our area, the tapping was not effective if the call originated outside the lata, or area, of our local phone company. No one was ever trapped or caught.

With the aid of Senator Conrad Burns' office, the FBI and state authorities were called in to the situation and again informed me that until something happened there was little that they could do. It was suggested that I carry a concealed weapon and that I teach my wife and children how to handle and fire a gun. What type of investigation was attempted of those who could be a threat to me and my family was never made clear. I was alerted on occasions where it was thought that I should "be careful" when giving speeches. For a "Cowboy/Logger Day Celebration" in Missoula, Montana, Rep. Marlenee and I were both told that there was reason to be concerned for our safety. Authorities in Sweet Home, Oregon, fitted me with a bulletproof vest for a speech in Oregon and my family was given protection on a tightly secured visit to the area.

Lincoln County, Montana, and other local authorities and the schools worked out a system of removal of my children from schools or home to safe houses when a threat was made. Our home, located in a sparsely populated area twelve miles south of our small town, was given additional security by the local state patrolmen. We purchased a large dog. We put security systems on our home. We went for periods of time where our children were not allowed to answer the phone for fear of them getting a direct link to the lunacy.

The impact of these acts upon my family have been marked. When the threats started my four children were aged three through twelve. We held numerous family meetings to determine whether or not we should continue our involvement in the debate over our future. We sought and got family and pediatric therapy to deal with the stress. The decision of my family has been consistent—faced with either shutting up as requested or speaking out so loudly that we make a highly visible and therefore, hopefully, poor target—we chose to speak out . . .

My family speaks openly and candidly with each other about our situation. We were assured by the authorities with experience that most terrorist threats were just that—threats—and that the odds of anyone actually carrying out one of the threats were minute.

Thankfully, the calls and threats have subsided. I wish I could say the same about the feelings of terror in my family. I believe, I desperately want to believe, that the authorities are right and that the hate-mongers feel satisfied by making simple and idle threats. But, what if some self-anointed Rambo of the ecoterror mind-set acts upon a threat and attacks more than just my logging equipment. It is in this one small word—but—that the power of terrorism is real and palpable in my life. "But" and "what if" are horrifying thoughts to have when you are hundreds or thousands of miles away from home.

As the father of four children I will go to my grave wondering if I have made the right decisions. Should I have let the terrorists win and gone quietly about the business of letting them run roughshod over my civil liberties? That seems unthinkable. . . but I question the wisdom of standing behind my six-year-old daughter, weeping quietly as I took the advice of the authorities and taught her and her siblings how to shoot. I wonder if I have made the right decision in speaking at this hearing. I am supposed to protect my children and exercising my first amendment right, speaking out on the environment—has exposed them to terrorists.

In a free country, those who perpetrate the acts that generate terror should be punishable by law. Please help make that possible . . .

SIGNIFICANCE

Ecoterrorism in the United States had its origins in England, where an organization called Hunt Saboteurs employed sabotage to interrupt fox hunting in the 1960s. In 1972, the organization evolved into the Band of Mercy, which took more militant action to protect animals. That organization, in turn, became the Animal Liberation Front (ALF) in 1976. ALF activities in the United States began in about 1979. ALF's most notorious action occurred in 1987, when it set fire to a University of California at Davis veterinary school laboratory, causing $3.5 million in damage.

After the 1992 bombing of a Michigan State University animal research laboratory, one of the leaders of ALF, Rod Coronado, was convicted for the crime and sent to prison. This was unusual, however, because the ALF, like most ecoterrorist groups, is not a formal organization that one can join; rather, it is a concept, and individuals gain "membership" in ALF simply by carrying out acts of ecoterrorism in the organization's name. Guiding them are Internet publications, including the *ALF Primer* and *Arson Around with Auntie ALF*, which provides readers with instructions for carrying out a "direct action."

While ALF tends to focus more on animal rights, the Earth Liberation Front, founded in 1992 by David Foreman, tends to focus more on the environment,

U.S. attorney Paul Warner holds a news conference September 28, 2004, in Salt Lake City, regarding two alleged ecoterrorism fires. AP/WIDE WORLD PHOTOS

opposing strip mining, mountain top removal mining, logging, and commercial development of public lands. In his testimony before the House of Representatives, Bruce Vincent alluded to Foreman's 1985 book *Ecodefense: A Field Guide to Monkeywrenching*. This is a how-to book for environmental sabotage and includes detailed instructions for such actions as tree spiking (driving metal spikes that will damage logging equipment into trees) and damaging equipment. The group makes available an Internet publication, *Setting Fires with Electrical Timers: An Earth Liberation Front Guide*.

In 1997, ELF made headlines when it burned down a ski resort near Vail, Colorado— at the time the costliest act of ecoterrorism in U.S. history, with damages totaling $12 million. On August 1, 2003, the group eclipsed that record when it burned down a housing development under construction in San Diego, California, causing $50 million in damages. Near the scene of the crime was an ELF banner that read, "If you build it, we will burn it." Three weeks later the group caused $2 million in damages when it firebombed a car dealership in West Covina, California, destroying or damaging Hummers and SUVs.

These organizations have historically caused property damage. However, in 1999, eighty Harvard researchers received letters booby-trapped with razor blades and containing this message: "You have until autumn 2000 to release all your primate captives and get out of the vivisection industry. If you do not heed our warning, your violence will be turned back upon you." Jerry Vlasak, a leader of the Animal Defense League, is reported to have said: "I don't think you'd have to kill too many [people]. I think for five lives, 10 lives, 15 human lives, we could save a million, 2 million, 10 million non-human lives." These and similar statements indicate what authorities see as a possible growing militancy among extremist envronmental groups.

FURTHER RESOURCES

Books

Long, Douglas. *Ecoterrorism (Library in a Book)*. New York: Facts on File, 2004.

McFall, Kathleen. *Ecoterrorism: The Next American Revolution?* High Sierra Books, 2005.

United States. *Acts of Ecoterrorism by Radical Environmental Organizations: Hearing before the Subcommittee on Crime of the Committee on the Judiciary, House of Representatives, Fifth Congress, second session,* 1998. Washington, D.C.: Government Printing Office, 2000.

Web sites

Anti-Defamation League, Law Enforcement Agency Resource Network. *"Ecoterrorism: Extremism in the Animal Rights and Environmentalist Movements."* <http://www.adl.org/Learn/Ext_US/Ecoterrorism.asp> (accessed June 1, 2005).

Missile Hits Home of British Intelligence

Attack on MI6 Snarls Central London

Newspaper article

By: Tom Buerkle

Date: September 22, 2000

Source: Newspaper article entitled "Attack on MI6 Snarls Central London: Missile Hits the Home Of British Intelligence," published in the *International Herald Tribune*, an English-language newspaper published in partnership with major newspapers in several locations around the world.

About the Author: Tom Buerkle was a correspondent for *International Herald Tribune* until April 2001. He is now European Editor of *Institutional Investor.*

INTRODUCTION

Four months after the Good Friday Agreement of April 1998 (a treaty signed by the Irish and British governments) had finally seemed to bring a political settlement to Northern Ireland, a 500-pound car bomb was set off at the height of shopping time on a Saturday afternoon in the small County Tyrone town of Omagh. The explosion on August 15, 1998 killed twenty-nine people (including a woman pregnant with twins) and injuring another 200.

The group that carried out act dubbed itself the "Real IRA", a splinter group created a year earlier after

The car used by suspected ETA separatists (who, like the IRA, are fighting for self-rule) to escape after exploding a car bomb in Madrid in 2002. AP/WIDE WORLD PHOTOS

the Irish republican Army (IRA) had implemented ceasefire. The ceasefire was intended to enable Sinn Fein, a political wing affiliated with the IRA, to partake in negotiations on power-sharing in government. The Real IRA comprised a score of IRA veterans, most from the Irish Republic, that were opposed the peace process.

Compared to the IRA proper, however, this dissident group lacked resources, political strength, and manpower. Rather than operate with a top-down leadership structure as the of IRA always had done, Real IRA members worked in splinter cells, carrying out attacks independent of a conventional command structure.

A series of minor attacks carried out by rebel republicans preceded the Omagh bomb—some of which were perpetrated by a rival dissident group, the Continuity IRA. After Omagh, most of the Real IRA's visible leaders were arrested by British and Irish authorities. MI5, Britain's domestic intelligence service and, in particular, Irish Guardian police worked diligently to infiltrate and track down Real IRA members.

Throughout 1999 and most of 2000, this strategy seemed effective—arrests were made, arms caches seized, and no further attacks followed.

However, on the night of September 20, 2000, a missile fired from somewhere in London hit the southern side of the headquarters of MI6, Britain's Secret Intelligence Service, in Vauxhall on the south bank of the River Thames. Damage to the fortress-like building—it is protected by bomb and bullet-resistant walls—was minimal and no one was hurt.

Suspicions that were initially directed towards Iraqi agents (at that time Britain was involved with the United States in bombing targets in northern Iraq) and Libya (Lybian leader Colonel Gadaffy had recently accused MI6 of planning to assassinate him) were quickly dismissed by police, who instead focused their search on Real IRA operatives.

PRIMARY SOURCE

A small missile smashed into the eighth floor of the headquarters of MI6, Britain's foreign intelligence service, and the London Metropolitan Police warned Thursday of a "genuine threat of terrorism" in London.

The attack, which occurred late Wednesday, was believed to be the work of a dissident wing of the Irish Republican Army. It caused no injuries and only minimal damage to the headquarters, an imposing concrete and green-glass building alongside the Thames a short distance upriver from the Houses of Parliament.

The incident was an embarrassment for an intelligence agency that has sought to keep its activity out of the public eye.

And like an IRA mortar shell that exploded in the garden of No. 10 Downing Street during a cabinet meeting in 1991, the blast demonstrated the vulnerability of major government institutions to terrorist attack.

'It was an audacious attack in a busy part of London,' said Alan Fry, deputy assistant commissioner and head of the Anti-Terrorist Branch of the police force.

'We will be looking to hunt down whoever was involved.'

The incident caused tremendous disruption during the morning rush hour as the police sealed off a wide area around the building to search for evidence.

Rail lines leading into Waterloo Station, which handles tens of thousands of commuters from southwest suburbs as well as Eurostar services from the Continent, were shut down until shortly after midday, while traffic was suspended on the Albert Embankment, the main artery into central London on the south side of the river.

Suspicion quickly turned to the Real IRA, a small group of dissidents who broke away from the Irish Republican Army because of their opposition to the peace process in Northern Ireland.

Like a small bomb blast at Hammersmith Bridge in southwest London in June that was believed to be the work of the group, the attack showed an ability to strike and create disruption without causing indiscriminate damage like the bombing in Omagh, Northern Ireland, in 1998, which killed 29 people and stirred up revulsion against the terrorists.

'This is right out of the Real IRA's playbook and consistent with what they've been doing lately,' said Steven Simon, assistant director at the London-based International Institute for Strategic Studies and a former counterterrorism expert at the National Security Council in the United States.

'They want to express contempt for the process, and they want to express contempt for Britain.'

Although the heavily fortified building withstood the attack easily, the incident raised fresh questions about the wisdom of the agency's move in 1994 to such a central and high-profile building.

Indeed, a bomb attack at the building featured in the opening sequence of the latest James Bond film, 'The World Is Not Enough.'

'As I have warned, we all need to be vigilant,' Mr. Fry said. 'We have a genuine threat of terrorism in London and that is against a number of targets, as we have seen.'

SIGNIFICANCE

The attack on the MI6 headquarters marked the end of an apparent ceasefire by the Real IRA. A further three mainland attacks followed over the next six months, but the very nature of their terrorism pointed to the weakness of the dissident group. As with the bomb fired at the MI6 headquarters, further targets were high profile (such as a car bomb outside the BBC (British Broadcasting Corporation) headquarters in White City), but the operations were low-tech, and disruptions and injuries minimal.

In August 2002, a booby trap at a Territorial Army British Army Reserves camp in County Londonderry killed a maintenance worker. It was the first life claimed by the Real IRA since the Omagh bombing. In October 2002, a message from the Real IRA's members in Portlaoise Prison in the Irish Republic, denounced the organization's leadership as corrupt, saying that it had "forfeited all moral authority," and called for its immediate disbandment.

A darker threat to the Good Friday agreement seemed to come from the reluctance of the IRA itself to disarm (even though a ceasefire remained in place). This was accompanied by a political shift by Northern Ireland's opposition Protestant community towards political parties who had rejected the Good Friday Agreement.

On October 14, 2002, the IRA's refusal to disarm led to the suspension of the Northern Ireland Assembly, the political body created by the Good Friday Agreement. Northern Ireland came back under the direct control of the British Government.

FURTHER RESOURCES

Books

McKittrick, David, David McVeigh. *Making Sense of the Troubles.* London: Penguin, 2003.

Web sites

Rowan, Brian. "Wars and Conflict: Paramilitaries—The Real IRA/32-County Sovereignty Committee." *BBC News.* <http://www.bbc.co.uk/history/war/troubles/factfiles/rira.shtml> (accessed June 27, 2005).

Sinn Fein. <http://sinnfein.ie/> (accessed June 27, 2005).

"How Did Eric Rudolph Survive?"

Newspaper article

By: Patrick Jonsson

Date: June 4, 2003

Source: *Christian Science Monitor.*

About the Author: Patrick Jonsson is a reporter and features writer for the *Christian Science Monitor*, an international daily newspaper.

INTRODUCTION

Eric Rudolph is one of the most infamous domestic terrorists in United States history. He masterminded the bombing at Atlanta's Centennial Olympic Park during the 1996 Summer Olympic Games, along with several other terrorist bombings. Rudolph was born in 1961 in Florida and lived throughout his life in the Southeastern United States. Rudolph briefly served in the U.S. Army, but was discharged for drug use.

Authorities claim that Rudolph was a supporter of the Christian Identity group, a racist extremist group that incorporates fundamentalist Christian ideology.

Christian Identity claims only white Aryans are members of God's chosen race. The group numbers about 50,000 believers in the United States. They closely identify with other neo-Nazi and White Supremacist extremists. Some officials suspect that Rudolph may have had contact with an anti-abortion terrorist group called Army of God. Rudolph denied association with any right-wing extremist groups, asserting that he always acted on his own.

On July 27, 1996, on the ninth day of the Olympic summer games held in Atlanta, Georgia, a bomb was placed near a stage in Centennial Olympic Park, amidst a crowd of thousands of visitors. The detonation of the bomb occurring at 1:20 A.M. killed Alice Hawthorne, an American citizen who had traveled with her daughter to watch the Games. A Turkish cameraman, Melih Uzonyol, died from a heart attack in his rush to record the devastation after the blast. Over one hundred other people were injured.

Despite the tragedy, Olympic officials and athletes decided that the Games should continue as scheduled. In the days following the attack, numerous media outlets named Richard Jewell, a security guard who had first located the bomb and attempted to evacuate the area, as the primary suspect in the bombing. Jewell was eventually cleared of all charges and won numerous libel suits against the media and government outlets on claims that they had tarnished his character.

On October 14, 1998, the Department of Justice announced that a thirty-two-year-old resident of North Carolina, Eric Rudolph, had been charged in the Olympic park attack. Rudolph was also charged with two other Atlanta-area bombings, one at an abortion clinic and a second at a lesbian nightclub. Rudolph also bombed a Birmingham, Alabama, abortion clinic, killing one person and critically injuring another.

On May 31, 2003, Rudolph was captured by a local law enforcement officer in Murphy, North Carolina, a mountain town where the suspect had been hiding out throughout what had become one of the most intensive searches in American history by a task force of numerous federal, state, and local agencies.

On April 8, 2005, in an attempt to avoid the death penalty, Rudolph plead guilty to his role in four separate bombings and was sentenced to four consecutive life sentences. In a statement released by Rudolph following his conviction, he said the purpose of the Olympic park attack was to "confound, anger, and embarrass the Washington government in the eyes of the world for its abominable sanctioning of abortion on demand."

Like Eric Rudolph, David Copeland's right-wing extremism led him to explode a series of nail-bombs in London in 1999.
AP/WIDE WORLD PHOTOS

PRIMARY SOURCE

Murphy, N.C.— He may have prayed for an apocalyptic race war, but in the end Eric Rudolph was just another neighbor—quiet, unobtrusive, slightly strange. For months, maybe years, the fugitive hid near a small valley of brick houses and trailers, leading a life so reclusive he was nearly invisible, though neighbors suggest it wasn't just the chipmunks stealing all that squash from their gardens.

"In retrospect, it doesn't bother me," says Mary Pickens, who lives nearby. "He hadn't ever hurt anyone around here." Since Mr. Rudolph's capture by a rookie cop on Saturday, this mountain town is coming to grips with

the ghost in its midst, wondering how the alleged terrorist went undetected, and whether he was helped by some of their own. Rudolph, painted by some as a modern Daniel Boone, apparently needed them. While evading a dogged five-year manhunt, he clung to the fringes of society in a neat ridge-top camp only 200 yards from two strip malls and the high school, and a half-mile from Murphy's blue-marble courthouse. In winter, he could likely see the town from his camp; in summer, he could have heard the roar of trucks on the Appalachian Highway.

Instead of retreating into the deep mountains or urban anonymity, he stayed in a "comfort zone" at the edge of society. Experts say that choice shows Rudolph's limits as a survivalist, but also a distaste for total isolation and, perhaps, a need to stay close to a network of conspirators. "I don't believe he was a good survivalist," says Kevin Reeve, director of the Tom Brown Tracking School in Asbury, N.J., who's studied the Rudolph case. "The analogy is of a scuba diver who's fine until his oxygen supply runs out, and then he has to come up for air." A real survivalist, says Mr. Reeve, would have taken off up through the Great Smokies.

Instead, Rudolph, with his "Regular Joe" looks, crossed a few ridges from Natahala Gorge, where the FBI found his truck five years ago, and planted himself in Murphy, a community that was changing from a close-knit town of jean-factory and saw-mill workers to a bustling retirement destination for Floridians.

Murphy may have been a logical choice for Rudolph's Butch-and-Sundance hideaway; rivers flush with bass and trout, there are lots of Dumpsters when the fish weren't biting, some sympathetic locals, and enough new residents so he wouldn't stick out as long as he stayed neat and nonchalant. His friendliness may have helped. Reports suggest that people spotted him, but "wanted" posters apparently didn't spring to mind.

Rudolph also might have known how politics ran in this mountain town. Some here may have shared his sentiments, at least enough to turn the other way. Even after his capture, the story is greeted as half scandal, half legend. At the Daily Grind coffee shop, women served up "Captured Cappuccinos" this weekend, and a sign outside town read "Pray for Eric Rudolph." After his arrest, Rudolph signed autographs of his "wanted" posters for sheriff's deputies.

"I'd like to say he was or he wasn't [helped]," says Officer Jeff Postell, the 21-year-old former Wal-Mart security guard who caught Rudolph behind the Save-A-Lot market early Saturday. "But I don't know."

The truth probably lies somewhere in between. Rudolph had skills, strong beliefs, and perhaps a small cadre of friends. At his camp he left behind a cache of pilfered bananas, onions, and tomatoes, and a pile of firewood. Small footpaths led into the mountains and to his secondary camp, what survivalists call the "castle keep," a refuge should the full-scale search resume.

With or without aid, he may have taken advantage of sleepy rhythms in a town "used to routines," says Wanda Stalcup, director of the Cherokee County Museum. While plenty of campers come through, she says, few would have trudged over the Appalachian Highway on a cowpath and climbed the hill to Rudolph's camp. Most likely, experts surmise, the former carpenter slept during the day and scavenged at night. "He became a nocturnal being," says Reeve.

Above all, he was a local boy who knew how to act in a changing mountain culture, where Toyota-driving kayakers live next to bearded mountain men and trading posts. Many

thought he was long gone. "I might've seen him a hundred times. I wouldn't know him from Adam," says Charles Franklin, a life-long valley resident mowing a park near Rudolph's camp on Fires Creek.

Mr. Franklin, like many locals, has scant sympathy for Rudolph's alleged misdeeds, which include bombing Centennial Park, a gay nightclub, and an abortion clinic, killing two and injuring over 100.

Rudolph was aligned with the radical Christian Identity movement, which posits that Jews and blacks are "polluting" America. But others trace his anger to his father's death and the government's failure to approve a cancer drug that Rudolph reportedly believes could have saved him.

People here knew Rudolph in his younger days as a quiet, well-mannered young man who lived with his mom, two brothers, and sister near Natahala Gorge. Those who hired him as a carpenter recall seeing him study the Bible during breaks, and some say he volunteered at a senior citizens' home on weekends. He also dabbled in drinking, with a twist: Caught for drunk driving in his 20s, he returned the next day to thank the officer who arrested him. But while he might have gleaned survival skills from fellow Christian Identity adherents in the mountains, some here insist he shared little with original settlers and the Indian tribes that found bounty in these temperate crags and valleys.

"Everybody's making him out to be some kind of Daniel Boone, but all he did was grow some dope up in the mountains," says a bearded hunter whittling cedar backscratchers on the stoop of Mason's Bait & Tackle. "People blame the FBI, which they say couldn't track a gut-shot buffalo through six feet of snow."

Law enforcement experts say the FBI deserves credit for flooding the media with pictures and publicizing Rudolph's alleged misdeeds. Still, the FBI itself may have been a reason why some here who nurse an old suspicion of the federal government looked the other way—even with a $1 million reward. "People here don't believe in killing, but there's lots of people who believe he may not have done it," says Harold Helton, owner of H&H Sports in Murphy.

Those who study how extremist movements integrate themselves into communities say Cherokee County, along with northern Idaho, is one of a few places in the country where a fugitive can find sympathy in eluding the long arm of Washington.

In fact, a few months before Rudolph was captured, police found militia leader Steve Anderson, former host of shortwave radio show "The Militia Hour," holed up in Cherokee County, three years after he allegedly shot at a Kentucky sheriff's deputy.

"He and Eric Rudolph were, in essence, neighbors," says Mark Pitcavage, national director of Fact Finding for the Anti-Defamation League. "It's an example of committed extremists being able to stay in western North Carolina for quite a long time, clearly with the help of somebody."

But the allure of living on the outskirts of society, albeit a society he rejected, may have worn thin. Many suggest that, after five years in the woods, Rudolph got lonely and basically gave himself up. True survivalism, total severance from society, might, at any rate, have eluded a man dogged by his past. "Being a fugitive would certainly cramp your style," says Reeve.

SIGNIFICANCE

The arrest of Eric Rudolph as the perpetrator behind the 1996 Olympic Park bombing reaffirmed for the people of the United States the danger posed by domestic terrorists. The fact that he was able to

evade capture for more than five years despite being placed on the FBI's Ten Most Wanted list and remaining in the United States, has led many to assume as this article suggests, that he may have hid with the aid of friends and supporters—despite the $1 million award which was promised to anyone who assisted in Rudolph's capture.

The article further exposes the relative ease with which a domestic terrorist can slip undiscovered into society and disappear for long periods of time in a way similar to how the Unabomber, Ted Kaczynski, succeeded in evading authorities for nearly two decades, while continuing to carry out terrorist attacks.

On April 8, 2005, the U.S. Justice department announced that Rudolph had agreed to a deal in which he would avoid a possible death sentence. Rudolph agreed to plead guilty to all charges against him. He also disclosed the location of his hidden weapons caches containing 250 pounds of dynamite, an already assembled bomb, detonators, bomb making materials, and guns. In July 2005, he was sentenced to life without the possibility of parole.

FURTHER RESOURCES

Books

Farrington, Jay. *Domestic Terrorism*. Philadelphia, Pennsylvania: Xlibris Corporation, 2001.

Schuster, Henry and Stone, Charles. *Hunting Eric Rudolph*. New York: Berkley, 2005.

Web sites

USA Today. Morrison, Tom. "Eric Rudolph tells how he eluded FBI." July 5, 2005. <http://www.usatoday. com/news/nation/2005-07-05-rudolph-cover-parttwo_x. htm?csp=34> (accessed July 10, 2905).

United States Department of Justice. "Eric Rudolph Charged in Centennial Park Bombing." October 14, 1998. <http://www.usdoj.gov/opa/pr/1998/October/477crm. htm> (accessed July 7, 2005).

Eric Rudolph, on June 22, 2004, as he is led into a federal courthouse for a trial in Huntsville, Alabama. AP/WIDE WORLD PHOTOS

"Hamas Rising From the Ashes"

Newspaper article

By: The Economist

Date: November 1, 2003

Source: The *Economist*.

A group of suicide bombers, with fake dynamite strapped around their chests, parade during an anti-Israel demonstration organized by Hamas. AP/WIDE WORLD PHOTOS

About the Author: The *Economist* is a weekly magazine based in London featuring world news and analysis. By tradition, articles written by staff writers and editors appear in the *Economist* with editorial backing, but without individual author attribution.

INTRODUCTION

Between 1987 and 1993, Palestinians protested Israeli occupation of the West Bank and Gaza through violence and civil unrest, a series of actions called the *Intifada*, or popular uprising. The Intifada ended in September 1993 as Palestinian leader Yasir Arafat and Israeli Prime Minister Yitzhak Rabin shook hands on the White House lawn and promised to bring an end to the conflict between Palestinians and Israelis by signing the Oslo Agreement. The Intifada and the failure of the agreement not only left the region in continued unrest, but also created conflict within Palestinian leadership.

The Intifada began as a spontaneous demonstration by rock throwing youths but later, under the leadership of groups like Hamas and Islamic Jihad, became increasingly more violent. Hamas, which means zeal, gained its popular support through its well-funded social actions, not just the violent actions against Israel during the Intifada. Grown out of the Muslim Brotherhood, Hamas sponsored the building of schools and hospitals, and ran other charitable and religious organizations. Through this work, Hamas established itself in Palestinian society.

During the Intifada, Yasir Arafat and other leaders of the Palestinian Liberation Organization (PLO) lived in exile. Israel wanted to give Palestinians an alternative to supporting the PLO and as a result, permitted Islamic groups to take control of civil institutions such as schools and health clinics. This allowed Islamic fundamentalism, promoted by the charity work of Hamas, to spread throughout the region. The PLO, a largely secular organization, tried to remotely control the extremist groups during the Intifada and eventually, with the signing of the Oslo Agreement in 1993, brought the unrest to a pause. Although the violence of the Intifada led by local extremists brought the Israelis to the negotiating table, the PLO acquired their political power from its success.

At its beginning, Palestinians widely supported the Oslo Agreement as it held the hope for an end to Israeli occupation of Gaza and the West Bank and the establishment of an open and democratic system of self-government. Support for violent protests declined sharply. As a condition of the agreement, exiled PLO leaders returned and established the Palestinian Authority (PA). In 1996, after the partial Israeli withdrawal from occupied Palestinian territory, national elections established the Palestinian Authority as a political power.

By 2000, however, the peace process initiated by the Oslo Agreement had stalled and economic and living conditions for the Palestinians continued to deteriorate. Although the agreement had held the promise to end the occupation of Gaza and the West Bank, Jewish settlements continued to expand and Palestinians were disappointed by the status of Palestinian democracy due to poor performance and charges of corruption. This perceived failure on the part of the Palestinian Authority once again created a vacuum of power that members of groups like Hamas sought to fill. The second Intifada, led by Hamas and Islamic Jihad, began and marked not only the struggle for independence from Israel, but also marked the struggles between the Palestinian Authority and Hamas.

PRIMARY SOURCE

It looks like the photograph of a bombed-out city in the Second World War. A 200-yard-wide swathe of gouged mud, crushed stone, and blasted skeletons of houses now defines the Gaza Strip's southern border with Egypt. It was once Block L of the Yebna refugee camp in the town of Rafah. Last month, the Israeli army destroyed 150 homes there to unearth arms-smuggling tunnels. Palestinians say it was the final act to "cleanse" them from an area that has long been one of the hottest front lines in their long war with Israel.

It stirs the most ominous of memories. "In 1948, the Israelis transferred us to the West Bank and Gaza. Now they're transferring us to places within the West Bank and Gaza," shrugs a Palestinian mother of seven whose house is now a pile of pulverised concrete covered by a carpet.

She is one of nearly 2,000 Palestinians displaced by this and two other recent Israeli incursions into Rafah. For relief the homeless turn mainly to two organisations. One is the United Nations Relief and Works Agency (UNRWA), which is responsible for Palestinian refugees. The other is the al-Salah Islamic Society, whose funds were frozen by the Palestinian Authority (PA) in August for its alleged links with the Islamist Hamas movement.

UNRWA is desperately seeking rented accommodation for the displaced in a town that already has 5,000 homeless due to earlier Israeli incursions, and where secure land on which to house them is dwindling. Al-Salah volunteers are busy doling out cash, blankets, and food. The PA, by contrast, is palpable by its absence. When its housing minister, Abdel Rahman Hamad, visited Rafah last week, he was confronted by locals outraged by the PA's inability to provide the barest of services.

Al-Salah admits that the freeze on funds has hindered its work. Employees go without salaries and recipients cannot cash cheques. But the charity struggles on. Its headquarters in Rafah is crammed with blankets, plastic kitchen utensils and school uniforms, all awaiting distribution.

How does al-Salah pay for all this stuff? "The banks give us credit. They know we can account for every penny we spend," says Nafiz Mansour, its director. He assumes the PA will eventually unfreeze the funds under popular pressure. He is probably right, for al-Salah's aid and activism are deeply appreciated by people who have rarely felt so abandoned.

There are other reasons, aside from welfare, for the Islamists' rising popularity in Gaza. On October 24th two fighters from Hamas and Islamic Jihad, the Palestinians' two biggest Islamist movements, infiltrated the Jewish settlement of Netzarim, in the Gaza Strip, killing three soldiers, two of them women. The settlement is home to 60 families and is a base for an army battalion. Its location south of Gaza City enables Israel to slice the strip in two, severing Palestinians in places like Rafah from their main hospitals, universities and businesses in Gaza City. In reprisal for the attack on Netzarim, the Israeli army demolished three unfinished 13-storey residential towers from which it said Palestinians had been firing on the settlement. The PA said that, once built, the apartments would have housed 5,000 Palestinians.

In September, Israel tried killing Hamas's leader, Sheikh Ahmad Yassin, aware of the movement's growing power in Gaza. He shrugs off talk that the attack on Netzarim augurs a new Islamist alliance ready to fill the PA's leadership vacuum. "We're not interested in ending the PA," he says.

"We're interested in ending the [Israeli] occupation." To this end, he justifies suicide bombings inside Israel as necessary responses to "Israel's crimes against our civilians" in the West Bank and Gaza.

Even so, he says he is ready to discuss another Palestinian ceasefire with Ahmed Qurei, the PA's new prime minister. "We're waiting to hear proposals from Abu Alaa [Mr Qurei's nom de guerre]," says the sheikh. "We observed a truce in summer and took some steps on the ground. But Israel refused to reciprocate. If it is in the Palestinian interest to have a ceasefire, we will have one. If not, we won't."

In practice, say other Hamas men, they won't sign another ceasefire unless Israel ends its policy of assassinating Islamist leaders, stops its incursions into the PA's areas, stops demolishing Palestinian homes and stops building new barriers cum borders. In these respects, Hamas is in tune with most Palestinians.

SIGNIFICANCE

The goals of the Palestinian Authority (PA) and Hamas are not in contention. Both groups desire the complete withdrawal of Israeli forces from the occupied territories in Gaza and the West Bank. The Palestinian Authority seeks a negotiated settlement that would allow them to remain in power. Hamas, on the other hand, seeks the destruction of Israel and the establishment of an Islamic state. As the popularity of the Palestinian Authority declines, the possibility for a negotiated settlement decreases. Hamas and its charitable entities continue to provide financial and religious support. Therefore, many Palestinians hold greater faith in Hamas than in the Palestinian Authority.

This rise in support for Hamas has greatly affected the PA. As the internationally recognized authority in Palestine, the Palestinian Authority is held responsible for managing the violence. Its ability to do so is impeded when it is viewed as ineffective by international leaders, due to its failure to secure the promises of independence and effective governance awarded by the Oslo Agreement. Hamas' popularity has also affected the PA's ability to negotiate internationally.

As the question of authority in Palestine continues to go unanswered, the Palestinian people are left in the balance and look to those who provide for their basic needs. Although many seek a peaceful solution to the conflict with Israel, the legacy of the first Intifada, the Palestinian Authority's perceived failures, and the continuing deterioration of living conditions create conflict for the Palestinian people and its leadership.

FURTHER RESOURCES

Periodicals

Shikaki, Khalil. "Palestinians Divided." *Foreign Affairs.* (2002): January/February.

Web sites

BBC News. Westcott, Katherine. "Who Are Hamas?" October 19, 2000. <http://news.bbc.co.uk/1/hi/world/middle_east/978626.stm> (accessed July 8, 2005).

NPR. Shuster, Mike. "The Mideast: A Century of Conflict Part 6: From the First Intifada to the Oslo Peace Agreement." October 7, 2002. <http://www.npr.org/news/specials/mideast/history/history6.html> (accessed July 9, 2005).

Members of an EPA and U. S. Coast Guard cleanup crew prepare to enter an office building where two people contracted anthrax through a letter. AP/WIDE WORLD PHOTOS

"Anthrax Detection"

Anthrax Contaminated Letters Sent to U.S. Capitol

Government document

By: The United States Government Accountability Office

Date: April 5, 2005

Source: "Anthrax Detection: Agencies Need to Validate Sampling Activities in Order to Increase Confidence in Negative Results," as published by the United States Government Accountability Office.

About the Author: The United States Government Accountability Office is the investigative arm of congress that examines government efficiency by evaluating federal programs, auditing federal expenditures, and issuing legal opinions.

INTRODUCTION

Shortly after the terrorists attacks of September 11, 2001, anthrax laced letters began appearing in the mailboxes of some U.S. senators, major U.S. news media personnel, and a few other individuals (who initially appeared as random receivers). At first, U.S. government and media reports asserted that these letters were connected with the al-Qaeda attacks on the United States, but the investigation of the anthrax source and initial mail drop of the letters substantiated the claim that the contaminated mail originated within the United States and from U.S. laboratories.

Anthrax is a bacterial disease that usually is transmitted from plant eating animals, and human infections in the United States are rare. Most commonly these infections occur from occupational hazards such as working in laboratories where the bacteria is created or handling infection-prone animals. Furthermore, a person can acquire anthrax by eating undercooked contaminated meat, having the bacteria enter the body through an open wound, or by inhaling airborne spores. Inhaling the spores is the most efficient way for anthrax to spread (especially among humans) because the spores can travel through the air, land on papers, and linger for a significant amount of time. While anthrax can be treated, victims can die if medical treatment is not sought in a timely manner. Anthrax is considered a weaponizable biological agent because of its airborne qualities and lethal implications.

The United States had considered the threat of anthrax long before the October 2001 letters that targeted media outlets and shut down the Hart Senate building in Washington, D.C. One Federal Bureau of Investigations (FBI) report states that in 2000, it dealt with 250 suspected cases of weapons of mass destruction and biological weapons, with about 200 of those cases concerning anthrax. These instances were deemed hoaxes, but the FBI initiated response programs to handle possible future anthrax threats.

Even though federal agencies had developed new strategic plans to deal with terrorism threats from biological agents, not all of the new counterterrorism measures had been put into place. The first anthrax letters began appearing a few weeks after the September 11 attacks. It was later disclosed that the letters were mailed on September 11. The first victims of anthrax were magazine publishers and postal workers, but this quickly changed when employees of the television network NBC New York tested positive for the bacteria. Then on October 15, 2001, letters sent to Senate majority leader Tom Daschle tested positive for anthrax, and on October 17, the U.S. capitol shut down (particularly the Hart Senate building) when thirty-one employees test positive. Most of the employees worked for Daschle. A similar letter was found addressed to Senator Patrick Leahy.

A federal investigation of the anthrax letter attacks immediately commenced. President George W. Bush labeled the anthrax letters as acts of terrorism. Initial reports connected the attacks to Bin Laden's al-Qaeda terrorist network, but FBI investigators quickly disclosed that al-Qaeda was most likely not responsible for the letters.

The 2001 anthrax letter attacks killed five people.

PRIMARY SOURCE

ANTHRAX DETECTION: AGENCIES NEED TO VALIDATE SAMPLING ACTIVITIES IN ORDER TO INCREASE CONFIDENCE IN NEGATIVE RESULTS

The first activity involved agencies' developing a sampling strategy, which included deciding how many samples to collect, where to collect them from, and what collection methods to use. The agencies primarily used a targeted strategy: They collected samples from specific areas considered more likely to be contaminated, based on judgments. Such judgments can be effective in some situations, for example, in determining (1) the source of contamination in a disease outbreak investigation or (2) whether a facility is contaminated when information on the source of potential contamination is definitive. However, in the case of a negative finding, when the source of potential contamination is not definitive, the basic question—Is this building contaminated?—will remain unanswered.

The targeted strategy the agencies used was reflected in their site-specific sampling activities. Sample sizes varied by facility and circumstances, increased over time, and excluded probability sampling. In the beginning, in each USPS facility, 23 samples were to be collected from specific areas relating to mail processing and up to 20 additional "discretionary" samples were to be collected, depending on the type and size of the facility. Later, USPS increased the number of samples required to a minimum of 55, with up to 10 additional discretionary samples for larger facilities. Consequently, the number of samples collected varied by facility, from a low of 4 to a high of 148. CDC's [Centers for Disease Control and Prevention] and

EPA's [Environmental Protection Agency] site-specific strategies were primarily discretionary. The number of samples CDC collected varied by facility, ranging from a low of 4 to a high of 202. The number of samples EPA collected ranged from a low of 4 to a high of 71.

According to CDC, a targeted sampling strategy may be effective in detecting contamination in a facility when sufficient site-specific information exists to narrow down the locations in which the release and contamination are most likely to have occurred. CDC's assumptions for this strategy are that at the outset, (1) a scenario where all locations have an equal chance of being contaminated is generally the exception rather than the rule; (2) information collected about the event, combined with technical judgment about exposure pathways, can be used to identify locations where contamination is most likely to be found; (3) contamination levels of the highest public health concern can usually be detected using a variety of available methods, despite their limitations; and (4) there is important public health value in quickly identifying contaminated locations. However, these assumptions may not always apply. For example, there may be limitations in the available information that restrict the ability to reliably identify target locations. The method of contamination spread could conceivably be via a mechanism where there is an equal chance of any area being contaminated. Lastly, all results may be negative, which will lead to a requirement for additional testing, as was the case in Wallingford. This, in turn, will result in the loss of the critical time needed for public health intervention.

CDC and USPS officials said that they used a targeted strategy for several reasons, including limitations on how many samples could be collected and analyzed. They also said that in 2001 they lacked the data necessary to develop an initial sampling strategy that incorporated probability sampling. We disagree with this interpretation. Probability sampling is statistically based and does not depend solely on empirical criteria regarding the details of possible contamination.

We consider probability sampling to be a viable approach that would address not only the immediate public health needs but also the wider public health protection, infrastructure cleanup, and general environmental contamination issues. We recognize that in a major incident, the number of samples that may need to be collected and analyzed may challenge available laboratory resources. Accordingly, there is a need to develop innovative approaches to use sampling methods that can achieve wide-area coverage with a minimal number of individual samples to be analyzed. For example, high-efficiency particulate air (HEPA) vacuum techniques, in combination with other methods, appear to be one such approach that could achieve this. In addition, because of limited laboratory capacity, samples may need to be stored after collection for subsequent analysis, on a prioritized basis.

The situation in 2001 was unique, and the agencies were not fully prepared to deal with environmental contamination. In the future, if the agencies decide to use a targeted rather than a probability sampling strategy, they must recognize that they could lose a number of days if their targeted sampling produces negative test results. In this case, additional samples would need to be collected and analyzed, resulting in critical time, for public health interventions, being lost. This was so at the Wallingford postal facility in the fall of 2001, when about 3 weeks elapsed between the time the first sampling took place and the results of the fourth testing, which revealed positive results. Furthermore, about 5 months elapsed between the time of the first sampling event and the time anthrax was found in the Wallingford facility's high-bay area.

Therefore, in the future, strategies that include probability sampling need to be developed in order to provide statistical confidence in negative results. Further, even if information on all the performance characteristics of methods is not yet available, a probability sampling strategy could be developed from assumptions about the efficiency of some of the methods. And even if precise data are not available, a conservative, approximate number could be used for developing a sampling strategy. This would enable agencies and the public to have greater confidence in negative test results than was associated with the sampling strategy used in 2001.

SIGNIFICANCE

In the aftermath of the anthrax letter attacks, the U.S. government strengthened security measures at all U.S. post offices. A new screening program was implemented for mail sent to Washington, D.C. These were just some of the precautions that legislators put into effect to possibly prevent future anthrax attacks using the postal system.

An elderly woman in Connecticut and a magazine employee in Florida both received anthrax letters because their mail was cross-contaminated during sorting and transport. These letters were processed through the same postal machines, held in the same barrels, and possibly transported in the same postal bags as the anthrax-laced letters sent to Washington, D.C. and New York.

There were limited copy-cat crimes on the heels of the anthrax letter attacks. However, none of the subsequent letters declaring that they contained biological

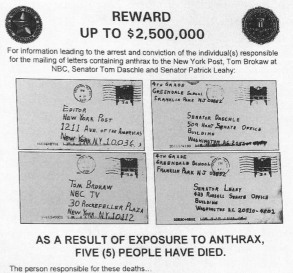

Flyer offering a reward for information leading to the arrest of those responsible for mailing anthrax-tainted letters in 2001. AP/WIDE WORLD PHOTOS

agents tested positive for such agents. When Senator Daschle received a second letter months after the initial attack, investigators quickly deemed it a hoax when tests confirmed the powdery substance in it to be talcum powder.

By mid-2005, the sender of the anthrax letters had not yet been identified, but U.S. government and law enforcement agencies continued to investigate the matter.

FURTHER RESOURCES

Books

Cole, Leonard A. *The Anthrax Letters: A Medical Detective Story*. Washington, D.C.: National Academy of Sciences, 2003.

Web sites

CNN.com. "Leahy letter 'as lethal' as one sent to Daschle." <http://archives.cnn.com/2001/HEALTH/conditions/11/20/senate.anthrax> (accessed July 6, 2005).

9 Counterterrorism

Introduction to Counterterrorism

Counterterrorism efforts, those acts or policies designed to prevent terrorism or immediately defeat its intended impact, range from the routine inspection of shoes at airports to sweeping legislation that touches at the very heart of cherished freedoms practiced in democratic states; from commando raids that free hostages, to the development of technologies designed to protect evolving uses of cyberspace. The purpose of counterterrorism efforts may be well defined and highly specific, such as with laws designed to restrict certain persons from possessing select biological agents or toxins. In contrast, some counterterrorism efforts, such as the use of profiling, are often argued to be so broad as to be both intrusive and ineffective.

A key challenge for any democratic state is how to effectively respond to terrorism in ways that conform to democratic principles. In many parts of the world, an alleged illegality in response to terrorism may be used to philosophically justify both the original terrorist act and to incite further acts.

The development of counterterrorism measures and policies forces societies to make difficult judgments about how to define terrorism. Moreover, the framing of those definitions forces societies to judge the intentions and motives of groups that often hold diverse and conflicting opinions.

For example, under provisions of the U.S. PATRIOT Act of 2001, the U.S. Secretary of State, in consultation with the Attorney General of the United States, may designate certain terrorist organizations on a terrorist exclusion list (TEL). Organizations listed on the TEL could be prevented from entering the country, and in certain circumstances, can be deported. Although the terms used in articulating criteria for including groups may also engender controversy, before the Secretary of State places an organization on the TEL, he or she must find that its members commit or incite terrorist activity, gather information on potential targets for terrorist activity, or provide material support to further terrorist activity. Under the terms of the statute, "terrorist activity means all unlawful activity that involves hijacking or sabotage of an aircraft, vessel, or vehicle; hostage-taking; a violent attack on a person protected under international law; assassination; or the use of firearms, biological or chemical agents, nuclear devices, or other weapons to endanger individuals or damage property, for purposes other than mere personal gain."

Above the horror of the actual acts of brutal terrorism that claim the lives of innocent people, the political and philosophical analysis of cause and motive—key elements in developing effective counterterrorism strategies—is usually a complex undertaking.

Although a myriad of government intelligence, security, and law enforcement agencies have counterterrorism responsibilities, there are only four common principles to stated U.S. counterterrorism policy (similar principles are articulated by other governments).

1. The government makes no concessions to, or agreements with, terrorists;
2. Terrorists must be brought to justice for their crimes;
3. States that sponsor terrorists and terrorism must be isolated and pressured so as to force a change of behavior;
4. The counterterrorism capabilities of countries allied with the United States, and those that require assistance in fighting terrorism, must be bolstered.

The editors leave to the judgment of the reader how well these principles are applied in each situation. The primary sources included in this chapter do demonstrate that the implementation of such policies are applied with varying degrees of vigor and are themselves, not wholly without controversy.

Burning of the Frigate *Philadelphia*

Barbary Pirates

Engraving

By: F. Kearney

Date: 1808

Source: *Burning of the Frigate Philadelphia in the Harbor of Tripoli*, February 16, 1804. The engraving was done in 1808 by F. Kearney.

About the Artist: F. Kearney was an artist who worked in the early 1800s.

INTRODUCTION

The first war fought by an independent United States was a war against terrorism, the Tripolitan War against pirates on the Barbary Coast of North Africa from 1801 to 1805.

From the fifteenth through the early nineteenth centuries, pirates from the Muslim kingdoms of Tripoli, Tunis, Morocco, and Algiers increased their kingdom's wealth and terrorized Europe by seizing merchant ships and their crews on the Mediterranean Sea and holding them for ransom. During the eighteenth century, a French Roman Catholic religious order called the Mathurins existed for the sole purpose of raising funds to ransom captives from Barbary pirates.

Before U.S. independence, American vessels in the Mediterranean received some measure of protection from the British navy. The British, in fact, could have crushed the Barbary pirates, but instead chose to buy protection while allowing the pirates to remain as a threat to Britain's maritime rivals. With independence in 1783, however, the United States became responsible for protecting its own merchant vessels, and in 1784, Congress appropriated $80,000 for tribute to the Barbary Coast states.

Thomas Jefferson, however, was a vocal opponent of appeasement. In 1785, Algerian pirates captured two American vessels and demanded tribute of $60,000. Jefferson, at the time U.S. ambassador to France, urged instead the formation of an international naval coalition to subdue the Barbary States, but his efforts were unsuccessful. Abroad, England and France found payment of tribute less expensive than military action. At home, the fledgling United States had no desire to go to war and instead signed a treaty with Morocco in 1786 guaranteeing annual payments. By 1797, similar treaties with the other Barbary kingdoms were in place.

Meanwhile, in 1795, the United States had paid nearly a million dollars in cash, supplies, and a ship to ransom 115 U.S. sailors from Algiers.

Matters took a new turn in 1801, when Jefferson became president. That year, the pasha of Tripoli reneged on its treaty with the United States, demanding an immediate large payment and annual tribute of $25,000. When Jefferson refused, Tripoli declared war on the United States on May 14, 1801. In response, Jefferson dispatched to the region a squadron of warships under the leadership of Commander Edward Preble, launching a four-year war, the Tripolitan War, with the Barbary Coast.

Jefferson met with considerable criticism at home for resorting to warfare. This criticism grew louder in 1803, when Tripoli seized the frigate *Philadelphia* and her crew. In February 1804, however, Lieutenant Stephen Decatur and a party of U.S. sailors managed to board the *Philadelphia* in Tripoli's harbor and, rather than allowing Tripoli to keep the vessel, destroyed it.

PRIMARY SOURCE

BURNING OF THE FRIGATE *PHILADELPHIA*
See primary source image.

SIGNIFICANCE

Commander Preble took aggressive action. He formed a naval blockade of the Barbary Coast, quickly subdued Morocco, and launched five bombardments of Tripoli. Hostilities continued until 1805, when a naval expedition under the command of Commodore John Rogers and a land force led by Captain William Eaton threatened to invade Tripoli and replace the pasha with his brother. Faced with overwhelming U.S. military power, Tripoli signed a treaty on June 4, 1805, requiring no further payment of tribute.

The United States, however, continued to pay tribute to Algiers until the outbreak of the War of 1812, when Algiers declared war on the United States and demanded an increase in its annual tribute. Again the United States responded with military force. A naval expedition led by Decatur, now a captain, and Commodore William Bainbridge was launched on May 10, 1815. After American forces quickly seized two Algerian ships, Algiers capitulated and signed a treaty on June 30 requiring no further tribute.

American vessels in the Mediterranean faced no further threats from the Barbary kingdoms. Several European nations continued to pay tribute until the 1830s.

PRIMARY SOURCE

Burning of the Frigate *Philadelphia* Photograph of the engraving *Burning of the Frigate Philadelphia in the Harbor of Tripoli, February 16, 1804,* by F. Kearney. © NEW YORK HISTORICAL SOCIETY, NEW YORK/BRIDGEMAN ART LIBRARY

Tripoli, the site of the first American overseas military action, was immortalized in U.S. military history in the opening line of the Marine hymn: "From the halls of Montezuma to the shores of Tripoli." One of the ships that led the bombardment of Tripoli, the USS *Constitution*, popularly known as "Old Ironsides," went on to further distinction in the War of 1812.

FURTHER RESOURCES

Books

Wheelan, Joseph. *Jefferson's War: America's First War on Terror 1801–1805.* New York: Carroll and Graf, 2003.

Web sites

Library of Congress: American Memory. The Thomas Jefferson Papers. "America and the Barbary Pirates: An International Battle against an Unconventional Foe."

<http://memory.loc.gov/ammem/collections/jefferson_papers/mtjprece.html> (accessed May 16, 2005).

Audio and Visual Media

Robbins, Jerry. *Old Ironsides and the Barbary Pirates.* Colonial Radio Theatre on the Air, 1996 (audiocassette).

Smith Act of 1940

Legislation

By: Howard W. Smith

Date: 1940

Source: 18 U.S. Code § 2385 (2000) Advocating Overthrow of Government.

About the Author: The Alien Registration Act of 1940, usually called the Smith Act after its author, Representative Howard W. Smith of Virginia, is the chief federal sedition law. The legislation makes it unlawful to conspire to advocate the violent overthrow of the government and to organize a group to do so. Smith, a conservative Democrat from Virginia, spent most of his political career opposing foreign radicals, labor unions, civil rights for African Americans, and most domestic spending. After heading the powerful House Rules Committee, Smith lost a reelection bid in 1966. He died in 1976.

INTRODUCTION

On the eve of World War II, with strong anti-foreign sentiment sweeping the country, the United States Congress passed the Smith Act in 1940. While alleged Nazi sympathizers were among the first charged under the law in 1943, the Smith Act was most often used to target communists. For several years the wartime alliance between the U.S. and Soviet Union protected American communists, but by 1948 Russian-American relations deteriorated when the Cold War began.

In 1948, the Truman Administration decided to shut down the Communist Party of the U.S.A. (CPUSA). The attorney general secured an indictment on July 20, 1948 charging the eleven members of the party's National Board with violation of the Smith Act. The CPUSA responded to this political prosecution with a political defense. It mounted a massive propaganda campaign, designed to mobilize the public behind a demand that the government drop the charges. When few people came to the defense of the communists, the CPUSA carried their struggle into the courtroom in an effort to criticize the suppression of dissent by American society and government.

Meanwhile, the Truman administration presented an equally political case, largely ignoring the defendants in an attempt to put the CPUSA on trial. The prosecution characterized the CPUSA as a disloyal, dangerous, and dishonest organization, whose disclaimers of intent to overthrow the government by violence could not be believed.

The communists were convicted on October 14, 1949. Influenced by the Cold War atmosphere, appellate courts confirmed the constitutionality of the Smith Act. The U.S. Supreme Court upheld the conviction on June 4, 1951, with the dissenting justices declaring the violence is rarely stopped by denying civil liberties to those advocating force. Following the Supreme Court decision, lower-level communist officers, editors,

and teachers were indicted in an effort to eradicate communism. As a result, the CPUSA essentially ended.

PRIMARY SOURCE

. . . Whoever knowingly or willfully advocates, abets, advises, or teaches the duty, necessity, desirability, or propriety of overthrowing or destroying the government of the United States or the government of any State, Territory, District, or Possession thereof, or the government of any political subdivision therein, by force or violence, or by the assassination of any officer of any such government; or

Whoever, with intent to cause the overthrow or destruction of any such government, prints, publishes, edits, issues, circulates, sells, distributes, or publicly displays any written or printed matter advocating, advising, or teaching the duty, necessity, desirability, or propriety of overthrowing or destroying any government in the United States by force or violence, or attempts to do so; or

Whoever organizes or helps or attempts to organize any society group, or assembly of persons who teach, advocate, or encourage the overthrow or destruction of any such government by force or violence; or becomes or is a member of, or affiliates with, any such society, group, or assembly of persons, knowing the purposes thereof—

Shall be fined under this title or imprisoned not more than twenty years, or both, and shall be ineligible for employment by the United States or any department or agency thereof, for the five years next following his conviction.

If two or more persons conspire to commit any offense named in this section, each shall be fined under this title or imprisoned not more than twenty years, or both, and shall be ineligible for employment by the United States or any department or agency thereof, for the five years next following his conviction.

As used in this section, the terms "organizes"and "organize," with respect to any society, group, or assembly of persons, include the recruiting of new members, the forming of new units, and the regrouping or expansion of existing clubs, classes, and other units of such society, group, or assembly of persons.

SIGNIFICANCE

The convictions of the eleven CPUSA leaders affected tens of thousands of other Americans, including rank and file communist members as well as those sympathetic to communism and those suspected of being sympathetic to communism. The convictions encouraged some judges, legislators, and other government officials to limit the constitutional rights of free speech of others not affiliated with the Communist Party. The House Committee on Un-American Activities and the Internal Security Committee in the Senate specialized in calling witnesses before them to answer questions concerning communism. These witnesses were confronted with the choice of either answering such questions, which usually involved the naming of other individuals and carried with it the danger of prosecution, or refusing to testify at all. Witnesses who failed to cooperate with these committees faced ostracism. It soon became customary to fire these people from their jobs, whether in factories, colleges, government, or business. Repression spread to the point where suspected communist sympathizers were banned from professional societies and denied housing.

The Smith Act had consequences outside of the United States. In its propaganda, the Soviet Union emphasized the contrast between American claims of democratic freedom and actual practice. In an era when the U.S. sought to present its best face to the world in order to win support, some foreign interests accused the U.S. of being driven by fear of free speech and retreating from fostering open, democratic debate.

A number of liberal organizations including the American Civil Liberties Union and the Southern California-Arizona Conference of the Methodist Church sought a Supreme Court review of the Smith Act. In 1957, in *Yates v. United States*, the Supreme Court handed down a decision which construed the Smith Act far more narrowly than had government attorneys conducting the attack on the CPUSA. The Court decided that the Smith Act did not prohibit the advocacy and teaching of forcible overthrow as an abstract principle, divorced from any effort to actually instigate action to that effect. The decision effectively halted Justice Department prosecutions of communists. The court freed five of the communists and ordered new trials for the rest in a six to one vote.

By the middle of 1962, the last of the convicted Communists had finished serving their prison sentences or had received commutations. By 1963, the Smith Act had fallen into disuse. It is still on the books, but it is regarded as a relic of the Cold War. Supreme Court opposition makes it unlikely that the government will again employ the conspiracy, advocacy, or membership provisions of the Smith Act against a dissident organization. Some provisions of the Smith Act have been superceded by the U.S. Patriot Act of 2001.

FURTHER RESOURCES
Books

American Civil Liberties Union. *The Smith Act and the Supreme Court: An American Civil Liberties Union Analysis, Opinion and Statement of Policy.* New York: American Civil Liberties Unions, 1952.

Belknap, Michal R. *Cold War Political Justice: The Smith Act, the Communist Party, and American Civil Liberties.* Westport, Conn.: Greenwood Press, 1977.

Starobin, Joseph R. *American Communism in Crisis, 1943–1957.* Berkeley: University of California Press, 1972.

McCarran-Walter Act

The Power to Ban or Deport "Subversives"

Legislation

By: Senator Patrick McCarran and Representative Francis Walter

Date: Legislation passed by the U.S. Congress on June 11, 1952; presidential veto overridden June 27, 1952; effective December 24, 1952.

Source: Immigration and Nationality Act, Public Law 82-414, U.S. Code, Title 8, Section 212 (a)(3)(B).

About the Author: Patrick Anthony McCarran (1876–1954) was a Democratic senator from Nevada. After a distinguished career as a lawyer and jurist, he was elected to the Senate in 1933, where he served until his death. Francis Eugene Walter (1894–1963) was a Democratic congressional representative from Pennsylvania from 1933 until his death.

INTRODUCTION

The Immigration and Nationality Act (INA) of 1952, generally called the McCarran-Walter Act after its congressional sponsors, was the product of Cold War (1945–1991) tensions and the emergence of African and Asian nations from colonialism in the wake of World War II.

The act created a quota system for immigration based on racial and ethnic categories and national origins, though it was not the first American law to do so. Beginning with the Chinese Exclusion Act of 1882 and continuing with the Asia Barred Zone Act of 1917 (directed primarily at Southeast Asians and Pacific Islanders), the National Origins Act of 1924 (directed primarily at the Japanese and eastern and southern Europeans), and the Tydings-McDuffie Act of 1934 (directed primarily at Filipinos), the United States had long tried to exclude some immigrant groups. In the early 1950s, with the growing influence of the Soviet

FBI Special Agent Edward Hegerty displays items captured during the arrest of four FLAN members. AP/WIDE WORLD PHOTOS

those with special employment skills. The second INA goal involved including provisions to address subversion, allowing the government to exclude or deport anyone whose activities or intentions were regarded as detrimental to U.S. security.

Accordingly, Section 212 of the act, a portion of which is reproduced below, defined "terrorist activity" that was grounds for exclusion or deportation.

PRIMARY SOURCE

Terrorist Activity Defined As used in this Act, the term "terrorist activity" means any activity which is unlawful under the laws of the place where it is committed (or which, if committed in the United States, would be unlawful under the laws of the United States or any State) and which involves any of the following:

(I) The highjacking or sabotage of any conveyance (including an aircraft, vessel, or vehicle).
(II) The seizing or detaining, and threatening to kill, injure, or continue to detain, another individual in order to compel a third person (including a governmental organization) to do or abstain from doing any act as an explicit or implicit condition for the release of the individual seized or detained.
(III) A violent attack upon an internationally protected person (as defined in section 1116(b)(4) of title 18, United States Code) or upon the liberty of such a person.
(IV) An assassination.
(V) The use of any

    (a) biological agent, chemical agent, or nuclear weapon or device, or
    (b) explosive or firearm (other than for mere personal monetary gain), with intent to endanger, directly or indirectly, the safety of one or more individuals or to cause substantial damage to property.

(VI) A threat, attempt, or conspiracy to do any of the foregoing.

The term "engage in terrorist activity" means to commit, in an individual capacity or as a member of an organization, an act of terrorist activity or an act which the actor knows, or reasonably should know, affords material support to any individual, organization, or government in conducting a terrorist activity at any time, including any of the following acts:

(I) The preparation or planning of a terrorist activity.
(II) The gathering of information on potential targets for terrorist activity.
(III) The providing of any type of material support, including a safe house, transportation, communications,

Union, the takeover by Communists in China in 1949, and the start of the Korean War in 1950, a major goal of U.S. immigration policy was to exclude potential subversives and communists perceived as a threat to American security.

In 1950, Senator Pat McCarran, head of the Senate Judiciary Committee's Internal Security Subcommittee, had sponsored the Internal Security Act, which required members of the Communist Party to register with the U.S. attorney general. President Harry Truman (1884–1972) vetoed the bill, but Congress overrode the veto. Then in 1952, McCarran joined Representative Francis Walter, later chair of the House Committee on Un-American Activities, in sponsoring the INA.

The INA had two goals. One was to update and codify existing immigration law, particularly the 1924 National Origins Act. The INA retained the quota system of the 1924 act while lifting exclusions directed at Asians and including preferences for the relatives of people already living in the United States as well as

funds, false documentation or identification, weapons, explosives, or training, to any individual the actor knows or has reason to believe has committed or plans to commit a terrorist activity.

(IV) The soliciting of funds or other things of value for terrorist activity or for any terrorist organization.

(V) The solicitation of any individual for membership in a terrorist organization, terrorist government, or to engage in a terrorist activity.

SIGNIFICANCE

Congress passed the McCarran-Walter Act on June 11, 1952. President Truman, who throughout his administration had expressed reservations about any bill or measure based on race or ideology, vetoed the bill, but Congress overrode the veto on June 27, and the law went into effect on December 24, 1952.

Almost immediately, opponents of the law called for its repeal or modification. They were concerned because, although the new law corrected some of the injustices of earlier immigration law, it still favored northern and western European immigrants over those from Asia and would exclude or deport people on the basis of opinions or beliefs rather than actions. Truman himself shared these concerns, so in September 1952, before the law even took effect, he created the Presidential Commission on Immigration and Naturalization, which recommended relaxing some of the security provisions of the act. In response, McCarran accused the commission of harboring communist sympathizers.

In time, some of the provisions of the McCarran-Walter Act would be repealed. In 1960, Congress eliminated ideological grounds for deportation, and the 1965 Immigration Act dismantled the quota system, creating a uniform cap of 20,000 immigrants from all countries.

Nonetheless, many provisions of the McCarran-Walter Act continue to guide U.S. immigration policy in the twenty-first century. In particular, the act is still used to define "terrorist activity," and the U.S. Secretary of State continues to cite the act in defining foreign terrorist organizations (FTOs). In October 2001, for example, in the wake of the September 11 terrorist attacks that year, the Office of the Coordinator for Counterterrorism cited the McCarran-Walter Act in defining twenty-eight FTOs and specifying procedures for adding to, or removing any such organization from the list. Al-Qaeda, the group responsible for the September 11 attacks, had been added to the list in 1999.

Thus, for example, the coordinator for counterterrorism stated that, under the provisions of the INA, "It is unlawful for a person in the United States or subject to the jurisdiction of the United States to provide funds or other material support to a designated FTO"; "Representatives and certain members of a designated FTO, if they are aliens, can be denied visas or excluded from the United States"; and "U.S. financial institutions must block funds of designated FTO's and their agents and report the blockage to the Office of Foreign Assets Control, U.S. Department of the Treasury."

FURTHER RESOURCES

Books

Tichenor, Daniel J. *Dividing Lines: The Politics of Immigration Control in America.* Princeton, NJ: Princeton University Press, 2002.

Periodicals

Campi, Alicia J. "The McCarran-Walter Act: A Contradictory Legacy on Race, Quotas, and Ideology." *Immigration Policy Briefs* (June 2004). Available online from <http://www.ailf .org/ipc/mccarranwalterprint.asp> (accessed May 16, 2005).

Cole, David D. "Enemy Aliens." *Stanford Law Review* 54 (2002): 953–1004.

Web sites

Immigration and Nationality Act. <http://uscis.gov/lpBin/ lpext.dll/inserts/slb/slb-1/slb-22?f=templates&fn= document-frame.htm#slb-act> (accessed May 16, 2005).

"Peru: Draconian Measures"

Magazine article

By: Latin American Newsletters

Date: December 13, 1974

Source: "Peru: Draconian Measures" as published by *Intelligence Research.*

About the Author: This news report was originally published as part of the Latin American News series from Lettres, UK (now Intelligence Research, Ltd.), a London-based news agency. Established in 1967, the *Latin American Newsletters* were written by Latin American specialists in London, writing about political and social events throughout Latin America as they unfolded. Printed in both English and Spanish, the *Latin American Newsletters* were a compilation from a variety of sources, without author attribution.

INTRODUCTION

In contrast to the right-wing military dictatorships that swept through Latin America from the late 1960s through the 1980s, Peru experienced a left-wing military dictatorship from 1968–1975, under the presidency of General Velasco Alvarado. The left-leaning general instituted a wide range of reforms in the country, including land reform, nationalization of private industry, and media censorship and control. Velasco sought out relationships with Cuba and the Soviet Union, a marked difference from fellow military-based governments in Latin America.

While the political violence that occurred during Velasco's administration was similar in scope to standard terrorist acts—bombings, assassinations and assassination attempts, destruction of symbolic property—the source was very different. In stark contrast to the leftist revolutionary opposition most military governments faced, revolutionary activities during Velasco's rule were from right-wing, conservative opponents. As a follower of the National Security Doctrine, holding that development and social reform were key to improving national security, Velasco represented a new kind of military leader. No longer would the military be a defender of the interests of the elite, but instead would use leftist means to achieve the "ends" of stability and security.

At the same time, Velasco faced massive opposition from rural unions. His Agrarian Reform Law of 1969 intended to eliminate large private landholdings and create cooperatives owned by the workers on the estates. The goal of this reform was to destroy the financial (and social) power of the elites in Peru, and to create a supposedly more cooperative society. This "third way" between socialism and capitalism, as designed by Velasco, still used military power, repression, and state control to accomplish its goals.

Rural unions were not pleased with the changes, as disputes broke out in the collectives. The lack of clear managerial authority created problems with production, and eventually led to the bankruptcy of many collectives. By 1974 Velasco faced major crises in Peru from angered elites, disgruntled rural workers, and alienated foreigners upset with nationalization of foreign investment.

PRIMARY SOURCE

Terrorist outrages and assassination attempts are comparatively new features of the Peruvian political scene. Government countermeasures should have the effect of strengthening the 'radical' tendencies within the armed forces.

Government spokesmen have been quick to interpret last week's unsuccessful attempt on the life of the prime minister, General Edgardo Mercado Jarrin, as a further escalation of the right-wing campaign to destabilize the revolution and, more immediately, to take the shine off this week's Ayacucho anniversary celebrations in Lima. Certainly this is not the first time the present government has been shown up in a repressive light in full view of assembled foreign dignitaries; in May 1971, for example, delegates to the annual meeting of the Inter-American development Bank were treated to front-page pictures of police beating ragged 'invaders' of urban land, and the unedifying spectacle of the auxiliary bishop of Lima being hustled off to jail on charges of subversion. In view of the unremitting campaign of harassment and boycott suffered by the Peruvian government over the past six years from disgruntled emigres and alarmed foreigners, it seems reasonable, even obvious, to see conspiracy behind these events. Right-wing activity since the expropriation of the Lima daily press in July has been on the increase, while the United States has a clear interest in isolating Peru from her neighbors and giving support to 'democratic' elements within the country.

However, there are some odd features about the recent wave of terrorism; and the severe government reaction, in decreeing the death penalty and summary trials for terrorists, should be seen in the context of the persistent political crisis over the future direction of the revolution. Some observers have noted that several of the recent acts of terrorism have clearly been intended to look like the work of leftists; the fire bomb attack on the Sheraton hotel, the bomb in the basement of Sears department store, and the dynamiting of the statue of a police officer killed by guerrillas in 1965—all these are the sort of things left-wing extremists might be expected to go in for, though what they might hope to gain from such acts is not clear. Whoever is behind these deeds, the tougher security measures and round-up of suspects considerably strengthens the government's hand in dealing with opposition of all kinds. There can be little doubt that in the long run the government is most concerned about the revolutionary process running out of its control, particularly as a result of activity by the militant unions in the country-side. At the same time, progressive elements in the armed forces will be anxious to prevent conservative officers from making a come-back on a wave of indiscriminate repression.

It appears that the decision to clamp down on the activities of rural unions had already been taken before the latest events, and in this respect, the recent appointments of Generals Gallegos and Hoyos to ministries dealing with the rural sector are particularly significant. As experienced and resolute leaders of the 'radical' tendency within the government, these generals can be expected to push for tighter central control over the rural sector, including disciplining the sugar cooperatives and eliminating opposition unions; the latter is a particularly pressing task in view of the failure of SINAMOS to cope with them even within the cooperatives. The way the government handled the Andahuaylas problem may give a foretaste of things to come. Following its apparent capitulation at the hands of the local peasant federation FEPCA, the entire leadership of FEPCA was arrested in September and October, together with the secretary general of the *Confederacion Campesina del Peru* (CCP), Andres Luna Vargas (only recently released from prison) and a well-known left-wing lawyer, Laura Caller.

The way should now be open for a more thorough implementation of the centralised model of development favoured by the 'radicals.' According to the Lima magazine *Caretas*, the scandal involving the state food marketing company EPSA came just in time to forestall an attempt, initiated by the new general manager, Alfonso Elejalde Zea, to wipe out the company's massive deficit by both opening it up to private investors and paying higher prices to rural producers. This plan, which goes completely contrary to current government policy on both counts, was apparently being supported by Mercado Jarrin, even after Elejalde died of a heart attack in September. The careful timing of the scandal, broken by the pro-government press, which explained EPSA's deficit and rural discontent in terms of corruption and smuggling, shows the 'liberal' tendency represented by Mercado Jarrin is still getting the worst of things. It is interesting to note that in recent speeches the prime minister has become the leading government exponent of participation and limiting the expanding role of the state and state enterprises. These points may also be played down in the near future. Certainly, no concessions to the private sector or foreign capital can be expected in the near future.

On the contrary, the political will that has produced a further radicalization of government policy following every crisis can be expected to push through the expropriation of private manufacturing industry some time next year. This seems to be the crucial point around which the current political debate within the government is revolving, and is being presented by the 'radicals' as the only way left to mobilize the private capital tied up in industry that four years of incentives and exhortations have conspicuously failed to touch. It seems that the 'national bourgeoisie,' like the rural capitalists before them, are about to get their comeuppance.

The outcome of the internecine struggle will presumably be known shortly after the new year, when Mercado Jarrin is due to retire. Already the radicals are occupying the key positions, and have their own men ready to take over the forthcoming vacancies; the new minister of education, for example, General Ramon Miranda Ampuero, is a former member of the president's advisory committee, COAP.

SIGNIFICANCE

As Velasco proceeded with his reforms, internal strife continued. New problems from foreign investors added to pressure on the military-controlled government. Right-wing elements within the military were carefully weeded out, state control of the press was enacted, and the stripping of rights during trials combined with widespread issuance of the death penalty terrorist acts were all part of Velasco's crackdown not only on violent political acts, but on most forms of political opposition.

Velasco reached out to communist regimes such as Cuba and the Soviet Union, actions that alarmed the United States. As Velasco nationalized industry and expropriated companies such as the International Petroleum Company, his policies alienated foreign investment. The United States took an active role in isolating Peru politically and economically in an effort to stem the spread of communism and socialism in Central and Latin America.

The attempt on Prime Minister General Edgardo Mercado Jarrin's life was the source of much speculation from political analysts and international observers. As one of the more fiscally conservative members of Velasco's government, Mercado pushed for more privative control than was the norm in Velasco's economic plan. In 1973, Vladimiro Montesinos became an aide to Mercado. That same year, General Augusto Pinochet removed socialist president Saldavor Allende from power in a military coup in Chile. Velasco's left-wing administration feared problems with Pinochet's right-wing dictatorship, and Peru began amassing war supplies in preparation for a possible conflict. The next year, Montesinos was accused of sharing military secrets with the United States; Mercado put an end to any investigation into Montesinos' involvement.

Velasco's use of traditional authoritarian tactics to achieve leftist goals angered the rural unions and began a process of leftist discontent that would stretch into the 1990s in the form of political violence. *Sendero Luminoso*, (Shining Path), a group of Maoist insurgents, formed during Velasco's administration. Future insurgent groups such as Tupac Amaru followed suit. Velasco's rule sowed the seeds of future insurgency.

In 1975 Velasco was removed from power. Most of his reforms were reversed as the country sought to attract foreign investment and to initiate free market policies. His employment of Montesinos and broad use of military and police power to thwart opposition foreshadowed Peru's experiences in future decades. Montesinos staged a comeback in the 1990s during Alberto Fujimori's presidency in Peru, becoming Fujimori's security advisor. He is widely considered, by political analysts, Peruvian prosecutors and investigators, and human rights observers worldwide, to be responsible for military and police policies that led to massive human rights abuses in Peru in the early 1990s.

FURTHER RESOURCES

Books

Starn, Orin. *The Peru Reader: History, Culture, Politics.* Durham, North Carolina: Duke University Press, 1995.

Web sites

The Center for Public Integrity. "The Spy Who Would Rule Peru" <http://www.publicintegrity.com/ga/report.aspx?aid=647 > (accessed June 29, 2005).

Entebbe Diary

Raid on Entebbe

Diary excerpt

By: Major (Res.) Louis Williams

Date: July 3–4, 1976

Source: Israeli Defense Force

About the Author: At the time Major Louis Williams wrote his daily commentary *Entebbe Diary*, concerning the raid on the Entebbe airport, he was a member of the Israeli Defense Force (IDF) in the Israeli Army.

INTRODUCTION

On June 27, 1976, ten armed terrorists, masquerading as Latin American tourists, from the Popular Front for the Liberation of Palestine (PFLP)—a Marxist-Leninist group originally from the Palestine Liberation Organization (PLO)—and the Baader-Meinhof Gang—a leftist revolutionary group from West Germany—hijacked Air France Flight 139 while in route from Athens, Greece, to Tel Aviv, Israel (also destined for Paris, France). PFLP leader Dr. Wadi Hadad, allegedly supported by Ilich Ramirez-Sanchez (Carlos the Jackal) and Ugandan dictator Idi Amin, planned the terrorist act.

With 246 passengers onboard, they forced the airplane to Entebbe International Airport in southern Uganda, near the northwestern shore of Lake Victoria. The terrorists released the non-Jewish and non-Israeli passengers and then threatened, on June 29th, to kill the remaining Jewish and Israeli hostages if fifty-three of their Palestinian comrades in Israeli, French, German, Swiss, and Kenyan jails were not released by July 1st.

Hostages return from Uganda after being rescued by Israeli forces at Entebbe airport in 1976. AP/WIDE WORLD PHOTO

At this time, with the realization that the other countries were not going to release their incarcerated Palestinians and with a three day extension given by the terrorists, Prime Minister Yitzhak Rabin secretly authorized the Israeli Defense Force (IDF) to plan a rescue mission for the hostages—a raid on Entebbe—under the name Operation Thunderbolt (later renamed Operation Yonatan); while at the same time publicly negotiating with the terrorists.

The IDF decided to fly four C-130 Hercules transport/cargo planes—one carrying about 200 IDF and Special Forces commandos and supplies; a second carrying Brigadier General Dan Shomron, a black Mercedes-Benz, and two Land Rovers, to resemble a high-ranking governmental Uganda caravan; a third with a demolition team to restrain Uganda's Russian-built MiG fighter jets; and a fourth carrying fuel for the others—to the Entebbe airport.

The assault began on July 4, 1976, when the IDF commandos killed the German terrorists and several Ugandan soldiers outside the Old Terminal's transit hall. Locating the hostages inside, the Israeli soldiers then killed the PFLP terrorists in a quick but deadly fight that lasted less than three minutes. Within an hour after the first airplane landed at the Entebbe airport, 103 surviving hostages were free and flying back to Tel Aviv. Three hostages were killed, along with Lieutenant Colonel Yonatan "Yoni" Netanyahu, the leader of the IDF Special Forces team.

PRIMARY SOURCE

Turning westward, the four Hercules headed into the African continent over Ethiopia. The weather was stormy, forcing the pilots to divert northwards close to the Sudanese frontier. However, there were no fears of detection. Firstly, it was doubtful that any alert radar operators would be able to identify the planes as Israeli and secondly, the storm would wreak havoc with incoming signals on the screens. On the approaches to Lake Victoria, they hit storm clouds towering in a solid mass from ground level to 40,000 feet. There was no time to go around, and no way to go above, so they ploughed on through. Conditions were so bad that the cockpit windows were blue with the flashes of static electricity.

Lt.Col. S. held the lead plane straight on course; his cargo of 86 officers and men and Dan Shomron's forward command post with their vehicles and equipment had to be on the ground according to a precise timetable. The other pilots had no choice but to circle inside the storm for a few extra minutes.

Yitzhak Rabin and some of the other ministers joined Shimon Peres in his office, and waited tensely for a sign of life from the radio link-up on his desk. Shortly before 23:00 hours, they heard a terse "over 'Jordan'" from Kuti Adam, confirming that the planes had reached Lake Victoria.

Lt. Col. S. held course southward, then banked sharply to line up on Entebbe main runway from the southwest. In the distance he could see that the runway lights were on. Behind him in the cargo compartment, Yoni Netanyahu's men were piling into the Mercedes and the two Land Rovers. The car engines were already running, and members of the aircrew were standing by to release the restraining cables. At 23:01, only 30 seconds behind the preplanned schedule, Lt. Col. S. brought the aircraft in to touch down at Entebbe. The rear ramp of the plane was already open, and the vehicles were on the ground and moving away before the Hercules rolled to a stop. A handful of paratroopers had already dropped off the plane to place emergency beacons next to the runway lights, in case the control tower shot them down. Lt. Col. S. switches on his radio for a second: "I am on 'Shoshana'".

The Mercedes, and its escorts, moved down the connecting road to Old Terminal as fast as they could, consistent with the appearance of a senior officer's entourage. On the approaches to the tarmac apron in front of the building, two Ugandan sentries faced the oncoming vehicles, aimed their carbines, and shouted an order to stop. There was no choice, and no time to argue. The first shots from the Mercedes were from pistols. One Ugandan fell and the other ran in the direction of the old control tower. The Ugandan on the ground was groping for his carbine. A paratrooper responded immediately with a burst. Muki and his team jumped from the car and ran the last 40 yards to the walkway in front of the building. The first entrance had been blocked off; without a second's pause, the paratroopers raced on to the second door.

Junior officers usually lead the first wave of an assault, but Muki felt it important to be up front in case there was need to make decisions about changes in plans. Tearing along the walkway, he was fired on by a Ugandan. Muki responded, killing him. A terrorist stepped out the main door of the Old Terminal to see what the fuss was about, and rapidly returned the way he had come.

Muki then discovered that the magazine of his carbine was empty. The normal procedure would have been to step aside and let someone else take the lead. He decided against, and groped to change magazines on the run. The young officer behind him, realizing what was happening, came up alongside. The two of them, and one other trooper, reached the doorway together—Amnon, the young lieutenant, on the left, Muki in the center and the trooper on the right. The terrorist who had ventured out was now standing to the left of the door. Amnon fired, followed by Muki. Across the room, a terrorist rose to his feet and fired at the hostages sprawled around him, most of whom had been trying to sleep. Muki took care of him with two shots. Over to the right, a fourth member of the hijackers' team managed to loose off a burst at the intruders, but his bullets were high, hitting a window and showering glass into the room. The trooper aimed and fired. Meanwhile, Amnon identified the girl terrorist to the left of the doorway and fired. In the background, a bullhorn was booming in Hebrew and English: "This is the IDF! Stay down!" From a nearby mattress, a young man launched himself at the trio in the doorway, and was cut down by a carbine burst. The man was a bewildered hostage. Muki's troopers fanned out through the room and into the corridor to the washroom beyond—but all resistance was over.

The second assault team had meanwhile raced through another doorway into a hall where the off-duty terrorists spent their spare time. Two men in civilian clothes walked calmly towards them. Assuming that these could be hostages, the soldiers held their fire. Suddenly one of the men raised his hand and threw a grenade. The troopers dropped to the ground. A machine-gun burst eliminated their adversaries. The grenade exploded harmlessly. Yoni's third team from the Landrovers moved to silence any opposition from the Ugandan soldiers stationed near the windows on the floor above. On the way up the stairs, they met two soldiers, one of whom was fast on the trigger. The troopers killed them.

While his men circulated through the hall, calming the shocked hostages and tending the wounded, Muki was called out to the tarmac. There he found a doctor kneeling over Lt. Col. Yoni Netanyahu. Yoni had remained outside the building to supervise all three assault teams. A bullet from the top of the old control tower had hit him in the back. While the troopers silenced the fire from above, Yoni was dragged into the shelter of the overhanging wall by the walkway.

The assault on Old Terminal was completed within three minutes after the lead plane landed. Now in rapid succession, its three companions came into touch down at Entebbe. By 23:08 hours, all of Thunderball Force was on the ground. The runway lights shut down as the third plane came in to land, but it didn't matter—the beacons did the job well enough. With clockwork precision, armored personnel carriers roared off the ramp of the second transport to take up position to the front and rear of Old Terminal, while infantrymen from the first and third plane ran to secure all access to roads to the airport and to take over the New Terminal and the control tower; the tower was vital for safe evacuation of the hostages and their rescuers. In a brief clash at the New Terminal, Sergeant Hershko Surin, who was due for demobilization from the army in twelve hours time, fell wounded. The fourth plane taxied to a holding position near the Old Terminal, ready to take on hostages. All the engines were left running. A team of Air Force technicians were already hard at work offloading heavy fuel pumps—hastily acquired by an inspired quartermaster one day earlier—and setting up to transfer Idi Amin's precious aviation fluid into the thirsty tanks of the lead transport—a process that would take well over an hour.

In Peres' crowded room in Tel Aviv, Kuti Adam's terse "Everything's okay " only served to heighten the tension. Motta Gur decided to contact Dan Shomron directly, but was little more enlightened by laconic "It's alright, I'm busy right now!"

Muki radioed Dan Shomron to report that the building and surroundings were secure and to inform him that Yoni had been hit. Though they were ahead of schedule, there was no point in waiting (possibly allowing the Ugandans to bring up reinforcements), particularly since Shomron now knew that refueling the aircraft in Nairobi was possible. The fourth Hercules was ordered to move up closer to Old Terminal. Muki's men and the other soldiers around the

building formed two lines from the doorway to the ramp of the plane; no chances would be taken that a bewildered hostage could wander off into the night or blunder into the aircraft's engines. As the hostages straggled out, heads of families were stopped at the ramp and asked to check that all their kin were present. Captain Bacos was quietly requested to perform the same task for his "family"—the crew of Air France 139. Behind them, Old Terminal was empty but for the bodies of six terrorists, among them a young European girl and a blond haired German called Wilfried Boese.

It was a mid-morning when a Hercules transport of the Israel Air Force touched down at Ben Gurion International Airport, rolled to a stop and opened its rear ramp to release its cargo of men, women and children into the outstretched arms of their relatives and friends and of a crowd of thousands. The ordeal was over.

SIGNIFICANCE

The raid on Entebbe to rescue hostages taken by international terrorists was highly significant to the counterterrorism activities of the United States, Israel, and other allies. The raid clearly brought to light the dangers inherent with global terrorism. The 1976 experience showed the world that when peaceful negotiations were

An Israeli soldier hugs a child who was a hostage on the Air France plane that was hijacked and held in Uganda.
AP/WIDE WORLD PHOTOS

unsuccessful, aggressive actions to rescue hostages could be quickly planned and successfully carried out with a minimum loss of life. Still today, the stunning raid on Entebbe is considered one of the most daring and successful raids in the recent history of the modern world.

Idi Amin was publicly embarrassed around the world by the surprise raid on Entebbe. When a government representative of Uganda condemned the Israeli raid in front of the United Nations (UN) Security Council as a violation of Ugandan independence, the Security Council rejected the criticism. From this point forward, Amin's military regime, which was widely known for carrying out human rights violations, began to crumble. Within two years he was forced into political exile in Saudi Arabia.

Of great political significance, Israel did not succumb to terrorist blackmail, but forcibly took matters into its own hands to free its citizens. At the time of the incident, the rescue symbolized to the world that Israel was willing and able to defend and protect its Jewish citizens from violence, regardless of the consequences, caused by terrorist acts. For the next several years the successful raid caused a great upsurge of pride for the people of Israel. Many of the Israeli soldiers that participated in the raid were later promoted to high-ranking positions in the military and political systems of Israel.

Ultimately, the members of the Security Council established an important precedent in international law when they enacted the principle of national self defense or the right of a country to protect itself and its citizens against violence or threatened violence with whatever force or means are reasonably necessary.

FURTHER RESOURCES

Books

Hastings, Max. *Yoni, Hero of Entebbe*. New York: Dial Press, 1979.

Netanyahu, Jonathan. *Self-Portrait of a Hero: From the Letters of Johathan Netanyahu, 1963-1976*. New York: Random House, 1980.

Ofer, Yehuda. *Operation Thunder: The Entebbe Raid: The Israelis Own Story*. Hamondsworth, Middlesex, U.K. and New York: Penguin, 1976.

Stevenson, William. *90 Minutes at Entebbe*. New York: Bantam Books, 1979.

Williams, Louis. *Israeli Defense Force: A People's Army*. Jerusalem and New York: Gefen Publishing House, 1996.

Web sites

BBC News. "1976: British Grandmother Missing in Uganda." <http://news.bbc.co.uk/onthisday/hi/dates/stories/july/7/newsid_2496000/2496095.stm> (accessed June 16, 2005).

United States Embassy in Tehran Seized

"U.S. Commando-Style Raid into Iran to Free Hostages Fails"

Photograph

By: The Associated Press

Date: April 24, 1980

Source: The Associated Press.

About the Photographer: Founded in 1848, the Associated Press claims to be the oldest and largest news organization in the world, serving as a news source for more than one billion people a day.

INTRODUCTION

Rising anti-Americanism had been one of the defining characteristics of the Iranian Revolution, which had led to the deposition of Iran's Shah Reza Mohammed Pahlavi in January 1979. Pahlavi had been America's closest ally in the Middle East during the 1960s and 1970s, and had come to power on the back of an American-led coup in 1953. Hostility towards the Shah had seemingly gone hand-in-hand with disaffection towards America, which had numerous military and oil interests in common with the Pahlavi regime.

This creeping tide of anti-Americanism had become a surge after the return from exile of Ayatollah Khomeini in February 1979. As the machinery of the Iranian state collapsed over the duration of that year, denunciations of America and Israel were frequently used by Khomeini to help bolster his own popularity in the midst of growing domestic chaos.

When the deposed Shah went to the United States in October 1979 to receive medical treatment for lymphoma, it caused consternation within Iran, and Khomeini called on his people to demonstrate against the U.S. Thousands gathered around the U.S. embassy in Tehran to protest on November 1, 1979. Demonstrations escalated over subsequent days and on November 4, a mob of around 500 students calling themselves the Imam's Disciples' seized the main embassy building, taking 66 staff captive.

Khomeini was unrepentant about the hostage taking, using the act as a demonstration that his government was capable of successfully opposing the United States. Even when President Jimmy Carter retaliated by freezing $8 billion of Iranian assets,

Khomeini merely turned around the sanctions, using them as the latest example of the United States acting against the interests of the Iranian people.

Although 13 hostages were released on November 19 and 20, 1979, the hostage crisis continued into the new year. In February 1980, Khomeini's government issued a set of demands in return for freeing hostages. This included the return of the Shah to Iran for trial and a number of diplomatic gestures, including American apologies for previous actions such as the 1953 coup. Carter refused to meet these conditions. Attempts to seek a diplomatic solution with Switzerland acting as a broker also failed.

Carter then ordered a secret rescue mission code-named "Operation Eagle Claw" on April, 25 1980. The mission failed, and resulted in the death of eight American soldiers.

Carried out during nighttime hours, transport aircraft preparing for a U.S. Special Forces landing in Tehran met at an airstrip in the Great Salt Desert in eastern Iran. Two helicopters had already pulled out of the mission with engine trouble, and a third was damaged as it landed on the airstrip, leaving five workable helicopters. The mission had become impossible before its full launch, at which point it was aborted on Carter's instructions.

As the aircraft took off to leave, however another helicopter crashed and burst into flames. Eight serviceman died, and another four suffered severe burns. The U.S. forces hastily retreated.

■ **PRIMARY SOURCE**

UNITED STATES EMBASSY IN TEHRAN SEIZED
See primary source image.

■ **PRIMARY SOURCE**

United States Embassy in Tehran Seized The remains of U.S. Marines amidst the wreckage of U.S. aircraft, after the failure of a Commando-style raid into the U.S. Embassy in Iran. AP/WIDE WORLD PHOTOS

SIGNIFICANCE

Operation Eagle Claw was a disaster for President Carter and merely added to the rising perception of his administration's inability to deal with the prevailing crisis. Additionally, America's European allies expressed shock that the mission had taken place without any consultation.

In Tehran, the mission's failure was greeted by jubilant scenes. Thousands of Iranian people hit the streets in celebration, and the bodies of the American soldiers were displayed in front of jubilant crowds. Intelligence documents were also uncovered in the wreckage and were flaunted by Iranian officials in front of the TV cameras.

Operation Eagle Claw, which was condemned by the Iranian Foreign Minister as "an act of war," all but doomed attempts to bring about a diplomatic solution to the hostage crisis. Domestically, Carter was engaged in a fight for re-election, and his rival Ronald Reagan used the crisis to his advantage, portraying Carter as unable to bring about a solution. The hostages were released after 444 days in captivity, on the day of Reagan's Presidential inauguration, January 20, 1981.

As President, Reagan characterized Khomeini's Iran as a terrorist state bent on damaging the interests of the American people. Iran was a backer of Hezbollah, an Islamist organization originating in Lebanon, and had strong ties to other extremist Shi'ite groups, such as Islamic Jihad. Between them, these organizations carried out a number of terrorist attacks against U.S. targets in Lebanon and across the Middle East during the mid-1980s.

Reagan also supplied military aid to Iraq, which was at war with Iran between 1980–1988. Further down the line, this contributed to an array of problems for subsequent U.S. administrations, including the 1991 Gulf War; the enforcement of sanctions against Saddam Hussein's regime; and ultimately, the U.S. led invasion of Iraq in March 2003.

FURTHER RESOURCES

Books

Cleveland, William L. *A History of the Modern Middle East.* Nashville, TN: Westview, 2000.

Sullivan, William H. *Mission to Iran.* London: W. W. Norton & Co., 1981.

Web sites

PBS. "People & Events: The Iranian Hostage Crisis, November 1979–January 1980." <http://www.pbs.org/wgbh/amex/carter/peopleevents/e_hostage.html> (accessed July 6, 2005).

Executive Order 13099

Prohibiting Transactions with Terrorists

Legislation

By: William Jefferson Clinton

Date: August 20, 1998

Source: Executive Office of the President (White House)

About the Author: William Jefferson Clinton (1946–) was the forty-second president of the United States (1993–2001). Before serving as president, Clinton served five terms as Arkansas' governor. During his presidency, Clinton helped to mediate the Israeli-Palestinian conflict—a disagreement over the status of the West Bank, Gaza Strip, and East Jerusalem. Negotiations between Israel and the Palestine Liberation Organization (PLO) resulted in a declaration of peace during September 1993; however, it did not stop the fighting. Clinton continued to push for peace in the Middle East throughout his eight years in office, but was never able to accomplish a final peace agreement.

INTRODUCTION

On October 28, 1977, the International Emergency Economic Powers Act (IEEPA) was enacted to give power to the U.S. president—in the event of a national emergency—to use various financial and commercial means to deal with abnormal threats to the United States with respect to its economy, foreign policy, or national security. Among his powers, the president has the right to restrict such activities as foreign travel, borrowing and lending, and fulfilling of contracts to citizens or governments of various countries.

On January 23, 1995, President Clinton issued Executive Order 12947, which declared a national emergency based on the IEEPA. Clinton stated that the executive order (EO) was necessary in order to counter serious violence by twelve terrorist organizations in their continuing attempts to destroy the Middle East peace process and to attack the United States and its allies. The EO, which enabled the United States to freeze terrorist's assets and to block their business transactions, also gave the U.S. Treasury Secretary the authority to add individuals and other terrorist groups to the EO list.

On August 20, 1998, Executive Order 13099, which was an amendment to EO 12947, was issued by President Clinton following the attacks on the U.S. embassies located in Tanzania and Kenya. With the issuance of EO 13099, under the title "Prohibiting

A U.S. ballistics investigator looks for clues in the burned-out wreakage of the U.S. Embassy in Tanzania, August 8, 1998.
AP/WIDE WORLD PHOTOS

Transactions With Terrorists Who Threaten To Disrupt the Middle East Peace Process," Clinton identified four additional terrorist individuals/groups—most importantly Osama Bin Laden—who had not been listed on any previous executive orders.

The three terrorist individuals and one terrorist group included in Executive Order 13099, which imposed broad economic sanctions against them as declared in EO 12947, were:

- Osama Bin Laden, a Saudi Arabian and founder of the Islamic Army, popularly called the al-Qaeda terrorist network.
- Islamic Army, the worldwide network of militant Islamist organizations under the leadership of Osama Bin Laden.
- Abu Hafs al-Masri (or, Mohammad Atef), the second in command of al-Qaeda before being killed in a U.S. missile attack in Afghanistan on November 15, 2001; since then, the Abu Hafs al-Masri Brigades were formed.

- Rifa'i Ahmad Taha Musa (or, Rifai al-Taha), a guerrilla leader of the Islamic Army (specifically, the militant faction of Al-Gama à al-Islamiyya) and top aid to Osama Bin Laden.

PRIMARY SOURCE

By the authority vested in me as President by the Constitution and the laws of the United States of America, including the International Emergency Economic Powers Act (50 U.S.C. 1701 et seq.), the National Emergencies Act (50 U.S.C. 1601 et seq.), and section 301 of title 3, United States Code,

I, WILLIAM J. CLINTON, President of the United States of America, in order to take additional steps with respect to grave acts of violence committed by foreign terrorists that disrupt the Middle East peace process and the national emergency described and declared in Executive Order 12947 of January 23, 1995, hereby order:

Section 1: The title of the Annex to Executive Order 12947 of January 23, 1995, is revised to read "TERRORISTS WHO

THREATEN TO DISRUPT THE MIDDLE EAST PEACE PROCESS."

Section 2: The Annex to Executive Order 12947 of January 23, 1995, is amended by adding thereto the following persons in appropriate alphabetical order:

> Usama bin Muhammad bin Awad bin Ladin (a.k.a. Usama bin Ladin)
> Islamic Army (a.k.a. Al-Qaida, Islamic Salvation Foundation, The Islamic Army for the Liberation of the Holy Places, The World Islamic Front for Jihad Against Jews and Crusaders, and The Group for the Preservation of the Holy Sites)
> Abu Hafs al-Masri
> Rifa'i Ahmad Taha Musa

Section 3: Nothing contained in this order shall create any right or benefit, substantive or procedural, enforceable by any party against the United States, its agencies or instrumentalities, its officers or employees, or any other person.

Section 4: (a) This order is effective at 12:01 A.M., eastern daylight time on August 21, 1998.

(b) This order shall be transmitted to the Congress and published in the Federal Register.

WILLIAM J. CLINTON
THE WHITE HOUSE,
August 20, 1998.

Passersby look at damaged buildings near the U.S. Embassy in Nairobi, Kenya, August 1998. AP/WIDE WORLD PHOTOS

SIGNIFICANCE

Executive Order 13099, in essence, made it illegal for any transaction in business or dealing in property (or interests in property) to be made by United States citizens or within the United States with regards to three terrorists and one terrorist organization listed in the executive order. The order also authorizes the Treasury Secretary to block the property of persons associated with any of the four persons designated in the order. In addition, the order also allowed U.S. law enforcement agencies to seize and hold any assets of these four terrorists that can be identified in the United States.

Executive Order 13099 is part of a concerted long-term plan by the United States government to prevent terrorism by destroying terrorist equipment, structures, finances, and other assets. The order, along with other similar executive orders, is significant to the U.S. war on terrorism because it permits the U.S. government to remove international financial funding that allows various foreign terrorist groups to pay for personnel, administration, supplies, information, training, and weapons. For example, the September 11, 2001 attacks on American soil were the result of an advanced, highly organized operation that required extensive use of intelligence, coordination, and training, and also necessitated significant amounts of money.

When this financial funding is removed, or at least substantially reduced, terrorist organizations have less direct ability to conduct their violent activities. For example, Bin Laden's al-Qaeda organization uses extensive private funding from around the world for its terrorist activities. Bin Laden uses his estimated $300 million in assets to fund many of the militant Islamic groups under the al-Qaeda network. However, it is difficult to locate or freeze these assets because many are not clearly tied to Bin Laden and other terrorists.

FURTHER RESOURCES
Books

Hafez, Mohammed M. *Why Muslims Rebel: Repression and Resistance in the Islamic World.* Boulder, CO: Lynne Rienner Publishers, 2003.

Junaid, Shahwar. *Terrorism and Global Power Systems*. Oxford and New York: Oxford University Press, 2005.

Linden, Edward V., editor. *Foreign Terrorist Organizations: History, Tactics and Connections*. New York: Nova Science, 2004.

Schanzer, Jonathan. *Al-Qaeda's Armies: Middle East Affiliate Groups and the Next Generation of Terror*. New York: Specialist Press International, 2005.

Web sites

Federal Register."Executive Order 12947."<http://frwebgate.access.gpo.gov/cgi-bin/getdoc.cgi?dbname=1995_register&docid=fr25ja95-126.pdf> (June 8, 2005).

Richelson, Jeffrey and Evens, Michael L., editors. "The September 11th Sourcebooks, Volume I: Terrorism and U.S. Policy" *The National Security Archive* <http://www.gwu.edu/~nsarchiv/NSAEBB/NSAEBB55/index1.html> (accessed June 8, 2005).

The National Security Archive. "The United States and Terrorism, 1968–2002: Threat and Response." <http://nsarchive.chadwyck.com/terr_essay.htm> (accessed June 8, 2005).

Clinton, William J. *Office of the Press Secretary, White House (United States Information Service)*. "Clinton's Letter to Congress on Freezing of bin Ladin Assets." <http://www.ict.org.il/documents/documentdet.cfm?docid=22> (accessed June 8, 2005).

National Commission on Terrorism (NTC) Report

"Countering the Changing Threat of International Terrorism"

Government report

By: The National Commission on Terrorism

Date: June 5, 2000

Source: "Countering the Changing Threat of International Terrorism," Report from the National Commission on Terrorism.

About the Author: The National Commission on Terrorism, a bipartisan body created by the United States Congress, released its report on June 5, 2000. The report warned of the increasing likelihood of terrorist attacks upon Americans and urged that the U.S. adopt a more aggressive strategy in pursuing terrorists. The commission recommended a more proactive counterterrorism policy, stronger state sanctions, and a better-coordinated federal counterterrorism response. Many of the commission's findings were not implemented until after the terrorist attacks on New York and Washington, D.C., on September 11, 2001.

INTRODUCTION

As the United States became a world power in the years following World War II (1939–1945) Americans increasingly became the targets of terrorism. In the 1990s, the threat of attacks creating massive casualties grew. In an effort to prevent a surprise attack in the manner of Pearl Harbor, Congress created the National Commission on Terrorism (NTC) in 1999.

The ten-member terrorism commission consisted of six members appointed by the Republican Congressional leadership and four by the Democratic minority. L. Paul Bremer, the chairman of the commission, had served as an ambassador at large for counterterrorism in the Reagan administration. In compiling its report, the NTC interviewed officials throughout the government, including at the State Department, Pentagon, National Security Council, Federal Bureau of Investigation (FBI), and Central Intelligence Agency (CIA).

The NTC stressed that the U.S. needed to develop effective counterterrorism policies that also respected constitutional protections of civil liberties. The members argued that terrorists sought to provoke a response that would undermine the democratic system of government. They premised their investigations on the notion that the U.S. would be more likely to succeed in striking a balance between effective counterterrorism policies and respect for civil liberties through careful planning rather than a rushed response in the highly charged atmosphere following catastrophic attack.

Despite its emphasis on the protection of civil liberties, the NTC unanimously recommended that the CIA drop its human rights guidelines on the recruitment of terrorist informants. In 1995, the CIA established new procedures for the agency's case officers to seek approval before recruiting informants who may have been involved in human rights abuses. The guidelines were put in place following charges that the CIA knowingly hired paid informers among Guatemalan military officers suspected of involvement in political killings, including those of an American citizen and a rebel leader married to another American. The NTC had heard testimony that such guidelines made it difficult to recruit agents within terrorist groups.

Rescue workers pull a man out of the remains of a building next to the site of the U.S. Embassy bombing in Nairobi, Kenya on August 8, 1998. KEN KARUGA/AP WIDE WORLD PHOTOS

PRIMARY SOURCE

EXECUTIVE SUMMARY

International terrorism poses an increasingly dangerous and difficult threat to America

This was underscored by the December 1999 arrests in Jordan and at the U.S./Canadian border of foreign nationals who were allegedly planning to attack crowded millennium celebrations. Today's terrorists seek to inflict mass casualties, and they are attempting to do so both overseas and on American soil. They are less dependent on state sponsorship and are, instead, forming loose, transnational affiliations based on religious or ideological affinity and a common hatred of the United States. This makes terrorist attacks more difficult to detect and prevent.

Countering the growing danger of the terrorist threat requires significantly stepping up U.S. efforts

The government must immediately take steps to reinvigorate the collection of intelligence about terrorists' plans, use all available legal avenues to disrupt and prosecute terrorist activities and private sources of support, convince other nations to cease all support for terrorists, and ensure that federal, state, and local officials are prepared for attacks that may result in mass casualties. The Commission has made a number of recommendations to accomplish these objectives.

Priority one is to prevent terrorist attacks. U.S. intelligence and law enforcement communities must use the full scope of their authority to collect intelligence regarding terrorist plans and methods

CIA guidelines adopted in 1995 restricting recruitment of unsavory sources should not apply when recruiting counterterrorism sources.

The Attorney General should ensure that FBI is exercising fully its authority for investigating suspected terrorist groups or individuals, including authority for electronic surveillance.

Funding for counterterrorism efforts by CIA, NSA, and FBI must be given higher priority to ensure continuation of important operational activity and to close the technology gap that threatens their ability to collect and exploit terrorist communications.

FBI should establish a cadre of reports officers to distill and disseminate terrorism-related information once it is collected.

U.S. policies must firmly target all states that support terrorists

Iran and Syria should be kept on the list of state sponsors until they stop supporting terrorists.

Afghanistan should be designated a sponsor of terrorism and subjected to all the sanctions applicable to state sponsors.

The President should impose sanctions on countries that, while not direct sponsors of terrorism, are nevertheless not cooperating fully on counterterrorism. Candidates for consideration include Pakistan and Greece.

Private sources of financial and logistical support for terrorists must be subjected to the full force and sweep of U.S. and international laws

All relevant agencies should use every available means, including the full array of criminal, civil, and administrative sanctions to block or disrupt nongovernmental sources of support for international terrorism.

Congress should promptly ratify and implement the International Convention for the Suppression of the Financing of Terrorism to enhance international cooperative efforts.

Where criminal prosecution is not possible, the Attorney General should vigorously pursue the expulsion of terrorists from the United States through proceedings which protect both the national security interest in safeguarding classified evidence and the right of the accused to challenge that evidence. . . .

The President and Congress should reform the system for reviewing and funding departmental counterterrorism programs to ensure that the activities and programs of various agencies are part of a comprehensive plan

The executive branch official responsible for coordinating counterterrorism efforts across the government should be given a stronger hand in the budget process.

Congress should develop mechanisms for a comprehensive review of the President's counterterrorism policy and budget.

Workers beside the crater left by a truck bomb explosion at a U.S. military facility in Saudi Arabia, June 26, 1996. AP/WIDE WORLD PHOTOS

SIGNIFICANCE

Upon its release, the NTC report met with resounding silence. The commission's warnings about the likelihood of an attack on U.S. soil that would result in mass casualties were not widely covered by the media. Despite an earlier attack on the World Trade Center and the increasing number of attacks on U.S. citizens and U.S. targets abroad, most Americans did not consider that a foreign terrorist attack on U.S. soil was very likely.

In 2004, the National Commission on Terrorist Attacks Upon the United States (commonly called the 9–11 Commission) released its report examining the September 11, 2001 attacks on the World Trade Center and the Pentagon. This second commission on terrorism made no references to the first commission, but it did take note of government faults first identified by the NTC. At least sixteen of the nineteen al–Qaeda hijackers of the planes that flew into the New York City and Washington, D.C. targets entered the country legally or remained in the United States on expired visas (immigration and temporary residence permits). The Immigration and Naturalization Service bore the responsibility to prevent suspected terrorists on the "watch list," a collection of databases from different federal agencies, from coming into the United Sates. The watch list, prepared primarily by the State Department, lacked access to FBI data. Contrary to NTC recommendations, government agencies were not cooperating in counterterrorism efforts by sharing information on a regular basis. No interagency comprehensive plan for counterterrorism had been put in place.

Following the findings of the 9–11 commission, the United States government began a wide-scale reorganization of the nation's intelligence services, immigration laws, and counterterrorism procedures. One of the major changes was the creation of the Department of Homeland Security, a new agency charged with directing and facilitating communication on terrorism and security issues among various government agencies.

FURTHER RESOURCES

Books

Flynn, Stephen. *America the Vulnerable: How the U.S. Has Failed to Secure the Homeland and Protect Its People from Terrorism.* New York: HarperCollins, 2004.

National Commission on Terrorist Attacks Upon the United States. *The 9/11 Commission Report: Final Report of the National Commission on Terrorist Attacks Upon the United States.* New York: WW Norton, 2004.

Pillar, Paul R. *Terrorism and U.S. Foreign Policy.* New York: Brookings Institution Press, 2001.

Web sites

Report of the National Commission on Terrorism. "Countering the Changing Threat of International Terrorism." <http://www.fas.org/irp/threat/commission.html> (accessed July 4, 2005).

Executive Order 13231

Critical Infrastructure Protection in the Information Age

Legislation

By: George W. Bush

Date: October 18, 2001

Source: Executive Order 13231, as recorded in the *Federal Register.*

About the Author: Executive Orders are directives issued by the President of the United States. The intent of this type of order, which has been in place since the first presidency of George Washington is usually to dictate specific action by officials or agencies working with the President on a specific issue. In more extreme cases of national emergency or threat to national security, an Executive Order can be used to impact upon specific members of groups within the general population. One famous case of this type of use of the directive occurred during the course of World War II (1939–1941), when President Franklin Roosevelt issued an Executive Order to intern American citizens of Japanese ancestry. On October 16, 2001, President Bush issued Executive Order 13231.

INTRODUCTION

With the world's increasing reliance on technology in all aspects of daily life, the threat posed by terrorists to use technology to interrupt the flow of information around the globe has grown more serious. There are few aspects of life in Western societies that are not directly connected to the information superhighway, as this flow of information around the globe has become known. The three tenets that help populations operate safely; free traffic of business and commerce, a strong government, and a national defense, could all be potentially crippled if the technological infrastructure supporting those institutions was compromised.

In the wake of the attacks of September 11, 2001, the United States government began to reassess all aspects of its national security including the potential threat to the nation's informational infrastructure posed by cyberterrorism.

Attacks launched over communications wires and computer networks can become manifest in numerous forms and with a large array of possible outcomes. Most commonly, information terrorists aim to introduce viruses into computer systems enabling them either to steal critical information or to destabilize public systems.

Cyber virus attacks can range from relatively harmless, in terms of human cost—such as those involving informational or commercial Internet sites being compromised—to attacks that could result in a large degree of human casualties. Such attacks include a cyber terrorist being able to shut down an electrical grid for an extended period of time, infiltrate national defense systems, or even destabilize nuclear power plants.

In addition to the countless benefits that information technology has offered, it has presented terrorists with the ability to wage their battles a world away from the site they plan to attack. A further danger involves the ease with which terrorists can communicate with one another without being detected.

Responding to this new reality required a coordinated response by the government and on October 16, 2001, President Bush issued Executive Order 13231 to protect the United States in the modern age of communications and technological reliance.

▌ PRIMARY SOURCE

By the authority vested in me as President by the Constitution and the laws of the United States of America, and in order to ensure protection of information systems for critical infrastructure, including emergency preparedness communications, and the physical assets that support such systems, in the information age, it is hereby ordered as follows:

Section 1: *Policy.* (a) The information technology revolution has changed the way business is transacted, government operates, and national defense is conducted. Those three functions now depend on an interdependent network of critical information infrastructures. The protection program authorized by this order shall consist of continuous efforts to secure information systems for critical infrastructure, including emergency preparedness communications, and the physical assets that support such systems. Protection of these systems is essential to the telecommunications, energy, financial services, manufacturing, water, transportation, health care, and emergency services sectors.

(b) It is the policy of the United States to protect against disruption of the operation of information systems for critical infrastructure and thereby help to protect the people, economy, essential human and government services, and national security of the United States, and to

ensure that any disruptions that occur are infrequent, of minimal duration, and manageable, and cause the least damage possible. The implementation of this policy shall include a voluntary public-private partnership, involving corporate and nongovernmental organizations.

Section 2: *Scope.* To achieve this policy, there shall be a senior executive branch board to coordinate and have cognizance of Federal efforts and programs that relate to protection of information systems and involve:

(a) cooperation with and protection of private sector critical infrastructure, State and local governments' critical infrastructure, and supporting programs in corporate and academic organizations;

(b) protection of Federal departments' and agencies' critical infrastructure; and

(c) related national security programs. . . .

Section 4: *Continuing Authorities.* . . . (b) National Security Information Systems. The Secretary of Defense and the Director of Central Intelligence (DCI) shall have responsibility to oversee, develop, and ensure implementation of policies, principles, standards, and guidelines for the security of information systems that support the operations under their respective control. In consultation with the Assistant to the President for National Security Affairs and the affected departments and agencies, the Secretary of Defense and the DCI shall develop policies, principles, standards, and guidelines for the security of national security information systems that support the operations of other executive branch departments and agencies with national security information. . . .

(c) Additional Responsibilities: The Heads of Executive Branch Departments and Agencies. The heads of executive branch departments and agencies are responsible and accountable for providing and maintaining adequate levels of security for information systems, including emergency preparedness communications systems, for programs under their control. Heads of such departments and agencies shall ensure the development and, within available appropriations, funding of programs that adequately address these mission areas. Cost-effective security shall be built into and made an integral part of government information systems, especially those critical systems that support the national security and other essential government programs. Additionally, security should enable, and not unnecessarily impede, department and agency business operations.

Section 5: *Board Responsibilities.* Consistent with the responsibilities noted in section 4 of this order, the Board shall recommend policies and coordinate programs for protecting information systems for critical infrastructure, including emergency preparedness communications, and the physical assets that support such systems. Among its activities to implement these responsibilities, the Board shall:

(a) Outreach to the Private Sector and State and Local Governments. In consultation with affected executive branch departments and agencies, coordinate outreach to and consultation with the private sector, including corporations that own, operate, develop, and equip information, telecommunications, transportation, energy, water, health care, and financial services, on protection of information systems for critical infrastructure, including emergency preparedness communications, and the physical assets that support such systems; and coordinate outreach to State and local governments, as well as communities and representatives from academia and other relevant elements of society. . . .

(ii) Consult with potentially affected communities, including the legal, auditing, financial, and insurance communities, to the extent permitted by law, to determine areas of mutual concern; and

(iii) Coordinate the activities of senior liaison officers appointed by the Attorney General, the Secretaries of Energy, Commerce, Transportation, the Treasury, and Health and Human Services, and the Director of the Federal Emergency Management Agency for outreach on critical infrastructure protection issues with private sector organizations within the areas of concern to these departments and agencies. In these and other related functions, the Board shall work in coordination with the Critical Infrastructure Assurance Office (CIAO) and the National Institute of Standards and Technology of the Department of Commerce, the National Infrastructure Protection Center (NIPC), and the National Communications System (NCS).

(b) Information Sharing. Work with industry, State and local governments, and nongovernmental organizations to ensure that systems are created and well managed to share threat warning, analysis, and recovery information among government network operation centers, information sharing and analysis centers established on a voluntary basis by industry, and other related operations centers. In this and other related functions, the Board shall work in coordination with the NCS, the Federal Computer Incident Response Center, the NIPC, and other departments and agencies, as appropriate.

(c) Incident Coordination and Crisis Response. Coordinate programs and policies for responding to information systems security incidents that threaten information systems for critical infrastructure, including emergency preparedness communications, and the physical assets that support such systems. In this function, the Department of Justice, through the NIPC and the Manager of the NCS and other departments and agencies, as appropriate, shall work in coordination with the Board. . . .

(e) Research and Development. Coordinate with the Director of the Office of Science and Technology Policy (OSTP) on a program of Federal Government research and development for protection of information systems for critical infrastructure, including emergency preparedness communications, and the physical assets that support such systems, and ensure coordination of government activities in this field with corporations, universities, Federally funded research centers, and national laboratories. In this function, the Board shall work in coordination with the National Science Foundation, the Defense Advanced Research Projects Agency, and with other departments and agencies, as appropriate.

(f) Law Enforcement Coordination with National Security Components. Promote programs against cyber crime and assist Federal law enforcement agencies in gaining necessary cooperation from executive branch departments and agencies. Support Federal law enforcement agencies' investigation of illegal activities involving information systems for critical infrastructure, including emergency preparedness communications, and the physical assets that support such systems, and support coordination by these agencies with other departments and agencies with responsibilities to defend the Nation's security, the Board shall work in coordination with the Department of Justice, through the NIPC, and the Department of the Treasury, through the Secret Service, and with other departments and agencies, as appropriate.

(g) International Information Infrastructure Protection. Support the Department of State's coordination of United States Government programs for international cooperation covering international information infrastructure protection issues. . . .

(i) Coordination with Office of Homeland Security. Carry out those functions relating to protection of and recovery from attacks against information systems for critical infrastructure, including emergency preparedness communications, that were assigned to the Office of Homeland Security by Executive Order 13228 of October 8, 2001. The Assistant to the President for Homeland Security, in coordination with the Assistant to the President for National Security Affairs, shall be responsible for defining the responsibilities of the Board in coordinating efforts to protect physical assets that support information systems.

SIGNIFICANCE

In the wake of September 2001, the government of the United States was forced to reconsider all possible threats that could be posed to the nation. This executive order outlines the commitment of the government in exposing the potential for further harm to be exacted against the United States. While this order by no means introduced the notion of the vulnerability of the nation's infrastructure in light of its reliance on technology, it used the attacks as a reason to strengthen defenses already in place.

In presenting this order, the government recognizes that terrorists are committed to discovering new ways of attacking their enemies, and recognizes that terrorist organizations have dedicated themselves towards enhancing their ability to bring down the information infrastructure of the United States.

The information age has made it extremely difficult, or even impossible, to create any physical barriers between the government and the outside world. Whereas in the past, secret documents were locked behind sealed and guarded doors, the nature of today's reliance on technology means that with enough motivation and the proper knowledge, criminals and terrorists can sometimes gain access to information at the highest levels of government and the defense community.

The primary action taken in light of this order was the creation of the President's Critical Infrastructure Protection Board, whose job it is to offer the recommendations for policies to protect the nation's critical systems from attack, and to provide an emergency plan for responding to such an attack. The board was created to work as a partner with the Office of Homeland Security.

FURTHER RESOURCES

Books

Ball, Kirstie and Webster, Frank. *The Intensification Of Surveillance: Crime, Terrorism and Warfare in the Information Age* . London: Pluto Press, 2003.

Web sites

Rand.com. "The Networking of Terror in the Information Age." <http://www.rand.org/publications/MR/MR1382/MR1382.ch2.pdf> (accessed July 4, 2005).

The Office of Homeland Security. "Research and Technology: Information and Infrastructure." <http://www.dhs.gov/dhspublic/display?theme=26> (accessed July 4, 2005).

Stockpiling Vaccine

"U.S. Seeks to Stock Smallpox Vaccine for Whole Nation"

Newspaper article

By: Sheryl Gay Stolberg

Date: October 18, 2001

Source: "U.S. Seeks to Stock Smallpox Vaccine for Whole Nation" as published by the *New York Times*.

About the Author: Sheryl Gay Stolberg is a journalist with the *New York Times*. Stolberg primarily writes on the subjects of politics and international affairs.

INTRODUCTION

Following the September 11, 2001 attacks on New York City and the Pentagon, the United States military and government increased efforts to shield Americans from the effects of terrorism. The September 11th attacks were followed shortly thereafter by anthrax-laced letters that were mailed to key political leaders and media personnel. Also, snipers located in the Washington D.C. area shot several randomly chosen individuals. Although The D.C. sniper was not connected to international terrorism, and authorities later concluded the anthrax attacks originated from within the United States, each of these actions led to federal legislation to increase the country's preparedness for a possible bioterrorism attack. One preparation included the purchase and stockpiling of smallpox vaccines. Smallpox is a disease caused by the variola virus and is often fatal, but the vaccine can prevent infection for several years, or if given after exposure can prevent or lessen the disease's impact. Smallpox was considered eradicated in 1979, but the possible threat of terrorists gaining access to existing stores of the virus for use in a bioterrorist attack prompted authorities to take action.

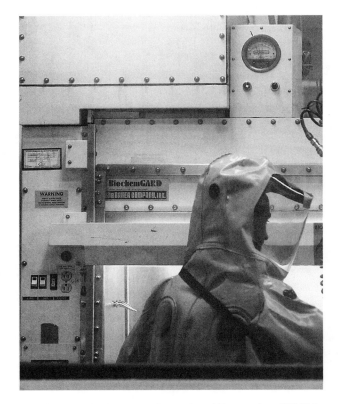

The Centers for Disease Control and Prevention (CDC) in Atlanta dedicated one of its two maximum-containment laboratories to smallpox-only research. AP/WIDE WORLD PHOTOS

PRIMARY SOURCE

Federal health officials are negotiating with four drug companies to buy 300 million doses of smallpox vaccine—enough for every American—and are gingerly discussing the possibility that ordinary Americans might someday once again be vaccinated against the disease.

While there are no immediate plans for vaccination, Tommy G. Thompson, the secretary of health and human services, said today that he was asking lawmakers for $509 million so that the government could stockpile enough vaccine to protect everyone in the nation against the potentially lethal smallpox vaccine.

"I can report to you that it looks very promising that we will have the 300 million doses by sometime next year," Mr. Thompson told reporters this evening. He said that he had met with representatives of two drug companies today, and that he would meet with two others on Thursday.

The decision to pursue more stocks of smallpox vaccine came as fears of attack with another biological agent, anthrax, spread across the country. Mr. Thompson did not say whether the recent spate of anthrax-laced letters, including one mailed to Tom Daschle, the Senate majority leader, influenced his decision.

Nor did he say whether the government was aware of any specific threat involving smallpox. Asked what prompted the policy shift, Mr. Thompson simply replied, "We thought we should go and see if we could get some other companies interested in the 300 million doses."

The health secretary and President Bush have been discussing bioterrorism preparedness since the Sept. 11 attacks on the World Trade Center and Pentagon, said Kevin Keane, a spokesman for Mr. Thompson. Sometime within the past week, Mr. Keane said, the White House gave Mr. Thompson the go-ahead to ask Congress to pay for the 300 million doses, so the country could be prepared for "the worst-case scenario."

Unlike anthrax, which is not transmitted from person to person, smallpox is highly contagious, and Mr. Thompson is clearly aware that it poses a potential menace. After the Sept. 11 attacks, he named Dr. Donald A. Henderson, who led the global effort that resulted in the eradication of smallpox in 1979, to lead a new advisory council on bioterrorism.

In June, a war game with the code name Dark Winter showed what chaos could erupt from a bioterrorist attack involving smallpox. The exercise, at Andrews Air Force Base, outside Washington, began with a report of a single case of smallpox in Oklahoma City. By the time it was over, the imaginary epidemic had spread to 25 states and killed several million people. As it unfolded, growing grimmer and grimmer, the government quickly ran out of vaccine.

Smallpox vaccine can be used not only to prevent infection with the smallpox virus but also to treat people exposed to the virus, and thus contain an epidemic.

But the United States abandoned smallpox vaccinations in 1972, because the disease had been virtually wiped out here. The vaccine itself carries serious health risks. It produced adverse reactions in roughly 1 in 13,000 vaccinated people, ranging from severe rashes to brain inflammation, which killed about one person in one million. So experts said that the risk of vaccination was greater than the risk of getting the disease.

Experts say that the chances that terrorists could lay hands on the smallpox virus—which officially exists now only in government laboratories in the United States and Russia—are remote.

But smallpox, which kills about one of three people infected with it, is a particularly worrisome threat because it is easily transmittable. Even those Americans who have been vaccinated are at risk, because the vaccine's protection is believed to last only 15 or 20 years.

And unlike anthrax, which would require that spores be prepared according to precise specifications to infect large numbers of people, a smallpox epidemic could begin with a single infected person—a "smallpox martyr," in the terminology of bioterrorism experts—simply walking through a crowd.

The two official laboratory repositories for smallpox, one at the Centers for Disease Control and Prevention in Atlanta and the other at a Russian government facility in western Siberia, are monitored by the World Health Organization, and are generally thought to be secure.

But, Dr. Tucker said, there are "suspicions that there are undeclared stocks of smallpox virus in Russia," particularly at a top-secret virology laboratory under control of the Russian Ministry of Defense. A federal intelligence report completed in 1998 concluded that clandestine stocks of smallpox virus probably existed in Russia, as well as in Iraq and North Korea.

The growing fear of bioterrorism has renewed the question of whether Americans should be vaccinated. Today, a higher proportion of the population than in the past may run the risk of being harmed by the vaccine. It could cause serious illness in people whose immune systems are suppressed, including organ transplant recipients and people with AIDS, a disease that was not even known the last time Americans were vaccinated for smallpox.

So a decision to vaccinate Americans would not be made lightly, and Mr. Thompson emphasized today that there are no plans to do so.

But he did suggest that the government would revisit the question, a startling comment in and of itself. "Sometime in the future there may be a discussion that may lead to voluntary vaccinations for the smallpox bug," he said.

Should that happen, it would constitute a huge shift in public policy. Mohammed N. Akhter, executive director of the American Public Health Association, has been publicly urging the administration to reopen the question of smallpox vaccination.

"My worry is that there will be a case in the U.S., we will rush to contain it, we will immunize some people but the level of public concern will be such that we will not be in a position to make a thoughtful decision," Dr. Akhter said today. He said the scientific community needed to "rethink the immunization priority for our people against smallpox."

The renewal of the immunization debate, said Dr. Irwin Redlener, president of a children's hospital at Montefiore Medical Center in the Bronx, "makes us really all pause in terms of what has happened to our country."

Dr. Redlener added, "If we have to go back to vaccinating people for smallpox, we are really about to turn back the hands of time."

SIGNIFICANCE

On 20 January 2004, the U.S. Congress amended the Public Health Service Act to provide additional avenues of support for countermeasures against chemical, radiological, and nuclear agents that may be used in a terrorist attack. Essentially, countermeasures include civil protections, vaccines, and defense plans to stop or prevent attacks by terrorists.

The United States sought to implement countermeasures for biological terrorist attacks when CIA and FBI intelligence reports stated it was possible that Iraq

The envelope in which an anthrax-laced letter was sent to the Senate Majority Leader Tom Daschle on October 23, 2001. © REUTERS/CORBIS

and other unauthorized countries had stockpiles of the smallpox virus. The only two countries authorized by the World health Organization to hold the smallpox vaccine are the United States and the former Soviet Union but intelligence reports asserted that the Soviet Union had possibly inadvertently supplied North Korea and Iraq with smallpox specimens.

The Soviet Union and the United States gained the right to store and research the smallpox virus because of post World War II peace accords and international political presences in organizations like the United Nations. Other major world powers also held stocks of the virus, but in 1978, the virus escaped from a British laboratory, infected a photographer in a nearby room, and she infected her parents. As a result of these actions, the World Health Organization passed a resolution to kill all remaining stocks of the virus except for those in the United States and Soviet Union.

The smallpox specimens were supposed to be destroyed in the 1990s under orders from the World Health Organization, but the U.S. successfully argued that samples of the smallpox virus were needed for future testing and for the possibility that researchers might one day need to vaccinate the general public again. The proposed destruction date of 1999 was postponed until 2002, but the September 11th terrorist attacks halted the destruction of the virus indefinitely. Opponents to storing the virus state that it is too dangerous to keep such a volatile disease on hand and assert that it can be obtained from other sources, such as from graves of smallpox victims or live animals infected with a similar virus in order to conduct research.

In 2003, U.S. officials sought to vaccinate frontline public health workers, state officials, and Pentagon workers against the virus with plans to extend the vaccination network outward. The vaccine can have serious side effects, although seldomly, and opponents to the program quickly voiced their opinions. Currently, the United States has halted mainstream vaccination plans, but is still acquiring smallpox vaccine.

FURTHER RESOURCES
Books

Laqueur, Walter. *The New Terrorism: Fanaticism and the Arms of Mass Destruction*. New York and Oxford: Oxford University Press, 2000.

Web sites

CNN.com. "Terrorism drill tests country's readiness." <http://www.cnn.com/2003/fyi/news/05/11/topoff/index.html> (accessed 22 June 2005).

cns.miis.edu. "Smallpox: Threat, Vaccine, and US Policy." <http://cns.miis.edu/pubs/week/030106.htm> (accessed 26 June 2005).

USA PATRIOT Act

Legislation

By: 107th U.S. Congress

Date: October 26, 2001

Source: USA Patriot Act

About the Author: President George W. Bush signed the USA PATRIOT Act, previously passed by the first session of the 107th United States Congress, into law on October 26, 2001.

INTRODUCTION

The United States Congress established the USA PATRIOT Act (Patriot Act) to improve the capabilities of law enforcement agents to prevent terror attacks, and to more effectively investigate and prosecute terrorists and would be terrorists. USA PATRIOT, is an acronym for, "Uniting and Strengthening America by Providing Appropriate Tools Required to Intercept and Obstruct Terrorism."

The United Sates Senate and House of Representatives created the Patriot Act to facilitate the work of investigators, so they would be better equipped to deal with the crimes labeled as terrorism. Because of their unconventional nature, terrorism-related crimes might not have been covered under laws prior to the Patriot Act.

President George Bush remarks on the Patriot Act in Buffalo, New York, 2004. AP/WIDE WORLD PHOTOS

The Act is intended to give investigators access to information and use of appropriate technology to monitor the movements of terrorists and to research suspected terrorist organizations, with the goal of stopping terrorist activities before they occur.

Information gathering is one area of focus of the Patriot Act. Previously, there were limitations to the instances when law enforcement could conduct electronic surveillance of terrorist related activities. The Act gives more authority to investigators to carry out surveillance of all terrorism-related activities, including chemical-weapons offenses, the use of weapons of mass destruction, the killing of Americans abroad, and the financing of terrorism.

The Act also helps law enforcement officials more easily obtain subpoenas for access to information records of suspected terrorists and terrorist organizations. The Act facilitates more functional sharing of information between government agencies and prosecutors, to improve efficiency, and eliminate duplicated efforts for solving terrorism-related crimes and prosecuting those involved.

Patriot Act legislation was officially signed by U.S. President George W. Bush on October 26, 2001. This was less than two months after the attacks of September 11th, when passenger planes were hijacked and flown into the Pentagon and the World Trade Center towers in New York City.

Much of the Patriot Act consists of additions, adjustments, and deletions to already existing laws so they can be applied to investigations involving terrorist activity. The Act is organized into ten different titles, with each title containing several sections describing different aspects of terrorism and how terrorism is to be dealt with in the United States.

▌ PRIMARY SOURCE

AN ACT

To deter and punish terrorist acts in the United States and around the world, to enhance law enforcement investigatory tools, and for other purposes.

Be it enacted by the Senate and House of Representatives of the United States of America in Congress assembled,

SECTION 1. SHORT TITLE AND TABLE OF CONTENTS.

(a) SHORT TITLE—This Act may be cited as the "Uniting and Strengthening America by Providing Appropriate Tools Required to Intercept and Obstruct Terrorism (USA PATRIOT ACT) Act of 2001".

Vince Dy right directs his search dog, Rexie, to sniff a passenger's bag at the United Airlines counter in Nashville, Tennessee. AP/WIDE WORLD PHOTOS

Sec. 1013. Expressing the sense of the senate concerning the provision of funding for bioterrorism preparedness and response.

Sec. 1014. Grant program for State and local domestic preparedness support.

Sec. 1015. Expansion and reauthorization of the crime identification technology act for antiterrorism grants to States and localities.

Sec. 1016. Critical infrastructures protection.

SIGNIFICANCE

According to the United States Department of Justice, the Patriot Act has been successful in providing expanded law enforcement powers that improve the federal government's efforts to identify and stop terrorism acts in the U.S. or against U.S. interests abroad. The Department of Justice calls attention to four significant aspects of the Patriot Act that highlight its success.

First, the Department of Justice says the Patriot Act allows terrorism investigators to use tools that have always been available for investigating organized crime and drug trafficking. These tools improve the ability of law enforcement agents to use surveillance measures for cases involving suspected terrorism crimes. Also, investigators are allowed the opportunity to delay notifying a person if a warrant has been executed to find out information about him or her. This is a method of collecting information without a suspect knowing, so the party does not destroy or hide pertinent information just prior to the arrival of investigators. Also, in some cases, investigators can be issued a subpoena for accessing information records more easily through a federal court than by going through a more complicated and timely grand jury hearing.

Secondly, the Department of Justice says the Patriot Act facilitates cooperation among government agencies allowing them to share information about individuals and specific cases. This is designed to allow prosecutors and intelligence officials to share evidence received from grand juries.

Third, the Patriot Act allows authorities to use up-to-date technologies to investigate terrorists who use highly sophisticated means of communication, and operate in many different locations. Authorities can monitor the activity of computer hackers on computer networks, as if they were physical trespassers on private property. In some cases, authorities can use a search warrant beyond the boundaries of the district where the search warrant was obtained. This is said to allow investigators to do their work in several districts without having to go through the lengthy process of obtaining multiple warrants where they want to follow specific terrorists.

Finally, the Department of Justice explains that the Patriot Act has increased penalties for those people who are involved in carrying out terrorist crimes. The law also specifically prohibits people from harboring terrorists. It increases the maximum penalties for crimes that would likely be carried out by terrorists, such as arson, destruction of energy facilities, and giving support to terrorist groups. The Act goes on to make penalties for specific types of terrorism, including terrorism on mass transit, bio-terrorism, and for conspiracy to carry out terrorist acts.

Despite the stated success from the U.S. government, there have been numerous critics of the Patriot Act, including the American Civil Liberties Union (ACLU). The ACLU, and other privacy and civil liberties advocates, assert that the Act violates too many individual freedoms and liberties, especially regarding privacy. They argue that the Act makes it too easy for law enforcement officials to collect personal information and monitor organizations and individuals, especially American citizens, under the auspices of terrorism-related investigation.

Critics also claim that the Patriot Act allows excessive monitoring of Americans who may or may not know they are being watched. The Act allows the Government to monitor records of Internet use, utilize roving phone taps, and monitor private records of individual participants of legal, legitimate protests.

It is argued that the Act minimizes the system of checks and balances between the legislative, judicial, and executive branches of government, by giving too much power to the executive branch. The executive branch has increased authority when search and surveillance powers are given to domestic and foreign law enforcement agencies. Critics say the judicial review and supervision of information gathering is therefore weakened. Critics also point out that the Attorney General has increased power to detain and deport non-citizens with minimized judicial oversight.

Supporters of the act disagree, claiming that authorities do not have free reign to do whatever they want, and that under the Act, the courts must still be included in the surveillance activities of law enforcement. They say the Patriot Act ensures the ease with which law enforcement agencies are able to obtain the mandatory court permissions for carrying out the necessary terrorism-related investigations.

In September 2004, a federal judge ruled that the Act did indeed violate the Constitution, by giving federal authorities unchecked powers to acquire private information.

Another common argument is that the Patriot Act oversteps its stated boundaries of working to eliminate terrorism, as many of the provisions in the ACT apply to all situations, not only those involving terrorist crimes.

Critics, who are found in both the Democratic and Republican political parties, say the Patriot Act is too large and complex, and that it was constructed in a rush shortly after the September 11th attacks in 2001. The goal then was to put legislation into place quickly in order to help ensure the prevention of additional terrorist attacks. Further debate and discussion may have produced a more acceptable set of provisions.

Numerous U.S. communities have debated in town hall and city council meetings as to whether or not the Patriot Act violates civil liberties. Resolutions stating an opposition to the Patriot Act have been passed in 389 communities in forty-three different states according to the ACLU. Of those, seven were statewide resolutions (including Colorado, Montana, and Idaho).

Many of the provisions in the Act expired at the end of 2005. Extension of, changes to, or permanent adoption of measures in the Act, are decided upon by the U.S. Congress, and ultimately must be signed into law by the President.

FURTHER RESOURCES
Periodicals

Julia Preston. "Judge Strikes Down Section of Patriot Act." *New York Times*. September 30, 2004.

James G. Lakely. "Conservatives, liberals align against Patriot Act." *Washington Times*. June 14, 2005.

Web sites

Jurist "The USA Patriot Act and the U.S. Department of Justice: Losing Our Balances?" <http://jurist.law.pitt.edu/forum/forumnew40.htm> (accessed July 4, 2005).

American Civil Liberties Union. "USA Patriot Act." <http://www.aclu.org/SafeandFree/SafeandFree.cfm?ID=12126&c=207> (accessed July 4, 2005).

United States Department of Justice. "The USA PATRIOT Act: Preserving Life and Liberty." <http://www.lifeandliberty.gov/highlights.htm> (accessed July 7, 2005).

G-8 Statement on WMDs

"The G-8 Global Partnership Against the Spread of Weapons and Materials of Mass Destruction"

Position statement

By: Group of Eight (G-8) industrialized nations

Date: June 27, 2002

Source: Available from the U.S. State Department at <http://www.state.gov/e/eb/rls/othr/11514.htm>.

About the Author: The Group of Eight, or G-8, began as the Group of Seven in 1975, when the leaders of the world's largest industrial democracies—Canada, France, Germany, Italy, Japan, the United Kingdom, and the United States—began meeting annually to discuss major political and economic issues. It became the G-8 when Russia joined the discussions in 1997, after having participated informally since 1994.

INTRODUCTION

When the Soviet Union collapsed in 1991, its former republics faced a monumental problem: what to do with the Soviet nuclear arms stockpile amassed during the Cold War, along with facilities for producing such weapons, enriching uranium, and storing nuclear materials. Many of these weapons and facilities were located in several of the old Soviet republics, including Kazakhstan, the Ukraine, and Belarus. Overnight, a number of new nations were, in essence, nuclear powers. Eventually, these nations responded to diplomatic pressure and economic incentives and returned the nuclear materials within their borders to Russia.

The ongoing problem, however, was the safety and security of Russian nuclear materials, as well as other weapons of mass destruction (WMD). The difficulties

The thirty-five feet deep crater made by a truck bomb at the Khobar Towers in Dhahran, Saudi Arabia, June 26, 1996.
AP/WIDE WORLD PHOTOS

were manifold. Rapid and momentous changes in Russia created political instability. Power vacuums led to the rise of Mafia-type organizations and corrupt officials willing to trade in arms, including nuclear weapons. Economic conditions deteriorated as the nation tried to make the transition from a communist to a market-based economic system. Russian infrastructure was crumbling, and little money was available to fix it. Rampant unemployment, especially among former communist research scientists in the weapons industry, made them susceptible to recruitment by terrorists.

These conditions exponentially increased the possibility that rogue nations or terrorist organizations, such as Al-Qaeda, could acquire unsecured Russian nuclear materials. Indeed, Al-Qaeda has attempted to acquire fissionable material, and in 2001, documents discovered in an Al-Qaeda safe house showed a grasp of nuclear weapons design.

The nuclear materials unaccounted-for included suitcase bombs (small, one-kiloton nuclear devices that could easily be smuggled into a major city), nuclear artillery shells, hundreds of metric tons of plutonium and highly enriched uranium that could be used to make a dirty bomb, and even full-scale nuclear bombs. The problem was not confined to so-called loose nukes. Also vulnerable was the Soviet stockpile of chemical, biological, and nerve agents. In 1995, the hypothetical threat became real when U.S. authorities, in a two-year investigation, uncovered and thwarted a credible plot to smuggle a stolen nuclear weapon into Miami, Florida.

Throughout the 1990s, the Western nations began to realize that the nuclear threat they faced came less from state actors than from terrorist organizations—and that the problem was international in scope. Accordingly, in 2002, in the wake of the September 11, 2001, terrorist attacks on the United States, the Group of Eight industrialized nations pledged $10 billion—$20 billion from the United States and $30 billion from the other nations—to help Russia secure its nuclear materials. Reproduced below is the G-8's statement announcing the program.

PRIMARY SOURCE

Statement by the Group of Eight Leaders

Kananaskis, Canada

June 27, 2002

The attacks of September 11 demonstrated that terrorists are prepared to use any means to cause terror and inflict appalling casualties on innocent people. We commit ourselves to prevent terrorists, or those that harbour them, from acquiring or developing nuclear, chemical, radiological

and biological weapons; missiles; and related materials, equipment and technology. We call on all countries to join us in adopting the set of non-proliferation principles we have announced today.

In a major initiative to implement those principles, we have also decided today to launch a new G8 Global Partnership against the Spread of Weapons and Materials of Mass Destruction. Under this initiative, we will support specific cooperation projects, initially in Russia, to address non-proliferation, disarmament, counter-terrorism and nuclear safety issues. Among our priority concerns are the destruction of chemical weapons, the dismantlement of decommissioned nuclear submarines, the disposition of fissile materials and the employment of former weapons scientists. We will commit to raise up to $20 billion to support such projects over the next ten years. A range of financing options, including the option of bilateral debt for program exchanges, will be available to countries that contribute to this Global Partnership. We have adopted a set of guidelines that will form the basis for the negotiation of specific agreements for new projects, that will apply with immediate effect, to ensure effective and efficient project development, coordination and implementation. We will review over the next year the applicability of the guidelines to existing projects.

Recognizing that this Global Partnership will enhance international security and safety, we invite other countries that are prepared to adopt its common principles and guidelines to enter into discussions with us on participating in and contributing to this initiative. We will review progress on this Global Partnership at our next Summit in 2003.

THE G8 GLOBAL PARTNERSHIP: PRINCIPLES TO PREVENT TERRORISTS, OR THOSE THAT HARBOUR THEM, FROM GAINING ACCESS TO WEAPONS OR MATERIALS OF MASS DESTRUCTION

The G8 calls on all countries to join them in commitment to the following six principles to prevent terrorists or those that harbour them from acquiring or developing nuclear, chemical, radiological and biological weapons; missiles; and related materials, equipment and technology.

1. Promote the adoption, universalization, full implementation and, where necessary, strengthening of multilateral treaties and other international instruments whose aim is to prevent the proliferation or illicit acquisition of such items; strengthen the institutions designed to implement these instruments.

2. Develop and maintain appropriate effective measures to account for and secure such items in production, use, storage and domestic and international transport; provide assistance to states lacking sufficient resources to account for and secure these items.

3. Develop and maintain appropriate effective physical protection measures applied to facilities which house such items, including defence in depth; provide assistance to states lacking sufficient resources to protect their facilities.

4. Develop and maintain effective border controls, law enforcement efforts and international cooperation to detect, deter and interdict in cases of illicit trafficking in such items, for example through installation of detection systems, training of customs and law enforcement personnel and cooperation in tracking these items; provide assistance to states lacking sufficient expertise or resources to strengthen their capacity to detect, deter and interdict in cases of illicit trafficking in these items.

5. Develop, review and maintain effective national export and transshipment controls over items on multilateral export control lists, as well as items that are not identified on such lists but which may nevertheless contribute to the development, production or use of nuclear, chemical and biological weapons and missiles, with particular consideration of end-user, catch-all and brokering aspects; provide assistance to states lacking the legal and regulatory infrastructure, implementation experience and/or resources to develop their export and transshipment control systems in this regard.

6. Adopt and strengthen efforts to manage and dispose of stocks of fissile materials designated as no longer required for defence purposes, eliminate all chemical weapons, and minimize holdings of dangerous biological pathogens and toxins, based on the recognition that the threat of terrorist acquisition is reduced as the overall quantity of such items is reduced.

THE G8 GLOBAL PARTNERSHIP: GUIDELINES FOR NEW OR EXPANDED COOPERATION PROJECTS

The G8 will work in partnership, bilaterally and multilaterally, to develop, coordinate, implement and finance, according to their respective means, new or expanded cooperation projects to address (i) non-proliferation, (ii) disarmament, (iii) counter-terrorism and (iv) nuclear safety (including environmental) issues, with a view to enhancing strategic stability, consonant with our international security objectives and in support of the multilateral non-proliferation regimes. Each country has primary responsibility for implementing its non-proliferation, disarmament, counter-terrorism and nuclear safety obligations and requirements and commits its full cooperation within the Partnership.

Cooperation projects under this initiative will be decided and implemented, taking into account international obligations and domestic laws of participating partners, within appropriate bilateral and multilateral legal frameworks that should, as necessary, include the following elements:

i. Mutually agreed effective monitoring, auditing and transparency measures and procedures will be required in order to ensure that cooperative activities meet agreed objectives (including irreversibility as necessary), to confirm work performance, to account for the funds expended and to provide for adequate access for donor representatives to work sites;

ii. The projects will be implemented in an environmentally sound manner and will maintain the highest appropriate level of safety;

iii. Clearly defined milestones will be developed for each project, including the option of suspending or terminating a project if the milestones are not met;

iv. The material, equipment, technology, services and expertise provided will be solely for peaceful purposes and, unless otherwise agreed, will be used only for the purposes of implementing the projects and will not be transferred. Adequate measures of physical protection will also be applied to prevent theft or sabotage;

v. All governments will take necessary steps to ensure that the support provided will be considered free technical assistance and will be exempt from taxes, duties, levies and other charges;

vi. Procurement of goods and services will be conducted in accordance with open international practices to the extent possible, consistent with national security requirements;

vii. All governments will take necessary steps to ensure that adequate liability protections from claims related to the cooperation will be provided for donor countries and their personnel and contractors;

viii. Appropriate privileges and immunities will be provided for government donor representatives working on cooperation projects; and

ix. Measures will be put in place to ensure effective protection of sensitive information and intellectual property.

Given the breadth and scope of the activities to be undertaken, the G8 will establish an appropriate mechanism for the annual review of progress under this initiative which may include consultations regarding priorities, identification of project gaps and potential overlap, and assessment of consistency of the cooperation projects with international security obligations and objectives. Specific bilateral and multilateral project implementation will be coordinated subject to arrangements appropriate to that project, including existing mechanisms.

For the purposes of these guidelines, the phrase "new or expanded cooperation projects" is defined as cooperation projects that will be initiated or enhanced on the basis of this Global Partnership. All funds disbursed or released after its announcement would be included in the total of

Libyan leader Moammer Gadhafi at a 2001 news conference after agreeing to halt his nation's drive to develop nuclear and chemical weapons. AP/WIDE WORLD PHOTOS

committed resources. A range of financing options, including the option of bilateral debt for program exchanges, will be available to countries that contribute to this Global Partnership.

The Global Partnership's initial geographic focus will be on projects in Russia, which maintains primary responsibility for implementing its obligations and requirements within the Partnership.

In addition, the G8 would be willing to enter into negotiations with any other recipient countries, including those of the Former Soviet Union, prepared to adopt the guidelines, for inclusion in the Partnership.

Recognizing that the Global Partnership is designed to enhance international security and safety, the G8 invites others to contribute to and join in this initiative.

With respect to nuclear safety and security, the partners agreed to establish a new G8 Nuclear Safety and Security Group by the time of our next Summit.

SIGNIFICANCE

The United States recognized early after the breakup of the Soviet Union that it was in its own interest to help its former cold war adversary secure its nuclear materials. Accordingly, in 1992, the U.S. Department of Defense provided Russia and other former Soviet republics with funds and expertise under the Cooperative Threat Reduction Program (often referred to as the Nunn-Lugar program after its congressional sponsors, Senators Sam Nunn and Richard Lugar).

The Nunn-Lugar program had some success in helping Russia dismantle portions of its nuclear arsenal, destroy missile silos and warheads, and secure remaining nuclear weapons storage sites. It also sponsored programs to convert Russia's military industries to peacetime applications. A dramatic moment occurred when the U.S. defense secretary and the Russian and Ukrainian defense ministers, who just years earlier had glowered at one another across an ideological divide, gathered to plant sunflowers over an old missile silo in the Ukraine.

But another dramatic moment occurred on January 25, 1995, when a Russian radar crew picked up a fast-moving object over the Barents Sea along Russia's northern border and was unable to identify it. Russian president Boris Yeltsin was literally one minute away from launching a retaliatory strike when the object disappeared from the radar. The object, it turned out, was a rocket launched from Norway to study the Northern Lights. Norway had notified Russia of the impending launch, but no one had notified the radar crew.

The Nunn-Lugar program was entirely a U.S. response to post-Cold War relations with Russia. Incidents such as the one in 1995, combined with the growing threat of global terrorism, made it the interest of all the world's powers to secure Russia's WMD. Cities such as London and Tokyo were just as vulnerable as New York and Washington, D.C. Knowing this, the G-8 took action.

Two years later, though, the G-8 pledge was not yet having the desired impact. The G-8 nations were $3 billion short on their pledges, and only a fraction of the $17 billion appropriated was spent. Disputes arose with Russia over tax and liability issues and access to sites. Political wrangling delayed, for more than three years, the construction of a plant for destroying Russia's WMD. Project completion dates under the G-8 program stretch well into the 2010s. As Senator Nunn himself noted, "The clock is ticking."

FURTHER RESOURCES
Books

Carter, Ashton B., and William J. Perry. *Preventive Defense: A New Security Strategy for America.* Washington, D.C.: Brookings Institution Press, 1999.

Periodicals

"Russia's Nuclear Arms Deemed Vulnerable; CIA Says 'Insider' Could Pose Threat." *Washington Times.* February 23, 2002.

Web sites

U.S. General Accounting Office. "Nuclear Nonproliferation: Security of Russia's Nuclear Material Improving; Further Enhancements Needed." February 2001. Available from <http://www.gao.gov/new.items/d01312.pdf> (June 30, 2005).

Audio and Visual Media

PBS. *"Russian Roulette: A Report on the Safety and Security of Russia's Nuclear Arsenal".* February 1999. Available online at <http://www.pbs.org/wgbh/pages/frontline/shows/russia/> (with video links) (June 30, 2005).

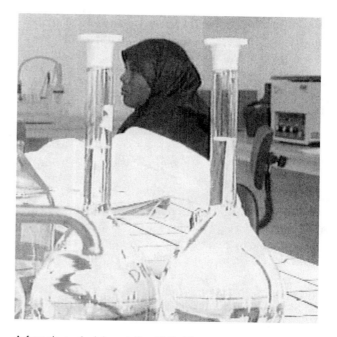

A female technician at the Shifa Pharmaceutical factory in Khartoum, Sudan, which was allegedly manufacturing chemical weapons. AP/WIDE WORLD PHOTOS

Terrorism and Technology

"Information Awareness Office Overview"

Speech

By: John Marlan Poindexter

Date: The text titled "Information Awareness Office Overview" contains remarks delivered by John Poindexter, then Director of DARPA's Information Awareness Office, at DARPATech 2002 Conference, Anaheim, Calif., August 2, 2002.

Source: Defense Advanced Research Projects Agency (DARPA).

About the Author: In 1958 John Marlan Poindexter graduated from the United States Naval Academy with a B.S. in engineering. In 1961, he earned his masters degree in physics from the California Institute of Technology and went on to earn his Ph.D. in nuclear physics in 1964. He served in the U.S Navy in various positions from 1958 to 1987. Under the Reagan administration (1981–1989) Poindexter went on to serve as Military Assistant, from 1981 to 1983, as Deputy National Security Advisor from 1983 to 1985, and as National Security Advisor from 1985 to 1986. He also briefly served as the Director of the Information Awareness Office (IAO) of the Defense Advanced Research Projects Agency (DARPA) in 2002. The DARPA is an agency of the United States Department of Defense responsible for the development of new technology for use by the military. In 2002, the IAO proposed the controversial Total Information Awareness Program (TIA), which was established after the September 11, 2001 attacks to gather intelligence data through electronic data surveillance and data mining techniques. Funding for the IAO was eventually eliminated and Poindexter retired from DARPA on August 12, 2003.

INTRODUCTION

The attack on the World Trade Center on September 11, 2001 propelled many organizations (that are a part of the United States Department of Defense) to take up initiatives for preventing future terrorist attacks. The Defense Advanced Research Projects Agency (DARPA) also introduced a number of programs to counter terrorism.

One such initiative that was introduced by the Information Awareness Office (IAO) was known as Total Information Awareness (TIA). TIA is now known as Terrorism Information Awareness. The text titled "Information Awareness Office Overview" is the transcript of the speech delivered by John Poindexter (then Director of IAO) at the DARPAtech 2002 Conference.

This speech was intended to provide a clear idea of the Information Awareness Office and the programs undertaken by DARPA. Poindexter discusses the implications and applications of various DARPA programs, such as Human Identification at Distance, Genisys, TIDES, EARS, Evidence Extraction and Link Discovery, War Gaming the Asymmetric Environment, Bio-Surveillance, Genoa II, and Total Information Awareness. The TIA Program was conceived to detect terrorists by analyzing huge resources of information. In his speech, Poindexter lays out the significance of the TIA program and why he considered it important to apply this program in the matters pertaining to national security.

Poindexter states that TIA is an all-encompassing program created to work in harmony with all the above mentioned DARPA programs.

PRIMARY SOURCE

The world has changed dramatically since the Cold War when there existed two super powers. During the years I was in the White House, it was relatively simple to identify our intelligence collection targets. It was sometimes hard to collect the intelligence, but the targets were clear. Today, we are in a world of asymmetries. The most serious asymmetric threat facing the United States is terrorism, a threat characterized by collections of people loosely organized in shadowy networks that are difficult to identify and define and whose goals are the destruction of our way of life. The intelligence collection targets are thousands of people whose identities and whereabouts we do not always know. It is somewhat analogous to the anti-submarine warfare problem of finding submarines in an ocean of noise—we must find the terrorists in a world of noise, understand what they are planning, and develop options for preventing their attacks. If we are to preserve our national security, we must figure out a way of combating this threat.

The Information Awareness Office at DARPA is about creating technologies that would permit us to have both security and privacy. More than just making sure that different databases can talk to one another, we need better ways to extract information from those unified databases, and to ensure that the private information on innocent citizens is protected. The main point is that we need a much more systematic approach. A variety of tools, processes, and procedures will be required to deal with the problem, but they must be integrated by a systems approach built around a common architecture to be effective. Total Information Awareness—a prototype system—is our answer. We must be able to detect, classify, identify, and track terrorists so that we may understand their plans and act to prevent them from being executed. To protect our rights, we must ensure that our systems track the terrorists, and those that mean us harm.

IAO programs are focused on making Total Information Awareness—TIA—real. This is a high level, visionary, functional view of the world-wide system—somewhat over simplified. One of the significant new data sources that needs to be mined to discover and track terrorists is the transaction space. If terrorist organizations are going to plan and execute attacks against the United States, their people must engage in transactions and they will leave signatures in this information space. This is a list of transaction categories, and it is meant to be inclusive. Currently, terrorists are able to move freely throughout the world, to hide when necessary, to find sponsorship and support, and to operate in small, independent cells, and to strike infrequently, exploiting weapons of mass effects and media response to influence governments. We are painfully aware of some of the tactics that they employ. This low-intensity/low-density form of warfare has an information signature. We must be able to pick this signal out of the noise. Certain agencies and apologists talk about connecting the dots, but one of the problems is to know which dots to connect. The relevant information extracted from this data must be made available in large-scale repositories with enhanced semantic content for easy analysis to accomplish this task. The transactional data will supplement our more conventional intelligence collection.

While our goal is total information awareness, there will always be uncertainty and ambiguity in trying to understand what is being planned. That's why our tools have to build models of competing hypotheses. That is, we need to bring people with diverse points of view together in a collaborative environment where there is access to all source data, discovery tools and model building tools. Collaboration has not been so important in the past when problems were less complex, but now it is essential. And tools have to make the analysis process more efficient, to properly explore the multiple possibilities. This is the analytical environment. I could have called it the intelligence community, but in the case of counter-terrorism, it is broader to include law enforcement, friendly allies, outside experts, etc. A similar environment exists for the policy and operations community, but the functions and tools are different. The mission here is to take the competing hypotheses from the analytical environment and estimate a range of plausible futures. The objective is to identify common nodes, representing situations that could occur, and to explore the probable impact of various actions or interventions that authorities might make in response to these situations.

The overarching program that binds IAO's efforts together is Total Information Awareness or TIA System. The primary goal of TIA is the integration and assured transition of components developed in the programs Genoa, Genoa II, GENISYS, EELD, WAE, TIDES, HumanID and Bio-Surveillance. TIA will develop a modular system architecture using open standards that will enable a spiral development effort that will allow the insertion of new components when they are available. We will produce a complete, end-to-end, closed-loop proto-type system in a realistic environment. To accomplish this we have established an organization whose structure is as diagramed here. We will supplement the programs in IAO with commercial and other government components to rapidly implement early versions of TIA system at our R&D laboratory. We have already begun a spiral development and experiment program in conjunction with Army partners. Over the next few years, we will continuously add functionality to the system as components become available.

SIGNIFICANCE

The Total Information Awareness program has been under constant scrutiny ever since it was in its primary stage of conception. The program proposed to make extensive use of advanced data-mining tools (tools that analyze data and create relationships based on the analysis) and a huge database to identify patterns of terrorist activities.

In a nutshell, the key goal of the TIA Program was to track and identify terrorists by collecting as much information about them as possible. The data collection would be accomplished by obtaining financial records, medical records, travel records, and communication records over and above other newer sources of obtaining personal information. This would form the basis of the "intelligence data" and would be used to track potentially harmful activities. The TIA tracking mechanism would then employ state-of-the-art data mining tools, computer-based surveillance tools, and human analysis of the intelligence data to establish preventive measures for countering terrorism.

Among other technologies, TIA also aimed at developing biometric technology along with its existing Human Identification at Distance program to facilitate a nationwide identification program that can track individuals that are identified by its data-mining tools.

In May 2003, DARPA issued its report regarding the Terrorism Information Awareness Program to the U.S. Congress, and renamed the TIA Program from Total Information Awareness to Terrorism Information Awareness. The main purpose of the report was to outline the components of TIA and discuss their accountability. However, the report failed to generate the required impact on Congress as well as the citizens of the United States. Many concerned citizens and lawmakers considered it inadequate in addressing critical issues such as privacy, security, civil liberties, as well as the accuracy of data obtained.

Simultaneously, organizations such as the Electronic Frontier Foundation (EFF), the Electronic Privacy Information Center (EPIC), and the U.S. Association for Computing Machinery (ACM) also criticized the TIA program. In January 2003, the U.S. Senate passed the Data Mining Moratorium Act of 2003, effectively ending all United States Department of Defense (DoD) and Homeland Security data mining activities similar to the Total Information Awareness program. Subsequently, in September 2003, the funding for the TIA program was stopped by the Congress resulting in the shut down of the Information Awareness Office.

Most experts at the time held that programs such as the TIA could be effectively used to counter terrorism

and there have been other technology initiatives taken by DARPA that have proved successful in various counterterrorism programs. These include DARPA technologies used in Operation Enduring Freedom and Operation Noble Eagle, which were especially useful in the aftermath of the September 11 attacks. DARPA's Tactical Mobile Robotics program, for example, developed small ground robots that were used in Afghanistan as part of Operation Enduring Freedom in 2002.

Operation Noble Eagle, the DoD's Homeland Security program, has extensively used DARPA's technologies since early 2002. One such technology is the tool known as LEADERS—a consequence management program that provided medical surveillance against biological warfare. This program was also used by the Centers for Disease Control and Prevention (CDC) to monitor specific symptoms observed in New York City hospitals (immediately after the WTC attack) and report them immediately to the CDC in Atlanta for instantaneous evaluation. DARPA technologies have also helped in the search and rescue operations following the WTC attack.

FURTHER RESOURCES
Web sites

Electronic Frontier Foundation. "Total Information Awareness." <http://www.eff.org/Privacy/TIA> (accessed July 01, 2005).

Electronic Privacy Information Center. "Total Terrorism Information Awareness (TIA)." <http://www.epic.org/privacy/profiling/tia> (accessed July 01, 2005).

IWS—The Information Warfare Site. "Terrorism Information Awareness (TIA) Program formerly known as Total Information Awareness." <http://www.iwar.org.uk/news-archive/tia/total-information-awareness.htm> (accessed July 01, 2005).

Sourcewatch. "Information Awareness Office." <http://www.sourcewatch.org/index.php?title=Information_Awareness_Office> (accessed July 01, 2005).

Homeland Security Act of 2002

Legislation

By: U.S. Congress

Date: November 19, 2002

Source: Homeland Security Act of 2002, as published in the *Federal Register*.

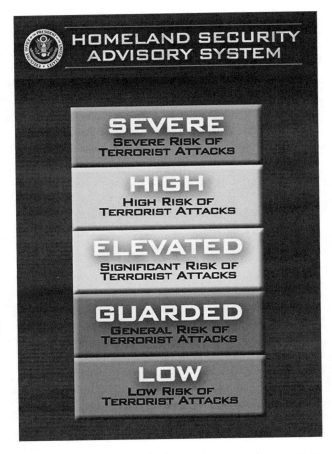

HOMELAND SECURITY ADVISORY SYSTEM

SEVERE
SEVERE RISK OF TERRORIST ATTACKS

HIGH
HIGH RISK OF TERRORIST ATTACKS

ELEVATED
SIGNIFICANT RISK OF TERRORIST ATTACKS

GUARDED
GENERAL RISK OF TERRORIST ATTACKS

LOW
LOW RISK OF TERRORIST ATTACKS

The five-level, color-coded terrorism warning system, enacted in 2002, to provide more information about terror alerts. AP/WIDE WORLD PHOTOS

About the Author: In reaction to the terrorist attacks of September 11, 2001, the United States government sought to establish a separate office within the federal system to address the needs and concerns for preventing future terrorists attacks. What ensued was a 484 page document known as the *Homeland Security Act of 2002* enacted by the 107th Congress (2nd session), and the creation of the Department of Homeland Security. In this act, Congress defines and outlines the purpose, scope, and responsibilities of the new office. Furthermore, it strengthens penalties for violating national security laws, and grants law enforcement personnel a higher degree of access to confidential records on individuals and corporations.

INTRODUCTION

The Department of Homeland Security's primary responsibilities include receiving and analyzing information pertaining to law enforcement, intelligence, and other information deemed pertinent to understanding the threat of terrorism. The Department is also intended to survey key U.S. resources and infrastructures to integrate relevant information into a cohesive and updated database of security information, to take necessary steps to prevent future terror attacks, and administer Homeland threat advisories when needed. The agency is responsible for connecting surveillance and law enforcement agencies like the Central Intelligence Agency (CIA) and Federal Bureau of Investigation (FBI). This integration stems from charges from federal law enforcement organizations and critics that a lack of communication between the agencies hindered prevention of the terrorist attacks of September 11, 2001, against the United States.

The development and implication of the Department of Homeland Security office is large and expansive. Initial proposals requested billions of dollars for the development of data tracking programs, the integration of software, and for the research for new technologies to help agencies investigate terror threats. Additionally, the office undertakes programs to challenge cyberterrorism, counter nuclear and biological threats, and other acts of terrorist warfare. Cyberterrorism comes in a variety of forms, but the best known avenues for this kind of warfare are computer viruses aimed at world financial structures, such as ATM machines, credit card companies, and even large global businesses.

The agency integrates twenty-two existing federal offices—like those mentioned and others, including the Secret Service, the Immigration and Naturalization Service, and many more. These offices still act as separate entities, within the federal system but they are now connected through communication networks and mandatory guidelines for the release of information.

Not since 1947 has the federal government seen such a large restructuring of its offices, when President Harry S. Truman established the Department of Defense. And the Office of Homeland Security stands to be a larger operation than the office of the military.

PRIMARY SOURCE

Sec. 2. Definitions

In this Act, the following definitions apply:

(1) Each of the terms "American homeland" and "homeland" means the United States.

(2) The term "appropriate congressional committee" means any committee of the House of Representatives or the Senate having legislative or oversight

jurisdiction under the Rules of the House of Representatives or the Senate, respectively, over the matter concerned.

(3) The term "assets" includes contracts, facilities, property, records, unobligated or unexpended balances of appropriations, and other funds or resources (other than personnel).

(4) The term "critical infrastructure" has the meaning given that term in section 1016(e) of Public Law 107–56 (42 U.S.C. 5195c(e)).

(5) The term "Department" means the Department of Homeland Security.

(6) The term "emergency response providers" includes Federal, State, and local emergency public safety, law enforcement, emergency response, emergency medical (including hospital emergency facilities), and related personnel, agencies, and authorities.

(7) The term "executive agency" means an executive agency and a military department, as defined, respectively, in sections 105 and 102 of title 5, United States Code.

(8) The term "functions" includes authorities, powers, rights, privileges, immunities, programs, projects, activities, duties, and responsibilities.

(10) The term "local government" means:

(A) a county, municipality, city, town, township, local public authority, school district, special district, intrastate district, council of governments (regardless of whether the council of governments is incorporated as a nonprofit corporation under State law), regional or interstate government entity, or agency or instrumentality of a local government;

(B) an Indian tribe or authorized tribal organization, or in Alaska a Native village or Alaska Regional Native Corporation; and

(C) a rural community, unincorporated town or village, or other public entity.

(11) The term "major disaster" has the meaning given in section 102(2) of the Robert T. Stafford Disaster Relief and Emergency Assistance Act (42 U.S.C. 5122).

(12) The term "personnel" means officers and employees.

(13) The term "Secretary" means the Secretary of Homeland Security.

(14) The term "State" means any State of the United States, the District of Columbia, the Commonwealth of Puerto Rico, the Virgin Islands, Guam, American Samoa, the Commonwealth of the Northern Mariana Islands, and any possession of the United States.

(15) The term "terrorism" means any activity that

(A) involves an act that (i) is dangerous to human life or potentially destructive of critical infrastructure or key resources; and (ii) is a violation of the criminal

laws of the United States or of any State or other subdivision of the United States; and

(B) appears to be intended (i) to intimidate or coerce a civilian population; (ii) to influence the policy of a government by intimidation or coercion; or (iii) to affect the conduct of a government by mass destruction, assassination, or kidnapping.

(16) (A) The term "United States", when used in a geographic sense, means any State of the United States, the District of Columbia, the Commonwealth of Puerto Rico, the Virgin Islands, Guam, American Samoa, the Commonwealth of the Northern Mariana Islands, any possession of the United States, and any waters within the jurisdiction of the United States.

(B) Nothing in this paragraph or any other provision of this Act shall be construed to modify the definition of "United States" for the purposes of the Immigration and Nationality Act or any other immigration or nationality law.

Sec. 3. Construction; Severability

Any provision of this Act held to be invalid or unenforceable by its terms, or as applied to any person or circumstance, shall be construed so as to give it the maximum effect permitted by law, unless such holding shall be one of utter invalidity or unenforceability, in which event such provision shall be deemed severable from this Act and shall not affect the remainder thereof, or the application of such provision to other persons not similarly situated or to other, dissimilar circumstances.

Sec. 4. Effective Date

This Act shall take effect 60 days after the date of enactment.

TITLE I—DEPARTMENT OF HOMELAND SECURITY

Sec. 101. Executive Department; Mission

(a) ESTABLISHMENT-There is established a Department of Homeland Security, as an executive department of the United States within the meaning of title 5, United States Code.

(b) MISSION:

(1) IN GENERAL: The primary mission of the Department is to:

(A) prevent terrorist attacks within the United States;

(B) reduce the vulnerability of the United States to terrorism;

(C) minimize the damage, and assist in the recovery, from terrorist attacks that do occur within the United States;

(D) carry out all functions of entities transferred to the Department, including by acting as a focal point regarding natural and manmade crises and emergency planning;

(E) ensure that the functions of the agencies and subdivisions within the Department that are not related directly to securing the homeland are not diminished or neglected except by a specific explicit Act of Congress;

(F) ensure that the overall economic security of the United States is not diminished by efforts, activities, and programs aimed at securing the homeland; and

(G) monitor connections between illegal drug trafficking and terrorism, coordinate efforts to sever such connections, and otherwise contribute to efforts to interdict illegal drug trafficking.

(2) RESPONSIBILITY FOR INVESTIGATING AND PROSECUTING TERRORISM: Except as specifically provided by law with respect to entities transferred to the Department under this Act, primary responsibility for investigating and prosecuting acts of terrorism shall be vested not in the Department, but rather in Federal, State, and local law enforcement agencies with jurisdiction over the acts in question.

SIGNIFICANCE

The Department of Homeland security stands to integrate the federal government and local law enforcement agencies to an unprecedented level. The use of new computer technologies, increased security forces, and increased national awareness to terrorist activities and threats have all factored into the creation of the office.

Opponents of the bill state that legalizing the U.S. government to track its citizens threatens to weaken civil liberties—particularly those outlined in the Bill of Rights. Critics further state that the employees transferred from the established twenty-two agencies should be left in place, and that existing agencies should be strengthened rather than creating a new "watchdog" organization.

In contrast, proponents of the bill argue that it is not establishing a watchdog organization. Rather, the Department of Homeland Defense will monitor existing agencies, smoothly connect them, and ensure that they communicate with one another in the future—so that another attack like September 11th does not happen again. In response to the tracking of data and the new governmental right to search and store information on individuals deemed a threat to the nation, proponents argue that only in rare instances would a common individual, with no security threat, accidentally appear in the system.

Other implications of the bill include limits on the information individuals can request under the Freedom of Information Act. (The Freedom of Information Act allows any U.S. citizen, researcher, or any other person deemed a viable source to obtain documents and data that has been declassified or deemed not a security threat to the United States.) Heightened criminal penalties for governmental employees who leak information to the general public have been increased, and governmental agencies have more freedom to meet in private, non-disclosed meetings. This last implication allows agencies and individuals who are dealing with information or goods directly connected to the security of the nation to keep their information private until declassification status has been issued. This process can take anywhere from ten to over one hundred years—depending on the threat level of the information.

Lastly, the bill allows for the development, storage, and procurement of weapons to counter bioterror attacks. One such example is the U.S. initiative to obtain mass quantities of the smallpox vaccine.

Accordingly, the Homeland Security Act of 2002 stands to drastically restructure the U.S. government. As this is such a large undertaking, with the possibility of misunderstandings regarding its purpose, the initial bill set out to clearly define and explain the new department. Since its initial signing, the Homeland Security Act of 2002 has been revised and amended.

FURTHER RESOURCES

Books

Etzioni, Amitai. *How Patriotic is the Patriot Act?: Freedom Versus Security in the Age of Terrorism.* New York and London: Routledge, 2004.

Web sites

whitehouse.gov. "Analysis for the Homeland Security Act of 2002." <http://www.whitehouse.gov/deptofhomeland/analysis/> (accessed 25 June 2005).

Ricin Found in London

"Terror Police Find Deadly Poison"

News article

By: BBC News

Date: January 7, 2003

Compounding the Ricin scare in London, a small vial of ricin was discovered at a U.S. Postal facility in 2003. AP/WIDE WORLD PHOTOS

Source: "Terror Police Find Deadly Poison" as published by *BBC News*.

About the Author: BBC News is a world-wide news gathering network headquartered in London and is sponsored by the government of the United Kingdom.

INTRODUCTION

The discovery by police of a substance believed to be ricin (a deadly poison) in a London flat in January 2003 came at a time when fears of a terrorism attack by al-Qaeda were particularly high in the United Kingdom. Since the major strike on the World Trade Center in the United States on September 11, 2001, there had been further terrorist attacks against western targets in Bali and in Kenya. In early 2003, Britain (alongside the U.S.) was preparing to go to war with Iraq and was therefore, thought to be a particularly vulnerable target for Islamic attacks in protest of the planned invasion of Iraq. War was being declared on Iraq due to its alleged possession of stockpiles of chemical or biological weapons and its failure to cooperate with United Nations (UN) weapons inspectors. In this context, the ricin discovery in north London gave rise to fears about possible links between the Iraqi president Saddam Hussein, and the terrorist network of al-Qaeda, particularly as UN inspections in the 1990s had revealed the existence of an Iraqi program for growing and processing castor beans for the production of ricin.

The fear of biological and chemical terrorism had been in the public eye since the mailing of anthrax spores to U.S. media and government offices in 2001, although no firm evidence has ever come to light that al-Qaeda had been involved in these mailings. There had also been a scare in the UK in November 2002, when the *The Sunday Times* claimed that a planned poison-gas attack by al-Qaeda on the London Underground (subway) had been thwarted by the security services.

The anti-terrorism police who raided the flat in January 2003 were acting on information from the Algerian authorities about a chemical terrorism plot in London, in which Kamel Bourgass was named as ringleader. The flat raided by the police was allegedly occupied by Bourgass. Although he was not found there, the police discovered equipment and instructions for making various poisons and a substance suspected of being ricin. The following week, the police and immigration officers raided another flat in Manchester, and found Bourgass there along with several other suspected terrorists. In a violent struggle, Bourgass stabbed to death a policemen. He was later sentenced to life in prison for the murder.

In September 2004, the trial began of Bourgass and four co-conspirators for the plot to launch a chemical terrorist attack on the UK. After a long court case, in April 2005, all four co-conspirators were acquitted. Bourgass was also acquitted of the most serious charge of conspiracy to carry out a chemical attack, but was found guilty of conspiracy to commit a public nuisance by the use of poisons or explosives to cause disruption, fear, or injury. Bourgass was sentenced to serve seventeen years in prison.

In the course of the trial it was revealed that examinations had shown that the substance found at the flat was not actually ricin. Only castor beans, apple pips, cherry pits, and a botched nicotine poison had been found. It was not clear when this information had been made available to the government.

■ PRIMARY SOURCE

Doctors have been warned to look out for signs of exposure to the potentially lethal poison ricin, after it was found by anti-terrorist police at an address in north London.

Six Algerian men are being questioned in connection with the discovery, made following an intelligence tip-off.

The men were arrested on Sunday morning and are in their late teens, 20s and 30s.

Tony Blair said the arrests showed the continued threat of international terrorism was "present and real and with us now and its potential is huge".

The intelligence services are said to be "shocked and worried" by the discovery and are looking at possible links with suspected Islamic extremists.

FORENSIC ANALYSIS

The arrests involved officers from the Anti-Terrorist Branch, Special Branch and the Security Service.

Castor oil beans, from which ricin is made, and equipment and containers for crushing the beans were found at a flat in Wood Green, north London, where one of the men was arrested.

Police said forensic analysis of the address, where a small quantity of material tested positive as ricin, was continuing, although they do believe the poison was made there.

It was identified by scientists at the Defence Science and Technology Laboratories at Porton Down in Wiltshire.

Police have not ruled out the possibility that some ricin may already have been distributed, although they believe it is highly unlikely.

They will also be looking at whether the group was part of a wider operation, possibly involving the manufacture of other chemicals.

'REAL EVIDENCE'

BBC home affairs correspondent Margaret Gilmore said: "For six months now MI5 and the anti-terrorist branch have been getting intelligence reports indicating that extreme groups want to launch a chemical, biological, or radiological attack. "Now we're being told this is probably the first real evidence they were trying to do this here in the UK."

It is thought that whoever made the poison did not have the capability to make a bomb, but they could have aimed to create panic by trying to kill small numbers of people.

Defence minister Geoff Hoon described the discovery of ricin as a "disturbing development".

Ricin is considered a potential biowarfare or bioterrorist agent and is on the Centre for Disease Control and Prevention's "B" list of agents considered a moderate threat.

It is relatively easy to manufacture in small amounts but would be considered an unusual agent to use for a mass attack as it must be ingested or injected to take effect.

It was also the toxin thought to have been used to murder dissident Bulgarian Georgi Markov, who was stabbed on Waterloo Bridge in London with a poisoned umbrella in 1978.

Mr Blair's official spokesman stressed there had been no specific intelligence about how the ricin was to have been used.

Deputy Chief Medical Officer Dr Pat Troop said, "While our message is still 'alert not alarm', we would re-iterate our earlier appeals for the public to remain vigilant and aware and report anything suspicious to police."

A Department of Health spokeswoman said all GPs and doctors had been told to look out for possible cases of ricin exposure. Sir Timothy Garden, former assistant chief of defence staff, told BBC News 24: "If it's a significant quantity then it's a worry because this is a poisonous agent which would require a lot of work to produce in a major quantity for use by terrorists."

SIGNIFICANCE

Biological and chemical warfare have been used in various forms since ancient times, but what is new is the growing fear that terrorists will employ biological or chemical agents in large-scale attacks against civilians.

At the time of the apparent ricin discovery, there was certainly mounting evidence that North African al-Qaeda cells in Europe were involved in the manufacture of chemical weapons for terrorist attacks. Shortly before Britain and the U.S. began their airstrikes on Iraq, ricin was discovered by French police in a luggage compartment at a rail station in Paris. Following so soon after the ricin discovery in London, this gave rise to new concerns of attack in both France and the UK.

However, none of the suspects brought to trial in the UK for the alleged plotting of a London Underground attack or for the manufacture of chemical weapons in the north London flat were convicted of terrorist charges. Overall, experts considered the attempts to produce poisons in the London flat as amateurish and unlikely to succeed.

FURTHER RESOURCES
Journal and Newspaper articles

Bird, Maryann. "A Poisonous Plot: Cops find a suspected al-Qaeda lab in London-but only traces of its lethal ricin. Inside the terror web." *Time*. January 20, 2003.

Carrell, Severin. "Special Report: Terror in the UK-Ricin: The plot that never was." *The Independent Sunday*. March 17, 2005.

Gibson, Helen. "The Algerian Factor: A murdered policeman. A series of arrests linked to the deadly ricin plot. And a race to uncover a web of North African terror cells in Britain." *Time*. January 27, 2003.

"Special report: Terror in the UK; Anatomy of a Conspiracy." *The Independent Sunday*. March 17, 2005.

"Abu Abbas Captured After Two Hours of Fighting"

PLF Leader Captured in Baghdad

News article

Date: April 16, 2003

Source: The Associated Press.

About the Author: The Associated Press is an international newswire service with regional offices and staff reporters positioned throughout the world.

INTRODUCTION

In October 1985, the Italian passenger ship *Achille Lauro*, carrying 680 passengers and 350 crew, was on a twelve-day cruise in the Mediterranean Sea. On Monday, October 7, the ship docked at Alexandria, Egypt, where most of the passengers disembarked for a sightseeing tour. Sixty to eighty people were still aboard when four armed Palestinian terrorists seized control of the ship to

A blindfolded Palestinian boy assembles an AK-47 assault rifle demonstrating what he learned at a warfare summer camp run by the Palestinian Authority. AP/WIDE WORLD PHOTOS

begin a fifty-two-hour hostage crisis. The terrorists sent a radio message in which they identified themselves as members of the Palestinian Liberation Front (PLF). They threatened to kill hostages if Israel did not release fifty Palestinians held in Israeli jails. Authorities in Italy, Israel, Egypt, and the United States were initially uncertain precisely which group the terrorists represented. PLF was a name loosely applied to a number of breakaway factions of the Palestinian Liberation Organization (PLO) led by Yasser Arafat. Some of these factions opposed Arafat's leadership, but the *Achille Lauro* terrorists were members of a pro-Arafat faction led by Abul (or Abu) Abbas, also known as Mohammad Abbas or by his birth name, Mohammad Zaidan, who masterminded the hijacking of the cruise ship and directed it via radio. U.S. officials were outraged when they learned that the terrorists had shot Leon Klinghoffer, a sixty-nine-year-old Jewish man from New York, and dumped his body, along with his wheelchair, overboard.

The *Achille Lauro* hijacking touched off a complex diplomatic situation. The terrorists, in the gunsights of at least three nations, surrendered to the Egyptian authorities in exchange for safe passage. The Egyptians then released them to the Palestinians and put them aboard an EgyptAir flight bound for Tunisia, the headquarters of Abbas's PLF faction. U.S. F-14 fighter jets, however, forced the plane down at a NATO base in Sicily, and after considerable diplomatic wrangling, it was agreed that the Italians would hold the hijackers, but that the United States would seek extradition.

Meanwhile, Abbas remained on the plane, claiming diplomatic immunity. The Italian government led by Prime Minister Bettino Craxi concluded that it had no legal grounds to detain Abbas because he held an Iraqi diplomatic passport and the plane was on a diplomatic mission, and Abbas was put on a plane and flown to Yugoslavia. In the late 1980s, he continued operating out of Tunisia but, under diplomatic pressure from Italy and the United States, Tunisia expelled him. In about 1994, he fled to Baghdad, Iraq, where he was given safe haven by Iraqi dictator Saddam Hussein.

Abbas remained a wanted man in both the United States and Italy for nearly two decades until April 14, 2003, when U.S. Special Forces of the 3rd Infantry Division in Operation Iraqi Freedom captured him in a compound in southern Baghdad. The following news article details the events surrounding his capture.

■ PRIMARY SOURCE

Baghdad, Iraq—Helicopters roared over at 4:30 A.M., and a few minutes later an explosion shattered the windows of the Faoud family home. For the next two hours, gunfire rattled around their one-story house; a desperate man tried to find haven by smashing his way inside. When it was over, American troops had grabbed one of the world's most wanted men, Abul Abbas, mastermind of the 1985 cruise ship hijacking during which 69-year-old Leon Klinghoffer was slain.

For the Faouds, the arrest was a revelation: No one knew the man down the street was anything more than an Arab volunteer fighting coalition forces, they said. "I didn't know who Abul Abbas was," said Ghada Butti, mother of the Faoud house. "I have never heard of him before."

On Wednesday, she and other neighbors provided a detailed account of the firefight Tuesday morning that led to the capture of the head of the Palestine Liberation Front.

The family was asleep when the helicopters swooped in at a low altitude, awakening everyone. Minutes later, the Faouds jumped from their beds, shocked by a window-shattering explosion, followed by two more blasts.

Abul Abbas was apparently hiding in one of the houses in alley No. 6 at al-Hurriya Square. Gunfire continued for more that two hours as Abul Abbas and his followers scurried around trying to escape the U.S. raiders.

Butti recalled hearing somebody in the garden of her home trying to break through a window in her children's room. Minutes later, someone pounded hysterically at the house's main door. "I wanted to open the door with my husband, Khaled, but before we did so I asked in English, 'Who's there?'" she recounted, saying she expected American troops to answer. " Khaled then opened the door for a few seconds, then closed it when he did not find anyone outside."

Neighborhood residents said they believed Abul Abbas was caught after taking refuge in an abandoned house. The house, which had no ceiling, was once an inn but was sold few years ago, one man said.

After Khaled Faoud closed the door, loudspeakers boomed out a message in Arabic: "Caution, caution, caution. Abul Abbas, surrender. Coalition special forces have surrounded the area. Follow the instructions and move forward toward the voice. Raise your hands up and walk slowly. We will not harm you. Think about your family."

The message, played repeatedly, terrified Butti. " I was afraid they might have thought we were his family, and they were about to storm our house," she said.

A little more than two hours after the helicopters came, American soldiers stormed the family's garden gate and approached the main door. Screaming "help, help," Butti let them inside.

The soldiers told the family not to worry, but asked them to leave the house as they searched every room. Her husband and two male neighbors were taken for "two hours of interrogation," Butti said. More than 24 hours later, none had returned.

At the house next door, Zareh Krekorian was one of those taken away with Faoud. Krekorian's wife, Hermenah, took a reporter from room to room, showing smashed windows and broken locks left by the Americans' search. The main door was so badly damaged that she had to summon workers to build a wall to keep thieves out.

Butti's eldest daughter, Hind, told of seeing a bloodied body wearing an olive green uniform, dangling from the wall of their backyard. She did not know if it was an American or one of Abul Abbas' men.

U.S. soldiers also came around showing a picture of Abul Abbas and asking neighbors if they had seen him, Butti said. She did not recognize him. Another announcement in Arabic followed, with the promise of a reward for information about Abul Abbas.

Later, an American came and gave Butti and her children a box filled with 12 meals. "I don't want food," she said she told the soldier. "I want my husband back." American troops stayed in the area for about three hours after the shooting stopped, she said.

Butti, who lives a few hundred yards from the heavily bombed Air Force Command, said the raid was the most frightening part of the war for her. "We did not feel at all that we will stay alive," she said, standing next to her 2-year-old son Faysal. "We surrendered to death that day . . . After we survived all these wars we were about to die in the battle of Abul Abbas."

SIGNIFICANCE

Abbas, who was born on December 10, 1948, joined the Popular Front for the Liberation of Palestine General Command in 1968. In 1977, when disagreements over policy led to rifts between the PFLP, the PLO, and other Palestinian factions, Abbas created the PLF. In turn, the PLF fragmented into various factions, but Abbas remained loyal to Yasser Arafat and, appointed to the PLO executive council in 1984, received support from the PLO. Throughout the 1980s the PLF planned and executed terrorist attacks primarily against Israeli civilians. In 1990, for example, Abbas planned an aborted speedboat attack on Israeli swimmers at a beach near Tel Aviv.

He was convicted *in absentia* in Italy and sentenced to five life terms for his role in the *Achille Lauro* hijacking.

In the 1990s, Abbas appeared to have undergone a kind of conversion. He claimed to support peace negotiations between Israel and Palestine, and the Israelis even gave him diplomatic immunity because he was apparently participating in the peace process. He also issued a statement about the murder of Leon Klinghoffer, saying that the shooting was a "mistake" and that the entire *Achille Lauro* incident was an operation that had gone sour. Nonetheless, he appeared on Iraqi television in 2001 to praise Saddam Hussein for inciting anti-Israeli sentiment in the Arab world.

U.S. officials regarded the capture of Abbas as a major victory in the war on terrorism. Abbas, however, was never brought to justice. On March 8, 2004, he died of an apparent heart condition while in American custody.

FURTHER RESOURCES
Books
Bohn, Michael K. *The "Achille Lauro" Hijacking: Lessons in the Politics and Prejudice of Terrorism.* Dulles, Va.: Brassey's, 2004.

Web sites
BBC News. "A Hijack on the High Seas," 2002. <http://www.bbc.co.uk/dna/h2g2/A730900> (accessed July 10, 2005).

CNN.com. Ensor, David. "U.S. Captures Mastermind of *Achille Lauro* Hijacking." CNN.com, April 16, 2003. <http://www.cnn.com/2003/WORLD/meast/04/15/sprj.irq.abbas.arrested/index.html> (accessed July 10, 2005).

Fartun Farah, whose husband—Mohammed Warsame—was arrested on suspicion of associating with al-Qaida, during a news conference in 2003. AP/WIDE WORLD PHOTOS

"Overstay Tracking"

GAO report on 13 of the hijackers involved in the September 11, 2001 terrorist attacks

Government report

By: United States Government Accountability Office (GAO)

Date: May 2004

Source: "Overstay Tracking: A Key Component of Homeland Security and a Layered Defense," as published by the United States Government Accountability Office.

About the Author: The United States Government Accountability Office is the investigative arm of congress that examines government efficiency by evaluating federal programs, auditing federal expenditures, and issuing legal opinions. Following the September 11, 2001, terrorist attacks on the United States, in-depth investigations probed the individuals that articulated the attacks. Soon investigators, and the American public, learned that thirteen of the fifteen hijackers were not interviewed before receiving visas to enter the United States and that their paperwork was not completed properly. This information, along with desires to prevent another terrorist attack, lead to several U.S. programs to track,

restrict, and more closely monitor visa holders and new entrants to the United States.

INTRODUCTION

Post-September 11 visa restrictions reflect U.S. and international attitudes on terrorism. The Governmental Accounting Office (GAO), the FBI, the Office of Homeland Security, and other federally headed agencies all agree that consulates issuing U.S. visas still have a wide range of options for denying an individual a visa into the United States. With mandated tracking software, mandatory interviews, and enforced paperwork, visa applicants will have to show clear evidence of who they are, their intentions for stay in the United States, and of any past activities that may be deemed a threat to U.S. national security. Alongside interviews, applicants will also be required to submit their fingerprints. These can then be entered into a database to compare and track them against fingerprints of known and suspected terrorists and other non-desirables. These tightened restrictions directly reflect the information received on the nineteen hijackers from the September 11, 2001, terrorist attacks.

The nineteen hijackers received a total of twenty-three visas from five different U.S. consulates between

April 1997 and June 2001, despite the fact that thirteen of the hijackers were never interviewed by U.S. officials and fifteen of them had not filled out their paperwork correctly. Their incorrect paperwork ranged from missing signatures, current and past addresses, place of departure, point of arrival, and various other mistakes. The applicants that did not have to submit to interviews were those from Saudi Arabia and the United Arab Emirates. Finally, two hijackers obtained third-party national visas from Berlin, Germany. Third-party national visas are those given to individuals holding residency (but not citizenship) in a nation other than their own, and often these visa holders are students. The two hijackers who received third-party visas from Germany were deemed acceptable entrants to the United States—those who would not stay illegally—because their studies in Germany showed them to be strong visa candidates.

The hijackers received their visas without interviews and extensive background checks because, prior to September 11, 2001, many U.S. consulates and the U.S. State Department were working under a philosophy to promote U.S. travel by expediting visas. Members of Congress also pushed for expedited visas as a means for expanding U.S. travel and to show good foreign relations to citizens of many countries—particularly those of the Middle East. Middle Eastern and Asian countries frequently received priority in visas because political maneuverings for trade initiatives could be increased if the United States showed friendly relations towards a nation's citizens. This tactic has been taken at various points in U.S. history; one example being the immigration and naturalization laws from the early twentieth century. President Theodore Roosevelt (1858–1919) established the Gentleman's Agreement with Japan so that U.S.-Japanese relations would benefit in trade and other economic avenues when Japanese citizens were allowed to obtain visas into the United States.

Just as the Gentleman's Agreement was later rescinded, angering Japan, in an era of post-September 11, the United States has rescinded many of its earlier visa granting policies. Tracking software, interviews, and governmental organizations aimed at monitoring visa holders have become more closely scrutinized in order to prevent future terrorist attacks. This intense monitoring of visa holders is also aimed at limiting those who overstay their visa, those who obtain one for illegal reasons, and to prevent double applicants.

PRIMARY SOURCE

Weaknesses in overstay tracking may encourage visitors and potential terrorists who legally enter the United States to overstay. Once here, terrorists may overstay or use other stratagems to extend their stay—such as exiting and reentering (to obtain a new authorized period of admission) or applying for a change of status. . . . Of the six hijackers who actually flew the planes on September 11 or were apparent leaders, three were out of status on or before September 11—two because of prior short-term overstaying.

Note: An overstay is an illegal alien who was legally admitted to the United States for a specific authorized period, but remained here after that period expired, without obtaining an extension or a change of status or meeting other specific conditions. Overstays who settle here are part of the illegal immigrant population.

Additionally, a number of current or prior overstays were arrested after September 11 on charges related to terrorism. For example:

- Two overstays pled guilty to separate instances of identity document fraud and were connected to different hijackers in the September 11 group. They were current, short-term overstays when the identity document fraud occurred.
- Four others with a history of overstaying (and variously connected to the September 11 hijackers, the Taliban, and Hezbollah terrorists) pled guilty to document fraud or weapons charges or were convicted of money laundering. One of these was also convicted of providing Hezbollah material support, including night vision devices and other weapons-related technology.

Last, the gunman who fired on several people at the El Al ticket counter of Los Angeles International Airport was identified (by DHS) as a prior overstay.

Terrorists who enter as legal visitors are hidden within the much larger populations of all legal visitors, overstays, and other illegals such as border crossers. Improved overstay tracking could help counterterrorism investigators and prosecutors locate suspicious individuals placed on watch lists after they entered the country. The director of the Foreign Terrorist Tracking Task Force told us that he considered overstay tracking data helpful. For example, these data—together with additional analysis—can be important in quickly and efficiently determining whether suspected terrorists were in the United States at specific times.

As we reported in 2003, between "September 11 and November 9, 2001 [that is, over the course of 2 months], . . . INS [Immigration and Naturalization Service] compiled a list of aliens whose characteristics were similar to those of the hijackers" in types of visas, countries issuing their passports, and dates of entry into the United States. While the list of aliens was part of an effort to identify and locate specific persons for interviews, it contained duplicate names and data entry errors. In other words, poor data hampered the government's efforts to obtain information in the wake of a national emergency, and it was necessary to turn to private sector information. Reporting earlier that INS data "could not be fully relied on to locate many aliens who were of interest to the United States," we had indicated that the Form I-94 system is relevant, stressing the need for improved change-of-address notification requirements. INS generally concurred with our recommendations.

DHS has declared that combating fraudulent employment at critical infrastructures, such as airports, is a priority for domestic security. DHS has ongoing efforts to identify illegal workers in jobs at various infrastructures (for example, airport workers with security badges). These sweeps are thought to reduce the nation's vulnerability to terrorism, because, as experts have told us, (1) security badges issued on the basis of fraudulent IDs constitute security breaches, and (2) overstays and other illegal aliens working in such facilities might be hesitant to report suspicious activities for fear of drawing authorities' attention to themselves or they might be vulnerable to compromise.

Operation Tarmac is a national multiagency initiative focused on screening employees working in secure areas of U.S. airports. Post-September 11 investigations of passenger-screening companies and other secure-area employers revealed substantial numbers of unauthorized foreign national employees. As a result, further sweeps began in 2001 with Washington, D.C., and Salt Lake City (in preparation for the Winter Olympics); these eventually became known as Operation Tarmac and are still ongoing. As of April 2004, DHS reported that 195 airports had been investigated and 5,877 businesses had been audited. Operation Tarmac investigators had checked the I-9 Employment Eligibility Verification forms or badging office records (or both) for about 385,000 employees and had found 4,918 unauthorized workers.

SIGNIFICANCE

Opponents to the enhanced visa tracking programs state that flaws in the tracking software can possibly prevent viable entrants from entering the United States, as well as still enabling potential terrorists to obtain U.S. visas. These concerns have been corroborated by the GAO and the U.S. State Department. Both agencies have admitted that biographical information on the hijackers in the Consular Lookout and Support System (CLASS) was incorrect: one hijacker's name was misspelled and another's birth date was wrong. CLASS contains information on individuals who are not eligible to obtain visas and passports into the United States.

The GAO and U.S. State Department consider the fear that visa tracking still has too many flaws and that

it will inhibit U.S. travel and tourism as a viable concern. Federal agencies governing visa tracking continually state that they are open to suggestions on how to improve the system, alleviate concerns about curbing U.S. tourism, and prevent individuals of national threat from entering the country. However, they assert that the U.S. government must accept responsibility for individuals who slip through the system, overstay their visas, violate its terms, and use falsified documents to enter the country. Thus, federal departments are continually revising visa terms, applications, and the generalized process in order to strengthen it and make it as user-friendly as possible.

FURTHER RESOURCES

Web sites

CNN.com. "US-VISIT Falls Short." <http://www.cnn.com/2005/US/03/28/visit.program/index.html> (accessed 6 July 2005).

CNN.com. "Eying Your ID." <http://www.cnn.com/2005/US/05/03/eying.identification/index.html> (accessed 6 July 2005).

E-Bomb

EMP as a Potential Terrorist Weapon

Congressional Research Report

By: Clay Wilson

Date: August 20, 2004

Source: Excerpt from "High Altitude Electromagnetic Pulse (HEMP) and High Power Microwave (HPM) Devices: Threat Assessments." Congressional Research Service Report written for Congress by Clay Wilson, August 20, 2004.

About the Author: Clay Wilson is a specialist in the Technology and National Security Foreign Affairs, Defense, and Trade Division for the Congressional Research Service. The Congressional Research Service (CRS), part of the Library of Congress, prepares it's reports for the U.S. Congress.

INTRODUCTION

An electromagnetic pulse (EMP) is capable of permanently disabling mechanical and electronic systems. As a potential weapon, the EMP was first recognized as an unintended consequence of nuclear explosions

The ability to generate EMPs from nuclear explosions could lead more countries to develop facilities like the one shown in this satellite image. AP/WIDE WORLD PHOTOS

missiles were used by U.S.-led forces in raids on Baghdad, Iraq in 1991 and in 2003.

At the same time, scientists and defense analysts warned that terrorists might be capable of building their own, much less sophisticated devices for a fraction of the cost to a superpower.

Following the terrorist attacks on the United States on September 11, 2001, lawmakers, policy planners, the military, the intelligence community, and the general public grew increasingly concerned about the nature and source of possible future terrorist threats, a fear compounded by the anthrax scare that began just weeks after September 11th. The government commission that investigated the attacks (the 9-11 Commission) concluded that in part they resulted from a failure of imagination on the part of the United States; that is, because no one imagined that terrorists could commandeer jetliners and fly them into buildings, no one took steps to prevent it from happening. In the years following the attacks, however, planners flexed their imagination, even to the point of hiring Hollywood scriptwriters as consultants to envision the form that future terrorist attacks might take.

One threat that received increasing attention is the "E-bomb," a bomb designed not to destroy targets or kill people, but rather to generate a powerful EMP that could knock out electronic circuitry, telecommunications systems, computers, satellites, electrical transformers, and anything that relies on or transmits electrical current. In 1925, American physicist and future Nobel laureate Arthur H. Compton (1892–1962) demonstrated that when a string of subatomic energy packets called photons were fired into atoms with a low atomic number—atoms with a relatively small number of protons in their nuclei—the atoms would eject electrons. This phenomenon, known as the Compton effect, is the principle underlying the E-bomb. If enough atoms eject enough electrons, which have a negative electric charge, the result is a massive electromagnetic pulse.

In a worst-case situation following a high energy EMP, hospitals would be unable to function, food supplies would rot, motorists would be unable to pump gas, lights and generators would not work—the resulting breakdown in social order could cause great damage to the nation and take years to repair.

Scientists concluded that a large nuclear explosion at very high altitude over the middle of the United States, or any other country, could instantly render the nation without vital communication links. In a 1985 report to the president, for example, the National Security Telecommunications Advisory Committee highlighted the vulnerability of the nation's telecommunications

during the 1950s, when the United States and the Soviet Union were conducting atmospheric nuclear tests. During one such test in the Pacific Ocean, EMPs knocked out streetlights in Hawaii and disrupted electrical systems as far away as Australia.

By the beginning of the twenty-first century, American and British scientists had the technology to develop E-bombs capable of generating EMPs. Carbon-graphite coils that are capable of generating an electromagnetic pulse which destroys electronics equipment—especially communications equipment— can be fitted to existing missiles. Carbon-graphite equipped cruise

infrastructure to a high-altitude EMP blast—one that would, in this instance during the Cold War (1945–1991), presumably be launched by the Soviets as a preliminary step in an all-out nuclear attack.

In the new century, planners are worried less about an EMP attack from a nation-state than about the threat posed by terrorists who could get their hands on a device that could generate a large EMP and who would be willing to use it. More concerning is the fact that it is not even necessary to possess nuclear technology to generate a devastating EMP.

In 2001, the Commission to Assess the Threat from High Altitude Electromagnetic Pulse was established by Congress to study the vulnerabilities of critical U.S. infrastructure to EMP attack. In 2004, the U.S. Congress House Armed Services Committee subsequently conducted hearings to assess the threat to the United States from electromagnetic pulse attack.

PRIMARY SOURCE

Electromagnetic Pulse (EMP) is an intense energy field that can instantly overload or disrupt numerous electrical circuits at a distance. Modern high technology microcircuits are especially sensitive to power surges, and the possible vulnerability of U.S. civilian computer systems to the effects of EMP has been discussed in the media. EMP can be produced on a large scale using a single nuclear explosion, and on a smaller, non-nuclear scale using a device with batteries or chemical explosives. Several nations, including reported sponsors of terrorism, may currently have a capability to use EMP as a weapon for cyber warfare or cyber terrorism, to disrupt computers, communications systems, or parts of the U.S. critical infrastructure.

The threat of an attack against the United States involving EMP is hard to assess, but some observers indicate that it is growing along with worldwide access to newer technologies and the proliferation of nuclear weapons. In the past, the threat of mutually assured destruction provided a lasting deterrent against the exchange of multiple high-yield nuclear warheads. However, now a single, specially-designed low-yield nuclear explosion high above the United States, or over a battlefield, can produce an EMP effect that results in a widespread loss of electronics, but no direct fatalities, and may not necessarily evoke a large nuclear retaliatory strike by the U.S. military. This, coupled with the possible vulnerability of U.S. commercial electronics and U.S. military battlefield equipment to the effects of EMP, may create a new incentive for other countries to develop or acquire a nuclear capability.

Policy issues raised by this threat include (1) what is the United States doing to protect civilian critical infrastructure

systems against the threat of EMP, (2) does the level of vulnerability of U.S. civilian and military electronics to large-scale EMP attack encourage other nations to develop or acquire nuclear weapons, and (3) how likely are terrorist organizations to launch a smaller-scale EMP attack against the United States?

SIGNIFICANCE

Based upon reports to Congress from experts, in early 2005 the Senate Judiciary Committee's Subcommittee on Terrorism, Technology, and Homeland Security, chaired by Senator Jon Kyl, conducted hearings on a wide range of threats to the United States. One threat was EMPs and the possibility that an organization such as al-Qaeda could develop an EMP, mount it on a missile bought from a rogue nation such as North Korea, and launch it from an oceangoing platform over the United States.

On March 8, 2005, for example, the committee heard testimony from Dr. Peter M. Fonash, acting deputy manager of the National Communications System (NCS), now part of the U.S. Department of Homeland Security. (The purpose of the NCS, established in 1963 by President John F. Kennedy, is to maintain and protect the nation's telecommunications infrastructure in the event of emergencies such as war or terrorist attack. Part of its mandate is to conduct tests on EMPs and devise ways to mitigate the devices' effects.) Fonash noted that the NCS took part in the congressionally sponsored Commission to Assess the Threat from High Altitude Electromagnetic Pulse in 2004. The conclusion of the committee and the NCS, based on tests conducted in the late 1980s through 2000, was that the nation's electrical grid was highly vulnerable to the effects of EMPs. The telecommunications infrastructure, however, was less so because of improvements that have been made in current telecommunications switches and because the structures in which they are housed provide some shielding.

Fonash, however, did not discount the threat and pointed out that evolving technologies require the United States and other nations to continue research efforts.

Based on reports and assessments, many analysts worry that the threat of an EMP attack against the United States increases as global access to new technologies increase and as the proliferation of nuclear weapons continues.

Recognizing that these powerful EMPs were a byproduct of nuclear explosions, for decades American and allied scientists set out to harden the defenses of

U.S. and NATO (North Atlantic Treaty Organization) electronic systems against disruption from nuclear explosions. As a specific response to terrorism, several U.S. agencies, including DARPA (Defense Advanced Research Projects Agency) and NIST (The National Institute of Standards and Technology), are continuing to conduct research on ways of protecting communications and computing infrastructure against the threat posed by EMPS.

FURTHER RESOURCES

Books

21st Century U.S. Military Documents: EMP Attack, Electromagnetic Pulse Threats, Report of the Commission to Assess the Threat to the United States from Electromagnetic Pulse, High-Altitude Nuclear Weapon EMP Attacks. Washington, DC: Progressive Management, 2004.

Web sites

Northwestern University. "Electromagnetic Weapons: Electromagnetic Pulse." 2001–2002. <http://www.physics.northwestern.edu/classes/2001Fall/Phyx135-2/19/emp.htm> (accessed May 16, 2005).

"Are Our Critical Systems Safe from Cyber Attack?"

National Infrastructure Systems Vulnerable

Newspaper article

By: Daniel Thomas

Date: April 21, 2005

Source: "Are Our Critical Systems Safe from Cyber Attack?," as published in the United Kingdom-based magazine *Computing* (U.K.).

About the Author: Daniel Thomas is a contributor to the weekly newspaper *Computing*, written primarily for those interested and working in information technology. *Computing* also publishes online and digital versions that have featured articles written by Thomas.

INTRODUCTION

Computers and electronic devices have become essential parts of most organizations and are necessary to provide transportation, financial services, medical services, and emergency services. The necessity of computers and electronic devices in providing everyday services makes cyber (computer-related) attacks a

potential terrorist action. While as of July 2005, there have not been any major terrorist actions involving cyber attacks, they remain a potential threat.

Of particular concerns are attacks that would affect the critical national infrastructure (CNI). The CNI refers to the assets, systems, and services that support economic, political, and social life to the extent that their complete or partial loss could either cause loss of life, have a serious impact on the economy, have significant social consequences, or be of major concern to the government.

The CNI in the United Kingdom is recognized as covering ten sectors. These are communications, emergency services, energy, finance, food, government, health, public safety, transport, and water. It is recognized that because these assets, systems, and services are necessary to society and everyday functioning, they become a potential target for terrorists. These systems, services, and assets are almost always controlled and operated by some type of computer or electronic device. The necessity of these systems combined with their reliance on computers or electronics makes cyber attacks a significant risk.

█ PRIMARY SOURCE

Last year, hundreds of organizations ground to a halt after the Sasser worm [a destructive computer program] spread rapidly around the world.

The worm severely disrupted UK coastguard stations; delayed 21 British Airways flights; infected IT [information technology] systems in Hong Kong hospitals and halted trains in Australia after affecting drivers' radio systems.

Created by an 18-year-old German student, Sasser has so far caused an estimated $3.5bn (GBP 1.8bn) in damage, according to analyst Computer Economics, and highlights just how much society relies on the internet and IT systems.

Most industries are heavily dependent on computers and electronic devices to carry out day-to-day activities and, as a result, are increasingly at risk from electronic attacks, be they viruses or deliberately orchestrated hacks.

In the UK, about 80 percent of organizations that are deemed critical to the continuity of everyday life are privately owned and mainly unregulated in terms of security, so most breaches have not been publicized. But, if evidence of attacks on publicly-owned systems in other countries is anything to go by, unless greater steps are taken to improve security, the UK's critical national infrastructure (CNI) could be the next to fall victim to malicious code, hackers and, in extreme circumstances, terrorism.

"If there was an explosion you would hear about it in the press," says Judy Baker, deputy director of the government's National Infrastructure Security Co-ordination Center (NISCC), which works to minimize electronic attacks in the UK. "But we don't hear about all the risks affecting companies, because they are concerned about their reputation or how it might affect shareholder confidence."

Cyber attacks on the UK's CNI—including government, emergency services, banks and transportation—is on the increase, says NISCC, although most come from viruses rather than terrorists.

"There's an increasing number of coordinated and sophisticated attacks, and they are targeting government, companies and individuals," says Baker.

"The unpleasant bottom line is that it may be impossible to totally mitigate the risks unless we stop the use of the technologies that many of our staff say they really need."

But that option is impractical, so NISCC is calling for businesses and home PC users to do more to safeguard their systems.

Firms maintaining services such as power stations, dams and trains need to be extra vigilant, as there is increasing evidence that terrorists are turning to hacking to create fear. Although terrorist organizations are only using IT for communications, fundraising and propaganda at the moment, denial of service (DoS) attacks and hacking could become more common, says Baker.

"There is not a current need to over-hype the risk of electronic attacks, but in the future it will be increasingly possible," she says. "Physical attacks will probably be the favored method, but electronic attacks are an option."

One of the biggest threats faced by multinational firms in charge of parts of the CNI is hackers taking control of supervisory control and data acquisition (Scada) systems, placed throughout energy plants, train networks and sewage treatment sites to automate operational processes.

There has been a tenfold increase in the number of successful attacks on Scada systems since 2000, according to research by PA Consulting and the British Columbia Institute of Technology, which also predicts that between 100 and 500 unreported industrial cyber attacks occur each year.

"For years managers have asked for standardized processes, easy-to-use operating systems and off-the-shelf applications," says Bernie Robertson, a member of PA Consulting's management group. "They are also asking for real-time information about production cycles, so they can integrate into enterprise resource planning systems.

"This means that if you're a hacker or virus writer it's easier to attack their systems."

Many of the networked Scada systems in industrial plants are out of date and insecure, he adds.

"If an IT department let an employee connect to their systems using an unprotected laptop they would be considered a fool," he says.

"But there are thousands of processors out there that don't have any anti-virus or firewalls, and they are controlling machinery that moves and manages critical industrial processes."

In extreme circumstances this could lead to hackers taking over parts of the CNI and holding them to ransom. Processing errors or acts of industrial espionage could also lead to food contamination, if control systems were used to change ingredients, adds PA consultant Peter Clay.

But while internal security is crucial, the CNI is also in danger from poor security practices by home PC users.

By protecting themselves properly, home users can help prevent the spread of damaging computer worms such as Sasser, and stop criminals from taking over their PCs to launch DoS attacks on company IT systems.

"We all need to play a part in securing cyberspace," says Howard Schmidt, former cyber security adviser to the White House.

"Simple things such as personal firewalls, anti-virus, email Spam filters and anti-spyware can all help.

"If we did this the police could focus on more important things, such as putting terrorists in jail."

International legislation also needs to be improved, to overcome the problem of criminals hacking into systems in one country while living in another region where it is not recognized as a crime, says Simon Perry, security strategist at Computer Associates.

"The fact that we have uneven legislation across countries plays into the hands of criminals. It's like trying to squeeze jelly in your hand; it just moves somewhere else," he says.

SIGNIFICANCE

Several computer viruses have swept around the world, creating serious problems in a range of countries. The Sasser worm, which spread worldwide and affected air flights, hospitals, and train systems, is one example. While the Sasser virus was not introduced as a terrorist act, its impact does show the potential threat that viruses and similar cyber attacks pose.

One of the significant problems of cyber attacks is related to managing the risk to CNI and protecting CNI from cyber attacks. This issue is a difficult one to manage because the majority of the organizations providing critical services are privately owned. This means that security for these systems is not regulated, which makes it difficult for the government to identify and minimize risks and take protective actions.

Another related issue is that cyber attacks are not widely publicized. Privately owned companies generally do not want to admit to shareholders, employees, the public, or competitors that their company has security problems. In addition, cyber attacks can easily be kept quiet, which is not true of more obvious forms of terrorism. This results in a general silence about cyber attacks—even if they are occurring, they tend not to be widely publicized. This creates problems in regard to assessing and understanding the risks and threats, while also making many organizations unaware that they are at risk from particular threats. Without knowledge of the potential threats or the risk level, organizations cannot recognize the need for protective action.

Even though data are limited due to the general silence regarding cyber attacks, cyber attack rates are increasing and attacks are becoming more sophisticated. At present, viruses are the major threat, while hacking and denial of service (DoS) attacks are becoming more common.

Hacking is a particular concern in regard to supervisory control and data acquisition (Scada) systems, which automate various processes by measuring data, inputting the data, and having the software make changes and adjust processes based on the data. Scada is commonly used in power plants, transportation, water control, and waste control. Scada systems are potential terrorist threats because hacking does not just change data, but has the potential to change the processes that occur. This could involve entering incorrect data to cause an explosion in a power station or a nuclear power plant. This could also involve inputting incorrect commands so that all trains increase speed or so that all water supply ceases. Since 2000, cyber attacks on Scada systems have increased by ten times. Successful cyber attacks have involved critical services including electricity, nuclear power, water, and transportation.

DoS attacks refers to criminal actions aimed at preventing users of a certain service from using the service. DoS attacks have the potential to crash computers, systems, or entire organizations.

Another concern is the possibility that terrorist groups will combine physical attacks with cyber attacks. An example would be detonating bombs to cause fires in a certain area while a simultaneous cyber attack prevents water from being available in that area. If a cyber attack were to be combined with a physical attack, the cyber attack might not involve disabling a major system, yet still cause major problems. This highlights the need to protect all systems from cyber attacks.

FURTHER RESOURCES

Books

Lukasik, S. J., S. E. Goodman, and D. W. Longhurst. *Protecting Critical Infrastructures against Cyber-Attack.* New York: Oxford University Press, 2003.

Verton, Dan. *Black Ice: The Invisible Threat of Cyber-Terrorism.* New York: McGraw-Hill/Osborne, 2003.

Web sites

Byrnes, Eric, and Justin Lowe. "The Myths and Facts behind Cyber Security Risks for Industrial Control Systems." <http://www.tswg.gov/tswg/ip/The_Myths_and_Facts_behind_Cyber_Security_Risks.pdf> (accessed June 22, 2005).

"Watchdogs Seek out the Bad Side"

Internet Vulnerability

Newspaper article

By: Ariana Eunjung Cha

Date: April 25, 2005

Source: Newspaper article published in the *Washington Post.*

About the Author: Ariana Cha writes for the *Washington Post.* She has written extensively on technology and related topics including space exploration, artificial intelligence, and social implications of the rise in online communication.

INTRODUCTION

The advent of the Internet has created a new set of tools that effortlessly circumvent national boundaries and radically alter the ways in which warfare is waged and reported. From the earliest days of the U.S.-led war on terror, the Internet has played a central role in the battle for mind-share around the world.

As the first major conflict fought in the online age, the war against terrorism has witnessed the use of cyberspace for a variety of purposes, and in support of a variety of causes. From the hours after the September 11, 2001 attacks, when online news servers were swamped with demands for updates, to the extensive online discussions of the war in Iraq, the Internet has been, for many Western citizens, the primary conduit through which war news is distributed.

While the U.S. and its allies have made extensive use of online resources in the campaign against terror,

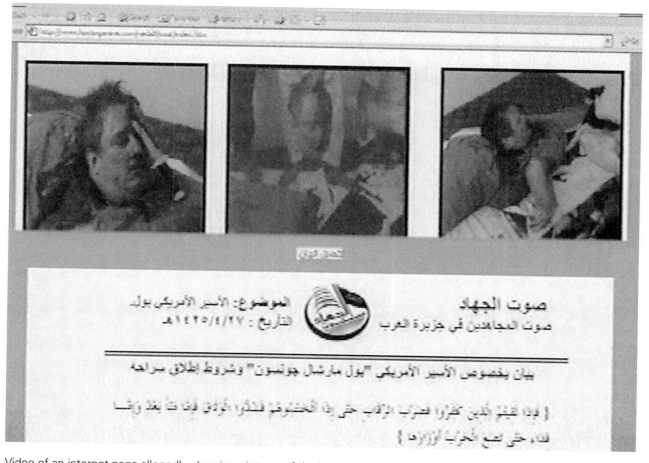

Video of an internet page allegedly showing pictures of the beheaded body of kidnapped American Paul M. Johnson, Jr. with a statement from a group of five Islamic extremists. AP/WIDE WORLD PHOTOS

the adoption of Internet tools has not been limited to one side of the conflict. Terrorist groups quickly learned to use the web for publicity. In 2004, when American Nick Berg was killed in Iraq, video of the grisly beheading spread over the Internet, providing free worldwide exposure to the kidnappers. As of July, 2005, Osama Bin Laden has managed to remain completely hidden, while releasing periodic video and audio messages on sympathetic web sites. In some cases, as with his 2002 "Letter to America," Bin Laden simply posted his message online in Arabic, knowing that it would be quickly translated and across the world at no cost to him.

The public's voracious appetite for information about Bin Laden and the war has also spawned other, more unusual incidents. In July 2004, an email message purporting to contain photos of Bin Laden's suicide began circulating; the message actually contained a computer virus. And in one of the more unusual incidents of the entire conflict, a militant group posted a picture claiming to show a captured U.S. soldier being held at gunpoint, along with a promise to kill him in 72 hours. However a U.S. toy manufacturer promptly identified the soldier as "Special Ops Cody," an action figure sold at U.S. military bases in the Middle East.

The inherent anonymity of the Internet has spawned a series of ethical dilemmas for businesses, as several American companies have found themselves unwittingly hosting websites for terrorist organizations. Given the hundreds of thousands of sites hosted by a typical ISP, locating such accounts among the masses would be a seemingly monumental task. And beyond this practical aspect lie even greater dilemmas: how does an Internet Service Provider (ISP) determine where free speech ends and national security begins? And how should it deal with sites that are deemed offensive, rather than threatening? And who decides? Americans debate the necessity to surrender some civil liberties in times of war, especially restrictions on free speech, making these questions more difficult to answer.

For one man, however, these dilemmas are not at all daunting. Policing the Internet has advanced from hobby to obsession, filling his days (and many of his nights) with an endless quest to locate and force anti-American sites off the web. For A. Aaron Weisburd, one line is clearly drawn.

PRIMARY SOURCE

A. Aaron Weisburd slogged up to his attic at 5 A.M. to begin another day combing through tips he had received about possible pro-terrorist activity on the Internet.

It did not take long for one e-mail to catch his attention: Ekhlaas.com was offering instructions on how to steal people's personal information off their computers. It was a new development for an Islamic discussion site accustomed to announcing "martyrdom operations," or suicide bombings, against U.S. troops and others in Iraq.

Weisburd quickly listed the discovery in his daily log of offensive and dangerous sites, alerting his supporters. A few days later, Ekhlaas experienced an unusual surge in activity, the hallmark of a hacker attack, forcing the company hosting the site to take it down.

It was another small victory for Weisburd, one of a new breed of Internet activists. Part vigilantes, part informants, part nosy neighbors, they search the Web for sites that they say deal in theft, fraud and violence.

Weisburd said he and his supporters are responsible for dismantling at least 650 and as many as 1,000 sites he regards as threatening, especially Islamic radical sites.

Like the foes they pursue, online crusaders like Weisburd are adept at using the Internet's unique characteristics— its anonymity, speed and ability to reach across nation-state boundaries. Some work alone and in secret; others like Weisburd have managed to put together well-organized operations that run almost like companies. Their causes can vary widely, be it stopping spam or holding large corporations accountable for poor products or service. There are groups that investigate murders and those that fight terrorism and other crimes.

The activists often operate at the boundaries of what is legal and illegal. For his part, Weisburd insists that he uses only legal means to go after his targets. A posting on his site explains that in fighting crime he does not think it proper to commit one, but he admits he cannot always control the actions of those who help him.

Government agencies and others are not sure what to make of him. Some law enforcement officials praise his efforts. Kenneth Nix, a police detective from Missouri who is on the Internet Crimes Task Force, said Weisburd often provides information that "we didn't have before."

But others say that he is making more trouble than he is doing good. Some U.S. officials think that they can learn more about terrorist operations by monitoring suspicious sites as they operate. Weisburd said an analyst from a federal agency recently wrote him a scathing letter calling him a "grave threat to national security" because his work was interfering with its investigations.

Marshall Stone, a spokesman for the FBI, said that while the agency encourages citizens to report alleged wrongdoing, it believes any attempt to stop criminals should be left to the government.

Without due process, evidence could be tainted and become unusable in court cases or, worse, targets could be condemned as guilty when they are really innocent, said Paul Kurtz, executive director of the Cyber Security Industry Alliance, a coalition of tech company chief executives. "When we all become 'law enforcement officers' justice becomes very blurry," he said.

Armed with three aging computers, Weisburd hunts what he describes as terrorists from his home.

Weisburd, 41, a half-Irish, half-Jewish New Yorker, said that like other Americans he was deeply affected by the Sept. 11, 2001, attacks. He wanted to enlist in the military, but his age and health issues made that impossible.

Then, about a year later, he saw a news story about a Web site that showed what appeared to be a kindergarten class in the Gaza Strip acting out terrorist attacks. He was outraged and went to his computer to do some research, eventually discovering the name of the company hosting the site. He e-mailed the owner of the Web-hosting company at 6 A.M. By 8 A.M. the site was down.

From that success, the former philosophy major from George Washington University set up "Internet Haganah,"— the latter word in Hebrew means "defense" and was the name of the underground Jewish militia in British-controlled Palestine from 1920 to 1948. The site, dedicated to fighting back against Islamic terrorist sites, has more than 30,000 unique visitors each month.

On another morning that same week in early April, Weisburd called up an e-mail informing him that someone on a Yahoo bulletin board was soliciting donations to go on a "jihad" somewhere. Within a few minutes, Weisburd is able to find three of the messages and trace their origin— from cable modems at someone's home and at a New England school district. He hit the forward button and sent the information off to a law enforcement contact.

Another message urged Weisburd to check out a Web site in Arabic rallying readers to pray to Allah for a volcanic eruption on the Canary Islands. The site surmised that, if large enough, the vibrations could trigger a tsunami that could wipe out the Eastern seaboard of the United States. The site even contained a map of the potential destruction. A bit absurd, Weisburd thought. He summarized the information, posted it on his site, and moved on to the next e-mail.

The site consumes so much of Weisburd's time that he gave up a steady job as a computer programmer. He now works part time as a high-tech consultant and he said he and his wife, who is a graphic artist, are just scraping by.

He said he has received thousands of dollars in donations, as well as some ominous death threats. One warning came in a handwritten letter mailed to Weisburd's house. Another letter on a Web site declared that he should be beheaded and it listed his address. For his protection, Weisburd keeps a loaded pistol in the house.

Weisburd is helped by a loosely organized group of volunteers. Among them are techies from Silicon Valley, Middle East experts, and more than a few women he described as "young grandmothers with high-speed Internet in rural areas."

In one case, Weisburd identified an Atlanta-based Web provider that appeared to be hosting a site that advocated attacks against the United States and its Western allies. The provider, however, seemed to be ignoring requests to remove it. So some Weisburd supporters figured out which church the owner went to and got his personal cell phone number and began lobbying him non-stop until he took down the site.

Some Web hosting providers who have dealt with Weisburd and his supporters said such groups place them in an awkward position. If they keep the sites up, they are in danger of being labeled as supporting terrorism. If they take down the sites, they could become targets of free speech advocates, and lose paying customers.

T. Griffin Conrad, vice president of marketing for iPowerWeb, Inc., the Santa Monica, Calif., company that hosted Ekhlaas, said the company shut down the site because it feared the surge in activity was in danger of triggering a ripple effect that could shut down the company's other clients. Conrad would not speculate on what caused the excess traffic and said he was unaware of the nature of the content on the site until contacted by a reporter.

Perhaps the most difficult question Weisburd faces is determining which sites qualify as promoting "jihad." Even some of his supporters are torn.

Brian Marcus, director of Internet monitoring for the Anti-Defamation League, said Weisburd deserves "a lot of praise." Marcus added that the line between a terrorist-support site and a discussion forum is often nebulous. "We are a civil rights group and freedom of speech means to lot of us," he said.

Weisburd does not read Arabic but uses a computer translator and relies on other volunteers who are fluent in other languages to assist him with more difficult text. But he said it is often clear from just the images and a few words on sites which ones deserve to be kept up and which ones should be made to disappear from cyberspace.

"I understand enough of what they say to know they are my enemy, and that's all I need to know," Weisburd said.

SIGNIFICANCE

Weisburd's methods raised multiple concerns to authorities. First, Weisburd's approach raises troubling questions about how and when citizens should begin enforcing their own ideas of right and wrong on other citizens. In the case of Weisburd's supporters who used harassing phone calls to a business man's personal wireless phone, the methods clearly violate the spirit, if not the letter of the law; yet Weisburd apparently feels no need to condemn this behavior.

A second question deals with whether Internet firms should be held responsible for the information and opinions they host on their servers. While U.S. law does prohibit a few specific types of speech, such as discussing plans to kill high government officials, most other speech is protected by the Constitution. And while some people argue that an ISP is responsible for what he distributes, U.S. libraries regularly acquire books and periodicals containing a variety of opinions which some might find distasteful or immoral. If such restrictions are enforced, some Internet users may find Weisburd's site offensive, spawning a new round of questions.

How much impact does Weisburd's approach really have? Is that impact positive or negative? Some government officials consider his work as interference with their investigations.

FURTHER RESOURCES
Books

Bergen, Peter I. *Holy War Inc.: Inside the Secret World of Osama Bin Laden*. New York: Touchstone, 2002.

Jenkins, Brian Michael. *Countering Al Queda: An Appreciation of the Situation and Suggestions for Strategy*. Arlington, VA: RAND Corporation, 2002.

Web sites

BBC News. "US Hostage Photo 'is doll hoax'." <http://inquirer.philly.com/packages/somalia/sitemap.asp> (accessed June 16, 2005).

CNN.com. "The Internet War: Terrorists Tap into Cyberspace." <http://www.cnn.com/2005/US/02/08/schuster.column/> (accessed June 16, 2005).

Guardian Unlimited. "Full text: Bin Laden's Letter to America." <http://observer.guardian.co.uk/worldview/story/0,11581,845725,00.html> (accessed June 16, 2005).

10 Terrorism and Society

Introduction to Terrorism and Society

Terrorists seek to change some facet of society, from freedom of religious expression to physical and political control over a region. Differences between societies, however, may result in shifting definitions of terrorism and dramatic differences in characterizations of groups or individuals as terrorists.

The September 11, 2001 attacks on the United States, for which the global terrorist group al-Qaeda claimed responsibility, were deadly international terrorist attacks with profound social consequences. Citizens of ninety countries perished in the September 11th terrorist attacks and there was an initial outpouring of sympathy from much of the world. In some Arab cities, however, there were jubilant street celebrations.

Societies around the world have long coped with terrorism, and the U.S. suffered an escalating string of terrorism over the past decades. Yet, the September 11th attacks brought the impact of terrorism on society into sharp focus for Americans. It also revealed solidarity and divisions between countries and within societies.

For example, French President Jacques Chirac was the first foreign leader to visit the World Trade Center site. He expressed French sorrow and solidarity with the American people. *Le Monde*, a leading French newspaper, ran a headline proclaiming solidarity with Americans. The two societies seemed synchronous in their attitudes toward terrorism. Within a few short years, however, differences over U.S. policy toward Iraq separated the longtime allies into feuding camps; both condemned terrorism, but severely differed on other points of policy.

New means of social communication, chiefly via the Internet, unfettered both articulate and profane discourse. Unfounded rumors and disinformation about the attacks on the U.S. vied for space with passionate debate over U.S. fears that Iraq might prove a conduit for terrorist acquisition of weapons of mass destruction. Anti-American sentiment in Europe grew while French wine was spilled into American streets. Two great societies founded on similar democratic ideals grew antagonistic toward one another and bitter divisions over U.S. and U.K. "war on terror" policies arose within those societies. In this climate, some critics maintained that by allowing such a division in Western society, terrorists could claim a victory.

Changes within a society also change definitions of terrorism. Shifts can be subtle, often based on rhetoric. For example, by mid–2005 the Bush Administration began to recharacterize the "war on terror" as a "global struggle against extremism." Most analysts agree that all terrorists are extremists, but the evidence is abundant that not all extremists are terrorists.

Terrorism is not genetic, or confined to one region, race, or group. Terrorism is a sickness of the individual and society. Just as xenophobia created violent and monstrous societies such as Nazi Germany, so too can intolerance, ignorance, and desperation fuel recruitment of suicide bombers.

Terrorism challenges and changes societies. Moreover, terrorism feeds upon society and uses its institutions of culture and media to propagate its impact and message. There are those who are quick to argue that acts of terrorism such as the attacks on September 11th, "forever changed society." It is arguable, however, that such perceptions hand terrorists the power they desire and so foster further terrorism. The true strength of a society may instead be measured by how little such barbarous acts are allowed to change the way people live, work, and relate to one another.

"Terrors of Brainwashing Ordeal"

"Tortures Imposed on Red Prisoners"

Speech

By: Harold William Rigney

Date: June 1, 1956

Source: "Terrors of Brainwashing Ordeal: Tortures Imposed on Red Prisoners," as published by *Vital Speeches of the Day*.

About the Author: Father William Rigney came to China in 1946 to serve as rector of the Fu Jen Catholic University in Peking (Beijing). Following the Communist takeover of the university in 1951, Rigney was arrested as an American spy. He spent more than four years in the prisons of Tsao Lan Tzu Hutung and Tzu Hsing Lu. Despite extensive reports of both physical and psychological torture, he refused to confess to being an agent of the United States government. He told the story of his ordeal in the book *Four Years in a Red Hell: The Story of Father Rigney*, published in 1956.

INTRODUCTION

The term "brainwashing" was coined by a journalist—who was purportedly also a CIA operative—named Edward Hunter. In 1951, he wrote a book called *Brainwashing in Red China: The Calculated Destruction of Men's Minds*. It was Hunter's assertion that agents of the communist Chinese government used a systematic and scientifically based program of mind control achieved through the use of drugs, hypnosis, classical (Pavlovian) conditioning, and repeated terrorist and anti-American philosophical propaganda to turn captive enemy citizens into supporters of their regime.

Hunter's book was a popular press favorite, and his statements achieved great belief and support among the masses; at the time, many people supported the notion that any communist use of propaganda constituted brainwashing. As a number of American military personnel, captured during the Korean conflict, publicly confessed to war crimes, there was an upsurge in popular belief that American servicemen were being brainwashed. Robert Jay Lifton, a psychiatrist and former professor turned terrorism expert for the media, published a groundbreaking book in 1961 entitled *Thought Reform and the Psychology of Totalism: A Study of "Brainwashing" in China*, which offered some support to the notion that something not completely unlike what was termed "brainwashing" was actually occurring. He inter-

A surveillance video of Patty Hearst (allegedly brainwashed by the Symbionese Liberation Army) during a SLA robbery at Hibernia Bank, San Francisco in 1974. AP/WIDE WORLD PHOTOS

viewed dozens of individuals who had been released from communist Chinese prisons and concluded that they had, indeed, been subjected to a multi-step program beginning with an assault on the identity of the prisoner through the use of humiliation and brutality (physical and emotional), and ending with either the admission of guilt, betrayal of friends, colleagues, total submission to the captors, and, sometimes, release. Some former prisoners reported confessing to extremely implausible, if not impossible, crimes.

However, in the view of Lifton, what was occurring in the communist Chinese prisons did not constitute mind control—it could, he felt, be more accurately termed group indoctrination and subjugation achieved through the use of torture, terrorism, physical brutality, and extreme intimidation. His support for that belief lay in the fact that less than 25 United States prisoners refused to be repatriated after the war, compared to more than 22,000 prisoners of war from communist countries.

PRIMARY SOURCE

I would like to make one remark to begin with, that I have not been brainwashed. I was subjected to the process of brainwashing, but I was never brainwashed. Now what do we mean by brainwashing? In the prisons of China, we use the term which in English you would translate by "changing your mind." Prisoners were told day in and day out that they must change their minds. . . it is a very simple concept. Brain-washing simply means a change of attitude and a change of mind from one of anti-communism to one of pro-communism . . .

To understand this awful process one must realize some of the psychological background.

The communists all over the world use two weapons wherever they have control and they are terror and deceit. They can't use terror in the free world, otherwise they would be arrested, but they can use deceit and they do. In America, they use deceit. In Communist China, they use the weapon of terror and the weapon of deceit. But please keep in mind that awful background of terror that every one in China, in Communist China, has in the background of his mind. It is an awful fear that he will be shot or she will be shot, or he or she will undergo even worse than being shot, being put into a wretched communist prison for life perhaps, or 30 years or 20 years, or 10 years.

The year I was arrested, in 1951, they were executing in Peiping alone, publicly, two to three hundred people every month, publicly taking them out with their hands bound behind their backs and their feet in chains, with a big slip of paper up each back, like a fish fin, with their crimes written on it.

They would be put on a truck and driven through the main streets of Peiping and taken out to the place near the Temple of Heaven, and there they had to get down on their knees, with a soldier behind their backs with a rifle, and they would be shot. People would be asked to come over to see these executions. Imagine the terror that went over the city! Any day you could see a truck-load of good Chinese (they weren't criminals, very few were real criminals: most of them were ordinary, honest business people like yourselves, who simply did not believe in the wretched, diabolical character of communism; that was their only crime) being driven up and down the streets of Peiping and taken out and shot. Think of the terror!

After '51, the executions were not so numerous, but still there were always public executions to keep in the mind of every good Chinese the terror, the fear that perhaps he or she would be shot.

I remember in prison how often we were told by the prison wardens that we were all supposed to be spies. I was arrested as a spy. I deny those charges; they were false charges. And most of the poor fellows in prison with me were also innocent, I'm sure. But we were told so often that the "big problem of you 'spies' is the problem of your thinking. You must change your thoughts. You must destroy your reactionary thoughts, and if you don't destroy your own reactionary thoughts, then the government will destroy those reactionary thoughts when the government destroys your body." I will tell you that meant something. . . .

SIGNIFICANCE

The communist Chinese regime maintained a large network of re-education camps, in which individuals who espoused "incorrect" ideology or dogma were subjected to systematic use of what is now termed a variant of "coercive persuasion." This is a practice still employed in many areas of the world when attempting to elicit information from suspected terrorists or prisoners of war. Essentially, it consists of repetitive use of police-style interrogation techniques, continual use of ideological propaganda, and physical intimidation. Sometimes, brutality, physical or emotional abuse, deprivation of food or sleep, and the use of extremes in temperature (from hot to cold, etc.) are employed as well. In the case of the prisoners held by the Chinese communists, the "coercive persuasion" utilized consisted of the systematic use of complete control over both information flow and the prisoner's environment, manipulation with the intent of eroding self-expression, criticism, humiliation and degradation, confession, peer pressure, renunciation of values, and coercion by physical force and threat.

The concept of brainwashing came to the forefront of the popular consciousness again in the 1970s, with the upsurge of radical cult activity. Although there were many assertions that brainwashing was an essential part of cult membership, or mass behaviors (as in the mass suicides at the People's Temple with Jim Jones in 1978), it was determined by some that this was not the case, because the element of physical coercion was notably absent during the process of cult indoctrination.

In November of 2003, Washington, D.C. area sniper suspect Lee Boyd Malvo's lawyer attempted to use the insanity defense during the teenager's first murder trial. It was potentially precedent-setting, as the defense contended that Malvo was "brainwashed to kill by his membership in a cult of two," by John Allen Muhammed, the other sniper suspect (Muhammed received the death penalty in a capital murder conviction for the same legal case).

Although there has been no compelling scientific evidence in favor of actual brainwashing, there is strong scholarly and popular support for the success of "coercive persuasion" techniques. In the American media, since the 1960s, there has been documentation of "brainwashing-like" activity, evidenced by the swastika carved foreheads and vacant stares of the Manson family murderers, the 912 member mass suicide at Jonestown, as well as that of the Heaven's Gate members. More recently, there has been much speculation about the use of coercive persuasion in extremist groups, in order to foment the willingness of members to become suicide bombers. Similarly, the families of Elizabeth Smart (kidnap victim who was held quite near her home for the duration of her captivity, but apparently never attempted an escape), "shoe bomber" Richard Reid, and American Taliban soldier John Walker Lindh have all asserted that their family members were "brainwashed."

There is progressively more evidence that behavior and attitudes can be strongly influenced by isolation, group mores, small group dynamics, information control, peer pressure, and obedience training—all of which are integral parts of extremist indoctrination.

FURTHER RESOURCES

Books

Rigney, H.W., S.V.D. *Four Years in a Red Hell: The Story of Father Rigney*. Henry Regnery, 1956.

Lifton, Robert Jay. *Thought Reform and the Psychology of Totalism: A Study of "Brainwashing" in China*. (Reprint Edition). University of North Carolina Press, 1989.

Hunter, Edward. *Brainwashing in Red China: The Calculated Destruction of Men's Minds*. Vanguard Press, 1951.

Web sites

PBS.org. "NOW Transcript: Bill Moyers Interviews Robert Jay Lifton." <http://www.pbs.org/now/transcript/transcript_lifton.html> (June 30, 2005).

"Violence and Xenophobia in Germany"

Anti-Turkish Attacks

Magazine article

By: Joachim Krautz

Date: October 1993

Source: "Violence and Xenophobia in Germany," written by Joachim Krautz and published in *Contemporary Review*.

About the Author: Krautz studied at the universities of Tübingen, Stuttgart and Massachusetts and holds a master's degree in literature and linguistics. He taught

for several years in the German and Philosophy Departments of University College, Cork.

INTRODUCTION

Nationalism, or pride in one's own country, is one of the more common sentiments expressed around the world. In many cases, specific slogans have summed up citizens' pride in their own nation. When Great Britain was at its zenith in the nineteenth century, its citizens boasted, "The sun never sets on the British Empire." As the United States rose to world power during the early twentieth century, some of its citizens summed up their feelings of manifest destiny (the term coined to describe the settlement of the West) with the slogan, "America, right or wrong."

Following Germany's humiliating defeat in World War I (1914–1918), nationalism became a powerful tool for the rising Nazi movement. As it took power in 1933, the Nazi party proclaimed the physical and intellectual superiority of white, Christian Germans. The Nazis passed discriminatory laws against Jews, Gypsies, and other groups, many of whom were German citizens. This era of persecution culminated in the murder of over six million Jews, Gypsies, political prisoners, Poles, and others during the Holocaust.

These historical roots underlie the German nationalistic slogan: "Germany for Germans." This extreme form of nationalism was largely purged with Germany's defeat in World War II (1939–1945) and the passage of strict laws against such forms of racism.

PRIMARY SOURCE

The arsonists came at night. Fully aware of the likelihood that people might be in their bedrooms they set fire to the apartment house, in which— according to the nameplates near the doorbells— a couple of Turkish families lived. The fact that Turks were the sole inhabitants of the house had been the precise reason for the murderer's choice of target. In the night from Saturday to Witsunday five people— all of them women and girls—became victims of this treacherous crime which took place in Solingen, a small, until then very ordinary town in the West of Germany. It was the climax of a whole series of violent attacks against foreigners since the reunification of Germany. A deadly series which claimed 49 lives so far. All these assaults had in common that the perpetrators were led by racist or right-extremist motives. Pictures went around the world showing young men with tattooed arms and closely shorn haircuts, instigated by beer and rock music with explicitly fascist texts, hurling petrol bombs at houses while honest citizens stood by and watched.

And the politicians, apparently, are not able or—as terrified foreigners in Germany claim— not willing to halt this development. Chancellor Helmut Khol did not even think it appropriate to be present at the memorial ceremonies. What is happening in Germany at the moment? Has Nazism risen from its grave? Or will Germany turn once more into the scourge of Europe?

The current events make up a very complex issue. Over the past few years facts and statistics with regard to foreigners, aggressors and right-extremism in Germany have been perpetually blurred and distorted—both at home and abroad—to serve various interest groups. Right-extremism, nationalism, and the ugly face of racism are by no means confined to Germany. But because of her historical peculiarity these phenomena have always been ascribed a specific significance in a country which made Auschwitz happen . . .

For the majority of young Germans who grew up in the sixties, seventies, and early eighties nationalism was out. And so were all its symbols like the national flag or the national anthem. It would have been unthinkable to sing the latter in school or play it in cinemas after the performance as is custom in some other countries. Intoxicated fans bawled the national anthem and waived the country's flag in football stadiums. But young (West) Germans who wanted to be politically fashionable defined their politics by the absence of patriotism and their national pride consisted of criticism of their country— if they were proud of it at all.

The situation in the other German state was different from the start. There the Communist government by definition had seen themselves as not having any links with the brown-shirted 'Nazi' past. As a result there had never been any attempt in dealing with the past as there had been in the West.

Consequently, the notion of the nation had retained its positive connotation for the people in the former German Democratic Republic. National pride for socialist achievements was not only condoned, but even encouraged by the government. After all, one lived in the better part of the two Germaines. The general public, however, saw it differently. After having been fed—or rather brainwashed—with West German advertisements and TV commercials for decades they, indeed, imagined paradise, the land of milk and honey, as the epitome of German ingeniousness—but on the other side of the Wall. Whether identifying themselves with or rebelling against the system and embracing the world view of the class enemy—none of the generations in East Germany ever felt obligated to suppress the sentiment of patriotism . . .

The damage right-wing extremism has done to Germany's image abroad is tremendous. Big business has long since realized that the current development runs against their interest. The tourist trade fears losses, export figures plummeted already, and Japanese investments fell

off to a record low in 1992. And they reacted swiftly: companies started to fire employees who molested foreign workmates in word or deed (measures which the women's rights movement has been fighting for years.) It was mainly their initiative which brought about the large turnout of concerned citizens protesting the xenophobia at the nationwide candle light vigils last December. All this reminded one of the 'public breast-beating contests,' as Max Horkheimer used to call the mass abjurations after World War II. And while honest middle-class citizens—in accordance with the government—call the perpetrators 'a few demented criminals,' the Left, in accordance with the press abroad, is busy conjuring the scare of reviving Nazism. Who is right?

Frustration and disappointment prevail with unemployment soaring in a country whose citizens had not known anything but full employment for 40 years and whose self-respect had always been based upon work. Only anti-social elements, who refused to work, used to be without a job. Furthermore, despite the snooper activities of the 'Stasi' (the East German Secret Service) there had been a sense of solidarity among the citizens against the bigwigs and the party bosses of the ruling SED. Now with jobs scarce and uncertainty everywhere mistrust and envy govern people's minds. Young people are deprived of any perspective for the future. Besides, now that the euphoria about the reunification has long since abated and its true costs are presented by an only too evasive government, East Germans feel more and more excluded as second-class citizens by West Germans. They in their turn exclude those whom they deem even further down the social scale. And so they fall back on the only identity which they think they can be sure of, i.e., their national identity: Germany for the Germans!

SIGNIFICANCE

The incident described in this magazine article was not an isolated incident. Figures compiled by the German Interior Ministry included more than 10,000 right-wing offenses during 2002, including 725 separate acts of violence. Given the stigma associated with such acts, there is likely a reluctance to report them, and the actual figure may well be much higher. Geographically, the incidents are concentrated in the East, though they occur throughout Germany.

A 2004 study of German attitudes toward various groups produced some unsettling findings. Germany's population includes about 6 percent foreigners (vs. 11 percent in the U.S.), yet a majority of Germans describe their country as "too foreign." With the Muslim population in Germany rapidly growing, more than two-thirds of Germans say the Muslims (mainly Turks) do not fit into German society. Some analysts attribute these attitudes to high unemployment, which leads unemployed workers to engage in immigrant-bashing.

German right-wing groups have adopted a variety of techniques to spread their message. In 2004 and again in 2005, neo-Nazis used the widely distributed Sober computer worm to email millions of nationalist German messages to computers around the world. The messages, which blamed immigrants, prisoners, and welfare recipients for Germany's problems, were the first known example of a political organization using Spam to distribute propaganda.

In 2004, the German state of Baden-Württemberg banned the wearing of Muslim headscarves by school teachers, calling them a "political" symbol in order to bypass Germany's legal guarantee of religious freedom. Backers of the ban were stunned when a German federal court ruled in October of 2004 that the ban must also be applied to Catholic nuns, requiring them to remove their habits before entering the classroom.

While far-right parties continue to gain some momentum, especially in the former East Germany, most Germans are beginning to take notice and voice their displeasure. In June 2005, right-wing marches were planned in two separate cities. In the town of Braunschweig, 280 neo-Nazi marchers gathered, but were met by more than 1500 protesters. And in the village of Halbe about 100 right-wing marchers were countered by more than 800 opposition protestors.

Anti-immigrant sentiment is not only directed against Germany's Turkish and Muslim populations, but also against the growing number of immigrants from Eastern European nations. Nor are such feelings limited to Germany. Many other European nations have also witnessed an increase in anti-immigrant activity from extremist groups.

Despite opposition to the influx, immigrants may prove to be an aid to the German economy. Germany's falling birth rates mean that it may soon be less-able to support its growing elderly population. Nevertheless, the persistence of unemployment and limited economic growth in Germany may continue to fuel anti-immigrant sentiment.

FURTHER RESOURCES
Books

Lieven, Anatol. *America Right or Wrong: An Anatomy of American Nationalism.* New York: Oxford University Press, 2004.

Smith, Helmut. *German Nationalism and Religious Conflict: Culture, Ideology, and Politics 1870–1914.* Princeton, NJ: Princeton University Press, 1995.

Web sites

Haaretz.com. "Neo-Nazi Opponents Arrested at German Far-Right Rally." <http://www.haaretz.com/hasen/spages/589374.html> (accessed June 24, 2005).

United States Holocaust Memorial Museum. "Inside History." <http://www.ushmm.org/;> (accessed June 24, 2005).

Washington Times. "Germans Intolerant of Immigrants." <http://www.nizza-thobi.com/washington_times_january_15.htm;> (accessed June 24, 2005).

"Terrorism in the United States"

FBI report excerpt

By: Federal Bureau of Investigation (FBI)

Date: 2001

Source: "Terrorism in the United States" is an unclassified report that has been published annually by the Federal Bureau of Investigation (FBI) since the mid 1980s. The report serves to inform the general public regarding the current status of terrorist activity in the United States and actions being taken by the federal authorities to deter future attacks. In 2001, the FBI for the first time released the report under the new name of "Terrorism" to reflect the new global environment of terrorism.

About the Author: Founded in 1908, the FBI is the investigative arm of the United States Department of Justice. It is charged with investigating federal crimes. The FBI often works in partnership with other law enforcement agencies both within the United States and around the world. Since the terrorist attacks of 2001, the FBI has changed its mandate to make the prevention of future terrorist attacks against United States citizens its primary goal. The FBI serves as the principal United States law enforcement agency charged with investigating terrorism in the United States. When attacks take place on U.S. interests abroad, the FBI works in an investigative capacity with local authorities.

INTRODUCTION

Following the attacks of September 11, 2001, the FBI's mandate was expanded by the October 26, 2001, USA PATRIOT Act (Patriot Act) which granted law enforcement agencies new provisions and freedoms to carry out their investigations into matters of national security and the threat of terrorism. On May

Iraqis scream as they fire their machine guns into the air during the funeral of slain Iraqi policemen in Fallujah. AP/WIDE WORLD PHOTOS

29, 2002, Attorney General John Ashcroft issued new investigative guidelines of operation for the FBI to further aid their efforts against terrorist activities in the United States.

The FBI investigation into the September 11 attacks, and the al-Qaeda network which carried out that attack as well as several other international attacks against United States interests has become the largest terrorism investigation ever carried out.

In addition to the newly expanded threat posed by international terrorism, domestic terrorists continue to operate within the United States, receiving considerable investigative attention from the FBI.

■ PRIMARY SOURCE

As the events of September 11, 2001, demonstrated with brutal clarity, the terrorist threats facing the United States are formidable. Between 1991 and 2001, 74 terrorist incidents were recorded in the United States. During this same time frame, an additional 62 terrorist acts being plotted in the United States were prevented by U.S. law enforcement. As troubling as these statistics are, they only hint at the full scope of the terrorist threat confronting U.S. interests. For every successful terrorist attack mounted in the United States, nearly 20 (19.83) anti-U.S. attacks are carried out around the world. Between 1996 and 2001, these overseas attacks killed 75 Americans and wounded an additional 606.

During the past two decades, the U.S. Government has expanded the FBI's authority to investigate terrorist activities against U.S. interests overseas. Specifically, the

Comprehensive Crime Control Act of 1984, the *Omnibus Diplomatic Security and Antiterrorist Act of 1986*, the *Antiterrorism and Effective Death Penalty Act of 1996*, and *Presidential Decision Directive 39* have served to extend FBI investigative authority beyond U.S. borders when U.S. interests are harmed or threatened. Since 1984, the FBI has carried out over 300 extraterritorial investigations, in close cooperation with the U.S. Department of State and with the assistance of host governments. These investigations include some of the FBI's most complex and high-profile cases, including investigations into the September 11 attacks, as well as the bombings of Khobar Towers in Saudi Arabia in 1996, two U.S. embassies in East Africa in 1998, and the USS *Cole* in the Yemenese port of Aden in October 2000.

The growing *internationalization* of crime, including the crime of terrorism, has led the FBI to expand its international presence. By the year 2001, the FBI had legal attaché (LEGAT) offices in 44 countries around the world. At the same time, the increasing scope of terrorist threats—from bombing plots of domestic and international extremists to threats involving weapons of mass destruction to the growing menace of computer intrusion crime and threat of cyberterrorism—led the FBI, in November 1999, to create the Counterterrorism Division to help focus its operational capabilities upon the full range of activities in which violent extremists engage.

Undeterred by its thwarted efforts to target U.S. and other interests in late 1999 during the millennial time frame, the Al-Qaeda terrorist network carried out two separate attacks against the United States in 2000 and 2001. The first of these, a suicide bombing of the U.S. naval destroyer USS *Cole* in the Yemenese port of Aden on October 12, 2000, claimed the lives of 17 U.S. sailors. The second, a coordinated suicide attack using four hijacked U.S. commercial aircraft as missiles on September 11, 2001, resulted in the deaths of 2,783 innocent people. The September 11 attack represents the most deadly and destructive terrorist attack in history and claimed more lives than all previous acts of terrorism in the United States combined. The attack of September 11 represented the first successful act of international terrorism carried out in the United States since the bombing of the World Trade Center in February 1993.

In response to the September 11 attack, the FBI launched the largest terrorism investigation ever conducted, working in close cooperation with other U.S. and foreign intelligence agencies. On October 7, 2001, the United States initiated military action against the Taliban regime in Afghanistan, which had provided safe-haven to Al-Qaeda leader Usama bin Laden and his followers since 1996. By year's end, U.S. forces were working with anti-Taliban Afghan fighters to target Al-Qaeda training camps in Afghanistan.

In keeping with a longstanding trend, domestic extremists carried out the majority of terrorist incidents during this period. Twenty of the 22 recorded instances of terrorism and the three terrorist preventions in the United States and its territories in 2000 and 2001 were perpetrated by domestic terrorists, predominantly by special interest extremists active in the animal rights and environmental movements. The acts committed by these extremists typically targeted materials and facilities rather than persons.

In contrast, the three major terrorist incidents of 2000 and 2001 continued a trend in terrorism tactics and methodologies that began in the 1990s, in which terrorists have sought to inflict massive and indiscriminate casualties within civilian populations. In the 1990s, this was evidenced in the 1993 bombing of New York's World Trade Center by international terrorists and the 1995 Oklahoma City bombing perpetrated by domestic terrorists, the latter of which received a measure of legal closure on June 11, 2001, with the execution of Timothy McVeigh. The three major terrorist attacks against U.S. interests during 2000 and 2001 also resulted in numerous deaths and serious injuries. Two of these were acts of international terrorism carried out under the auspices of the Al-Qaeda terrorist network, which already in the mid 1990s had emerged as the most pressing international terrorist threat worldwide. These attacks by Al-Qaeda were the suicide bombing of the U.S. naval destroyer USS *Cole* and the coordinated suicide attack using four hijacked U.S. commercial aircraft as missiles on September 11, 2001. The attack on September 11, which claimed more lives than all previous acts of terrorism in the United States combined, was the first successful act of international terrorism carried out in the United States since the bombing of the World Trade Center in February 1993. The third lethal terrorist incident during this period involved the sending of the biological agent anthrax through the U.S. postal system during fall 2001. These anthrax mailings represented the first fatal terrorist use of a biological agent in the United States. The investigation into the anthrax mailings continues, and they as yet remain unclassified as either a domestic or international terrorist incident.

These major incidents, and the continued commitment of terrorist groups like Al-Qaeda to attempt acts of mass destruction, led the FBI and U.S. Government to strengthen existing counterterrorism measures and initiate new procedures at the end of 2001. On October 7, the U.S. Government initiated military action in Afghanistan to destroy the Al-Qaeda training facilities in that country and to overthrow the illegitimate Taliban regime that had provided Al-Qaeda with support and safe haven since 1996. On October 10, the FBI established a Most Wanted Terrorists List of 22 names to focus global attention on indicted terrorist suspects involved in the commission of acts of terrorism against the United States. On October 26, the U.S. Government enacted the USA PATRIOT Act—legislation that has been instrumental in helping law enforcement counter

the terrorist threat. On October 29, the interagency Foreign Terrorist Tracking Task Force was created to deny known terrorists and their supporters entry into the United States and to track them should they gain entry. In December 2001 the FBI merged the analytical resources of its Investigative Services Division into the Counterterrorism Division to improve its ability to gather, analyze, and share critical national security information with the broader Intelligence Community and the FBI's law enforcement partners. At the beginning of the 21st century, the problem of terrorism has become a global one, and the FBI continues to improve the capacity of its counterterrorism program to accurately assess and effectively counter the dynamic variety of domestic and international terrorist threats.

SIGNIFICANCE

The growing internationalization of criminal activity in general and terrorism in specific has led to an increased need on the part of the FBI to expand their investigative focus beyond the borders of the United States. With increased technology, and a growing reliance of terrorists on media and the internet, the ease of planning terror attacks from afar has led to greater challenges for law enforcement.

The most controversial aspects of the new policies following the attacks of 2001 revolve around the expansion of policing powers offered to investigators through the Patriot Act. As this report details, the Act, together with other similar legislation, provides law enforcement agencies with increased latitude in who they are able to detain for suspected involvement with terrorist activities. The report further established that despite the international terrorist attacks being the most costly in terms of their targets, the majority of attacks carried out in the United States in 2000 and 2001 were perpetrated by domestic terrorists, who were responsible for twenty of the twenty-two terrorist incidents that took place during this period.

The conclusions of the report indicate that the events of 2000 and 2001, including the bombings of the USS *Cole* in Yemen and then the September 11 attacks, have exposed the seriousness of the threat to United States citizens. The report also notes the increased ability of global terrorist groups to inflict mass civilian casualties with strategic attacks. The report also highlights new counterterrorism measures adopted after the attacks on the World Trade Center and the Pentagon.

FURTHER RESOURCES
Books

Thompson, Paul. *The Terror Timeline: Year by Year, Day by Day, Minute by Minute: A Comprehensive Chronicle of the*

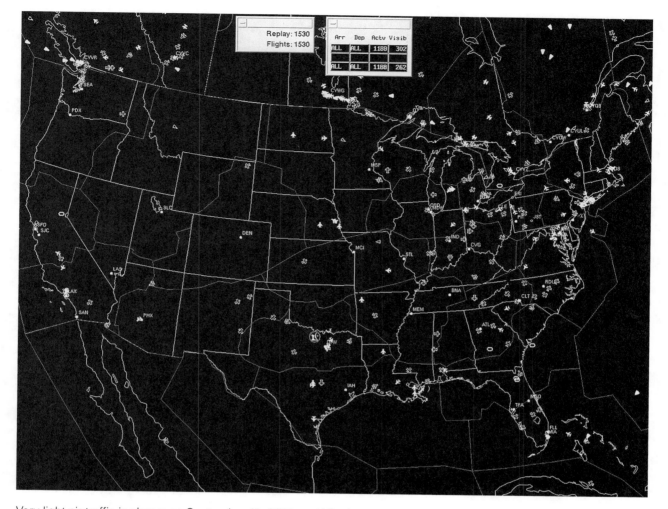

Replay: 1530
Flights: 1530

Arr	Dep	Actv	Visib
ALL	ALL	1188	302
ALL	ALL	1188	262

Very light air traffic is shown on September 11, 2001, as U.S. airspace was closed after the terrorist attack on the World Trade center and Pentagon. AP/WIDE WORLD PHOTOS

Road to 9/11—and America's Response. New York: Regan Books, 2004.

Web sites

Federal Bureau of Investigation. <www.fbi.gov> (accessed July 11, 2005).

The Terrorism Research Center. <www.terrorism.gov> (accessed July 11, 2005).

Terrorist Use of News Media

Osama Bin Laden tape shown on Al-Jazeera

Video still

By: The Associated Press

Date: October 7, 2001

Source: The Associated Press.

About the Author: Founded in 1848 in New York, the Associated Press serves as a news source for more than one billion people a day worldwide.

INTRODUCTION

Launched in 1996, Al-Jazeera has established a reputation as the leading independent news source across the Arab world. With a mix of snappy graphics, gripping reporting and aggressive interviews, not to mention an array of stunning scoops, Al-Jazeera has come to dominate the Arab airwaves.

Backed by the Emir of Qatar, Sheikh Hamad, the tiny Gulf state where the network is based, Al-Jazeera was founded by Arab journalists trained by the British Broadcasting Corporation (BBC) to run the British network's abortive Arab TV channel. To the annoyance of many of his neighbors, the Qatari leader gave

PRIMARY SOURCE

Terrorist Use of News Media Image of Osama Bin Laden taken from an al-Jazeera broadcast. AP/WIDE WORLD PHOTOS

Al-Jazeera's editors a free rein to report what they liked, which, combined with the principles honed at the BBC, made for explosive television in a region otherwise gripped by censorship and state-run channels.

At various times, Al-Jazeera has been banned in a number of different Middle Eastern countries because of the nature of its open reporting (though this has seldom stopped individuals in the banned countries from illegally viewing Al-Jazeera via their own private satellites). Most notable amongst these was Saudi Arabia, about whose royal family Al-Jazeera routinely reported; and Bahrain, who accused Al-Jazeera of being too "pro-Zionist," or favorable to the state of Israel.

Al-Jazeera's journalistic independence soon fostered a trust with dissident groups across the region, some with extremist convictions. As most other Arab media outlets are state run and state censored, there was a likelihood that, for instance, a Hezbollah activist giving an interview to Egyptian TV would be revealed to the relevant authorities. Al-Jazeera often maintained the confidentiality of its sources when they requested, and this practice handed Al-Jazeera a number of exclusive news stories, adding to its burgeoning reputation.

Acclaim started to give way to notoriety after the September 11 attacks, however, when al-Qaeda first passed on tape recordings purporting to take responsibility for the attacks to Al-Jazeera. Then, four weeks after the atrocities, Al-Jazeera broadcast (and also sold to Western media outlets) a video recording of Osama Bin Laden warning the United States of further attacks.

PRIMARY SOURCE

TERRORIST USE OF NEWS MEDIA
  See primary source image.

SIGNIFICANCE

The broadcast of Osama Bin Laden on Al-Jazeera provoked outrage from the United States government. The National Security Advisor, Condaleeza Rice denounced the station and Colin Powell, the U.S. Secretary of State, accused Al-Jazeera of passing on coded messages in the broadcast.

When U.S. officials asked Sheikh Hamad to stop Al-Jazeera from giving terrorists a voice, Hamad reminded them that for years, they had been asking Arab governments to eliminate censorship in the media.

The Bush administration repeatedly called into question Al-Jazeera's journalistic principles, but journalists across the world still debate the broadcasts. Despite the Bush administration's dislike of Al-Jazeera, Powell, Rice, and Secretary of Defense Donald Rumsfeld all made appearances on the network.

In December 2001, during the war in Afghanistan, the United States bombed Al-Jazeera's Kabul bureau. The U.S. government claimed the event was a wartime accident.

In 2003, the U.S. military launched a military attack on Al-Jazeera's Baghdad bureau, killing Tariq Ayoub, a correspondent for the station. There were no military sites nearby and the BBC reporter Rageh Omaar, who was stationed in the nearby Palestine Hotel, described the bombing as "suspect." He said: "We were watching and filming the bombardment and it's quite clearly a direct strike on the Al-Jazeera office. This was not just a stray round. It just seemed too specific."

Al-Jazeera continued to draw fierce criticism from the U.S. government throughout the Iraq war, in particular when the channel aired graphic footage, provided by Iraqi television, of American soldiers and dazed American prisoners of war being questioned in broken English. By 2003, bolstered by its coverage of events in Iraq, Al-Jazeera was regularly drawing forty-five million Arabic speaking viewers, and had plans for an English language channel.

In November 2004, Al-Jazeera unexpectedly broadcast another message from Osama Bin Laden, his first appearance in more than two years. In this tape, Bin Laden explicitly took credit for killing nearly 3,000 Americans in the September 11, 2001 terrorist attacks on the World Trade Center and the Pentagon.

FURTHER RESOURCES

Books

Miles, Hugh. *Al Jazeera*. London: Abacus, 2005.

Web sites

Al-Jazeera Online. <http://english.aljazeera.net/HomePage> (accessed 11 July 2005).

Peer Pressure Spurs Terrorists, Psychologists Say

Psychology of Terrorism

Newspaper article

By: Shankar Vedantam

Date: October 16, 2001

Source: "Peer Pressure Spurs Terrorists, Psychologists Say," as published by the *Washington Post.*

About the Author: Shankar Vedantam is a staff writer for the *Washington Post* who has also been published in periodicals and newspapers worldwide. His written works on mental health earned him the prestigious Rosalynn Carter Fellowship for Mental Health Journalism. In addition to his prolific newspaper writings, he contributed to a book of essays on terrorism entitled *Violence or Dialogue.*

INTRODUCTION

Terrorists have used themselves as suicide weapons since the beginning of recorded history: Jewish Zealots used suicide terrorists against the Romans in first century Judea; the Islamist Order of Assassins reportedly used this technique in the Middle East from the ninth to the fourteenth centuries. In more recent times, Japanese Kamikaze pilots flew their planes into enemy ships during World War II (1939–1945).

In the latter half of the twentieth century, the modern era of suicide terrorism came to worldwide consciousness in April of 1983 when Hezbollah, under the cover name of Islamic Jihad, employed a truck bomb to attack the United States Embassy in Beirut with a truck-bomb, killing sixty-three people. The tactic of using suicide bombers has since been used by dozens of groups around the world, most prolifically by Hamas and the Liberation Tigers of Tamil Eelam (otherwise know as the Tamil Tigers). The media has reported more than five hundred suicide attacks around the world since 1980.

What propels young people to use the act of committing suicide as a means of killing others? Particularly since the attacks on American soil on September 11, 2001, psychologists and anthropologists have been closely researching suicide attacks. These researchers have come to some de-mythologizing conclusions. First, more suicide bombers came from the middle classes of their cultures and from well-educated families, than from poor or minimally educated families. Second, suicide bombers overall have

A poster on a wall in Jenin refugee camp in the West Bank glorifies Palestinian suicide bomber Shadi Zakaria. AP/WIDE WORLD PHOTOS

not been found to be fundamentalist religious zealots, but have been from more secular, politically motivated extremist groups.

Suicide bombers do not act impulsively, by and large. They are recruited, cultivated, indoctrinated, and prepared over a period of weeks or months (sometimes years, as in the case of some September 11th terrorists), by efficient, well-organized extremist organizations, who give them social support and encouragement as they are prepared for their ultimate acts. In Western societies, this type of social support is referred to as *peer pressure*, which vastly understates the power and influence of the organization over the individuals who are recruited for suicide missions.

The majority of suicide bombers are young and impressionable; most are between early adolescence (around fourteen years old) and early adulthood (twenties to around thirty). Terrorist groups are typically rooted in societies perceived as oppressed, so the impressionable youth is surrounded by evidence of the

negative conditions catalyzing development of extremist ideology, giving a social context to the future suicide bomber's belief in the group. The youth is usually also drawn into a political structure comprised of older individuals who are capable of using psychological manipulation to encourage not only the development of a radical belief system, but the ability to envision using death as a means of furthering the interests of the larger group.

PRIMARY SOURCE

The 19 men who carried out the Sept. 11 attacks may have been motivated by a force more powerful than religious zeal or hatred for the United States: Peer pressure, according to psychological experts who have analyzed the backgrounds of the terrorists.

Although only sketchy information is available about most of the men, it's become increasingly clear in the four weeks since the attacks that the terrorists did not meet the profile of the prototypical suicide bomber—young, uneducated, poor and disaffected.

A number of experts who have analyzed what is known about the men and studied the long history of suicide bombers that precedes them have concluded that the roots of the attacks lie less in the men's personalities and beliefs than in group psychology.

"The power of the group over the individual is what's important," said Martha Crenshaw, a professor at Wesleyan University who studies political psychology and terrorism. "People may be more loyal to the group than the cause. The cause is long-term; the group is tangible."

Some of the Sept. 11 hijackers appear to have been extremely religious, leading to speculation that they may have committed their acts as part of a religiously motivated "jihad," believing that as martyrs a paradise awaited them in the afterlife.

While those beliefs may have played a role, psychologists, psychiatric profilers and terrorism experts who have been studying the Sept. 11 attacks—including some experts who have worked in law enforcement or consulted with the federal government on national security issues—said religious zeal isn't necessary to become a suicide bomber, and cannot by itself explain the behavior.

"Two thirds of suicide attacks in Lebanon were carried out by secular organizations," said Ariel Merari, a psychologist at Tel Aviv University in Israel who has puzzled over the psychological makeup of the Sept. 11 hijackers and has spent years studying suicide attacks around the world. "Religion is neither necessary nor a sufficient cause."

"Suicidal terrorist attacks are not a matter of individual whim," said Merari. "I don't know of a single case in which an individual decided on his or her own to carry out a suicidal attack. In all cases—it certainly is true in Lebanon and Israel and Sri Lanka and the Kurdish case—it was an organization that picked the people for the mission, trained them, decided on the target, chose a time, arranged logistics and sent them."

The role of group dynamics may have played an especially important role in the Sept. 11 attacks because they were far more complex than strapping on a backpack of explosives and walking into a pizza parlor, or driving a truck laden with explosives into an enemy building. The terrorists had lived for weeks, months or even years far from the main groups that had inspired and chosen them. They had to blend in with their neighbors as they learned to fly large commercial planes at U.S. flight schools, acquiring drivers' licenses and booking airline tickets over the Internet.

"These people were living in the midst of Western life. No beard, no Koran, and yet they carry with them laser-like beams focusing on their ultimate missions. I see them as fully formed psychological adults who have subordinated their individuality to the group," said Jerrold Post, a former CIA psychological profiler now at George Washington University.

Because the desire to participate in high-risk or suicidal missions fluctuates with time, said Merari, suicide attackers are usually sent hurtling toward their targets soon after they are selected and indoctrinated. Most groups do not allow prospective attackers to mingle with anyone outside the group's inner circle before an attack—certainly not with the "enemy."

"With all the groups who are willing to kill themselves . . . they have yielded their authority to the group. They will give their lives to the group," said Post, who has served as a government consultant on national security matters.

One of the reasons for the large number of hijackers involved in the Sept. 11 mission may have been the extension of this group psychology—the hijackers reinforced each other's beliefs and deterred an individual who wanted to back out at the last moment: He would have not only faced the wrath of the shadowy leaders who planned the operation, but would have been letting down his immediate circle of friends, peers and comrades. Groups that prepare suicide attackers are keenly aware of this psychology.

"I see Mohamed Atta as like a coach before the big game. He has them pray a lot to keep their minds on what they are doing." Post said.

Many organizations make recruits videotape their intentions, and are told that the videotape will be released to their families and the public after the attack, Merari said. Backing out of the operation now becomes difficult, and besides the fear of retaliation from the group, comes the prospect of shame and dishonor.

"Suicide candidates, when they are chosen by an organization, enter into one end of a production process and in the other end they come out as complete, ready suicides," he said. "There is a psychological process of preparation that consists of boosting motivation, pep talks and the creation of points of no return."

The Sept. 11 hijackers wrapped themselves in each other's company. They traveled together, planned together, ate together. Even when they partook of Western temptations—bars, drinking and pornography—they probably reinforced each other's contempt for America, said Washington psychologist Rona Fields, much like men who "go to strip shows and get involved with prostitutes but have tremendous contempt for women."

The group psychology tactics, said the experts, are an extension of military preparations. Soldiers join armies to fight for king, God and country, but soldiers under fire fight to the death for their buddies in the nearby trenches. Whole regiments in World War I have been immortalized for charging artillery positions, knowing that death was certain. Japanese kamikaze pilots in World War II wrote notes before their missions saying they hoped that by crashing a plane into a U.S. ship they would slow the allied advance by a single day and bring honor to themselves and their squadrons, said Mako Sasaki, a Washington area researcher.

Most modern groups that rely on terror have similarly astute psychological training: The Tamil Tigers have suicide recruits compete to be chosen for missions. The "winners" eat "celebratory" final meals with the charismatic leader of the movement—and photos of the celebrations are later released to local magazines. Merari said he thought it was likely that the 19 hijackers of the Sept. 11 attacks had made such formal commitments.

The fact that the Sept. 11 terrorists did not fit the usual profile makes tracking terrorism more difficult, experts said.

"This is what I'm increasingly afraid of," said Ehud Sprinzak, dean of the school of government at the Interdisciplinary Center in Herzliya, Israel. If educated, older men could "go into the suicide cycle, why not professors, doctors, lawyers who go through conversion and become very, very committed? . . . It's going to be increasingly difficult to characterize psychologically."

Some experts suggested the answer, again, may be found in studying the groups that produced these individuals, because they are more identifiable.

Fields, who has studied the Sept. 11 attacks and suicide terror movements in Palestine, Israel, Lebanon, Northern Ireland and South America, said groups on the fringes of societies—both abroad and in the United States—offer an opportunity for the desperate to feel good about themselves.

"One of the things that typify high school kids and gangs is they have to be with their identity groups in order to feel vindicated and reinforced," she said. "If you take militias that operate in the U.S.—like Tim McVeigh's bunch, what you find is they engage in only one kind of social interaction. That is their vocation, their avocation, their social life, religious life, everything."

Members of Hezbollah's suicide bomber squad during a rally to mark the death of guerrillas and civilians killed during the Israeli blitz in Lebanon. AP/WIDE WORLD PHOTOS

SIGNIFICANCE

Terrorists who become suicide bombers almost always come from oppressed societies, and that tends to be where the stereotypic characterizations generally end. Recent research by anthropologists, psychologists, and sociologists indicates that these individuals are not psychotic, or even demonstrably mentally ill. They are generally well-educated, not typically fundamentalist religious zealots, and frequently come from middle class families. "They are like you and me," according to Rohan Gunaratna, who is the head of terrorism research at the Institute of Defence and Strategic Studies at Nanyang Technological University in Singapore.

In a study of Hamas and Palestinian Islamic Jihad suicide terrorists from the late 1980s to 2003, Claude Berrebi, an economist at Princeton University, concluded that only 13 percent came from a poor background compared with 32 percent of the Palestinian population in general. In addition, more than half of the suicide bombers had at least some post-secondary education, compared with just 15 percent of the general population.

Ariel Merari, a psychologist at Tel Aviv University in Israel, who has extensively studied Middle Eastern terrorism in general—and suicide bombers in particular—reports that individuals who take their own lives in an effort to kill others are not suicidal by nature or by proclivity. Merari studied the background and circumstances of suicide bombers in the Middle East between 1983 and 2004, and arrived at an unexpected conclusion: "In the majority you find none of the risk factors normally associated with suicide, such as mood disorders or schizophrenia, substance abuse or history of attempted suicides." Scott Atran, an anthropologist at the Institute for Social Research at the University of Michigan in Ann Arbor, agrees: "There is no psychological profile whatsoever for suicide terrorists." There have been highly disturbed suicide bombers—twenty-one year old Reem Raiyshi, the mother of two small children, aged one and a half and three years, who blew herself up in Gaza in January of 2004, had been ostracized by her parents and family and was depressed, according to Eyad El Sarraj, chairman of the Gaza Community Mental Health Programme—but they are not the norm.

What drives a person to become a suicide bomber? Most published research seems to suggest that the key lies with the extremist organization that recruits them. Modern suicide terrorism history indicates that each mission has been authorized and planned by a terrorist core group. "Suicide terrorism is an organisational phenomenon," confirms Merari. "An organisation has to decide to embark on it."

The decision to engage in suicide terrorism is generally considered to be both political and strategic, with a singular aim: to coerce or destroy a government, through force of popular opinion created as a result of the establishment of a climate of fear and distrust of the prevailing political regime.

FURTHER RESOURCES
Web sites

Foreign Policy Research Institute. "E-Notes: Radical Islam and Suicide Bombers." <http://www.fpri.org/enotes/20031021. americawar.radu.islamsuicidebombers.html> (accessed February 5, 2005).

LSA; University of Michigan, Department of Psychology. "Guilt by Association: What's the Difference Between Suicide Bombers and Normal People?" <http://www.military. com/NewContent/0,13190,Brookes_011904,00.html> (accessed June 25, 2005).

National Review Online, Goldberg File. "The Ultimate in Peer Pressure: the Palestinian road to vaporization." <http://www.nationalreview.com/goldberg/goldberg 200403260842.asp> (accessed June 22, 2005).

Military.com. "Peter Brookes: Suicide Psyche, January 19, 2004." <http://www.military.com/NewContent/0,13190, Brookes_011904,00.html> (accessed February 5, 2005).

SignOnSanDiego.com. The San Diego Union Tribune. "Many suicide bombers are educated, come from well-off families." <http://www.signonsandiego.com/uniontrib/20041009/ news_1n9peer.html> (accessed February 5, 2005).

"Harsh Detention for Afghan Prisoners"

Terrorism, law, and social values

Newspaper article

By: BBC News

Date: January 16, 2002

Source: "Harsh Detention for Afghan Prisoners," as published by the British Broadcasting Corporation (BBC News), and available online at: <http://news.bbc.co.uk/ 1/hi/world/south_asia/1752863.stm>.

About the Author: BBC News is a world-wide news gathering network headquartered in London and is sponsored by the government of the United Kingdom.

INTRODUCTION

On January 11, 2002 Camp X-Ray in Guatanamo Bay, Cuba, became the temporary detention center for suspected members of the Taliban government and al-Qaeda terrorist group members who were captured during the United States invasion of Afghanistan. Camp X-Ray stirred debate about the role of the Geneva Conventions (an international agreement barring torture, abuse, and indeterminate detention of prisoners of war) in modern warfare.

The human rights of detainees was complicated because they were not granted prisoner of war status. Individuals with prisoner of war status are protected by the Third Geneva Convention, which defines the humanitarian rights and the required treatment of prisoners of war (POWs). The U.S. government classified Taliban (Taleban) members as prisoners of war and followed the Geneva Convention, releasing them from custody. However, they classified most captured al-Qaeda members as illegal combatants, claiming that they are not soldiers or guerrillas, nor part of an army or militia.

Humanitarian groups have argued that if they are not protected under the Third Geneva Convention, then they should be protected under the Fourth Geneva Convention, which describes the required treatment of civilians in enemy hands. The United States government

U.S. Army military police lead a Taliban detainee through Camp X-Ray, Guantanamo, Cuba. AP/WIDE WORLD PHOTOS

asserts that all enemy combatants in its custody are treated in accordance with standing international human rights agreements.

PRIMARY SOURCE

Taleban and al-Qaeda prisoners flown from Afghanistan to an American naval base in the Caribbean are being held in tough conditions of detention.

A temporary detention centre called Camp X-Ray has been set up at the base in Guantanamo Bay, an isolated US outpost on the edge of Fidel Castro's Cuba.

The prisoners are being housed in cells measuring 1.8 by 2.4 metres (six feet by eight feet) with open, chain-link walls, a concrete floor and wooden roof.

They face intense interrogation by US officials anxious to track down Osama Bin Laden, the alleged mastermind behind the 11 September suicide attacks on New York and Washington.

The US authorities have not granted the detainees prisoner-of-war status, meaning they are not protected by the Geneva Convention.

Washington wants military tribunals to try the prisoners, and the cases are expected to be heard outside the U.S.

As the base is located outside sovereign territory, the prisoners have no legal rights under the US constitution, and no right of appeal to federal courts.

Jeffrey Kofman, an American journalist who has visited the base, said the facility was "very, very minimal."

The cells had concrete floors, wooden roofs and wire mesh walls. Prisoners had a foam mat to sleep on, two towels—one for washing, the other to use as a prayer mat, and some form of chamber pot, he said.

"It was a far more bares bones facility than frankly I expected to see. They say they will be holding the detainees in cells, but really they are cages . . .

"One person said: 'Are they kennels?', to which one of the military staff in charge said: 'No they're not kennels, they are cells, and they're within the bounds of the Geneva Convention. What we are operating is humane treatment, but we're not offering comfort."

The human rights group Amnesty International voiced concern about the "cages" used for accommodation, saying they would "fall below minimum standards for humane treatment."

The first group to arrive—20 prisoners described by U.S. military officials as "the worst elements of al-Qaeda and the Taleban"—wore goggles covered with tape and had their hands tied. Some also wore leg shackles.

They wore surgical masks as some prisoners had tested positive for tuberculosis and at least one prisoner was sedated.

They will spend most of their time separated, although they will be allowed out of their cells in small groups for meals, showers, and some recreation.

They will be allowed to pray according to their faith.

The camp gets chilly at night and there are swarms of mosquitoes.

The base—known by U.S. servicemen as "Gitmo" is surrounded by mangrove swamps, salt marshes, and dense bush—and the sea is shark-infested.

The camp perimeters, lit up at night, has watchtowers and two fences topped with razor wire constantly patrolled by heavily armed marines.

At night the camp is lit up with halogen floodlights.

Members of a movement that tried to prevent women from working may be disconcerted to find that some of their guards are women.

"We have no intention of making it comfortable," Marine Brigadier-General Michael Lehnert told Reuters news agency. "It will be humane."

Hundreds of marines and military police have been flown to Guantanamo Bay to expand the compound to house up to 2,000 prisoners.

American marines landed in Guantanamo during the Spanish-American War in 1898, and the base was established under a 1903 treaty.

After Fidel Castro led the Communists to power in Cuba in 1959, then U.S. President Dwight Eisenhower refused to relinquish the base despite strong objections from Havana.

Although Washington continues to pay the rent, set 100 years ago at 2,000 gold coins a year, and now worth about $4,000, Castro refuses to cash the cheques.

Cuban Frontier Battalion troops continue to watch their U.S. counterparts along the 28-kilometre fence, but tension has diminished since the end of the Cold War.

American officials have named al-Qaeda and Taleban leaders killed or captured as frustration grows that some senior Taleban figures are reportedly slipping through the net.

Among those who have not been questioned by the U.S. military are three former Taleban ministers who turned themselves into the new Afghan authorities—only to be allowed to return to their homes.

The most important is former Justice Minister Mullah Nuruddin Turabi—known to be close to Taleban leader Mullah Omar, former Defense Minister Mullah Ubaidullah and former Industry Minister Mullah Saadudin.

U.S. officials are eager to question the three, who they believe may have vital clues about the whereabouts of Mullah Omar and Osama Bin Laden.

The hunt continues for Bin Laden himself and Mullah Omar, who is believed to have escaped by motorbike as thousands of Afghan soldiers closed in on his suspected hideout.

Suspected Taliban and al-Qaida detainees in a holding area at Camp X-Ray, Guantanamo Bay, Cuba. AP/WIDE WORLD PHOTOS

Also on the wanted list are many more of Bin Laden's top lieutenants who are believed to have evaded capture. They include Ayman al-Zawahri, the Egyptian Islamic Jihad leader who is Bin Laden's close adviser and personal doctor.

SIGNIFICANCE

On April 29, 2002, Camp X-Ray was closed and prisoners were transferred to Camp Delta, a newly constructed detention center in Guatanamo Bay, Cuba. While the new facility offered improved accommodations for detainees, issues continued to be raised about the detainees' human and legal rights.

In 2003, Human Rights Watch released a report stating that the United States ignored human rights standards in its treatment of detainees at Camp X-Ray and that the United States did not comply with the requirements of the Geneva Conventions. The report stated that the United States should have granted prisoner of war status to Taliban soldiers and followed the standards of the Third Geneva Convention in regards to Taliban members. The report also stated that the United States should have convened a tribunal to determine the status of al-Qaeda members, as is described in the Geneva Conventions.

The legal rights of detainees also continued to be an issue. On November 10, 2003 the Supreme Court of the United States stated that it would hear appeals by detainees who considered that they were being held unlawfully. On June 28, 2004 the Supreme Court of the United States ruled that some enemy combatants could legally challenge their detention. However, the Supreme Court also ruled that detainees could be held without charges. On January 31, 2005, the federal court found that the military trials used to classify detainees as illegal combatants were unconstitutional. Legal challenges over detainment at Guantanamo Bay have continued.

FURTHER RESOURCES

Periodicals

Lewis, N.A. "Red Cross Finds Detainee Abuse in Guantanamo." *New York Times.* November 30, 2004: A1.

Web sites

Amnesty International. "Memorandum to the US Government on the rights of people in US custody in Afghanistan and Guantanamo Bay." <http://web.amnesty.org/library/Index/ENGAMR510532002?open&of=ENG-313> (accessed July 3, 2005).

Human Rights Watch. "World Report 2003: United States." <http://www.hrw.org/wr2k3/us.html> (accessed July 3, 2005).

Biological Counterterrorism

Research Laboratories, Selected Agents, and Restricted Persons

Government report

By: The Centers for Disease Control and Prevention

Date: March 18, 2005

Source: The Centers for Disease Control and Prevention

About the Author: The Centers for Disease Control and Prevention (CDC) regulates "the possession, use, and transfer of select agents and toxins that have the potential to pose a severe threat to public health and safety. The CDC Select Agent Program oversees these activities and registers all laboratories and other entities in the United States of America that possess, use, or transfer a select agent or toxin." The U.S. Departments of Health and Human Services (HHS) and Agriculture (USDA) published final rules for the possession, use, and transfer of select agents and toxins (42 C.F.R. Part 73, 7 C.F.R. Part 331, and 9 C.F.R. Part 121) in the Federal Register on March 18, 2005.

INTRODUCTION

The USA PATRIOT Act (commonly called the Patriot Act) is an acronym for the Uniting and Strengthening America by Providing Appropriate Tools Required to Intercept and Obstruct Terrorism Act of 2001. The bill was signed into law by President George W. Bush on October 26, 2001. According to the Act, research facilities that handle certain chemical and biological agents were required to institute new employee screening and security procedures.

The Patriot Act was introduced to improve counterterrorism efforts by providing law enforcement with new tools to detect and prevent terrorism. Section 817 of the USA Patriot Act is titled "Expansion of the Biological Weapons Statute" and expands on chapter 10 of title 18 in the United States Code, providing new laws designed to prevent terrorist acts involving biological weapons.

The specific changes made by the Patriot Act include making it unlawful to possess biological agents, toxins, or delivery systems unless there is a reasonably justified purpose and making it unlawful for a restricted person to possess biological agents, toxins, and delivery systems that are classified as select agents.

The Patriot Act defines a biological agent as any microorganism or infectious substance that: can cause death or disease to humans, plants, or animals; can cause deterioration of food, water, supplies, or other material;

HHS and USDA Select Agents and Toxins
7 CFR Part 331, 9 CFR Part 121, and 42 CFR Part 73

HHS SELECT AGENTS AND TOXINS
Abrin
Cercopithecine herpesvirus 1 (Herpes B virus)
Coccidioides posadasii
Conotoxins
Crimean-Congo haemorrhagic fever virus
Diacetoxyscirpenol
Ebola viruses
Lassa fever virus
Marburg virus
Monkeypox virus
Ricin
Rickettsia prowazekii
Rickettsia rickettsii
Saxitoxin
Shiga-like ribosome inactivating proteins
South American Haemorrhagic Fever viruses
    Flexal
    Guanarito
    Junin
    Machupo
    Sabia
Tetrodotoxin
Tick-borne encephalitis complex (flavi) viruses
    Central European Tick-borne encephalitis
    Far Eastern Tick-borne encephalitis
    Kyasanur Forest Disease
    Omsk Hemorrhagic Fever
    Russian Spring and Summer encephalitis
Variola major virus (Smallpox virus)
Variola minor virus (Alastrim)
Yersinia pestis

OVERLAP SELECT AGENTS AND TOXINS
Bacillus anthracis
Botulinum neurotoxins
Botulinum neurotoxin producing species of *Clostridium*
Brucella abortus
Brucella melitensis
Brucella suis
Burkholderia mallei (formerly *Pseudomonas mallei*)
Burkholderia pseudomallei (formerly *Pseudomonas pseudomallei*)
Clostridium perfringens epsilon toxin
Coccidioides immitis
Coxiella burnetii
Eastern Equine Encephalitis virus
Francisella tularensis
Hendra virus
Nipah virus
Rift Valley fever virus
Shigatoxin
Staphylococcal enterotoxins
T-2 toxin
Venezuelan Equine Encephalitis virus

USDA SELECT AGENTS AND TOXINS
African horse sickness virus
African swine fever virus
Akabane virus
Avian influenza virus (highly pathogenic)
Bluetongue virus (Exotic)
Bovine spongiform encephalopathy agent
Camel pox virus
Classical swine fever virus
Cowdria ruminantium (Heartwater)
Foot-and-mouth disease virus
Goat pox virus
Japanese encephalitis virus
Lumpy skin disease virus
Malignant catarrhal fever virus
    (Alcelaphine herpesvirus type 1)
Menangle virus
Mycoplasma capricolum/ M.F38/*M. mycoides capri*
    (contagious caprine pleuropneumonia)
Mycoplasma mycoides mycoides
    (contagious bovine pleuropneumonia)
Newcastle disease virus (velogenic)
Peste des petits ruminants virus
Rinderpest virus
Sheep pox virus
Swine vesicular disease virus
Vesicular stomatitis virus (Exotic)

USDA PLANT PROTECTION AND QUARANTINE (PPQ) SELECT AGENTS AND TOXINS
Candidatus Liberobacter africanus
Candidatus Liberobacter asiaticus
Peronosclerospora philippinensis
Ralstonia solanacearum race 3, biovar 2
Schlerophthora rayssiae var *zeae*
Synchytrium endobioticum
Xanthomonas oryzae pv. *oryzicola*
Xylella fastidiosa (citrus variegated chlorosis strain)

This information current as of July 12, 2005

PRIMARY SOURCE

Biological Counterterrorism A list of the Select Agents and Toxins from the Centers for Disease Control and Prevention.

INFORMATION OBTAINED FROM THE CENTER FOR DISEASE CONTROL (WWW.CDC.GOV)

or can cause damage to the environment. A toxin is defined as any toxic material or infectious substance. A delivery system is defined as any apparatus, equipment, device, or means of delivery specifically designed to deliver or disseminate a biological agent, toxin or vector. By limiting possession of biological agents, toxins, and delivery agents, the Patriot Acts seeks to prevent terrorist acts involving biological weapons.

The Patriot Act defines a restricted person as anyone who: (A) is under indictment for a crime punishable by imprisonment for a term greater than one year; (B) has been convicted of a crime punishable by imprisonment for a term greater than one year; (C) is a fugitive from justice; (D) is an unlawful user of any controlled substance; (E) is an alien illegally or unlawfully in the United States; (F) is mentally defective or has been committed to any mental institution; (G) is an alien who is a national of a country that the U.S. Secretary of State has determined to be a repeated provider of support for acts of international terrorism; or (H) has been discharged from the Armed Services of the United States under dishonorable conditions.

PRIMARY SOURCE

BIOLOGICAL COUNTERTERRORISM
See primary source image.

SIGNIFICANCE

Section 175 of Chapter 10 of the United States Code describes the prohibitions related to biological weapons. Section 175 of the statute states that, "Whoever knowingly develops, produces, stockpiles, transfers, acquires, retains, or possesses any biological agent, toxin, or delivery system for use as a weapon, or knowingly assists a foreign state or any organization to do so, or attempts, threatens, or conspires to do the same, shall be fined under this title or imprisoned for life or any term of years, or both."

The Patriot Act did not change the above section of the statute. However, it did add an additional offense, which states that, "Whoever knowingly possesses any biological agent, toxin, or delivery system of a type or in a quantity that, under the circumstances, is not reasonably justified by a prophylactic, protective, bona fide research, or other peaceful purpose, shall be fined under this title, imprisoned not more than 10 years, or both."

The expansion that is made with the USA Patriot Act is that it becomes unlawful to possess biological agents, toxins, or delivery systems if that possession is not for a justified purpose. In contrast, the previous United

States Code made it unlawful to possess biological agents, toxins, or delivery systems for use as a weapon. This change places a demand on organizations to ensure that the possession of any biological agents, toxins, or delivery systems is justified.

The USA Patriot Act also added Section 175b, which limits the possession of select agents by restricted persons. This states that, "No restricted person shall ship or transport in or affecting interstate or foreign commerce, or possess in or affecting interstate or foreign commerce, any biological agent or toxin, or receive any biological agent or toxin that has been shipped or transported in interstate or foreign commerce, if the biological agent or toxin is listed as a select agent in Appendix A of part 72 of title 42, Code of Federal Regulations." This addition to the law places demands on organizations possessing select agents to ensure they are not accessed by restricted persons.

Laboratories that operate within the United States or that are funded by the United States must comply with the new regulations regarding prohibiting access to selected agents by restricted persons. Each organization is required to develop their own screening or application forms to obtain the required information on persons working (or seeking work) in their laboratories in order to certify their right to access selected agents.

FURTHER RESOURCES

Books

Ball, Howard & Vasan, Mildred. *The USA PATRIOT Act: A Reference Handbook.* New York: ABC-Clio, 2004.

Web sites

Office of the Law Revision Counsel. 18 USC CHAPTER 10 "BIOLOGICAL WEAPONS." <http://uscode.house.gov/download/pls/18C10.txt> (accessed July 2, 2005).

Library of Congress. "H.R.3162: Uniting and Strengthening America by Providing Appropriate Tools Required to Intercept and Obstruct Terrorism (USA PATRIOT ACT) Act of 2001." <http://thomas.loc.gov/cgi-bin/query/D?c107:4:./temp/~c107rEAiyQ:> (accessed July 2, 2005).

Tamim Ansary Interview

Growing up bicultural: An interview with Afghan-American Tamim Ansary

Interview

By: Alexis Menten

Date: July 10, 2002

Source: Tamim Ansary was interviewed for *Asia Source*. The interview is available online at: <http://www.asiasource.org/arts/tamimansary.cfm>.

About the Author: Tamim Ansary was born in Afghanistan and moved to America to study when he was just sixteen. He settled in Portland, Oregon and made his living writing children's books. In the aftermath of the September 11, 2001 terrorist attacks on the United States, Ansary sent an email to friends suggesting that the Taliban should be removed from power by American ground forces. Ansary has become a regular figure on talk shows and in newspaper columns throughout the United States. *AsiaSource* is an online publication of the Asia Society, a nonprofit international organization headquartered in New York and dedicated to strengthening relationships and understanding among the peoples of Asia and the United States. Alexis Menten, a writer and media producer specializing in near Eastern issues and archaeology, contributed this interview to *AsiaSource* in 2003.

INTRODUCTION

In September 2001, Tamim Ansary was in a prime position to comment on the events that unfolded in the aftermath of the attack on the World Trade Center in New York. Ansary's Afghan roots and American

Carrying a grenade launcher and its ammunition, a Taliban fighter talks on a radio near the front-line of Jalrez, Afghanistan, June 1, 1997. AP/WIDE WORLD PHOTOS

schooling gave him an almost unique insight into both worlds. Ansary's response to the crisis was a short email to his closet friends, in which he outlined his intention to "tell anyone who will listen how it all looks from where I'm standing." He went on to explain that "the Taliban and Bin Laden are not Afghanistan. They're not even the government of Afghanistan. The Taliban are a cult of ignorant psychotics who took over Afghanistan in 1997. Bin Laden is a political criminal with a plan. When you think Taliban, think Nazis. When you think Bin Laden, think Hitler." Ansary made his thoughts clear regarding the removal of the regime, rejecting the idea of "bombing Afghanistan back to the Stone Age" and instead, advocated that "the only way to get Bin Laden is to go in there with ground troops." His email was quickly circulated on the Internet and was soon read by millions of people all over the world.

The events of September 11th and the attention his subsequent email brought, affected Ansary deeply. Not unsurprisingly for an author, his response was to turn to the written word and the construction of a memoir of his life in Afghanistan. Ansary insisted that the book, *West of Kabul, East of New York: An Afghan American Story*, was planned prior to September 11, 2001, but the events served to convince him that the time was right for him to examine his own "bicultural identity." Ansary attempted to portray the peaceful Muslim society of his youth, and therefore, show the American people how the majority of Muslims lived.

■ PRIMARY SOURCE

Alexis Menten: . . . You describe your September 12 email as a time when you "spoke for Afghanistan with my American voice." But due to the volatility of the period immediately after September 11, and also due to the immediacy of the Internet, your email addressed a very specific moment in time that has now passed. What was a clearly stated analysis of a situation in Afghanistan that few Americans knew about now reads as common knowledge. Do you see this book as an extension of this "American voice speaking for Afghanistan" from your email?

Tamim Ansary: To some extent that certainly is true. In the whole first part of the book where I describe my childhood in Afghanistan, I'm speaking in my American voice about not just my Afghan self, but also the context that gave rise to that Afghan self. I feel that the culture of Afghanistan in those days before the war was something that nobody had been situated to describe in a way that could make Americans really see it. One reason was, those who experienced it didn't speak English, and beyond that, even those who did experience it, while being very literate like my father, had literary impulses that expressed themselves through poems that were epic or lyric but not through a descriptive evocation of a time and a place.

I think I am using whatever voice I have to speak for not just Afghanistan, but also for a certain kind of cultural and social coherence that has passed away in a lot of places, especially in the parts of the world we now describe as the developing world. I think it is only recently that secular Western civilization, thoroughly industrialized and technology-driven, has come in contact with cultural frameworks that are much more traditional and more ancient. I was using what voice I had to describe that older culture and what it was like to experience it, and maybe to try to evoke what was lost.

But having written this book, I discovered two things are true: Afghans who talk to me say, "Oh yeah, that's really how it was. You got it." They like what I said and they like me for having said it. So I'm discovering to my own delight that I did speak for Afghans in that way. And then I have also heard from many Americans who have read the book that they are very interested in this portrait and that it shows them and tells them something about Afghans and Afghanistan they find likable. Then I think, "Wow, I did speak for Afghans." So surprisingly enough to myself, the answer is yes.

Alexis Menten: Despite America's strong desire and need to learn more about Afghanistan's history and culture, we have heard from relatively few Afghan writers. How do you think other Afghans will be able to start to speak for themselves?

Tamim Ansary: I think you're going to see that coming. One of the reasons I say that is because now that I've published a book and I've been reading from it, I've been meeting lots of Afghans who are interested in writing and who are writing here in America.

Afghans came here relatively recently; most of them came 20 years ago or less, and most of these people spent maybe the first 10 years just trying to figure out how to survive. Now, for the first time in the last couple of years, there are Afghans who are articulate in their second tongue, or they're young Afghans for whom English has become their first language. There is a large enough pool of such people that sophisticated writing can begin to emerge.

Alexis Menten: The difficulties you describe in growing up bicultural are resolved differently by each of the Ansary children. Your younger brother embraces an orthodox interpretation of Islam, while your older sister settles into a wholly secular American life. You, the middle child, try to "straddle the crack in the earth" between both cultures, although, as a non-practicing Muslim,

you remain more firmly on the American/ Western side. Do you think that your siblings' struggles to reconcile themselves with the differences between both Islamic and Western ways of life mirror the struggles many Muslims feel about this issue?

Tamim Ansary: Definitely. I think that the Islamic world has been going through a period of self-examination for at least a century or more that has to do with its encounter with the West, in a way that the West hasn't been doing because of its encounter with Islam. I would say that most of the West as an overall entity has been almost unaware of Islam. It has overwhelmed Islamic civilization and barely noticed it was there. But Islamic civilization is very much aware of the West, and has been asking for these several centuries, "Wait a minute, what's going on here? We're the world's civilization, what are we doing wrong? No, it can't be our fundamental premises that are wrong, so what is it?"

They've been going through this, and there have been movements arising in Islam that at some times said, "Okay, we can be Muslims, but we have to accept technology." And then other movements have said, "The problem is all the new social ideas, let's smash those and get rid of them." I think that going back and forth and trying to figure out a stance is certainly a part of what's been going on in the Muslim world and also of what has ended up generating these troublesome sects.

Alexis Menten: You write in your book of the difficulty in growing up between Islamic and Western lifestyles; "When you're in two worlds so different, your mind is forced to say that one is legitimate and the other is a crock." Do you think it is possible to live in both cultures in a way that is simultaneously acceptable to both, without necessarily declaring one a crock?

Tamim Ansary: I think that is a difficult question. I want to say, "Yes, of course." I don't want to say it isn't possible. I think where I come down is that in terms of the world, it is important for the West to be able to somehow step back and let go, and let societies whose overall impulse is to discover their own way become Islamic societies. We in the West have to allow some societies to be Islamic if they want to be, and many do want to be. And what that would mean in some places, possibly in Afghanistan, is that they wouldn't be pluralistic and kaleidoscopic societies, because I think there is something in the vision of Islam that demands that a society have a certain uniform pattern; Islam is not solely about personal conduct.

It's a different question when you come to Muslims living in America, however. America has its own vision, one that I subscribe to, and if a Muslim comes here, they have to find a way to satisfy their religious life and also become part of America's pluralistic, multicultural society, with tolerance for all others and without demanding anything of the society that's special for Muslims. I think they have to be able to accept that you might go to a restaurant and the guy at the next table might be eating pork while the guy at the table after that might be drinking martinis. I think the two systems ought to be able to coexist in the world, and there also has to be a way for purely Islamic societies to exist in the world.

Alexis Menten: A reviewer wrote that your book was "highly useful for anyone seeking to understand the Muslim world's hatred for the West." It could be said, however, that your book could be more useful in helping the West understand the peaceful and benevolent Islam of your youth, before the growth of extremist Islam in Afghanistan and other Islamic countries. What understanding of Islam did you hope to bring with your book?

Tamim Ansary: I think I wanted to bring both, because I see that there are two angles to this. I think that in portraying the peaceful Muslim society of my youth, I did want to bring this vision of Islam to Americans and show that this is how a lot of Muslims live and want to live. At the same time, I became aware that there was an emerging political ideology in the world that had its roots in Islam. That is to say, it was finding in the myths and narratives of Islam a way to justify and to rally people for a political purpose. Because this political ideology has been emerging in the Islamic world, I think it's important to see the people that are behind it and how they're managing to construct such effective propaganda. It's important because, in my view, we are actually in competition with that Islamist, extremist point of view. And the competition is for the minds and hearts and allegiance of most of the Muslim world.

I would say we're not at war or in conflict with the Muslim world; it's not a done deal whatsoever. I would not even say of fundamentalists that they are our enemies. Because when you speak purely of religious fundamentalism, of somebody who wants to pray five times a day and live exactly as the Prophet Muhammad and not wear western clothes and so on—well, so what? Let them. Why would we have to go kill that guy? And we would be wrong to assume that someone who does all those things is a militant, much less a terrorist. But the militant and the terrorist are busy trying to convince the religious fundamentalist that you cannot do those things without being against Americans, because they're not going to let you do them. So we're in competition with

somebody who is trying to tell millions of fundamentalists such a thing. Not to mention all the Muslims who are devout but not fundamentalist, or who are secular but not devout. I wanted to probably speak about both of these things in my book.

Alexis Menten: There is much discussion about the need for the return of the intellectual middle-class to Afghanistan during this time of rebuilding. Do you think that is what the country needs, and if so, do you have any plans to return?

Tamim Ansary: I'm about to take a trip that's going to end up, I hope, in Afghanistan. I personally don't plan to go back to Afghanistan to live because my life is here in the West. However, since September 11, it has become clear that my life is very much involved with Afghanistan. This wasn't a one-shot deal. I think for the rest of my life I'll be heavily concerned with what happens in Afghanistan.

I know that lots of people who have been living in the West are talking of going back. And I think one of the things that I'm going to be interested in seeing for myself when I go there is how things are going between the people who stayed and the people who are coming back. I think it's an interesting dilemma that the country desperately needs the skills and the sophistication of those who have been living in the West, and yet, when they go back to try to contribute their skills (with very idealistic and warm impulses in all instances I've seen), they will instantly be the upper class because they'll be running things. And will the people who have been there all along be able to take orders from people who didn't suffer?

Right now, from all I've heard however, there's nothing but tenderness and warmth between those two groups. When I went to Pakistan two months ago to distribute aid in the refugee camps along the border, I was bringing blankets gathered by the American Friends Service Committee. That was my first visit back, and I felt that the people in the camps would very justifiably look at me with a certain hostility. They would say, "Wait, where were you all this time? We've been here in these camps, and yeah, now you bring some blankets, great." But it wasn't like that at all. Their attitude was, "You didn't even have to come back, you were in the States. And yet you came back; you didn't forget us. Oh, you're so good." It was a very heartwarming experience.

SIGNIFICANCE

The interview with Tamim Ansary helps to illuminate the complicated issue of bicultural identity. This is an issue that is further compounded by the state of conflict that exists between the two cultures and ignorance in the West of much of the Islamic world and experience. The events of September 11th have forced many citizens to look outside their boundaries and examine the motivations of a world alien to them. Ansary argues that the Afghan culture did itself few favours in helping to bridge this gap. He explains that the tendency for Afghans to use cultural expressionism—such as epic or lyric poems—makes their culture less accessible to Western minds.

Ansary notes that only in the last twenty years have significant numbers of Afghan people moved to the United States. However, for the first ten years many young Afghans where simply trying to survive and adjust to Western life. It is only now that they have found the confidence and voice to be heard. Importantly, Ansary identifies the recent emergence of Islamic fundamentalist terrorism as an extreme reaction to the meeting of Western and Islamic worlds. However, he recognizes that both worlds must find a way to co-exist.

FURTHER RESOURCES

Books

Ansary, Tamim. *West of Kabul, East of New York: An Afghan American Story*. Picador USA, 2003.

Web sites

Tamim Ansary. "Biography." <http://www.mirtamimansary.com/index1.php?p=3 > (accessed July 7, 2005).

"The Psychology of Terrorism"

Essay excerpt

By: Clark R. McCauley

Date: 2002

Source: Social Science Research Council: After September 11th Essay Archive.

About the Author: Clark R. McCauley, a professor of psychology at Bryn Mawr College in Pennsylvania, is the Director of the Solomon Asch Center for the Study of Ethnopolitical Conflict at the University of Pennsylvania. He began studying terrorism in the 1980s, while he was a consultant for the Frank Guggenheim Foundation in New York. He joined the faculty of Bryn Mawr College in 1970.

INTRODUCTION

It is Clark McCauley's opinion that "terrorists are neither crazy, nor suicidal. The vast majority, more than 90 percent, of all terrorists are perfectly normal, psychologically speaking." He assumes that individual citizens may be drawn to terrorist activities when they feel that a cherished group is threatened. When that occurs, average citizens may become so involved in the intensity of the small-group dynamics that their allegiance to the group supersedes their normal inhibitions against violence. In short, they may be willing to harm or kill others, or to be killed themselves, rather than risk disappointing their peers.

McCauley views the acts of terrorism and the state's response to those acts as parts of a dynamic system that must be considered together in order to be understood. McCauley uses the metaphor of the pyramid to explain the concepts of terrorism: the base of the pyramid contains all of those individuals who sympathize or intellectually support the goals of the terrorists. Those at the base of the pyramid may not necessarily agree with the means used by the terrorists; they may, in fact, be morally opposed to violence as a means of achieving political or even religious goals. The apex of the pyramid is composed of the extremist members of the terrorist group. Between the base and the apex lie the varying groups of supporters whose allegiance lies with the cause represented by the terrorists. The closer to the apex, the greater is the individuals' identification with the ideology and philosophy of the extremist group. The structure of the pyramid affords cover, multiple sources of support, and an ample supply of potential new recruits for the terrorist group.

The paradox of terrorist violence lies in the typical reaction from the targeted location: the country (or state, or group, or whatever the targeted area is) typically responds to violence with the perpetration of retaliatory violence, followed by the persecution, or at least marginalization, of individuals associated with the terrorist group (either actual group members or simply citizens of the same country, or members of the same, or similar, religious, ethnic or cultural group). In so doing, the victim may, in effect, expand the support system for the terrorists. Secondary violence (retaliatory actions) could strengthen the belief system of terrorist sympathizers in the rhetoric espoused by the terrorists (that the victims are, in fact, the aggressors and are deserving of the acts perpetrated against them).

McCauley suggests that the best possible response to a terrorist act is to maintain a stance of non-violence, as that will ultimately separate terrorists from their support systems.

A Tamil man garlands the portraits of Black Tigers, the suicide bomber squad of the Tamil Tiger rebels on Black Tigers Day in Sri Lanka, July 5, 2004. AP/WIDE WORLD PHOTOS

PRIMARY SOURCE

. . . A common suggestion is that there must be something wrong with terrorists. Terrorists must be crazy, or suicidal, or psychopaths without moral feelings or feelings for others. Thirty years ago this suggestion was taken very seriously, but thirty years of research has found psychopathology and personality disorder no more likely among terrorists than among non-terrorists from the same background. Interviews with current and former terrorists find few with any disorder found in the American Psychiatric Association's Diagnostic and Statistical Manual. Comparisons of terrorists with non-terrorists brought up in the same neighborhoods find psychopathogy rates similar and low in both groups.

Another way to think about this issue is to imagine yourself a terrorist, living an underground existence cut off from all but the few who share your goals. Your life depends on the others in your group. Would you want someone in your group suffering from some kind of psychopathology?

Someone who cannot be depended on, someone out of touch with reality? Of course there are occasional lone bombers or lone gunmen who kill for political causes, and such individuals may indeed suffer from some form of psychopathology. But terrorists in groups, especially groups that can organize attacks that are successful, are likely to be within the normal range of personality.

Indeed, terrorism would be a trivial problem if only those with some kind of psychopathology could be terrorists. Rather we have to face the fact that normal people can be terrorists, that we are ourselves capable of terrorist acts under some circumstances. This fact is already implied in recognizing that military and police forces are eminently capable of killing non-combatants in terrorism from above. Few suggest that the broad range of military and police involved in such killing must all be abnormal.

No one wakes up one morning and decides that today is the day to become a terrorist. The trajectory by which normal people become capable of doing terrible things is usually gradual, perhaps imperceptible to the individual.

In too-simple terms, terrorists kill for the same reasons that groups have killed other groups for centuries. They kill for cause and comrades, that is, with a combination of ideology and intense small-group dynamics.

The cause that is worth killing for and even dying for is personal, a view of the world that makes sense of life and death and links the individual to some form of immortality. We have to, because, unlike other animals, we know that we are going to die. We need something that makes sense of our life and our death. The closer and more immediate death is, the more we need the group values that give meaning to life and death. These values include the values of family, religion, ethnicity, and nationality-the values of our culture. Dozens of experiments have shown that thinking about our own death leads us to embrace more strongly the values of our culture ("terror management theory").

The group values represented in the cause are focused to a personal intensity in the small group of like-minded people who perpetrate terrorist violence. Most individuals belong to many groups—family, co-workers, neighborhood, religion, country—and each of these groups has some influence on the beliefs and behavior of the individual. These groups tend to have different values and the competition of values reduces the power of any one group over its members. But members of an underground terrorist group have put this group first in their lives, dropping or reducing every other connection. The power of this one group is now enormous, and extends to every kind of personal and moral judgment. This is the power that can make violence against the enemy not just acceptable but necessary . . .

. . . In brief, the psychology behind terrorist violence is normal psychology, abnormal only in the intensity of the group dynamics that link cause with comrades.

Psychologists recognize two kinds of aggression, emotional and instrumental. Emotional aggression is associated with anger and does not calculate long-term consequences. The reward of emotional aggression is hurting someone who has hurt you. Instrumental aggression is more calculating—the use of aggression as a means to other ends. Terrorist aggression may involve emotional aggression, especially for those who do the killing, but those who plan terrorist acts are usually thinking about what they want to accomplish. They aim to inflict long-term costs on their enemy and to gain long-term advantage for themselves.

Terrorism inflicts immediate damage in destroying lives and material, but terrorists hope that the long-term costs will be much greater. They want to create fear and uncertainty far beyond the victims and those close to them. They want the enemy to spend time and money on security. In effect the terrorists aim to lay an enormous tax on every aspect of the enemy's society, a tax that transfers resources from productive purposes to anti-productive security measures.

Terrorists particularly hope to elicit a violent response that will assist them in mobilizing their own people. A terrorist group is the apex of a pyramid of supporters and sympathizers. The base of the pyramid is composed of all those who sympathize with the terrorist cause even though they may disagree with the violent means that the terrorist use. The pyramid is essential to the terrorists for cover and for recruits. The terrorists hope that a clumsy and over-generalized strike against them will hit some of their own side who are not yet radicalized and mobilized, will enlarge their base of sympathy, will turn the sympathetic but unmobilized to action and sacrifice, and will strengthen their own status at the apex of this pyramid . . .

. . . A violent response to terrorism that is not well aimed is a success for the terrorists. . .

. . . Terrorists also hope for a reaction of stereotyping and prejudice in which the terrorists are seen as typical members of the cause they say they are fighting for. Usually the terrorists are only a tiny splinter of the group they aim to lead. Their most dangerous opposition is often from their own side, from moderates who see alternatives other than violence. If the response to terrorist attack is to lump together all who sympathize with the cause the terrorists claim to serve, to see a whole ethnic or religious group as dangerous and violent, then the moderates are undermined and the terrorists win . . .

. . . Since the first bombing attack on the World Trade Center, the U.S. response to terrorism has shifted from criminal justice—finding, trying and punishing perpetrators—to waging war. This shift has psychological consequences.

Framing terrorism and response to terrorism as "war" implies a movement from individual blame to group blame. This is just what the terrorists want. They want to be seen as representing all who feel that the U.S. has since WWII dominated, humiliated, and helped to kill Muslims. They want responsibility for their actions projected to all who sympathize with their cause. It should be our business not to accept the terrorists as leaders of a billion Muslims. Rather we should inquire into the policies of the U.S. that could create so much anti-American feeling around the world . . .

. . . The domestic costs of increased security are the costs of a more centralized state that can become the enemy of its own people. In the U.S., the government has already assumed new powers without consulting Congress. Polls taken in years preceding the terrorist attack on 11 September indicate that about half of adult Americans saw the federal government as a threat to the rights and freedoms of ordinary Americans. No doubt fewer would say so in the aftermath of the recent attacks, a shift consistent with the adage that "war is the health of the state." But if more security could ensure the safety of the nation, the Soviet Union would still be with us.

The response to terrorism can be more dangerous than the terrorists . . .

SIGNIFICANCE

Contrary to the commonly held belief that terrorists must be experiencing significant psychopathology (mental illness), research conducted during the latter half of the twentieth century suggests that those individuals (members of terrorist groups) would be unlikely to be given a diagnosis of psychopathology if assessed. In fact, those with significant psychopathology are unlikely to be able to function within a small, cohesive group of like-minded individuals acting together to achieve a common goal (as in an extremist group). In order to achieve a terrorist act or attack, it is necessary to be able to calmly and logically create a plan of action, envision the probable outcomes, and carry out the scenario to successful fruition.

Psychological theory defines two types of aggression: emotional and instrumental. Emotional aggression is akin to the "fight" aspect of the "fight or flight" theory. Emotionally aggressive behavior is the "hurting back" of a perceived aggressor. It is aggression that does not calculate the long-term outcome of events; it is a response born of anger and fear, and it is often impulsive and poorly thought out. The goal of emotional anger is to inflict harm and pain on the perceived aggressor, in at least the measure in which it was received. Instrumental aggression also perpetuates violence, but it is violence with a long-term goal. The aggressive act is viewed as a catalyst for other events. It is those events that, in the long run, achieve the ultimate goals of the perpetrators.

Although terrorism and terrorist acts of violence causes damage and pain (and often death and the destruction of significant amounts of material or property) in the immediate aftermath of the initiating act, the goal of the terrorist group is far more long-term. Most terrorist organizations aim to achieve a climate of fear and suspicion far beyond the immediate moment. The group anticipates that the acts of the moment will have the long-term effects of causing the target to expend large amounts of time and money on broadened and increased security, ramping up military personnel and training, and generally expending vast, unplanned, sums of money on measures associated with security. A primary goal of terrorist acts, then, is actually a financial one: necessary resources are diverted from practical, social, and humanitarian uses (fruitful use of funds) to those associated with perceived protection and security.

FURTHER RESOURCES

Books

Worchel, S., McCauley, C., Lee, Y-T, and F. Moghaddam, eds. *Psychology of Ethnic and Cultural Conflict.* Praeger Publishers, 2004.

Web sites

Social Science Research Council: After September 11 Essay Archive. "The Psychology of Terrorism." <http://www.ssrc.org/sept11/essays/mccauley.htm> (accessed May 11 2005).

S&T Bryn Mawr College Newsletter on Science and Technology. "Understanding the Psychology of Terrorism." <http://www.brynmawr.edu/sandt/2004_may/terrorism.htm> (accessed June 9, 2005).

Solomon Asch Center for the Study of Ethnopolitical Conflict. "The Psychology of Terrorism: An Interview with Clark McCauley, Co-Director of the Solomon Asch Center for Study of Ethnopolitical Conflict (September 11, 2001)." <http://www.psych.upenn.edu/sacsec/online.Intervue.htm> (accessed June 11 2005).

Islam Denounces Terrorism

Book cover

By: Harun Yahya

Date: 2003

Source: *Islam Denounces Terrorism* was produced by Global Publishing (United Kingdom) and Okur Productions (Turkey).

About the Author: Global Publishing is a British-based publishing house. Okur Productions is a group of Turkish-based publishers specializing in Islamic literature.

INTRODUCTION

In *The Clash of Civilizations*, his seminal 1993 book, the academic Samuel Huntington argued that America's main global challenges over the coming decades would come not from a resurgent east, or post-Soviet Russia. Instead, he wrote, that as people defined themselves increasingly by ethnicity and religion, the West would find itself more and more at odds with civilizations that reject its ideals. In particular, Huntingdon predicted that a confrontation between Islamists and the West was inevitable.

After the terrorist attacks of September 11, 2001, Harun Yahya (a penname used by Adnan Oktar), a prominent Turkish thinker, set about demolishing the myths that a clash of civilizations was in some way inevitable, and that jihad (holy war) was not only a fallacy, but also incompatible with Islam. Already the author of more than one hundred books—which have been translated into more than twenty languages and include such varied subject titles as *Islamic Denounces Anti-Semitism, Jesus will Return, Darwinism Refuted, Islam and Buddhism,*—*Islam Denounces Terrorism* was a polemic against those who tried to justify terrorist atrocities by grounding their acts in religious terms.

"Religion commands love, mercy, and peace," Yahya wrote in its introduction. "Terror, on the other hand, is the opposite of religion; it is cruel, merciless, and demands bloodshed and misery. This being the case, the origins of the terrorist action must be sought in disbelief rather than in religion. . . 'Islamic terror' is an erroneous concept which contradicts the message of Islam. The religion of Islam can by no means countenance terrorism. On the contrary, terror (i.e., murder of innocent people) in Islam is a great sin, and Moslems are responsible for preventing these acts . . ."

Islam Against Terrorism, like many of Yahya's other works is available free over the Internet. In 2003, a film was made of the work.

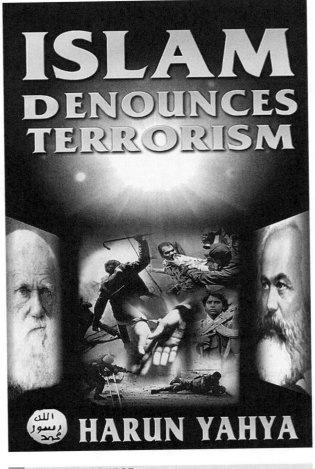

PRIMARY SOURCE

ISLAM DENOUNCES TERRORISM
See primary source image.

SIGNIFICANCE

Though a sometime contributor to such august publications as *National Geographic* and *New Scientist*, Harun Yahya and his work remain best known throughout the Moslem world in general, and within his own country in particular. Like the written version of this work, the film was made available on the Internet.

America's invasion of Iraq in 2003 halted the threat of a dictatorial regime in the Middle East, but it also served to ignite insurgent attacks against American servicemen and Iraqi civilians. Again, the perpetrators cited Jihad as justification for the violence. Mainstream Islamic leaders worldwide have voiced concern that the religion of Islam continues to be increasingly associated with violence.

FURTHER RESOURCES
Web sites

Yahya, Harun. *Islam Denounces Terrorism.com.* <http://www.islamdenouncesterrorism.com/> (accessed July 10, 2005).

PRIMARY SOURCE

Islam Denounces Terrorism Book cover from Harun Yahya's work *Islam Denounces Terrorism.* COURTESY OF WWW. HARUNYAHYA.COM

Audio and Visual Media

Harun Yahya Islam Denounces Terrorism. <http://www. harunyahya.com/m_video_terrorism.php> (accessed July 10, 2005).

"Linkage Logarithms"

Newspaper column

By: Mark Steyn

Date: October 19, 2003

Source: "Linkage Logarithms," published by the *Washington Times.*

About the Author: Mark Steyn is a journalist, columnist, and film and theater critic. He is a senior contributing editor for a large number of Hollinger, Inc. Publications, a senior North American columnist for the United Kingdom's Telegraph Group, the North American editor for *The Spectator*, a writer for the *Jerusalem Post*, the *Irish Times*, and the *National Review*, as well as *Western Standard*.

INTRODUCTION

Mark Steyn's syndicated columns appear internationally, and he has been published in dozens of periodicals and newspapers worldwide. His political leanings are strongly conservative, and he is known for his sharp wit and cutting satire. He often writes on foreign policy issues. He has been vocally, and prolifically opposed to the Canadian Liberal Party policies, including multiculturalism, public healthcare, gun control, high taxation, secession of Quebec, and anti-Americanism. He was an outspoken proponent of the 2003 invasion of Iraq, and continues to voice his support of military actions in that global region; he is an outspoken critic of the United Nations, which he has favored disbanding. If that does not occur, he has suggested that the United States should withdraw from membership or participation in UN-related activities. He is scornful of nations that have opposed the war in Iraq.

It is his contention that "the media aren't interested in showing you images that might rouse the American people to righteous anger, only images that will shame and demoralize them." Steyn asserts that the Internet is the most honest source of real-world information about political and world events at present. He has contended that the media has become so fond of fictionalized sensationalism, and so wary of offending extremist groups, that there is a strong tendency to report what is likely to achieve a predictable reaction, rather than suggesting a more frightening truth: it is easier to hypothesize that a sniper might be a stereotypic white loner than to contemplate a connection between the sniper and extremist religious group members linked to recent acts of terrorism in the United States.

PRIMARY SOURCE

A year ago, when the self-regarding buffoon Chief Charles Moose was bungling the Washington sniper investigation and the cable-news shows were full of endless psychological profiles of "white male loners," a few of us columnists entertained the notion that the killer was linked to Islamist terrorism.

The Chicago Sun-Times' Richard Roeper thought this was so absurd he very kindly apologized to readers on my behalf. "An awful lot of conservatives really, really wanted the snipers to be terrorists," explained Richard. "But they were wrong. I'll say that because they never will."

Even at the time, the Roeper position required a certain suspension of disbelief. John Allen Muhammad was a Muslim, a supporter of al Qaeda's actions, a man who marked the events of September 11, 2001, by changing his name to "Muhammad" and a man who marked the first anniversary of September 11 by buying the Chevy Caprice subsequently used in the sniper attacks. Coincidence? Of course. It's only a handful of conservative kooks who would even think otherwise.

Interesting item from the London Evening Standard last week:

"Evidence has emerged linking Washington sniper John Allen Muhammad with an Islamic terror group. Muhammad has been connected to Al Fuqra, a cult devoted to spiritual purification through violence. The group has been linked to British shoe bomber Richard Reid and the murderers of American journalist Daniel Pearl in Pakistan last year."

Hmm. Might be nothing. Might be just another coincidence. Lot of them around at the moment—like that Saudi Cabinet minister who coincidentally stayed in the same hotel on the night of Sept. 10 as some of the September 11 terrorists. Just one of those things. But the authorities seem to be taking the links more seriously than when they first surfaced a year ago.

Here's another coincidence: The guy who heads up the organization that certifies Muslim chaplains for the U.S. military was arrested at Dulles Airport last month and charged with illegally accepting money from Libya. The month

Investigators believe that this tanker vessel was hit by an al-Qaeda-linked terrorist attack off the coast of al-Mukalla, Yemen, 2002. AP/WIDE WORLD PHOTOS

before that, Abdurahman Alamoudi was caught by the British trying to smuggle some $340,000 into Syria.

Think about that for a minute. Ten years ago, at an American military base, at a ceremony to install the first imam in this country's armed forces, it was Mr. Alamoudi who presented him with his new insignia of a silver crescent star. And the guy's a bagman for terrorists.

Infiltration-wise, I would say that's pretty good. The arthritic bureaucracy at the CIA say oh, no, it would be impossible for them to get any of their boys inside al Qaeda. Can't be done. But the other side has no difficulty getting their chaps set up in the heart of the U.S. military.

What kind of chaplains did Mr. Alamoudi's American Muslim Armed Forces and Veterans Affairs Council pick out to serve our men and women in uniform? Well, among them was Capt. James "Yousef" Yee, recently detained under suspicion of spying at Guantanamo Bay. Also arrested were two Arabic translators, found with classified documents from Gitmo on their CDs, etc.

Infiltration-wise, that's also pretty good. The CIA say, sorry, folks, the best we can do with all the gazillions of dollars we get is monitor phone calls from outer space. But the other side has no difficulty getting their boys inside America's most secure military base and principal terrorist detention center.

The Pentagon, of course, is taking this subversion of its chaplaincy program seriously. It's currently reviewing all its chaplains. By "all," I mean not just all the Muslim chaplains, but also all the Catholic, Episcopalian, Jewish ones. After all, it might just be another one of those coincidences that the chaplain detained for spying is Muslim and that the organizations that certified him are Muslim. Best to investigate the Catholics just to be on the safe side.

If the Democrats hadn't decided to sit out the war on terror by frolicking on Planet Bananas for the duration, they could be seriously hammering the administration on this. Richard Reid, the shoe-bomber, while in prison was converted to radical Islamism by a chaplain who came to Britain under a fast-track immigration program for imams set up by Her Majesty's Government. They felt they had a shortage of Muslim chaplains, and not knowing much about the business or where to look for 'em felt it easiest to put up a big neon sign at Heathrow saying, "Hey, mullahs, come on down." It all seemed to be working well until they noticed that these guys seemed to be the spiritual mentors of a lot of the wackiest terrorists.

So how come, two years after September 11, groups with terrorist ties are still able to insert their recruiters into America's military bases, prisons and pretty much anywhere else they get a yen to go? It's not difficult to figure out: Wahhabism is the most militant form of Islam, the one

followed by all 19 of the September 11 terrorists and by Osama bin Laden. The Saudis—whose state religion is Wahhabism—fund the spread of their faith in lavishly endowed schools and mosques all over the world and, as a result, traditionally moderate Muslim populations from the Balkans to South Asia have been dramatically radicalized. How could the federal government be so complacent as to subcontract the certification of chaplains in U.S. military bases to Wahhabist institutions?

Here's an easy way to make an effective change: Less Wahhabism is in America's interest. More Wahhabism is in the terrorists' interest. So why can't the U.S. introduce a policy whereby, for the duration of the war on terror, no organization directly funded by the Saudis will be eligible for any formal or informal role with any federal institution?

That would also include the pro-Saudi Middle East Institute, whose "adjunct scholar" is one Joseph C Wilson IV. Remember him? He's the fellow at the center of the Bob-Novak-published-the-name-of-my-CIA-wife scandal. The agency sent him to look into the European intelligence stories about Saddam trying to buy uranium in Africa. He went to Niger, drank mint tea with government flacks, and then wrote a big whiny piece in the New York Times after the White House declined to accept his assurances nothing was going on. He was never an intelligence specialist, he's no longer a "career diplomat," but he is, like so many other retired ambassadors, on the House of Saud's payroll. And the Saudis vehemently opposed war with Saddam.

Think about that. To investigate Saddam Hussein's attempted acquisition of uranium, the United States government sent a man in the pay of the Saudi government. The Saudis set up schools that turn out terrorists. They set up Islamic lobby groups that put spies in our military bases and terror recruiters in our prisons. They set up think tanks that buy up and neuter the U.S. diplomatic corps. And their ambassador's wife funnels charitable donations to the September 11 hijackers.

But it's all just an unfortunate coincidence, isn't it? After all, the Saudis are our friends. Thank goodness.

SIGNIFICANCE

Significant concern has been expressed through some media, particularly conservative political Internet sites, that the Saudi influence in the United States is being used as a potential incubator of terrorist cells, or, at least, of strong anti-American sentiment. At the Institute of World Politics in Washington, D.C., the influence of Saudi Arabia on the prison and military populations has been extensively researched. Those studies suggest that many millions of dollars have been allegedly spent by the Saudi Arabian government on the

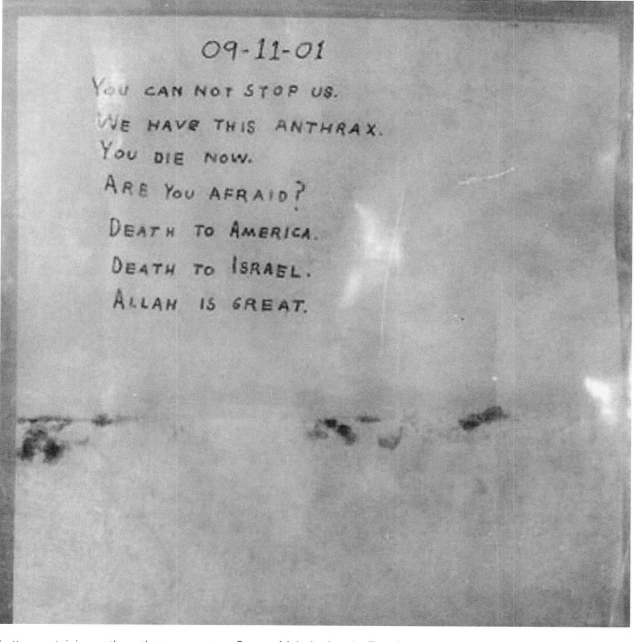

Letter containing anthrax that was sent to Senate Majority Leader Tom Daschle which, despite reference to Allah, investigators believe was not linked to al-Qaeda or Islamic terrorists. AP/WIDE WORLD PHOTOS

spreading of pro-al-Qaeda doctrine among United States prison inmates and military personnel. The recruitment and organization of ideological and political extremist groups among those two captive populations has been reported throughout recorded history.

Dr. Michael Waller asserted in his testimony before the United States Senate Committee on the Judiciary in October of 2003, that "Islamist terrorists view conversions of non-Muslims—and even moderate Muslims to

Islamism as vital to their effort. U.S. counterintelligence is vigilant against recruitment of American military personnel by foreign intelligence services, but has been blind toward the possible recruitment of American officers into Wahabi political extremism or Islamist terrorist networks."

According to the research reported by the Institute of World Politics, not only did the Muslim Brotherhood limitedly infiltrate the United States military, but as many as nine of the fourteen Islamic chaplains (imams) in the U.S. military (in 2003) received some religious training from the Graduate School of Islamic and Social Sciences in Leesburg, Virginia, which receives its major financial support from Saudi Arabia.

Finally, the same research report cited by Waller in his Senate Committee testimony, concluded that Saudi-sponsored Wahabi organizations are predominant among the Muslim prison recruiting agents in the United States. Wahabists in the prison system typically espouse strong anti-American sentiments.

FURTHER RESOURCES

Books

Steyn, Mark. *The Face of the Tiger*. Stockade Books, 2002.

Steyn, Mark. *Mark Steyn From Head To Toe: An Anatomical Anthology*. Stockade Books, 2004.

Kimball, R., and Kramer, H. eds. *Lengthened Shadows: America And Its Institutions In The Twenty-First Century*. Encounter Books, 2004.

Web sites

GlobalSecurity.org. "Testimony, United States Senate Committee on the Judiciary—Terrorist Recruitment and Infiltration in the United States: Prisons and Military as an Operational Base. October 14, 2003. Dr. Michael Waller, Annenberg Professor of International Communication, The Institute of World Politics." <http://www.globalsecurity.org/security/library/congress/2003_h/031014-waller.htm> (accessed July 4, 2005).

9/11: Long-term Health Monitoring

World Trade Center Health Registry Quarterly Report

New York City Government Report

By: New York City Department of Health and Mental Hygiene (DOHMH)

Date: May 13, 2004

Source: New York City Department of Health and Mental Hygiene

About the Author: In 2003, the New York City Department of Health and Mental Hygiene (DOHMH) began to recruit people that had lived and worked in Lower Manhattan during and after the World Trade Center attacks of September 11, 2001, to participate in a long-term study of health effects: the World Trade Center Health Registry (WTCHR).

United Airlines Flight 175 flies into the South Tower of the World Trade Center during terrorist attacks on September 11, 2001. © ROB HOWARD/CORBIS

INTRODUCTION

Persistent smoke and fumes from the nation's longest burning commercial fire contaminated the air over Manhattan and parts of New Jersey in the months following the September 11, 2001 attacks on the World Trade Center. The New York City and federal governments were faced with mounting pressure from environmental groups such as the Sierra Club to explore the long-term health effects of the fire. Health effects had to be determined not only for emergency personnel, firefighters, police, cleanup and construction workers and volunteers active at Ground Zero, but also for hundreds of thousands of people that lived and worked in Lower Manhattan. Air contamination by dust from the disaster persisted even after the fire was extinguished as windblown particulate matter that had not been cleaned up continued to circulate around the area.

Early claims by the United States Environmental Protection Agency (EPA) that it was safe to live and work in the area were met with skepticism by environmental and public health critics. Additionally, the formation of the World Trade Center registry was not simply a response to political and popular pressure; in fact individuals within city government had initiated plans to study the effects soon after September 11, 2001. New York Senator Hilary Rodham Clinton was outspoken in her determination to hold the EPA accountable for monitoring any potential long-term health effects.

The city, backed with federal government funding, hired Research Triangle Institute (RTI), a major governmental consulting firm, to administer a disease registry that would enroll as many residents and workers in the target area as possible. The operating epidemiological assumption has been that many of the health effects of the airborne toxins from the fire at Ground Zero would be of low frequency and would not be detected unless tens of thousands of people were tracked over the long term. The source document excerpts cited in this article offer insight into the complex issues involved in maintaining this study and making sure that it does what it purports to do—detect the incidence and prevalence of long-term respiratory problems, cancers, and other conditions that could be attributed to toxins in the smoke from Ground Zero. Some adverse health effects, such as respiratory disorders, are already being discovered.

PRIMARY SOURCE

EXCERPT 1: EXECUTIVE SUMMARY OF THE PROCEEDINGS: EXPERT PANEL ON PUBLIC HEALTH REGISTRIES

Immediately following the World Trade Center terrorist attacks of September 11, 2001, the New York City Department of Health and Mental Hygiene (DOHMH) and other environmental health experts became concerned about several health issues of the exposed populations.

First, it was not immediately known what environmental toxins were released from the building collapse and ensuing fires, and how such toxins or irritants would affect the health of residents and office workers in the vicinity, and emergency responders. Second, there was equal concern about the mental health needs of the population attacked as well as those responding. Additionally, there were concerns about the injuries suffered by survivors and responders. After deliberations between NYC DOHMH, the Environmental Protection Agency (EPA), the Agency for Toxic Substances and Disease Registry (ATSDR), and the Federal Emergency Management Agency (FEMA), it was decided that a registry of persons exposed to the dust, airborne particulates, and fumes from the fires and the events of 9/11 was necessary to document baseline health and mental health status; and would be an investment in the City's ability to understand any long term health effects.

Registries have been used for over 30 years to study the extent of health problems from exposures to environmental contamination and disasters. A registry, unlike most epidemiological studies, allows participation of all exposed persons willing to enroll. Registries can enable long-term evaluation of health effects, since subjects for more structured studies can be selected from the registry cohort.

After extensive careful planning and expert consultation on the development of the scientific approach the WTCHR began data collection on September 5, 2003. Data collection continued through November 20, 2004. Over 70,000 persons were registered . . .

SIGNIFICANCE

In the aftermath of September 11, 2001, many people in New York and on the Jersey Shore, where the smoke plume from the World Trade Center most often settled, talked about "the World Trade Center Flu," a complex of symptoms that included cough and hyper-reactivity. Although many people reported such symptoms, others experienced no symptoms, even on September 11. Therefore, the EPA initially asserted that the air quality in Lower Manhattan presented no known long-term health risks.

A presentation by scientists at the American Chemical Society (ACS) convention in 2003 concluded that rescue workers, volunteers, and others close to Ground Zero in the months after September 11 were exposed to dangerous pollutants and that these same pollutants posed little threat to people in New York and New Jersey away from the neighborhood of Ground Zero. Conditions were toxic for workers at the site without respirators and slightly less so for people living and working in adjacent buildings. The study focused on the persistent fires at Ground Zero that burned until mid-December. Tests were conducted in October from a rooftop site a mile from Ground Zero. High readings were recorded only on days when the wind was blowing directly toward the test site.

The ACS presentation came only a week after the Inspector General of the EPA released a statement that the agency had bowed to pressure to tone down public warnings about air quality, to refrain from issuing cautions and cleanup instructions, and to issue a claim that the air was safe to breathe. The inspector general said that the EPA lacked data to make such a claim.

Former EPA Administrator Whitman said EPA testing revealed similar high spikes of pollutants based on wind shifts, but they always dissipated rapidly, a position that was supported by the scientists' study. She reiterated that no study had disproved what the agency had said from the beginning.

The University of California at Davis study, based on 8,000 air samples, collected from the rooftop at 201

Varick St. in Manhattan, showed that the smoke and dust cloud contained:

- fine toxic metals that interfere with lung chemistry
- sulfuric acid, which attacks cilia and lung cells
- fine glass particles
- high temperature organic matter, possibly carcinogenic.
- It is clear that residents and workers near Ground Zero were exposed to erratic but sometimes high levels of poisonous pollutants. New studies by epidemiologists are revealing that toxic chemicals in the smoke plume over Lower Manhattan are indeed having at least short-term health effects on worker and resident populations exposed to the smoke and dust from the destruction of the World Trade Center.

FURTHER RESOURCES

Periodicals

Geyh AS, Chillrud S, Williams DL, et al. "Assessing Truck Driver Exposure at the World Trade Center Disaster Site: Personal and Area Monitoring for Particulate Matter and Volatile Organic Compounds during October 2001 and April 2002." *Journal of Occupational and Environmental Hygiene.* 2:179–193(2005).

Lin S, Reibman J, Bowers JA, Hwang SA, et al. "Upper Respiratory Symptoms and Other Health Effects among Residents Living Near the World Trade Center Site after September 11, 2001." *American Journal of Epidemiology.*

Reibman J, Lin S, Hwang S.A., et al. "The World Trade Center Residents' Respiratory Health Study: New Onset Respiratory Symptoms and Pulmonary Function." *Environmental Health Perspectives.* 113:406–411(2005).

Chambers S. "Ground Zero air study shows a 'chemical factory.' Series: 9/11 Two Years Later." The *Newark Star-Ledger.* September 11, 2003, page 8.

Rich, M., "Ground Zero Health Worries Linger Amid More Questions." The *Wall Street Journal*, Feb 10, 2003.

Web sites

World Trade Center (WTC) Health Registry. <http://www.nyc.gov/html/doh/html/wtc/index.html> (accessed July 6, 2005).

"Nobody Is Going to Live Forever"

Recruitment of Suicide Bombers

Interview

By: James Reynolds

Date: July 16, 2004

Source: BBC News

About the Author: Hussam Abdo is a Palestinian boy living in the Machifa district of the West Bank town of Nablus. He told his story to James Reynolds, a BBC correspondent based in Jerusalem.

INTRODUCTION

On March 24, 2004, the al-Aqsa Martyrs' Brigade claimed responsibility for a failed suicide-bombing attempt, citing the action as retaliation for the assassination of the Hamas leader Sheikh Ahmed Yassin. Israeli soldiers stopped the bomber, Hussam Abdo, before he could reach his target at the Huwarra checkpoint south of Nablus in the West Bank. After his surrender, the soldiers directed the young man by radio

Reem Raiyshi, a mother of two from Gaza, poses holding a gun before she blew herself up at the major crossing point between Israel and the Gaza Strip AP/WIDE WORLD PHOTOS

how to dismantle his belt of explosives. At the time of the suicide bombing mission, Abdo was fifteen years old. Abdo was poised to become the youngest suicide bomber in the Israeli-Palestinian Conflict. The lure of martyrdom entices some people, such as Abdo, to undertake suicide bombings, but they are not lone zealots. Suicide bombers are low-cost, high-yield instruments of terror in a larger network intent on creating fear and generating political change.

PRIMARY SOURCE

It was an unforgettable image. A teenager standing alone at a checkpoint, explosives strapped to his chest, confused, trying to follow Israeli orders to get him to dismantle his bomb.

That afternoon, in March 2004, 15-year-old Hussam Abdo took up his own small place in the imagery of this conflict.

Since his arrest he has been in an Israeli prison.

We were let inside a high security jail in the north of the country and told to wait in a meeting room.

Minutes later, Hussam Abdo was brought in to see us.

He was wearing a brown prison uniform and handcuffs. He was tiny; he didn't even reach my shoulder.

He sat down, smiled and talked readily. A prison guard sat at the end of the room watching our conversation.

Below is a transcript of the interview:

James Reynolds: Everyone saw the TV pictures of you at the checkpoint that day. Can you tell me what you did that day?

Hussam Abdo: In the morning at 6:00 A.M. I prayed and kissed my mother goodbye and told her I was going to school.

Then I went to my friend's house at 6:00 A.M.

He took me to some guys in Nablus. I sat with them and spoke to them. And then they took pictures of me and put on the bomb belt.

And then I went off to the checkpoint. I got to the checkpoint at 1:00 P.M.

The army caught me at 1:30 P.M. I stayed with the soldiers at the checkpoint till 9:00 P.M. and then they took me to the military base.

JR: When you went out with your bomb belt what was your target?

Hussam: They told me to go to a checkpoint. They told me you blow yourself up at the checkpoint.

They showed me a videotape of it.

JR: When you put on that belt did you really know—as a 15-year-old—that you were going to go and murder

people, that you were going to go and cause great suffering to mothers and fathers, that you were going to be a mass murderer? Did you really know that?

Hussam: Yes. Just like they came and caused our parents sadness and suffering they too should feel this. Just like we feel this, they should also feel it.

JR: Were you excited?

Hussam: I was a little bit nervous. But not to the point that I was very scared. I was kind of normal.

JR: Were you scared of dying?

Hussam: No. I'm not afraid of death.

JR: Why not?

Hussam: Nobody is going to live forever. We're all going to die.

JR: But you were only 15 years old at the time.

Hussam: I wanted to be relieved of school.

JR: When the army caught you, how did you feel?

Hussam: I was a bit scared. The soldiers came to me and there were many of them so I was a bit scared.

I was afraid that they would beat me but I wasn't afraid that they'd shoot me.

They were nice to me; they treated me well.

JR: Are you sad that you didn't manage to blow yourself up and kill many Israelis?

Hussam: I feel normal. But I thank God that the operation didn't go through.

JR: You thank God that you didn't die—why?

Hussam: It's just the way it is. God doesn't want me to die.

JR: Who sent you?

Hussam: My friend Nasser. He's 16. He was my classmate.

JR: How did he tell you about it?

Hussam: I was sitting with a friend of mine and he comes to me and says can you find me a martyr bomber?

Then I told him I'll do it. My friend says—really? And I answer—yes I'll do it.

So he agreed and he took me to see another guy.

The guy's name was Wael. He was from Al Aqsa Martyrs' Brigades. He was 21.

Then he took me to another guy who put the bomb belt on me and they took pictures of me.

The pictures were on the day before. Of course he asked me a lot of questions.

He asked me who I was and why I wanted to do this. I answered all of his questions. I told him I wanted to do it because of my friend who was killed and he agreed to let me do it.

JR: Did the people who sent you—the people from the Al Aqsa Brigades—did they promise you anything?

Hussam: Of course they did. They told me, once you carry out the operation and the soldiers come and demolish your home, we'll stand by your parents and rebuild your house and give them money.

JR: What are your feelings towards the people who sent you?

Hussam: I feel normal. One of them is my friend and he will stay my friend because, just like me, he's also in prison.

JR: Did you ever talk to your family about what you were going to do?

Hussam: I didn't tell my parents.

JR: Why not?

Hussam: Because if I'd told my mother she wouldn't have let me leave the house.

She'd have yelled at me, cried and told me not to do it.

JR: Have you spoken to them since your arrest?

Hussam: I spoke to them shortly after I was arrested. I was at the army base and the doctor there was checking me and I told him I wanted to speak to my mother, so he lent me his mobile phone.

He let me speak to my mother. She began to cry—she'd seen what happened on TV.

Then the doctor took the phone away from me and he spoke to my mother.

He said don't worry about your son, he's fine, we'll take care of him.

JR: How did you feel when you spoke to your mother?

Hussam: I felt relieved.

JR: Some teenagers want to be footballers, others want to be singers. You wanted to be a suicide bomber. Why?

Hussam: It's not suicide—it's martyrdom.

I would become a martyr and go to my God. It's better than being a singer or a footballer. It's better than everything.

JR: What was the main reason for you deciding to become a suicide bomber? The one reason in particular.

Hussam: The reason was because my friend was killed.

The second reason I did it is because I didn't want to go to school.

My parents forced me to go to school and I didn't feel like going.

JR: Are you saying that one of the reasons you wanted to become a suicide bomber was because you didn't like your teacher?

Hussam: That and because of my friend Sabih, who was killed.

JR: It seems extreme that if you don't like your teacher it could partially propel you towards murder and suicide.

Hussam: The thing is my parents forced me to go to school and I didn't want to go.

So I used to go there and run away. Then I had problems with the teachers. The principal took me to the police because I got into a fight with the teachers.

JR: Let's say there's another kid your age—15 or 16—and he wanted to go and blow himself up and kill Israelis. Would you stop him?

Hussam: I would stop him because if he got caught he would go to prison and it's not a nice place and he shouldn't be away from his parents.

JR: If you could turn back time and go back to that morning would you do it again?

Hussam: No.

JR: You wouldn't do it again? Why not?

Hussam: Because of prison. And also in the end there'll be peace.

JR: You really think in the end there will be peace?

Hussam: Yes.

JR: Do you know how long you will be here in an Israeli prison?

Hussam: The lawyer told me two-three years.

JR: What do you want to do with your life when you get out of prison?

Hussam: I want to go home and be with my parents and work in my father's shop.

SIGNIFICANCE

The willingness to use suicide as a weapon is not a new concept nor is it exclusive to the Israeli-Palestinian conflict. In recent history, suicide attacks have occurred in various political struggles. In 1983, suicide bombers from the group Hezbollah in Beirut, Lebanon killed 241 U.S. Marines and 58 French paratroopers, members of a multinational peacekeeping force. Members of the separatist group Liberation Tiger of Tamil Eelam (LTTE) assassinated two heads of state, Prime Minister Rajiv Gandhi of India in 1991 and Sri Lankan President Ranasinghe Premadasa in 1993 using suicide bombers. In Turkey, members of the Kurdistan Workers' Party (PKK), a Marxist separatist group executed suicide bombing missions between 1995–1999 in their efforts to create an independent Kurdish state. The most notorious and destructive suicide mission occurred on September 11, 2001 with the attacks on the World Trade Center and the Pentagon.

Suicide bombings provide an organization a mission that usually provides high impact relative to its cost. Though such missions carry a high cost of human life,

A would-be suicide bomber, Palestinian youth—Hussam Abdo— stares at journalists following his arrest near the northern West Bank city of Nablus. AP/WIDE WORLD PHOTOS

suicide bombings do not require high-priced weapons and expensive training. A successfully planned and executed suicide bombing not only inflicts damage to property and mass casualties, but also creates a psychological impact by creating a sense of uncertainty in the affected community.

For Palestinian groups, such as al-Aqsa Martyrs' Brigade, organizers use the cultural admiration of martyrdom (which they and other extremist groups helped to create) to inspire would-be bombers. Although members of the Palestinian Authority do not openly support suicide bombings, operations against Israeli targets allegedly continue with permissive support. Community groups led by the Palestinian leaders offer financial incentives and support to the family members of suicide bombers. Extremist groups in the region also seize upon a sense of distress, a perception of victimization, hatred toward the enemy, and avenging the death of a comrade as means of psychologically motivating would-be suicide bombers.

FURTHER RESOURCES

Periodicals

Atran, Scott. "Mishandling Suicide Terrorism." *The Washington Quarterly*. 27:3 pp. 67–90.

Sprinzak, Ehud. "Rational Fanatics." *Foreign Policy*. September 2000: p. 66.

Web sites

BBC News. "Profile: al-Aqsa Martyrs Brigade." July 1, 2003. <http://news.bbc.co.uk/2/hi/middle_east/1760492.stm> (accessed June 28, 2005).

The *Guardian Unlimited*. MacAskill, Ewan. "He Began Running: He Would Have Killed Them All." March 25, 2004. <http://www.guardian.co.uk/israel/Story/0,2763, 1177325,00.html> (accessed June 28, 2005).

Sources Consulted

Abanes, Richard. *American Militias: Rebellion, Racism, and Religion*. Downers Grove, IL: InterVarsity Press, 1996.

Ainsworth, Peter B. *Offender Profiling and Crime Analysis*. Portland, OR: Willan, 2001.

Alexander, John B. *Future War: Non-Lethal Weapons in Twenty-First Century Warfare*. New York: St. Martin's Press, April 1999.

Alexander, Martin S. *Knowing Your Friends: Intelligence Inside Alliances and Coalitions from 1914 to the Cold War (Cass Series-Studies in Intelligence)*. London; Portland, OR: Frank Cass, 1998.

Alexander, Yonah, and Michael S. Swetnam. *Cyber Terrorism*. Ardsley, NY: Transnational, 2001.

Allen, George W. *None So Blind: A Personal Account of the Intelligence Failure in Vietnam*. Chicago: Ivan R. Dee, 2001.

American Civil Liberties Union. *The Smith Act and the Supreme Court: An American Civil Liberties Union Analysis, Opinion and Statement of Policy*. New York: American Civil Liberties Unions, 1952.

Amuzegar, Jahangir. *The Dynamics of the Iranian Revolution*. NY: New York University Press, 1991.

Anderson, Terry A. *Den of Lions*. New York: Crown 1993.

Andreason, N.C., and D.W. Black. *Introductory Textbook of Psychiatry*. Washington, DC: American Psychiatric Press, Inc. 1991.

Ansary, Tamim. *West of Kabul, East of New York: An Afghan American Story*. Picador USA, 2003.

Anti-Defamation League, Law Enforcement Agency Resource Network. "*Ecoterrorism: Extremism in the Animal Rights and Environmentalist Movements*," 2005. <http://www.adl.org/Learn/Ext_US/Ecoterrorism.asp> (accessed June 1, 2005).

Atherton, Louise. *Top Secret: An Interim Guide to Recent Releases of Intelligence Records at the Public Record Office*. London: PRO Publications, 1993.

Aubrac, Lucie. Konrad Bieber and Betsy Wing (trans.). *Outwitting the Gestapo*. Lincoln: University of Nebraska Press, 1994.

Austs, Stefan. *The Baader-Meinhof Group: The Inside Story of a Phenomenon*. London: Bodley-Head, 1987.

Avrich, Paul. *Sacco and Vanzetti: The Anarchist Background*. Princeton, NJ: Princeton University Press, 1991.

Avrich, Paul. *The Haymarket Tragedy*. Princeton, NJ: Princeton University Press, 1986.

Bailey, Kathleen C. *Iraq's Asymmetric Threat to the United States and U.S. Allies*. Fairfax, VA: National Institute for Public Policy, December 2001.

Baird-Windle, Patricia, and Eleanor J. Bader. *Targets of Hatred: Anti-Abortion Terrorism*. New York: Palgrave Macmillan, 2001.

Ball, Kirstie and Webster, Frank. *The Intensification of Surveillance: Crime, Terrorism and Warfare in the Information Age*. London: Pluto Press, 2003.

Baram, Daphna. *Disenchantment: "The Guardian" and Israel*. London: Politico's Publishing, 2004.

Baritz, Loren, ed. *The American Left: Radical Political Thought in the Twentieth Century*. New York: Basic, 1971.

Bar-Joseph, Uri. *Intelligence Intervention in the Politics of Democratic States: The United States, Israel, and Britain*. University Park: Pennsylvania State University Press, 1995.

Becker, Jillian. *Hitler's Children: The Story of the Baader-Meinhof Terrorist Gang*. Philadelphia: Lippincott, 1977.

Beckwith, Charlie A., and Donald Knox. *Delta Force*. San Diego: Harcourt Brace Jovanovich, 1983.

Belknap, Michal R. *Cold War Political Justice: The Smith Act, the Communist Party, and American Civil Liberties.* Westport, Conn.: Greenwood Press, 1977.

Bergen, Peter I. *Holy War Inc.: Inside the Secret World of Osama Bin Laden.* New York: Touchstone, 2002.

Bergen, Peter. *Holy War, Inc.: Inside the Secret World of Osama bin Laden.* Free Press, 2002.

Berkowitz, Bruce D., and Allan E. Goodman. *Strategic Intelligence for American National Security.* Princeton, NJ: Princeton University Press, 1989.

Bessell, Richard. *Political Violence and the Rise of Nazism: The Storm Troopers in Eastern Germany, 1925–1934.* New Haven, CT: Yale University Press, 1984.

Bickerton, Ian J., and Carla L. Klausner. *A Concise History of the Arab-Israeli Conflict,* 4th ed., updated. Upper Saddle River, NJ: Prentice Hall, 2005.

Black, Jeremy *War Since 1945.* London: Reaktion Books, 2004.

Blunden, Bob. *The Money Launderers: How They Do It, and How to Catch Them at It.* Chalford, England: Management Books, c. 2001.

Bodziak J., Jon J. Nordby *Forensic science: An Introduction to Scientific and Investigative Techniques.* CRC Press, 2002.

Boghitchevitch, M.; edited by André Delpeuch; translated by Marvin Perry. *Le Procès de Salonique, Juin 1917.* Paris, 1927.

Bohn, Michael K. *The* Achille Lauro *Hijacking: Lessons in the Politics and Prejudice of Terrorism.* Dulles, VA: Brassey's, 2004.

Boll, Michael M. *National Security Planning Roosevelt Through Reagan.* Lexington: University Press of Kentucky, 1988.

Bolz, Frank, et al. *The Counterterrorism Handbook: Tactics, Procedures, and Techniques.* Boca Raton, FL: CRC Press, 2002.

Bonds, Ray, ed. *The Modern U.S. War Machine: An Encyclopedia of American Military Equipment and Strategy.* New York: Military Press, 1987.

Bose, Atinkranath. *A History of Anarchism.* Calcutta: World Press, 1967.

Bosworth, Seymour (ed.) and Michel E. Kabay. *Computer Security Handbook.* New York: John Wiley & Sons, April 2002.

Boulton, David. *The Making of Tania Hearst.* London: New English Library, 1975.

Bowden, Mark. *Black Hawk Down: A Story of Modern War.* New York: Atlantic Monthly Press, 1999.

Browning, Christopher R. *Ordinary Men.* New York: Harper Perennial, 1993.

Busby, Robert. *Reagan and the Iran-Contra Affair.* Chippenham, Wiltshire, Great Britain: Macmillan, 1999.

Bushart, Howard L. *Soldiers of God: White Supremacists and Their Holy War for America.* New York: Kensington, 1998.

Butler, Richard. *The Greatest Threat: Iraq, Weapons of Mass Destruction, and the Crisis of Global Security.* New York: Public Affairs May 22, 2001.

Cabinet Office. *National Intelligence Machinery.* London: HMSO, 2000.

Calhoun, Frederick S. *The Trainers: The Federal Law Enforcement Training Center and the Professionalization of Federal Law Enforcement.* Washington, D.C.: U.S. Government Printing Office, 1996.

Cameron, Gavin. *Nuclear Terrorism: A Threat Assessment for the 21st Century.* New York: St. Martin's Press, 1999.

Campbell, Christy. *Fenian Fire.* New York: HarperCollins, 2002.

Campbell, James B. *Introduction to Remote Sensing (3d edition).* New York: Guilford Press, 2002.

Campbell, Kurt M., and Michele A. Flournoy. *To Prevail: An American Strategy for the Campaign Against Terrorism.* Washington, D.C.: CSIS Press, 2001.

Carney, John T., and Benjamin F. Schemmer. *No Room for Error: The Covert Operations of America's Special Tactics Units from Iran to Afghanistan.* New York: Ballantine, 2002.

Carter, Ashton B., and William J. Perry. *Preventive Defense: A New Security Strategy for America.* Washington, D.C.: Brookings Institution Press, 1999.

Cefrey, Holly, et al. *Epidemics: Deadly Diseases Throughout History (The Plague, AIDS, Tuberculosis, Cholera, Small Pox, Polio, Influenza, and Malaria).* New York: Rosen Publishing Group, 2001.

Chalk, Peter. *The Response to Terrorism as a Threat to Liberal Democracy.* The Australian Journal of Politics and History. September 1, 1998.

Chalmers, David M. *Hooded Americanism: The History of the Ku Klux Klan.* Durham, NC: Duke University Press, 1981.

Chapman, Robert, et. al. *COPS Innovations: A Closer Look: Local Law Enforcement Responds to Terrorism: Lessons in Prevention and Preparedness.* Washington, D.C.: U.S. Department of Justice Office of Community Oriented Policing Services.

Chase, Alston. *Harvard and the Unabomber: The Education of an American Terrorist.* New York: Norton, 2003.

Cheswick, William R., Steven M. Bellovin, and Aviel D. Rubin. *Firewalls and Internet Security: Repelling the Wiley Attacker, Second Edition.* Boston: Addison Wesley Professional 2003, February 24.

Cigar, Norman. *Genocide in Bosnia: The Policy of Ethnic Cleansing.* Texas: A&M University Press, 1995.

Clark, Wesley K. *Waging Modern War: Bosnia, Kosovo, and the Future of Combat.* New York: Public Affairs, 2001.

Cleveland, William L. *A History of the Modern Middle East.* Boulder, CO: Westview Press, 2000.

Coben, Stanley. *A. Mitchell Palmer, Politician.* New York: Columbia University Press, 1963.

Cohen, Susan, and Daniel Cohen. *Pan Am 103: The Bombing, the Betrayals, and the Bereaved Families' Search for Justice.* New York: Signet, 2001.

Colby, William E. with McCarger, James. *Lost Victory: A Firsthand Account of America's Sixteen-Year Involvement in Vietnam.* Chicago: Contemporary Books, 1989.

Cole, Leonard A. *The Eleventh Plague: The Politics of Biological and Chemical Warfare.* New York: WH Freeman and Company, 1996.

Cole, Leonard A. *The Anthrax Letters: A Medical Detective Story.* Washington, D.C.: National Academy of Sciences, 2003.

Coll, Steve. *Ghost Wars: The Secret History of the CIA, Afghanistan, and Bin Laden, from the Soviet Invasion to September 10, 2001.* New York: The Penguin Group, 2004.

Colliers, A., et al. *Microbiology and Microbiological Infections,* vol. 3. London: Edward Arnold Press, 1998.

Collin, Richard H. *Theodore Roosevelt's Caribbean: The Panama Canal, the Monroe Doctrine, and the Latin American Context.* Baton Rouge: Louisiana State University Press, 1990.

Combatting Terrorism: How Five Foreign Countries Are Organized to Combat Terrorism. Washington, D.C.: General Accounting Office, April 2000.

Conaghan, Catherine M. *Fujimori's Peru: Deception In The Public Sphere.* Pittsburgh: University of Pittsburgh Press, 2005.

Conboy, Kenneth J. *Feet to the Fire: CIA Covert Operations in Indonesia,* Annapolis MD: Naval Institute Press, 1999.

Conroy, John. *Unspeakable Acts: The Dynamics of Torture.* New York: Alfred A. Knopf 2000.

Cook, David. *Understanding Jihad.* Berkley: University of California Press, 2005.

Cordesman, Anthony H. *Terrorism, Asymmetric Warfare, and Weapons of Mass Destruction: Defending the U.S. Homeland.* Westport, CT: Praeger, 2002.

Cordesman, Anthony H., and Justin G. Cordesman. *Cyber-Threats, Information Warfare, and Critical Infrastructure Protection: Defending the U.S. Homeland.* Westport, CT: Praeger, 2002.

Coughlin, Con. *Hostage: The Complete Story of the Lebanon Captives.* New York: Warner Books, 1993.

Cronin, Audrey. *Foreign Terrorist Organizations.* Washington, D.C.: CRS, 2004.

CSIS Homeland Defense Project. *Combating Chemical, Biological, Radiological, and Nuclear Terrorism: A Comprehensive Strategy : A Report of the Crisis Homeland Defense Project.* Washington, D.C.: Center for Strategic and International Studies, 2001.

Cuban-American National Foundation. *Castro's Puerto Rican Obsession.* Washington, D.C.: Cuban-American National Foundation 1987.

Dalton, Patricia A. *Combating Terrorism: Enhancing Partnerships through a National Preparedness Strategy.* Washington, D.C.: General Accounting Office, 2002.

Dando, Malcolm. *Biological Warfare in the 21st Century.* New York: Macmillan, 1994.

Daughtery, William J. *In the Shadow of the Ayatollah: A CIA Hostage in Iran.* Annapolis, MD: Naval Institute Press, 2001.

Davies, Barry. *Terrorism: Inside a World Phenomenon.* London: Virgin, 2003.

Davis, Brian L. *Qaddafi, Terrorism, and the Origins of the U.S. Attack on Libya.* New York: Praeger, 1990.

Davis, James Kirkpatrick. *Spying on America: The FBI's Domestic Counterintelligence Program.* New York: Praeger, 1992.

Dobson, C. and Payne, R. *War Without End: The Terrorists, An Intelligence Dossier.* London: Harrap Limited, 1986.

Downing, David. *The War on Terrorism: The First Year.* Chicago: Raintree, 2004.

Drell, S.D. *The New Terror: Facing the Threat of Biological and Chemical Weapons.* Stanford, CA: Hoover Institute Press, 1999.

Duiker, William. *Ho Chi Minh: A Life.* New York: Hyperion, 2000.

Dunn, Robert W. *The Palmer Raids.* New York: International Publishers, 1948.

Dunnigan, John P. *Deep-Rooted Conflict and the IRA Cease-Fire.* Lanham, MD: University Press of America, 1995.

Durant, Michael J. *In the Company of Heroes.* New York: G.P. Putnam's Sons, 2003.

Dutton, David. *The Politics of Diplomacy: Britain, France and the Balkans in the First World War.* International Library of Historical Studies, 13. London: I.B. Tauris, 1998.

Dwyer, Jim. *Two Seconds under the World: Terror Comes to America.* New York: Crown Publishers, 1994.

Edwards, Francis. *Guy Fawkes: The Real Story of the Gunpowder Plot.* London: Hart-Davis, 1969.

Elliott, Michael. *Time.* "The Shoe Bomber's World." February 16, 2002. <http://www.time.com/time/world/article/0,8599,203478,00.html> (accessed July 8, 2005).

Elliston, Jon (introduction) *InTERRORgation: The CIA's Secret Manual on Coercive Questioning, Second Edition.* San Francisco: AK Press, May 1999.

Emerson, Steven, and Brian Duffy. *The Fall of Pan Am 103.* New York: Putnam, 1990.

Eshed, Haggai. *Reuven Shiloah: The Man Behind the Mossad: Secret Diplomacy in the Creation of Israel*. Portland, OR: F. Cass, 1997.

Etzioni, Amitai. *How Patriotic is the Patriot Act?: Freedom Versus Security in the Age of Terrorism*. New York and London: Routledge, 2004.

Farrington, Jay. *Domestic Terrorism*. Philadelphia, Pennsylvania: Xlibris Corporation, 2001.

Ferguson, Amanda and Stair, Nancy L. *The Attack on U.S. Servicemen at Khobar Towers in Saudi Arabia on June 25, 1996*. New York: Rosen Publishing Group, 2003.

Feuerlicht, Roberta Strass. *America's Reign of Terror: World War I, the Red Scare, and the Palmer Raids*. New York: Random House, 1971.

Finkelstone, Joseph. *Anwar Sadat: Visionary Who Dared*. Portland: Frank Cass, 1996.

Fire Protection Publication. *Final Report: Alfred P. Murrah Federal Building Bombing April 19, 1995*. Oklahoma City: City of Oklahoma City Document Management, 1996.

Fisher, Jack. *Stolen Glory: The McKinley Assassination*. La Jolla, CA: Alamar Books, 2001.

Fisk, Robert. *Pity the Nation: Lebanon at War*. Oxford Paperbacks, 2001.

Fites, Philip, Peter Johnston, and Martin Kratz. *The Computer Virus Crisis*. New York: Van Nostrand Reinhold, 1992.

Flynn, Stephen. *America the Vulnerable: How the U.S. Has Failed to Secure the Homeland and Protect Its People from Terrorism*. New York: HarperCollins, 2004.

Follain, John. *Jackal: The Complete Story of the Legendary Terrorist, Carlos the Jackal*. New York: Arcade Publishing 1998.

Fraser, Nicholas. *The Voice of Modern Hatred : Tracing the Rise of Neo-Fascism in Europe*. New York: Overlook TP, 2002.

French, Scot. *The Rebellious Slave: Nat Turner in American Memory*. Boston: Houghton Mifflin, 2004.

Friedman, Thomas L. *Longitudes and Attitudes: exploring the world after September 11*. New York: Farrar, Straus and Giroux, 2002.

Frist, W.H. *When Every Moment Counts: What You Need to Know About Bioterrorism from the Senates only Doctor*. Lanham, MD: Rowman & Littlefield, 2002.

Fritz, Sandy, and Jack Brown. *Understanding Germ Warfare (Science Made Accessible)*. New York: Warner Books, December 2002.

Fromkin, David. *Europe's Last Summer: Who Started the Great War in 1914?* New York: Knopf, 2003.

Gall, Carlotta, and Thomas De Waal. *Chechnya: Calamity in the Caucasus*. New York: New York University Press, 1998.

Ganguly, Sumit. *The Crisis in Kashmir: Portents of War, Hopes of Peace*. Cambridge: Cambridge University Press, 1999.

Gavish, Dov. *A Survey of Palestine during the Period of the British Mandate, 1918–1948*. Routledgecurzon Studies in Middle Eastern History. London: Routledge, 2005.

Gellately, Robert. *The Gestapo and German Society*. Oxford: Oxford University Press, December 1991.

George, John, and Laird Wilcox. *American Extremists: Militias, Supremacists, Klansmen, Communists, and Others*. Amherst, NY: Prometheus Books, 1996.

Geraghty, Tony. *The Irish War: The Hidden Conflict Between the IRA and British Intelligence*. Baltimore: Johns Hopkins, 2000.

Gerson, Allan, and Jerry Adler. *The Price of Terror*. New York: HarperCollins, 2001.

Gerson, Allan, and Jerry Adler. *The Price of Terror*. New York: HarperPerennial, 2002.

Gilbert, Martin. *Israel: A History*. New York: William Morrow, 1998.

Goldstein, Donald M., et al. *Spanish-American War: The Story and Photographs*. Dulles, VA: Potomac, 2000.

Gordon, Nathan J., William L. Fleisher, and C. Donald Weinberg. *Effective Interviewing and Interrogation Techniques*. New York: Academic Press, November 2001.

Gowers, Andrew. *Behind the Myth: Yasser Arafat and the Palestinian Revolution*. London: W.H. Allen, 1990.

Gowers, Andrew. *Inside the PLO: Covert Units, Secret Funds, and the War Against Israel and the United States*. New York: Morrow, 1990.

Gowers, Andrew, and Walker, Tony. *Arafat: The Biography*. Virgin Books, 2005.

Goya y Lucientes, Francisco. *The Disasters of War*, edited by Philip Hofer. New York: Dover, 1967.

Grandin, Greg. *The Last Colonial Massacre: Latin American in the Cold War*. Chicago: University of Chicago Press, 2004.

Greenberg, Kenneth S. *Nat Turner: A Slave Rebellion in History and Memory*. New York: Oxford University Press, 2003.

Griswold, Terry, and D. M. Giangreco. *Delta, America's Elite Counterterrorist Force*. Osceola, WI: Motorbooks International, 1992.

Guenena, Nemet. *The "Jihad": An Islamic Alternative in Egypt*. Cairo: American University in Cairo Press, 1986.

Gunaratna, Rohan. *Terrorism in the Asia-Pacific: Threat and Response*. Singapore: Eastern Universities Press, 2003.

Hafez, Mohammed M. *Why Muslims Rebel: Repression and Resistance in the Islamic World*. Boulder, CO: Lynne Rienner Publishers, 2003.

Hamilton, Richard F., and Holger H. Herwig, eds. *The Origins of World War I*. Cambridge, UK: Cambridge University Press, 2003.

Hamzeh, Ahmad Nizar. *In the Path of Hizbullah*. Syracuse, NY: Syracuse University Press, 2004.

Haney, Eric L. *Inside Delta Force: The Story of America's Elite Counterterrorist Unit*. New York: Delacorte Press, 2002.

Harik, Judith P. *Hezbollah: The Changing Face of Terrorism*. London, NY: I.B. Tauris, 2004.

Hastings, Max. *Yoni, Hero of Entebbe*. New York: Dial Press, 1979.

Haugen, David M. *Biological and Chemical Weapons*. San Diego: Greenhaven Press, 2001.

Hearst, Patricia. *Every Secret Thing*. Garden City, NY: Doubleday, 1982.

Heikal, Mohammed. *Autumn of Fury: The Assassination of Sadat*. London: AndrÈ Deutsch, 1983.

Hewitt, Vernon Marston. *Reclaiming the Past: The Search for Political and Cultural Unity in Contemporary Kashmir*. London: Portland Books, 1995.

Heyman, D.A., J. Achterberg, and J. Laszlo. *Lessons from the Anthrax Attacks: Implications for U.S. Bioterrorism Preparedness: A Report on a National Forum on Biodefense*. Washington, DC: Center for Strategic and International Studies. May 2002.

Heymann, Philip B. *Terrorism and America: A Commonsense Strategy for a Democratic Society*. Cambridge, Mass.: MIT Press, 1998.

Hoffman, Bruce. *Inside Terrorism*. New York: Columbia University Press, 1999.

Holman, Virginia. *Rescuing Patty Hearst: Growing Up Sane in a Decade Gone Mad*. New York: Simon and Schuster, 2004.

Hughes, Robert. *Goya*. New York: Knopf, 2003.

Hunter, Edward *Brainwashing in Red China: The Calculated Destruction of Men's Minds*. Vanguard Press, 1951.

Hyun-Hee, Kim. *The Tears of My Soul: The True Story of a North Korean Spy*. New York: William Morrow and Company, 1993.

Inglesby, Thomas V. *Bioterrorist Threats: What the Infectious Disease Community Should Know about Anthrax and Plague. In:* Emerging Infections 5. Washington, DC: American Society for Microbiology Press, 2001.

Jacobs, Ron. *The Way the Wind Blew: A History of the Weather Underground*. London: Verso, 1997.

Jacquard, Roland. *In the Name of Osama Bin Laden: Global Terrorism and the Bin Laden Brotherhood, Revised and Updated Edition*. Durham: Duke University Press, 2002.

Jenkins, Brian Michael. *Countering Al Queda: An Appreciation of the Situation and Suggestions for Strategy*. Arlington, VA: RAND Corporation, 2002.

Juergensmeyer, Mark. *Terror in the Mind of God: The Global Rise of Religious Violence*. Berkeley: University of California Press, 2000.

Junaid, Shahwar. *Terrorism and Global Power Systems*. Oxford and New York: Oxford University Press, 2005.

Katz, Samuel M. *Relentless Pursuit: The DSS and the Manhunt for the al-Qaeda Terrorists*. New York: Tom Doherty Associates, 2002.

Kenny, Kevin. *Making Sense of the Molly Maguires*. New York: Oxford University Press, 1998.

Kimball, R., and Kramer, H. eds. *Lengthened Shadows: America And Its Institutions In The Twenty-First Century*. Encounter Books, 2004.

Kimura, Rei. *Aum Shinrikyo: Japan's Unholy Sect*. Charleston: Booksurge LLC, 2002.

Kite, Marsha, editor. *Forever changed: Remembering Oklahoma City April 19, 1995*. Amherst, New York: Prometheus Books, 1998.

Kline, Harvey F. *Colombia: Democracy Under Assault*. Boulder: Westview, 1995.

Knezys, Stasys, and Romanas Sedlickas. *The War in Chechnya*. College Station: Texas A&M University Press, 1999.

Korn, David A. *Assassination in Khartoum*. Bloomington, IN: University Press, 1993.

Kropotkin, Peter. *Anarchism: A Collection of Revolutionary Writings*. Mineola, NY: Dover, 2002.

Kruse, Warren G., II., and Jay G. Heiser. *Computer Forensics: Incident Response Essentials*. Boston: Addison Wesley Professional 2001, September 26.

Laqueur, Walter. *A History of Zionism: From the French Revolution to the Establishment of the State of Israel*. New York: Schocken, 2003.

Laqueur, Walter. *The New Terrorism: Fanaticism and the Arms of Mass Destruction*. New York and Oxford: Oxford University Press, 2000.

Latifa. *My Forbidden Face: Growing Up under the Taliban: A Young Woman's Story*. New York: Miramax Books, 2003.

Lavoy, Peter R., Scott D. Sagan, James J. Wirtz. *Planning the Unthinkable: How New Powers Will Use Nuclear, Biological, and Chemical Weapons*. Cornell: Cornell University Press, December 2001.

Lederberg, Joshua, and William S. Cohen. *Biological Weapons: Limiting the Threat (BCSIA Studies in International Security)*. Boston: MIT Press 1999, May 7.

Lemarchand, René. *Political Awakening in the Belgian Congo*. Berkeley: University of California Press, 1964.

Lentz, Harris M. *Assassins and Executions: An Encyclopedia of Political Violence, 1865–1986*. Jefferson, NC: McFarland, 1988.

Lerner, K. Lee. and Lerner, Brenda Wilmoth. *Encyclopedia of Science* 3rd ed. Detroit: Gale Group, 2003.

Lerner, K. Lee. and Lerner, Brenda Wilmoth. *World of Microbiology and Immunology*. Detroit: Gale Group, 2002.

Lesser, Ian O. *Countering the New Terrorism*. Santa Monica, CA: RAND, 1999.

Levine, Michael. *Deep Cover: The Inside Story of How DEA Infighting, Incompetence, and Subterfuge Lost Us the Biggest Battle of the Drug War*. New York: Delacorte Press, 1990.

Lidin, Harold J. *History of the Puerto Rican Independence Movement.* Puerto Rico: Hato Ray, 1981.

Lieven, Anatol. *America Right or Wrong: An Anatomy of American Nationalism.* New York: Oxford University Press, 2004.

LIFE *One Nation: America Remembers September 11, 2001.* Boston: Little, Brown and Co. 2001.

Lifton, Robert Jay. *Thought Reform and the Psychology of Totalism: A Study of "Brainwashing." in China.* University of North Carolina Press (Reprint Edition), 1989.

Linde, Erik J. G. van de. *Quick Scan of Post 9/11 National Counter-terrorism Policymaking and Implementation in Selected European Countries: Research Project for the Netherlands Ministry of Justice.* Santa Monica, CA: RAND Europe, 2002.

Linden, Edward V., editor. *Foreign Terrorist Organizations: History, Tactics and Connections.* New York: Nova Science, 2004.

Lindroth, David. *First In: An Insider's Account of How the CIA Spearheaded the War on Terror in Afghanistan.* New York: Presidio Press, 2005.

Lockman, Zachary and Joel Beinin, eds. *Intifada: The Palestinian Uprising Against Israeli Occupation.* Cambridge, MA: South End Press: 1989.

Long, Douglas. *Ecoterrorism (Library in a Book).* New York: Facts on File, 2004.

Lukasik, S. J., S. E. Goodman, and D. W. Longhurst. *Protecting Critical Infrastructures against Cyber-Attack.* New York: Oxford University Press, 2003.

Lynd, Staughton. *Intellectual Origins of American Radicalism.* London: Faber and Faber, 1969.

Maldonado, A. W. *Teodoro Moscoso and Puerto Rico's Operation Bootstrap.* Gainesville: University Press of Florida, 1997.

Mamdani, Mahmood. *Good Muslim, Bad Muslim: America, the Cold War, and the Roots of Terror.* Academic Literature, Pantheon Books, 2004.

Mamdani, Mahmood. *When Victims Become Killers: Colonialism, Nativism, and the Genocide in Rwanda.* Princeton University Press, 2002.

Marenches, Count de Alexandre. *The Fourth World War: Diplomacy and Espionage in the Age of Terrorism.* New York: William Morrow and Company, 1992.

Markvart, T., ed. *Solar Electricity.* Chichester, UK: John Wiley, 1994.

Marsden, Peter. *The Taliban: War, Religion and the New Order in Afghanistan* Oxford: Oxford University Press, 1971.

Marshall, Jonathan, Peter Dale Scott and Jane Hunter. *The Iran-Contra Connection: Secret Teams and Covert Operations in the Reagan Era.* Boston: South End Press, 1987.

Marshall, Jonathan, Peter Dale Scott, and Jane Haapiseva-Hunter. *The Iran-Contra Connection: Secret Teams and Covert Operations in the Reagan Era.* Boston: South End Press, 1987.

Marx, Karl, and Friedrich Engels. *The German Ideology,* translated by S. Ryazanskaya. Moscow: Progress, 1964.

Marx, Karl, and Friedrich Engels. *The Holy Family, or, Critique of Critical Critique,* translated by R. Dixon. Moscow: Foreign Languages Publishing House, 1956.

Mason, Carol. *Killing for Life: The Apocalyptic Narrative of Pro-Life Politics.* Ithaca, NY: Cornell University Press, 2002.

Matar, Khalil R., and Robert W. Thabit. *Lockerbie and Libya: A Study in International Relations.* Jefferson, NC: McFarland, 2003.

Mayer, Arno J. *The Furies: Violence and Terror in the French and Russian Revolutions.* Princeton: Princeton University Press, 2002.

McCormick, Charles H. *Seeing Reds: Federal Surveillance of Radicals in the Pittsburgh Mill District, 1917–1921.* Pittsburgh: University of Pittsburgh Press, 1997.

McCullough, David. *Truman.* New York: Simon & Schuster, 1992.

McDermott, Terry. *Perfect Soldiers, the Hijackers: Who They Were, Why They Did It.* New York: HarperCollins 2005.

McDowell, Jim. *Godfathers: Inside Northern Ireland's Drugs Racket, Dublin, Gill & Macmillan,* 2003.

McFall, Kathleen. *Ecoterrorism: The Next American Revolution?* High Sierra Books, 2005.

McKittrick, David and McVeigh, David. *Making Sense of the Troubles.* London: Penguin, 2003.

McLellan, Vin, and Paul Avery. *The Voices of Guns: The Definitive and Dramatic Story of the Twenty-Two-Month Career of the Symbionese Liberation Army.* New York: Putnam, 1977.

Meier, Andrew. *Chechnya: To the Heart of a Conflict.* New York: Norton, 2004.

Michel, Lou, and Dan Herbeck. *American Terrorist: Timothy McVeigh and the Oklahoma City Bombing.* New York: ReganBooks, 2001.

Micheletti, Eric. *Special Forces in Afghanistan 2001–2003: War against Terrorism.* Paris: Historie and Collections, 2003.

Miles, Hugh. *Al Jazeera.* London: Abacus, 2005.

Millard, Mike. *Jihad in Paradise: Islam and Politics in Southeast Asia.* Armonk, NY: M.E. Sharpe, 2004.

Miller, Stuart Creighton. *Benevolent Assimilation: The American Conquest of the Philippines, 1899–1903.* New Haven, CT: Yale University Press, 1982.

Mooney, John and Michael O'Toole. *Black Operations: The Secret War Against the Real IRA.* Ashbourne, Ireland: Maverick House, 2003.

Mooney, John and O'Toole, Michael. *Black Operations: The Secret War Against the Real IRA.* Dunshaughlin: Maverick House, 2003.

Moore, Robin. *The Hunt for Bin Laden.* New York: Random House, Inc., 2003.

Moriarty, Laura J., and David L. Carter. *Criminal Justice Technology in the 21st Century*. Springfield, IL: Charles C. Thomas, 1998.

Morris, Benny. *Righteous Victims: A History of the Zionist-Arab Conflict, 1881–1999*. New York: Alfred A. Knopf, 1999.

Moya Pons, Frank. *The Dominican Republic: A National History*. New York: Marcus Weiner Publishers, 1998.

Murakami, Haruki. *Underground: The Tokyo Gas Attack and the Japanese Psyche*. New York: Random House, 2000.

Mylroie, Laurie. *Study of Revenge: The First World Trade Center Attack and Saddam Hussein's War Against America*. Washington, D.C.: AEI Press, 2001.

Naden, Corinne J. *Muammar Qaddafi (Heroes and Villains)*. San Diego: Lucent Books, 2004.

Nanavati, Samir, Thieme, Michael, Nanavati, Raj. *Biometrics: Identity Verification in a Networked World*. New York: Wiley and sons, March 2002.

National Commission on Terrorist Attacks Upon the United States. *The 9/11 Commission Report: Final Report of the National Commission on Terrorist Attacks Upon the United States*. New York: WW Norton HarperCollins, 2004.

National Commission on Terrorist Attacks. *The 9/11 Commission Report: Final Report of the National Commission on Terrorist Attacks Upon the United States*. New York: Norton, 2004.

Netanyahu, Jonathan. *Self-Portrait of a Hero: From the Letters of Johathan Netanyahu, 1963–1976*. New York: Random House, 1980.

O'Balance, Edgar. *The Congo-Zaire Experience, 1960–98*. New York: St. Martin's Press, 2000.

O'Balance, Edgar. *The Algerian Insurrection, 1954–1962*. London: Faber & Faber, 1967.

Oberfohren, Ernst. *The Oberfohren Memorandum: What German Conservatives Thought about the Reichstag Fire; Full Text, with an Introduction and the Findings of the Legal Commission of Inquiry on Its Authenticity*. German Information Bureau, 1933.

Ofer, Yehuda. *Operation Thunder: The Entebbe Raid: The Israelis Own Story*. Hamondsworth, Middlesex, U.K. and New York: Penguin, 1976.

Oklahoma Today. The Official Record of the Oklahoma City Bombing. Norman: University of Oklahoma Press, 2005.

Oliver, Anne Marie and Steinberg, Paul. *The Road To Martyrs' Square: A Journey Into The World of The Suicide Bomber*. Oxford University Press, 2004.

O'Neal, Michael. *The Assassination of Abraham Lincoln*. San Diego, CA: Greenhaven Press, 1991.

Orr, Michael. *Russia's Wars with Chechnya 1994–2003*. UK: Osprey Publishing, 2005.

Payne, Leslie. *The Life and Death of the SLA*. New York: Ballantine Books, 1976.

Pelossof, Noa Ben-Artzi. *In The Name of Sorrow and Hope*. Schocken Trade Paperback, 1997.

Perry, M., Peden, J.R., and T.H. Von Laue. *Sources of the Western Tradition. Volume II. 5th ed.* Houghton Mifflin 2003.

Petit, Michael. *Peacekeepers at War: A Marine's Account of the Beirut Catastrophe*. Boston: Faber and Faber, 1986.

Pillar, Paul R. *Terrorism and U.S. Foreign Policy*. New York: Brookings Institution Press, 2001.

Politkovskaia, Anna. *A Dirty War: A Russian Reporter in Chechnya*. London: Harvill, 2001.

Politkovskaya, Anna. *The Dirty War*. New York: Harvill Press, 2004.

Poolos, J. *Nerve Gas Attack on the Tokyo Subway*. Rosen Publishing Group Inc., 2002.

Pope, Daniel, ed. *American Radicalism*. Malden, MA: Blackwell, 2001.

Preston, Julia, and Samuel Dillon. *Opening Mexico: The Making of a Democracy*. New York: Farrar, Straus and Giroux, 2004.

Preston, R. *The Demon in the Freezer*. New York: Random House October 8, 2002.

Quandt, William B. *Revolution and Political Leadership: Algeria, 1954–1968*. Cambridge, MA: Massachusetts Institute of Technology, 1969.

Rafferty, Oliver P. *The Church, the State and the Fenian Threat, 1861–1875*. New York: Palgrave Macmillan, 1999.

Randel, William Peirce. *The Ku Klux Klan: A Century of Infamy*. Radnor, PA: Chilton Book Company, 1965.

Rashid, Ahmad. *Taliban. The Story of the Afghan Warlords*. Appendix l. London: Pan Books, 1971.

Reeve, Simon. *One Day in September: The Full Story of the 1972 Munich Olympics Massacre and the Israeli Revenge Operation "Wrath of God"*. New York: Arcade Publishing, 2001.

Reeve, Simon. *The New Jackals: Ramzi Yousef, Osama bin Laden, and the Future of Terrorism*. Boston: Northeastern University Press, 1999.

Reichert, William O. *Partisans of Freedom: A Study in American Anarchism*. Bowling Green, OH: Bowling Green Popular Press, 1976.

Reynolds, David S. *John Brown, Abolitionist: The Man Who Killed Slavery, Sparked the Civil War, and Seeded Civil Rights*. New York: Alfred A. Knopf, 2005.

Rice-Maximin, Edward. *Accommodation and Resistance: The French Left, Indochina and the Cold War, 1944–1954*. Westport, Conn.: Greenwood Press, 1986.

Rigney, H.W., S.V.D. *Four Years in a Red Hell: the Story of Father Rigney*. Henry Regnery 1956.

Riley, Kevin Jack, and Bruce Hoffman. *Domestic Terrorism: A National Assessment of State and Local Preparedness*. Santa Monica, CA: RAND Corporation, 1995.

Rivers, Gayle and Hudson, James. *The Teheran Contract* Garden City, New York: Doubleday & Company, Inc., 1981.

Roberts, Brad. *Biological Weapons: Weapons of the Future?* Wahington, D.C.: Center for Strategic and International Studies, 1993.

Rogers, Paul. *Political Violence and Asymmetric Warfare*. (U.S.-European Forum Paper) Washington: Brookings Institution, 2001.

Rossbach, Jeffery S. *Ambivalent Conspirators: John Brown, the Secret Six, and a Theory of Black Political Violence*. New York: Brookings Institution Press, 2001.

Royster, Jacqueline Jones, ed. *Southern Horrors and Other Writings: The Anti-Lynching Campaign of Ida B. Wells, 1892–1900*. Boston: Bedford Books, 1997.

Rubin, Barry M., and Rubin, Judith Colp. *Yasir Arafat: A Political Biography*. Oxford University Press, 2003.

Sadar, Ziauddin, and Mervyn Wynn Davies. *Why Do People Hate America?*. London: Icon Books, 2003.

Sagan, Scott D. and Kenneth N. Waltz. *The Spread of Nuclear Weapons: A Debate Renewed*, Second Edition. New York: W W Norton & Co., 2003.

Sageman, Marc. *Understanding Terror Networks*. Philadelphia, PA: University of Pennsylvania Press, 2004.

Salem, Elie Adib. *Violence and Diplomacy in Lebanon: The Troubled Years, 1982–1988*. London and New York: I.B. Tauris, 1995.

Saxton, Alexander. *The Indispensable Enemy: Labor and the Anti-Chinese Movement in California*. Berkeley: University of California Press, 1971.

Schanzer, Jonathan. *Al-Qaeda's Armies: Middle East Affiliate Groups and the Next Generation of Terror*. New York: Specialist Press International, 2005.

Schmidt, Gustav, ed. *A History of NATO: The First Fifty Years*. New York: Palgrave, 2001.

Schneider, Ronald M. *The Political System of Brazil: Emergence of a Modernizing Authoritarian Regime, 1964–1970*. 1973.

Schneier, Bruce. *Secrets and Lies: Digital Security in a Networked World*. New York: John Wiley, 2000.

Schulze, Kirsten E. *The Arab-Israeli Conflict*. London: Longman, 1999.

Schuster, Henry and Stone, Charles. *Hunting Eric Rudolph. New York: Berkley*, 2005.

Seagrave, Sterling *Yellow Rain: A Journey Through the Terror of Chemical Warfare*. New York: M. Evans and Company, Inc., 1981.

Seberry, J. and J. Pieprzyk. *Cryptography: An Introduction to Computer Security*. New York: Prentice Hall, 1989.

Seibert, Jeffrey W. *"I Done My Duty": The Complete Story of the Assassination of President McKinley*. Bowie, MD: Heritage Books, 2002.

Sells, Michael. *The Bridge Betrayed: Religion and Genocide in Bosnia*. Berkley: University of California Press, 1996.

Semple, Robert B. *Four Days in November: The Original Coverage of the John F. Kennedy Assassination*. New York: St. Martin's Press, 2003.

Shai, Shaul. *The Axis of Evil: Iran, Hizballah, and Palestinian Terror*. New Brunswick, NJ: Transaction Publishers, 2005.

Sheehan, Sean. *Anarchism*. London: Reaktion, 2003.

Shepherd, Naomi. *Ploughing Sand: British Rule in Palestine, 1917–1948*. Piscataway, NJ: Rutgers University Press, 1999.

Simon, Jeffrey D. *The Terrorist Trap: America's Experience with Terrorism*. Bloomington and Indianapolis: Indiana University Press, 1994.

Simons, Geoff. *Libya: The Struggle For Survival*. New York: Macmillan, 1993.

Smit, Ferdinand. *The Battle for South Lebanon: The Radicalization of Lebanon's Shi'ites, 1982–1985*. Amsterdam: Bulaag, 2000.

Smith, Colin. *Carlos: Portrait of a Terrorist*. New York: Holt, Rinehart and Winston, 1977.

Smith, G. Davidson. *Combating Terrorism*. New York: Routledge, 1990.

Smith, Helmut *German Nationalism and Religious Conflict: Culture, Ideology, and Politics 1870–1914*. Princeton, NJ: Princeton University Press, 1995.

Smith, Paul J. *Terrorism and Violence in Southeast Asia: Transnational Challenges to States and Regional Stability*. Armonk, NY: M.E. Sharpe, 2005.

Snyder, Rodney A. *Negotiating with Terrorists: TWA Flight 847*. Pew Case Studies in International Affairs. Washington, DC: Institute for the Study of Diplomacy, School of Foreign Service, Georgetown University, 1994.

Soesastro, Hadi, Anthony Smith, and Han Mui Ling, eds. *Governance in Indonesia: Challenges Facing the Megawati Presidency*. Singapore: Institute of Southeast Asian Studies, 2003.

Spignesi, Stephen J. *In the Crosshairs: Famous Assassinations and Attempts*. New York: New Page Books, 2003.

St. John, Ronald B. *Qaddafi's World Design: Libyan Foreign Policy 1969–1987*. London: Saqi Books, 1987.

Starn, Orin. *The Peru Reader: History, Culture, Politics*. Durham, North Carolina: Duke University Press, 1995.

Starobin, Joseph R. *American Communism in Crisis, 1943–1957*. Berkeley: University of California Press, 1972.

Stevenson, William. *90 Minutes at Entebbe*. New York: Bantam Books, 1979.

Steyn, Mark. *Mark Steyn From Head To Toe: An Anatomical Anthology*. Stockade Books, 2004.

Steyn, Mark. *The Face of the Tiger*. Stockade Books, 2002.

Stirner, Max. *The Ego and His Own*, translated by Steven Byington, revised and edited by David Leopold. Cambridge: Cambridge University Press, 1995.

Streitmatter, Rodger. *Mightier Than the Sword: How the News Media Have Shaped American History*. Boulder, CO: Westview Press, 1997.

Sullivan, William H. *Mission to Iran*. London: W. W. Norton & Co., 1981.

Taylor, Diana. *Disappearing Acts: Spectacles of Gender and Nationalism in Argentina's "Dirty War"*. Durham, North Carolina: Duke University Press, 1997.

Testrake, John, and David J. Wimbish, Triumph. *Over Terror on Flight 847*. New Jersey: Old Tappan, 1987.

Testrake, John, and David J. Wimbish. *Triumph over Terror on Flight 847*. Old Tappan, NJ: Fleming H. Revell, 1987.

The Centralia Case: Three Views of the Armistice Day Tragedy at Centralia, Washington, November 11, 1919: The Centralia Conspiracy. Civil Liberties in American History. New York: Da Capo Press, 1971.

The Jemaah Islamiyah Arrests and the Threat of Terrorism: White Paper. Singapore: Ministry of Home Affairs, 2003.

The Terrorism Reader: A Historical Anthology, edited by Walter Laqueur and Yonah Alexander. New York: Penguin, 1987.

Thompson, Paul. *The Terror Timeline : Year by Year, Day by Day, Minute by Minute: A Comprehensive Chronicle of the Road to 9/11—and America's Response*. New York: Regan Books, 2004.

Tichenor, Daniel J. *Dividing Lines: The Politics of Immigration Control in America*. Princeton, NJ: Princeton University Press, 2002.

Topp, Michael M. *The Sacco and Vanzetti Case: A Brief History with Documents*. Boston: Bedford/St. Martin's, 2005.

Tourgée, Albion Winegar. *The Invisible Empire*. Baton Rouge, LA: Louisiana State University Press, 1989.

Trager, Oliver, ed. *The Iran-Contra Arms Scandal: Foreign Policy Disaster*. New York: Facts on File, 1988.

Trelease, Allen W. *White Terror: The Ku Klux Klan Conspiracy and Southern Reconstruction*. Baton Rouge: Louisiana State University, 1999.

Tripp, Charles. *A History of Iraq*, London: Cambridge University Press, 2002.

Tripp, Charles. *A History of Iraq*. Cambridge: Cambridge University Press, 2002.

U.S. Government. *21st Century U.S. Military Documents: EMP Attack, Electromagnetic Pulse Threats, Report of the Commission to Assess the Threat to the United States from Electromagnetic Pulse, High-Altitude Nuclear Weapon EMP Attacks*. Washington, DC: Progressive Management, 2004.

United States. *Acts of Ecoterrorism by Radical Environmental Organizations: Hearing before the Subcommittee on Crime of the Committee on the Judiciary, House of Representatives, Fifth Congress, second session*, June 9, 1998. Washington, D.C.: Government Printing Office, 2000.

Van der Kiste, John. *The Romanovs, 1818–1959: Alexander II of Russia and His Family*. Gloucester, UK: Alan Sutton, 2000.

Varon, Jeremy. *Bringing the War Home: The Weather Underground, the Red Army Faction, and Revolutionary Violence in the Sixties and Seventies*. Berkeley: University of California Press, 2004.

Vaugh, Bruce, et al. *Terrorism in Southeast Asia*. Washington, D.C. CRS, 2005.

Verton, Dan. *Black Ice: The Invisible Threat of Cyber-Terrorism*. New York: McGraw-Hill/Osborne, 2003.

Walsh, Lawrence E. *Final Report of the Independent Counsel for Iran/Contra Matters*. Washington, D.C.: U.S. Court of Appeals for the D. C. Circuit, 1993.

Walsh, Lawrence E. *Firewall: The Iran-Contra Conspiracy and Cover-Up*. New York: Norton, 1997.

Wheelan, Joseph. *Jefferson's War: America's First War on Terror 1801–1805*. New York: Carroll and Graf, 2003.

Wiesel, Eli. *Night*. New York: Bantam; Reissue edition, 1982.

Williams, Louis. *Israeli Defense Force: A People's Army*. Jerusalem and New York: Gefen Publishing House, 1996.

Wirsing, Robert G. *India, Pakistan, and the Kashmir Dispute*. New York: St. Martin's Press, 1998.

Wittke, Carl Frederick. *Against the Current: The Life of Karl Heinzen (1809–80)*. Chicago: University of Chicago Press, 1945.

Wolff, Leon. *Little Brown Brother: How the United States Purchased and Pacified the Philippine Islands at the Century's Turn*. Garden City, NJ: Doubleday, 1961.

Woodworth, Paddy. *Dirty Wars, Clean Hands: ETA, the GAL and Spanish Democracy*. Cork University Press, 2001.

Woodworth, Paddy. *Why do they Kill? Violence in Spain's Basque Country*. World Policy Journal 2001, March 22.

Worchel, S., McCauley, C., Lee, Y-T, and F. Moghaddam, eds. *Psychology of Ethnic and Cultural Conflict*. Praeger Publishers, 2004.

Wright, Joanne. *Terrorist Propaganda: The Red Army Faction and the Provisional IRA, 1968–86*. New York: St. Martin's Press, 1990.

Yallop, David A. *To the Ends of the Earth: The Hunt for the Jackal*. London: Jonathan Cape, 1993.

Yasgur, Batya Swift. *Behind the Burqa: Our Life in Afghanistan and How We Escaped to Freedom* Wiley, 2002.

Zwickel, Jean Wiley. *Voices for Independence: In the Spirit of Valor and Sacrifice*. Pittsburg, CA: White Star Press, 1988.

Index

IWW. *See* Industrial Workers of the World

Izetbegovic, Aliza, 249

Izzeddin Al-Kassam, 149

J

Jacobins, 4–5

Jaish-e-Mohammed (JeM), 220–21

Jamaat-e-Islami, 315

James Bond, 353

Jammu, independence for, 220–21

Japanese Embassy, Peruvian forces and, 73

Japanese Red Army, 139

Jarrah, Ziad, 305–6

Jarvis, James, 298

Jefferson, Thomas, 334, 366

Jemaah Islamiyah (JI), 311–13, 317, 318

Jerusalem Railway Station bombing, 119

Jess, Mervyn, 307–10

Jewell, Richard, 344, 345, 354

"The Jewish Cemetery" (Sarajlic), 248–50

Jews, extermination of, 234–36

JI (Jemaah Islamiyah), 311–13

Jihad

  9/11 hijackers and, 305

  Bin Laden, Osama and, 268–69, 278, 279–80

  meaning of, 277–80

Jihad Fardh al Ein, 278

Jihad Fardh al Khafiya, 278

"John Brown's Body," 89–90

Johnson, Andrew, 94, 108

Johnson, Lyndon B., 30–34, 35, 40

Johnston, David, 313–16

Jones, Cristina, 294

Jones, Jim, 427

Jonsson, Patrick, 354–57

Joseph, King of Spain, 87–88

J.P. Morgan Building, bombing, 19

June 2 Movement, 51

Justice Department (U.S.), 18–19, 395–96

K

Kabret, Shamsu, 146 (ill.)

Kach movement, 203–5

Kaczynski, David, 341

Kaczynski, Theodore, 338–41

Kadyrov, Akhmad, 171

Kahan Commission, 62

Kandahar, Afghanistan, 297–98

Karadzic, Radovan, 249–50

Karzi, Hamid, 214

Kashmir, independence for, 220–21

Kasper, John, 334

Kataeb Regular Forces, 61

Kayibanda, Gregore, 254

Kearney, Dennis, 328

Kehoe, John "Black Jack," 331, 332

Kennedy, Jacqueline, 30, 30 (ill.)

Kennedy, John F., 337

  assassination of, 30–34, 30 (ill.)

  National Communications System and, 415

Kennedy, Robert F., 133 (ill.)

Kenya bombing, 269, 270–71, 272, 278

Kerr, Malcolm, 101

Khaled, Leila, 338 (ill.)

Khalifa, 279

Khallad. *See* Bin Attash, Walid Muhammad Salih

Khanum, Qudsia, 315

Kherchtou, L'Houssaine, 271, 278

Khomeini, Ayatollah

  anti-Americanism, 236, 377–79

  former students, 67

  Lebanese civil war and, 144

  return to Iran, 188–90

Khomeini, Rohollah Ayatollah, 191

Khuddam-ul-Islam. *See* Jaish-e-Mohammed (JeM)

"The Kidnappers Strike Again," 39–41

Kidnappings

  Baader-Meinhof Gang, 51–52

  Buckley, William, 197–99

  diplomatic, 39–41

  Hearst, Patricia, 44–46, 47–48

  Hezbollah, 62–64

  Lebanon, 67–72, 142

  Moro, Aldo, 52–54

  Peron, Isable, 50

  Shpigun, Gennady, 170

Kilburn, Peter, 68

Kilgore, James, 47–48

King David Hotel bombing, 117–19, 118 (ill.)

King Fahd (Saudi Arabia), 267

KKK. *See* Ku Klux Klan

Klee, Ernst, 234

Klinghoffer, Leon, 142, 147–48, 409, 411

Kluiters, Nicolas, 68

Knights of the White Kamelia, 335

Kopp, James, 344

Kopp, Magdalena, 139

Korean Air Lines Flight 858, 241–43, 241 (ill.)

Koresh, David, 78

Kropotkin, Peter Alexeievich, 11–13

KSM. *See* Mohammed, Khalid Sheikh

Ku Klux Klan (KKK), 329–30, 332–35

Kunar Camp, Afghanistan, 266

Kuta, Bali, 310–13, 310 (ill.)

Kuwait Airlines Flight 221, hijacking of, 142

Kyl, Jon, 415

L

La Belle disco bombing, Berlin, 65–67

Labor movement, 331–32

Labor Party, 154, 288–90

Labor strikes. *See* Strikes, labor

Labor unions

  Industrial Workers of the World, 21, 24

  suspicions of, 10

Labor unrest, 10, 23–25

Lange, Herbert, 235

LaPensee, Kenneth Travis, 284–88

Laqa, Mah, 315

Latin American Newsletters, 41–43

League for Vietnamese Independence, 122–23

League of Nations, 115–16

Leahy, Patrick, 361

Lebanese Revolutionary Brigades, 149

Lebanon

  bombings, 62–63, 95–101

  civil war, 60–62, 143, 144–46

  hostage crisis, 67–70

Lee Un Hae, 242–43

Legionnaires, Wobblies and, 24–25

Leif, Louise, 260–61

Lemkin, Raphael, 252

Lemont, Illinois, 10

Lenin, Vladimir, 12 (ill.), 13

Leopold II, King of Belgium, 126

Leopoldville mutiny, 127

Letters, from Timothy McVeigh, 77–79

  See also Anthrax letters

Liberation Tiger of Tamil Eelam (LTTE), 460

Libya

  disco bombing, 65–67

  terrorism sponsors, 143, 225

Libyan People's Bureau, 66

"Life as 'Tania' Seems so Far Away" (Orth), 43–47

Lifton, Robert Jay, 426